INVITATION TO

CHURCH HISTORY
World

INVITATION TO

CHURCH HISTORY

World

JOHN D. HANNAH

Kregel
Academic

Printed in the United States of America
18 19 20 21 22 / 5 4 3 2 1

DEDICATION

THE SCARIEST THING ABOUT being a communicator in any medium, though here I am primarily speaking of oral and literary artistry, is the realization that the one who assumes that role is undertaking the endeavor of interpreting reality to his or her hearers. I think as a teacher this is not only scary; it is a daunting responsibility. It seems that Gotthold Lessing had a valuable insight several centuries ago that between the past and the present is an "ugly ditch," an insurmountable chasm. The sources that appear to authenticate the past are often few and riddled with myopic perspectivalism by those who handle them. The scholars, who study these historical artifacts, seeking to authentically represent the past, are themselves not without prejudice and blindness is endemic.

As a teacher in the academy, I wonder not so much about the art of teaching as the wonder of learning. I am often amazed and shocked that students learn far more than I am capable of teaching. How is it that a student can understand the past and translate it into a usable present for themselves as well as tools to help others? It is not that the thin stream of knowledge acquired through study and reflection becomes an even thinner extract when it is communicated. As a Christian teacher I wonder how I can be of help to students whose giftednesses, personalities, and ministerial aspirations are so contrary to those possessed by the type of person who is inspired by silence and isolation, revels in books and archival materials, and lacks the social skills of those who aspire to profit from my instruction. As a teacher, I do not desire students to be like me; my goal is to make them what I, as a teacher, am not.

That said, this volume is dedicated to those who have sat under my tutelage for over forty years at the same institution, the Dallas Theological Seminary. Countless men and women have graduated from the school and are standing strong for Christ and the sacred gospel of divine grace in lecterns, pulpits, missions organizations, and secular endeavors all over the world. The treasure of a teacher is not found in professional activities; it is found in his or her students. It is a vicarious life that finds the deepest satisfaction in the accomplishment of others. A teacher lives in quietness, diligence, and hope. Our students are our surrogates; they have sat with us for a short time, but we go with them as graduates and find our deepest delight and joy in their successes, share their sorrows and disappointments, and always seek to be a source of encouragement in the work to which each has been called.

Enriched immensely by wonderful men and women who have sat in my classes, this dedication is a small token of my gratitude to you. A passion for God should be the driving impetus behind the Christian teacher's work and that should structure and inform the teaching task. I am thankful that God has allowed my passion for Christ and the gospel to be reincarnated in the lives of men and women far more gifted than me.

—John D. Hannah

CONTENTS

PREFACE

THE ENDEAVOR TO WRITE and publish a book on a subject that has witnessed the publication of several commendable volumes of recent vintage requires some justification. The reason for such a consuming and complex labor should rise above the desire to add another voice on church history even though the story may deserve endless repetition. Market interests alone appear equally unsatisfactory. There must be some uniqueness in approach or interpretative insight that inspires and warrants an additional contribution.

With so many impressive compilations of the history of Christian churches, how is this a unique contribution? The answers are several. First, the story of the Christian church is set in a theological context, a blatant spiritual metanarrative. Writing from within the educational establishment of the modern pluralistic university has certain advantages for careful and reflective discourse with the voices of the past, as well as the best of contemporary scholarship, but a conservative, theological perspective, though seen by some as having the scent of precritical bias, also has value. Rationalistic approaches to knowledge, particularly post-modernist deconstructionist views despair of the possibility of unifying knowledge, but the presuppositional assumptions of this study are those of the conservative church and the educational edifices that exist to serve them. While religion has not been excluded from the secular academy, it does not have the value it once occupied, now being a category within the social sciences. This book is written from the advantages that the conservative religious academy affords in valuing subjective perceptions of truth, but hopefully with the astuteness of research and care of scholarly awareness reflective of the contribution of the secular academy.

The bias of this work is not merely awareness that God orchestrates the course of history, even the affairs in the minutest detail, but that history is fundamentally the manifestation and outworking of a divinely directed and God-centered purpose. Just as time and human existence had a beginning at some point in the past; it will have an end in some near or distant event in the second advent of Jesus Christ into human history. The story of religious experience began before the beginning of time in the interTrinitarian love of God and the unnecessitated effusive love manifested to those who both reflect it and delight in it.

God's creative and constant providential power and love finds its purpose and end in a divine display of himself. God created the tree, the marvelous beauty of the Grand Canyon, and the regularity of the rising sun to reveal the symmetry and majesty of himself for his own beholding and delight. He made human kind for the same reason, but endowed them with greater capacity to fulfill the divine intent. The blight that was occasioned by the devolution of our first parents not only blemished the potential of humans to reflect and cherish God's goodness and mercies, it also marred the human habitat and its divine purposes for existence. God is rebuilding the "garden," a dwelling among his people so that they might recognize and adore his beauty, not merely by one couple but by myriads. Recorded history is the story of God gathering his "new people."

This is not to suggest, however, that it is possible to understand the actions of God in human affairs. The particularities of human existence is neither predictable nor explainable; God has not revealed his orchestration as much as his purposes. John Owen (1616–1683), perhaps the greatest of Puritan writers expressed the point well: "Hath God intrusted [sic] the ministers of the Gospel with His intentions, purposes or counsels, or with His commands and promises?" (*The Death of Death in the Death of Christ, Works*, 10:281).

The providence of God is a mystery far beyond finding out. Adversity and benefit are gifts from God; the "winners" might claim the smile of divine mercy with the recognition of some favorable outcome, but God may have a greater purpose, having little to do with answered prayer or personal piety. Defeat and the burden of consequent circumstances may have a greater, even far greater purpose, than the triumph of one particular party over another.

William Cowper (1731–1800), the inseparable friend of John Newton at Olney, England, captured the thought in a timeless poem:

God moves in a mysterious way,
  His wonders to perform;
He plants his footsteps in the sea,
  And rides upon the storm.

Deep in unfathomable mines
  Of never failing skill,
He treasures up his bright designs,
  And works his sovereign will.

Ye fearful saints, fresh courage take,
  The clouds ye so much dread
are big with mercy, and shall break
  In blessings on your head.

Judge not the Lord by feeble sense,
  But trust him for his grace;
Behind a frowning providence,
  He hides a smiling face.

His purposes will ripen fast,
  Unfolding every hour;
The bud may have a bitter taste,
  But sweet will be the flower.

Blind unbelief is sure to err,
  And scan his work in vain;
God is his own interpreter,
  And he will make it plain.

This is not to suggest the God is capricious or that pain and disappointment should be met with a cavalier attitude of distance and callousness. Fears are real; tragedies abound in our families, nation, and world. Holocausts and natural disasters have brought words like "nine eleven" and "tsunami" into our daily vocabulary just as previous generations had "Rwanda," "Pol Pot," "Joe Stalin," and "Adolph Hitler." The issue of the existence of evil is a difficult problem that often leads to the questioning of divine sovereignty, if not his benevolence. The tension between sovereignty and care has led to a false dichotomy suggesting that either God truly cares but lacks the power to effect his caring—and hence we have a world out of control and humanity left to their own contrivances—or, what might be more frightening, God controls the affairs of humanity but is callous and uncaring. Are ineptitude with care or care without power the only options? The answer is an emphatic "No!" God does care for his creation and lacks no power to accomplish his design. The benefit of human kind is not the primary purpose of God; it is the manifold manifestation, perception, and recognition of his glory that will one day find its ultimate fruition in a new "garden."

Humans are simply finite, rationally limited, and full of self-interest. Stephen Charnock (1628–1680), the English Puritan, made the point persuasively when he noted, "But what if the knowledge of God, and the liberty of the will cannot be reconciled by man? Shall we therefore deny a perfection in God to support liberty in ourselves? Shall we rather fasten ignorance upon God, and accuse Him of blindness, to maintain our liberty?" *(Discourse on the Existence and Attributes of God*, 450).

Second, this work purposes to be an introductory description of the history of our Lord's church. To undertake such an endeavor is daunting in light of the intense scholarship that has preceded this synopsis. The issue of material selection, as well as exclusion, and the manner of description is a matter of bias that this writer recognizes and confesses its blighting affect in undertaking any literary endeavor. The story of the professing church shows evidence of the author's field of study in various graduate programs. The emphasis in the book, evident by space utilization, is upon the impact of the Renaissance in shaping the modern era. While this perspective is clearly valid, it is my hope that the volume will be a

tool for knowledge-acquisition through all the centuries of the church.

Third, this work has been assembled with a variety of learning enhancement devices to hopefully promote comprehension, not merely a literary story. Each chapter is prefaced with instructional objectives so that the reader can more readily conceptualize the content and the major focuses of each chapter. Maps are frequently employed to help the reader grasp the geographical dimensions of the story; sidebars function to provide biographical summaries, definitions of important terms and movements, and descriptive quotations elucidating major points in the text; pictures of prominent personages and selected scenes of historical events and figures are provided to demonstrate the vitality of the past by depicting real-life, influential people and important instances. At the end of each major section of the book is found a list of bibliographical entries designed to provide an avenue for further inquiry in a variety of subjects the reader may desire to pursue. These sections are divided into primary or original source materials that are the actual documentary materials behind and determinative of the structure of the story as well as a host of secondary sources that will allow the reader an opportunity to more readily gain an increased depth in understanding various people, crucial movements, and defining moments. Glossaries defining key terms and events appear at the end of each chapter and collectively at the end of the book. A unique feature of the book is its color throughout, which adds a vitality not possible in black-and-white print.

In every endeavor in life, research and writing being not an exception, there is a mountain of indebtedness that has been incurred. A word suggestive of the depth of appreciation for the sacrifice and kindness of so many seems a very small tribute. It is hard to know where to begin because a sequential rehearsal of important contributors may suggest that some may be more important than others and someone may be inadvertently left out.

Perhaps the starting point should be the recognition of those who helped me in the assembly of this work. My friend, Bill Petro (alias "Doc Rock") has remained an encouragement in a brother-like relationship for years; his particular contribution to this work was in the assembly of numerous sidebars that appear throughout the book. His love for the past should impress scholars and encourage the untrained to be "lay history buffs." There were several graduate students who caught the vision of this book, helping me immensely. Foremost among them is Dan Roeber, one of my recent graduate students and a teaching assistant. He sacrificed significantly to assist in the creation of the instructional objective in each chapter, the glossaries of terms, and the indexes.

There was a sabbatical graciously and sacrificially granted by the institution of my primary employment for which recognition and thanks are due. I was able to finish a writing project that had essentially languished due to classroom and administrative duties and begin this one. Secretaries are rather specially gifted people in administrative techniques and people management. I have been graced with a wonderfully caring "executive," Mrs. Beth Motley. She is one of those rare persons who not only does her work well but shares in my professional projects as if they were her own. Then, I would be remiss if I did not mention the staff of Turpin Library, Dallas Theological Seminary, and in particular Mr. Jeff Webster. Their helpful kindnesses expressed in response to my interests and inquiries have been both gracious and professional. Jeff's gentle interest and work has never been tainted by the least hint of irritation or hurry. I am thankful for a dear professional, an adept friend, and a colleague.

The hours writing requires in the context of the duties of teaching mandates sacrifice of time from family and friends. Though we are now empty nesters, a writing project at the institution I serve makes it a second or third job, executed in the evenings and on weekends, and even during vacations and trips to see the grandchildren. I am thankful for a wife who understands that in the ministry of serving the churches there is really no forty- or sixty-hour work week and yet with little resistance has been a consummate companion, friend, and counselor. My children, now mature ladies with their own little broods, remain my joy and comfort, even from a distance. Their husbands are fine, godly men who make a father-in-law thankful and proud. Our grandchildren are both a challenge to my quest for quiet and an inspiration filling me with delight, joy, and hope. I am blessed with a wonderful family that has made my continuance in teaching possible. Words cannot capture my sense of gratitude to them, however important words may be.

Lastly, in what seems to be a common refrain in many prefaces, I must confess my fallibility. It was some old Puritan long ago who commented, "Lord do not lead me into error, for thou doest know how hard it is to change my mind." For errors in writing, I accept full responsibility; for misjudgment and distortion of the perimeters of interpretative permissibility, I render my apologies. I have sought to be fair and knowledgeable with my comments both in tone and presentation, but recognize that I, like others, am bound by the restrictions of perspectivalism and prejudice.

OUTLINE OF BOOK

PROLOGUE

Isaiah 40:12–26

¹²Who has measured the waters in the hollow of his hand,
    or with the breadth of his hand marked off the heavens?
Who has held the dust of the earth in a basket,
    or weighed the mountains on the scales
    and the hills in a balance?
¹³Who can fathom the Spirit of the LORD,
    or instruct the LORD as his counselor?
¹⁴Whom did the LORD consult to enlighten him,
    and who taught him the right way?
Who was it that taught him knowledge,
    or showed him the path of understanding?

¹⁵Surely the nations are like a drop in a bucket;
    they are regarded as dust on the scales;
    he weighs the islands as though they were fine dust.
¹⁶Lebanon is not sufficient for altar fires,
    nor its animals enough for burnt offerings.
¹⁷Before him all the nations are as nothing;
    they are regarded by him as worthless
    and less than nothing.

¹⁸With whom, then, will you compare God?
    To what image will you liken him?
¹⁹As for an idol, a metalworker casts it,
    and a goldsmith overlays it with gold
    and fashions silver chains for it.

²⁰A person too poor to present such an offering
    selects wood that will not rot;
they look for a skilled worker
    to set up an idol that will not topple.

²¹Do you not know?
    Have you not heard?
Has it not been told you from the beginning?
    Have you not understood since the earth was founded?
²²He sits enthroned above the circle of the earth,
    and its people are like grasshoppers.
He stretches out the heavens like a canopy,
    and spreads them out like a tent to live in.
²³He brings princes to naught
    and reduces the rulers of this world to nothing.
²⁴No sooner are they planted,
    no sooner are they sown,
    no sooner do they take root in the ground,
than he blows on them and they wither,
    and a whirlwind sweeps them away like chaff.

²⁵"To whom will you compare me?
    Or who is my equal?" says the Holy One.
²⁶Lift up your eyes and look to the heavens:
    Who created all these?
He who brings out the starry host one by one
    and calls forth each of them by name.
Because of his great power and mighty strength,
    not one of them is missing.

Romans 1:18–32

¹⁸The wrath of God is being revealed from heaven against all the godlessness and wickedness of people, who suppress the truth by their wickedness, ¹⁹since what may be known about God is plain to them, because God has made it plain to them. ²⁰For since the creation of the world God's invisible qualities—his eternal power and divine nature—have been clearly seen, being understood from what has been made, so that people are without excuse.

²¹For although they knew God, they neither glorified him as God nor gave thanks to him, but their thinking became futile and their foolish hearts were darkened. ²²Although they claimed to be wise, they became fools ²³and exchanged the glory of the immortal God for images made to look like a mortal human being and birds and animals and reptiles.

²⁴Therefore God gave them over in the sinful desires of their hearts to sexual impurity for the

degrading of their bodies with one another. [25]They exchanged the truth about God for a lie, and worshiped and served created things rather than the Creator—who is forever praised. Amen.

[26]Because of this, God gave them over to shameful lusts. Even their women exchanged natural sexual relations for unnatural ones. [27]In the same way the men also abandoned natural relations with women and were inflamed with lust for one another. Men committed shameful acts with other men, and received in themselves the due penalty for their error.

[28]Furthermore, just as they did not think it worthwhile to retain the knowledge of God, so God gave them over to a depraved mind, so that they do what ought not to be done. [29]They have become filled with every kind of wickedness, evil, greed and depravity. They are full of envy, murder, strife, deceit and malice. They are gossips, [30]slanderers, God-haters, insolent, arrogant and boastful; they invent ways of doing evil; they disobey their parents; [31]they have no understanding, no fidelity, no love, no mercy. [32]Although they know God's righteous decree that those who do such things deserve death, they not only continue to do these very things but also approve of those who practice them.

Hebrews 2:1–10

[1]We must pay the most careful attention, therefore, to what we have heard, so that we do not drift away. [2]For since the message spoken through angels was binding, and every violation and disobedience received its just punishment, [3]how shall we escape if we ignore so great a salvation? This salvation, which was first announced by the Lord, was confirmed to us by those who heard him. [4]God also testified to it by signs, wonders and various miracles, and by gifts of the Holy Spirit distributed according to his will.

[5]It is not to angels that he has subjected the world to come, about which we are speaking. [6]But there is a place where someone has testified:

[7]"What is mankind that you are mindful of them,
    a son of man that you care for him?
[8]You made them a little[a] lower than the angels;
    you crowned them with glory and honor
    and put everything under their feet."

In putting everything under them, God left nothing that is not subject to them. Yet at present we do not see everything subject to them. [9]But we do see Jesus, who was made lower than the angels for a little while, now crowned with glory and honor because he suffered death, so that by the grace of God he might taste death for everyone.

[10]In bringing many sons and daughters to glory, it was fitting that God, for whom and through whom everything exists, should make the pioneer of their salvation perfect through what he suffered.

Introduction Outline

The Benefits of the Study of the Christian Church

The Structure of History: The Views from the Academy

A Structure of History: A View from the Church

The Meaning of History: The Glory of God

The Structure for the Study of Church History
    Ancient Church
    Medieval Church
    Modern Church
    Postmodern Church

The Scope and Limitations of This Study

Introduction Objectives

- That the reader will describe why the study of church history is useful for the present and the future

- That the reader will distinguish between circular, linear, and progressive views of history

- That the reader will identify major figures in the study of history

- That the reader will describe the structure and meaning of history from the perspective of the church

- That the reader will identify the four main periods of church history by name and time period

- That the reader will identify the three major expressions of the Christian faith

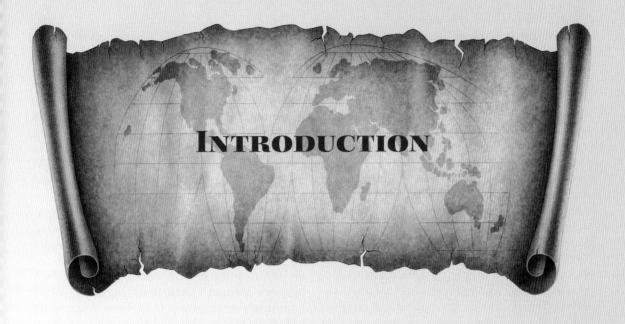

INTRODUCTION

T HE APOSTLE JOHN ENDED his account of the claims of the Lord Jesus by stating that, if all that Jesus did had been recorded, the libraries of the world would not have the shelf space to house them (John 21:25). That is an amazing assertion.

Centuries have passed since that remarkable person entered the world that he had created; in fact, though he lived among us briefly, he spawned a movement that is truly unexplainable from natural perspectives. It has always appeared a frail movement. Hostile political states have severely persecuted it; armies have relentlessly endeavored to crush it; zealous visionaries from within have proven disastrous pied-pipers; heretics have attempted to redefine and control it; and friends have shown themselves, at times, to be as dangerous as its enemies. Yet, from a small band of fearfully distraught followers, the story of the Christ has been told with remarkable courage and sacrifice over and over through the centuries. Christianity has spread to the nations of the world with tremendous vitality. The Christian faith quickly became a global movement that has ebbed and flowed through the pages of the centuries. It has conquered nations, been conquered by them, and yet has sustained an undeniably enduring quality.

It is that story, or shall we say "his story," that is the focus of this study. As a discipline, history is the study of the recorded past with the goal of presenting it to contemporaries; it is learning through historical inquiry, the gathering of records with a view to telling a story. Ultimately, it is an attempt, through the search of the past, to explain the meaning and function of the present while providing hope and direction for the future. Church history, the focus of this inquiry, is the story of the "body of Jesus Christ," the people of God fashioned through the atoning death of the incarnate Son of God, infused with the Spirit of God, overwhelmed with a sense of divine forgiveness, and motivated to live life in such a way as to represent him in society at large, the home, the visible church, and to neighbors near and distant from no other motive than to respond intellectually, physically, and emotionally to such great fortune. This is a love story; it is a narrative of a people who have sought and seek to love the Lord their God with all their heart, soul, and mind and their neighbors as they do themselves (Matt. 22:37, 39). It is a movement that is blind to ethnicity, nationalism, economic status, and educational accomplishments. It is found in the poorest of cultures and in the economic wealth of the advanced western nations. It is red, yellow, black, white, and brown. It transcends all these things because they are not the most important issues in life. There is emptiness in the human soul, restlessness in the spirit of mankind, and only satisfaction and delight in the Lord Jesus will transcend the deepest human needs and social differences.

The Benefits of the Study of the Christian Church

Though it may be impossible to cross "the ugly broad ditch," to know the past accurately, because it cannot be duplicated, the sources are biased, and the human mind cursed with prejudice, is there no benefit in the attempt? Gotthold Ephraim Lessing (1729–1781), a prominent figure in the development of the **Enlightenment**, a movement whose principal assumptions were that the rational facilities are a more sure guide to truth than any ancient, external authorities, believed new insights would offer hope for peace, harmony, and the perfectibility of mankind through rational reflection, progress in the sciences, and the inevitability of social progress. Lessing argued that history is not a sufficient guide for contemporaries because it cannot be accurately re-represented. This is evident in the emergence of the Hobbesian despair of certainty. Lessing contended that the past is an uncertain guide to truth because most of it has been inaccurately recorded and transmitted.

This, he and others argued, is clearly applicable to Christian truth claims, which are based upon fallible eyewitnesses (since all people are error prone). For example, the Christian assertion of miracles, he stated, is the product of more mistruth than truth because people commonly exaggerate. It is more reasonable to believe that people lied about miracles happening than that they actually happened.[1]

The assumption that reason alone can discover what is true has been turned upside down by postmodernist scholars; it is an absolutist claim that cannot be absolutely proven. Further, the rationalist denial of the possibility of the supernatural has led western civilization to the twilight of despair. It has produced failed materialistic-political approaches to life, huge governmental attempts to organize social cohesiveness, and the loss of personal and corporate meaning. By despairing of past solutions to complex human problems, the Enlightenment enterprise put its hopes for the betterment of mankind in restructuring social and cultural structures through the sciences. Man became mind, progress became quantifiable **materialism**, aesthetics was lost, and the spiritual was crushed.

The ground for this study, this retelling of a story, is that the past is valuable for the present and it has something to offer to lead us into

---

1. This is based on the assertion that all truth is empirically verifiable through observation and repetition. Christian faith is rooted in the reality of one-time occurrences, such as the incarnation and the resurrection, and the truth of the possibility of divine intervention.

the future with hope. Time is a seamless garment; it can only be compartmentalized with great loss. Most particularly, knowledge of the history of Christianity, for those who cherish it, must be constantly retold because the lessons garnered from the past are invaluable. Let me list a few of those lessons before we proceed. Here are a few.

First, the story of Christianity is a powerful argument for the validity of Christian truth claims. The place to begin, it seems, is to broach the question of the nature of knowing or certainty. When it is said that something is true, it means that it is *more reasonable* that it is true than false. That is, arguments can be amassed that hopefully entitle an affirmation as valid. It does not mean that arguments cannot be presented against a truth-claim; it is that the claim is reasonable. The criterion of reasonableness is not concerned that a belief system begins with several unprovable assumptions; it is that the worldview developed from those assumptions explains the world as it is, broken and dysfunctional, and offers hope. Christianity, which assumes the existence of God and his communication to humankind, most poignantly in the Bible, claims to do just that; it explains the problems in society and offers peace and hope. This is where the story of Christianity becomes important. Though the history of Christianity has regrettable episodes and derelictions have abounded at times, the centuries of its existence bear proof that it is true. It has brought hope to the hopeless, peace to the forsaken, strength to the weakened, and purpose to the downtrodden. Christian faith is not true because of this; these things suggest that it is true.

Second, a knowledge of the history of the church not only provides a potent argument, it allows us to understand why the church today thinks the way it does, why it uses the language it does, why it worships as it does. Prejudices and insights have historic roots that are helpful to plumb in order to understand current issues and, thereby, help us to have a sense of stability in changing times.

Third, a knowledge of church history gives perspective to our own times. These are neither the worst of times nor the best of times! The knowledge of church history suggests that some things are timeless, but much is not. It preserves the church from fads and novelty. We have the tendency to perceive new programs and methods as having messianic promises of success, thus falling into the trap of thinking that novelty, accompanied with zeal, is *the* catalyst for church growth. History teaches that there are few great events or life-changing moments; on the contrary, change is very gradual. It is the little things that bring about significant alteration in culture. In short, knowledge of the past can be a preventative; it can help us separate the merely exciting, but temporary, from the enduring and eternal.

Fourth, it reminds us that we are part of the body of Christ that is far more extensive than our private beliefs or denominational affiliations. It should deliver us from provincialism, pride, and arrogance borne of the idea that any one church or ecclesiastical tradition stands in the exclusive heritage of first-century orthodoxy. It should help all to realize that the church of Jesus Christ is a global community that easily transcends the boundaries of ethnicity, nationality, economic status, or intellectual progress.

Fifth, knowledge of the history of the church will preserve the church from error; it provides apologetic weapons against deception. The accumulated wisdom of the church can provide an arsenal of arguments as we struggle to preserve the church today from opponents within and without. History exhibits patterns in the work of God that may be applicable today.

LESSONS OF CHURCH HISTORY

1. Validates Christian truth claims

2. Provides rootedness

3. Gives perspective

4. Prevents pride and provincialism

5. Arms against error

6. Offers hope

7. Provides inspiration

8. Presents knowledge and wisdom

in triumphal anticipation of the day when the kingdoms of this world will be put under Christ's feet, and the bride, without spot or wrinkle, will be given to the king. Such knowledge can dispel the sense of loneliness and isolation that is characteristic of the present times with its stress on the temporal, peripheral, and sensational.

Seventh, throughout the history of the church, women and men have provided a rich literary depository with regard to the spiritual life. The lives of many, recorded in their writings or biographies, have inspired and directed subsequent generations of saints. Numerous books on Christian spirituality in the annals of the church offer counsel, solace, and insight.

Finally, history can be a sourcebook of knowledge. To guide our path the Lord has given his people a rich heritage. The sources of helpful information are several: the *Bible*, which is the supreme authority for life and the corrective for the errors perpetuated by other sources; *reason*, though it is subject to misperception and bias; *natural history*; *experience*; and the *collective memory of the past*, which historians of the church call tradition. Knowledge of the past provides stability in the uncertain present and hope for the future. How the church has gone about its work in the past, how it faced its challenges, how it has understood the Bible are all aids as we seek to serve our generation.

The Structure of History: The Views from the Academy

The study of history is as old as Herodotus, the fifth-century BC[2] Greek who described the Per-

Sixth, an understanding of the past can give us a sense of calm in turbulent times and assurance that the Lord's church will ultimately triumph. The devil has employed every strategy to destroy the church, armies have marched against it, faithless scholarship has relentlessly assaulted it, internal bickering has rent it, and martyrdom has depleted its ranks from time to time. Yet the church marches forward

---

2. A recent trend in the scholarly designation of the past has been to refer to the era before Christ as "Before the Common Era [BCE]" and the period after Christ as the "Common Era [CE]," a not-so-subtle attempt, at least it may be argued, to express the point that Christ is not the centerpiece of human history. Such a movement is consistent with the secularizing trends in literary arts that became obvious in the previous century within academic circles. I have chosen to use the traditional designations for the division of history based on the assumption that the incarnation of Jesus Christ is the central focus of redemptive history, that the story of time is that of the promise, advent, and return of Jesus.

sian Wars, and Thucydides, an Athenian who later described the Peloponnesian Wars. The earliest view of history, whether from China, India, Persia, or the Greeks, was to see it as cyclical or circular. Nations, dynasties, cultures have a rise, maturity, and decline (though often the cycle was seen as retrogression from a "golden era" or the harbinger of rebirth from a dull one [the **Renaissance** view]). Perhaps the most famous, recent exponents of such a view were Oswald Spengler (1880–1936), *The Decline of the West*, and Arnold Toynbee (1889–1975), *A Study of History*. The latter, however, combined a cyclical view with a linear view of progress in time. Though Toynbee did not see Christianity as the final truth, he adopted the Christian notion of history as the embodiment of progress toward a goal; he embraced the idea of cycles, but not endless cycles. The cyclical/linear combination view is, perhaps, best illustrated in the work of the American Christian historian, Kenneth Scott Latourette (1884–1968), whose massive histories of the Christian church and Christian missions, combined the ideas of successive waves of declension, followed by ever-longer waves of progress, culminating in an endless wave of the dominance of Christian faith, a **postmillennial**, progressive **idealism**.

As Christianity emerged into the Roman world with its message of profound hope, the naturalistic or spirited, often fatalistic, circular theory of history was displaced. For Christians, history is one of linear progress toward a goal orchestrated by the Lord, who directs the events of this world by providential care and intervention. History is inexorably on a path that will end in the triumph of God over his enemies and reign over his own people forever. At times of perceived Christian triumph, such as during the reign of Constantine in the fourth century and several Frankish and Carolingian kings of the medieval era, the sixteenth century Reformations (particularly in England), and among the late nineteenth century and early twentieth century liberal progressivists, the kingdom of

the king and that of earthly kings seemed to have blurred. In times of political uncertainty, hostility, and persecution, the two kingdoms were separated. Both views appear to be overstated expressions of contemporary myopia.

In articulating a theory of history from a Christian perspective, Augustine (354–430) has had an immense influence. Writing to explain how an empire that embraced the Christian faith could be in the death throes of pagan invasion (Alaric's pillage of Rome in 410), the bishop of Hippo articulated a general theory of the flow of history, a history of nations, and a theodicy. To explain why the empire was crumbling, he argued for a divinely orchestrated and providentially secured notion of the rise and fall of nations. In brief, he argued that God rises up nations for a divine purpose (such as the emergence of the Christian faith) and preserves

A portrait (c. 1480) of Augustine by Sandro Botticelli (1445–1510). At Church of Ognissanti, Florence. Courtesy of the Yorck Project.

them according to his purposes by curbing their lawlessness and granting them success. When his purpose for a nation ends, he withholds his preserving mercies, allowing them to voluntarily devolve into exploitation and selfishness, and then justly condemns and destroys them.

Augustine also postulated a providential theory of cosmic history, a theory that is more linear than progressive (though it had components of both), interventionist, and eschatological. Since the fall of humankind, the world, argued Augustine, is composed of two entities, each characterized by love, but having vastly different objects of love. The City of Man, the Earthly City, is characterized by self-love, false gods, envy, strife, and brute strength. The City of God, the Heavenly City, is the creation of the true God and partakes of his character. These two cities, intertwined in existences, share the same joys and afflictions in this life though they have different faith-objects, expectations, loves, and ends (*The City of God*, 14.28, 18.54). The inhabitants of the "heavenly city" use the good of the world to enjoy God; citizens of the "earthly city" use God that they might enjoy the world (15.7). At the end of time (though there is no end to existence), the two kingdoms will be dissolved in a divine judgment: the righteous will be received into a spiritual kingdom that Christ purchased, and the wicked will be received into an existence devoid of divine blessing and comfort forever (20.6).

The general theory of history delineated by Augustine was embraced with variations through the Christian era (400–1750) until the secularizing tendencies of the Enlightenment emerged in the eighteenth century. The empirical and materialist approaches taken by many eighteenth-century scholars and churchmen precluded the possibility of the supernatural, interventionist assumptions of historic Christianity. Instead, the forces for change were increasingly deposited in natural causes and God was relegated to "the-watch-presupposes-a-watch-maker" theory of a distant god who operates the universe by the law he imposed on it at

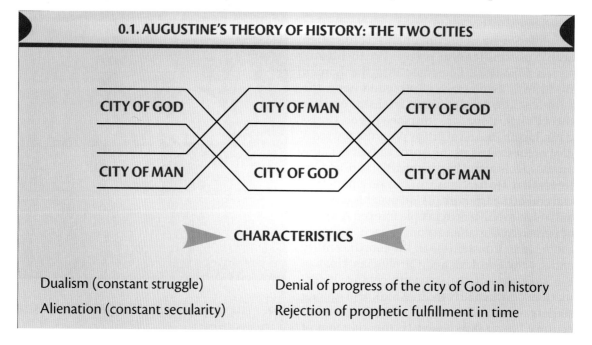

0.1. AUGUSTINE'S THEORY OF HISTORY: THE TWO CITIES

| CITY OF GOD | CITY OF MAN | CITY OF GOD |
| CITY OF MAN | CITY OF GOD | CITY OF MAN |

CHARACTERISTICS

Dualism (constant struggle)   Denial of progress of the city of God in history

Alienation (constant secularity)   Rejection of prophetic fulfillment in time

creation, never to intervene again. Natural processes replaced miracles, mere earthly progress replaced the *eschaton*, and the hope of a better human existence preempted the promise of heaven.

Integral to the rejection of divine interventionism was the emergence of a more optimistic assessment of human moral and spiritual abilities and, its corollary, the embrace of the notion of the perfectibility of man. Historic Christian faith has strenuously argued that the human species is irreparably blighted by sin. The hope of retrieval is only partial in this life through the Savior of the world, but complete when time will be no more. Enlightenment advocates announced a new, more favorable assessment of the human condition and turned a future heaven into the not-yet of scientific and moral advance.

While Christians have asserted moral and spiritual responsibilities to improve the plight of the neighbor, they have tempered their enthusiasm for progress, not the endeavor itself, with the realization that perfection awaits another realm of existence. The worst demonstrations of human behavior can be ameliorated by social, economic, and political action, but they cannot be eradicated. Simply stated, human nature is educatable, but the evil of it is not eradicable.

In the history of philosophy, no one is more central than Georg Hegel (1770–1831). Hegel argued that time and human nature is not static, but is subject to advance through the convergence of conflicting opposites, creating new syntheses that push humankind in a forward, ascending spiral of degrees of perfectibility. Spiritual forces, the impersonal *Geist*, propel the quest of humankind for freedom or self-consciousness. Christianity is reduced to a primitive, now archaic, steppingstone of humankind on the way to perfectibility.

The elasticity of Hegel's historical and philosophical theory was applied to sociology by August Comte (1798–1857). Comte, the father of modern sociology, argued that humankind has progressed through three stages on the road to perfectibility: the religious stage, the philosophical stage, and the sociological stage. For Comte, sociology was the key to progress with the philosophical and theological stages inferior steppingstones. Hegel also influenced Karl Marx, Herbert Spencer, Adolph Hitler, and others. Truth became relative, temporary perceptions in the upward march of time.

A reaction to the philosophical school of historical development can be seen in the rise of nineteenth-century **historicism**. Advocates of historicism rejected the notion of human perfectibility and progress through rationalism, moving historical change even further from

Oil painting of Georg Hegel by Jakob Schlesinger in 1831. Courtesy of FreeArt1.

Christian assumptions. Historicists, such as R. G. Collingwood, argued that each age is an age unto itself, created and advancing through its own unique intuitive powers. The approach is rooted in nineteenth century **Romanticism** that infused nationalistic pride with a spiritual pietism. In brief, historicism, emergent in Germany, took the form of radical nationalism. The state was elevated to the status of redeemer, not the individual or, in the case of Christianity, the Christ. Historicism offered immediate gratification by arduous application of its principles. The Christian's hope is in a temporally shadowed, but ultimately deferred, fulfillment of expectations. Both made significant impact upon our world, but the promises of enlightened progress and nationalistic pride have failed; they have proven empty and destructive. Christianity argues that hope deferred is real hope that awaits realization; that this world, being only a shadow of reality, an imperfect one at that, at its best moments only prefigures a better world to come.

While historicists found the clue to progress in national character, Marxists offered a more extreme explanation of the progress of history, its nature, and cause. Often denominated as **Marxist materialism**, it is, perhaps, more accurately described as economic materialism. Indebted to Hegel for the thought that man participates in the historical process as an active, causative agent of change, Marx rejected Hegel's **idealism**, viewing man as only material. He, therefore, saw man's highest potential blunted by the lack of material equality or the disproportionate control of it by an elite. Marx and Engel saw economic disparity as the origin of humanity's failure to reach its potential. They believed this could be reversed by social and economic equalitarianism (unfortunately imposed by force should the need arises to do so). Like historicism, Marx's economic materialism, as an explanation of the human dilemma and a source of hope, has proven disastrous for those who have been forced to embrace it.

The cenotaph of Karl Marx, East Highgate Cemetery, London. Courtesy of Paasikivi.

Postmodern historiography has rejected the possibility of a cosmic pattern in history and has found comfort in individualized hopes and private aspirations. Sadly, postmoderns can detect no plan or purpose in the universe. Time is not circular, linear, or progressive. It is erratic and unpredictable. It makes no sense! They correctly see that the brilliant rhetoric of the historians and philosophers of the Enlightenment whose "messianic" promises of the improvement of the human race has proven empty in the heartrending devastations brought to our world by the most advanced nations. The idea of the improvement of human nature through economic and social progress has become a delusion. Postmoderns have seen the folly of technological redeemers, but they have turned inward to find meaning. Perhaps, it is wiser to argue that redemption is not in this world, that intellectual redeemers can only give us vaporous illusions of hope that time and experience dash into tiny pieces. It could be that the assertion of the Christian faith that hope came to us in the person of the Christ is worthy of renewed consideration. Because the enormous advances of the applied sciences cannot grasp "heaven," it may be time to reconsider the Augustinian maxim that "heaven" will always be elsewhere!

A Structure of History: A View from the Church

From a Christian perspective, physical existence is a created phenomenon. We believe that God created the universe by speaking it effortlessly into existence (Ps. 33) and constantly sustains it by his moment-by-moment power. It had a beginning and will have an end (2 Pet. 3). Viewing the centuries from that perspective, from the pages of the Bible, it is appropriate to ask the question, what is the purpose of the creation? Having raised the issue, it might prove helpful to situate church history into the larger panorama of the history of the world. In essence, the Christian perspective on history, at least in part, is a divine stage on which the wonder of redemption is enacted. The Bible explains the redemptive drama from the beginning of time to its end, though there are significant gaps in the story (i.e., the Bible does not provide a history of the centuries, though some have viewed the book of Revelation as a divine time line of the centuries between the advents of the Christ). The history of humankind involves a huge plot that exists as a "golden thread" through the story of nations and families. As Augustine argued, God is calling out of the "City of Man" the "City of God." Though the two cities share many of the same vicissitudes of life, they are distinct cities because of separate goals, motives, and ultimate objects. The Bible describes this grand metanarrative. It explains how a pristine creation became corrupted and how it is being, and will be, restored.

The Christ is the focal point of all history (Heb. 1:1). He created the world and sustains it

(John 1:3; Col. 1:16–17; Heb. 1:3, 2:10). He is also the end of history. There will come a day when Christ will bring time to a conclusion. At that moment, he will be the centerpiece for eternity. He is the "alpha and omega," the beginning and the end. However, there is something more. He is the center of history. Jesus, who is called the Lord and the Christ, is the most important figure of all times; he alone is central. Before secularism divided history into two "common" eras, it was normal to segment history before Christ (BC) and after Christ (AD); Christians embrace a third era to follow the second called "fulfillment" in which all of God's promises will find fruition. The Old Testament Scriptures anticipated his incarnation; the New Testament Gospels describe it; the Epistles of the New Testament delineate the proclamation of his message in the first century; and Revelation describes its culmination in the "new heavens and new earth." The Hebrew Scriptures, rightly interpreted, have a christocentric focus. Luke tells us that Jesus on the Emmaus road "beginning with Moses and with all the Prophets . . . explained to them what was said in all the Scriptures" (24:27). Jesus said on another occasion, "You study the Scriptures diligently because you think that in them you have eternal life. These are the very Scriptures that testify about me" (John 5:39). Christians today look back upon what the prophets of old longed for, the coming of the Christ (1 Pet. 1:10–12). We look back to the first century and also anxiously anticipate the return of the king the prophets anticipated. When he comes a second time, time will end and a new world will begin that will last forever.

Though the Christian Bible is composed of two unequal parts, the Hebrew Scriptures and the Greek Scriptures, the Old Testament and the New Testament, it is unified by one, single promise, the promise that God made to Abraham to bless all the nations of the earth through his greater progeny, Jesus Christ (Gen. 12, 15, 17). The promise to Abraham was threefold: a land, a seed, and a blessing. The ultimate fulfillment of the land promise is spiritual in nature though the shadowed fulfillments are physical. This is evident in that the "seed" promised to him is interpreted by the Apostle Paul (Gal. 3:16) as a reference to Christ. The blessing itself in its final fulfillment will be the redemption of the nations through the Christ in the eternal state.

The Bible's central theme is redemption. Redemption was anticipated in the Old Testament writings, procured in the New Testament Gospel accounts through Christ, and applied in the other books of the New Testament down to the end of time through the preaching of the gospel. It reached its penultimate fulfillment at the conclusion of the book of the Revelation, the description of a world with remarkable parallels to the original creation in Gen. 1–2.

The Old Testament contains what is described as the Old Covenant, the promises to the ancient people of God; the New Testament gives us the New Covenant, the promises to the new people of God. The Old Covenant is presented to us in Exodus 19 and repeated in Deuteronomy 5. The New Covenant is promised in Jeremiah 31 and instituted in Christ's death (Matt. 26, Heb. 8). The differences between the two great covenants are made clear in Hebrews, a book whose central concern is to explain the superior qualities of the New Covenant over the old one. In essence, the New Covenant is superior because it is based on better promises through a superior priest, Christ, and his superior once-for-all-times sacrifice. The Passover lamb is a figure of Christ, the true Lamb that takes away sin forever.

The Old Testament is a book of shadows (Heb. 10:1) that anticipates the promised seed of Abraham, Christ. In figure and ceremony, the Old Testament taught the believer to expect a greater One to come who would bring a greater deliverance. It is the great era of anticipation! The Old Testament progressively reveals two things to the inquiring reader. First, it reveals the person who would bring redemption to his people.

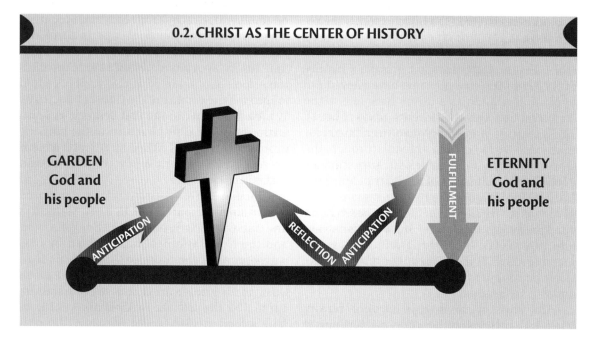

0.2. CHRIST AS THE CENTER OF HISTORY

GARDEN
God and
his people

ANTICIPATION

REFLECTION ANTICIPATION

FULFILLMENT

ETERNITY
God and
his people

- Genesis 3:15: a male child born of a woman

- Genesis 9:26: a male Semite (a son of Shem)

- Genesis 12:3: a son born of the Semite Abraham

- Genesis 49:10: a son born of Isaac's son Jacob, and of Jacob's son Judah

- 2 Samuel 7:14: a son of David of Judah's descendants, a king

- Isaiah 7:14: a son born of a virgin in Israel

- Micah 5:2: a son born in Bethlehem whose days are from eternity.

Second, the Old Testament progressively reveals what this person would do to accomplish the redemption of his people. In this capacity the roles of priest and king were combined; he has the character and station to represent his people being a divine mediator and royal prince!

- Genesis 3:15: the redemption involved violence

- Exodus 12:1–28: the redeemer is a "lamb" whose blood will protect from death

- Leviticus 16:1–34: the redeemer is a slain "goat" that covers sin, making expiation

- Isaiah 52:13–53:12: the redeemer is an astonishing (52:13–15), misunderstood (53:1–3), vicarious (53:4–6), submissive (53:7–9), and a righteously-bruised-exalted deliverer (53:10–13).

The New Testament gospel writers identify that the One promised in the Old Testament who came to suffer and die for his people is Jesus. He is the long-anticipated One. First, it tells us who this one would be, Jesus Christ the Lord (Matt.1:21, 23). Second, the New Testament tells us he did what was foretold of him. He is the fulfillment of Old Testament prediction. For example, Jesus commented that the prophets anticipated his arrest ("How would the Scriptures be fulfilled that say it must happen in this way" [Matt. 26:54]). The Christ is the fulfillment of the sacrificial lamb-figure of the Hebrew Scriptures.

- John 1:29: "the Lamb of God"

- 1 Corinthians 5:7: "For even Christ our passover has been sacrificed for us."

- 1 Peter 1:18–19: "the precious blood of Christ, a lamb"

- 1 John 1:17: "the blood of Jesus, his Son purifies us from all sin"

The Gospels and the Epistles of the New Testament tell us what Jesus accomplished; Revelation describes its completion. All the nations will be blessed in Abraham through his greater Son, who will reign over all peoples forever. Thus, the Old Testament is a book of *shadows*; the New Testament is a book of *light*. What was *enfolded* in the Old Testament is *unfolded* in the New Testament; what was *promised* in the Old has been *realized* in the New. However, to this day we "see through a glass darkly," but in a future day we will see more clearly. The Gospels and the Epistles are replete with fulfillment and anticipation. Salvation has come; sin has been judged, but it has not been removed. When Christ comes again, he will destroy his enemies and welcome his children into a final, forever rest. That period is the time of the ultimate fulfillment of the promises given after the fall of mankind (Gen. 3:15) to Abraham (Gen. 12:1–3).

The Bible envisions three eras of history. Biblical scholars commonly speak of the Old Testament era, the New Testament era, and the Kingdom; or, a period that was, a period that is, and a period that will be. Hebrews 1:1-2 speaks of a time long ago when God spoke "to the fathers . . . by the prophets" ("past . . . ignorance," Acts 17:30) and "in these last days he has spoken to us by his Son." In this Hebrews passage, the writer is indicating that the Jews thought of only two ages—former times and latter times. They thought they were living in the former times, because they did not think the "latter times" had come in the spiritualized kingdom inaugurated by Christ. The latter times are divided into two parts: the time between Christ's two advents and a period of his full reign as the triumphant king after his second coming. Hebrews refers to the time between the two advents of Christ as the "last days" (1:2) and the "time of the new order" (9:10) that will end when Christ appears a "second time (this time in judgment) at the "consummation of the ages" (9:26). Peter, in his sermon recorded by Luke (Acts 3:19–24), says that the prophets from Samuel announced "these days," the latter days, and that Jesus will not return to earth "until the time comes for God to restore everything" (v. 21), or the latter part of the latter days. The Jews envisioned only two eras in all of history, the former days and the latter days, the promise of Messiah and the advent of Messiah. They saw Messiah as reigning politically and religiously, not crucified and resurrected. They did not see the latter days in two parts, thereby segmenting history into only two eras, with Messiah reigning most fully at its end and forever.

The study of church history focuses on the "new people of God"; it concerns itself with the events between the two advents of Christ. It is the story of the redemptive purposes of God in the second great period of all time, the period when God's people look back to

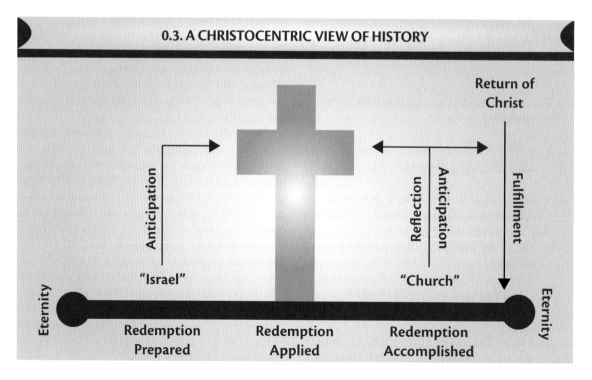

0.3. A CHRISTOCENTRIC VIEW OF HISTORY

Return of Christ

Anticipation

Reflection Anticipation

Fulfillment

Eternity

"Israel"

"Church"

Eternity

Redemption Prepared

Redemption Applied

Redemption Accomplished

celebrate the coming of the One the Old Testament prophets promised and who live in anticipation of his return when the redemption of humankind will be complete, the earth restored to its pristine beauty, and a people will have been gathered from the nations through the centuries to worship and adore the "Lamb" forever and ever. The history of the church is the story of the proclamation of the gospel: its defense, clarification, and extension for over twenty centuries since our Lord commanded us to make disciples of all the nations through going and baptizing, accompanied with the comforting promise that the endeavor will not fail because he, through his Spirit, will be with us until the task is complete (Matt. 28:19–20).

There have been times of great external success in going, telling, and receiving; the Christian faith has made significant strides among the nations. At other times, the fortunes of the church have been crushed under the persecuting blows of its enemies, even supposed friends. Sometimes in the name of the church, its leadership has persecuted the church. The Christian movement is so varied and different than others. When it is numerically strong, it has proven to be spiritually weak and culturally ineffective; when it has suffered alienation, it has risen with great impact. The story of the Christian church is not an easy story to tell because it is not the same as institutions, movements, and denominations. It is an invisible movement, the most "real" entity in this world of the surreal and shadows. This is a real world, and ought not be minimized, yet there is a coming world more "real" than this one, a city whose builder and maker is God!

The Meaning of History: The Glory of God

To gain an even deeper perspective of the meaning of history from a Christian perspective, it is important to grasp that though a re-demptive metanarrative threads through the Bible, it is not, in itself, the final or ultimate purpose in God's creative and recreative activity. Redemption is a wonderfully profound, but secondary reason for the creation, the sustaining of it, and the restoration of humankind and the universe. What, then, is the deepest reason God created the universe, placed humans on a sphere called the earth, witnesses the violence and inhumanity of his creatures, and some day will return it all to uprightness?

In short, the answer is that God's fundamental interest is his own glory (Rom. 11:36). God delights in himself alone, for who is the measure of his worth and beauty but he himself alone! For God to take delight in less than himself is to delight in inferiorities. Further, God not only shares mutual love and delight in his Trinitarian existence, he delights in exuding that delight so as to delight even more in beholding his beauty. God made the world so as to behold his own beauty and humans to reflect that beauty. God delights in himself and in the extension of himself. He delights in the praise emanating from his own creation. Praise does not make God better, nor does its refusal cause deletion. He alone is the all-sufficient, self-sufficient God, needing nothing. He simply delights in praise!

Why, then, did God make the world and inhabit it with animals and humans? He did it so that he could behold himself in his workmanship. He made a realm of symmetry and beauty because he is symmetry and beauty. The biblical fall has marred that world so that the capacity to accomplish its divine purpose has become severely encumbered. Peace and harmony have been replaced by avarice and war. The animal kingdom is in rebellion; creation groans for a day when thistles and weeds will no longer limit flowers from blooming at full strength and trees from foliating in abundance. Humanity is a wrecked vestige of his created potential. God is now glorified to a lesser degree by a twisted, rebellious world, but that will not be the case forever.

What then is God doing in the world that has lost so much of its potential to reflect his beauty? He is creating it anew day-by-day, year-by-year, and century-by-century. God is redeeming a people; he is reversing the effects of the great retrogression (Gen. 3). Some day creation will be liberated and that day draws closer with every passing one. History is not aimless; it is progressing toward a goal, though that progress seems to flux, sometimes being more apparent than at other times, though that is a merely human perception. The goal will be realized when creation rejoices and the people of God worship him in a new heaven and earth.

God is seeking his own glory, and he is doing it by shaping the destiny of nations and people. The study of church history can tell part of that story, the story of a redeemed people living in a blighted world with their eyes and hearts set on non-earthy values and motives. It is the narrative of a people who have been caused to see the world in a different way from many around them, yet with a love for the world that has not been diminished, only refocused, with an other-worldly perspective. So church history, like universal history, is the story of how it is that God is glorifying himself now and will do so until the kingdoms of this world become the kingdom of God's Son, Jesus Christ. To God be the glory!

The Structure for the Study of Church History

As scholars approach ways to convey the history of the period between the advents of Christ, the age of the church, the task is not at all easy. The records available from the past are incomplete, the sources blighted by prejudice and jaundice, as well as that of the interpreter, and the context of statements cannot be fully reconstructed. An added dilemma for the historian is that Christianity is not always to be identified with institutional structures, whether Orthodox, Roman Catholic, or Protestant. A movement is not necessarily Christian because it professes attachment to pious ideals, makes prominent display of religious symbols, claims historic connections to a fertile past, possesses a large and obedient following, or has a record of religious sacrifice and zeal for the cause. Christianity is more than institutional identity; it is a matter of an invisible heart-attachment that may or not be expressed in quantifiable ways. The center of Christianity is a devotion to a person whose claims and accomplishments are revealed in the Christian Bible.

With that caveat, the scholar studies the outward manifestations of Christian faith to uncover an inner meaning and dynamic. Organizational structure, though somewhat arbitrary at times, is important in making complex material more readily understandable. Accordingly, scholars divide the centuries of Christian history into large units of time and subdivide them into a variety of subjects integral to each period. Generally, church history is divided into four periods: the ancient church, the medieval church, the modern church, and the postmodern church.

Ancient Church
The early church, often called the ancient church or the patristic period, stretches from the beginning of the life and ministry of Christ, and the birth of the church, to the decline of the Roman Empire in the West (33–600), revealing a western perspective on the story. It is the story of the expansion of the Christian faith, the hostilities of the pagan state seeking to crush it, attempts at explaining the faith and the writing of creeds, and the unexpected triumph of the church in the fourth century through the benevolence of Constantine.

Medieval Church
The medieval period (600–1500) begins with the collapse of the Roman Empire in the West

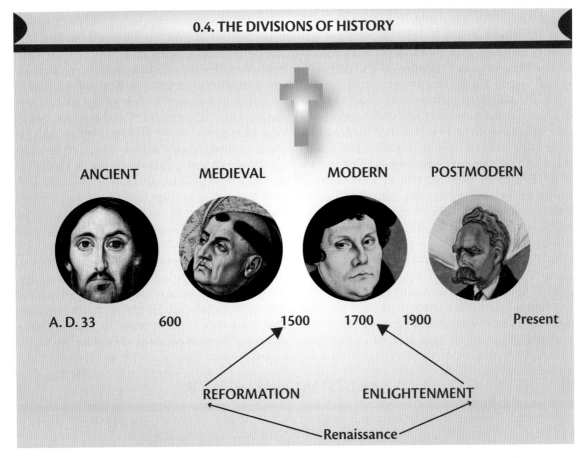

0.4. THE DIVISIONS OF HISTORY

ANCIENT   MEDIEVAL   MODERN   POSTMODERN

A. D. 33   600   1500   1700   1900   Present

REFORMATION   ENLIGHTENMENT

Renaissance

and ends with the demise of the same empire in the East, the time of the great Western Renaissance. It was a remarkable era, an unprecedented millennia of the dominance of Christianity. In the West, the pagan tribes were progressively christianized from Ireland to the steppes of Russia, though the rise of Islam presented a powerful reminder that the true kingdom of God is "not and not yet," the "garden" has weeds and thistles in it. Perhaps the greatest stories of the period is that of the rise of the papacy, the unresolved clashes between church and state for temporal supremacy, and the corruption of the church, morally and spiritually, that became the background for the sixteenth-century reformations. The outward unity of the church was shattered in the eleventh century as the churches in the West and the East divided into separate entities, each claiming to be the more ancient and original (the Orthodox churches in the East and the Catholic church in the West).

Modern Church

The modern era (1500–1900) is generally divided into two parts: early modern and late modern. The former (1500–1650) is typically denominated as the era of the great reformation or early modern Europe, again revealing the bias of western historians. Like its successor, the late modern period (1650–1900), the early modern period was characterized by a rejection of medieval ecclesiastical authoritarianism as expressed in church councils, papal decrees, and the Bible if inappropriately used (it was not a rejection of external authority, but a type of it). Both eras are rooted in the European Renaissance of the fifteenth century with its emphasis on revisiting the past. The sixteenth century witnessed the rise of several reformations or renewal movements, attempts to redirect a church that for a variety of reasons had lost its way. The two most prominent of these were the Protestant movement (itself frightfully divided into various contentious parties) and the Roman Catholic Church, though lesser reformist movements such as pietistic, rationalistic, and political reform movements also appeared.

At this point it is instructive to state an assumption, though it will be argued in subsequent chapters. The Protestant movement and the Roman Catholic Church had their creedal beginnings in the sixteenth century. Each is a reaction to the other; each is an attempt to reform late medieval Catholicism. Both movements have sought to use the past as justification for their existence, though the Roman Catholic Church has more decisive and developed arguments; both selectively use the past to erect their viewpoints. This is why Protestants have argued for the priority of the sacred canon over tradition; history can be used to demonstrate contradictory views. Abelard, the late medieval scholar, made this point in *Sic et Non*, and Calvin's massive *Institutes of Christian Religion* is, at least in part, an attempt to correct misuses of a shared past. I am arguing that Protestants and the Roman Catholic Church share fourteen centuries. Though the issues that separate the two movements are serious, the two movements embrace together a rich heritage, doctrinally and institutionally. Both are part of the "catholic church," a universal community that professes the Christian faith (the differences will be subsequently delineated).

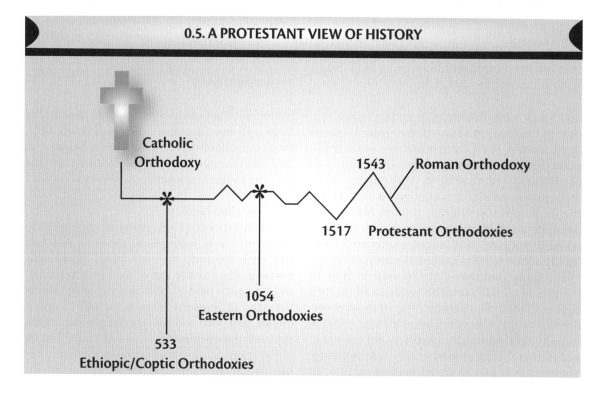

0.5. A PROTESTANT VIEW OF HISTORY

Catholic Orthodoxy

1543 Roman Orthodoxy

1517 Protestant Orthodoxies

1054
Eastern Orthodoxies

533
Ethiopic/Coptic Orthodoxies

The Protestant reformations created a movement, a renewal of the Christian faith, whose influence can be seen in its impact on nations such as Germany, the Swiss Republic, France, Holland, England, Scotland, the colonial empires of many of these countries, and eventually the United States of America and Canada. It produced the great Protestant missions movement of the eighteenth and nineteenth centuries, a countermovement to the Roman Catholic global missions thrust of the Franciscans from the sixteenth century.

A third major expression of the Christian faith, the Orthodox churches, would see themselves as the original first-century expression of Christianity and the other two as schematic divisions. The argument is largely historical in nature. Constantinople did become a center of Christian faith in the fourth century; the Christian faith did emerge in the East and the sites of our earliest Christian communities are there. I will argue that none of the three major branches of the confessing Christian church has a singular grip upon the initial centuries and that such a claim based on history is weak (particularly if it is not warranted by the Scriptures that all three traditions share). The initial centuries of the church were simply "catholic." The precarious unity of the "catholic church" was evident as early as the fourth century with Constantine's administrative division of the church between Rome in the West and Constantinople in the East. Significant cultural and social differences between the West and East, as well as historical experiences, created a wedge of separation that has been seen generally as occurring in the eleventh century, creating a Western Catholic Church and the Eastern or Orthodox churches. Subsequently, over entirely different issues, the Western Catholic Church divided into the Protestant churches and the Roman Catholic Church.

The late modern era (1650–1900) marked the beginning of the end of the cultural and intellectual dominance of Christianity in the Mediterranean and western worlds, an era that stretched from the time of Theodosius I in the late fourth century to the twentieth century. The intellectual root of the era was the great Renaissance of the fifteenth century in Western Europe. The movement sought to return to the past as a guide to the present, the assumption being that present authoritarian structures (i.e., the medieval church) were no longer beneficial, as they had become corrupted. The reformers, children of the Renaissance spirit, imbibed the critical institutional ethos of the times, but found refuge in the sources of first-century Christianity and sought to reduplicate them. The emergent Roman Catholic Church endeavored to curb the moral and religious excesses of the late medieval church. As a renewal movement, Protestants claimed that their Roman Catholic opponents did not address the weightier issues of the means of redemption and the nature and cause of divine grace. Others, however, found in a more distant past than the first century, sources for the renewal of Western culture that had, in their judgment, become bedraggled by an oppressive and perverse authoritarianism, an im-

> "Studying church history . . . is like being at a Bible study with a great company of people who thought about those questions that were bothering you and others" (Alister McGrath, "The State of the Church Before the Reformation," *Modern Reformation* [January/February 1994]: 11).

posed authority, whether Protestant or Roman Catholic, over the minds and consciences of men and women. The evil was not religion per se, but an external authority (the church, the Bible, or both). The inspiration for the movement, the Enlightenment, was drawn from pre-Christian sources, Greco-Roman culture, with its focus on human potential, on mankind as the measure of all things.

The emphasis upon the rational competencies of mankind to create a world safe from oppression emerged as a philosophical movement, suggesting its secular-source orientation, but rapidly brought about vast religious, political, and cultural changes as its assumptions concerning the nature and sources of truth were adopted. In short, it gave birth to the late modern era with its great confidence in human perfectibility through education that appeared to be validated by the scientific and technological advances of the time. It was truly a remarkable era, but its many success stories were its own undoing. It brought economic prosperity, yet, in so doing, precipitated a crisis in Western culture.

While the West prospered materially, it suffered a denouement of social and cultural cohesiveness. The promises of the late modern era simply did not come to fruition; science, the new savior of the race, instead contributed its knowledge to world wars and holocausts. The atom could be divided, but the human soul could not be united; it was restless with new venues for its tragic expression.

Postmodern Church
The postmodern era (1900–present)[3] is difficult to describe, but it stands in sharp antithesis to the optimism, a supposed societal corporate

ethic, and faith in progress that characterized the previous era. Postmoderns have lost faith that reason and science have redemptive potential; instead, the quest for meaning has turned inward toward self, individualness, and the private viewpoint. Absolutes are unimaginable in this "new world" except in a frail, often vague, utilitarianism.

However, Christians, live in another "city" with distinctly different values and goals, as Augustine so wonderfully stated centuries ago. In all the eras of the history of the church, and however more there may be, God is building a community that someday from out of all the peoples of the world will assemble to worship him forever. Something far more "real" than what can be observed is occurring. This world is the outward shell of an amazingly invisible story. It is a stage and upon it a divinely orchestrated story is unfolding. It is His story!

The Scope and Limitations of This Study
The goal of the literary effort that follows is the production of a tool that accurately tells something of the story of the Christian heritage, though this writer is limited by impartial information, distortive ignorance, and biased blindness.

I have structured the volume to enhance comprehension. First, I have chosen not to place in the text an abundance of footnotes with a view that the text be as uncluttered as possible. Source verification can be obtained in some cases by citations within the text, particularly if direct quotations are used. In other cases, substantiation has been provided by the addition of a list of "Further Readings" at the end of each section. The readings will provide

---

3.   The beginning of the postmodern era appears to have been about 1900 in Western Europe, but not so in the United States. Until the post World War II era, Americans embraced the assumptions and promises of the Enlightenment. The disillusionment with rationalism became observable in the 1960s with the status-quo rebellion expressed in the hippie movement, the shock of the assassination of a president, and the social disruptions caused by American military intervention in Southeast Asia, the Vietnam War.

a great depth of knowledge. They are selective, being either recognized, time-certified sources or more recent works reflecting the contemporary state of scholarship, interpretation, and bibliographical sources.

Second, to facilitate learning, the text is interspersed with illuminating sidebar comments and quotations, each documented, as well as descriptive diagrams and pictures. Pur-posed to be a learning tool, as well as a descriptive story of a movement, hopefully this work will prove beneficial for learning.

Third, in regard to learning, a glossary of terms can be found at the end of each chapter and a complete glossary of terms at the end of the volume. Terms are highlighted when they first occur in the text.

GLOSSARY OF TERMS

Enlightenment (Age of Reason): a movement begun in eighteenth-century Europe that emphasized the inner capacities of man (rational reflection, intuition) as opposed to external authority sources such as the church or the Bible to improve social and society performance. Strenuously opposed by the religious community as well as secular materialists, the Enlightenment spawned the modern era, a three-century experiment in the redemptive values of science and technology. Though highly successful in the technical realms, the venture collapsed under the weight of holocausts and wars, suggesting that the blight of human discord could not be remedied by social advances alone. The movement filled life with opportunities but emptied it of meaning, creating postmodernism.

Historicism: a view of history that emphasizes the role of context, largely cultural forces, in the understanding of events. Prominently proposed by Hegel and later borrowed by Karl Marx, who used the theory in a materialistic direction, the theory argues, opposed to rationalist theories of progress, that cultural forces shape and determine the direction of the history of nations and peoples.

Idealism (see German Idealism): a philosophical approach to the nature of knowledge arguing that the structure of reality is immaterial or mentally constructed.

Marxism (Marxist Materialism): a philosophy developed by Karl Marx that centers around a materialist interpretation of history and the Hegelian dialectic model of social change. Marx and Lenin argued that the blight of the human condition is attributable to social

and economic disparity, clearly the antithesis of the capitalistic, free enterprise approach to societal organization.

Materialism (Philosophical): a term that suggests that all existence is subject to the categories of volume, shape, and proportion; that is, only matter exists and only the observable is real. This view of existence can easily be invoked to deny the existence of God and the spiritual since such cannot be observed. The view, however, does not take into account such recognized realities as gravity, an invisible force.

Postmillennialism: a view of "end times" that understands that the church through Christ is progressively triumphing, that the reign of Christ is in the church, not in a geopolitical rule in space-time history. This rule, rather than a literal reign, will be brought to consummation in Christ's literal return to judge the nations, triumph over all his enemies, and share in the eternal state. In this view Christ's return to judge and redeem will take place after the millennium, the reign of Christ through the church.

Renaissance (Renaissance Humanism): a cultural and educational reform emphasis that emerged in the fourteenth and fifteenth centuries in reaction to medieval scholasticism, emphasizing personal affirmation of truth through a study of the sources of belief-structures, as well as the engagement in civic life through speaking and writing with eloquence and clarity. Its focus was on the study of the humanities with the new curriculum of university education, a shift from the scholastic preoccupation with rational explanation of the medieval faith to the readoption and prominence of the Aristotelian method.

Romanticism (Romantic Movement, Romantic Philosophy): a movement in the latter half of the eighteenth century in reaction to the dangers of Enlightenment rationalism and the Scientific Revolution with their quest for truth primarily in the cognitive faculties at the denigration or diminution of the affective and emotional faculties of the human makeup. Like its counterparts, the Romantic movement, expressed religiously in transcendentalism and mysticism, finds the quest for meaning in humankind in the emotive, intuitional, and the balance or harmony with nature.

Further Readings:
General Introduction to Church History

Bebbington, D. W. *Patterns in History: A Christian View.* Downers Grove, IL: InterVarsity Press, 1979.

Bradley, James E. and Mueller, Richard A. *Church History: An Introduction to Research, Reference Works, and Methods.* Grand Rapids: William B. Eerdmans Publishing Co., 1995.

Chesterton, G. K. *Orthodoxy.* New York: Image Books/DoubleDay, 1959.

Clouse, Robert G. *The Church From Age to Age: A History from Galilee to Global Christianity.* St. Louis, MO: Concordia Publishing House, 2011.

Edwards, Jonathan. *The Works of Jonathan Edwards. Vol. 9. A History of the Work of Redemption.* New Haven, CT: Yale University Press, 1989.

_____, *The Works of Jonathan Edwards. Vol. 8. Ethical Writings. Dissertation I: Concerning The End For Which God Created The World,* New Haven, CT: Yale University Press, 1989.

Frend, W. H. C. *The Rise of Christianity.* Philadelphia, PA: Fortress, 1984.

Gonzalez, Justo. *The Story of Christianity: The Early Church to the Present Day.* Peabody, MA: Prince Press, 1999.

Johnson, Marshall D. *The Evolution of Christianity: Twelve Crises that Shaped the Church.* London: Continuum, 2005.

Leith, John. *Creeds of the Churches. Garden City,* NY: Doubleday & Co., 1963.

MacCulloch, Diarmaid. *Christianity: The First Three Thousand Years.* New York: Viking, 2010.

McDermott, Gerald R. The Great Theologian: A Brief Guide. Grand Rapids: InterVarsity Press, 2010.

Nichols, Stephen J. *Pages From Church History: A Guided Tour of Christian Classics.* Phillipsburg, NJ: P&R Publishing, 2006.

Noll, Mark A. *Turning Points: Decisive Moments in the History of Christianity.* 2nd Ed. Grand Rapids: Baker Books, 2000.

Tucker, Ruth and Walter Liefeld. *Daughter of the Church: Women and Ministry from the New Testament to the Present.* Grand Rapids: Zondervan Publishing House, 1987.

Schaff, Philip. *The Creeds of Christendom.* 3 vols. Reprint. 1877. Grand Rapids: Baker Book House, n.d.

Wright, Jonathan. Heretics: *The Creation of Christianity, from the Gnostics to the Modern Church.* Boston, MA: Houghton Mifflin Harcourt, 2011.

PART
1

THE ANCIENT
CHURCH (AD 33–600)

Chapter 1 Outline

The Early Church (33–90).
The Setting of the Church
   The Roman Influence
   The Greek Influence
   The Jewish Influence
The Importance of Jesus, called the Christ,
* now the Lord Jesus Christ.*

The Birth of the Church, the Age of the Spirit
The Structure of the Churches
The Worship of the Churches

The Earliest Fathers (90–150).
The Earliest Fathers and Their Work
The Earliest Fathers and Their Teachings

Chapter 1 Objectives

- That the reader will identify the four main periods of the early church by name and time period

- That the reader will describe the origin of the church: its historical and social setting

- That the reader will describe early church structure and practices

- That the reader will identify major writers and records of the early church period

- That the reader will describe perspectives on the Trinity, Eucharist, and church leadership in the early second-century church

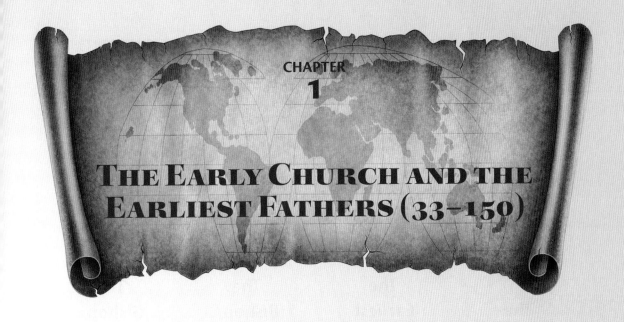

THE EARLY CHURCH AND THE EARLIEST FATHERS (33–150)

T HE PERIOD OF BEGINNINGS, or the Ancient Church, stretches from the birth of the Christian faith to the collapse of the **Roman Empire** in the West. These several centuries of Christianity can be divided around the reigns of Constantine I and Theodosius I in the fourth century. Prior to the reigns of these emperors, Christianity received no political sanction and was frequently persecuted; the Christ was often portrayed as a donkey on a cross. The fortunes of the church changed suddenly from hostility to toleration, and later the church emerged as the sole expression of **religion** in the empire. Paganism was suppressed. Apart from the story of the emergence of the faith, the political acceptance of Christianity was, most likely, the most important political event in the period.

Scholars have generally divided the period from the perspective of the developing fortunes within the church, rather than from issues between the church and state. Though arbitrary, the era will be divided into four parts based upon the criteria of the prominence of spokesmen and their literary productivity: the period of the apostles (33–100), the period of the earliest fathers (100–150), the period of the apologists (150–300), and the period of the bishops (300–600).

The age of the apostles embraces the birth of the church ("the time of the new order," Heb. 9:10) through the era of the creation of the new canonical writings, the Greek Scriptures.

The period of the earliest fathers is demarcated by the uniqueness of their literary production. The writings are pastoral in tone and quality in contradistinction to the more polemic writings that followed them. They collectively provide our first glimpse into the emerging church after the apostolic writings of the first century.

The age of the apologists is characterized by

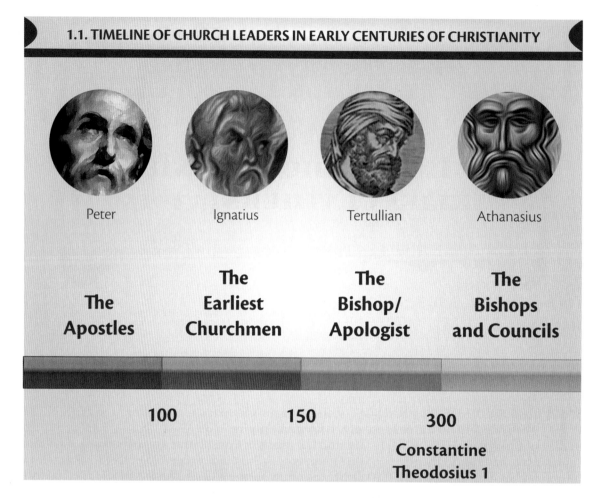

1.1. TIMELINE OF CHURCH LEADERS IN EARLY CENTURIES OF CHRISTIANITY

Peter	Ignatius	Tertullian	Athanasius
The Apostles	**The Earliest Churchmen**	**The Bishop/ Apologist**	**The Bishops and Councils**

100   150   300
                              Constantine
                              Theodosius 1

writings that reflect conflict in the empire and theological dissension in the churches. In the process of answering a rising tide of critics, the bishops began the task of the orderly explanation of the Christian faith. The age of the bishops is defined by the triumphant emergence of the church through political patronage and the great ecumenical councils that defined Christian orthodoxy.

The Early Church (33–90)

As Christians reflect upon their movement, it is appropriate to speak of the church as beginning with the advent of the age of the Holy Spirit that was predicted by the prophet Joel

(2:28–32) and fulfilled in Acts 2 (cf. Acts 11:15). However, it is not valid to speak of the people of God in that manner. The church represents the new people of God, the "new Israel," distinct from the prevarications of Judaism in our Lord's day (Matt. 15:1–14, 23:1–36) and in fulfillment of the religion of Moses and the prophets. The religion of the Hebrew Scriptures stands in continuity with the religion of Jesus and the writers of the Greek Scriptures (Matt. 5:17). Jesus came to explain the age of shadows, the time of anticipation, and bring it to a conclusion, though important distinctions remain between the spiritual lives of the ancient people of God and the new people of

God (Heb. 8:1–13), for example, in the age of the promised Holy Spirit (John 14:26, 15:26). Though the promises made to God's ancient people will be fulfilled, the people of God, having been gathered through the once-for-all sacrifice of the priest-king, Jesus, are, in a sense, a single people, being the fulfillment of every Old Testament temporal sacrifice. Christianity and ancient Judaism is one seamless thread. Since the curtain of the temple was split from top to bottom (Matt. 27:51), the tabernacle and temple sacrificial system ended because the "true temple," the embodiment of the presence of God for and with his people, had offered the final sacrifice (Heb. 10:1–18). The eternal promises of God have to do with the redemption of a people. The unfolding of those promises dwelt first with a people who failed though redeemed from the land of bondage through the shedding of blood, and, second, with a new people, composed of Jews and Gentile as one new entity (Eph. 2:11–22) with new and better promises.

> "But when the set time had come, God sent his Son, born of a woman, born under the law, to redeem those under the law that we might receive the adoption to sonship" (Galatians 4:4–5).

The Setting of the Church

The "Apostle Paul" described the time of the incarnation of Christ as a special time ("the set time" (Gal. 4:4). When the time was exactly as God planned it, Christ came into our world, lived and died among us, and a vast movement began after his resurrection. Scholars who have pondered the phrase, "the fullness of time," have explained its meaning by speaking to the historical context of the advent of Christ and the beginning of "the Way" (Acts 19:23).

A profound assumption of the Christian faith is that God is the supreme director of all events (Gen. 50:20; Acts 2:23–24), which he shapes according to the counsels of his incomprehensible purposes. Though we are often perplexed by circumstances that bring joys and

tears to us, we refuse to limit understanding by the incompleteness of our human knowledge. God has revealed himself to us as the all-wise, all-powerful and covenant-faithful God. He works all things according to his purposes in Christ Jesus both in the Scriptures and in our experience of the truths revealed through them by the Holy Spirit (most centrally, the wonder of divine forgiveness through a divine substitute!).

The Roman Influence

Divinely appointed circumstances, gradually put in place over centuries, became the cradle for the birth of the most enduring movement in the history of humankind. Christ came into a Roman world and the church rapidly was disseminated throughout it. It was the time of the *Pax Romana*, the Roman peace, an iron-fisted military control that offered the opportunity of travel and protection to Roman citizens particularly, and others as well, across an empire that spanned from the Atlantic Ocean in the west to Asia in the east, from the Rhine and Danube rivers in the north to Africa above the Sahara in the south. In this enormous expanse, a network of well-maintained roads interconnected, guaranteeing the swift movement of commerce and soldiery. These roads also provided a means for the spread of news concerning Christ by the apostles and countless others. Along those roads, connecting major cities, the gospel was taken and, as a result, churches sprang up. Paul would utilize his Roman citizenship to extend gospel proclamation (Acts 16:11–40, 22:22–29) though he endured much adversity (2 Cor. 4:7–18, 6:1–13, 11:23–28).

From the perspective of religion, the Romans were eclectic, embracing the deities of conquered peoples into an ever-increasing pantheon of gods and goddesses, the ruins of Rome's ancient forum bearing a silent witness today. As polytheistic Romans pursued the gods of the nations, they also adopted the deification of the emperors (it appears that a major polemic in

1.2. THE IDEOLOGICAL SETTING OF THE CHURCH

Galatians 4:4
In the fullness of time
God sent forth His Son . . . .

The Influence of Rome—POLITICAL

The Influence of Greece—INTELLECTUAL

The Influence of the Jews—RELIGIOUS

the Revelation is that Jesus alone, not Domitian, was "King of Kings" and "Lord of Lords" [19:16]). Allegiance to the many deities was lapsing and people lost hope in their efficacy. Paul tailored his preaching in Athens around the observation of an inscription "to an unknown God" (Acts 17:19–31). The church was born into a world that was as empty of hope as it was abundant in religions and gods, a fertile circumstance for Christians to preach Christ and demonstrate the validity of the message by a redeemed lifestyle.

The Greek influence
The unique influence of the Greek world was be-

cause of a universal trade language. Though the Romans conquered the Greeks in the second century BC militarily, they adopted much of the Greek intellectual culture. For a few centuries, from the second century before Christ to two centuries after Christ, Greek was the common language of the empire. Knowledge of Koine Greek, the language of commerce, allowed Paul to speak to merchants and political figures throughout the empire. For example, the apostle spoke to a Greek merchant, Lydia of Thyatira, in Philippi, Macedonia, proclaiming the gospel by a river in a city where there appears to have been no local synagogue to serve as a pulpit (Acts 16:11–15). The sacred writings produced by the early churchmen were all in Koine Greek, a witness to the universality of the language and the eastern origins of "the Way."

The Bible of the early Christians was a Greek translation of the Hebrew Scriptures completed in Alexandria, Egypt, by Jews of the **Diaspora**. This was called the Septuagint, a term referring to the legend that it was the work of seventy scholars working independently (the LXX). As the Christian witness spread throughout the Roman Empire, this was the Bible they carried; it is clearly the text used often by the writers of the canonical Scriptures. The collection of books in the Septuagint includes several intertestamental texts that the Protestant movement would come to reject as canonical, but the Roman Catholic Church would embrace a selection of them, and the Orthodox Church all of them.

Another important impact of Greek culture is that its presence forced the church to accommodate the message to non-Jewish audiences. In some salient ways, the Jewish scholar Philo (20 BC–AD 50) and Christian scholars had to demonstrate that the Bible was compatible with Greek philosophical thought. To do so, early Christian exegesis in the great intellectual centers, following the lead of Philo, adopted an allegorical approach to biblical interpretation. Later, apologists such as Justin Martyr tried to demonstrate that Moses predated the Greeks

so that a "true philosopher" should become a follower of Moses and the Scriptures. The insights of Greek philosophical idealism became a powerful tool through which to state the invisible supernaturalism of Christianity.

The Jewish influence

The roots and connectedness between ancient Judaism and Christianity are profound. The Christian faith is the outworking of a divine promise to Abram, an ancient Semite, that he would become the father of many nations (Gen. 15, 17) through his seed, Jesus Christ (Gal. 3:7–16). That is a momentous contribution to the Christian faith; however, Judaism shaped Christianity in other ways.

First, Judaism in Christ's day manifested a deep hope in the soon advent of the Messiah figure. Simeon, a person described as "waiting for the consolation of Israel," recognized in Jesus at his dedication that his "eyes . . . [had] seen" God's "salvation" (Luke 2:25–30). Zachariah (Luke 1:67–79), Elizabeth (Luke 1:42–43), Mary (Luke 1:46–55), and Anna (Luke 2:38) witnessed to the expectancy of the redeemer. For most of the leadership of the nation of Israel, the hope was not in the fulfillment of spiritual promises; it was in a faith that the real deliverer would be a political champion and would lead a subjected people to the reestablishment of its national sovereignty. The nation had experienced a renewal under the Persians following the Babylonian captivity, and they had gained freedom from the yoke of Greek oppression in the revolt of the Maccabees in 168 BC, as well as political sovereignty. The nation existed as a free state until the rising shadow of the Romans crept over the land, first in the form of vassalship under Pompey (64–37 BC) and then in complete subjugation under Rome's client-king, Herod the Great (37–4 BC). In Christ's day, the political repercussions of Roman hegemony were wearing thin and hope of deliverance, as of old, preoccupied many in the nation. The hope, however, for most was not a "lamb-figure," but military leadership that would throw off the Roman yoke. Jesus was out of step with the expectations of most.

Second, the scattering of the Jews in the Diaspora following the destruction of the nation under the Babylonians cast them across the Mediterranean world, the largest concentrations being in Babylon and Alexandria, though Jews could be found in many cities. Separated from the temple, Jews began to gather in synagogues, houses for prayer and Torah study. The synagogue figured prominently into early missionary strategy as Paul focused on preaching in the synagogues to Jews and God-fearing Gentiles before gathering elsewhere (Acts 13:5, 14; 14:7; 17:1, 10, 17; 18:1–4, 19; 19:8–10). Philippi, apparently having no synagogue, caused Paul to shift from his normal strategy and preach outdoors (Acts 16:12–13); the case is likely also true of Perga (13:14). The synagogues were the initial contact points in early evangelistic work and out of them grew the churches. Paul's preaching strategy was to demonstrate that the Hebrew Scriptures, so cherished by the Jews, announced the coming of the Messiah and were fulfilled in Jesus Christ. He did this by profusely quoting Jewish Scriptures (Acts 13:32–42).

The Importance of Jesus, Called the Christ, Now the Lord Jesus Christ.

The most important event in all human history, the event that will be celebrated in adoring worship for all eternity, the event that will be remembered when all other events through the centuries of time fade into insignificance, centers on the person of Jesus: his incarnation, ministry, crucifixion, resurrection, and ascension. His life changed the world forever! Perhaps, Karl Barth was correct when he identified John 1:14 as the central text on the incarnation ("The word became flesh and made his dwelling among us"). Further, Philippians 2:5–11 is a wonderful summary of his person, work, and exaltation. In the birth narratives, it was Simeon in the temple who connected him with Isaiah's prophecies as "a light of revelation to the Gentiles, and the glory of your people Israel" (Luke 2:32). John, the apostle, summarized what he had learned from him this way: "In him was life, and that life was the light of all mankind" (John 1:4).

Jesus came as Israel's priestly redeemer king (Matt. 22:41–46) but was renounced and denounced by the nation's leadership. They rejected his claim to be all that the prophets of old anticipated, though verified by numerous miracles, including raising the dead (Luke 7:11–17;

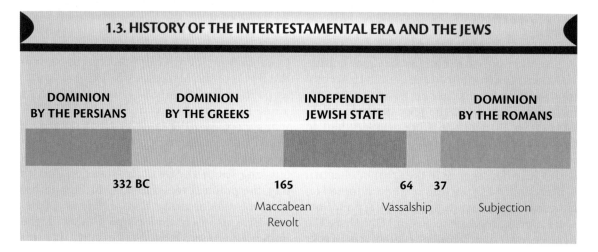

1.3. HISTORY OF THE INTERTESTAMENTAL ERA AND THE JEWS

DOMINION BY THE PERSIANS	DOMINION BY THE GREEKS	INDEPENDENT JEWISH STATE	DOMINION BY THE ROMANS
	332 BC	165	64 37
		Maccabean Revolt	Vassalship Subjection

"The Adoration of the Shepherds" (25 December 1622) by Gerard van Honthorst (1590–1656). Courtesy of the Yorck Project.

John 11:38–44), and his words (Matt. 26:55–56; John 6:25–59, 8:12–20, 10:7–30, 11:17–29). They were blinded by the shortsightedness that the most pressing, urgent need was a physical, military deliverance by an earthly leader prefigured in David of old and Judas Maccabeus of more recent vintage. Jesus's claim to be a spiritual deliverer from heaven, the Son of God, was simply too much; it was blasphemy, a claim worthy of death (John 10:31–39). The proof of the falsity of his claims, in their judgment, was that he broke the Law of Moses (Matt. 5:21–48, 12:1–14). Not able to kill him in the most grotesque way (John 19:30–31), they fabricated the charge of political insurrection and he was crucified under the accusation: "This is Jesus the King of the Jews" (Matt. 27:37).

A king he was, but, at that time, Jesus's kingdom was not an earthly one ("You say that I am a king" [John 18:33–37]). Jesus came to establish a kingdom that would have both spiritual and earthly dimensions by means of the ministry of the Holy Spirit (John 16:7–11). That kingdom, emerging now through the centuries, will be consummated when his body, the church, is complete. He conquered death through his own death; he satisfied divine justice in suffering the curse of sin, paying its penalty on the cross (Rom. 3:21–30). The Jewish leadership thought the Romans were killing a societal menace; but, indeed, Jesus died to redeem society. He did not die a hopeless, pathetic figure overwhelmed by circumstances but majestically (John 19:11) in the eternal plan and will of God (Acts: 2:23–24, 33). The resurrection of Christ (Matt. 28:6) is the proof that he conquered death. His instructions to the disciples were that they should wait in Jerusalem for inducement, for power, evidenced by the coming of the Holy Spirit (Luke 24:44–49; Acts 1:4–5, 8) and his baptizing work of placing

An 1870 painting of Christ on the cross by Carl Heinrich Block (1834–1890). Courtesy of Goose.

believers in Jesus into a new organism, the church, the body of Christ.

The apostles, infused by the Spirit of God, on the Day of Pentecost, the Day of First Fruits or Ingathering (an ancient religious celebration that foreshadowed a great spiritual truth), were charged to proclaim the resurrection, that there is profound hope through one who conquered death (Rom. 1:1–7; 1 Cor. 15:3–5, 51–58). The instructions given to the church, the Christ followers, were that "repentance for the forgiveness of sins should be preached in his name to all nations, beginning at Jerusalem" (Luke 24:47). The apostle Matthew laid down clear instructions for us with the command "make disciples of all nations" through the actions of going, baptizing, and teaching what he has taught us, all with the promise that however long before his return "I am with you always, to the very end of the age" (Matt. 28:18–20).

The Birth of the Church, the Age of the Spirit

The events recorded in Acts 2 inaugurated the new age. Peter, explaining the phenomena of the Spirit's coming, argued that the new age was prophesied of old by Joel and was grounded in the ministry of Jesus who is "both Lord and Messiah" (Acts 2:36).

The preponderance of sources for our knowledge of the early years of the church is found in the canonical writings, particularly the book of Acts, which provides the context for many of the letters to the churches. Luke's account of the expansion of the church covers the initial thirty years. It is a selective recounting that emphasizes the expansion of the witness of the gospel to the Jews, later to the Samaritans, and then to the Gentiles. The focus appears to be on the irrepressible surge of the witness of the church culminating in the center of the great empire, Rome.

The rapid dissemination of the message of the resurrection of Christ is impressive. On the

1.4. THE BEGINNING OF THE CHURCH

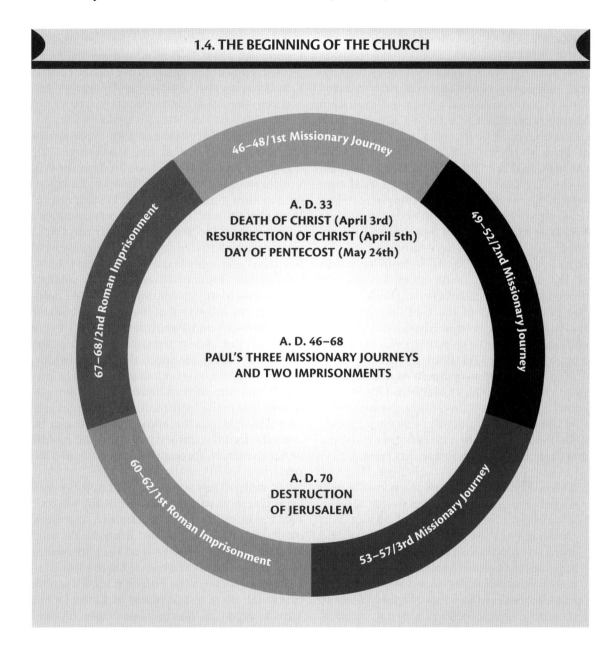

46–48 / 1st Missionary Journey

49–52 / 2nd Missionary Journey

67–68 / 2nd Roman Imprisonment

A. D. 33
DEATH OF CHRIST (April 3rd)
RESURRECTION OF CHRIST (April 5th)
DAY OF PENTECOST (May 24th)

A. D. 46–68
PAUL'S THREE MISSIONARY JOURNEYS
AND TWO IMPRISONMENTS

A. D. 70
DESTRUCTION
OF JERUSALEM

60–62 / 1st Roman Imprisonment

53–57 / 3rd Missionary Journey

Day of Pentecost, Jews and proselytes from fifteen geographical areas (Acts 2:9–11) heard Peter's stirring message. Some 3,000 believed in Jesus (2:41), and the numbers in Jerusalem swelled quickly to about five thousand (4:4). Later, Luke tells us that "more and more men and women were added to their number" (5:14) and that "the word of God spread [and] the number of the disciples in Jerusalem increased rapidly" (6:7). The churches experienced peace and prosperity throughout Israel (9:31) though persecution was not precluded, which only served to expand the churches' witness (8:1, 11:19, 12:1–2).

Paul emerges in Luke's account as the central, pioneering church planter who endured three arduous missionary tours in the eastern Mediterranean. With a large Christian concentration in Antioch, Syria, where followers of Jesus were first called Christians (11:26), churches had been established from Jerusalem to the Adriatic Sea. It is clear that Paul considered his work in the area completed when he wrote to the Christians in Rome in the late 50s, little more than ten years after his first missionary journey. In his estimation, his pioneering work was finished ("So from Jerusalem all the way around to Illyricum, I have fully proclaimed the gospel of Christ." [Rom. 15:19]). The financial gifts of the Gentiles for needy saints in Jerusalem from Macedonia, Achaia, and Galatia were the crowning evidence of the completion of the task (Rom. 15:26, 1 Cor. 16:1–4). Paul set his sights on Spain as his new mission field (Rom. 15:24, 28). Little did the apostle know that in taking the gifts to Jerusalem he would face imprisonment in Caesarea for two years before his removal to another two-year imprisonment in Rome before his release.

"The new birth in those days was a new birth; it kindled in the soul thoughts and feelings to which it had hitherto been strange; it brought with it the consciousness of new powers; a new vision of God; a new love of holiness; a new insight into the Holy Scriptures, and into the meaning of man's life; often a new power of ardent, passionate speech. In the first Epistle to the Corinthians Paul describes a primitive Christian congregation. There was not one silent among them. When they came together every one had a psalm, a revelation, a prophecy, an interpretation. The manifestation of the Spirit had been given to each one to profit withal; and on all hands the spiritual fire was ready to flame forth. Conversion to the Christian faith, the acceptance of the apostolic gospel, was not a thing which made little difference to men: it convulsed their whole nature to its depths;

they were never the same again; they were new creatures, with a new life in them, all fervor and flame" (Denny, James, "The Epistles to the Thessalonians" in The Expositor's Bible, ed. W. R. Nicoll [London: Hodder & Stoughton, 1903], 234).

While the story of the earliest expansion of Christianity, then called "the Way" (Acts 9:2)," was given broadly in the book of Acts, most of the chronicles of the early Christian faith otherwise have gone unrecorded. We are not informed of the impact of the Ethiopian eunuch's conversion on the beginnings of African Christianity (Acts 8:26–39), the missionary work of Barnabas and John Mark (Acts 15:26); the impact of the contact between Roman soldiery with Jesus (Matt. 8:5–13, Mark 15:33–39, John 18:1–11), the full extent of the activities of Peter (Acts 10:1–48) and Paul (Phil.1:12–14), or the work of the other ten apostles. (Legends emerged, likely with some degree of validity, concerning the other apostles because it was important in early Christian polemics to demonstrate the continuity of the message that Jesus gave to the apostles.) What can be argued is that the Christian faith spread rapidly and extensively throughout the Roman Empire.

Details of the spread of Christianity become even sketchier with the advent of the 60s and Paul's release from the first Roman imprisonment. Piecing together data from the Pastoral Epistles, scholars believe that Paul labored in Spain, considered then the end of the world, as Ireland would be in the fifth century. Returning from that labor to the island of Crete, he left Titus to organize the churches (Titus. 1:5) and returned to Asia Minor. There he was arrested, taken to Rome, and martyred along with Peter in the 60s. The only other canonical lens into first-century Christianity is the Revelation, written by the Apostle John most likely during the reign of Domitian (81–96), though some scholars date it earlier. According to that book, persecution appears to be the lot of the seven

The conversion of Saul (apostle Paul) on the way to Damascus (c. 1600–1601) by Caravaggio (1573–1610). At Santa Maria del Popolo, Rome. Courtesy of Masur.

churches; some were healthy and prospering, while others were stumbling badly.

There are few references to the Christian faith outside of the biblical writings in the first century, suggesting that Christianity did not penetrate the cultured classes. The Roman view of Christianity was that it was another of the endless fractures in Judaism. There is a reference by the Roman historian Suetonius (ca.70–ca.130) to a controversy in Rome among the Jews over "Chrestus" during the reign of Claudius (ca. 49 AD) that caused the expulsion of the "Jews." If this was a clash over Jesus's claims, it may be an allusion to Jews such as Aquila and Priscilla (Acts 18:2) who left the city for Corinth at that time. This "Chrestus" many recognized as a reference to Christ (*Lives of the Caesars*, Claudius, 25). The Roman historian, Tacitus (ca. 59–ca. 117) details the persecution of Christians in Rome following the burning of the city in AD 64. Nero blamed the Christians, the followers of "Christus," for various unspecified "abominations" (*Annals*, 15:44). Writing at the end of the first century, the Jewish historian, Josephus (37–ca.100), mentions Christ, his death and resurrection story, and his followers "at this day" (*Antiquities of the Jews*, 18.3.3). A most insightful lens into the spread of the church was the letter of the governor of Bithynia, Pliny, to Emperor Trajan inquiring what to do with the Christians because "this superstition is spread like a contagion." The emperor replied that unless accused formally, they should be left alone.

The Structure of the Churches

The presence of the apostles in Jerusalem in the embryonic days of the church made for a unique organizational pattern that would change of necessity as the churches multiplied across the empire. The apostles appear to have exercised a jurisdictional role in those earliest days. The earliest gathering site of the saints was in the porticos of the renovated Second Temple in Jerusalem (Acts 5:12) where the apostles, John and Peter, often preached and the believers gave attention to the teaching of the apostles described as "fellowship" and the "breaking of bread" (the Lord's Supper or Eucharist), accompanied with prayer (Acts 2:42). In addition, believers gathered in private homes (Acts 5:42). In those stirring days, the apostles worked numerous miracles by the power of the Spirit, as in the days of Elijah and Jesus, calling attention to and verifying their truth claims (Acts 2:43). What seems clear is that the apostles were the leaders in the Jerusalem church, as well as James, the brother of Jesus (1 Cor. 15:7; Gal. 1:19, 2:9); they had received the most intimate and sustained tutelage from the Lord. Serving under the apostles in the Jerusalem churches was a group called elders (Acts 15:4, 6).

The rapid growth of the church burdened the apostles beyond their ability to serve effectively (Acts 6:3-4), so the saints, "the whole congregation," created an office of assistants, seven godly and gifted men, which the apostles approved (Acts 6:3, 5–6). The function of these assistants involved more than remedying the problem that occasioned their appointment. Stephen and Philip were gifted heralds of the claims of Christ (Acts 6:8; 8:12, 25, 26–27, 40). It is interesting that the apostles became important links as non-Jewish people embraced the gospel (Peter and John among the Samaritans [8:14-16] and Peter among the Gentiles [10:44–48]), suggesting that the unity of the church rested in their office and their understanding of the gospel.

As churches sprang up beyond Jerusalem, apart from the immediacy of the apostles, (except, perhaps, aside from visits or greetings through letters), the authority structure of the churches had to change (2 John 1, 12; Rev. 2–3). After preaching through the cities of southern Galatia, Paul and Barnabas returned to the new groups of believers and "they appointed elders for them in every church" (Acts 14:23, 20:17). This pattern of leaderhship for the local churches is

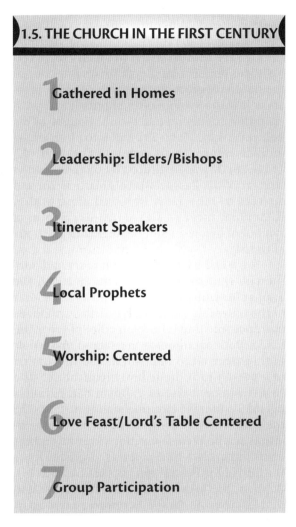

1.5. THE CHURCH IN THE FIRST CENTURY

1 Gathered in Homes

2 Leadership: Elders/Bishops

3 Itinerant Speakers

4 Local Prophets

5 Worship: Centered

6 Love Feast/Lord's Table Centered

7 Group Participation

cifically delineated, the churches also had deacons. Since the term means "one who serves or ministers," it is likely that they assisted the elders/bishops, perhaps somewhat like the seven chosen in Acts 6 to assist the apostles. Like elders/bishops, they appear in the plural and in parity (Phil. 1:1). Women may have served as deaconesses (Rom. 16:1–2, 1 Tim 3:11, see Pliny's *Letter*). Though disputable in the earliest churches, it is an office that is present later.

At the local level, the churches were led by a plurality of elders/bishops and teachers (shepherds would teach, yet there seems to be a separate office also). However, the churches had the benefit of itinerate ministries as well. The nonlocal gift-ministries were apostles, prophets, and evangelists (Eph. 4:11). Together with the bishops and teachers, these are officers charged with the maturing of the believers for the works of service. Paul indicates that the foundation of the church universal could be found in the New Testament apostles and prophets (Eph. 2:20).

"Those who were members of the church met from time to time in assembly. At these meetings, prophecy and speaking with tongues were practiced, and each member had some sort of contribution to make to the proceedings: a word of knowledge or of wisdom, a piece of teaching or revelation, given as prophecy or in a tongue (xii. 8; xiv. 26). Paul's instructions suggest that the meetings were sometimes tumultuous, even chaotic; they were certainly not dull. They were not confined to members of the church; unbelieving outsiders might find their way in (xiv. 23). The extent to which women were permitted to take part is hard to assess because it is difficult to reconcile xi. 5 and xiv. 34; see the notes on these passages" (C. K. Barrett, *The First Epistle to the Corinthians* [New York: Harper & Row, 1968], 25).

The Worship of the Churches

Writing to the emperor, Pliny described the meetings of Christians. He learned that they gathered before daylight to sing hymns to

replete in the letters of the Greek Scriptures. The terms "elder" and "bishop" ("overseer") were used interchangeably on several occasions (Acts 20:20, 28; Titus 1:5, 7). The term "elder" appears to emphasize the spiritual maturity prerequisite for the office, while "bishop," meaning shepherd, emphasizes the function of the office. The elders/bishop function never appears in the singular, one person the head of a singular church, in the New Testament writings; the churches were led by a group of men who functioned as equals in the house churches.

Though the function of the office is not spe-

Christ "as a god," making promises of mutual moral fidelity, and taking a meal together. The Greek Scriptures provide a much fuller picture. The place of meeting appears to have been in private homes (Acts 2:46, 16:40; Romans 16:5, 14, 15 [there apparently were several house-churches in Rome]; Col. 4:15). The preferred day of meeting appears to have been on Sunday (Acts 20:7, 1 Cor. 16:1–2), though it was not an apostolic custom at the time (Col. 2:16–17). Singing (Eph. 5:19), thanksgiving to God (Eph. 5:20, and mutual exhortation and encouragement were part of the worship gatherings (1 Cor. 14:1–40, esp. v. 26). Instruction of the flock was a central component of gathering (Acts 20:7; 2 Tim. 4:2–4; Titus 1:9) as well.

The center of the house-church worship was the Lord's table (1 Cor 10:21), called the "breaking of bread" (Acts 2:42)," the Lord's Supper (1 Cor. 11:20)," and the "Eucharist," or "Thanksgiving." The Supper was to be done as a "remembrance" of Christ (1 Cor. 11:24–25)," through a demonstration of the unity of the body of Christ. While the Supper has been a subject of considerable scrutiny, even division, through the centuries, the Greek Scriptures do not focus on the manner of Christ's presence or the nature of grace in the mystery of his presence. It was a symbol of the Lord's "real" presence that he commanded on the night of his betrayal (Matt. 26:26–29), and is to be observed until his return for his people (1 Cor. 11:16–17, 11:23–28). It was instituted by the Lord in the context of the Passover meal (Matt. 26:26) and appears to have been observed along with a communal meal (1 Cor. 11:20–21). It was a symbol of fellowship, of belonging to the body of Christ.

The Lord gave the church a second sacrament, that of baptism (Matt. 28:19). If the Supper is symbolic of fellowship as a member of the assembly of saints, baptism symbolizes entrance into that fellowship, the sphere of the saved. Both sacraments are sacred mysteries. Luther referred to baptism as the welcoming of a person into the fellowship of Christ. The New Testament rite of baptism had parallels in Old Testament circumcision (Col. 2:11-12); the latter was a shadow of the former. Circumcision symbolized separation and finds fulfillment in baptism that pictures cleansing from the filth of the flesh (Rom. 6:1–6; Col. 2:12–14). Baptism pictures the new life in Christ, and that is why the Greek Scriptures connect it with genuine repentance (Acts 2:38). There is a connection between the invisible work of the Spirit in saving and its outward demonstration in water baptism (Acts 8:12, 36; 10:47; 22:16; Titus 3:5).

This is not to say that the first-century was the "best of times," and that subsequent centuries have somehow retrogressed. There were tragic behavioral flaws in the early saints (1 Cor. 5:1; 6:1–2, 12–20; 8:1–6; 11:21, 30) and doctrinal perversion was evident (Gal. 1:6). In that sense, the first century has proven to be little different from subsequent ones.

Reflecting on the churches of the first cen-

1.6. EARLY CHURCH WORSHIP

The aim of those who speak

edification

exhortation

consolation

1.7. WORSHIP IN THE EARLY CHURCH

1 COR. 14:26

When you assemble each one has:

A psalm (song)
A teaching
A revelation
A tongue
An interpretation

tury and the churches through the early centuries, one has to be struck with their simplicity. The churches met once weekly under a plurality of leaders for worship symbolized most pointedly in the Lord's Supper; it was a sacred community of the faithful who covenanted together to mutually instruct one another in the faith and share that faith in word and deed with others. The complexity of organization gradually evident in subsequent centuries was simply not there. As will become evident, the complexity of organization, as well as increased explanations of the church's message and function, came about as a function of the growth of the church in the empire. There were challenges to be met, saints to be protected, adversaries to denounce, explanations of the faith to strengthen the saints, and heresies to identify.

Is the church free to adopt methods and strategies that are not specifically delineated in the Scriptures? This has certainly happened, but is it justifiable? How can one be faithful to the Scriptures and address issues not directly addressed by them? It is my judgment that the Bible left a lot of things to human ingenuity and rational reflection, that the church is freed from the contextual restrictions of the first century, and is, thereby, enabled to adjust to any social, cultural, or political exigency it might encounter until the Lord returns at the end of the age. The church understands that the deposit of divine truth has been once for all delivered to the saints (Jude 3); however, our understanding and explanation of it is an ever ongoing process. To remain biblical means never to deviate from the directives of Holy Scripture, the apostolic commands; it does not mean that the practices of the early churches are incumbent upon the churches today or that they must limit us. We must never act in contradistinction to them. Simply put, there is a lot of "gray" every generation must negotiate that requires a diligent study of the Scriptures so that we listen to the voice of God as well as learn when that voice is silent. To be a biblically based community means that we conform our lifestyle, church practices, and beliefs to the Bible, yet we are not limited to the Bible. There is a sphere of creativity that is necessary for every generation of saints who seek to be faithful.

"The Apostles received the gospel for us from the Lord Jesus Christ; and Jesus Christ was sent from God. Christ, therefore, is from God, and the Apostles are from Christ. Both of these orderly arrangements, then, are by God's will. Receiving their instructions and being full of confidence on account of the resurrection of our Lord Jesus Christ, and confirmed in faith by the word of God, they went forth in the complete assurance of the Holy Spirit, preaching the good news that the Kingdom of God is coming. Through countryside and city they preached; and they appointed their earliest converts, testing them by the spirit, to be the bishops and deacons of future believers. Nor was this a novelty: for bishops and deacons had been written about a long time earlier. Indeed, Scripture somewhere says: 'I will set up their bishops in righteousness and their deacons in faith'" (Clement of Rome, *To the Corinthians*, 42).

The Earliest Fathers (90–150).

The terms, "church father" and "fathers of the church" generally refer to the writers and writings of the Christian church through the fifth century, though the term can be used to signify any writer throughout the history of the church. The earliest of the "fathers," those within two generations or so of the era of the canonical writers, have been designated as **apostolic fathers** or post-apostolic fathers ("earliest fathers") will be used to designate this group of writers because their works later were deemed inferior in quality to the canonical writings). As such, "earliest fathers" is being used to designate those writers or anonymous writings that appeared in the churches after the apostolic writings and before the middle of the second century. The small coterie of works is generally pastoral and moral in tone; they are not polemical, nor are they strident. The concern of these early churchmen is for the unity and purity of the church in following Christ (to these people discipleship meant martyrdom) in humbleness and humility. Here there are not defenses of the faith proclaimed in the churches, adversaries appearing either within or without, and attempts to demonstrate the truth claims of Christianity. The tone of the writings is exhortatory. This is an unique period in the history of our Lord's church and provides us with the first glimpse outside the canonical writings of the church.

1.8. EARLY CHURCH LEADERS

Apologists

Fathers

Apostles

The Earliest Fathers and Their Work

The corpus of the earliest fathers is composed of the works of five known writers and four anonymous works, one of which, the Epistle of Diognetus, has traditionally been misplaced among these writings but belongs to a later period. Little is known of these men. With the exception of Clement of Rome and Hermas, the writings emerge from the eastern portion of the empire suggesting that the church was numerically stronger there. All of the writings are in Greek, the universal language of the day. Two of the writers, Polycarp and Papias, were disciples of the Apostle John.

"And when our iniquity had been fully accomplished, and it had been made perfectly manifest that punishment and death were expected as its recompense, and the season came which God had ordained, when henceforth He should manifest His goodness and power (O the exceeding great kindness and love of God), He hated us not, neither rejected us nor bore us malice, but was long-suffering and patient, and in pity for us took upon Himself our sins, and Himself parted with His own Son as a ransom for us, the holy for the lawless, the guileless for the evil, the just for the unjust, the incorruptible for the corruptible, the immortal for the mortal. For what else but His righteousness would have covered our sins? In whom was it possible for us lawless and ungodly men to have been justified, save only in the Son of God? O the sweet exchange, O the inscrutable creation O the unexpected benefits; that the iniquity of many should be concealed in one Righteous Man, and the righteousness of One should justify many that are iniquitous! Having then in the former time demonstrated the inability of our nature to obtain life, and having now revealed a Saviour able to save even creatures which have no ability, He willed that for both reasons we should believe in His goodness and should regard Him as nurse, father, teacher, counselor, physician, mind, light, honor, glory, strength and life" (*The Epistle of Diognetus.* 2:4–6).

Clement of Rome (ca. 30–ca. 100) was a leader in the church of his city. Later tradition argues that he was the fourth bishop of the Roman See, but evidence does not suggest that a hierarchical form of church government had emerged in Rome at this early date (the tradition appears to emerge from Irenaeus in the late second century and was created to support the claim of the truthfulness of the gospel). The writing itself provides no clues that Clement viewed himself in any papal role. What is known is that he wrote a letter to the church in Corinth urging harmony and obedience among the believers (ca. 96–98), a situation not unlike Paul had earlier addressed in several letters (two being in our canon and at least one lost). Tradition states that Clement was martyred under Trajan.

"Let us fix our eyes on the blood of Christ and understand how precious it is unto His Father, because being shed for our salvation it won for the whole world the grace of repentance" (Clement of Rome, *To the Corinthians*, 7).

Ignatius of Antioch, also known as The-

Clement I icon in the city of Ohrid in the republic of Macedonia. From the thirteenth to fourteenth century.

ophorus, the God-bearer (ca. 35–ca. 110), was the bishop of his city (hierarchical government in the churches replaced plural rule in the East earlier than it did in the West, but for much the same reasons. See below.). On his way to Rome, where he would be martyred in the arena under Trajan, he wrote six letters to various churches and one to Polycarp, a fellow bishop. Among his many contributions, Ignatius was the first to use the term "catholic" to refer to the church as a whole (*To the Smyrneans*, 8:7), as well as a defense of Sunday as the day of Christian worship ("fashioning their lives after the Lord's Day, one which our life also arose through Him and through His death" [*To the Magnesians*, 9:1–2]).

A painting of Ignatius (c. a. 1000) of Antioch from the *Menologion* of Basil II. Courtesy of Miadifilozof.

"My spirit is devoted to the Cross" (Ignatius of Antioch, *To the Ephesians*, 18:10).

Polycarp (ca. 69–155) was a disciple of John and bishop of Smyrna. Having taught Irenaeus, perhaps the most significant of the later apologists, he is a link from the first century to the third. He suffered martyrdom under Emperor Antoninus Pius. His legacy is a letter to the church in Philippi. Papias (ca. 60–ca. 135), bishop of Hierapolis, was a hearer of John and a friend of Polycarp. His writings remain only in fragments recorded by the later writers, Irenaeus and Eusebius.

Little is known of Hermas of Rome. He appears to have composed *The Shepherd* in the early second century which is a heavily allegorical presentation consisting of a series of visions, mandates or commands, and similitudes or parables. It is the story of a slave in the home of a Christian whose freedoms won in Christ were lost by dereliction and regained; it was a highly prized exhortation to obedience. Among its many treasured features is insight into the governmental structure of the Roman church of his time. It is clear that the apostolic pattern of a plurality of elders and deacons was in operation; the concept of a single leader or monarchical bishop over the church is foreign to Hermas (*The Shepherd of Hermas*, 2.2.6, 2.4.3, 3.9.7).

The remaining writings are anonymous. *The Epistle of Barnabas* is unique in the literature of this period because of its strident polemic against Judaism (4:6–10) as well as its use of allegory to mine the "true" meaning of the Hebrew texts. These two features of the epistle have caused some scholars to think that its audience was the large Jewish community in Alexandria, Egypt. *2 Clement,* a homily, was once attributed to Clement of Rome and is now recognized as anonymous. It provides us a sampling of mid-second century preaching. *The Didache (The Teaching of the Twelve)* is a manual of church order; it provides a glimpse into rituals of the church, the conduct of laity, and the structure of leadership in the early second century. The book begins with basic instruction on Christian conduct (1–6), the Two Ways; turns to church ritual (7–10) such as baptism, the Eucharist, and prayer; and ends (11–16) with instruction for teachers, itinerant and local. The final work, *The Epistle of Diognetus,* is late second century and belongs in the corpus of the apologists, though it was initially placed in the work of the earliest fathers and remains so.

The Earliest Fathers and Their Teachings

Understanding a people in another culture and distant circumstances through contemporary perspectives and formulas is precarious. It is easy to forget that the way we look at things, determine priorities, and organize knowledge is often the result of various social and cultural factors. It is unwise to impose current viewpoints and perspectives on the past. Though it is difficult to imagine, the insights, circumstances, and interests of a distant people may not be ours. All of this to indicate that it is precarious to demand of the earliest fathers the theological interests that shaped subsequent centuries of theological discussion. Systematic

1.9. THE EARLIEST CHURCH FATHERS

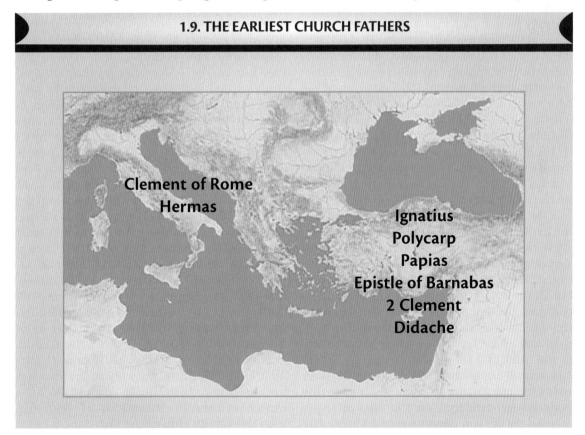

Clement of Rome
Hermas

Ignatius
Polycarp
Papias
Epistle of Barnabas
2 Clement
Didache

theology, divided into its several branches and answering questions developed over centuries of discussions, does not formally emerge until the late medieval era with the rise of the university, the scholastic community, and the formal classroom. The earliest fathers were neither speculative nor rationalistic in their approach to the faith, as is much later theology.

The Bible of the earliest Fathers was the Hebrew Scriptures. The sayings of Jesus and the apostles of Christ were given a place of importance, though the issue of collecting books to be read in the churches to the exclusion of others was not broached. The earliest line of defense in the churches was the concept of "apostolic succession," not a person in an office but the truth of the gospel passed through the office (2 Tim. 2:2). Christians argued that God gave his gospel to his son who brought it to the apostles. The apostles passed that message to their successors, such as John to Polycarp and Papias. Thus the churches became zealous to establish continuity with the apostles as proof of the genuineness of their proclamation. It became important later to argue that Clement of Rome was the fourth "bishop" after Peter and Ignatius was the third bishop after Peter in Antioch. Clement writes that the apostolic genealogy progressed from God, to Christ, to the apostles, and to the bishops and presbyters, not a single bishop at Rome (*Epistle to the Corinthians*, 42, 47).

The unspeculative, pastoral perspective of the earliest fathers is apparent in their understanding of the Trinity, a term coined later by Tertullian, and of the person of the incarnate Christ. They embraced the Trinitarian formula, but showed no evidence of explaining how it could be (for example: Hermas, *The Shepherd*, III.9.1). Central to their understanding was that Christ was "God in man, true life in death, son of Mary and son of God" (Ignatius, *To the Ephesians*, 72). The death of Christ on the cross was a foremost concept in the writings of this period, suggesting that the churches interests focused on the wonder of the incarnation, the procurement of life through Christ's death, and assurance through the resurrection. In *To the Trallians*, Ignatius exhorts his readers to remember "Jesus Christ who died for our sins, that believing on his death you might escape death" (7:1). Clement writes, "Let us fix our eyes on the blood of Christ and understand how precious it is unto His Father, because being shed for our salvation it won for the whole world the grace of repentance" (*Epistle to the Corinthians* (7:4). Ignatius is adamant before his detractors that "the official record is Jesus Christ; the inviolable record is His cross, His death, and His resurrection, and the faith which He brings about" (*To the Philadelphians*, 8).

In the life of the church two sacraments (the term means a "mystery," a shadowed figuring of profound realities) remained the focus of church worship: baptism and the Eucharist (the Lord's Supper). Baptism is viewed as the outward sign of inward spiritual life; it signified entrance into the invisible family of God and the visible family, the church. The *Didache* states that after instruction and fasting candidates are to be baptized in running water or by pouring water in the persons of the Godhead (7). The churches looked upon the act of water baptism as the simultaneous occurrence of cleansing; people came believing in the message to be saved (*The Epistle of Barnabas*, 11:11, *The Shepherd*, II.4.3.1).

The Lord's Supper or the Thanksgiving (the meaning of the term "Eucharist") was viewed as the "mystery" of the real presence of Christ among and for his people; it was a celebration of life through Christ. It was spiritual food. Ignatius speaks of it as "a the medicine of immortality and antidote that we should not die but live forever in Jesus Christ" (*To the Ephesians*, 20:2). The *Didache* provides two prayers to be spoken at the celebration (9–10); the second, in part, reads, you "bestow [ed] upon us spiritual food and drink and eternal life through thy Son" (10:5). The *Didache* also instructs the churches to observe "this sacrifice" when they assemble on the Lord's Day (14:1–5).

The manner of governing the churches gradually changed throughout the empire in the early second century beginning in the eastern churches. The *Didache* mentions the itinerant service to the churches of apostles, teachers, and prophets, but states that local churches were presided over by bishops and deacons, chosen by the congregations (15:1). Hermas indicates that presbyters presided over the church at Rome (I.2.6, 4:3). Clement of

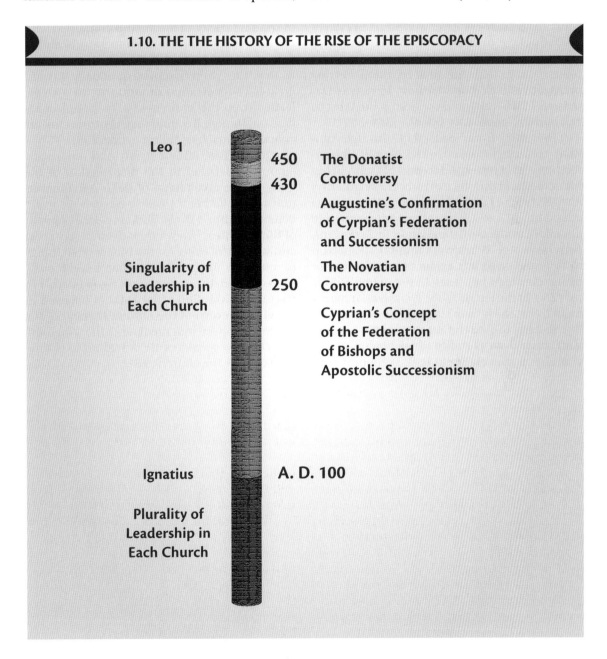

1.10. THE THE HISTORY OF THE RISE OF THE EPISCOPACY

Leo 1

450   The Donatist
430   Controversy

Augustine's Confirmation
of Cyrpian's Federation
and Successionism

Singularity of
Leadership in
Each Church

The Novatian
250   Controversy

Cyprian's Concept
of the Federation
of Bishops and
Apostolic Successionism

Ignatius   A. D. 100

Plurality of
Leadership in
Each Church

Rome urges the saints to obey the presbyters (*To the Corinthians*, 57:1). The rise of a monarchical bishop, a single leader over the church, in Rome appears late in the second century. The first certain date of a single bishop in Rome dates from Urban I (ca. 222–230); the first to claim the primacy of Peter was Stephen I (254–257); the first to claim that all the churches were answerable to the bishop of Rome was Julius I (337–352); the first to claim Petrine prerogatives based on Matthew 16:18 was Damascus I (366–384); and the first in the West to call himself "pope" was Siricus I (384–399).

The shift from leadership through plurality to a single leader in the church (the interchangeable terms, elders and bishops, being bifurcated and the office of bishop a singularity) emerged in the East and is found in the writings of Ignatius of Antioch. Ignatius's letters provide abundant evidence of the change. In *To the Trallians* he wrote, "When you submit to the bishop as to Jesus Christ it is evident that you are not living after men but Jesus Christ, who died for us" (2:1). In the letter, *To the Ephesians*, Ignatius argued that the bishop is to rule the flock (4).

Seeking to find the reason for the gradual shift away from plurality of leadership in the churches is speculative at best. Perhaps it is as simple as the insight that a monarchy is easier to administrate that an oligarchy. The concentration of authority, particularly in certain kinds of gifted people, might have been envisioned to be a better bulwark for the protection of flocks from false teachers. The concept of the singularity of leadership combined with the idea of apostolic succession most likely became acceptable for this reason. What is clear is that the church moved gradually toward greater concentration of authority in a single leader over the churches, a quasi-episcopalianism, though it would take centuries for the concept to reach its fullest expression.

The earliest fathers firmly and universally embraced a belief in the resurrection of the body as the great hope of believers. Ignatius notes, "The Father . . . will so raise us also who believe on Him" (*To the Trallians*, 9:2). Clement of Rome writes, "Do we then deem it any great and wonderful thing for the Maker of all things to raise up against those that have piously served Him in the assurance of a good faith" (*To the Corinthians*, 26:1). The Fathers believed in the visible return of the Lord at the end of the age resulting in judgment and the kingdom. The *Didache* speaks of the kingdom as a time prepared for the church (9:8).

GLOSSARY OF TERMS

Apostolic Fathers (Church Fathers, Earliest Fathers): the small group of writers or anonymous writing that came within two generations or less of the era of the canonical writers, giving the first glimpses of church life outside the New Testament writings.

Diaspora: a word that generally means "scattering." In reference to the Bible, and most particularly to the Jewish people, it refers to the dispersal of the Jews into the nations of the world by the Assyrians, Babylonians, and Romans.

Greco-Roman Tradition: a term used to express the influence of the "Mediterranean World," the cultures of ancient Greece assimilated into Roman culture that has subsequently impacted later Western conceptions of religion, government, language, and culture.

Mystery Religions: religious cults that flourished in the Greco-Roman era and in the early Christian period, each having its own sacred rites and rituals. Secrecy characterized religious expressions with disclosure made available only to the "enlightened." Many of these were eventually persecuted when the Roman Empire under Theodosius I made Christianity the sole religion.

Religion: A set of values, perspectives, and assumptions about life and human destiny that shapes the ordering of our lives, explains the array of human experiences, and provides hope. For the ancients, however understood, it was expressed in the firm postulate of a transcendent being, called god, or beings, called gods.

Roman Empire: The geographical, political ,and social hegemony of authorities extending from the city of Rome. At its height it stretched from England to the north of the Sahara, from the Atlantic Ocean to the Indus Valley.

Chapter 2 Outline

Chapter 2 Objectives

- That the reader will identify major periods of persecution under the Roman Empire

- That the reader will identify and define the heretical views that plagued the early church

- That the reader will identify the major apologists of the early church and their contributions to Christian doctrine

- That the reader will describe the development of the Biblical canon

- That the reader will gain insight into the development of the structure of the church

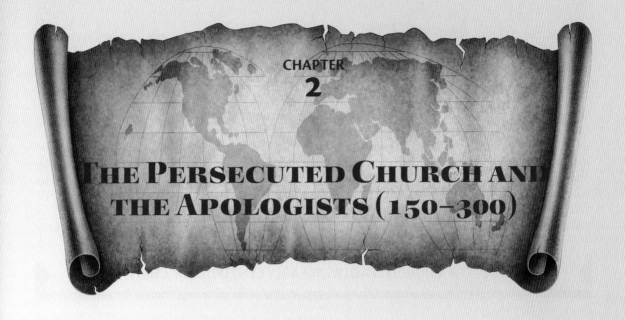

THE PERSECUTED CHURCH AND THE APOLOGISTS (150–300)

A S THE SECOND CENTURY unfolded, the number of Christians increased throughout the empire, but mounting accusations, threats, and persecution from those outside the church and false teachers within it accompanied this progress. The tone of the literature, as well as the sheer volume of it, changed; churchmen felt compelled to defend the church by answering its critics. The nature of much of the literature of the era, being largely polemical and strident, marks it as unique. In the course of answering the churches' opponents, these apologists/churchmen/bishops gave greater attention to explaining the nature of the Christian profession than the earlier fathers.

The Context for the Rise of Apologetic Literature

The difficulties the church encountered emerged from its unsanctioned place in the empire, where it was viewed as a political threat to social cohesiveness. Further, danger encroached from religions within the empire and doctrinal perversions in the churches that attracted a following; they led many naive and untaught people away from the church with partial truths, seeming answers to difficult questions, and attractive claims. To complicate matters, the churches attracted few from the learned classes, being composed largely of the lower strata of society, who were often poor and illiterate. (This is one of the accusations made by Celsus, an early critic of Christianity, that was valid [Origen, *Against Celsus*, 3.44]).

The existence of the church in the empire was tenuous; the threat of hostility was always present. Generally, Trajan's advice to Pliny, to leave Christians alone unless accusations were made against them, was followed. This being the case, persecution of the church throughout the early period was sporadic and localized. The danger of Christianity, it was supposed, was that it bred social divisions (here is the hint of class prejudice). The bond between state and religion was inseparably intertwined so that even failure to attend the theater or sporting events was seen as a threat to both. It might incur the wrath of the gods who would judge the empire. This insight led to Christians being blamed for droughts, floods, and military setbacks.

"This is the reason, then, why Christians are counted public enemies: that they pay no vain, nor false, nor foolish honors to the emperor; that, as men believing in the true religion, they prefer to celebrate their festal days with a good conscience, instead of with the common wantonness" (Tertullian, *Apology*, 35).

Celsus, an intellectual critic of the second century, whose writings are found in quotations from Origen's rebuttal, *Against Celsus*, argued that the incarnation of Jesus is a lie perpetuated by deluded followers. The "truth," he contended, is that the virgin birth was invented

2.1. TIMELINE OF CHURCH LEADERS IN EARLY CENTURIES OF CHRISTIANITY

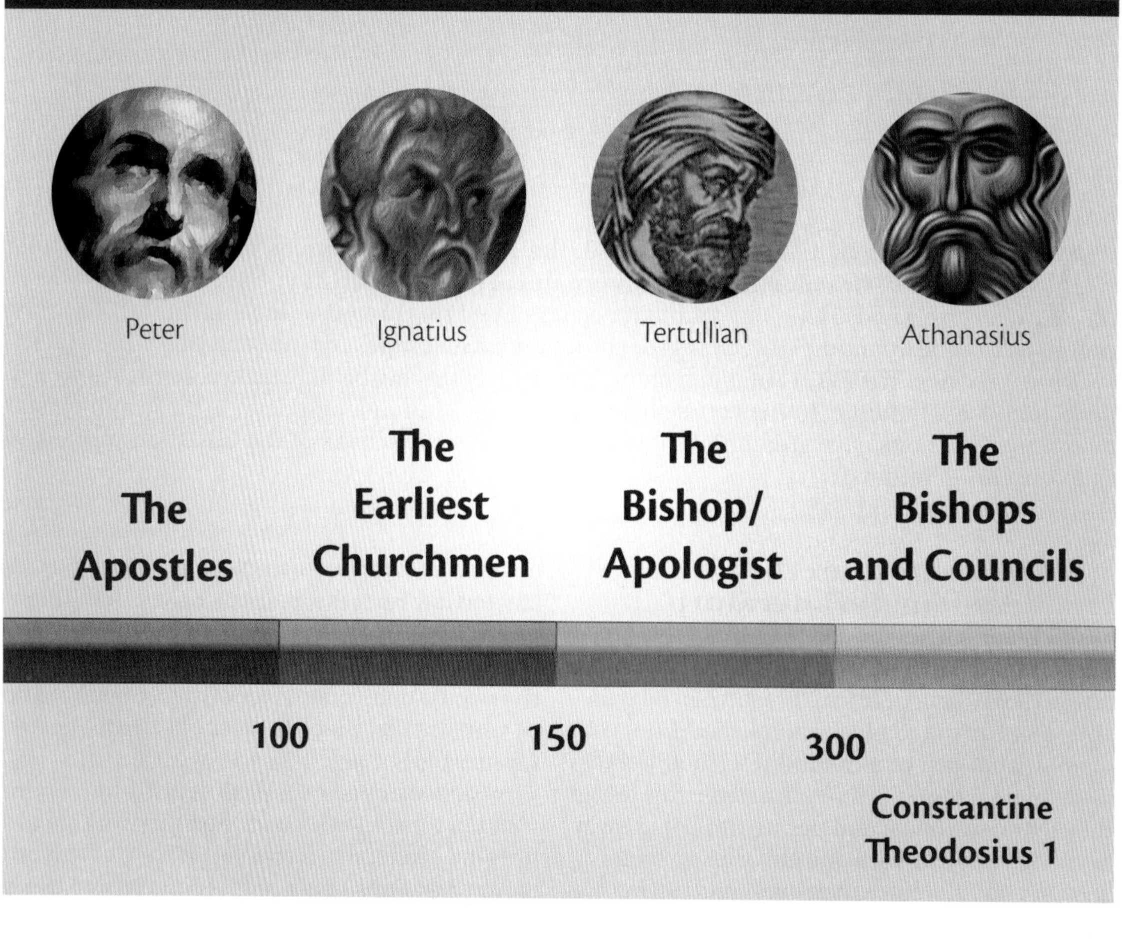

Peter — Ignatius — Tertullian — Athanasius

The Apostles — The Earliest Churchmen — The Bishop/Apologist — The Bishops and Councils

100 — 150 — 300

Constantine
Theodosius 1

to enhance Christ's importance. Jesus was born out of an adulterous affair and learned his magical powers from Egyptians (1.28). That the incredulous, irrational story of an incarnate god (4.64) had been concocted is proven by the fact that only the ignorant and gullible embrace it (3.55). There were two further accusations: first, if the story of a loving God who sent a merciful son into our world is true, why did he come to so few of them (6.78)? And, second, Christians are a danger to the state because of their antisocial traits and their stubbornness, their insistence that Jesus alone is God (8.55).

The State and the Church

The wrath of the state is a theme throughout the early centuries. The ravages of Domitian, who exiled John, followed the tradition of Peter and Paul's martyrdoms under the diabolical Nero. In the second century, the celebrated Ignatius of Antioch in the reign of Trajan and Polycarp in the reign of Antoninus Pius were killed. In the third century, Septimius Severus outlawed conversions to the Christian faith and likely extended the edict to those who sought to convert others. (This edict was imposed on Christians and Jews as the emperor mandated

Execution of Hippolytus in medieval miniature. According to legend, he was dragged to death by wild horses at Ostia, Rome's seaport. Provided by Polylerus.

religious **pluralism**). This may be the reason that bishops, such as Irenaeus, Hippolytus, and Cyprian were targeted. Perhaps, the most well-known martyrs of the period were Perpetua and Felicitas of Carthage. Perpetua was of the aristocratic class and Felicitas, her slave (there was another female slave and two men in the group). All were **catechumens**, recent converts, preparing for baptism. Refusing to denounce the faith, the two young mothers, along with the others, were killed.

The persecution under Decius (249–251) was the first of two that was enforced empire wide. The fortunes of the empire were on a downward spiral with economic unrest at home and increased military incursions on the borders. It was also the millennial anniversary of the founding of Rome. Decius's notion was that the restoration of prosperity depended upon national unity; Christians were blamed as perpetrators of social, religious, and political disruption. The focus on the persecutions

Emperor Traianus Decius (c. 201–June 251). Courtesy of Mary Harrsch.

was not to discourage conversion to Christianity; it was to retrieve people from Christianity so as to restore the prosperity of Rome. This persecution brought unexpected division in the churches, particularly in North Africa, over those who had lapsed in their faith and returned to sacrifice to the gods, only to seek repentance after the crisis passed. The division was over the policy of restoration, some advocating leniency and others a rigorist refusal to sanction readmittance.

Cyprian, the bishop of Carthage, who was

later martyred, took a conservative policy of readmission, bringing criticism from the strict exclusivists, a party led by Novatian of Rome. The issue of admission or exclusion was ultimately a question of the churches' understanding of the nature of divine grace. The **Novatian** party stressed the importance of obedience, the austerity of God, and that forgiveness for some sins should not be granted because it is wrong and leads to further moral laxity. Cyprian argued that God is by nature forgiving and loving, understanding human frailty. More importantly, he argued that the church is the conduit of salvation. To deprive

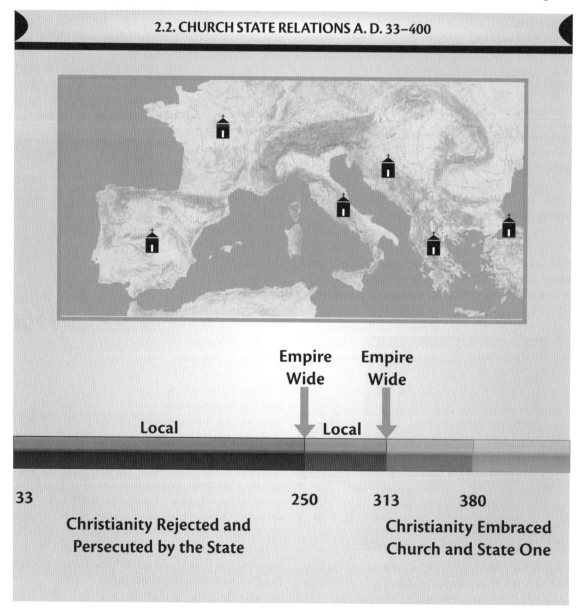

2.2. CHURCH STATE RELATIONS A. D. 33–400

Empire Wide

Empire Wide

Local

Local

33

250

313

380

Christianity Rejected and Persecuted by the State

Christianity Embraced Church and State One

a person of the grace that flows through the church is to sever them from Christ. The discussion divided the church at Rome. Novatian rejected Cornelius (251–253) and set up a rival bishopric, but Novatian was excommunicated by a local council and probably martyred under Valerian in 258).

> "For as for us, we reckon that no evil can be done us, unless we be convicted as evil-doers or be proved to be wicked men; and you, you can kill, but not hurt us" (Justin Martyr. *The First Apology*. 2).

Restoration received greater attention in the Diocletian persecution and in the writings of Augustine who defended Cyprian's less severe policies toward the lapsed. In part, these restorationists attempted to admit the lapsed but not promote moral laxity; the subsequent influence of this issue had much to do with the development of the medieval penitential system.

Severe persecution came to the church at the beginning of the fourth century under Diocletian (284–305). In the majority of his reign, Diocletian was not hostile to the Christian faith; his wife and a daughter embraced it. He was also an astute administrator. In an effort to stabilize the empire, he arranged for four leaders, two with the title of "Augustus" (himself in the East and Maximian in the West) and two subordinates with the title of "Caesar" (Constantius Chlorus in the West and Galerius in the East), to govern a portion of the empire with Diocletian supreme. A measure of peace and prosperity came to the empire except for conflict with the tribes along the Danube. Galerius viewed the ambivalent attitudes of Christians toward military service a threat and secured from Diocletian the authority to expel them from the army and to later force them to denounce the faith. A fire in the imperial palace, blamed on Christians, caused a change of perspective by the emperor, and he ordered sacrifices to the gods, churches destroyed, and

sacred writings burned. Those who refused to deny the faith faced death by hideous torture; many fled. Galerius forced the abdication of Diocletian in 305 and Maximian in 308, lifting the aggressive policies against the church to new heights of terror. With death nearing, Galerius ended the persecutions, allowing churches to again flourish so long as they did not become a social nuance.

> "The blood of the martyrs is the seed of the church" (Tertullian, *Apology*, 50).

Reaction to the decree forcing Christians to sacrifice to the gods and surrender sacred writings, or face torture and death brought several responses. Some, like the emperor's wife and daughter, renounced the faith but

Laureate bust of Diocletian at Museum of Archeology, Istanbul, Turkey. Courtesy of G. Dall'Orto.

Invitation to Church History: World

others remained steadfast in their allegiances. A problem emerged, as it had a half-century earlier, concerning the proper response of the church to the lapsed who later repented and sought the mercies of the church. It led to a schism in the North African churches that would endure for several centuries. The rigorists, led by Donatus (originally by Majorinus), argued that the efficacy of a bishop's work was related to the unsullied purity and perpetuity of his confession, which, in Donatus's judgment, disqualified many bishops from office and discredited their ministerial efficacy. When Felix of Aptunga, who had surrendered sacred writings in the persecution, appointed Caecillian as bishop, a group from Carthage rejected the appointment. The question they posed is an intriguing one: does the spirituality of the servant of God determine the benefit of his work, in this case to serve the sacraments and ordain to ministry? The Council of Arles in Gaul (314), called by Emperor Constantine, decreed that the validity of baptism or ordination does not depend on the merit of the administrator, though they did decree that a bishop who proved unfaithful in the persecutions should be exposed. A permanent schism resulted from the decree in 317. By the fifth century Donatists outnumbered Orthodox Christians in North Africa. That is, when Augustine used his literary and argumentative powers against them. The Donatist and the **Orthodox churches** suffered eclipse with the coming of the Muslims in the seventh century.

The State of the Church

The churches were beset with the potential problem of religious perversion from within, as well as political and intellectual attacks from without. Some of the teachings about the church were easy to refute. Athenagoras, for example, in *Pleas for Christians* answers the charges of atheism (to refuse sacrifices to the emperor was tantamount to the worship of no god), cannibalism in secret orgies, and inces-

tuous activity (3). The defense he proposed was the evidence of ethics, an appeal to the standards of conduct exhibited by early Christians. To the first charge, he replies that Christians worship the one true God: the Father, the Son (who is the idea or expression of the Father), and the Spirit (who is the power of God expressed), one in being, three in manifestations (11). To the other charges, he appeals to the superior morals of Christians, even those who may lack in the ability to carefully articulate their faith (12, 32). Beyond this, Athenagoras explained the absurdity of polytheism and, in the process, showed what Christians believed in contradistinction to the pagans.

Accusations from opponents, outside the community, did not have the immediate impact upon the churches as much as the distorted teachings that found some acceptance within the churches. To answer critics, who firmly stood outside the pale, was one thing; to counter the subterfuge of well-meaning "friends," though confused, deceived, or misled, is another. Further, as Athenagoras concedes, the Christian faith was embraced by the intellectually weak and uninstructed:

> Among us you find uneducated persons, and artisans, and old women, who, if they are unable in words to prove the benefit of our doctrine, yet by their deeds exhibit the benefit arising from their persuasion of its truth; they do not rehearse speeches, but exhibit good works; when struck, they do not strike again; when robbed, they do not go to law; they give to those who ask of them, and love their neighbours as themselves (11).

The most destructive threat that infiltrated the churches from outside the community of faith was **Gnosticism**. The fact that Gnostics often appealed to the same authority sources as did the Christian community (the standard of authoritative texts not yet determined), used much of the same language, and appeared to have cogent answers to troubling questions made their views acceptable. It was only when what they surrendered of Christianity became apparent that their assertions were shown to be untenable.

Gnostics asserted that the world was an evil place, created by a god other than the supreme God of the universe. After all, how could the sovereign and holy God create or permit a world so evil? And was not salvation as an escape from the world's evils simply an environmental explanation of dysfunctional behavior? An inferior god, a mixture of good and evil, created this world; material is evil; and deliverance is through the higher teachings of the true God delivered by his messiah, the Jesus-figure. In essence, Jesus is not God; Jesus is not human; Jesus did not die on a cross; Jesus did not rise from the dead. He was a moral teacher who came, not to be the way of life, but to show us the way to life. His higher life, his way of righteousness, was by way of avoidance. All Gnostics were dualists; all Gnostics believed a lesser god made the world and a less-than-God was sent as "redeemer," making salvation a secret for the "chosen" or enlightened. The fact that Gnostics appealed to the same writings as Christians caused the defenders of the church to think through the issue of authority. Were the words of the ancients enough?

A potent threat that arose from within the churches was the teaching of Marcion (ca.100–ca.160). Marcion was the son of a bishop in Sinope, Asia Minor, who appears to have acquired considerable wealth and came to Rome about 140. His teachings led to his excommunication in 144, the first schism among the churches, but his personal finances allowed his movement to continue. Marcionism was a blend of gnostic insights, anti-Jewish bias, and Christian teachings. Marcion struggled to find a solution to the discrepancies he observed between the God of the Hebrew Scriptures and the God of the Greek Scriptures and found a

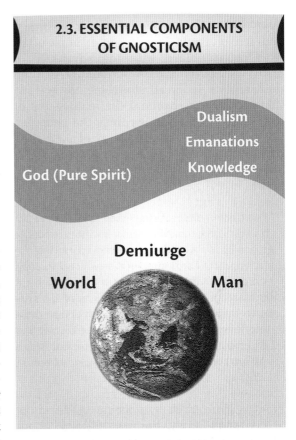

2.3. ESSENTIAL COMPONENTS OF GNOSTICISM

Dualism
Emanations
Knowledge

God (Pure Spirit)

Demiurge

World   Man

solution in two gods and two messiahs. The God of the Hebrew Scriptures was evil and cruel in contrast to the God of the Greek Scriptures who was merciful and kind, Driving a wedge between them, he envisioned a lesser, more materialistic god who made the world through a still lesser god and a good God who sent his son to deliver us from the confines of earthy imprisonment. Borrowing from the Gnostics, the incarnation was inconceivable; Jesus only appeared in human flesh and only appeared to die and rise from the dead. Further, Marcion took this set of assumptions and went about determining which of the Greek Scriptures were authoritative and which were not. Books that were "overly influenced" by the Hebrew Scriptures were rejected, leaving him with a mutilated body of writings (only an abridged

Luke among the gospel writers, no Hebrews, and ten of Paul's letters, for example). His teaching, combined with the advantage of his wealth, posed a most serious threat than the Gnostics. It forced churches, however, to think constructively about the relationship of the Hebrew and Greek writings the churches revered; about the compatibility of such attributes of God as wrath and mercy, generosity and justice; and the centrality of the physical life of Christ.

> "[Marcion], moreover, mutilated the Gospel according to Luke, removing all that is written about the generation of the Lord; and he removed much of the teaching of the Lord's utterances, in which the Lord is recorded as confessing most clearly that His Father is the Maker of the universe. He also persuaded his followers that he himself was more truthful than those Apostles who have handed down the Gospel; and he furnished them not with the Gospel but with a small part of the Gospel" (Irenaeus, *Against Heresies*, 1.27.2).

It is more difficult to assess the teaching of Montanus. Several things can be said about it. First, Montanists did not deny the orthodox faith at any major point. In fact, it could be argued that **Montanism** was a reforming movement though it added emphases that were rejected by most churchmen. Second, it did not bring about a schism in the church; it did cause polarization of churches that identified with Montantist emphases. Third, it did not appear to have been a uniform movement. In some areas, such as Asia Minor, it appears more radical than in North Africa.

Montanus emerged from Asia Minor after the middle of the second century; little is known about him. He claimed to be the mouthpiece of the Spirit of God, the promised Paraclete, as did two prophetess followers, This assertion implied that his insights, ecstatic revelations, were superior to the Scriptures and that a new age was beginning, the age of the Spirit, the

final age. Some of his followers appear to have been more extreme than he. However, the emphasis on moral purity within the movement was attractive to many who perceived that the church was adrift somewhat. This appears to have been the case with Tertullian, who embraced the movement and became its greatest defender. Montanism, which continued for several centuries in varying degrees, forced the church to reflect on the idea of its authority sources.

The Major Apologists and Their Contributions

The majority of the writers in the era of the apologists of the second and third centuries emerged from the eastern portion of the empire and North Africa. Some scholars have divided the apologists by their various approaches to the task of defending the church. The North African, Alexandrian apologists in the East sought to defend the faith by approaching it through a strong philosophical and spiritualizing perspective. Those in Asia Minor tended to approach their task in a grammatical, christocentric way. In the West a literal realism prevailed in approaching the Scriptures (admittedly these divisions are arbitrary).

Justin Martyr (ca.100–ca.165)

Likely born of either Greek or Roman parentage in Roman Palestina, Martyr was raised a pagan and educated in philosophy. On the Mediterranean seacoast at Caesarea about 130, he met a man who pointed him to Christ through the Hebrew prophets. Immediately, "a flame was kindled in my soul," he wrote (*Dialogue with Trypho*, 8). Justin was martyred in Rome under Marcus Aurelius. Martyr had given the church three major treatises: *The First Apology*, written to Emperor Antoninus Pius and his sons; *The Second Apology*, addressed to the Roman Senate, and the *Dialogue with Trypho*, an attempt at winning a Jew to the Savior.

2.4. THE MAJOR APOLOGISTS

▶ **Justin Martyr (ca.100–ca.165)**

▶ **Irenaeus (ca.140–ca. 202)**

▶ **Tertullian (ca.160–ca. 225)**

▶ **Clement of Alexandria (ca. 150–ca. 211/16)**

▶ **Origen (185–ca. 253)**

▶ **Cyprian of Carthage (ca. 205–258)**

"When he had spoken these and many other things, which there is no time for mentioning at present, he went away, bidding me to attend to them; and I have not seen him since. But straightway a flame was kindled in my soul; and a love of the prophets, and of those men who are friends of Christ, possessed me. And whilst revolving his words in my mind, I found this philosophy alone to be safe and profitable. Thus and for this reason I became a philosopher, and I could wish that all men were of the same mind as myself, not to turn from the doctrines of the Savior" (Justin Martyr, *Dialogue with Trypho*, 8).

Among Martyr's many insights in the defense of his faith, three are unique. First, he developed an approach to reaching those enamored with Greek philosophy, not unlike later Alexandrians. He posed the question: How do you account for truthful insights, though only partially so, in the great Greeks? He answered by arguing that the divine word, the logos, has been infused in everyone. It was partially distributed to the Greek philosophers, fully to Moses who antedates them, so that, if one wants to become a philosopher in the deepest sense, he should follow Moses and the Hebrew Scriptures that speak of the true redeemer, Christ. Justin wrote:

Mosaic of the beheading of Justin Martyr, Mount of the Beatitudes. Courtesy of Poletniy.

Invitation to Church History: World

"Moses is more ancient than all the Greek writers. And whatever both philosophers and poets have asserted concerning the immortality of the soul or punishment after death, or contemplation of heavenly things, or doctrines of similar kind, they have received such suggestions from the prophets, as have enabled them to understand and interpret these things, and hence there seem to be seeds of truth among all men" (*First Apology*, 44).

Second, Justin sought to explain the relationship between God the Father and God the Son. The question often posed to Christians was this, If God is one and Jesus is also God, how do you avoid two gods? Justin speaks of Jesus as the reason of God, meaning the one through whom God is known. This divine word, or logos, is the creator of the material universe and the revealer of God, being the incarnate Son of God.

Third, in Justin's attempt to speak meaningfully to Trypho, he employed an argument not unlike that he used with philosophers. In essence, he argued that to be a "real" Jew is to

be a follower of Jesus because the "real" Israel is the church. The nation, in effect, had been destroyed after the great Bar Kochba Rebellion (132–135), the Second Jewish Revolt. Justin saw tremendous continuities between the Old and New Covenants, insights not mined prior to his writing and in sharp contrast to Marcion in the West. For Justin, the Hebrew Scriptures point to Christ, the sacred writings being a seamless garment with one theme.

"I, Justin, the son of Priscus and grandson of Bacchius, natives of Flavia Neapolis in Palestine, present this address and petition in behalf of those of all nations who are unjustly hated and wantonly abused, myself being one of them. . . . For we have come, not to flatter you by this writing, nor please you by our address, but to beg that you pass judgment, after an accurate and searching investigation, not flattered by prejudice or by a desire of pleasing superstitious men, nor induced by irrational impulse or evil rumors which have long been prevalent, to give a decision which will prove to be against yourselves. For as for us, we reckon that no evil can be done us, unless we be convicted as evil-doers or be proved to be

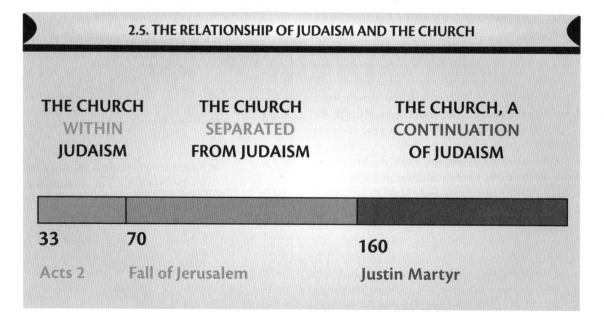

2.5. THE RELATIONSHIP OF JUDAISM AND THE CHURCH

THE CHURCH WITHIN JUDAISM	THE CHURCH SEPARATED FROM JUDAISM	THE CHURCH, A CONTINUATION OF JUDAISM
33	70	160
Acts 2	Fall of Jerusalem	Justin Martyr

wicked men; and you, you can kill, but not hurt us" (Justin Martyr, *The First Apology*, 1–2).

Irenaeus (ca.140–ca. 202)

In the "School of Asia Minor," the most outstanding apologist/bishop was Irenaeus. Raised in a Christian family, most likely in Smyrna, and a disciple of Polycarp, he later emerged as a priest in Lyon, Gaul. After the martyrdom of Photius, Irenaeus succeeded him as the second bishop of the city and remained there the remainder of his life. Irenaeus's concerns are that of a pastor called to defend and nourish his flock. Two complete compositions from his collective writings have been preserved, *Against Heresies* and *Demonstration of Apostolic Preaching*. The former is composed of five books in which Irenaeus refutes the validity of various gnostic groups; it is a masterpiece. The latter is an attempt to set forth the apostolic message.

"And not by the aforesaid things alone has the Lord manifested Himself, but also by means of His passion. For doing away with that disobedience of man which had taken place at the beginning by the occasion of a tree, 'He became obedient unto death, even the death of the cross;' rectifying that disobedience which had occurred by reason of a tree, through that obedience which was upon the tree" (Irenaeus, *Against Heresies*, 5.16.3).

As Irenaeus sought to discredit the gnostic claims to biblical authority, he realized that using Scripture was not adequate because many of his opponents claimed the same sources. Therefore, the *accurate interpretation* of the sacred writings became important to him. To build his case, Irenaeus appealed to apostolic tradition, the apostolic succession of the bishop, and the priority of the Roman bishop.

"He summed up in Himself the long roll of the human race, bringing to us a compendious salvation, that what we lost in Adam, namely, being in the

Stained glass image of the second-century saint is in Mansfield College chapel, Oxford. Courtesy of Lawrence OP.

image and likeness of God, we might regain Christ Jesus" (Irenaeus, *Against Heresies* 3.18.1).

Apostolic tradition is what has been taught about the Bible, commonly called the Rule of Faith. It is the oral transmission in propositional form of what is taught about the Christian message. It is the collective wisdom and teachings of the church that is a bulwark against private interpretations of the sacred writings. It is what has been passed down by those who taught us the Christian faith (2 Tim. 1:13–14, 2:2, 3:14; 2 Thess. 2:15, 3:4). Scripture and tradition formed in Irenaeus's mind a non-contradictory, seamless garment of truth; Irenaeus did not envision a time when the two would conflict.

A second line of the defense of the faith was the presence of a bishop in each of the churches who could trace a lineage of succession back to an apostle. From this concept grew the need for every church to demonstrate a linkage to an apostle or someone known to them. This, it was thought, would ensure the continuity of the church's message with Christ who passed it to his disciples, and from the disciples to their successors.

In the third line of the defense of the apostolic message, particularly expressed by Irenaeus, was the prioritizing of the bishopric of Rome as the custodian of the gospel. For example, Irenaeus says:

> "Tradition derived from the apostles, of the very great, the very ancient, and universally known church founded and organized at Rome by the two most glorious apostles, Peter and Paul, as also [by pointing out] the faith preached to men, which comes down to our time by means of the succession of the bishops. For it is a matter of necessity that every Church should agree with this Church, on account of its preeminent authority, that is, the faithful everywhere, inasmuch as the apostolic tradition has been

preserved continuously by those [faithful men] who exist everywhere" *(Against Heresies, 3.3.2).*

Irenaeus about 177 created the first genealogical connection between the Apostle Peter and subsequent bishops. Rome was an ideal illustration of the universality of the church's true teachings because the capital city had people from all over the empire. Thus, there is some guarantee that the faith taught at Rome faithfully reflected the apostolic tradition. The crucial issue is the truth, not geographic supremacy or prominent leaders. Hence a succession of truth, not men.

The contributions of Irenaeus are largely from the perspective of his pastoral concerns in the education and nourishment of his flock. What is remarkable about his writings is the Christ-centered, gospel-focused grid through which he understood the sacred writings. In answering the Gnostics, including Marcion, Irenaeus emphasized the unity of the Scriptures and, therefore, the singularity of God, the oneness of the God/man, Jesus Christ, and unity of the people of God. His sense of the unity of the Scriptures is evidenced in his understanding of the wonder of Christ's redemption. He connected Christ to Adam (Rom. 5:12–21) as the second Adam, who secured salvation through his obedience ("what we lost in Adam, namely, being in the image and likeness of God, we might regain in Christ Jesus" [*Against Heresies*, 3.18.1]).

Tertullian (ca.160–ca. 225)

Sometimes called the "father of the Latin church," he was the first major writer to compose his treatises in Latin, Tertullian was the son of a Roman centurion and grew up in Carthage, North Africa. He appears to have been trained in literature and rhetoric. He lived some time in Rome, where he was converted in his 30s. It is unlikely that he occupied a church office. He joined the Montanists in his later years, perhaps drawn to them by their moral rigor. His association with them and his separation from the mainstream of the church, likely accounts for the fact that his contributions to the church were not immediately recognized. He was a voluminous writer, producing over thirty extended works. Many of the terms he used in explaining the Christian faith in Latin have entered our theological vocabulary, such as the term *Trinity*.

> "What indeed does Athens have to do with Jerusalem?" (Tertullian. *Prescription against Heretics*, 7).

Though Tertullian's understanding of the faith differs little from the Alexandrian Apologists, his failure to appreciate the contribution of Greek philosophy stands in sharp contrast. For him, the Greek philosophers offer nothing, except danger, to the Christian. In contrast to the Scriptures, they can only offer tentative conclusions and speculation. "What indeed does Athens have to do with Jerusalem? What concord is there between the academy and the church? asked the great apologist (*Prescription Against Heretics*, 7). His point requires careful study, because, as is often supposed, he does not oppose philosophy or a rational methodology. His concern is the use of non-biblical sources to determine the content of the Christian faith. The opposition to philosophy is that it is a fallible truth source in contrast to the Bible. Christians should consult the sacred writings, not the pagan scholars when it comes to understanding the faith. Reason and faith are opposite truth sources. The one produces heresies and the other truth. Tertullian's razor sharp mind is at its best when he writes:

2.6. THE RECAPITULATION OF THE ACCOMPLISHMENT OF THE ATONEMENT

FIRST ADAM
Law Broken
Lost Eternal
Life for Man

SECOND ADAM
Law Obeyed
Regained for Man
What Adam Lost

But yet, if I have believed what I am bound to believe, and then afterwards think that there is something new to be sought after, I of course expect that there is something else to be found, although I should by no means entertain such expectation, unless it were because I either have not believed although I apparently have become a believer, or else have ceased to believe (*Prescription Against Heresies*, 11).

Clement of Alexandria (ca. 150–ca. 211/16)

In unknown circumstances, Clement came to Christ, but he sought for a teacher who might help him in deepening his understanding of the faith. This he found in the city of Alexandria, Egypt, under the tutelage of Pantaenus. He remained there most of his life, succeeding his mentor as the head of a catechetical school. He was forced to leave his post because of the persecutions under Septimius Severus; he then traveled to the East. Unlike Irenaeus, his concerns were related more to the defense of the faith before a pagan world than the shepherding of a flock. Unlike Tertullian, he embraced philosophical idealism, using it as a tool in defense of the faith. Three works are his major ones: *Exhortation to the Heathen*, *The Instructor*, and the *Miscellanies*.

"For many reasons, then, the Scriptures hide the sense. First, that we may become inquisitive, and be ever on the watch for the discovery of the words of salvation. Then it was not suitable for all to understand, so that they might not receive harm in consequence of taking in another sense the things declared for salvation by the Holy Spirit. Wherefore the holy mysteries of the prophecies are veiled in the parables preserved for chosen men, selected to knowledge in consequence of their faith; for the style of the Scriptures is parabolic" (Clement of Alexandria, *Misellanies*, 6.15).

A dominant feature of Alexandrian apologetics was to view truth through the embrace of the epistemological viewpoint of Platonism or **Platonic** idealism. Because the world was understood as a prefiguring of a greater reality, it was not difficult to apply the theory to the interpretation of Scripture, creating levels of learning or insight; the physical or literal sense was a shadow of a deeper non-physical reality to which it pointed. This shadow-versus-ultimate-reality dichotomy was applied by the Alexandrian tradition to Scripture as a tool to explain troublesome passages or to illustrate biblical truth in its unclear form in the Hebrew Scriptures.

Clement believed that there were levels of spiritual maturity related to levels of interpreting the Scripture. For the "simple believer," the sacred writings were to be taken at face value. For the "true gnostic" believer, the mature saint, there are deeper, non-literal meanings in Scripture (*Miscellanies*, 6.15). The embrace of platonic philosophy led to the use of the allegorical method of interpretation, which at times proved serviceable to the church and, at other times, allowed churchmen to devalue the sacred text, unaware perhaps that they had crossed the bridge into fantasy.

Origen (185–ca. 253)

Of all the apologists, Origen is the most confusing and most prolific. He was a defender of the faith and was gravely tortured during the reign of Decius. Though he was a prolific commentator on the sacred texts, he was non-orthodox in many ways. Unlike his mentor, Clement of Alexandria, Origen was raised in a Christian family and as a teen witnessed his father's martyrdom. He became a teacher in his native city, but after a dispute with his bishop over his unauthorized ordination as a priest, he moved to Caesarea Maritima where he taught, preached, and wrote for twenty years. His literary output was stupendous. In addition to compiling the *Hexapla* (a six-column work comprising the Hebrew Scriptures, a Greek transliteration of the Hebrew, and four other Greek translations), he composed commentaries on many of the biblical texts, wrote a defense against the critic Celsus (*Against Celsus*), and a theology text (*First Principles*).

> "One must therefore portray the meaning of the sacred writings in a threefold way upon one's own soul, so that the simple man may be edified by what we may call the flesh of the Scripture, this name being given to the obvious interpretation; while the man who has made some progress may be edified by its soul, as it were; and the man who is perfect and like those mentioned by the apostle. . . . this man may be edified by the spiritual law, which has "a shadow of the good things to come." For just as man consists of body, soul and spirit, so in the same way does the Scripture, which has been prepared by God to be given for man's salvation" (Origen, *First Principles*, 4.2.4).

In his philosophical approach, Origen was a **Neoplatonist**. This dualist theory of the seen, being only a pointer to the actual and ultimate, led him to interpret the sacred writings through various senses or levels, in the tradition of Clement of Alexandria. Origen embraced the doctrine of the Trinity of God (the Father, Son, and Spirit), though he appears to not have fully grasped their unity and equality. Profoundly devoted to the Scriptures and the tradition of the church, his understanding of them, at times, is truly amazing.

Origen believed that where Scripture ceases to speak, rational inquiry is warranted. For example, perceiving two creation accounts, he did not seek to correlate them. Instead he saw a spiritual creation (Gen. 1:1–2:3) and a physical creation (Gen. 2:4–25). The second creation was occasioned by a heavenly angelic rebellion; some became demons and others humans. Thus, he appears to have believed in the preexistence of the soul, pure spirits now encased in the limitation of mortal bodies. This led Origen to see the death of Christ as procuring release from the bondage of the devil, sometimes referred to as the ransom-to-

Satan view. He believed in the transmigration of the soul, rebirths, a progressive trek toward an eventual restoration and deification in the presence of God that is universal in scope.

Origen rejected the notion of an eternal judgment awaiting anyone. He argued that each soul stands before God in its fallen state with it own abilities and disabilities so that there is no single standard of response to God, ability being relative to knowledge and willingness. It appears that progressive enlightenment through the mind and will are the keys to redemption (*First Principles*, 1.6.2–3). His theory of time is progressive, rather than a redemptive discourse, anticipating the work of Georg Hegel.

Though it is not difficult to see Origen as a follower of Christ, he is an example of runaway enculturation, despite a profound interaction with the sacred writings. He sought to fit the faith into a Platonic and Gnostic worldview instead of seeing the faith as "truly" otherworldly. Epistemological assumptions shape the contours of the perception of what is valid and true.

Cyprian of Carthage (ca. 205–258)

Born into wealth, Cyprian was educated in rhetoric in his native city and was later very attracted to Tertullian. After his conversion, and the distribution of many of his possessions to the poor, he rose to become a bishop in the tragic times of the Decian persecutions. During the Decian fury, Cyprian through a vision left his city, fearing for his life, and went into seclusion to direct the affairs of the church. Some, including the bishop of Rome, viewed this action as cowardice. Several years later during the persecutions under Valerian, Cyprian refused sacrifice to the gods and did not flee. He faithfully prepared his flock for martyrdom and sacrificed his life for Christ. Cyprian's interest centered on the church and on being a faithful shepherd of the flock in difficult times; his writings are not of the polemical nature of either an

Irenaeus or an Origen. Among his works, the most important are *The Lapsed* and *On the Unity of the Church*. These works provide a lens to show how the churches functioned in relationship to each other in the third century.

> "The spouse of Christ cannot be adulterous; she is uncorrupted and pure. She knows one home; she guards with chaste modesty the sanctity of one couch. She keeps us for God. She appoints the sons whom she has born for the kingdom. Whoever is separated from the Church and is joined to an adulteress, is separated from the promises of the Church; nor can he who forsakes the Church of Christ attain to the rewards of Christ. He is a stranger; he is profane; he is an enemy. He can no longer have God for his Father, who has not the Church for his mother. If any one could escape who was outside the ark of Noah, then he also may escape who shall be outside of the Church. The Lord warns, saying, 'He who is not with me is against me and he who gathers not with me scattereth.' He who breaks the peace and the concord of Christ, does so in opposition to Christ; he who gathereth elsewhere than in the Church, scatters the Church of Christ. The Lord says, 'I and the Father are one;' and again it is written of the Father, and of the Son, and of the Holy Spirit, 'And these three are one.' And does any one believe that this unity which thus comes from the divine strength and coheres in celestial sacrament, can be divided in the Church, and can be separated by the parting asunder of opposing wills? He who does not hold this unity does not hold God's law, does not hold the faith of the Father and the Son, does not hold life and salvation" (Cyprian, *On the Unity of the Church*, 6).

Cyprian became embroiled in the controversy over the lapsed, the ones who had sacrificed to the gods and who had renounced the faith during persecution, but who sought later to return to the church, to be rebaptized, when the dark clouds had passed. He presided over several North African councils in Carthage to reach a consensus on the divisive matter. Those who could certify that they had not sacrificed

Head Reliquary of Saint Cyprian in the St. Kornelius chapel of the abbey church of Kornelimünster Abbey in Kornelimünster, Germany. Courtesy of ACBahn.

to the gods would be readmitted; those who had would be allowed to do so on their deathbeds unless they chose martyrdom before; and those who did not repent would be refused admittance. Others in North Africa and Rome, principally Novatus's party, conceived the policy as too lenient.

Cyprian argued for a degree of leniency based upon the nature of the church and the relationship of the bishops to the church. In essence, Cyprian answered the rigorists by stating that the unity of the church resided in the episcopate, the bishop of each church (a view propagated by Ignatius of Antioch in the East and repeated by Irenaeus in the West). The bishops were the successors of the apostles, and their authority, according to Cyprian, derived from the validity of that succession, the same that Christ granted to the apostles. Each bishop, presiding over his church in succession from the apostles, was autonomous in the affairs of his jurisdiction. The point was that authority resided in the bishop in ecclesiastical matters, not those who had survived the persecutions ("confessors") or another bishop. Though Cyprian recognized the priority of Rome among the churches ("the throne of Peter, the chief church whence priestly unity takes its source" [*Letter*, 54:14]), it was a historical precedent, a unifying precedent, not a jurisdictional precedent. After quoting from the Petrine restoration passage in John 21, Cyprian wrote,

> "He founded a single Chair, that He might set forth unity. He established by His authority the origin of that unity, as having its origin in one man alone. No doubt the others were all that Peter was, but a primacy was given to Peter, and it is thus clear that there is but one Church and one Chair" (*On the Unity of the Church*, 4).

The reason for Cyprian's insistence on the restoration of the lapsed is his understanding that salvation is only possible if one is in the church of the apostles, the faith expressed by that church. Said the bishop, "He who does not hold this unity does not hold God's law, does not hold the faith of the Father and Son, does not life and salvation" (*On the Unity of the Church*, 6)." Because the gospel is where the church is, where the bishop resides as the church, there can be no salvation outside the church, which is the gospel!

Other Apologists

Though the writers above were particularly prolific in the defense of the church in the second and third centuries, they were not alone in undertaking the task of responding to the critics of the church.

The *Letter of Methetes to Diognetus*, a work often misclassified among the earliest fathers, is an anonymous work written to a pagan of-

ficial who sought "to learn the mode of worshipping God prevalent among the Christians . . . what God they trust in, and what form of religion they observe. . ."(1).

Aristides of Athens wrote one of the earliest defenses of the faith and presented it to Emperor Hadrian. He stated, "But the Christians . . . while they went about and made search, have found the truth " (*Apology*, 15).

> "Christians trace their origin to the Lord Jesus Christ. He that came down from heaven in the Holy Spirit for the salvation of men is confessed to be the Son of the Most High God. He was born of a holy Virgin without seed of man, and took flesh without defilement; and He appeared among men so that He might recall them from the error of polytheism. When He had accomplished His wonderful design, by His own free will and for a mighty purpose He tasted of death on the cross. After three days, however, He came to life again and went up into the heavens" (Aristides of Athens, *Apology*, 2).

An intriguing apologist was Hippolytus of Rome (ca. 170–ca. 236). He appears to have been a disciple of Irenaeus, a prolific writer, a presbyter, an antagonist of the bishop of Rome, and a reconciled martyr. During the bishopric of Zephyrinius (199–217), he became disturbed by the bishop's unwillingness to stamp out a christological heresy known as **Modalism**, a denial of the distinction of the persons in the Godhead. When his successor, Callistus I (217–222), supported Modalism (Hippolytus, *The Refutation of All Heresies*, 9.2), Hippolytus set up a rival communion and served as bishop. Among his writings are *The Refutation of All Heresies*, *The Apostolic Tradition*, and *On Christ and The Antichrist*.

Melito of Sardis was a prominent bishop in Asia Minor in the second century; his works, though valuable and voluminous, are only available in fragments scattered in later works. It is known that he wrote an apology to Emperor Marcus Aurelius challenging him to examine the claims of the Christians and put an end to the persecutions.

Tatian (ca.110–ca.180) was born on the frontier between the empire and Parthia in the East and trained in Greek philosophy. Repelled by the immoralities within the culture, he was attracted to the integrity of Christians and became a member of the church in Rome. There he heard Justin Martyr and served as a teacher. After the death of Justin, according to Irenaeus (*Against Heresies*, 1.28), Tatian renounced the Christian faith, amalgamating Christian and gnostic beliefs, and returned to the East. His major works are two: *Address to the Greeks,* a description of Christian beliefs accompanied by a ridicule of paganism, and the *Diatessaron*, the latter being a harmony of the four Gospels.

Athenagoras of Athens (ca.133–ca.190) lived in the latter half of the second century and trained in Greek philosophy before converting to the Christian faith. Little is known about him except what can be gathered from his writings, *A Plea for Christians* and *A Treatise on the Resurrection.* The former was written to Marcus Aurelius, the emperor. Athenagoras answers at length the charge that Christians are atheists (4) and makes a case for the truthfulness of Christian claims based on the superior morality of believers. For example, in answer to the charges of murder and cannibalism, he answered with a stinging rebuke.

> Who does not reckon among the things of greatest interest the contests of gladiators and wild beasts, especially those which are given by you? But we, deeming that to see a man put to death is much the same as killing him, have abjured such spectacles. How, then, when we do not even look on, lest we should contract guilt and pollution, can we put people to death? And when we say that those women who use drugs to bring on abortion commit murder, and will have to give an account to God for the abortion, on what principle should we

> commit murder? For it does not belong to the same person to regard the very fetus in the womb as a created being, and therefore an object of God's care, and when it has passed into life, to kill it; and not to expose an infant, because those who expose them are chargeable with child-murder, and on the other hand, when it has been reared to destroy it (35).

Lactantius (ca. 240–ca. 320) was a North African Latin rhetorician. At the behest of Diocletian, he moved to Nicomedia in the East and served as a teacher. Sometime after entering imperial service, he was converted to the Christian faith. Diocletian's persecution of Christians forced Lactantius to leave his post. Through a later friendship with Constantine, he was restored to imperial service and died in Trier in Gaul at Constantine's palace, where he served as tutor to the emperor's son, Crispus. His most important work was *The Divine Institutes*; it has been hailed as the first Latin systematization of theology. It is more than that, however; it is an apology for the faith pointing out the shortcomings of paganism. Though a work of rhetorical beauty, it lacks scriptural depth. A second notable work is *On The Deaths of the Persecutors*. It chronicles the horrible deaths of the Roman emperors that persecuted the church, from Nero in the first century through Galerius in the fourth. Lactantius is recognized as the last of the apologists.

The Church in the Age of the Apologists

Justin Martyr described to Emperor Marcus Aurelius the manner of worship by Christians. He noted that they gather on Sunday, the day of the resurrection, in scattered local assemblies. In their meetings, the Hebrew Scriptures are read as well as the "memoirs of the apostles" followed by exhortation and instruction by the leader. Afterward there is prayer, the celebration of the Lord's Table, and a collection is

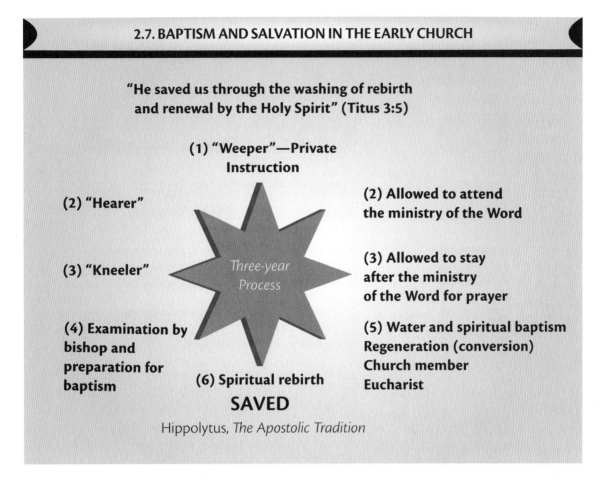

2.7. BAPTISM AND SALVATION IN THE EARLY CHURCH

"He saved us through the washing of rebirth
and renewal by the Holy Spirit" (Titus 3:5)

(1) "Weeper"—Private Instruction

(2) "Hearer"

(3) "Kneeler"

(4) Examination by bishop and preparation for baptism

Three-year Process

(2) Allowed to attend the ministry of the Word

(3) Allowed to stay after the ministry of the Word for prayer

(5) Water and spiritual baptism Regeneration (conversion) Church member Eucharist

(6) Spiritual rebirth
SAVED

Hippolytus, *The Apostolic Tradition*

taken up for the widows, orphans, and the otherwise needy (*First Apology*, 67). He explains, further, that the Christians find their roots in the patriarchal promises and that the revelation of God is revealed through two covenants, an old and a new. The old has been abolished in Christ and replaced by the new. Christians are the new people of God (*Dialogue with Trypho*, 11).

Aristides speaks of the Christians as the fourth race, distinguishing barbarians, Jews, and Greeks from the saints. Irenaeus speaks of the church as the "glorious body of Christ," meaning it is one composed of many churches across the empire, the fulfillment of the promises to Abraham of children (*Against All Heresies*, 4.33.7; 5.32.2). Origen states that the church is the body of Christ because it is animated by him and consists of all who are believers in him (*Against Celsus*, 6.48).

Central to the worship in the church was the celebration of and participation in the gospel through symbol as well as instruction through the Word. Two symbolic ceremonies were common to the churches: baptism and the Lord's Table or Eucharist (the Thanksgiving). The former was the means of entrance into the church; it was a welcoming into the family, the body of Christ.

Justin Martyr, for example, states rather clearly that those who are "persuaded and believe" the message of Christ are to be brought,

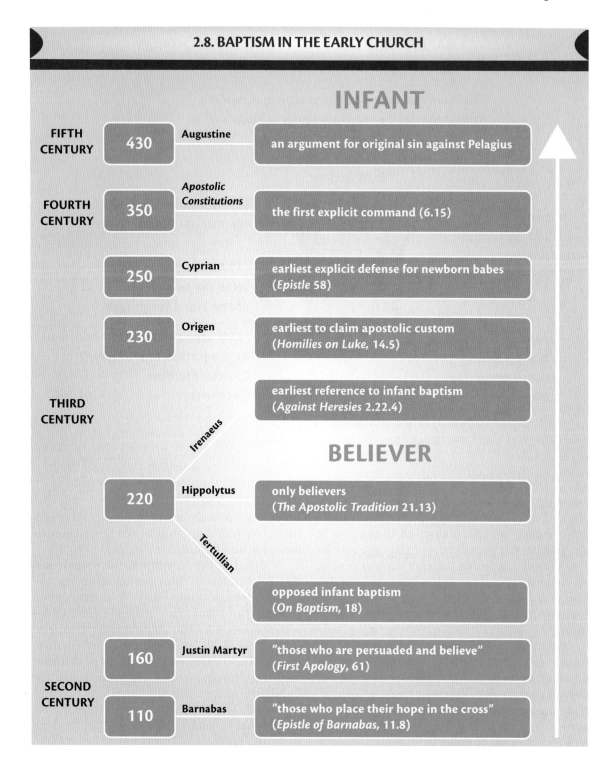

2.8. BAPTISM IN THE EARLY CHURCH

INFANT

| FIFTH CENTURY | 430 | Augustine | an argument for original sin against Pelagius |

| FOURTH CENTURY | 350 | Apostolic Constitutions | the first explicit command (6.15) |

| | 250 | Cyprian | earliest explicit defense for newborn babes (*Epistle* 58) |

| | 230 | Origen | earliest to claim apostolic custom (*Homilies on Luke*, 14.5) |

| THIRD CENTURY | | Irenaeus | earliest reference to infant baptism (*Against Heresies* 2.22.4) |

BELIEVER

| | 220 | Hippolytus | only believers (*The Apostolic Tradition* 21.13) |

| | | Tertullian | opposed infant baptism (*On Baptism*, 18) |

| | 160 | Justin Martyr | "those who are persuaded and believe" (*First Apology*, 61) |

| SECOND CENTURY | 110 | Barnabas | "those who place their hope in the cross" (*Epistle of Barnabas*, 11.8) |

2.9. THE LORD'S SUPPER IN THE EARLY CHURCH

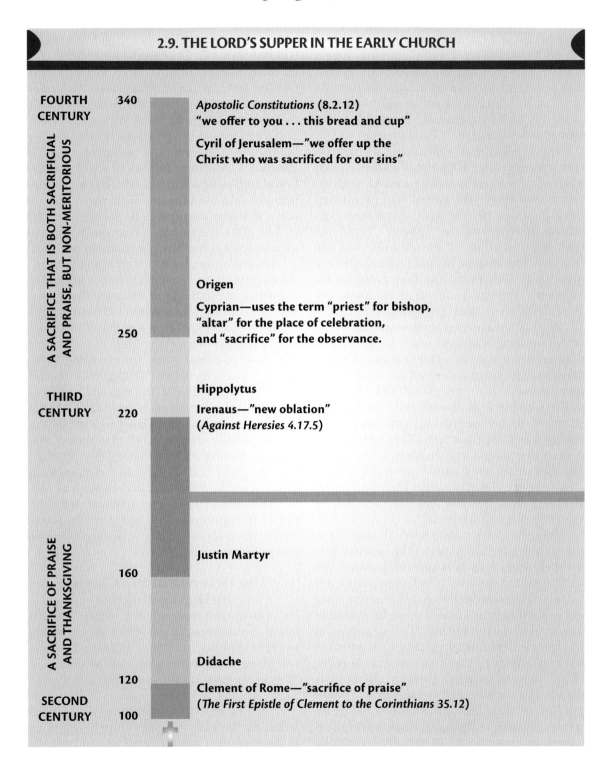

FOURTH CENTURY

340

Apostolic Constitutions (8.2.12)
"we offer to you . . . this bread and cup"

Cyril of Jerusalem—"we offer up the Christ who was sacrificed for our sins"

A SACRIFICE THAT IS BOTH SACRIFICIAL AND PRAISE, BUT NON-MERITORIOUS

Origen

Cyprian—uses the term "priest" for bishop, "altar" for the place of celebration, and "sacrifice" for the observance.

250

THIRD CENTURY

Hippolytus

Irenaus—"new oblation"
(*Against Heresies* 4.17.5)

220

A SACRIFICE OF PRAISE AND THANKSGIVING

Justin Martyr

160

Didache

120

Clement of Rome—"sacrifice of praise"
(*The First Epistle of Clement to the Corinthians* 35.12)

SECOND CENTURY

100

after prayer and fasting, to water where in receiving the "washing of water" they are "regenerated" (*First Apology*, 61). Clement of Alexandria speaks of baptism as an illumination, "a washing by which we cleanse away our sins; grace by which the penalties accruing to transgressions are remitted." (*The Instructor*, 1.6).

The process that culminated in baptism was a lengthy one. Hippolytus indicates that a learner, a catechumen, received instruction over a three-year period and progressed through stages (the "weeper," permitted only private instruction; the "hearer" could attend the preaching of the church, and the "kneeler" was allowed to hear prayers after the preaching). Only then were they prepared for baptism. Baptisms occurred on Sundays; the candidates were naked (*The Apostolic Tradition*, 17, 20, 21). Though the church looked upon the reception of salvation and water baptism as simultaneous, it was not water that saved. It was the gospel message witnessed to in the water that cleansed. The early church did not separate the reality from the symbol. Though it is strange to us, believers came to the water to be saved (Acts 2:38; Titus 3:5). Hippolytus makes it clear that should catechumens be martyred for their faith, they would inherit salvation (*The Apostolic Tradition*, 19.2). Therefore, in the strictest sense, baptism was not required for salvation, but only a true faith.

There has been considerable discussion in the church over age issues. That baptism was withheld from infants is unclear because the word used for children is not age-specific. Infants were baptized in the church, but that does not in itself help us know if those incapable of instruction were baptized. The structure of the catechetical format leading to baptism is a strong argument that those incapable of instruction were excluded. However, Hippolytus does have a statement that children who could not express their faith, for whatever unknown reason, could have their parents do so for them (*Apostolic Tradition*, 21.4). Tertullian cautions against baptizing too quickly and too young (*On Baptism*, 18). Cyprian delineated the case for the baptism of infants based, in part, on the Old Testament ritual of circumcision. He makes it clear that, in his view and the judgment of a council of bishops in North Africa, that newborns can receive divine grace (*Epistle*, 58). The baptism of true infants is commanded in the *Apostolic Constitution* (6.15) and appears as the first record to do so (this particular chapter appears to date from the middle of the third century). It seems reasonable to conclude by the middle of the third century that the baptism of incapables was becoming a common practice.

Immediately after baptism through the catechetical method, the baptized were permitted to participate in the Lord's Supper, the Eucharist. The Supper was a symbol of being in the family of God, baptism a symbol of entrance. The bread symbolized the body of Christ and the "bowl of mixed wine," the shedding of his blood "for all who believe" (Hippolytus, *The Apostolic Tradition*, 23, 27). The fruit of the Eucharist was the cleansing of the conscience. Justin Martyr understood that Christ was present in the eucharistic elements, but also speaks of it as a nourishing remembrance (*First Apology*, 66). The early church held to an ambivalent position on the Eucharist, perceiving it as real, yet symbolic; memorial, yet spiritual. The comments of Hippolytus indicate that the Lord's Table was a joyous event with much singing and a communal meal.

The Defense of the Church by the Apologists

To protect and instruct the saints, bishops found it important to construct means to answer the church's critics and insure that correct teachings were promulgated in the churches. Thus in the early centuries three protective devices emerged.

The first of these is the rise of the bishop's office. By the early second century, beginning in the East, the churches gravitated away from a plurality of leadership in the house churches. This trend was coupled with the concept that the message of the gospel had been transmitted from God the Father to Christ the Son who diligently taught it to his disciples. In turn, they passed it on to others, creating a notion of truth succession. In answering their critics, churchmen pointed to an unbroken message passed from heaven. The bishops became increasingly important in apologetic pursuits because they were the ones through whom the truth was preserved. People could point to the successions of their bishops back to an apostle with the assurance that they were in the truth, the gospel. The church, the bishop, and the gospel were one. In this context, the comment of Cyprian that there is no salvation outside the church, or the bishop makes sense. Among the churches, four had direct contact with the apostles. These then became the principal churches that others looked to for apostolic connection.

The first of these was Jerusalem where Peter, James, and John were described as "pillars," but the church had been disseminated in the Jewish revolts and was no longer a hub of Christian activity. The second was Antioch where Syrian Christianity flourished and Peter and Paul ministered. The third was Alexandria, Egypt, which according to tradition had early contact with John Mark and was the most prominent city in the eastern world. The fourth was Rome, the capital of the empire in the early Christian era. Though not founded by Paul, the Rome church was blessed with the witness of the two most prominent apostles, Peter and Paul, and both were martyred there. There was a fifth, Constantinople, but it only emerges in the fourth century. It was built by Constantine and became the second capital of the empire after the decline of the empire in the West. Churches looked to these metropolitan churches for advice and assistance.

A second line of protection was the catechetical method developed to prepare people for recognition as Christians. The process encompassed three years of instruction and the careful monitoring of the candidate's lifestyle. "When they are chosen who are to receive baptism, let their lives be examined, whether they have lived honorably while catechumens, whether they honored the widows, whether they visited the sick, and whether they have done every good work" (Hippolytus, *The Apostolic Tradition*, 20).

As a catechumen came for baptism, he or she would affirm their faith by answering a series of questions as a statement of faith. This method was the precursor of the Old Roman Symbol, a second-century formula, and forerunner of the Apostles' Creed. The creed begins with the words, "I believe." It is a confession of personal faith. The emphasis on the incarnation of Christ would have been a powerful repudiation of Docetism, the denial that Christ came in human flesh, embraced by Gnostics and Marcionites.

A third line of defense was the gradual realization of the necessity of recognizing the writings of the apostles, or those sanctioned by contact with an apostle, to be read in the churches. The churches readily recognized the Hebrew Scriptures, generally the Greek translation of them, (the Septuagint), which had been done in Alexandria, Egypt, However, the recognition of a volume of newer writings took some time, though the works of the apostles were elevated and revered in the churches. Further, the writings were carried from church to church, and given the spread of churches throughout the empire and the limitations of travel, many were unaware of some of them. The inroads of the Gnostics with their own writings, as well as the destructive opinions of Marcion and the expansive concept of continuing words from the Lord as practiced by the Montanists, caused churchmen to shore up the issue of what the Lord's people should be exposed to in the churches.

The earliest collection of Greek texts dates from the late second century and is commonly called the Muratorian canon after an eighteenth century historian who discovered the manuscript. The list includes the four gospels, all the epistles of Paul, and Acts by Luke; Hebrews, the two epistles of Peter, and James are not included. The Apocalypse of John and two other epistles by John are included. The writer adds that the Apocalypse of Peter is read in some churches, though not all of them, and the Wisdom of Solomon, an intertestamental Greek text, is received.

The first translation of the apostolic books was done in Syriac, the Peshitta or "simple version," in the second century. The fact that the first translation of the Bible outside the orig-inal language was in Syria bears witness to the growth of the church in Syrian Antioch. This early version included all the books as we have them with the exception of 2 Peter, 2 and 3 John, Jude, and Revelation.

The issue of the list of authoritative books to be read in the churches emerged slowly. The gospels and the writings of Paul and Acts by Luke, were received very early. The smaller books or those that created controversy were not as readily made a part of the church's worship.

In 363 about thirty churchmen gathered at Laodicea in Asia to discuss the health of the churches. Emperor Julian (331–363), the Apos-

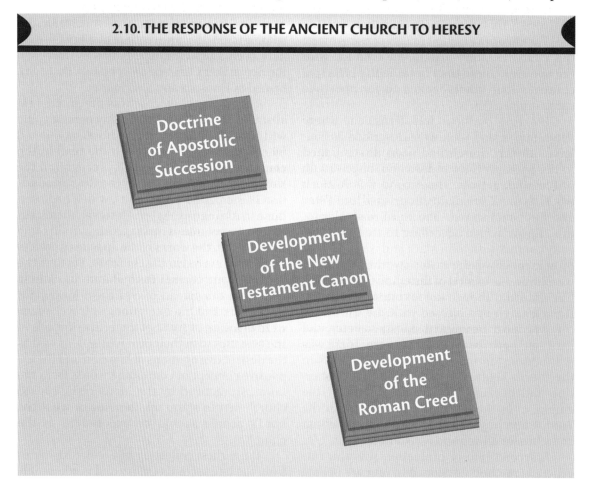

2.10. THE RESPONSE OF THE ANCIENT CHURCH TO HERESY

Doctrine of Apostolic Succession

Development of the New Testament Canon

Development of the Roman Creed

tate, had lost his life in fighting the Persians, but strenuously had sought to bring about a revival of traditional Roman religion, causing a regression of Christian fortunes. Part of the approach of these bishops was to strengthen the churches by restricting the books to be read in the churches. The fifty-ninth canon of the council listed the Old Testament books consistent with later Protestant lists, but included two additional books, Baruch and the Letter of Jeremiah. The sixtieth canon listed the New Testament books, with the exception of the book of Revelation.

In 367 the bishop of Alexandria, Athanasius, published a festal letter for the churches and monasteries in Egypt. The annual letter set the date for Easter and the beginning of the Lenten season and, in so doing, established the times of all festivals for the year. The bishop was concerned that unauthorized, fraudulent books might circulate in the churches upsetting the faith of some. Accordingly, he listed the books authorized in the churches; his list comprised the twenty-seven books of the Orthodox canon as we have it today. The Old Testament canon included Baruch and the Letter of Jeremiah, but excluded Esther, which he listed along with the Wisdom of Solomon, Wisdom of Ben Sirach, Tobias, Judith, the Shepherd of Hermas, and the Didache as "fabrications of heretics."

Athanasius wrote in AD 367 his thirty-ninth Festal Letter on the occasion of Easter, in which he identified the twenty-seven books of the New Testament, the same twenty-seven we use today. He was the first person to identify these and by doing so established a high-water mark in the canon of the New Testament books. Fifteen years later, at the Council of Rome in 382, Pope Damascus I, bishop of Rome, distributed a similar list with the same twenty-seven books as Athanasius. In 397 the Third Council of Carthage reiterated this same list in the "Festal Letter" of AD 366/7.

The bishop of Rome, Damascus I, convened a council in his city in 382. In the canons of the council there is a list of the canonical books. Of the New Testament books there are twenty-seven, the same in all Orthodox churches. However, the list of Old Testament Scriptures, forty-six in number, contained seven books later rejected by Protestants (Wisdom of Solomon, Wisdom of Ben Sirach, Judith, 1 and 2 Maccabees, and Tobias). Baruch is included with Lamentations as one book).

From this time, the books of the New Testament were solidified. Subsequently, the Council of Hippo, North Africa, in 393 and the Council of Carthage, 397, confirmed the New Testament canon at twenty-seven books. The Old Testament canon received no consensus within the churches, at least until the sixteenth century. Jerome's masterful translation of the sacred writings, the Latin Vulgate, had three sections of books: thirty-nine Old Testament books, twenty-seven New Testament books, and thirteen others arranged in the back of the volume, not considered by him as worthy to be read in the churches. While later Protestants will protest the use of all thirteen, Roman Catholics will place seven of them among the Hebrew texts as equally canonical. The extent of the Old Testament canon was not resolved in these early centuries.

GLOSSARY OF TERMS

Catechumen: in early Christianity the term meant a person who was willing to receive instruction in the faith with the eventual possibility of baptism, the symbol of true Christian profession.

Gnosticism: a second century heresy that elevated obscure and mystical knowledge over faith. A potent threat to the church, Gnostic faith reflects each teacher though common characteristics can be discerned: a radical dualism of spirit from matter; emanationism, a belief in a plurality of gods with one semigod creating the material world; salvation through secret knowledge, involving asceticism; and a denial of the incarnation of Christ.

Marcionism: a second-century heretical group that combined some of the teachings of Christianity and Gnosticism with a dose of anti-Jewish religious appreciation. Led by Marcion, the sect accepted a series of dichotomies that sharply divided the Old Testament from the New Testament writings as well as disparaging Jewish-flavored books in the latter. Marcion argued for two gods in the writings, one good and one evil and a docetic, merely spiritual Christ. He made the church think about the creator-redeemer unity as well as the canon of sacred writings.

Modalism (Patripassionism, Sabellianism): the attempt to explain the Trinitarian existence of God by arguing for a strict singularity of God in person and attributes, but in a threefold manifestation. Often designated by a major proponent, Sabellius, God is seen as threefold in manifestation but singular in person. This explanation of the divine Trinity was consistently condemned in the fourth and fifth-century ecumenical councils of the church.

Montanism: a second-century movement in the church that sought to restore it to its first-century purity—the assumption being the church had drifted morally and spiritually, by emphasizing the extraordinary spiritual gifts of healing and perhaps ecstatic utterances and ecstasy. Some Montanists embraced the concept of continuative revelation through prophets, forcing the church to take up the issue of canon, or books to be read in the churches. The movement was condemned in the church, but it did have a prominent supporter in the great Tertullian.

Neoplatonism (Neo-platonists): a philosophically religious movement that arose in the third century, a synthesis of Platonic thought with Gnostic insights and Jewish theology in the tradition of the Alexandrian Philo. In essense it was a type of theistic monism. Neoplatonists, in contrast to Platonists who saw this world as a merely shadow of a greater invisible reality, envisioned ultimate reality in the infinite world of experience, thus eliminating the gap between form or substance and reality, by combining them.

Novatianism (Novatian Party, Rigorism): a third-century crisis in the early church caused by division of opinion concerning the treatment of Christians who had faltered in faith during the Decian persecutions. While Cyprian favored the readmission of such because he considered that the church was the only ground of salvation, the Novatians favored exclusion because they viewed the lapsed in violation of the qualifying characteristic of holiness.

Orthodox Church (the Eastern Church): a major expression of the Christian faith, along with Roman Catholicism and Protestantism, that resulted from a separation from the Western Catholic churches, in the Great Schism, a devastating division in 1054, largely over the issue of the intrusion of the Western church in Eastern church affairs.

The Orthodox community is composed of several independent churches, recognized along ethnic lines (for example, the Antiochian Orthodox Church, the Greek Orthodox Church, and the Serbian Orthodox Church) with leadership placed in the Patriarch of Constantinople, the second capital of the former Roman Empire, though the patriarchs in the various churches are seen as equal.

When the term "Orthodox church" is used prior to the 1054 schism, it means those churches that possess what is considered correct faith and practice. In the fourth century and beyond, it refers to the affirmation of the findings of the ecumenical councils.

Platonism (Platonic Idealism): a philosophical school of thought developed by Plato concerning the nature of reality, central to which is the distinction between what is perceptible, but not intelligible, and that which is intelligible but imperceptible. Plato argued that reality existed most fully before the forms and substance. The observable functioned as shadows or figurements of that greater, more real reality. Platonist thought has proved both a handmaid to Christian theology as well as a detriment in the hands of monastistics, mystics, and transcendentalists who disparaged substance and form as less than real.

Pluralism: a perspective integral to postmodern, deconstructionist approaches to the nature of truth, it is a counter-response to the progressive optimism and utopian idealism of Enlightenment thought. Truth is private and individualized, a non-corporate concept of reality with all values as relative.

Chapter 3 Outline

The Prominent Bishops

The Trinitarian Controversy
Adoptionism
Modalism
Arianism
Nicene Othodoxy

The Christological Controversies
Apollinarianism
Nestorianism
Eutychianism
Monophysites and Chalcedonians

The Development of Monasticism
Saint Anthony
Simon the Stylite
Cenobites

The Augustinian-Pelagian Controversy
Augustine, Bishop of Hippo
Augustine and the Pelagian Controversy
The Post-Augustine Pelagian Controversy
The Synod of Orange (529)

The Crisis in the Western Empire

Missions among the "Barbarians"
Ulfilas
Martin of Tours
Gregory of Tours
Patrick of Ireland

The Church at the End of the Ancient Period

Chapter 3 Objectives

- That the reader will provide the reasons for the improving relations between Christianity and the Roman Empire

- That the reader will define the Trinity as well as alternative models declared to be heretical

- That the reader will describe the major accomplishments of the Councils of Nicaea, Constantinople, Ephesus, and Chalcedon

- That the reader will define the orthodox view of Christology as well as alternative models declared to be heretical

- That the student will delineate between the perspectives of Augustine and Pelagius on the effect of sin on humanity

- That the student will understand the importance of the revisionist Cassianian approach to salvation as well as the ramifications of the Synod of Orange in the medieval period

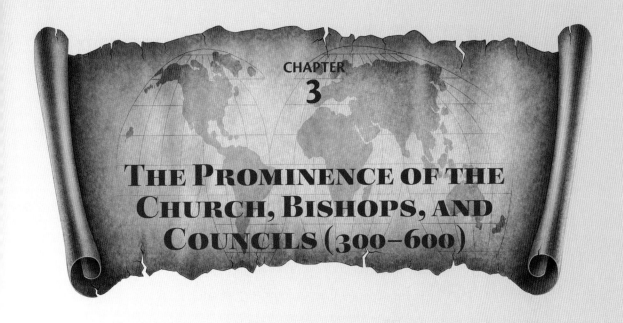

CHAPTER
3
THE PROMINENCE OF THE CHURCH, BISHOPS, AND COUNCILS (300–600)

T HE FOURTH CENTURY BROUGHT an unexpected turn of events. Who would have thought an emperor would be sympathetic to the Christian faith? Since the times of Claudius and Nero, the church had felt the hostility of the state. Christians were perceived as a low, illiterate class whose unwillingness to participate in the community threatened the unity of the empire by incurring the wrath of the gods.

Diocletian had divided the administration of the empire between himself in the East and Maximian in the West with two subordinates (Galerius and Constantine Cholorus respectively). Galerius forced the abdication of Diocletian and Maximian with military threat and installed puppets. When Constantine Cholorus died, the legions sided with his son, Constantine, who controlled the Western portion of the empire (North Africa, Spain, Gaul, and Britannia). Galerius, the last of the persecuting emperors before Constantine's rise to complete power, died and was replaced by Licinius.

Licinius (who married Constantine's sister), Constantine, and Maximinus Daia considered Maxentius's appointment as the successor of Maximian illegitimate.

Constantine defeated Maxentius in 312 at Milvian Bridge, entered Rome, and annexed his territories. It was at this time that Constantine, either through a vision or dream, adopted the Christian symbol, the *chi/rho* (the first two letters in Greek for Christ), placing it on his standards. In 313 Constantine and Licinius agreed to the Edict of Milan, which ended the persecution of Christians in their realms, permitted

3.1. TIMELINE OF CHURCH LEADERS IN EARLY CENTURIES OF CHRISTIANITY

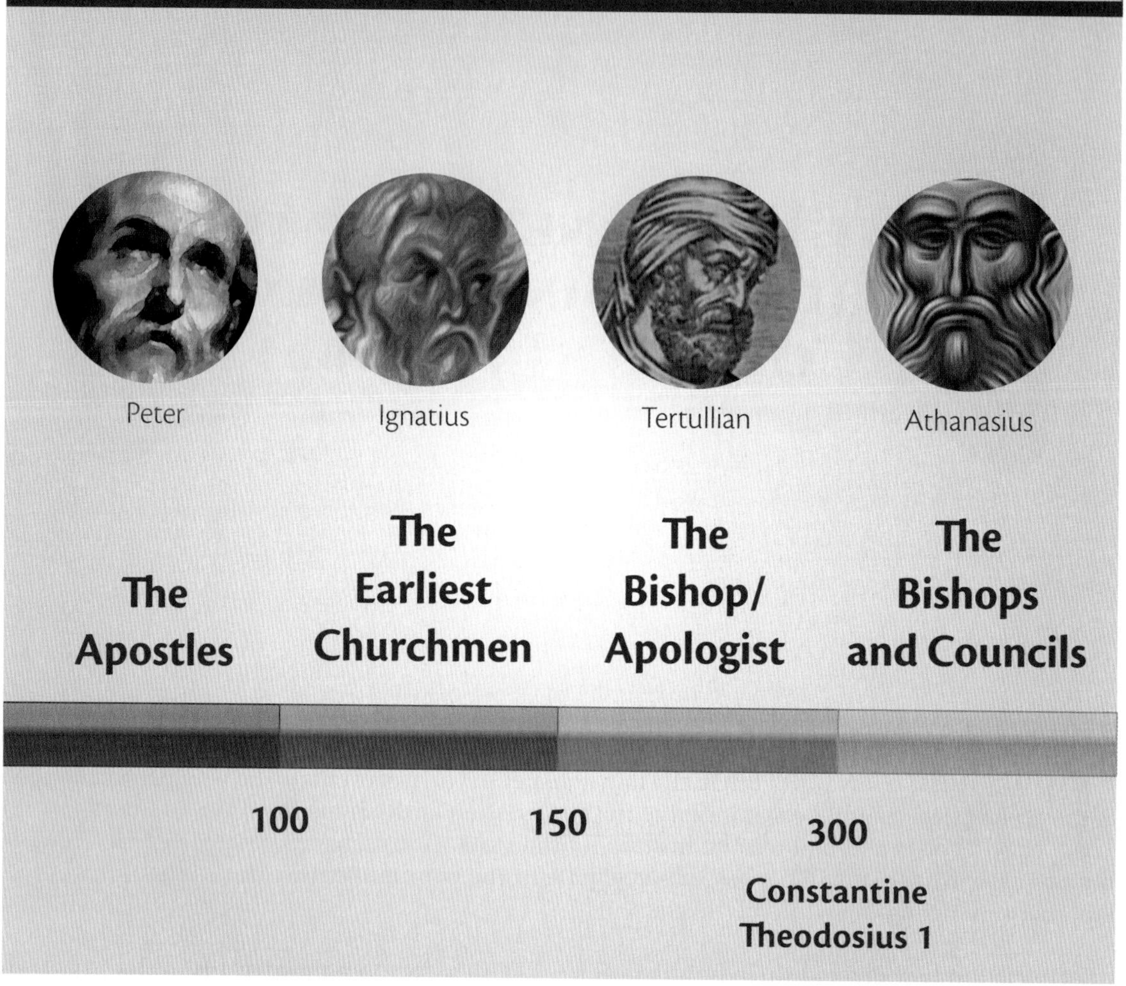

Peter   Ignatius   Tertullian   Athanasius

**The
Apostles**

**The
Earliest
Churchmen**

**The
Bishop/
Apologist**

**The
Bishops
and Councils**

100   150   300

**Constantine
Theodosius 1**

places of worship, and returned confiscated properties. Maximinus Daia's attempt to invade Galerius's territory and conqueror Byzantium led to his defeat in 313. The empire was then divided under the control of Constantine in the West and Licinius in the East. After several years of an uneasy peace between them, Constantine defeated Licinius in 324 and consolidated the empire.

The relationship of Constantine to the Christian church is easier to discern than his relationship to Christianity. Was he merely a clever opportunist who seized the moment? Did he recognize that his legionnaires, many of whom were Christians, were supportive of his rise to power? Whatever the motive, or complex of motives, his support of the Christian faith was truly remarkable. The persecution of Christians ended; pagan temples, like the pantheon in Rome, were converted into churches; grand basilicas were built at government expense; Christians were appointed

Invitation to Church History: World

Statue of Constantine, Capitol Museum, Rome, Italy. Courtesy of Jean-Christophe Benoist.

to high positions in the empire; those who took church offices were allowed tax exemptions; and Sunday became a day of rest with markets and offices closed. Death by crucifixion was abolished, the gory gladiatorial games ended, and branding on the face was outlawed because humankind was made in the image of God. Further, Constantine took an interest in the affairs of the church, arbitrating controversies and calling councils at his own expense. His mother, St. Helen, was singularly devoted to the recovery of the holy sites in Roman Palestina.

Constantine's embrace of Christianity did not preclude his attachment to pagan worship. and he did not submit to Christian baptism until on his deathbed. Did he seek to amalgamate Mithraism and sun worship with Christian worship? He gained tolerance for the Christian faith, not its supremacy. He aspired to headship in his new religious affiliations claiming to be "bishop of the bishops" and at the same time continued worshipping the "unconquered sun."

The result of Constantine's approach was a Christian faith that became unmistakably etched by political embraces and remained so for over a millennium and a half (this is sometimes called "**ceasaropapism**" by critics, the distorting influence of the state upon the church). The church, in some cases, degenerated into a religious arm of the state and, at times, would succumb to the largesse of political advantage. Being a beneficiary of the state, churches became more complex in their operations, whether it was expressed in expensive garments worn by clerics, elaborate processionals of pomp and circumstance, complex rituals, or the emergence of choirs. The churches took on the image of secular statecraft. In effect, the church became governed by a professional class and laity participation declined to the role of observer. Bishops became very powerful political figures, at times ambassadors of state.

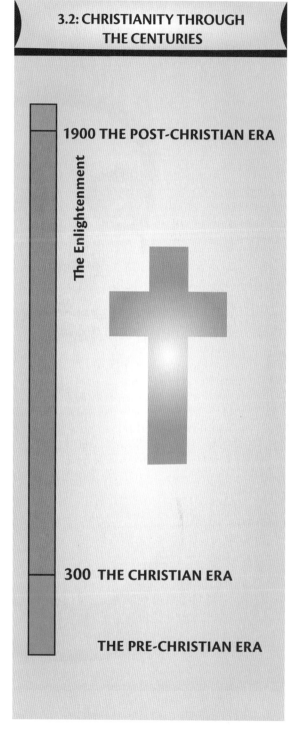

3.2: CHRISTIANITY THROUGH THE CENTURIES

1900 THE POST-CHRISTIAN ERA

The Enlightenment

300 THE CHRISTIAN ERA

THE PRE-CHRISTIAN ERA

The Prominent Bishops

There were many significant and influential churchmen of the era whose lives and writings subsequently influenced the church, some for centuries and others to this day. Two of the most important were Athanasius (ca. 296–373), the bishop of Alexandria, and Augustine (354–430), bishop of Hippo. The latter perhaps being the singularly most influential churchmen of all time. Others, besides these two, are threads in the story of the church, figuring prominently in some significant event or controversy (these will be discussed below).

Some, while important, were not as central to the story. For example, John of Chrysostom (ca. 347–ca. 407), archbishop of Constantinople, was likely one of the most eloquent preachers of the age, known for his denunciations of power, wealth, and avarice (his name literally means, the golden-mouthed orator). Jerome (ca. 342–420), a scholar and ascetic with a combative personality, is most celebrated for his monumental translation of the Bible, the Latin Vulgate, the Bible of the medieval era. Ambrose (ca. 338–397), the bishop of Milan, was a prolific writer, an accomplished preacher, opponent of **Arianism**, and father of Latin hymnody (he introduced rhymed, metric singing from the East and promoted antiphonal singing of the Psalms in worship).

Perhaps a lens for viewing the content of Christian faith in the era can be seen in Cyril of Jerusalem (ca. 315–386), bishop of Jerusalem, whose work, *Catechetical Lectures*, contains instructions on the basics of Christianity. His greatest strength appears to have been his pastoral care for his flock. His delineation of the sacred writings was the books later recognized as the Protestant list of canonical books, though he also included Baruch and the Letter of Jeremiah in the Old Testament (4.35, 36).

"Believe that this only-begotten Son of God came down from heaven to earth on account of our sins, and took humanity of a like condition to ours, and was born of the Holy Virgin and of the Holy Spirit; and was made man, not in appearance or phantasy, but in truth. Neither did He pass through the Virgin as through a channel, but was truly made flesh of her, and was truly nourished with her milk, and did truly

The conversion of Saint Augustine by Fra Angelico (1395–1455). At the Musée Thomas-Henry, Cherbourg-Octeville, France. Courtesy of Drolexandre.

An early Byzantine mosaic of John Chrysostom of Antioch from the Cathedral of Hagia Sophia, Istanbul. Courtesy of Valentinian

eat as we eat, and truly did drink as we drink. For if the incarnation was a phantasm, so too is salvation a phantasm. The Christ was twofold: man in what was seen, but God in what was not seen. As Man, He truly ate as we do, for His flesh was of a condition like to ours; and as God, He fed the five thousand with five loaves" (Cyril of Jerusalem, *Catechetical Lectures*, 4.9).

Responding to the Arian Controversy that marked his century, Cyril embraced the Nicene faith, instructing his parishioners in this matter:

> Believe also in the Son of God, One and Only, our Lord Jesus Christ, Who was begotten God of God, begotten Life of Life, begotten Light of Light, Who is in all things like to Him that begat, Who received not His being in time, but was before all ages eternally and incomprehensibly begotten of the Father (4.7).

Cyril's descriptions of the redemption purchased by Christ are captivating and rapturous; he has to be ranked among the greatest of our gospel preachers and teachers. His lectures on Christ's sacrifice are replete with scriptural citations and majestically powerful descriptions:

> And wonder not that the whole world was ransomed; for it was no mere man, but the only-begotten Son of God, who died on its behalf. Moreover one man's sin, even Adam's, had power to bring death to the world; but if by the trespass of the one death reigned over the world, how shall not life much rather reign by the righteousness of the One? And if because of the tree of food they were then cast out of paradise, shall not believers now more easily enter into paradise because of the Tree of Jesus? If the first man formed out of the earth brought in universal death, shall not He who formed him out of the earth bring in eternal life, being Himself

the Life? If Phinnes [sic], when he waxed zealous and slew the evil-doer, staved the wrath of God, shall not Jesus, who slew not another, but gave up Himself for a ransom, put away the wrath which is against mankind? (13.2).

When discussing the meaning of faith, he seems to have been overwhelmed because he confessed to his hearers, "There is much to tell of faith, and the whole day would not be time sufficient for us to describe it fully" (5.5). He explains that the word faith has two nuances. The first concerns the assent of the soul to right teaching. The second concerns the heart-felt grace bestowed by Christ through the Spirit:

> For if you shall believe that Jesus Christ is Lord, and that God raised Him from the dead, you shall be saved, and shall be transported into Paradise by Him who brought in thither the robber. And doubt not whether it is possible; for He who on this sacred Golgotha saved the robber after

Saint Cyril of Jerusalem, a fourteenth-century fresco at a Greek Orthodox church. Courtesy of Bocachete.

one single hour of belief, the same shall save you also on your believing (5.10).

"Let us then not be ashamed of the Cross of our Saviour, but rather glory in it. For the word of the Cross is unto Jews a stumbling-block, and unto Gentiles foolishness, but to us salvation: and to them that are perishing it is foolishness, but unto us which are being saved it is the power of God. For it was not a mere man who died for us, as I said before, but the Son of God, God made man. Further; if the lamb under Moses drove the destroyer far away, did not much rather the Lamb of God, which taketh away the sin of the world, deliver us from our sins? The blood of a silly sheep gave salvation; and shall not the Blood of the Only-begotten much rather save? If any disbelieve the power of the Crucified, let him ask the devils; if any believe not words, let him believe what he sees" (Cyril of Jerusalem, *Catechetical Lectures*, 13.3).

Cyril's description of baptism is utterly as fascinating as it is garnered with figurative language. The recipient was first stripped of clothing suggesting separation from defilement, "an image of putting off the old man with his deeds. Having stripped yourselves, you were naked; in this also imitating Christ, who was stripped naked on the Cross, and by His nakedness put off from Himself the principalities and powers, and openly triumphed over them on the tree" (20.2). Anointed with oil, symbolizing the fullness of Christ's mercies (20.3), the candidate was led to water ("as Christ was carried from the Cross to the Sepulchre" [20.4]) where, upon confession of faith in Christ, he or she would be immersed three times signifying death to sin and resurrection to new life. Taking up Solomon's words in Ecclesiastes 3:2 he noted, "There is a time to bear and a time to die; but to you, in the reverse order, there was a time to die and a time to be born; and one and the same time effected both of these, and your birth went hand in hand with your death" (20.4).

The Lord's Table represented to Cyril the spiritual presence of Christ among his people. "Consider therefore the Bread and the Wine not as bare elements, for they are, according to the Lord's declaration, the Body and Blood of Christ" (22.6). Though the manner of Christ's presence is described as spiritual, not physical (23.8), he does not explain himself further. What is clear is that for Cyril, it is a thanksgiving feast, a celebration of an accomplished redemption. "For verily we are bound to give thanks, that He called us, unworthy as we were, to so great grace; that He reconciled us when we were His foes; that He vouchsafed to us the Spirit of adoption" (23.5).

The Trinitarian Controversy

The roots of the controversy over the relationship of the Father to the Son are found in the unfathomable mystery of the simultaneous unity and diversity of the Godhead, as well as the early eastern approach to apologetics that sought to find parallels between earthly shadows and ultimately realities. The success of these churchmen led to an explanation of Christ that emphasized the oneness of God, denigrated diversity, and seemed to imply some degree of subordination or inequality between the Father and the Son. Apologists such as Justin Martyr, Clement of Alexandria, and Origen argued for a beginning of the Son prior to creation, one who participated with God as the agent of the creation ("this Offspring, which was truly brought forth from the Father, was with the Father before all the creatures, and the Father communed with Him" [*Dialogue to Trypho*, 62]).

The tendency in the eastern empire was to come dangerously close to subordinating the Son to the Father in their drive to demonstrate the continuity between Platonic monism and the Christian God. The extreme of this tendency to emphasize the oneness of God is evident in teachers that saw the Son as the adopted inferior of the Father; others, stressing unity in another direction, saw the Son as the Father.

Invitation to Church History: World

Adoptionism

The first of these eastern views of the Trinity is often called **Adoptionism**; the Son acquired the status of sonship. For example, Hippolytus described the teachings of Theodotus of Byzantium, who had recently come to Rome this way:

> Jesus was a (mere) man, born of a virgin, according to the counsel of the Father, and that after he had lived promiscuously with all men, and had become preeminently religious, he subsequently at his baptism in Jordan received Christ, who came from above and descended (upon him) in the form of a dove (*Refutation of all Heresies*, 7.23).

A more prominent early adoptionist was Paul of Samosata, bishop of Antioch. Paul argued that Christ is not God who became man, but he was a man that progressively matured to the status of divinity. He was condemned by a council of bishops in Antioch in 269 (Eusebius, *Ecclesiastical History*, 7.30), continued in his office, and was deposed in 272 by imperial edict (the first such in the history of the church).

"A certain Theodotus, a native of Byzantium, introduced a novel heresy, saying some things concerning the origin of the universe partly in keeping with the doctrines of the true Church, in so far as he admits that all things were created by God. Forcibly appropriating, however, his idea of Christ from the Gnostics and from Cerinthus and Ebion, he alleges that He appeared somewhat as follows: that Jesus was a man, born of a virgin, according to the counsel of the Father, and that after He had lived in a way common to all men, and had become preeminently religious, He afterward at His baptism in Jordan received Christ, who came from above and descended upon Him" (Hippolytus, *Refutation of All Heresies*, 7).

Modalism

Another early attempt to explain the relationship of the Father and Son, **Modalism**, identified the two so intimately that the Father became the Son. This is why the view is also called Patripassionism. The Father suffered on

3.3. THE GREAT EARLY COUNCILS AND THE ORTHODOX FAITH: ACCOMPLISHMENTS

THE EXPLANATION OF THE PREINCARNATE CHRIST

THE EXPLANATION OF THE INCARNATE CHRIST

THE EXPLANATION OF SIN IN MAN AND THE GRACE OF CHRIST

the cross, and the persons within the Godhead were dissolved. Noetus, who taught in Rome, and led two bishops, Callistus and Zephyrinus, into sympathy with his views, alleged that the "Father and Son, so called, are one and the same (substance), not one individual produced from a different one, but Himself from Himself; and that He is styled by name Father and Son, according to vicissitude of times" (Hippolytus, *Refutation of All Heresies*, 9:5).

The modalist, Praxeas, incurred Tertullian's literary wrath saying he thinks "that one cannot believe in One Only God in any other way than by saying that the Father, the Son, and the Holy Ghost are the very selfsame Person" (*Against Praxeas*, 1.2). The most influential of the modalists was Sabellius of Pentapolis who brought the teachings to Rome.

"In various ways has the devil reviled truth. Sometimes his aim has been to destroy it by defending it. He maintains that there is one only Lord the Almighty Creator of the world, that of this doctrine of the unity he may fabricate a heresy. He says that the Father Himself came down into the Virgin, was Himself born of her, Himself suffered, indeed, was Himself Jesus Christ. . . . Praxeas did two pieces of the devil's work in Rome: he drove out prophecy and he brought in heresy; he put to flight the Paraclete and he crucified the Father" (Tertullian, *Against Praxeas*, 1).

Arianism

The lingering discussion of the relationship of the Father to the Son culminated with the emergence of the teachings of a presbyter in Baubalis, Arius, under bishop Alexander of Alexandria. Arius (ca. 256–336) followed the teachings of Lucan of Antioch, an adoptionist, who followed the thought of Sabellius, his predecessor. Lucan established a school that attracted Arius, and Lucan's martyrdom in 311 further added to the prestige of his views. Arius not only adopted the view his mentor, he would gain the sympathy of two powerful bishops, Eusebius of Caesarea and Eusebius of Nicomedia.

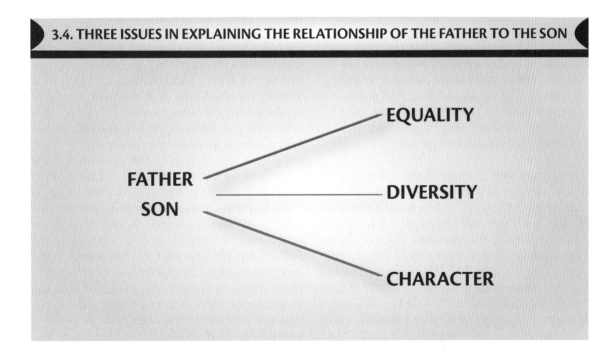

3.4. THREE ISSUES IN EXPLAINING THE RELATIONSHIP OF THE FATHER TO THE SON

FATHER

SON

— EQUALITY

— DIVERSITY

— CHARACTER

Arius's teaching was different than Lucan's though it remained only a subordinationistic variation. Arius argued that Christ was from eternity one with the Father, but that he had a beginning in eternity from the Father. Athanasius quotes from Arius's *Thalia* where he states:

> The Son was not always; for, whereas all things were made out of nothing, and all existing creatures and works were made, so the Word of God Himself was made out of nothing, and once He was not, and He was not before His origination, but He as others had an origin of creation (*Orations Against the Arians*, 2.1).

Arius found support for his view from Proverbs 8:2 by identifying created "wisdom" with Christ by referring to 1 Cor. 1:24, 30 where Christ is called the "wisdom of God." He also believed he had support for his view from Psalm 45:7 and Isaiah 1:2 as well as in the meaning of the term, "only begotten" in John 1:14, 18. To Eusebius of Nicomedia, he wrote:

> We are persecuted, because we say that the Son has a beginning, but that God is without beginning. This is the cause of our persecution, and likewise, because we say that He is of the non-existent. And this we say, because He is neither part of God, nor of any essential being (quoted by Theodoret, *Ecclesiastical History*, 1.4).

Charges and counter charges were made. Arius accused his bishop Alexander of succumbing to Modalism by overstating the unity of God, and Alexander accused his presbyter Arius of denying the complete deity of Christ. Consequently, Alexander had Arius condemned at the Synod of Alexandria in 320, but his subsequent reception by Eusebius of Caesarea and Eusebius of Nicomedia, and not a few others, meant the divisive issue remained unresolved.

When Constantine defeated Licinius and emerged as sole emperor over the great empire, the extension of his interest in political unity extended to the turbulent religious issue that threatened the peace of his domain, He instructed Hosius of Cordova (ca. 256–ca. 358), a personal confidant, to correspond with the two protagonists, bishop Alexander of Alexandria and bishop Eusebius of Nicomedia. Hosius advised Constantine that a council of the church's bishops would be necessary to resolve the issue.

Consequently, Constantine called a council of the bishops throughout the empire to gather in Nicaea, a summer residence near the city that he was building as his new capitol, Constantinople. It was epic making, the first of a series of universal councils. Though the exact number of bishops that gathered is a matter of speculation; it appears to have been several hundred. The central issue, though not the only one, was Arianism. Arius was not permitted to be present since he was not a bishop, so Eusebius of Nicomedia represented his view. Alexander led the anti-Arian faction. The majority of the bishops viewed the issue of division more dangerous to the health of the church than either party's views. They sought conciliation thinking that Tertullian's affirmation of the Trinity (*Against Praxeas*, 12), a term Tertullian coined, that God is "one in substance in three coherent inseparable [persons]" was sufficient. Eusebius of Caesarea, the church historian, represented this position as well.

At the conclusion of the deliberations, a creed was formulated as representative of the orthodox position. Christ was described as "begotten not created, of the same essence [the term used here is *homoousia*, the same in essence, not *homoiousia*, like in essence] as the Father." Though the creed was impressive, it did not come with an interpretation of how it was to be read and understood. Some felt that the emphasis on unity in the Godhead did not sufficiently enumerate the distinction of persons and was a veiled concession to Modalism. This

3.5. ARIANISM

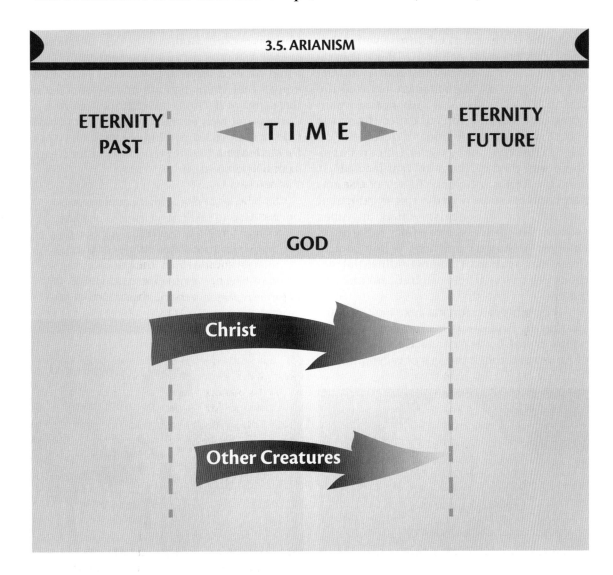

ETERNITY PAST

◀ T I M E ▶

ETERNITY FUTURE

GOD

Christ

Other Creatures

explains why Arius was not immediately expelled from the church. In a profound sense, Nicaea did not resolve the conflict. Arianism continued to have a large following in the empire; Constantine seemed not to grasp the seriousness of the issue and was baptized by Eusebius of Nicomedia, and his successor son, Constantius II, was Arian.

The Nicene Creed of 325: "We believe in one God, the Father All Governing, creator of all things visible and invisible; and in one Lord Jesus Christ, the Son of God, begotten of the Father as only begotten, that is, from the essence of the Father, God from God, Light from Light, true God from true God, begotten not created, of the same essence as the Father, through whom all things came into being, both in heaven and in earth; Who for us men and for our salvation came down and was incarnate, becoming human. He suffered and the third day he rose, and ascended into the heavens. And he will come to judge both the living and the dead. And in the Holy Spirit."

As the issue remained unresolved, Athanasius (ca. 296–373), called the "Black Dwarf," succeeded Alexander of Alexandria in 328, the same year that Constantine revoked the ban on Arius. For his views, Athanasius would experience several forced exiles from his church, including one under Constantine to Trier in the West and another time to Rome. There was even a charge of murder against him. The Arians, who had the ear of the emperor and his sons, waged a smear campaign against their opponents, which at times seemed to prove successful. Athanasius emerged a stalwart defender of the Nicene Creed and, perhaps, the most influential, orthodox churchmen between Irenaeus and Augustine.

The approach Athanasius took in answering the Arians was neither academic nor philosophical; it was pastoral. He saw the issue of Arianism through the lens of redemption. If Christ is not fully God, and the demands of God are consistent with his divine perfections, how could he ever atone for our sins? Justice demands that the substitute and justifier be of the same perfections as the one justified; if Christ is not truly all that God is, he would have failed as our redeemer. In his marvelous work, *On the Incarnation*, he states the matter clearly from his perspective:

> So here, once more, what possible course was God to take? To demand repentance of men for their transgression? For this one might pronounce worthy of God; as though, just as from transgression men have become set towards corruption, so from repentance they may once more be set

Icon from the Mégalo Metéoron Monastery in Greece, representing the First Ecumenical Council of Nicaea, 325 A.D., with the condemned Arius depicted beneath the feet of Emperor Constantine and the bishops (though Arius was not actually there). Courtesy of Jjensen.

A seventeenth-century icon of Athanasius in Varna Archaeological Museum, Varna, Bulgaria. Courtesy of Nk.

Invitation to Church History: World

in the way of incorruption. But repentance would, firstly, fail to guard the just claim of God. For He would still be none the more true, if men did not remain in the grasp of death; nor, secondly, does repentance call men back from what is their nature—it merely stays them from acts of sin . . . But if, when transgression had once gained a start, men became involved in that corruption which was their nature, and were deprived of the grace which they had, being in the image of God, what further step was needed? Or what was required for such grace and such recall, but the Word of God, which had also at the beginning made everything out of nought? For His it was once more both to bring the corruptible to incorruption, and to maintain intact the just claim of the Father upon all. For being Word of the Father, and above all, He alone of natural fitness was both able to recreate everything, and worthy to suffer on behalf of all and to be ambassador for all with the Father (7).

Athanasius was allowed to return to Alexandria with the ascension of Julian the Apostate because Julian had no interest in the controversy and hoped to use the controversy to weaken the fortunes of Christianity. Through his second major work, *Against the Arians*, Athanasius was able to convince many bishops to his view at the same time that Arian assertions were becoming more extreme. In 362 he convened a synod in Alexandria, secured the readmission of some of the moderate Arians, and convinced the bishops that Christ had to be accorded the status of absolute deity (though the language was left indefinite). The synod proved to be an important step toward the final resolution, though Athanasius was banished again from his church shortly after the synod by Julian.

At the same time the church was moving toward resolution of the relationship between the Father and the Son, the question of the relationship of the Spirit to the Father and Son came into focus. The Council of Nicaea did not take up the relationship of the Spirit to the Father and Son, though it spoke in a triadic manner. The creed recognized the existence of the Spirit, but no more ("And in the Holy Spirit"). Appointed as the bishop of Constantinople in 342 for his pro-Arian sympathies by Constants II, Macedonius led a party that denied the deity of the Spirit (the *Pneumatachi* or "Combaters against the Spirit"). Athanasius wrote against his views using the same scriptural logic that he used with the Arians. If the Spirit is the one who sanctifies, and sanctification means bring us into conformity with the character of God (the term he used was "deification," or "paradosis"), how could one less than God do it?

Nicene Othodoxy
The final victory for the Nicea Party came through the literary endeavors of three very remarkable bishops from Cappodocia (modern Turkey), designated as the "Cappodocian Fathers": Basil, bishop of Caesarea (ca. 330–379), called Basil the Great; Gregory, bishop of Nyssa (ca. 335–ca. 386) (the brother of Basil and sister of the saintly Macrina); and Gregory, bishop of Nazianzus (329–389). Their work comprised a careful definition of terms used to express the Trinitarian nature of God so that the confusion over terminology in the discussion ended.

"And when I speak of God you must be illumined at once by one flash of light and by three. Three in Individualities or Hypostases, if any prefer so to call them, or persons, for we will not quarrel about names so long as the syllables amount to the same meaning; but One in respect of the Substance—that is, the Godhead. For they are divided without division, if I may so say; and they are united in division. For the Godhead is one in three, and the three are one, in whom the Godhead is, or to speak more accurately, Who are the Godhead. Excesses and defects we will omit, neither making the Unity a confusion, nor the division a separation. We would keep equally far from the confusion of Sabellius and from the division of Arius, which are evils diametrically opposed, yet equal in their wickedness. For what need is there heretically to fuse God together, or to cut Him up into inequality" (Gregory of Nazianzus, *Oration on the Holy Lights*, 11)?

For example, Basil was able to make the important distinction between "essence" and "persons," enabling him to speak of three per-

sons who share a single set of defining characteristics equally.

We must, therefore, confess the faith by adding the particular to the common. The Godhead is common; the fatherhood particular. We must therefore combine the two and say, "I believe in God the Father." The like course must be pursued in the confession of the Son; we must combine the particular with the common and say

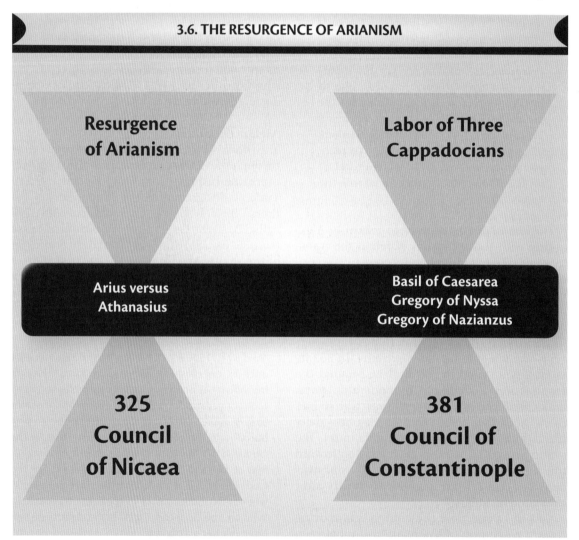

3.6. THE RESURGENCE OF ARIANISM

Resurgence of Arianism

Labor of Three Cappadocians

Arius versus Athanasius

Basil of Caesarea
Gregory of Nyssa
Gregory of Nazianzus

325
Council of Nicaea

381
Council of Constantinople

"I believe in God the Son," so in the case of the Holy Ghost we must make our utterance conform to the appellation and say "in God the Holy Ghost" (*Epistle,* 236.6).

The clarifying contribution of Gregory, bishop of Nazianzus, was in making the point that the nomenclature used to express the triune persons in the Godhead (the Father, the Son, and the Spirit) are functional designations, not ontological descriptors:

This is what we mean by Father and Son and Holy Ghost. The Father is the Begetter and the Emitter . . . The Son is the Begotten, and the Holy Ghost the Emission; for I know not how this could be expressed in terms altogether excluding visible things (*Oration,* 29.2).

The exile under Julian was the last for Athanasius; he returned to his church and experienced peace in his final seven years of ministry. For his resolve to persevere through enormous difficulties and his insightful defenses of the faith has earned him the titles "Pillar of the Church," "Father of Orthodoxy," and "Champion of Christ's Divinity."

When Theodosius I became emperor in 379, he declared Christianity the sole religion of the empire. As a champion of Nicene orthodoxy, he deposed the pro-Arian bishop of Constantinople and chose Gregory of Nazianzus as his successor. Theodosius abolished pagan festivals, destroyed temples and erected churches, ended the Olympic Games, demolished the great library in Alexandria, and actively persecuted pagans for which Ambrose, bishop of Milan, excommunicated him.

Theodosius called for a second empire-wide council of the bishops to categorically state the faith, discrediting Arianism. The council, attended by 150 bishops, largely from the eastern portion of the empire, affirmed the Nicene Creed and enlarged it into

Gregory of Nazianzus (1408) by Andrei Rublev (1360–1430). Courtesy of Bakharev.

3.7. TRINITARIANISM (ERROR AVOIDED)

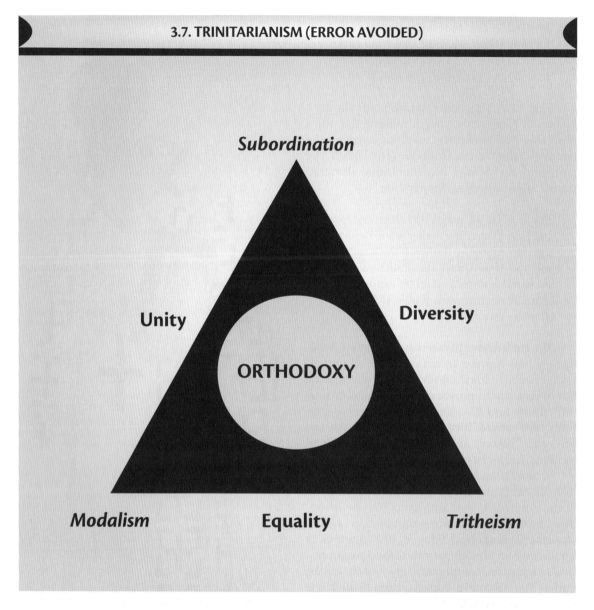

Subordination

Unity   ORTHODOXY   **Diversity**

Modalism   **Equality**   *Tritheism*

the Nicene/Constantinople Creed by expanding the statement on the Holy Spirit. They officially endorsed the doctrine of the Trinity and affirmed a canon that Constantinople was the "New Rome," first in honor after Rome; the bishops of the two churches were equal in authority. For whatever reason, bishop Damascus I of Rome did not attend the council so that its status as a universal council was questionable until affirmed as such by the Council of Chalcedon in 451. The doctrine of Trinity remained a foundation stone in the church without significant challenge for over twelve hundred years, until the rise of Michael Servetus and the Socinians of the sixteenth century.

Emperor Theodosius on the Disco de Teodosio at the National Museum of Roman Art, Madrid. Courtesy of Manuel Parada López de Corselas.

The Christological Controversies

The sudden change of fortunes, the change of status from a destructive pest to solitary triumph, brought its own problems, as well as enormous benefits. The persecutions ended and the church, throughout the empire, received favored status. It could declare the faith and worship without fear or hindrance. In fact, unity in the empire was perceived through the lens of doctrinal cohesiveness in the churches. The era began in a crisis of how to explain the relationship of the Father to the Son, which was extended to their relationship to the Holy Spirit, leading to an official explanation of the teachings of the sacred writings on the subject. It is difficult from the current culture and religious milieu to imagine a time when the Christian faith was considered so crucial to life that debates would threaten the peace and unity of an empire. However, such was the situation in the fourth century.

In the earliest centuries of the church, the struggle against the gnostic denial that the Christ came to us in a real body, true flesh, caused the church to make that point clear as is evidenced in the early baptismal formulas. The Nicene triumph over Arianism made it equally evident that Christ was also very God, not merely like God. If the incarnate Christ was truly God and man at once, how is that to be explained? (Churchmen were not seeking to invent the faith; they were seeking to understand the faith as delivered to us in the Holy Scriptures.). The earlier fathers had spoken of Christ as God and man, but they did not endeavor to state an explanation beyond that. Tertullian, for example, had stated in effect what would become the Orthodox explanation:

> We see plainly the twofold state, which is not confounded, but conjoined in One Person—Jesus, God and Man. . . . the property of each nature is so wholly preserved (*Against Praxeas*, 27).

Apollinarianism

The bishop of Laodecia, Apollinarius (ca. 310–390) sought to explain the relation of humanity and deity in one, incarnate Christ and in doing so caused considerable conflict among the churches. Apollinarius was determined to maintain the unity and unchangeableness of Christ by appealing to passages of sacred scripture such as "the Word became flesh" (John 1:14) and "that which is born of the flesh is flesh" (John 3:6). These texts, among others, he argued, supporting the case that the humanity of Christ consisted of his visible appearance, not the totality of his invisible soul. Christ was fully God, but he was not truly human; he brought a "celestial humanity" with him and was joined with flesh. The bishop's Christ was more divine than human.

The condemnation was quick in coming, particularly from Gregory of Nazianzus. In a letter to Cledonius, in the manner of Irenaeus and Athanasius, he viewed religious truth through the lens of redemption. If Christ came to heal us through identity with us, how could

3.8. RELATIONSHIP OF HUMANITY AND DIVINITY IN THE INCARNATE CHRIST

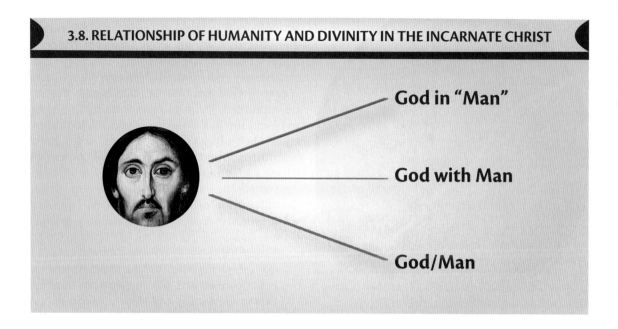

God in "Man"

God with Man

God/Man

he be our redeemer if he was not entirely like us?

> If anyone has put his trust in Him as a Man without a human mind, he is really bereft of mind, and quite unworthy of salvation. For that which He has not assumed He has not healed; but that which is united to His Godhead is also saved. If only half Adam fell, then that which Christ assumes and saves may be half also; but if the whole of his nature fell, it must be united to the whole nature of Him that was begotten, and so be saved as a whole. Let them not, then begrudge us our complete salvation, or clothe the Savior only with bones and nerves and the portraiture of humanity (*Epistle*, 101).

Apollinarius's views were condemned at two local synods by bishop Damascus I of Rome paving the way for the issue to be resolved by a broader council of the church. The bishops, with Arianism uppermost on their agenda, gathered at Constantinople in 381 to convene the second "ecumenical" or universal council, sometimes called the First Constantinople Council. In appealing to phrases in the Nicene/Constantinople Creed, they also condemned **Apollinarianism** ("from the Holy Spirit and the Virgin Mary" and "became human").

Nestorianism

The condemnation of Apollinarius's view did not resolve the controversy; it advanced it. The accomplishment of the council, however, was the recognition that any explanation of the incarnate Christ that denigrated his complete humanity rendered human redemption impossible. How could he take our debts for us if he was not one with us? Though Apollinarius's view did preserve the unity of the two natures, it did not resolve the issue because it did not delineate the relationship between the two natures. The stage was set for an enhanced discussion when Nestorius, newly appointed bishop of Constantinople, preached a sermon denying that Mary could be the mother of God (the Greek word is "theotokos," the bearer of God).

3.9. APOLLARIANISM (A DENIAL OF THE HUMANITY OF CHRIST)

Nestorius, who zealously attacked the heterodox (Apollinarians, Arians, Macedonians, and Novatians), argued that Mary, being only mortal and capable of producing only in kind, birthed Christ but not God. She bore the human Christ only, and he became the vessel that housed God. In so doing, he severed the integrity of the two natures of Christ and seemed to denigrate the unity of the one Christ. Cyril (ca. 396–444), bishop of Alexandria, entered the fray exchanging a series of letters with his opponent and chairing a council at Alexandria in 430 condemning his views. In one of the twelve anathemas issued by the council, the second of them, the opposition to Nestorius was stated most clearly.

> If anyone shall not confess that the Word of God the Father is united hypostatically to flesh, and that with that flesh of his own, he is one only Christ both God and man at the same time: let him be anathema.

Cyril appealed to the bishop of Rome,

3.10. NESTORIANISM (A DIVIDED CHRIST: DENIAL OF UNITY)

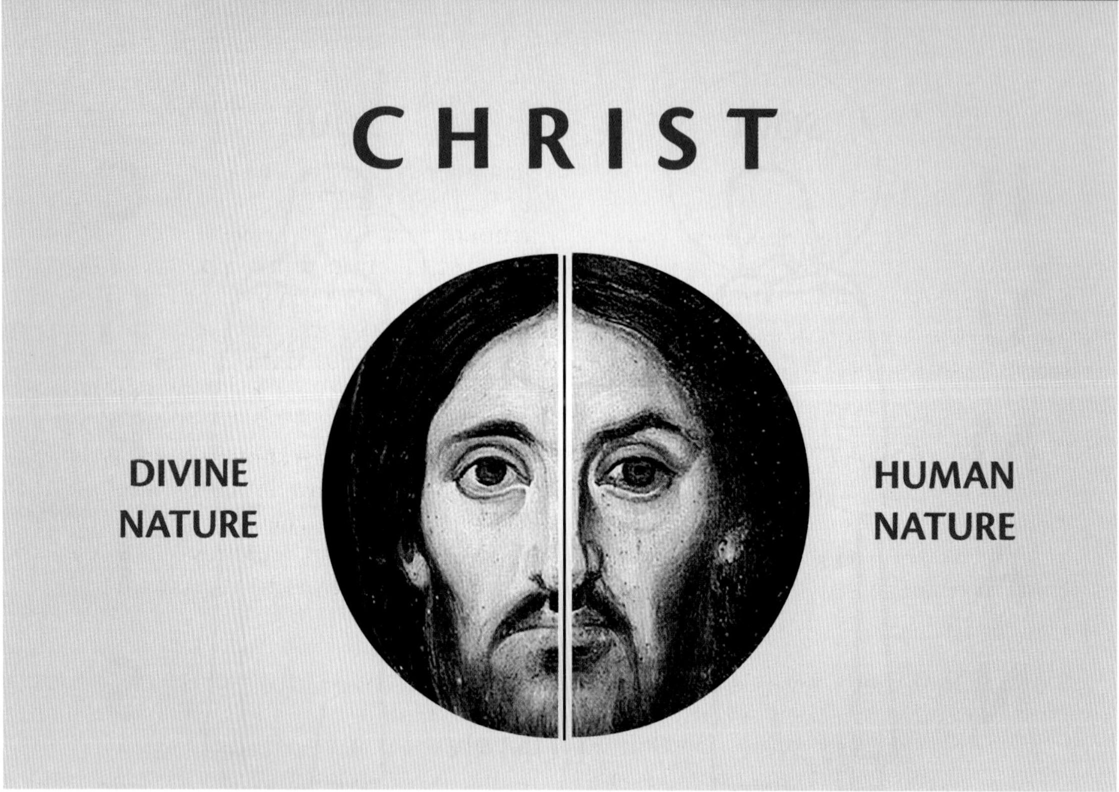

CHRIST

DIVINE
NATURE

HUMAN
NATURE

Celestine I, for support in the condemnation of Nestorius, which he provided in 430. Celestine supported Cyril for several reasons: (1) the undesirable emergence of Constantinople as the "New Rome," (2) Nestorius's light treatment of Pelagius, the troubling western issue at the time, and (3) the historical policy of Rome to support Alexandria. With tension at a feverish pitch, emperor Valentinian III called a general council for 7 June 431, the Third Ecumenical Council, to gather in Ephesus. With Nestorius not present, Cyril convened the council and immediately condemned him.

The anathemas of Cyril accepted by the Council of Ephesus, 431, condemning Nestorius: "If anyone divides in the one Christ the hypostases after the union, joining them only by a conjunction of dignity or authority or power, and not rather by a coming together in a union by nature, let him be anathema" (3).

"If anyone distributes between the two persons or hypostases the expressions used either in the gospels or in the apostolic writings, whether they are used by the holy writers of Christ or by him about himself, and ascribes some to him as to a man, thought of separately from the Word from God, and others, as befitting God, to him as to the Word from God the Father, let him be anathema" (4).

Four days later Nestorius arrived in the city,

gathered a countercouncil, and condemned Cyril and the previous council. The emperor settled the issue by confirming the correspondence that had been read from Cyril and Celestine, affirmed by the original council presided over by Cyril. Valentinian declared as orthodox faith the statements of Cyril. One of these letters read:

> Confessing the Word to be made one with the flesh according to substance, we adore one Son and Lord Jesus Christ: we do not divide the God from the man, nor separate him into parts, as though the two natures were mutually united in him only through a sharing of dignity and authority (for that is a novelty and nothing else), neither do we give separately to the Word of God the name Christ and the same name separately to a different one born of a woman; but we know only one Christ, the Word from God the Father with his own Flesh.

Though Nestorius's view is not entirely clear, the council insisted that you cannot preserve the integrity of his person, "very God and very God," at the cost of his oneness. One Christ hung on the cross. Being only man or only God would not do; it required a human being and a divine being, a God/man.

As for Nestorius, he was sent away to a monastery in Antioch, later to Petra, and then to a desert oasis in Libya. He did live beyond the Council of Chalcedon (451 A.D.) and believed that in the findings of that council his own doctrine was vindicated.

Though Nestorius was banished and his understanding of the incarnate Christ declared heterodox, **Nestorianism** did not cease to exist and survives in Iran to this day. The center of Nestorianism was their school in Edessa in southeastern Turkey, but, after it was closed by imperial edict in 489, Nestorians migrated into Persia where they established a school at Nisibis and then spread into India in the sixth cen-

tury. With the Arab conquest of Persia in the seventh century, the Nestorians were granted legal protection and they flourished. Nestorian communities could be found in Egypt and China from the seventh to the tenth centuries. They became dominant in Central Asia where the vast majority of the Tartar tribes embraced Nestorian Christianity. Persecution subsequently led to near extinction, with a remnant joining the Roman Catholic Church in the sixteenth century and others, the Russian Orthodox Church and the Syrian Jacobite Church. The Nestorian schism, as it relates to the Western Roman Catholic Church, ended in 1993 when John Paul II nullified its excommunication.

The controversy continued to simmer in the empire on a more technical point. What is the nature of the oneness of Christ? If Christ is truly God, truly man, and truly one, what is the relation of the two natures in that oneness?

Eutychianism
The controversy swirled around the teachings of a leader of a monastery in Constantinople, Eutyches (ca. 378–454). He acquired a reputation for his staunch rejection of Nestorius's claims at the Council of Ephesus in 431 and expressed his own interpretation saying that the two natures of Christ in the one person amalgamated or fused together so that the two became one.

Flavian, the bishop of Constantinople, convened a council of forty churchmen to investigate the views of his popular monastic in 448. At the conclusion of the council Eutyches was condemned. When asked the question: "Do you or do you not confess that our Lord, who is of the Virgin, is consubstantial and of two natures after the incarnation?" he replied by saying, " I confess that our Lord was of two natures before the union but after the union one nature. . . ."

In Eutyches's confession, he implicated the see of Alexandria by saying that his view was that of Athanasius and Cyril. This was too much

3.11. EUTYCHIANISM (MONOPHYSITISM)—A UNITED CHRIST: DENIAL OF DUALITY

CHRIST

DIVINE NATURE

HUMAN NATURE

Two natures meshing to create a third, single nature

for Dioscurus, then bishop of Alexandria, who not only sided with Eutyches, but appealed to Rome and Leo I to settle the dispute among the bishops (the precedent of appealing to Rome for adjudication of important issues in the East is, in part, the ground for the later claim of Roman supremacy. Further, and on a sad note, the bishops often did not rise above their humanity and seemed to care more for the predominance of their bishopric than truth).

To resolve the mounting crisis, Theodosius II called for what was to be a fourth universal council, the Second Council of Ephesus. The council was to determine if the council of the previous year in Constantinople was correct in condemning Eutyches. Dioscurus convened the council with 130 other bishops in 449, refused to seat Flavian and six bishops. The council mistreated Flavian in deposing him (he died shortly thereafter), letters from Leo of Rome were not read, and Eutyches was vindicated. The findings of the council were later overturned and the council itself was dubbed "the Robbers Council."

The emperor, Theodosius II, sympathized with Eutyches and approved the council's conclusions. Fortunes quickly changed, however, when Theodosius died and Pulcheria, his sister, became empress in the East. She and her husband, Marcian, now emperor, opposed the teachings of Dioscurus and Eutyches and called for another universal council, the fourth, to settle the issue. It seems also that Leo I's letter, which was not read at the Council of Ephesus in 449, had influenced many eastern bishops away from Eutyches view. In part his famous letter to Flavian read:

> So the proper character of both natures was maintained and came together in a single person. Lowliness was taken up by majesty, weakness by strength, mortality by eternity. To pay off the debt of our state,

Bishop Leo 1 of Rome by Francisco de Herrera el Mozo (1622–1685). At Prado Museum in Madrid, Spain. Courtesy of Magnificus.

invulnerable nature was united to a nature that could suffer; so that in a way that corresponded to the remedies we needed, one and the same mediator between God and humanity the man Christ Jesus, could both on the one hand die and on the other be incapable of death. Thus was true God born in the undiminished and perfect nature of a true man, complete in what is his and complete in what is ours.

The council convened in 451 in Chalcedon, today a part of Constantinople. Over 500 bishops from over the empire attended; it was truly ecumenical or universal. The council condemned **Eutychianism** and issued a definition of faith, perhaps the greatest ecumenical creed in the history of the church. The creed affirmed that the incarnate Christ was truly God, truly man, in one person without confusion or mixture. Jesus was not God in man or God and man; he was (and is) the God/man. The letter of Leo to Flavian was mentioned in the findings of the council as the expression of Orthodox faith.

In addition to its primary work, the council produced a series of disciplinary canons or instructions. The Council of Constantinople (381) was recognized as ecumenical and clarified the status of Constantinople and Rome that they were equal (the Roman bishop did not accept this assertion [Canon 28]).

The Creed of Chalcedon (451): "Following, then, the holy fathers, we unite in teaching all men to confess the one and only Son, our Lord Jesus Christ. This self-same one is perfect both in deity and also in humanness; this self same one is also actually God and actually man, with a rational soul and a body. He is of the same reality [homoousion] as we are ourselves as far as his humanness is concerned; thus like us in all respects, sin only excepted. Before time began he was begotten of the Father, in respect of his deity, and now in these "last days," for us and on behalf of our salvation, this self same one was born of Mary the virgin, who is God-bearer [*theotokos*] in respect of his humanness."

Monophysites and Chalcedonians

The condemnation of Eutychianism in 451 did not silence the controversy in the empire, as numerous churches in the East were uncomfortable with the Chalcedonian formulation of Christology. Advocates of dissent agreed in the condemnation of Eutyches, but objected to the phrase "in two natures." These Monophysites, or single-nature Christologists, argued that a person is a single nature so that Christ had to have a single nature since he was one person. The Monophysites affirmed the truth of Chalcedon in rejecting both Nestorianism and Eutychianism, but reacted to "two natures" as implying "two persons." Severus of Antioch (ca. 465–538) categorically affirmed the perfect deity and humanity of Christ, but insisted on a single nature in Christ.

A revival of Monophysites fortunes came in 476 when Basiliscus usurped the imperial throne and reversed the findings of Chalcedon. When Zeno (ca. 425–491) was restored to the throne of the empire in the East (the western

empire collapsed during his reign), he attempted to placate the religious controversy by working out a compromise between the Chalcedonians and Monophysites. This ended in failure and caused a break in relations between the East and Rome. When Justin I (450–527) came to the throne in 518, he was able to heal the schism with Rome assuring bishop Hormisdas that he affirmed the Chalcedonian Creed. The ascendancy of Chalcedonianism had the effect of dividing the Monophysites into those who favored the substance of the creed but objected to the language (**Verbal Monophysites**), the followers of Severus of Antioch, and those who adopted Eutychianism entirely (Real Monophysites), led by John of Harlicarnassus.

The greatest of the rulers in the Justinian Dynasty was the nephew of Justin I, Justinian I, the Great (ca. 482–565). It is rare that a strong political figure would be accorded the status of sainthood by the church, but such was the contribution of this man that the honor was accorded him. Justinian's dream was to restore the Roman Empire to its former greatness by reclaiming the western portions that had succumbed to tribal invasion. His interests ex-

3.12. THE DEBATE OVER CHRISTOLOGY: THE RENDING OF THE CATHOLIC CHURCH

The (Monophysite) Catholic Church

THE CATHOLIC CHURCH ·········· **553** ························

The (Chalcedonian) Catholic Church

Justinian 1 (before 547) at Basilica of San Vitale in Ravenna, Italy. Courtesy of the Yorck Project.

affirming the condemnation of the "Three Chapters"). The council produced a series of anathemas; the eighth states in part:

> If anyone confesses a belief that a union has been made out of the two natures, divinity and humanity, or speaks about the one nature of God the Word made flesh, but does not understand these things according to what the fathers have taught, namely that from the divine and human natures a union was made according to subsistence, and that one Christ was formed, and from these expressions tries to introduce one nature or substance made of the deity and human flesh of Christ: let him be anathema.

The condemnation delivered by the council resulted in a permanent schism in the Catholic Church, creating the Chalcedonian Catholic Church and the Monophysite Catholic Church. Monophysite Catholics have survived the centuries, today being represented by the Jacobite Church of Syria, the Coptic churches of Egypt and Ethiopia, and the Armenian churches.

Another side to the tensions between the Monophysites and the Chalcedonians was the Monothelete Controversy of the seventh century, an attempt to end the schism in the church following the Constantinople Council of 553. The conciliatory move was set within the context of a political exigency. Emperor Heraclitus, being militarily pressured by Persians in the northeast of the empire and Saracens (another name for Arab Muslims) in Egypt, hoped to bring the divided factions in the empire together. Damascus was lost to the empire in 635, Jerusalem in 636, and Alexandria in 640. The eastern Mediterranean Sea was rapidly becoming a Muslim sea as naval power declined. Patriarch Sergius of Constantinople sought, as a means of rapprochement, the formula "one energy" with "two natures." The bishop of Alexandria reconciled **Seve-**

tended to the church as he hoped to end the divisions caused by the Monophysites. He sought to console the Verbal Monophysites and condemn the Real Monophysites.

Justinian called the fifth of the great universal councils of the church, the second in Constantinople, in 553. The tact of the 150 bishops, mostly from the East, was to condemn what were considered the formulators of Monophysite doctrine, the teachers of Antiochene theology: Theodore of Mopsuestia, Theodoret of Cyrus, and Ibas of Edessa (this appeared in a document called "the "Three Chapters"). This created confusion and frustrated any hope of conciliating the Verbal Monophysites (in fact, Justinian, at one point, deposed the bishop of Rome, Vigilius, for not

rians, Verbal Monophysites, with the formula, "a single hypostatic energy." As opposition from Chalcedonians mounted to these concessions, Sergius proposed **Monothelitism**, a single will in Christ, as a solution. Sergius secured the approval of Honorius I of Rome of "one will in our Lord Jesus Christ."

While many were succumbing to the urge for reconciliation, Maximus the Confessor, sometimes called Maximus the Theologian (580–662), adamantly refused. Maximus was amazing, like Athanasius who had struggled for Orthodoxy when most thought him to be foolish. With his friend, Pyrrhus, the deposed bishop of Constantinople, Maximus fled to Rome where he staunchly defended Dyothelitism, two wills in Christ. Pyrrhus recanted of his views and returned to Constantinople. Maximus was forced to return, was severely tortured (his tongue was removed so that he would no longer speak his errors and his right hand severed so that he would no longer write them), and he was exiled from the empire. His views triumphed at the sixth universal council (the third Constantinople Council) in 680–681.

The council was called at the behest of emperor Constantine IV who had previously asked the bishop of Rome, Donus, who was succeeded by Agatho to prepare a statement condemning Monotheletism. Convening a synod in Rome of 125 bishops in 680, Agatho prepared a profession of faith and sent it with delegates to the council. The council adopted the profession sent by Agatho. In part, it reads:

> And we proclaim equally two natural volitions or wills in him and two natural principles of action which undergo no division, no change, no partition, no confusion, in accordance with the teaching of the holy fathers. And the two natural wills are not in opposition, as the impious heretics said, far from it, but his human will following, and not resisting or struggling, rather in fact subject to his divine and all powerful will.

Honorius of Rome, Sergius of Constantinople, Pyrrhus of Constantinople, and Macarius of Alexandria were condemned for "the heresy of a single will."

The Development of Monasticism

When the era of persecution ended throughout most of the empire, many in the churches were presented with an unanticipated dilemma. How is one to "take up the cross," the symbol of a sacrificial, deprecatory lifestyle, as wealth and peace brought the detrimental complements of spiritual sloth and self-centered living?

The answer for some was the celibate life. It had precedent in the sacred writings as the Apostle Paul made the point that marriage presents limitations in the service of Christ (1 Cor. 7:8), as well as the perception of the nearness of the Lord's return to establish a kingdom where marriage will not exist. The monastic movement appears in the late third century and takes a more distinct form in the fourth century. It appears to have begun in Egypt, the desert providing isolation and solitude, where the godly life could be pursued without the distractions common to towns and cities. The term *monk* is derived from a Greek word meaning "solitary." The earliest monks were also called hermits or anchorites, the latter term meaning "one who withdraws."

Saint Anthony

The first of the "**desert fathers**," at least according to Athanasius and Jerome, were Saint Anthony and Paul of Thebes, though others were before them. The biographies of these men did much to promote the monastic lifestyle. Anthony (ca. 251–356) was raised in a Christian family, but after the death of his parents, though yet a teenager, he found in such scriptures as Matthew 19:21 and 6:34 the warrant to leave his siblings and learn the solitary

3.13. THE DEVELOPMENT OF MONASTICISM

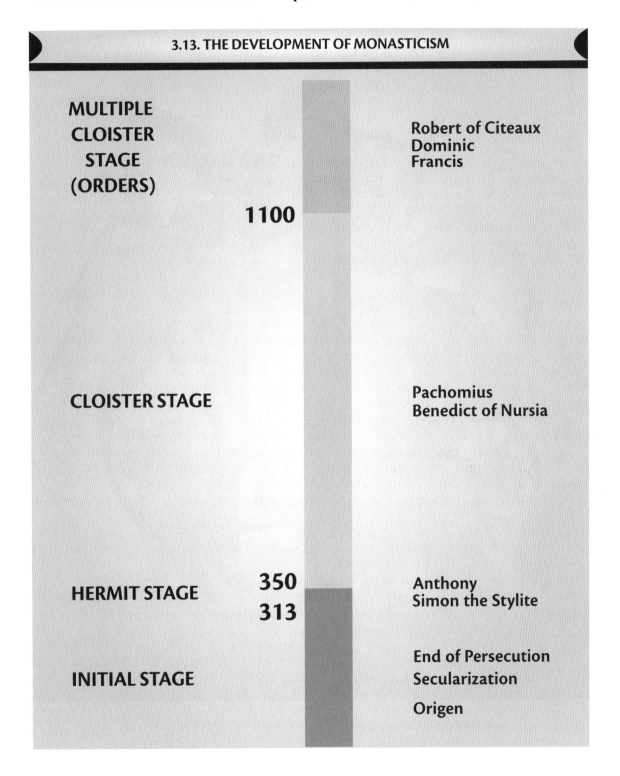

MULTIPLE CLOISTER STAGE (ORDERS)

Robert of Citeaux
Dominic
Francis

1100

CLOISTER STAGE

Pachomius
Benedict of Nursia

350

313

HERMIT STAGE

Anthony
Simon the Stylite

INITIAL STAGE

End of Persecution
Secularization

Origen

"The Torment of Saint Anthony" by Michelangelo (1475–1564). A depiction of his trials in the desert. At Kimbell Art Museum, Fort Worth. Courtesy of DcoetzeeBot.

Invitation to Church History: World

life from a hermit who lived nearby (Athanasius, *Life of St. Anthony*, 2–3). After twenty years of wrestling with the devil to gain separation from worldliness, and the clamoring of many to be benefited by his instruction, he emerged from isolation. "His soul was free from blemish, for it was neither contracted as if by grief, nor relaxed by pleasure, nor possessed by laughter or dejection" (14).

Anthony lived the life of a hermit, giving instruction to an increasing number of disciples, and longed for martyrdom (46). Failing in that regard after going to Alexandria, he returned to his cell in a desert mountain (47) to pray, counsel, instruct, and perform miracles. Athanasius exclaimed, "And the fame of Anthony came even unto kings. For Constantine Augustus, and his sons Constantius and Constans the Augusti wrote letters to him, as to a father, and begged an answer from him" (81). Upon his death Anthony was buried secretively by Amathas, a disciple, and his only clothing, a tunic, was sent to Athanasius.

During a stay in the deserts of Syria, Jerome composed a biography of Paul of Thebes (d. ca. 341), a predecessor to Anthony. Paul was born into wealth to parents that lost their lives during the Decian persecutions. He retired to a cave "and there in prayer and solitude spent all the rest of his life" (6). Paul's life intertwines with Anthony's as Jerome unfolds the narrative. The biography extols the beauty and virtues of the solitary life and ends with an exhortation:

> Your tunics are of wrought gold; he had not the raiment of the meanest of your slaves. But on the other hand, poor though he was, Paradise is open to him; you with all your gold will be received into Gehenna. He though naked yet kept the robe of Christ; you, clad in your silks, have lost the vesture of Christ. Paul lies covered with worthless dust, but will rise again to glory; over you are raised costly tombs, but both you and your wealth are doomed to the burning (17).

Simon the Stylite

Simon the Stylite (ca. 390–459) was unique even among the ascetics. Troubled by people who interrupted his solitude for prayer and advice, he spent nearly forty years of his life perched on small platforms on top of pillars of increased heights in the Syrian dessert (the Greek word, *stylo*, means "pillar"). There solitude eluded him and his fame increased. From his elevated separation from the "world," he preached to those who would gather below, corresponded with inquirers, and advised emperor Theodosius and the Council of Chalcedon. He inspired a generation of pillar sitters or "pillar saints" called Stylites.

Cenobites

As time passed, and the number of hermitic

Simon the Stylite in sixteenth-century icon. At the base of the pillar is his mother's body. At the Historic Museum, Sanok, Poland. Courtesy of Pleple2000.

monks grew, a new form of the monastic life emerged—communal living. The first cenobite, a term used for communal, monastic individuals, was Pachomius (ca. 292–348). He gathered hermits into hierarchically structured communities to practice the spiritual disciplines. He called himself "father." Over monasteries of men, the leader was called an abbot and those over women, abbotesses. The ascetic form of spirituality, which included manual labor and devotional exercises, became immensely popular. By the fifth century, it had spread across the empire and claimed over 7,000 monastic communities. Cenobites refused church orders, preferring to remain aloft from the establishment, with Jerome being a notable exception. They found silence to be the best context for meditation of the Scriptures that they cherished beyond all other books. These men and women sought to take the Bible seriously: to pray without ceasing (1 Thess. 5:17), to be solicitous in the use of the tongue (Prov. 18:21), and to live detached from the lure of materialism (1 Tim. 6:17).

It appears that **cenobitism**, or communal monasticism, took one of two directions. One observable tendency was to emphasize the cultivation of individual spirituality (Vertical Cenobitism). The other tendency was to view spirituality more from a relational perspective (Horizontal Cenobitism).

An example of the first type can be seen in the instructions of Pachomius. In Pachomius (ca. 292–348), the focal point of spiritual was union with God. The emphasis in this type of spirituality was on Bible reading and meditation privately, instruction in the Bible, and two meetings daily to hear Bible readings accompanied with prayers (all in the context of poverty, manual labor, and obedience).

Mention should be made of Martin of Tours (ca. 316–397), a man who was both a cenobite and simultaneously a bishop. His biographer, and hagiographer, Sulpicius Severus

indicates that Martin was raised in a pagan military family. Later he was a cenobite for ten years near Tours before being chosen as the successor to Lidorius, though he lived an austere life dressed in rags and disheveled in appearance. He built a primitive cell near his church for his residence. The most oft-repeated legend of Martin was a vision. During military service, he met a naked beggar near Amiens and gave him half of his cloak (called a "capella," from it comes the term *chapel*). In a dream that night he saw Jesus clothed in half of his cloak.

Several churchmen through the fourth and fifth centuries assembled rules for monastic conduct and spirituality. Among these was Basil the Great, the defender of Nicene Orthodoxy, who founded a monastery in Pontus; John Cassian (360–435), who introduced monastic practices into the West, and Augustine.

Benedict of Nursia (480–547) was founder of the monastery at Monte Cassino. Sometimes called the father of Western Monasticism, he gathered many of these various monastic instructions together in the sixth century. Now known as the *Rule of St. Benedict* (ca. 530), it contained seventy-three instructions to regulate monastic life. The twelve steps to true humility, as a ladder that leads to heaven, say much about Benedictine spirituality (7).

The Augustinian-Pelagian Controversy

Of the three great controversies that rent the Catholic churches in the period, the issues raised in the Augustinian-Pelagian controversy had not been accorded a universal resolution in council that brought the Trinitarian and christological controversies to a conclusion. The church did condemn the extreme teachings of Pelagius at the third ecumenical council (Ephesus, 431), half-hearted though it may have been as the church strove for unanimity on a christological issue. Yet the points of contention were not completely resolved by the

3.14. THE AUGUSTINIAN-PELEGIAN CONTROVERSY OF SIN AND GRACE

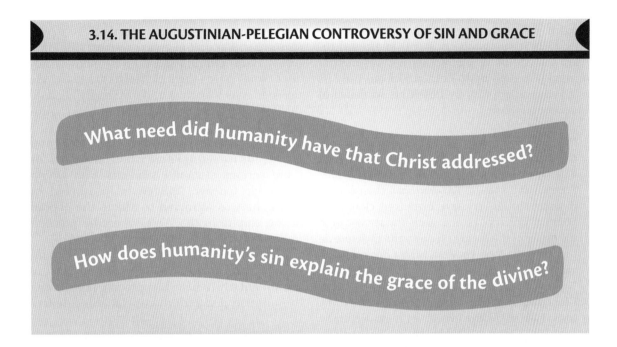

What need did humanity have that Christ addressed?

How does humanity's sin explain the grace of the divine?

churches' bishops. It is this failure that divided the churches in the sixteenth-century West.

The issues are of monumental gravity if the theme of history, as is being assumed here, is the growth of that kingdom of God that in a future day will culminate in the restoration of a "garden." In the matter of humankind's dilemma (all are agreed that humankind has experienced a devolution to some degree), two issues are foremost: the extent of the problem and the solution to the problem. The nature of the need determines the nature of the solution; the nature of the solution presupposes the nature of the need it addresses regardless of the field or social science (be it psychology, psychiatry, or religion) that seeks to establish the roots of dysfunctional behavior and ameliorate it. The sin that is in humankind determines the extent of grace from God. They are the two threads that are woven together that lead to the "garden."

This issue is intricately connected to the Trinitarian discussion. Athanasius rightly understood that the coequality of the Father and Son is demanded by the truth of a divine redemption of sinners through Christ. This is also true of the christological discussion, which dealt with the relationship of deity to humanity in the incarnate, preexistent Son of God. If he did not identify with us in our fallenness, how could he redeem us? The question here is the nature of man and the kind of grace required from God through Christ by the Spirit to effect our restoration.

Augustine, Bishop of Hippo
It is not too much to say that Augustine is the most influential bishop in the history of the church. Not only was he a powerful figure in his own day, his ideas have shaped the church through the centuries, even today. His writings are monumental, his explanation of the faith often compelling, and his continuing influence on pastors, teachers, and laity phenomenal. The life story of Augustine can be gathered from two of his writings and the biographical statements of a friend. From his *Confessions* (397), a work addressed to God in the form of a

lengthy prayer, we learn of his spiritual struggles; from his *Retractions* (428*)*, composed toward the end of his life, we learn of his mental struggles in coming to faith, and from the *Life of St. Augustine* (439) by Possidius we learn of his pastoral work.

> "Narrow is the mansion of my soul; enlarge Thou it, that Thou mayest enter in. It is ruinous; repair Thou it. It has that within which must offend Thine eyes; I confess and know it. But who shall cleanse it? or to whom should I cry, save Thee? Lord, cleanse me from my secret faults, and spare Thy servant from the power of the enemy. I believe, and therefore do I speak. Lord, Thou knowest. Have I not confessed against myself my transgressions unto Thee, and Thou, my God, hast forgiven the iniquity of my heart? I contend not in judgment with Thee, who art the truth; I fear to deceive myself; lest mine iniquity lie unto itself. Therefore I contend not in judgment with Thee; for if Thou, Lord, shouldest mark iniquities, O Lord, who shall abide it?" (Augustine, *The City of God*, 1.6).

The man who would dominate the thought of the medieval era grew up in Tagaste, North Africa, near Carthage (now Tunis, Algeria), the land of the once-powerful Hannibal. Augustine was born in 354 to a couple with variant religious beliefs. His father, a minor Roman official, embraced the gods of the empire; his doting mother, Monica, was a follower of Christ. In his youth he was attracted to the morals of his pagan culture, finding pleasure in sensuality. In a long-term, faithful relationship with a mistress, likely a slave or former slave, he fathered a son, Adeodatus.

He was educated in Carthage (unfortunately he spurned the study of Greek because of a brutal teacher and regretted it later) where he became a student of rhetoric, the art of persuasive speaking and writing. Realizing that truth was not to be found in the rhetorical arts, he turned to philosophy. He became enamored by Manichaeism, a dualistic, gnostic religion,

(which, promising to be the final religion, possessed a stellar cast of great prophets [Buddha, Jesus, Mani] offering salvation through avoidance and psychological self-assurance). He pursued it as a learner, and eventually became disillusioned by its contradictions and ignorant teachers.

He determined to leave Carthage and pursue his career in Rome where he hoped for more serious students, students who would pay their teacher. Though he prospered in Rome, he was attracted to Milan, the capital of the empire in the West, where he excelled under the influence of Bishop Ambrose.

Impressed with Ambrose's character and explanation of the Christian faith, Augustine went regularly to hear him preach. In listening to Ambrose, a superb rhetorician, his intellec-

Painting of Augustine of Hippo and his mother Monica of Hippo (1846) by Ary Scheffer (1795–1858). At the National Gallery, London. Courtesy of Jfhutson.

tual doubts concerning Christianity slowly dissolved. He learned that **Platonism** and Christianity were, in some significant ways, compatible. Both took a spiritual, as opposed to a material, outlook on religion; both espoused an ultimate and supreme being; both explained the origin of evil as a human, willful choice of departure from God; and both viewed spirituality as a voluntary abandonment of sensual pleasures. With his intellectual doubts of Christianity removed, the remaining obstacle was the issue of the moral implications of becoming a Christian or even remaining a Neo-Platonist, the new twist on classic Platonism. His mother pressed him to marry; but his mistress was sent back to Africa, and he could not handle his passions and fell into promiscuity. One of his most quoted lines from the *Confessions* is "Grant me chastity . . . but not yet" (8.17).

In this troublesome time of torment, Augustine experienced God's forgiving, transforming grace in a Milan garden, hearing children at play say, "Take up and read it" (*Confessions*, 8.12), as his eyes fell upon Romans 13:14 ("make not provision for the flesh to fulfill the lusts thereof" [KJV]).

Converted in 386 and baptized the following year by Ambrose, Augustine returned to North Africa in 397 where he hoped to pursue the life of a monastic scholar within a cenobite community that he established, but he was thrust into the limelight as a priest and eventually as a bishop.

Not only a powerful preacher and shepherd of the flock of God, Augustine excelled as a polemicist. His writing interests form something of a time line of his mature years: polemics against the Manichees (385–400), polemics against the Donatists (390–410), and polemics against the Pelagians (410–430). He also wrote such important works as *The City of God*, *On the Trinity*, *On Christian Doctrine*, and numerous homilies and expositions.

The City of God is Augustine's monumental attempt to explain the sacking of Rome in 410

by Alaric the Goth when many thought it was evidence of the judgment by the ancient gods of the empire for the embrace of the Christian faith. Rome was mighty when pagan but invaded when Christian. Such a tragedy caused many to loose hope. Augustine's response was cast in the form of an entire philosophy of history and nations, a theodicy, the first attempt to produce such from a Christian perspective.

> "The good use the world that they may enjoy God; the wicked, on the contrary, wish to use God that they may enjoy the world" (Augustine, *The City of God*, 15.7).

As he looked across the ages, Augustine envisioned two intertwined kingdoms, two loves, the kingdom of man and the kingdom of God. Interestingly, he did not equate the latter with the church, believing that even it consisted of the two kingdoms. These two worlds, simultaneously existing, are in constant conflict until the end of times when the kingdom of God will triumph.

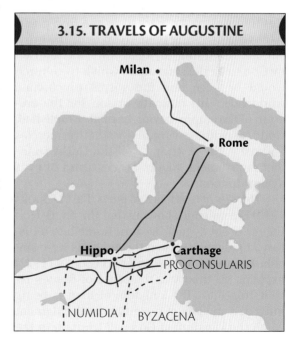

3.15. TRAVELS OF AUGUSTINE

Milan

Rome

Hippo   Carthage
          PROCONSULARIS

NUMIDIA   BYZACENA

"We see then that the two cities were created by two kinds of love: the earthly city was created by self-love reaching the point of contempt for God, the Heavenly City by the love of God carried as far as contempt of self. In fact, the earthly glories in it- self, the Heavenly City glories in the Lord. The former looks for glory from men, the latter finds its highest glory in God, the witness of a good conscience. The earthly lifts up its head in its own glory, the Heavenly City says to its God; 'My glory; you lift up my head.' In the former, the lust for domination lords it over its princes as over the nations it subjugates; in the other both those put in authority and those subject to them serve one another in love, the rulers by their counsel, the subjects by obedience. The one city loves its own strength shown in its powerful leaders; the other says to its God, 'I will love you, my Lord, my strength'" (Augustine, *The City of God*, 14.28).

God, says Augustine, raises up nations using them for his purposes, preserving sta- bility in them against their natural tendencies to accomplish divine intentions, and judges them when they have fulfilled the purposes of their creation by withholding preserving mer- cies, mercies never merited in the first place, so as to justly bring them to an end. The great empire, according to Augustine, was chosen by God to be the stage upon which the church would be born and the gospel proclaimed worldwide. This ultimate reason for the cre- ation of the empire having been accomplished, God was withdrawing his protective mercies and using the instrument of the Goths to in- flict punishment, finally, for centuries of evils against his church.

The *City of God* has two parts. Part I (Books 1–10) is a polemic showing that the angry God theory is not cogent because Rome had a his- tory of judgments when the old gods were sin- gularly revered. The second part (Books 11–22) explains his theory of the cause of Rome's re- cent tragedies. The kingdom of man is being judged, a shadow of a coming final judgment when the kingdom of God will triumph in the last day. This work, like his writings against the Donatists, profoundly shaped his under- standing of the church.

The **Donatists**, like the **Novatians** before them, represented a serious ecclesiastical crisis. In fact, in Augustine's time, the Donatists were larger in number than the Orthodox Church in much of North Africa. The questions that the Donatists posed struck at the heart of the nature of the church and the nature of the efficacy of the church's sacraments. Con- trary to Augustine, the Donatists were purists in their approach to the church, defining it as composed of "wheat" only, not a mixture of tares also. Further, Donatists believed that the benefit of the function of clerical practices was a direct fruit of clerical purity.

Augustine's response to the Donatists is found in seven books he composed in the 390s, collectively entitled *On Baptism*. His ar- guments against them are three. The first line of argument was historical; he retraced the history of the movement to show their many travesties, particularly their misuse of Cyprian. The second line of refutation was doctrinal. He argued that there was but one true church and that was the Catholic Church. The church traced its origins to the primacy of Peter in Rome and an unbroken succession from him to Augustine's day. The Roman Church was the embodiment of the one true, Catholic Church that was spread throughout the empire. Here he also argued that the validity of pastoral function does not depend on the sanctity of the office holder, but upon the purity and sanctity of the office. His third argument was logical. He showed the rational inconsistency of Donatist argumentation.

Augustine and the Pelagian Controversy
Perhaps no single question has occupied the church more over the centuries as the issue of free will and human inability. The denial of the latter seems to militate against the truth of creaturely responsibility and culpability

(praiseworthiness and just condemnation); the denial of the former seems to destroy responsibility, making the creature little more than a puppet on a string of divine caprice. The great question is this: How can the two important doctrines be preserved, or should one be entirely abandoned? If one affirms human inability, what is the basis of divine wrath? Do not the commands of Scripture presuppose the ability to perform them? If so, how does the grace of God, his unmerited favor, remain unmerited?

> "Such passages do they collect out of the Scriptures,—like the one which I just now quoted, "Turn ye unto me, and I will turn unto you"—as if it were owing to the merit of our turning to God that His grace were given us, wherein He Himself even turns unto us. Now the persons who hold this opinion fail to observe that, unless our turning to God were itself God's gift, it would not be said to Him in prayer, 'Turn us again, O God of hosts;' and, 'Thou, O God, wilt turn and quicken us'; and again, 'Turn us, O God of our salvation,' with other passages of similar import, too numerous to mention here" (Augustine, *On Grace and Free Will*, 10).

These are the issues that came to the forefront when Augustine encountered the teaching of a monk from Roman Britannia and his followers. Pelagius (ca. 354–ca. 424) was a studious acetic, fluent in Latin and Greek (thus linguistically superior to Augustine) who came to Rome about 380 as a teacher. A man of saintly demeanor, he gathered about him a group of influential students: Coelestius, a lawyer; Refinius; and Julian of Eclanum. Pelagius's concern was the rapid moral deterioration of the churches, and he believed that the antidote was an emphasis on moral responsibility. He objected to Augustine's stress on human inability because he thought it led to a justification of moral dereliction.

The tensions between Pelagius and Augustine emerged about 405 with the publication of the former's commentary on Paul's epistle to the Romans. With Alaric's impending invasion of Rome in 409, Pelagius left the city with Coelestius hoping to meet Augustine in Carthage. After a brief meeting, Pelagius left for the East where he hoped to gain support for his views.

To preserve moral responsibility, as the basis for praise and judgment, Pelagius denied the doctrine of innate, inherited moral and spiritual depravity. His most fundamental assumption was human ability and influence of outside, social factors to do all that God commands. According to Pelagius, each person is born into the state that Adam enjoyed before the fall, all sinning is voluntary, and Adam's sinning is merely the setting of a bad example (cf. Rom. 5:12, 2 Cor. 5:21, Eph. 2:3). Freedom of choice is the grace that is possessed of all humans; nothing was lost for anyone in Adam's first transgression. Sacred teaching such as election and predestination are explained by defining foreknowledge as foresight on the part of God. God's choice of humans was predicated of God's knowledge of our choice of him.

> "This grace, however, of Christ, without which neither infants nor adults can be saved, is not rendered for any merits, but is given *gratis*, on account of which it is also called *grace*. 'Being justified,' says the apostle, 'freely through His blood.' Whence they, who are not liberated through grace, either because they are not yet able to hear, or because they are unwilling to obey; or again because they did not receive, at the time when they were unable on account of youth to hear, that bath of regeneration, which they might have received and through which they might have been saved, are indeed justly condemned; because they are not without sin, either that which they have derived from their birth, or that which they have added from their own misconduct. 'For all have sinned'—whether in Adam or in themselves—'and come short of the glory of God'" (Augustine, *On Nature and Grace*, 4).

In 415, Pelagius was able to convince John

3.16. THE ANTHROPOLOGY OF PELAGIUS

Plenary Ability

Denial of Depravity

Sin does not corrupt a human's

mind
emotion
will

He or she is spiritually alive

of Jerusalem that his views were not heterodox, though he was neither condemned nor exonerated by a local council; later the same year the Synod of Diopolis acquitted him. After hearing of this news through a disciple, Orosius, whom he had sent to the East to press charges against Pelagius, Augustine called a provincial council in Carthage (416) where Pelagius's views were condemned. However, since local councils were not binding without the sanction of the bishop of Rome, Augustine appealed to Innocent I and secured Pelagius's condemnation. When Bishop Zosimus succeeded Innocent I, Pelagius pled his case and won a reversal of the decision. Augustine reacted by continuing his literary assault and by condemning Pelagius at a second council in Carthage (418). Subsequently, Augustine appealed to Emperor Honorius, whose subsequent action brought Zosim-

us's retraction and all the bishops in the West were forced to agree with the Council of Carthage.

At the universal Council of Ephesus (431), called to adjudicate the Nestorian controversy, bishops in the East agreed to condemn Pelagius. It appears that the decision was motivated by more of a compromise to preserve unity in the churches than a profound conviction over the importance of the issues. The East was gripped with profound Trinitarian and christological issues, not the issues that concerned the Western churches. Nonetheless, and for whatever motives, **Pelagianism** was condemned.

Augustine argued that Pelagius's attempt to preserve human responsibility and culpability threatened the Catholic faith; that scriptural integrity allowed for an entirely different

3.17. THE ANTHROPOLOGY OF AUGUSTINE

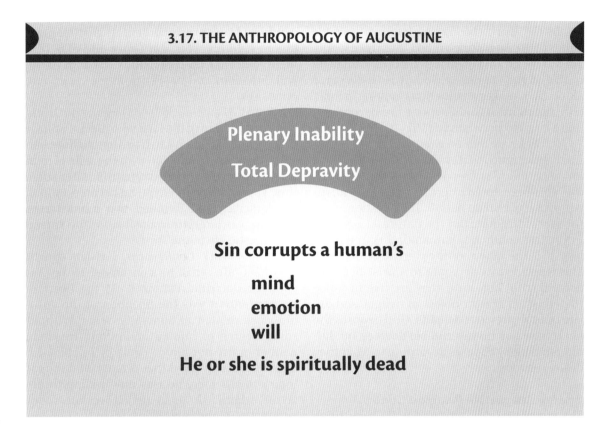

Plenary Inability

Total Depravity

Sin corrupts a human's

mind
emotion
will

He or she is spiritually dead

approach. Praise and blame could be preserved without Pelagius's distortions of Holy Scripture. Augustine felt that Adam's first sin brought on the race not only the loss of moral rectitude, but also a spiritual separation from God. Mankind lost the grace of a virtuous state and any hope of its restoration. Thus, salvation has to begin in God as the only hope, grace has to be without merit, and electing grace has to be rooted in divine love.

Augustine's response to the Pelagian crises first came in *On the Merit and Forgiveness of Sins and the Baptism of Infants* (412). There he argued that death was not the result of a depraved nature in the race, but was the penalty of sin for the loss of original righteous over the entire race in Adam (condemnation precedes actions; actions are the evidence of condemnation). Consequently, through baptism infants have

the hope of heaven, not because of any righteousness of their own, because baptism effects a cleansing from the penalty of Adam's first sin, not having the consequences of any sin of their own (Augustine's view seems to explain why infants die, but it does not explain the fact people, cleansed of the cause of sinning, universally sin if they live long enough to do so).

His second work, *On the Spirit and the Letter* (414), Augustine argues that divine grace is an absolute necessity since compliance to the law brings only condemnation. The law can only judge; it cannot acquit! Good works flow from the priority of grace, never grace from the works of the law (11).

In *Nature and Grace* (415) Augustine argued that grace by its very nature is opposed to works; grace would not be grace if it were a reward.

In the work *On the Predestination of the Saints* (418), Augustine argued that since works are not the ground of divine election, it must be rooted in the actions of God. It is God's grace alone that makes distinctions among people (10); the roots of God's actions are beyond the finite mind to understand (16).

In *On Grace and Freedom of the Will* (427), Augustine argued that grace and free will are not incompatible (31). Freedom is not destroyed by the fall, nor restored by grace; freedom is an integral part of human nature. The question is not the fact of freedom, but the nature of freedom. In the lost condition, humankind is free to be lost. It is the object of their greatest delights. The redeemed freely come to Christ because, according to Augustine, they are free by grace to perceive a greater object of delight and desire than all previous delights. God deposes the heart based on his inscrutable decrees, but humankind freely chooses according to what they desire the most.

The Post-Augustine Pelagian Controversy

The controversy did not end with Augustine's clash with Pelagius; many viewed his solutions as overstated. They sought a moderate position, between the two supposed extremes, which has been subsequently described as semi-Pelagian. (The term first appears in the late sixteenth century because of the perception that Pelagius's views were resurfacing. The monks who embraced views similar to Cassian's modification of Augustine's views originally were called Massilians, those from Marseilles or southern Gaul).

Vincent of Lerins (d. 450), answered Augustine, seeking to distinguish heresy from orthodoxy, by arguing that truth is what the church always and everywhere teaches (*Commonitory*, 28). However, Augustine's explanations, according to Vincent, were often not found in the history of the church. Hence, Augustine was accused of being an innovator. Faustus of Rhegium (ca. 410-ca. 490), also of

southern Gaul, was an ardent Augustinian antagonist. In his work, *On Grace and Free Will*, he argued that faith demands freedom of the will. Freedom and necessity, in his view, were opposites.

John Cassian (ca.360–435) was by birth and education a man of the East who did not appear in the West until 405, when he went to Rome on some business connected with the exile of John Chrysostom, his friend and patron. After some time as an ascetic in Egypt, he became a monk in Marseilles and founded two monasteries. Cassian was largely responsible for the spread of monastic life in the West.

In his work *Conferences*, Cassian sought to ameliorate what he considered to be Augustine's doctrinal extremes. At the heart of his contention was the rejection of the absolute enslavement of humanity to sin. Without some degree of human ability and freedom, neither praise nor blame could be established. While Cassian argued that Adam's fall brought injury to the race, he was only willing to describe Adamic sin as incurring weakness, not complete impotency. Consequently, humankind needs grace in the sense of assistance or helping grace. Strength a person possesses, but not enough to fulfill God's demands. God calls us to

> the way of salvation either by His own act, or by the exhortations of some man, or by compulsion; and that the consummation of our good deeds is granted by Him in the same way: but that it is in our own power to follow up the encouragement and assistance of God with more or less zeal, and that accordingly we are rightly visited either with reward or with punishment (3.19).

Cassian felt compelled to defend freedom in such a way that it destroyed absolute necessity. Grace was surely important and needed, but it alone was not enough. "Our free will al-

3.18. PELAGIUS AND AUGUSTINE: A STUDY IN CONTRAST

	PELAGIUS	**AUGUSTINE**
Original Sin	Denied	Affirmed
Natural Will	Plenary Ability	Inability
Grace	Gracious, Not Necessary	Absolute Necessity
Predestination	Based on Knowledge (Foresight)	Based on Love (Foreknowledge)

ways has need of the help of the Lord" (3.22). Cassian, like many others after him, felt that responsibility could only be established if humankind had some control over his/her moral choices (he was working with unruly monks). He did not realize that freedom does not require the ability to make unlimited choices. It only requires the ability to freely choose among available options.

In response to Cassian's understanding of freedom, Prosper of Aquitaine (ca. 390–ca. 460) rose to Augustine's defense (hence, he is sometimes called "the first Augustinian"). He appears to have been an educated layman who corresponded with Augustine. His works are primarily two: *The Call of All the Nations*, a defense of Augustine's doctrine of grace, and *Divine Grace and Free Will*, a refutation of Cassian's concept of free will.

The Synod of Orange (529)

The controversy continued into the sixth century. Faustus of Rhegium was so persuasive that two provincial councils in 475, Arles and Lyons, formally supported his position. While southern Gaul remained fertile soil for the cultivation of **Cassianism**, Rome's bishops were unwilling to depart from Augustine. It is clear also that the churches universally rejected Pelagius's understanding of salvation (his understanding of sin was simply too facile). However, would the churches embrace Augustine's rebuttal? The answer is "no," but the moderate position the churches adopted is important in understanding the medieval discussion of sin and grace.

In 529, on the occasion of the dedication of a church at Orange in Gaul, fourteen bishops and several lay notables gathered. Caesarius of

Arles, who presided, presented a series of eight articles against the Massilians that had been prepared by Bishop Felix of Rome, largely drawn from the works of Augustine and Prosper of Aquitaine. These articles became the basis of the twenty-five issued by the synod. Though the council was only a provincial gathering, Boniface II approved its findings in 530, giving its conclusions universal status in the churches.

> "If anyone affirms that we can form any right opinion or make any right choice which relates to the salvation of eternal life, as is expedient for us, or that we can be saved, that is, assent to the preaching of the gospel through our natural powers without the illumination and inspiration of the Holy Spirit, who makes all men gladly assent to and believe in the truth, he is led astray by a heretical spirit, and does not understand the voice of God who says in the Gospel, 'For apart from me you can do nothing' (John 15:5), and the word of the Apostle, 'Not that we are competent of ourselves to claim anything as coming from us; our competence is from God'" (2 Cor. 3:5) (The Synod of Orange, Canon 7).

The conclusions of the council would have been disappointing to the Cassian position because it was condemned and to the Augustinans because several important features were neglected. What prevailed at Orange, and into the medieval era, with some exceptions, was a weakened Augustinianism, which affected the theological landscape.

The synod affirmed the perversion and corruption of all the human facilities (1, 8), Adamic unity (2, 15), denial of human merit (even prayer) (3, 13,18), the priority of grace even before faith (4, 6, 7, 14), and the absolute necessity of the gift of grace (5, 16, 21, 22).

3.19. THE CONTROVERSY OVER SOTERIOLOGY IN THE EARLY CHURCH

AUGUSTINE	SYNOD OF ORANGE		CASSIAN	PELAGIUS
		SALVATION		
Totally and Causatively of God	Originates in God, Proceeds by God and Man		Originates in Man, Proceeds by Man and God	Inability
AUGUSTINIANISM ⟵			⟶ **PELAGIANISM**	

"If anyone says that the grace of God can be conferred as a result of human prayer, but that it is not grace itself which makes us pray to God, he contradicts the prophet Isaiah, or the Apostle who says the same thing, 'I have been found by those who did not seek me; I have shown myself to those who did not ask for me'" (Rom 10:20, quoting Isa. 65:1). (The Synod of Orange Canon 3).

What is decidedly not Augustinian is the notion that free will is restored though in a weakened state (13); that the grace of God comes, at least in part, in the manner of assistance (19, 20); that grace is resistible. The Augustinian doctrines of election, foreknowledge, and predestination had been left out. To Augustine, the only explanation for grace, since it is unmerited, is the doctrine of God's eternal love for his chosen. If predestination (the divine directives) is eliminated, and the nature of

sin weakened, as happens in the late medieval period, there is no recourse but a retreat to an unbiblical gospel. This will be the claim of the sixteenth-century, Protestant reformers.

The great error of the medieval church was the movement away from the anthropology of the Synod of Orange, though the precedent was laid out for it at that very council. With all of this said, however, the Synod of Orange bears witness to a church that embraced many of the doctrinal truths of Augustine.

The Crisis in the Western Empire

The Roman Empire was gigantic. It stretched from Hadrian's Wall, even Antonius's Wall, in Britannia to Africa north of the Sahara, from the Atlantic to Roman Palestina. North of Hadrian's Wall were the Picts, West of the Rhine River the Germanic tribes, North of the Danube the Goths and the Huns, and be-

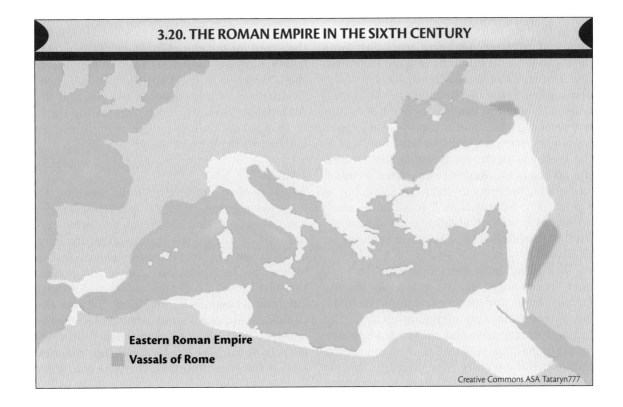

3.20. THE ROMAN EMPIRE IN THE SIXTH CENTURY

■ Eastern Roman Empire
■ Vassals of Rome

Creative Commons ASA Tataryn777

Invitation to Church History: World

yond the eastern fringes of the empire were the Persians. The great Roman legions held the barbarians out of its boundaries by the sheer might of its military, mostly infantry. However, in 378 the empire showed the first signs of ineffectiveness. Pushed by the barbarian Huns, the Goths sought refuge within the Roman Empire. When refused a haven, the Goths defeated a huge Roman army at the Battle of Adrianople on the border of modern Greece and Bulgaria, killed the Roman emperor Valens, and pushed as far as the gates of Constantinople before being turned back by Theodosius I.

This ringing defeat by the Goths was the first major military setback in four centuries. Suddenly the great empire was vulnerable. It changed many things within the empire: the Goths, as an uncertain ally in the empire, the employment of mercenaries because of the depleted army, and emphasis on cavalry rather than infantry in warfare.

In the late fourth century, Roman legions appeared to have departed from Britannia for the defense of interests in Italy. Germanic tribes crossed the Rhine River in 406. The Visigoths sacked Rome in 410, a pillage that lasted three days, and the Vandals sacked the city for two weeks in 455. What is clear is that Roman hegemony over its extensive land holdings in the West was declining. It seems best to view the decline of the Western empire not so much as a grand, sweeping military endeavor, but as a gradual transformation. It was not so much a "fall," as it was an adaptation or mutual assimilation of cultures (the toga was replaced by trousers!).

The tribal incursions appeared to have been occasioned by the quest for fertile farming lands and greater economic stability. The Romans, needing mercenaries to fill the ranks of an expensive and challenged military, allowed gradual settlement of some tribal factions in the empire. The Visigoths, for example, established themselves in southern

Gaul as protectors of Roman interests. The Franks moved into the north of Gaul and the Alemanni, central Gaul. The Vandals, pushed by the Visigoths, crossed from southern Spain into North Africa. In the push and pull of borderless conflicts, Romans allied with some of the tribes to ward off other tribes. Over time, the Roman Empire simply blurred out of definable existence in the chaos of collapsing perimeters and the establishment of new ones. In 476, a date often identified as the end of the western empire, Odoacer, a Goth, deposed Augustus Romulus, the last Roman emperor, by besieging Ravenna, the "new" capital after Rome was not longer deemed defensible.

Missions among the "Barbarians"

The story of the penetration of the gospel among the tribes is tantalizingly meager. From the witness of unknown Christians, the tribes gradually embraced the faith and produced leaders of their own for the churches. Many of these early tribes embraced the Arian Christian faith rather than Nicene faith (perhaps the attraction was its disconnection from Rome, the fact that the Arian Jesus was a warrior [a conquering man], or that Arians took the story of the Christian faith across the Roman borders to them).

Ulfilas

The story of missions to the Goths concerns the work of a missionary, Ulfilas (ca. 310–383). The sources suggest that Ulfilas was of Gothic heritage; he came into the empire about the time of the Arian Controversy and was ordained a bishop by the Arian Eusebius of Nicomedia. He subsequently returned to his people and labored successfully among them. Because the Gothic chieftain, Athanaric, persecuted the believers, Ulfilas received permission from Constantius II to move the believers into the area known today as Bulgaria. There he devised a Gothic alphabet and translated the Bible, called the "Silver Bible" because it is written in silver and gold letters on purple vellum. The Goths, sometimes called Visigoths ("Noble" or "Good" Goths) once ruled a vast land east of the Black Sea to the Dnieper River but were pushed by the Huns into the Western empire where they dominated for some time. In his confession, recorded in the Letter of Auxentius, Ulfilas says of the Holy Spirit, "Neither God nor Lord, but the faithful minister of Christ; not equal, but subject and obedient in all things to the Son. And I believe the Son to be subject and obedient in all things to God the Father."

Martin of Tours

Martin of Tours (ca. 316–397) is credited with the founding of the first monastery in Gaul. He was influenced by Hilary of Poitiers and staunchly defended Nicene Christianity among the Arian Goths. He was appointed by the people of Tours as their bishop and aggressively traveled witnessing to the gospel from house to house and appointing priests or monks over communities of new believers. It is difficult to separate legend and truth in the life of Saint Martin, as hagiography dominates Sulpicius Severus's biography of the great man, bordering, at times, on the surreal.

Gregory of Tours

Gregory of Tours's (ca. 538–594) most important contribution to the history of missions is the recording of the conversion of the Frankish tribe to Nicene Christianity. The Franks crossed the Roman frontier and settled in northeastern Gaul and were assimilated into the empire by the middle of the third century. Gradually the Franks extended their lands and in 481 established the Merovingian dynasty of kings that lasted into the eighth century. In 509 the Frankish chieftain, Clovis I (465–511), defeated the Goths, pushing them into the Iberian Peninsula; he declared himself the "King of the Franks" occupying most of Gaul. The Franks became the dominant tribe controlling terri-

tory from the Atlantic Ocean to the Elba River, from the North Sea to central Italy.

Of importance to the story of Christianity is the conversion of Clovis I. Raised to embrace pagan religion, he married Clothilde, the niece of the king of the Burgundians, and she sought to convert her husband to the Christian faith. The occasion came in the context of the invasion of the Alemanni into his territory. He promised his wife that, if he came out of the conflict victorious, he would become a Christian. Returning from battle the victor, he kept

Clovis 1 by François-Louis Dejuinne (1786–1844). At the Musuem and National Estate of Versailles and the Trianon. Courtesy of Romain0.

Invitation to Church History: World

his promise, submitted to Christian baptism, and encouraged his people to do the same.

Gregory states in his *History of the Franks* (II.31), "Another Constantine advanced to the baptismal font, to terminate the disease of ancient leprosy and wash away with fresh water the foul spots that had long been borne." Over three thousand in his army were also baptized as well as two of his sisters. His commitment to Nicene Christianity and the expansion of his hegemony insured the decline of Arian Christianity (II. 37), though it continued among the Goths across the Pyrenees and the Vandals in North Africa.

Clovis established his capital in Paris and there he and his queen built the Church of St.

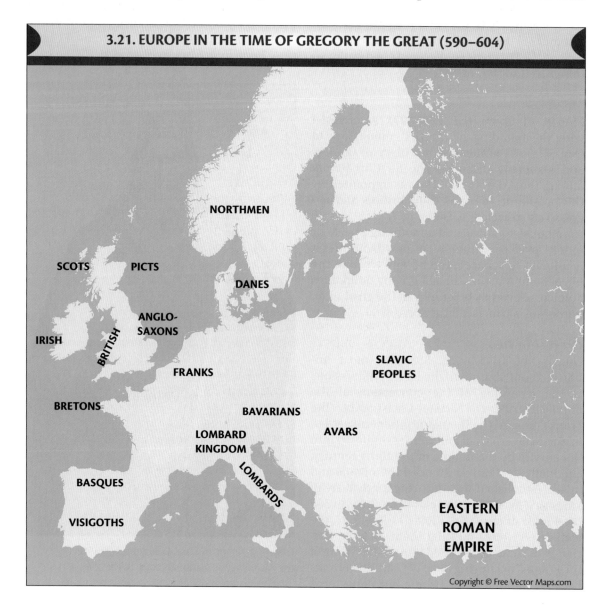

3.21. EUROPE IN THE TIME OF GREGORY THE GREAT (590–604)

NORTHMEN

SCOTS   PICTS

DANES

IRISH   BRITISH   ANGLO-SAXONS

BRETONS

FRANKS

SLAVIC PEOPLES

BAVARIANS

LOMBARD KINGDOM   AVARS

LOMBARDS

BASQUES

VISIGOTHS

EASTERN ROMAN EMPIRE

Invitation to Church History: World

Genevieve, where he was buried. Genevieve (422–511) was an ascetic, who inspired the citizens of Paris during the siege of Attila the Hun in 451 and Childeric the Frank in 486 with deeds of compassion and daring. She later became a counselor to Clovis I and the patron saint of the city.

Patrick of Ireland

Though the information is less than curious eyes would delight in beholding, our knowledge of Patrick of Ireland is more substantive than that of most early missionaries. Further, his life is a lens into the turbulent consequences occasioned by the withdrawal of the Roman legions from Britannia, as well as into the nature of the gospel that he preached and the church embraced.

The conventional picture of Saint Patrick presents him as a modern bishop with miter and pastoral staff, banishing snakes from Ireland, teaching the Trinity by the example of the shamrock, overcoming the opposition of the high king of Ireland, holding conversations with a guardian angel, and climbing mountains to commune with God. Not a single one of these details is historical: miters were not invented until at least over 500 years after his death, the snake story emerges 300 years after his death, and the shamrock example a millennium later.

> "I was like a stone that lies in the deep mud, and he who is mighty came and in his compassion raised me up and exalted me very high and placed me on the top of the wall" (Patrick, *Confession*, 12)..

> "Because I truly am a debtor to God, who gave me so much help that many people were reborn into God through me and afterwards were confirmed and that clergy were ordained everywhere for them for a people who had recently come to belief whom God chose from the ends of the earth as long ago he had promised through his prophets" (Patrick, *Confession*, 38).

Patrick was raised in pre-Anglo-Saxon Britain; the Romans who ruled most of the island called it Britannia. The Roman Empire circled the Mediterranean and stretched across modern Europe south of the Danube, west of the Rhine. Julius Caesar made punitive raids against Britannia during the Gallic Wars, but it was Emperor Claudius whose legions conquered and Romanized it after AD 43, though they were not able to subject the northern portions of the island nor Scotland (now Ireland, "Irish" translates a word which is literally "Scots"; it is the word used throughout Europe for the Irish until the ninth century). The empire began to crumble in the third century due to internal decay, rampant inflation, unstable leadership, and military setbacks. Roman fortunes revived in the fourth century beginning with Constantine, but fractured once more by century's end. This decline was the setting of Patrick's life.

Little is known of the Christian movement in Britannia. Roman soldiers and settlers likely brought Christianity to the island in the first century. It grew to sufficient strength to send three bishops to the Council of Arles in Gaul in 314 (Eborius, Restitutus, and Adelfius). Pelagius came from Britannia at the end of the same century.

Patrick was born in Britannia, likely in the western or southwestern coastal area, of upper-class or aristocratic parents. His father (Calpornius) was a deacon in the church; his grandfather, a presbyter. Calpornius also appears in the record as an administrator responsible for raising the taxes for the imperial government in the area. Since Patrick indicated that he was not raised in a religiously devoted home, scholars have suggested that his father's attachment to the church was to avoid taxation (Constantine's devotion to Christianity was expressed positively in not taxing the clergy. Consequently, there was a rush of wealthy upper-class people into Holy Orders). At the century's end, there was a move to close this loophole in the tax laws by forcing wealthy churchmen to surrender a good portion of their estates. This may indicate that Calpornius (who was a church officer, owned a villa with a large staff, and was an administrator) could be all these things because the hold of the empire was lessening in Britannia at this time.

The date of Patrick's birth is uncertain, but there are several important clues that point to ca. 390. We know that the Roman educational system broke down as the empire began to shrink in 408 under the onslaught of tribal intrusion. In this context Patrick's education was suddenly halted when a raiding party from Scotland (Ireland) captured him. His lament of educational deficiency (writing skills and oratory) suggests that he was not able to complete the rhetor stage of the three-tiered Roman educational system (*ludus* to age twelve comprised reading skills and some mathematics, *ludus grammaticus* to age seventeen included grammar and literature, and *rhetor*). It appears that Patrick was a captive from 405–411 in Ireland and returned there as bishop about 430. We know from his writing that he was a slave, a herder, for six years. It is fairly certain that he was held captive in the northwestern part of the island because upon his escape he traveled 200 miles to the eastern coast. This would suggest that he found a ship returning to Britannia on the southeast coast of the island.

Contrary to tradition, the evidence suggests that Patrick was not trained in Gaul, but in Britannia for the missionary task. His linguistic ability would certainly have been more advanced had he been trained in Gaul. He seems to have spent the time before his return in Britannia and was sent by his native church.

Patrick returned to Ireland in 430 and spent the remainder of his life there. The inhabitants of the island were Celtic; there were no towns. The political organization was that of numerous tribal units with ruling kings. Irish law was not a written one because there was no writing at all in ancient Ireland. Patrick indicates that there were pockets of British settlers on the island and that a missionary named Palladius preceded him.

In the *Letter to Coroticus*, Patrick described himself this way:

> I Patrick, a sinner, very badly educated, in Ireland, declare myself to be a bishop. I am quite certain that I received from God that which I am. I live among barbarian tribes as an exile and refugee for the love of God; God Himself is the witness that this is true . . . I am compelled by zeal for God and the truth of Christ has aroused me out of affection for my neighbors and children for whom I have given up country and kinsfolk and my own life even unto death.

In the same letter he confesses, "I am a slave in Christ to an outlandish nation because of the unspeakable glory of eternal life which is in Jesus Christ our Lord."

Christianity flourished on the island in a semimonastic setting, and from it missionaries would reach into the former western portion of the Roman Empire. Patrick wrote of his work:

> I must teach from the rule of faith of the Trinity, without fear of danger to make known the gift of God and eternal comfort, to promulgate the name of God everywhere fearlessly and faithfully, so as to leave after my death a legacy to my brothers and my children whom I have baptized in the Lord, so many thousands of people (*Confession*, 14).

An understanding of his gospel can be gleaned from the fact that the most quoted of the sacred writings was the book of Romans, as well as his practical grasp of the salvation message:

> For the sun which we see rises every day for our benefit at his behest, but it will never

reign nor will its radiance endure, but all who worship it will come to a bad end in wretched punishment as well. But we who believe in and adore the true son, Christ, who will never die, nor will anyone who has done his will, but he will last forever just as Christ lasts forever, Christ reigns with God the Father Almighty and with the Holy Spirit before ages now and for all ages of ages. Amen (*Confession*, 60).

It is also interesting that Patrick saw his missionary activities through the lens of end times and the coming of Christ to judge the nations. He believed that he was called of God to preach the gospel to the last nation to be evangelized before the end of the world. The Romans viewed Ireland as the end of the world much as first-century Romans viewed it to be Spain. Thus to Patrick his ministry was inspired by a great eschatological passion that also provided great comfort.

The Church at the End of the Ancient Period

Reflecting on the initial five hundred years of the Christian movement is mind-boggling, even though so little is available from preserved sources of all that happened during the period. Its embryonic beginnings provided no clue to the greatness of its expansion, at least to outsiders. From a small coterie of disappointed intimates and a small group of other followers, the movement was energized by the events of Acts 2 and rapidly spread through a hostile Jewish world and a threatening Roman one. Who could have ever imagined a persecuted sect called "The Way," largely drawn from the poor, illiterate, and enslaved classes, would be capable of sustaining a movement that eventually would be embraced by kings and emperors? In the dark days of Decius's and Diocletian's intolerance, who would have thought that the church would have not only survived but triumphed? Who could have en-

visioned a Constantine, Theodosius I, or Clovis I so providentially given and directed as to embrace Christianity in troublesome times? In the beginning of the era, it was a small sect; at the end of the era it was the religion of the civilized world. In the beginning, the Roman Empire was unified under a Caesar; at the end it no longer existed in the West yet Christianity continued to flourish. In the beginning, the Romans killed their king; at the end, kings embraced him as their resurrected and living Lord.

All this appears to have transpired without mass meetings, conferences, emphasis on technique, or mass advertising. It was a people's movement; people shared with their family members and neighbors. The word spread in the slums, shanties, and villas, inspiring hope and fierce devotion among those who experienced the meaning of the message.

With growth came the necessity of change and with error the necessity of explanation, comfort, and reproof. The combination of these two factors caused the church to gradually move from an oligarchy, a leadership by a few (elders/bishops) to a single leader in each of the churches. Over time with the increase of churches, bishops took on, in addition to their own pastoral roles, increased administrative functions in the care and supervision of other churches. All the bishops across the empire were considered as possessing equal authority, giving a united voice at the great councils of the fourth and fifth centuries. Bishops in the most prestigious cities in the empire were given a special place of judicatory importance and were called Metropolitan Bishops or archbishops, though at this time titles were not uniformly used or defined (Council of Nicaea, 325, Canons 4–6). The term *pope* is used of various bishops such as the bishops of Carthage, Alexandria, or Rome.

There were also noticeable changes in the churches, particularly the more wealthy and prestigious ones, as the fourth century progressed. The pomp and circumstance of the state became a part of the liturgy of the churches. Bishops adopted the tradition from the state of wearing toga-like attire; services began with processional ritual, including choirs. Large edifices were constructed, shaped in the form of a cross with sacred altars that only the leaders could access. The segmentation of the clergy and laity widened to reflect the separation of common citizen from political leader. Ritual and ceremony became the focus of worship. This, however, is not to imply that the Bible became less important and true worship marginalized.

Generally, bishops were caring shepherds of their flocks who fed their hearers on the teaching of sacred scripture and pastoral care. The homilies of Ambrose, Chrysostom, Jerome, and Augustine (to name a few) bear witness to a church leadership that loved and taught the Bible. The catechetical instruction of Cyril of Jerusalem and the pastoral emphases Martin of Tours (in spite of the incrustations of legend and myth) indicate the presence of devoted leaders who cared for the spiritual health of the flocks of God.

The monastic movement, like the martyrs of the initial centuries, demonstrated a willingness to follow Christ in a self-denying manner, as well as a profound longing for intimacy with the one they loved and discovered through the crucible of devotional piety and sacrifice.

The presence of error in the churches appears to have been a factor in the movement away from plurality of leadership to the bishop's office. Before recognition and collection of the new sacred writings, the church developed several lines of protective devices: the idea of an identifiable succession of bishops in a church with connections to an apostle (that is, apostolic succession), the Rule of Faith (those teachings that have always had a universal existence in the churches), and the identification of the true gospel, the bishop, and the church as one. Such appeals to history and uniformity seemed helpful and comforting, though subject to misuse, overstatement, and bias as later centuries demonstrate. As time passed, churchmen recognized that collecting the sacred writings and authorizing them alone to be read in the churches was another bulwark against false teachings. The "Bible" was there from the earliest decades of the church, having been written by churchmen, but it took time to recognize, properly admire, and use the treasure.

Though the church should be cautious of naturalistic explanations for spiritual phenomena (nor should it over-spiritualize nature), it must take them into account. Culture and context are shaping factors. While it might be argued that we have become "resident aliens," having been translated out of the kingdom of darkness into the kingdom of God's Son, we are still citizens. We live in the same environment, breathe the same air, as all human beings do. Because culture and context shape perception, even spiritual perception, there are natural causes that influence the perception of what is truth. The apologists' stress on unbounded freedom of the will in battling their gnostic critics, who accused Christians of fatalism, is a case in point. Influenced by that criticism the early church tended to be slow in recognizing the witness of Holy Scriptures to human inability and insufficiency. The presence of false teachers with their own sacred writings caused the church in reaction to, perhaps, overstate the concept of bishop succession. Nor can the role of greed for position be overlooked in the struggles over the Trinitarian and christological controversies. The golden, invisible thread through history is the providential care of God by incomprehensibly directing the affairs of humankind.

Of significant importance in the history of the Christian movement is the progress made in understanding and explaining the faith in the era. One thing is clear: churchmen did not invent teachings to silence critics or quiet the constituency. Their role was not that of innovator; it was that of explainer. This is evident from the fact that they sought to conform their explanations to what was revealed, and therefore permissible, within the limitations of the sacred writings. Though it was Tertullian who was the first to refer to the members of the Godhead as the *Trinity*, and another, as a *triad*, he did not invent a concept by using those terms that are alien to the Bible. Athanasius's insistence on the deity of Christ or the Cappadocians' distinction of such terms as *essence* and *persons* are explanations of the biblical witness. Augustine's understanding of sin and grace (however one may look upon his understanding of foreknowledge and predestination) are valid and warranted explanations from the perspective of Scripture. The ancient churchmen did not invent Christianity; they served us in seeking to understand and explain it.

While the Bible is of a heavenly origin, it did not come to us with an index or glossary of terms. It is a remarkable book, assembled by writers over sixteen centuries; it has a central theme (the triumph of God through Christ by the Spirit over death and hell to redeem a new people to inhabit the new garden), but it has required the best of enlightened thinking, prayer, and determination for an understanding of the incomprehensible God. Though we can know God truly, we cannot know him exhaustively! The work of explaining, the task of the theologian, will and should continue because the knowledge of God is inexhaustible. We are free to explore the Bible, but we can never stand in contradistinction to it.

In general, and in particular, the expanding role of the church and the meaning of the sacrament of baptism in particular are important in understanding later trends and abuses in the church. In conflict with the Novatians and the Donatists, Cyprian and Augustine developed a unique understanding of the church. They argued that separation from the one, true (hence catholic) church would disconnect followers from apostolic origins and its understanding of the true gospel of Jesus Christ. The gospel is where the church is; the gospel is where the bishop is; and, therefore, there is no salvation outside the teachings of the church or the bishop. If you understand that the issue is the gospel, not an institution or its clerics, there is much truth in such assertions. Unfortunately, over the centuries the teachings of the church will, at times, contradict Scripture. The church, the bishop, and the gospel will not speak with the same voice. The church will lead its constituents astray by suggesting that it only teaches what always and everywhere has been taught.

Augustine's insistence that the validity of the sacraments does not depend on the piety of the administrator, an argument he used against the Donatists, hides the potential of terrible consequences. While personal piety does not determine the efficacy of clerical function, the piety and purity of the churchmen cannot be lost. Furthermore, it could be potentially hazardous to argue that validity of clerical function finds its origins in the church and its apostolic succession rather than in the gospel.

Also, Augustine's definition of the church, being composed of sheep and goats, though a sad reality, is not an operative theory for church practice. The church is the assembly of professing saints who have been brought together through the waters of baptism. It seems that circumstances brought about by the creation of state-sponsored Christianity forced churchmen to broaden definitions in this regard. Success always has a dark side, I suppose!

To redefine the makeup of the church, Augustine had to redefine the role of catechesis. Catechesis did not prepare one to enter the assembly of the saints; it prepared a person to confirm the rightness of their membership (hence the origin of confirmation). Change in itself is neither valuable nor invaluable; the issue is permissibility of belief without contradicting the Holy Scriptures.

The struggle with the Pelagians caused

Augustine to develop a doctrine of baptism that may be scripturally unwarranted, but it is consistent with a view that the church with its offices and sacraments is life-giving. To answer the Pelagian charge that inability cannot be consistent with blame and praise and that it contradicts justice to condemn those without ability, Augustine had to take up the question of the infant and judgment. His solution was found in the function of infant baptism. Infant baptism cleanses from the inherited stain of Adam's first sin. If a child by virtue of the sacrament is cleansed in this manner, and the child has no actual sins since it is incapable of sinning (at least that is how it is explained), the child is safe even though it may die. One wonders if Augustine would have ventured down this path had it not been for the Pelagians. He laid the foundation for the medieval distinction between implied faith and actual or implicit faith.

Augustine greatly influenced the medieval era in his understanding of the church and the function of baptism. Also, Augustine understood that justification was a progressive action, not a declarative act. He made justification progressive sanctification, putting justification off until glorification. Again, this concept will flourish in the medieval era alongside the intense development of sacramental theology.

The shadow of Augustine was cast long and deep over the medieval era. His insights into the church, redemption, and grace were not uniformly embraced by any in the subsequent divisions of the Catholic Church in the sixteenth century. Protestants applauded his insights in some areas and were strangely silent on what they considered his weaknesses. Roman Catholics seem to have a similar capacity for selectivity. The Orthodox Churches appear to think that both parties overstate the issues. The central focus, from the perspective of the Orthodox community of churches, is misplaced in either case by a misuse of Roman legal language imposed on the sacred writings.

Christianity entered an unprecedented era with the benevolences of Constantine and Theodosius I, a period of dominance of a Christian view of values that would prevail in Mediterranean and northern European cultures for fourteen hundred years. In terms of the unity of Christendom, the medieval era was a remarkable millennium. The seeds sown, or at least some of them, would flower into variegated landscapes of beautiful displays and grotesque distortions of scriptural truth.

GLOSSARY OF TERMS

Adoptionism: a second-century heresy that believed that Jesus was adopted as God's son at his baptism.

Apollinarianism: a fourth-century heresy that believed that Jesus had a human body and lower soul but did not possess a human mind. The view was condemned at the second ecumenical council (Constantinople, 381) under the direction of Theodosius I.

Arianism: the late third-century heresy that Jesus is inferior to God the Father and was not eternally preexistent. Such an understanding of the incarnate Christ was condemned at the ecumenical councils held at Nicaea (325) and Constantinople (381) only to reemerge in the church in the sixteenth century as Socinianism and in the eighteenth century as Deism and Unitarianism.

Caesaropapism: a view of the relationship of the church and the state that combined secular government with spiritual authority into a single power structure under the bishop of Rome. It has commonly been designated as the theory of the "two Swords," initially proposed by Gelasius I in the late fifth century and frequently supported by the use of Matthew 16:18. Both Roman Catholics and some Protestants embraced the concept in various forms.

Cassianism: also known as semi-Pelagianism, is frequently understood as a mediating anthropological and soteriological position between the views espoused by Augustine and Pelagius. John Cassian, from whom the term is derived, argued that divine grace can begin in human sincerity and be finalized by causative cooperativeness between human efforts and

divine ones. The Roman Catholic Church is often defined as Cassian by Protestant critics, but the church officially advocates the primacy of grace, though mandating human obedience in cooperation with God to obtain heaven.

Cenobitism: a monastic tradition that emphasizes life in community, as opposed to living as a hermit in solitude. This form of isolated spiritual experience became predominant eclipsing an earlier form, the single hermit living alone in a cave, on a pole, or in some other barren environment.

Desert Fathers: hermits, ascetics, and monks who retreated to isolated, unpopulated areas beginning in the third century in Egypt. In so doing, they provided a model for the later development of Christian monasticism.

Donatism: a North-African Christian schematic sect that emerged after the Diocletian persecutions over the issue of church readmission for those who recanted of their faith but subsequently sought reinstatement. The dispute was most importantly over the nature of the church. Donatists argued that the mark of the church was holiness and "traitors" forfeited membership privilege; Augustine argued that the redemptive nature of the church required readmission since the efficacy of the church's offices came from God and did not depend on the grace of its officers.

Eutychianism: a fifth-century attempt to explain the relationship of the humanity and deity of Christ in the incarnate state. Eutychians argued that Christ was of two natures, human and divine, but they existed in a compound unity of a single nature. Condemned at the Council of Chalcedon (451), the persistence of the view in Monophysitism led to the first permanent schism in the professing church.

Macedonianism: an interpretation of the relationship of the Holy Spirit to God the Father that did not recognize ontological equality, much as Arianism rejected the equality of the Father and Son. The view was condemned at the Council of Constantinople (381) where it was asserted that the triunity of Godhead was fully expressed in the Trinitarian formula.

Manichaeism: an early formidable threat to the Christian faith that combined elements of Christianity, Zoroastrianism, and Buddhism, and that thrived from the third through the seventh centuries. The influential Saint Augustine embraced the dualistic ideals of Mani prior to his acceptance of the Christian faith and subsequently those wrote against their teachings.

Modalism (Patripassionism, Sabellianism): the attempt to explain the Trinitarian existence of God by arguing for a strict singularity of God in person and attributes, but in a threefold manifestation. Often designated by a major proponent, Sabellius, God is seen as threefold in manifestation but singular in person. This explanation of the divine Trinity was consistently condemned in the fourth-and-fifth century ecumenical councils of the church.

Monothelitism: a view of the incarnate Christ suggesting that he possessed a single will, not two (one human and one divine). It seems to have appeared as an attempt to bring the eastern churches together against the formidable threat of Muslim insurgency. At the Council of Constantinople, the Third Constantinople Council (668), the Catholic Church condemned the view.

Nestorianism: a teaching in the fourth-century church concerning the relationship between Christ's two natures in the incarnation. Nestorius accepted the full humanity and deity of Christ, but seemed to reject the concept of his unity, disjointing the natures and giving Christ two natures joined morally but not organically. The view was condemned at the third ecumenical council held at Ephesus (431). Advocates of this view continued in existence for several centuries, extending their teaching into the Far East.

Novatianism (Novatian Party, Rigorism): a third-century crisis in the early church caused by division of opinion concerning the treatment of Christians who had faltered in faith during the Decian persecutions. While Cyprian favored the readmission of such because he considered that the church was the only ground of salvation, the Novatians favored exclusion because they viewed the lapsed as in violation of the qualifying characteristic of holiness.

Pelagianism: a teaching promulgated in the fifth-century church concerning the nature of humankind and the human factor in salvation. Pelagius taught that Adam's first sin affected only himself and not the race except by setting a precedent that has been subsequently and voluntarily pursued universally. Rejecting original sin and inherent birth depravity, sin was defined as moral selfishness, remedied by resolve. Further, Pelagius rejected the divine initiatives of predestination, election, and foreknowledge, redefining the terms as predicated on human action. The view was condemned in the Catholic Church through the writings of Augustine and at the Synod of Orange (529).

Platonism (Platonic Idealism): a philosophical school of thought developed by Plato concerning the nature of reality, central to which is the distinction between what is perceptible but not intelligible, and that which is intelligible but imperceptible. Plato argued that reality existed most fully before the form and substance observable functioned as shadows or figurements of that greater, more real reality. Platonist have proved both a handmaid to Christian theology as well as a detriment in the hands of monastistics, mystics, and transcendentalists who disparaged substance and form as less than real.

Real Monophysitism: see *Eutychianism*

Severians (Monphysites, Monophysitism): another designation for those in the Eastern Empire who embraced a single nature in Christ, opposing the findings of Chalcedon. They were more generally known as verbal Monophysites, in distinct from ontological Monophysites, Severians were so named because the principal advocate of the position was Severus, patriarch of Antioch (512–519).

Semi-Pelagianism (Cassianism): a view concerning the issues of sin and grace in the church often identified with the teachings of the fifth century cleric/monastic John Cassian. Cassian struggled to explain the relationship between ability, responsibility, and culpability (as well as freedom and sovereignty) by arguing for a matrix of causative, cooperative factors. He suggested that when God detects religious sincerity, clearly deficient to cause redeeming mercies, God can act in grace to supply what human effort can conceive but not accomplish. The view is a compromise of sorts between Augustinian inability—the necessity of uncaused, unmerited divine initiative in salvation—and the Pelagian view that humankind has the capacity to effect salvation by moral resolve and rectitude. The view was condemned at the Synod of Orange (529), but reemerged in the medieval church.

Subordinationism: a view espoused in the early church by Origen, among others, prior to the Nicaea (325) and Constantinople (381) ecumentical councils, claiming that the Son is ontologically inferior to the Father, though not the view of Tertullian and Aristides. The latter spoke of a "triade of equal glories" and the former coined the term *Trinity*.

Verbal Monophysites (Severians): a view concerning the incarnate Christ. The Monophysites rejected the dual nature Christology decreed at the Council of Chalcedon (451), arguing that a person is a single nature and that Christ was not two persons (Nestorianism) and, therefore, possessed a single nature. Monophysites of this variety agreed in substance with the findings of Chalcedon, but disagreed with the language used in the Chalcedonian Creed.

Further Readings:
The Ancient Church (33–600)

Primary Sources from the Ancient Church

[Numerous Christian classics can be accessed at http://www.ccel.org]

Athanasius. *St. Athanasius on the Incarnation.* Translated by Archibald Robertson. 2d ed. London: D. Nutt, 1891.

Augustine. *The City of God.* New York: Fathers of the Church. 1950.

_____, and Carolinne White. *The Confessions of St. Augustine.* Grand Rapids: William B. Eerdmans Publishing Co., 2001.

Bettenson, Henry Scowcroft. *The Early Christian Fathers: A Selection from the Writings of the Fathers from St. Clement of Rome to St. Athanasius.* New York: Oxford University Press, 1956.

_____ . *The Later Christian Fathers: A Selection from the Writings of the Fathers from St. Cyril of Jerusalem to St. Leo the Great.* New York: Oxford University Press, 1970.

Holmes, Michael W. *The Apostolic Fathers: Greek Texts and English Translations.* 3rd ed. Grand Rapids: Baker, 2007.

Richardson, Cyril Charles, ed. *Early Christian Fathers.* The Library of Christian Classics, v. 1. New York: Macmillan, 1970.

General Surveys of the Ancient Church

Boer, Harry R. *A Short History of the Early Church.* Grand Rapids: William B. Eerdmans Publishing Co., 1976.

Crocker III, H.W. *Triumph: The Power and Glory of the Catholic Church.* New York: Three Rivers Press, 2001.

Drobner, Hubertus R. *The Fathers of the Church: a Comprehensive Introduction.*

Peabody, MA: Hendrickson Publishers, 2007.

Ferguson, Everett. *Christianity and Society: The Social World of Early Christianity.* New York: Garland Publishers, 1999.

Guy, Laurie. *Introducing Early Christianity: a Topical Survey of Its Life, Beliefs, and Practices.* Downers Grove, IL: InterVarsity Press, 2004.

Harvey, Susan Ashbrook. *The Oxford Handbook of Early Christian Studies.* Oxford: Oxford University Press, 2008.

Jefford, Clayton N. *The Apostolic Fathers: An Essential Guide.* Nashville, TN: Abingdon, 2005.

Lampe, Peter. *From Paul to Valentinus.* Minneapolis, MN: Fortress Press, 2003.

Litfin, Bryan. *Getting to Know the Church Fathers.* Grand Rapids: Brazos Press, 2007.

Lynch, Joseph H. *Early Christianity: A Brief History.* New York: Oxford University Press, 2010.

Pratscher, Wilhelm, ed. *The Apostolic Fathers: An Introduction.* Trans. Elisabeth G. Wolfe. Waco, TX: Baylor University Press, 2010.

Important Topics and People of the Ancient Church

Anatolios, Khaled. *Athanasius.* New York: Routledge, 2004.

Barnes, Timothy D. *Athanasius and Constantius: Theology and Politics in the Constantinian Empire.* Cambridge, MA: Harvard University Press, 1993.

Chadwick, Henry. *Augustine of Hippo: A Life.* Oxford: Oxford University Press, 2009.

Chadwick, Owen. *Western Asceticism.* Philadelphia: Westminster Press, 1958.

Hardy, Edward Rochie. *Christology of the Later*

Fathers. Philadelphia: Westminster Press, 1954.

Jefford, Clayton N. *The Apostolic Fathers and the New Testament*. Peabody, MA: Hendrickson, 2006

Johnson, Douglas W. *The Great Jesus Debates: 4 Early Church Battles About the Person and Work of Jesus*. St. Louis, MO: Concordia Publishing House, 2005.

Johnson, Lawrence J. *Worship in the Early Church: an Anthology of Historical Sources*. Vol. 1. Collegeville, MN: Liturgical Press, 2009.

Nichols, Stephen J. *For Us and for Our Salvation: The Doctrine of Christ in the Early Church*. Wheaton, IL: Crossway, 2007.

Osborn, Eric. *Irenaeus of Lyons*. New York: Cambridge University Press, 2001.

Polman, A.D.R. *The Word of God According to St. Augustine*. Grand Rapids: William B. Eerdmans Publishing Co,, 1961.

Rusch, William G. *The Trinitarian Controversy*. Philadelphia: Fortress Press, 1980.

Stephenson, Paul. *Constantine: Roman Emperor, Christian Victor*. New York: Overlook Press, 2010.

Weaver, Rebecca Harden. *Divine Grace and Human Agency: A Study of the Semi-Pelagian Controversy*. Macon, GA: Mercer University Press, 1996.

Williams, Michael Stuart. *Authorised Lives in Early Christian Biography: Between Eusebius and Augustine*. Cambridge: Cambridge University Press, 2008.

Workman, Herbert B. *Persecution in the Early Church*. New York: Oxford University Press, 1980.

PART
2

THE MEDIEVAL CHURCH
(600–1500)

Chapter 4 Outline

The Growth of Ecclesiastical Authority

The Roman Empire and the Church in the Sixth and Seventh Century

The Church and the Carolingian Empire

Missionary Activity in the Early Middle Ages

The Rise of the Islamic Faith

Chapter 4 Objectives

- That the reader will identify the causes and course of the growth of ecclesiastical authority in the early medieval church

- That the reader will describe why authority for the church came to be centered in Rome

- That the reader will define the iconoclastic controversy

- That the reader will describe the development of missionary activity in the early medieval church

- That the reader will recognize the influence of Islam on the development of Christianity

CHAPTER 4

THE EARLY MEDIEVAL CHURCH (600–900)

T HE IMAGES THAT THE **Middle Ages** conjure in our minds are those of magnificent castles, princes and princesses, and valiant knights off on one or another crusade, mostly against Saladin and his Turkish hordes, or sitting around King Arthur's table. Sometimes we think of jousting matches where thunderous horses gallop with their ironclad warriors and decorative decor toward a violent clash of lances. It is seen as an era of crossbows, court jesters, and hideous instruments of torture. Ultimately, it is frequently viewed as a time when not a great deal of significance happened, a time when darkness rather than light shown across a landscape of lords, fiefdoms, and impoverished, illiterate serfs. Though the period included an oppressive and derelict church, blackened by the moral stench of greed and gross neglect of spiritual office, consigning the souls of men and women to a spiritual darkness, the time was not as dark as generally imagined.

The terms, "Middle Age" or "Medieval Period," seems strange to post moderns who no longer believe that it was a transitional time between two others. The designations may have outlived their usefulness, or so it seems. The term, "medieval," is derived from a Latin word that means, "middle." Generally, the perimeters of the medieval era stretch from the collapse of the Western Roman Empire (the end of the classical era) to the rise of the fifteenth-century Renaissance (there is no agreement on the precise dates that frame the period).

It is also common to refer to the period as the "**Dark Ages**." The term seems to have been first used by Francesco Petrarch (1304–1374), sometimes called the "Father of **Humanism**," who shared a disdain for the decline of culture that followed the demise of Greco-Roman dominance and hoped that the Renaissance, which showed promise of restoring an ancient past, would usher in a modern era. Leonardo Bruni (ca. 1369–1444), called the first modern historian, devised the conceptual framework for a division of history into three parts (antiquity, middle, and modern) though the actual naming of the second period, the Middle Age, is accredited to Flavio Biondo (1392–1463) in 1442.

While the emergent Renaissance movement has an element that sought the restoration of **Greco-Roman culture**, originating in southern Europe, northern European humanists criticized the middle period as dark for generally religious reasons. Humanists, like Desiderius Erasmus (ca.1469–1536), the greatest of the northern humanists, viewed the middle period as the Dark Age because of the state of the church in the period. Whereas it was common to refer to antiquity as a age of darkness and the coming of Christianity as the Age of Light, Erasmus, and many others including Martin Luther, viewed early Christianity as the age of light and the Middle Ages as the age of darkness. The reform minded people like Erasmus and Luther sought not to reduplicate Greco-Roman culture but to substitute a robust and biblically centered Christian faith. To these men the church had drifted in the intervening centuries from a biblically astute and caring community to the corrupting dominance of an oppressive ecclesiastical hierarchy that promoted ignorance, immorality, and avarice.

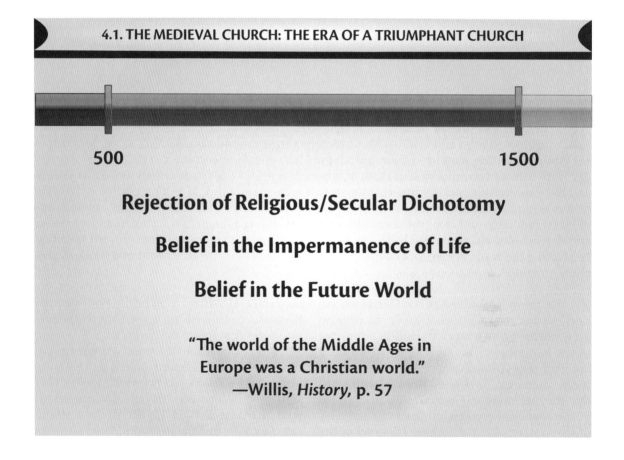

4.1. THE MEDIEVAL CHURCH: THE ERA OF A TRIUMPHANT CHURCH

500   1500

Rejection of Religious/Secular Dichotomy

Belief in the Impermanence of Life

Belief in the Future World

"The world of the Middle Ages in
Europe was a Christian world."
—Willis, *History*, p. 57

In many respects, it was an era like most. It was a time, at least in the high Middles Ages of advances in science and technology, the rise of the universities, the emergence of a market economy with burgeoning towns and cities, and the recovery from the torment of invasions, either from the "barbarians," the berserk **Vikings**, or the Islamic hordes. It was the era of the creation of the modern nation-states. It was a remarkable era in terms of the prominence of the Christian faith.

The wall separating the sacred from the secular, so prominent in the modern era, was unknown. Religion and culture were a harmonious whole. In this respect, it was the unprecedented era for the triumph of Christianity as a worldview. The lens through which people determined values was rooted in the church. People in the Middle Ages viewed themselves as moderns (though the term only became into our vocabulary in the nineteenth century) and embraced a heavenly perspective on life. Life was viewed as an impermanent gift in which the priority in the use of time was to prepare the soul for heaven. As foreign as it sounds to our very earth-oriented perspective, the medievalist person's primary striving was to reach beyond the temporary purgation of an interim state after death (a view popularized by Augustine) and acquire the beatific vision. It was a world that had its vices, but its virtues were outstanding!

The Growth
of Ecclesiastical Authority

In the chaos of the last vestiges of the Western Roman Empire, the capital was moved from Rome to Ravenna, where its marshes offered some illusion of protection from the pillaging and provided a respite for a defenseless people. For the population the church was a stable force. With the dethronement of Augustus Romulus in 476, the Western empire became a distant memory. Though churches were destroyed, precious relics carried off, and people

4.2. HISTORY OF CHRISTIAN CHURCH

THE CHURCH DIFFUSE

1500

THE CHURCH TRIUMPHANT

500

THE CHURCH EMERGENT

33

massacred, the church at Rome was providentially spared from Attila the **Hun's** ravages by the pleading of bishop Leo I in 452. Three years later the bishop was not able to prevent the city from being sacked by the **Vandals**, but his urgings prevented Genseric from utterly destroying the city. In 476 Odoacer (ca. 435–493), a former Roman general but then part of a tribal confederation, deposed the last western emperor and declared himself king of Italy (a title later confirmed by Constantinople); his rule appears to have been kind toward his subjects.

Zeno, emperor in the East, conspired with Theodoric of the (Goths were divided into eastern and western [Visigoths] tribes) to invade Italy and depose Odoacer, which they did in 493. This extended Byzantine rule into Italy for a short time. However, the **Lombards**, a Germanic tribe, invaded and displaced the Ostrogoths, establishing a kingdom in Italy that would last into the eighth century as eastern Byzantine armies gradually withdrew. When the Lombards threatened Rome in 579, Pelagius II was able to end the siege by offering a large sum of money. Roman bishops became the protectors of the city. Since military assistance could no longer be expected from Constantinople, bishops made alliances with the Franks to ward off the Lombards.

In the midst of the uncertainties and disillusionment, as well as the pain, the church at Rome maintained a profoundly stabilizing role. Other cities such as Rheims, Mainz, and Worms were completely devastated. It is interesting that though the Roman Empire in the East was largely unchallenged by the invading tribes, the emperors in Constantinople did not feel constrained to defend and preserve the western territories (the only attempt came under Emperor Justinian in the sixth century). This, most likely, bears witness to the fact of a gradual transmutation rather than a cataclysmic diminution of the Western empire,

In the wake of growing political, social, and cultural instability in the West, the churches, particularly the church at Rome, assumed an increasing role in bringing a sense of security and hope. It is in this context that the bishop of Rome, Gregory I (Gregory the Great, ca. 540–603), appears to be the first bishop to claim religious hegemony over all the churches, a claim never embraced within the Eastern empire. The term **pope** means, "father." It was used in a non-technical sense by the bishop of Carthage, Cyprian, and the bishop of Alexandria, Athanasius, prior to the sixth century, as well as some Roman bishops (the first Roman bishop to do so was Marcellinus [d. 304]).

Though titles can be disputed, roles cannot. Roman bishops assumed the function of head over the western churches, and they did so based on **Petrine priority** over the

Pope Gregory the Great from the Registrum Gregorii (Trier, Stadtbibliothek, Hs. 171/1626). Courtesy of Sailko.

4.3. THE EMERGING POWER OF THE MEDIEVAL CHURCH

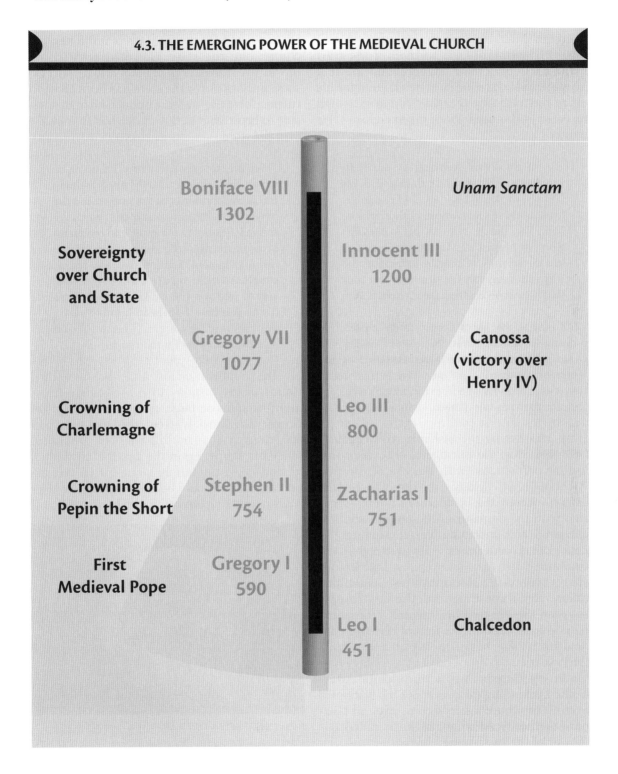

Boniface VIII
1302

Unam Sanctam

Sovereignty
over Church
and State

Innocent III
1200

Gregory VII
1077

Canossa
(victory over
Henry IV)

Crowning of
Charlemagne

Leo III
800

Crowning of
Pepin the Short

Stephen II
754

Zacharias I
751

First
Medieval Pope

Gregory I
590

Leo I
451

Chalcedon

churches (Matt. 16:18). In the bishopric of Leo I (440–461), a time of social turmoil, he assumed it was his duty to meet temporal and spiritual needs among the churches. He claimed for his office the authority that God alone extended to Peter in the capacity of his successors. He wrote:

> . . . if we obtain anything by our daily supplications from God's mercy, it is his [Peter's] work and his merits, whose power lives in his see and whose authority is so high. For, dearly beloved, his confession won this reward . . . which transcended all the uncertainty of human judgment and was endowed with the firmness of a rock that no assault could shake (*Letters*, 3.3).

"As early as the age of Gregory there existed, evidently, some seeds of this evil. . . . We have fallen into outward busyness, and we undertake one thing, but perform another. . . . For men have become so insane as to consider it beneath the bishop's dignity to preach to the people" (Calvin, *Institutes*, 4.5.12).

It was during the bishopric of Gelasius I (492–496) that the prestige of the office was further perpetuated with the use of the title "vicar of Christ." Gelasius, the last of three Africans to occupy the bishopric of Rome, struggled with the emperor of the empire and the patriarch of Constantinople, continuing the policy of his predecessor, Felix III, who had excommunicated Acacius over his conciliatory efforts toward the **Monophysites**. Sometimes called "the Three Chapters," the controversy between the Western bishop and the eastern patriarch resulted in the formal division. The Acacius Schism began in 484 and lasted for thirty years.

In 494 Gelasius wrote to Emperor Anastasius I extending the powers of his bishopric over all the churches, as well as over all temporal authority. In what has been called the "power of the two swords" or two realms, Ge-lasius argued for two spheres of authority, the church and the state. God had granted authority over the church to Peter and his successors; authority over the state has been given to rulers. However, the state under God is answerable to Peter; that is, the church has supremacy over the state:

> There are two powers, august Emperor, by which this world is chiefly ruled, namely, the sacred authority of the priests and the royal power. Of these that of the priests are the weightier, since they have to render an account for even the kings of men in the divine judgment. You are also aware, dear son, that while you are permitted honorably to rule over human kind, yet in things divine you bow your head humbly before the leaders of the clergy . . . that you should be subordinate rather than superior.

The political chaos and the ascending claims of the bishops to a two-sphere hegemony explains, in large measure, the claims of Gregory the Great, who emerged as a bishop in 590. Gregory appears to have been a political official in Rome. Upon the death of his father, he converted the family home into a monastery, St. Andrews, and became a monk. He later was appointed a deacon in the church, an am-

Pope Gelasius I from the Basilica of Saint Paul, outside walls, Rome. Courtesy of Wikipedia.

bassador of Pelagius II to the imperial court in Constantinople, and a secretary to the Roman bishop.

Though Gregory did not assume the title of "pope," willing only to call himself "the servant of the servants of God," his bishopric witnessed the formal end of the concept of a federation of egalitarian bishops that had prevailed in the churches from the second century, though it had slowly faded as the churches grew more numerous and administration more complex. As the leader, Gregory sought to restore the churches by extending the ecclesiastical power and prestige of Rome. In the absence of the Roman senate or prefect, as a head of city government, he assumed the duties of leadership in both church and state.

Gregory was able to strengthen the church by increasing revenues and using them to meet the pressing needs of the poor. In his official capacity, he reached out to the western churches offering aid and counsel, binding them close to Rome. In his *Dialogues*, he upheld the claims of Rome as the head of all the churches against Constantinople (5.44). He argued that Rome is supreme among all the churches and responsible alone for them, which the Council of Chalcedon (following the Council of Constantinople I, Canon 3) confirmed by decreeing that Rome was first among the churches. Further, he argued that ecumenical councils had no authority without the affirmation of his apostolic see. Needless to say, the eastern churches did not share Gregory's opinions!

Above all else, Gregory was a shepherd of the flock of God who cared deeply for his people and fed them on the Holy Scriptures in a very practical manner. His sermons, as well as his commentary on the book of Job (*The Moralia*), reveals an interpreter of the Bible who extended Augustine's threefold method: the literal, the allegorical, and the moral. The first approach reveals the historical facts; the second, the spiritual meaning; and the third,

our duties (*Moralia*, Preface, 3). Gregory's pastoral concerns are revealed in a work entitled *Book of Pastoral Rule*. The short work is divided into two parts: rules concerning a pastor's personal demeanor and those for the conduct of his work. He stated the following at one point:

> The pastor should always be a leader in action, that by his living he may point out the way of life to those who are put under him, and that the flock, which follows the voice and manners of the shepherd, may learn how to walk rather through example than through words. For he who is required by the necessity of his position to speak the highest things is compelled by the same necessity to do the highest things.

Though Gregory did not possess the intellectual or literary brilliance of Augustine, he did transmit many of his ideas to the Middle Ages and in the process elaborated and distorted his mentor, often with a questionable use of the miraculous. His gifts were more evident in the administrative realm than at the scholar's desk. His contribution to the fabric of the medieval church is crucial to understanding the church's development.

"Guilt can be extinguished only by a penal offering to justice. But it would contradict the idea of justice, if for the sin of a rational being like man, the death of an irrational animal should be accepted as a sufficient atonement. Hence, a man must be offered as the sacrifice for man; so that a rational victim may be slain for a rational criminal. But how could a man, himself stained with sin, be an offering for sin? Hence a sinless man must be offered. But what man descending in the ordinary course would be free from sin? Hence, the Son of God must be born of a virgin, and become man for us. He assumed our nature without our corruption (culpa). He made himself a sacrifice for us, and set forth for sinners his own body, a victim without sin, and able both to die by virtue of his

4.4. THE RISE OF EPISCOPACY AND PAPACY IN THE CHURCH

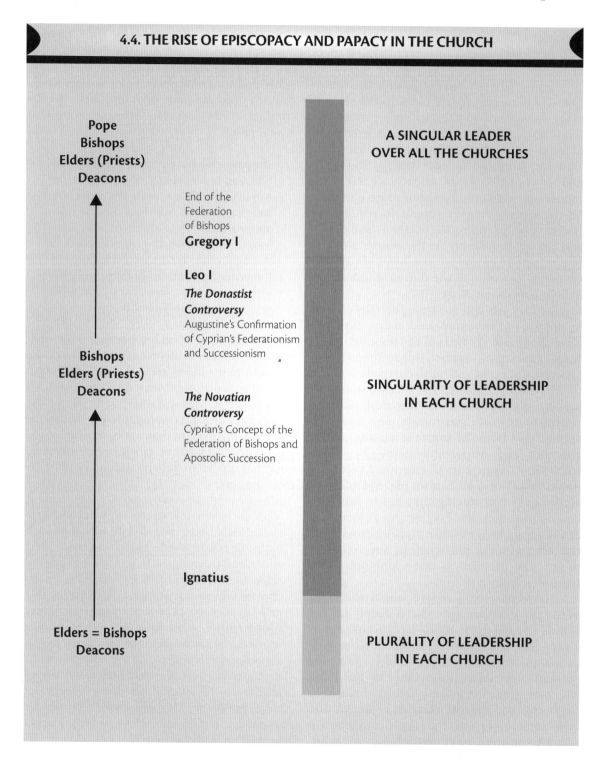

Pope
Bishops
Elders (Priests)
Deacons

End of the
Federation
of Bishops
Gregory I

A SINGULAR LEADER
OVER ALL THE CHURCHES

Leo I

The Donastist
Controversy
Augustine's Confirmation
of Cyprian's Federationism
and Successionism

Bishops
Elders (Priests)
Deacons

The Novatian
Controversy
Cyprian's Concept of the
Federation of Bishops and
Apostolic Succession

SINGULARITY OF LEADERSHIP
IN EACH CHURCH

Ignatius

Elders = Bishops
Deacons

PLURALITY OF LEADERSHIP
IN EACH CHURCH

humanity, and to cleanse the guilty, upon grounds of justice" (*The Moralia*, 17).

An example of Gregory's development of earlier thought into a more clear and rigid teaching is his influence on the concept of an interim state between death and entrance into heaven for the saints. The idea seems to have emerged in the churches in the third century apologists based on 1 Cor. 3:11–15 ("saved—even though only as one escaping through the flames"). The Western churches under the lead of Augustine and Jerome seemed to view the interim as a time of judgmental purgation of residual sinfulness. The Eastern churches showed a tendency to spiritualize the same passages emphasizing a progressive positive transformation in life (a concept called deification). It was Gregory who elevated such thinking into a formal teaching of the churches. By the late medieval era the idea of purgatory will have developed into a horrifying obsession as seen in Dante's *Divine Comedy*.

Gregory's desire to help the struggling saint progress toward the beatific vision opened new possibilities of how to satisfy God for daily sins. At the same time, Gregory deemphasized such foundational Augustinian insights as predestination and foreknowledge and viewed redemption from a horizontal perspective more than a vertical one. Unfortunately, Gregory continued Augustine's idea of justification as a progressive, continual action of "making one righteous." Grace was still truly grace to Gregory, but he gave a "new" Augustine to his day, with the starting points and primary foci changed.

Interest in a healthy temporal state led to an increased emphasis of the role of the cleric, the priest, and the daily life of the parishioner, heaven being less certain. Confession of sins to priests was encouraged in new ways leading to absolution and acts of penance. Later church scholars will describe confession/penance as the "**second plank**" to secure the soul, the first being baptism. The Lord's Supper, the **Mass**, became a vehicle of temporal grace in a miraculous transformation of the host and cup into the real Christ who was sacrificed anew in an unbloodied manner effecting forgiveness of temporal sins (*Dialogues*, 4. 59–62) (While Gregory was singing the Mass, Christ is said to have appeared to him above the altar confirming its real, transformational significance). Though Gregory can be criticized for some of the changes and trends he occasioned, his reasons seemed to be valid, although frequently temporally clouded ones.

Commenting on Matthew 12:32 Gregory states (*Dialogues*, 4.39), "In this sentence it is given to understand that many sins can be remitted in this world, but also many in the world to come."

The Roman Empire and the Church in the Sixth and Seventh Centuries

Though the Western portions of the Roman Empire ceased as a viable political entity in the fifth century, only to be the empty illusions of later Frankish and German kings, the Roman Empire continued into the fifteenth century in

A coin of Byzantine Emperor Justinian. Provided by Maximus Rex.

the East. Of its many emperors none exceeded Justinian I (ca. 482–564). His legal reforms, the codification of Roman law, became the basis for the Western legal system; his building programs, most spectacularly evident in the rebuilding of Hagia Sophia, the Church of Holy Wisdom, and in the great expansion and embellishment of Constantinople. His capital became the center of commerce throughout the Mediterranean.

In keeping with the desire to reclaim lost territories in the West, he defeated the Vandals of North Africa, recovered the southern Iberian Peninsula and the islands of Corsica and Sardinia. In 540, Justinian's armies entered Italy and defeated the Ostrogoths, taking their capital of Ravenna (they were unsuccessful in taking Rome). After quailing a revolt of the Persians on his northeast frontier, who had apparently created a diversionary alliance with the Ostrogoths, a second campaign in Italy brought the final victory, the recovery of Rome, and the conquest of Sicily. Justinian's dream was only partially realized, but it came at a huge financial cost that contributed to the empire's decline as the population was decimated by epidemics. Eventually, the Lombards conquered most of Italy within three years after the Ostrogoth defeats, and much of North Africa was reclaimed by the Vandals.

The shadow of Justinian was cast over the Roman churches for several centuries as subsequent emperors continued his policy of political hegemony over the bishops of Rome. The great urgency to placate the Monophysites after military options proved unsuccessful, causing Justinian to force Roman bishops to compromise their **Chalcedonian** convictions. Heraclius, for example, compelled Bishop Honorius (d. 638) to accept monothelitism (a fact not over looked by those who opposed the granting of papal infallibility in the nineteenth century).

A Hagia Sophia mosaic with Justinian on the left offering a model of the Hagia Sophia to the Virgin Mary and the Christ child. On the right Constantine I offers a model of Constantinople. Courtesy of Myrabella.

When Martin I ascended to the papal office in 649, he condemned monthelitism and the patriarch of Constantinople at the First Lateran Council (a gathering of over 100 western bishops at the papal residence, the Lateran Palace [named for a wealthy family that owned the area of the city in Nero's reign] in the Cathedral of St. John, which was built by Constantine in the fourth century). The emperor, Constans, subsequently had the pope arrested, taken as a prisoner to Constantinople, and banished from the empire along with Maximus the Confessor. For over two hundred years the election of a pope had to be confirmed by Constantinople before it could be recognized as official.

What became clear to the Roman see was that the cost of political stability came at the price of religious supremacy by Roman emperors. The presence of the Ostrogoths, only to be replaced by the Lombards, made the tolerance of a subservient role a practical necessity. However, the ascendancy of the Frankish kingdom opened new political options for the Roman popes. Alliances with the Franks would be useful in defeating Rome's adversaries and eliminate the need for Eastern interference, especially since that option was questionable with new military threats arising in the East.

The Frankish tribes were united under Clovis I and the Merovingian dynasty of kings (the name is derived from an earlier Frank, Merovech). The dynasty was hereditary, but equally divided among a king's surviving sons. This lent itself to political instability, intertribal warfare, and weakness. In the eighth century the Merovingian dynasty, by then largely ceremonial in nature, was replaced by another hereditary office within the kingdom called "Mayor of the Palace." The first of these "Mayors" was Pepin I (ca. 580–640). It was under Pepin II (ca. 635–714) that the office assumed dynastic proportions gradually displacing the Merovingians. Charles Martel (ca. 686–741) dropped the façade of mayor and took the title of king. With Charles, the Carolingian dynasty

The statue of Charles Martel at the Palace of Versailles. Provided by Arnuad 25.

was fully established. His expansionist militarism consolidated the empire and stopped the aggressive Muslim hordes that had crossed the Pyrenees at the Battle of Tours in 732, earning him the title "Charles the Hammer."

The Church and the Carolingian Empire

The dominance of the emergent Carolingians with the first standing army in northern Europe since the Romans, the integration of heavily armored infantry with wooden shields, and a similarly armored cavalry in close coordination appealed to the popes who sought relief from dependence on Constantinople. The loss of the Visigoths to the Muslim invaders on the Iberian Peninsula only accentuated the need for another political alliance. Relations began between the two parties in 750 when Zacharius (d. 752) agreed with Pepin III, or Pepin the Short (ca. 714–768) that the Merovingian dynasty had become dysfunctional. Three years later Zacharius's successor, Stephen II (d. 757), crowned Pepin III king and his two sons "Patricians of the Romans" granting them the duty of protecting papal interests. Pepin came to the pope's aid in 751 and 754 when the Lombards posed serious threats . In exchange, he received additional titles. Pepin, in turn, in the "**Donation of Pepin**" gave the church extensive territories in central Italy (these papal states remained in the church's possession until the nineteenth century).

In the era of papal struggles with the Lombards, as well as the attempt to gain the favors of the Carolingian kings without losing papal power and influence, a document emerged called the *Donation of Constantine*. The essence of the work was the claim that Constantine had relinquished jurisdiction over the Western empire, church and state, to the Roman popes when he established his new capital in the

A 13th-century fresco of Sylvester and Constantine, showing the purported Donation of Constantine. In San Silvestro Chapel at Santi Quattro Coronati, Rome. Courtesy of Ras67.

East. What is clear is that the writer sought to defend papal interests over the Byzantine Empire and the Carolingian kings. In the fifteenth century an Italian humanist, Lorenzo Valla, demonstrated through textual analysis that the document was fraudulent, though the church responded initially by rejecting Valla's claim and placing his work on the list of prohibited books. The *Donation of Constantine* was later included in a massive collection of false documents called the *Isidorean Decretals*. Though inauthentic, the documents had a pervasive influence on the solidification of papal preeminence in the medieval era.

Upon Pepin's death in 768, his two sons, Carloman and Charles, jointly ruled the empire. The death of Carloman three years later reunited the empire under Charles, or Charlemagne (742–814), the greatest of the Carolingians. He was a man of robust habits, tall in stature, and a warrior's warrior. In over fifty military campaigns that extended over thirty years, he subdued his adversaries and extended the borders of his empire across Europe. His dress was plain and unassuming; he wore a blue cloak and always carried a sword.

Almost immediately upon becoming king, Charlemagne received the urgent request of Adrian I, whose territories (the Donation of Pepin) were threatened by the Lombards. Disiderius, the Lombard king, attempted to bring pressure on the pope to recognize Carloman's sons as claimants to the throne of his father. Charlemagne crushed the Lombards, renewed the promise to Adrian of the Papal States (even enlarged them), and was crowned "Patrician." He engaged the Muslims on the Iberian Peninsula gaining back territory, conquered the **Avars** in modern-day Austria and Hungary, attacked the Slavs beyond the Elbe River, and subdued **Saxons** and fought the Danes.

Throughout his imperial reign, Charlemagne remained a loyal protector of the church. At the behest of Leo III, Charlemagne went to

Charlemagne on the front side of the Shrine of Charlemagne in Aachen, Germany. Courtesy of ACBahn.

Rome to end rioting that threatened the pope. While kneeling in prayer at a Mass in St. Peter's Basilica, Christmas Day, 800, Leo crowned the king, "Emperor of the Romans," a title reserved for the Byzantine emperors. By such an act, Leo was announcing that the church was no longer tied to Eastern interests because the Western empire had been revived. This event is often looked upon as one of the most monumental in the medieval era.

The Significance of the Crowning of Charlemagne
By crowning Charlemagne as Holy Roman Emperor on Christmas Day AD 800, Pope Leo III signified that Charlemagne was to be the defender of Rome. At a time when the duty of protecting the pope was usually reserved by Constantinople, the Western empire was thus regarded with greater political influence by the pope. At the same time, this act of coronation declared that the church had the authority to crown temporal rulers.

Charlemagne often viewed his reign as an attempt to incarnate Augustine's *City of God* in a "**Carolingian renaissance**." His economic and monetary reforms unified and strengthened the empire. Though he apparently did not learn to write, he could speak several languages. At meals he preferred scholars to read learned works to him rather than be entertained by court jesters. He promoted education and scholarship by creating an educational system and gathering scholars from across his empire to his capital at Aachen, including Alcuin (ca. 735–804) from York (called the greatest scholar of a crude era), as well as Einhard (ca. 775–840), who wrote the *Life of Charlemagne*, and Paul the Deacon (ca. 720–799) of the Lombard kingdom, who wrote a history of the Lombards.

As head of state, Charlemagne functioned as head of the churches by appointing bishops, as well as other churchmen in his realm, and entering into church disputes. Charlemagne had a particular interest in church music and the improvement of liturgy. At the Synod of Aachen in 803, Charlemagne instructed his bishops to open schools for music training. His biographer, Einhard, wrote, "He was at great pains to improve the church reading and psalmody, for he was well skilled in both although he neither read in public nor sang, except in a low tone and with others" (*Life*, 26). He often forced the conquered to embrace Christianity or face immediate death.

Charlemagne called significant councils of the church to adjudicate theological issues. In 792 Charlemagne called together the Synod of Regensburg (Ratisbon) to address the teachings of two Spanish churchmen: Elipandus (ca. 716–ca. 805), archbishop of Toledo, and Felix (d. 818), bishop of Urgell. Elipandus seems to have embraced a form of **subordinationism** ("we confess and . . . believe that He was made from a woman, under the law, that He is the Son of God not by generation but by adoption, and not by nature, but by grace" [*Epistle to Francia*, 3.3]). Charged with denying the Chalcedonian conception of the two perfect natures in a single person (they seemed to denigrate Christ's humanity relative to his deity), the defendants could not be persuaded to relinquish their views; so Charlemagne gathered a second synod at Frankfurt in 794. At a third synod in 799 at Aachen, Alcuin was unable to convince Felix of his error and Felix was exiled; Elipandus remained unconvinced of Alcuin's view but remained secure in his ecclesiastical position.

The **iconoclastic controversy** caused considerable unrest in the Eastern Empire from 726–843, but the discussion of the issue in the Western churches is a suggestive lens of the prominence of Charlemagne in theological issues. The issue revolved around the propriety of portable pictorial images executed in wood, or of mosaics and frescos (not so much statuary) of religious figures: the Savior, the holy Mother, angels, and saints. Was this a violation of the second mosaic commandment forbidding physical representations of God in worship? Did not representationalism distort worship in "spirit and truth"?

In 726, Leo III, emperor of the empire, issued a series of edicts forbidding the use of icons. This led to conflict with the popes in Rome, particularly Gregory II (d. 731) and Gregory III (d. 741), who refused to enforce his

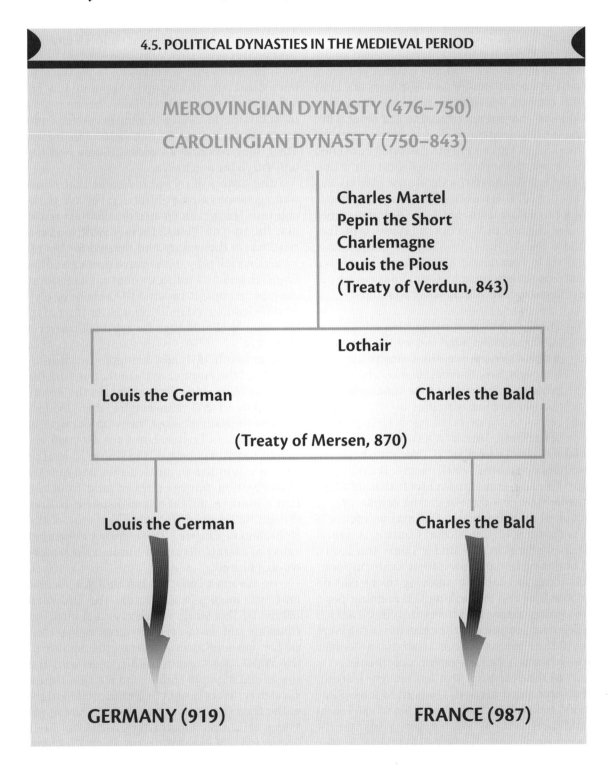

4.5. POLITICAL DYNASTIES IN THE MEDIEVAL PERIOD

MEROVINGIAN DYNASTY (476–750)

CAROLINGIAN DYNASTY (750–843)

Charles Martel
Pepin the Short
Charlemagne
Louis the Pious
(Treaty of Verdun, 843)

Lothair

Louis the German   Charles the Bald

(Treaty of Mersen, 870)

Louis the German   Charles the Bald

GERMANY (919)   FRANCE (987)

ban on images. Leo's successor, Constantine V, continued the imperial policy and called an ecumenical council in 754, the Council of Hieria, to have it condemn the use of images of Christ (the council, sometimes called the "Headless Council," was not recognized as ecumenical because the patriarchical chair was vacant at the time). In 787 an ecumenical council convened in Nicaea, the seventh, at the behest of the emperor, Leo IV, and the moderate use of icons was sanctioned. This was largely through the efforts of John of Damascus, (ca. 676–749), sometimes called the last of the church fathers, and Theodore the Studite (759–826), a Byzantine monastic. In *Fountain of Knowledge,* John drew a distinction between a pictorial image as an educational tool and an object of worship:

> Often, doubtless, when we have not the Lord's passion in mind and see the image of Christ's crucifixion, His saving passion is brought back to remembrance, and we fall down and worship not the material but that which is imaged (4.16).

In the West, Adrian I approved the findings of the Nicene Council of 787; however, he did so without consulting Charlemagne. The power of the Frankish emperor was such that he overturned the pronouncement of Adrian at the Council of Frankfurt in 794 and condemned the findings of the Nicene Council. A synod held in Paris in 825 under Louis the Pious, Charlemagne's successor, went further by condemning the pope for agreeing to the Nicene Council of 787 and asking the reigning pope to censor Adrian I for his errors. The Frankish judgment prevailed in the churches of the West until the eleventh century when the moderate use of icons became generally acceptable.

In the year prior to Charlemagne's death, he summoned his son, Louis the Pious (778–840), before the chief men of his whole realm and designated him as coregent and ultimate successor. (Charlemagne had four wives in succession that gave him eleven children and five concubines who gave him seven more. Louis was the third son, a surviving twin, born to his second wife, Hildegarde.) Appointed by his father at the age of three, Louis became king of Aquitaine following the unsuccessful campaign on the Iberian Peninsula in 778. Though other sons received kingdoms, Louis was the only surviving son in 813.

The historical record indicates that Louis was a generous monarch, though not a remarkable one. His beneficence to the church earned him the title of "Pious." He was swift to crush rebellion in the empire and revered for his reforms, but fell prey to the consequences of the Frankish policy of ruling through subkingdoms allotted to sons. It became the source of civil conflict leading to Louis's abdication, forced by his sons, in 833, though he regained power a year later.

The death of Louis brought the disintegration of the empire, civil conflict among his three surviving sons for territory. In the Treaty of Verdun in 843, the empire was divided. Charles the Bald received the western portion, roughly today's France. Louis the German acquired territories east of the Rhine River. Lothair was granted an indefensible, and quickly disintegrating, narrow strip of land from the Low Countries to the Papal Estates in Italy though he retained the title, "Emperor of the Holy Roman Empire." These events coincided with the Viking intrusions through the waterways of Europe.

In this era of political instability, a second medieval forgery was written, the *Isidorean Decretals.* This work, which also included the *Donation of Constantine,* has been recognized as the most influential literary deception of the Middle Ages, again having to do with the sustaining of papal claims in uncertain times. Though scholars cannot be certain of the origin of the forgeries, it may have been in the monastery at Corbie, Picardy, by Paschasius Radbertus (ca. 786–ca. 860), a monk and scholar,

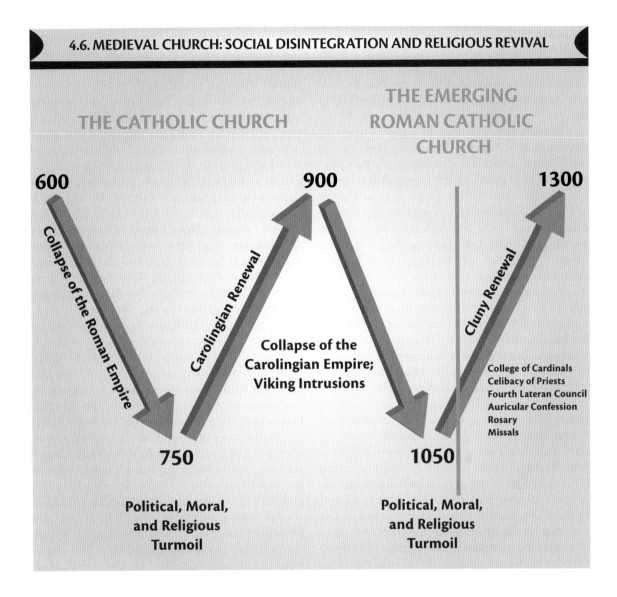

4.6. MEDIEVAL CHURCH: SOCIAL DISINTEGRATION AND RELIGIOUS REVIVAL

THE CATHOLIC CHURCH

THE EMERGING ROMAN CATHOLIC CHURCH

600

900

1300

Collapse of the Roman Empire

Carolingian Renewal

Collapse of the Carolingian Empire; Viking Intrusions

Cluny Renewal

College of Cardinals
Celibacy of Priests
Fourth Lateran Council
Auricular Confession
Rosary
Missals

750

1050

Political, Moral, and Religious Turmoil

Political, Moral, and Religious Turmoil

because documents were used from the monastery in the fraudulent work. Within the extensive collection of works that span over seven hundred pages decorated with beautiful artistry, are about one hundred letters allegedly written by Roman popes of the first three centuries establishing rules that protected church officials from political incrimination.

The decretals' major influence came in the tenth and eleventh centuries when the church, after debilitating losses through moral ineptitude and political infringement, sought to reestablish its prominence in an era called the **Cluny Reform Movement**, a resurgence of papal claims. In the fifteenth century Cardinal Nicholas of Cusa questioned the validity of the documents, though it was in the seventeenth century that the French Calvinist David

Blondel (1591–1655) proved them to be forgeries. Though Roman Catholic scholars sought to rebut Blondel's claims initially, the Roman Church has unquestionably recognized the decretals as fraudulent since the nineteenth century.

Though the Carolingian Empire suffered diminution in the ninth century, the robust intellectual renaissance inaugurated by Charlemagne continued to have significant influence. In the Benedictine monastery at Corbie in Picardy, founded in 657, and at New Corbie established ca. 820 by Louis the Pious, scholarship and missionary preparation was combined with piety and emerged as a leading center of learning.

Paschasius Radbertus distinguished himself as a scholar and abbot. In a work entitled *On the Body and Blood of the Lord* (831), he became the first churchman to explicitly teach the doctrine of a transubstantiation of the bread and wine in the Mass, though the term itself was coined centuries later. Charles the Bald, skeptical of Radbertus's conclusions asked another monk in the monastery, Ratramnus (d. ca. 868), to respond. In *On the Body and Blood of the Lord*, Ratramnus agreed that Christ is truly present in the Eucharist, but argued that the nature of that presence is spiritual, not material. The church, as yet, had not singularized the interpretation of the presence of Christ in the Supper. Two scholars in the same monastery took opposite views without remonstration on the part of the state or church. Though Radbertus's view was new, it would prevail in subsequent centuries. Ratramnus's understanding was consistent with the church's teachers through the centuries, but his work would later be banned.

A second disagreement between Radbertus and Ratramnus occurred over the manner of explaining Mary's perpetual virginity (early churchmen took two tacks in this regard: Jesus's siblings were Joseph's from a previous marriage [Epiphanius] or they were his cousins [Jerome]). The discussion was not over the fact of perpetual virginity, but the question of whether or not Jesus's birth compromised Mary's virginal integrity. Was Mary's womb altered by the birth? Did her womb actually open? Radbertus argued that Mary's womb remained closed making it a miraculous conception and a miraculous birth. His biblical text was Ezekiel 44:2. Ratramnus argued that the womb was altered in the birth process. Though there was a miraculous conception, it was a natural birth.

An interesting look into the changing tolerable perspectives within the church is the case of Gottschalk (ca. 800–868) and the response of his superiors. Gottschalk, "God's servant," was an oblate, a child dedicated to monastic life by his parents, and lived in the Benedictine monastery at Fulda. After completing his education, he asked to be released from his monastic vow, since it was imposed without his sanction; he won a temporary release (829), but Louis the Pious rescinded it and he was sent to the monastery at Orbais (835). In the interim, Gottschalk met Ratramnus, a student of Augustine's works at Corbie, Gottschalk became convinced of Augustine's **double predestinarianism**. Gottschalk appears to have traveled extensively, even to the Balkans, preaching Augustine's views without permission to do so.

He was condemned for his actions by Hrabanus Maurus, the archbishop of Mainz who was his former abbot at Fulda, and transferred to the jurisdiction of Hincmar of Rheims who had him condemned, separated from the priesthood, flogged nearly to death, and imprisoned for the remainder of his days in solitary confinement. In 849 Gottschalk requested a second trial, which did not take place, and Hincmar responded to his views with his own document and appealed to scholars for affirmation of his position against Gottschalk.

The appeal created controversy when several scholars replied that Gottschalk correctly interpreted the great church father. Gottschalk's old nemesis, Hrabanus Maurus, refused to speak to the issue, but Charles the Bald, the emperor, demanded a resolution. Ratramnus of Corbie defended Gottschalk's views while Hincmar, archbishop of Rheims; opposed them fearing that it would devalue the place of good works. The issue was clearly divisive.

John Scotus Erigena (ca. 815–877), an influential scholar and head of the Palatine Academy of Charles the Bald's, proposed a compromise by arguing that Gottschalk correctly interpreted Augustine, but pressed the logic of it beyond Augustine's actual conclusions. That is, Augustine was a double predestinarian but not a **supralapsarian** (the view that God's determinative actions precede man's actions). Erigina argued for **infralapsarianism**, defending a **single predestinarianism** (God did not predestine the reprobated to their state, but in choosing the elect, he passed over the others who did as they pleased, meriting condemnation). He was a Christian universalist, being influenced in his opinions by Greek churchmen, particularly Origen. Ratramnus argued for a double predestinarianism, a strictly determinist position, but refused the suggestion that the position necessitated that God be the author of evil actions. Erigena's compromise was condemned at local synods, particularly by churches in Lyon in 855 and 859 respectively.

Hincmar, who was in the good graces of Charles the Bald, called the Synod of Chiersy (853), and arrived at four conclusions. First, the synod decreed a single predestination of the elect based upon foresight, not foreknowledge (the latter insight distorts Augustine's view). Second, that the wording of human freedom is such that it is open to either an Augustinian or semi-Pelagian interpretation. The third is an affirmation of the universal, nondiscriminatory desire of God for all to be saved without delimitation from the divine perspective. And, fourth, is the affirmation of a universal atonement without a universal application described as a mystery. The third and fourth con-

clusions are not Augustinian. The weakening of Augustinianism is the connecting link between catholic orthodoxy and a developing **semi-Pelagianism** that would gradually ascend to greater degrees of dominance in the churches. The fact that this issue was not resolved and the papacy affirmed neither view, allowing variance of opinion to coexist in the church, anticipated the dramatic schisms and defining polarizations of the sixteenth century.

Missionary Activity in the Early Middle Ages

The introduction of Christianity to the tribes that brought the disintegration of the western portion of the Roman Empire was the focus of considerable missionary endeavor in the years prior to the breakup of the Carolingian Empire in the ninth century, first in the British Isles and then on the continent. Christianity in Ireland flourished in the sixth century, having been firmly rooted by Saint Patrick Finnian (ca. 495–589), who is regarded as the father of Irish monasticism and the founder of a school at County Down about 540. There he wrote rules for monks, as well as the first of the penitential books (rules governing penance for various sins).

Finnian's most illustrious student was Saint Columba (521–597), who, along with eleven others, founded the monastery at Iona on an island off the west coast of Scotland in 563 and served as its abbot. It became one of the most influential monasteries in western Europe as a training center for missionaries and for the copying of the Scriptures. After Columba labored at Iona for some time, he left the island and did missionary preaching in Scotland among the **Picts**.

The Life of Columba. Also known as Colum Cille (Old Irish: dove of the church), Columba was born in Donegal, Ireland, in AD 521 and preached the gospel to the Picts (Scots). He studied at Clonard Abbey in County Meath under St. Finian and was known along

> with eleven other students as the Twelve Apostles of Ireland. Later as a priest, he founded the monasteries of Kells, Durrow, Derry, and Swords. Following a battle resulting from his copying a psalter manuscript at Movilla Abbey, he went into exile as a missionary in Scotland where he operated from his monastery on the Isle of Iona.

The monastery on the craggy island at Iona became both an intellectual center and a missionary training school. The masterpiece of Iona was the production of the Book of Kells, a Latin translation of the four gospels with elaborate calligraphy based on Jerome's Latin Vulgate (a copy of Jerome's Vulgate was brought from Rome by Finnian). Like most monasteries in the period, Iona was a center for the duplication of the Bible, a major task of monks. From Iona, missionaries spread the gospel into Scotland, England, and the continent as far as Switzerland. Among the missionaries was Aidan (d. 651). Trained at Iona, he came to Northumbria where he founded the monastery at Lindis-

West wall of St Columba's church, Gartan, Donegal; Gartan is said to be the birthplace of Columba. Courtesy of Kay Atherton.

farne off the northeast coast of England about 635.

Through the efforts of Irish missionaries, King Oswald was converted and that led to the Christianizing of his people. In the eighth century the Lindisfarne Gospels were completed, composed of a beautifully illustrated Latin text. In the ninth century, the earliest Old English text of the gospels was produced at Landisfarne. With twelve monks, Columbanus (543–615) crossed from Ireland to England and then to France where they labored, establishing over one hundred monasteries as far away as Switzerland and Northern Italy. Characteristic of Irish Christianity at this time was an emphasis on the private confession of sin to superiors, as well as **penitential regulations**.

A second missionary thrust towards England came from Rome. Tradition suggests that Gregory the Great became burdened for a people he saw auctioned as slaves in Rome, the Angles. In 597 Gregory sent a contingent of missionaries led by missionary Augustine (d. 604) to the south of England. Their labors were initially discouraging, even though the wife of Ethelbert, ruler in Kent, was a Christian and a Frankish princess. Gregory insisted that the work continue, and the king was converted. A number of other kingdoms came into the Christian fold. Missionary Augustine established the first bishopric in England in the capital of the kingdom of Kent, Canterbury. He served as the first archbishop of Canterbury, the hub of Christianity on the island.

Irish or Ionian Christianity had some marked dissimilarities with Roman Christianity that caused controversy as missionaries interfaced. Prominent among these was the celebration of Easter, the highest of the church festivals. Ionians followed the Jewish pattern and celebrated Easter on the fourteenth of the first month in the Jewish calendar, the day of Passover. Those who followed this pattern in the early church were called **Quartrodecians**. At the Council of Nicaea (325) the bishops changed the date in several significant ways. The celebration of Easter was to be on a Sunday and the day was to be determined by a solar, not lunar calendar (the first Sunday after the fourteenth day of the spring equinox).

Things became exacerbated when King Oswy of Northumbria and his queen celebrated Easter on different days; one fasted while the other feasted! Should the celebration focus on Christ's death or his resurrection? The two factions gathered at the Council of Whitby to decide the issue in 664. Evidence also exists that in Ionan Christianity monastic life did not require celibacy; leaders were chosen from within the monastic communities, and monastic tonsure took different forms (Roman tonsure involved the shaving of the head except for around the base of the skull, forming a crown. Ionians shaved the head back to the ears and allowed it to grow long in the back). Though influenced by Ionan Christianity, King Oswy determined to follow the Roman pattern, being persuaded that the bishop of Rome possessed the keys to heaven and hell. This council signaled the eclipse of Ionian Christianity and the triumph of Roman Christianity.

Significant missionary activity occurred on the continent in addition to the work of the Irish Christians as missions activity flourished in the Frankish kingdom following the conversion of Clovis I in the late fifth century. Of particular note is the labor of Willibrord (ca. 658–739), a Benedictine monk. Trained in an abbey, he was sent along with twelve others at the behest of Peppin, to labor in Frisia, over which he exercised nominal control in 695. Willibrord established a monastery at Utrecht and became the city's first bishop. A later revolt by a pagan king brought the destruction of many churches and the killing of the missionaries. Willibrord was able to return to his work under the protection of Charles Martel.

Boniface (ca. 672–754), the apostle to the Germans and **Frisians**, a Benedictine, was trained in England and served in missionary

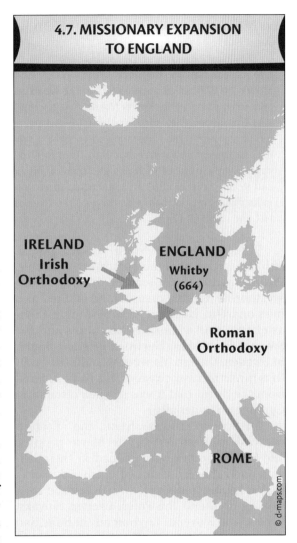

4.7. MISSIONARY EXPANSION TO ENGLAND

IRELAND
Irish Orthodoxy

ENGLAND
Whitby (664)

Roman Orthodoxy

ROME

© d-maps.com

work on the continent. In 722 he felled the Oak of Thor in an Elijah-like confrontation with paganism, marking the beginning of Germanic christianization and the destruction of pagan shrines. Under the protective graces of the Carolingian empire, Boniface became the archbishop of lands east of the Rhine River with the ecclesiastical center in Mainz. He was killed attempting to bring the resistant Frisians into the fold. Charlemagne conquered the Germanic tribes to the Elbe River in the east and brought Christian faith with the arm of militarism.

> **Life of Missionary Boniface.** Born in England around AD 672, he was a missionary to the Germans and was the first archbishop of Mainz. A legend persists that he invented the Christmas Tree when he found a group of men preparing to sacrifice a boy in Geismar near an oak tree sacred to Thor. Boniface cut down the oak tree with a single stroke of his ax and stopped the sacrifice. A small fir tree sprang up in its place. He told them that this was the "tree of life" and stood for Christ.

"The Apostle of the North" was Ansgar (ca. 801–865). Trained in the monastery in Corbie, Picardy, he became a teacher in New Corbie, Westphalia. A gifted preacher, he labored as a missionary in Hamburg, establishing a monastery. He worked among the **Danes** and the Swedes, establishing the first Christian church in Sweden, though his work was destroyed in those areas on two occasions. His work suffered from the threat that it was a veiled attempt at Carolingian imperialism.

Missionary efforts from the Eastern churches reached out to the Slavic peoples. The Slavic peoples were divided in their religion and culture, but united in their devotion to Methodius and Cyril, two Byzantine missionary brothers. The Poles, Czechs, Slovaks, Croats, and Slovenes are Roman Catholic and western in culture; the Russians, Bulgarians, and Serbs are in the Orthodox Church and eastern culture. This is largely due to the historical setting. Two great nations emerged to dominate the Slavs in the ninth century: the Carolingian Empire in the West and the Byzantine Empire in the East.

The term, *Slav*, appears to have come into our English language because marauding tribes settled in the Balkan region and northward between clashing empires only to often fall into slavery (a "Slav" was a slave). The Slavs were polytheists and linked various festivals to the

Saint Boniface memorial in Fritzlar, Germany. Provided by Benutzer:AxelHH.

agricultural cycle. They seemed to be ruthless people; for example, widows were sacrificed on the funeral pyre of their husbands.

The earliest missionaries to the Slavs were Frankish and German. Their success was marginal due to the tie with Carolingian imperialism. This caused some Slavic tribes to turn to the Byzantine Empire to embrace Christianity.

"The Apostles to the Slavs," Methodius and Cyril, were born in Thessalonica (northern Greece) of nobility; Leo, their father, was connected to the Imperial Byzantine court. Methodius (ca. 825–885) and Cyril (ca. 827–863) were trained in law and prepared for administrative careers; both later entered a monastery and were ordained as priests.

> **Life of Methodius**. Along with his brother Cyril, who developed the Glagolithic (later Cyrillic) alphabet to translate the Bible into Slavic languages, Methodius worked as a missionary to the Slavs. Cyril, after ministering to the Jews and Muslims, ultimately became professor at the University of Magnaura. Pope Adrian II named Methodius archbishop of Greater Moravia and Pannonia to which he brought the Slavonic liturgy that enabled the spread of Christianity throughout Eastern Europe. He died in AD 885.

Methodius was initially sent to the Bulgarians, the imperial court of King Boris. Cyril, because of his skill in debate was sent to the **Saracens** (Muslims). Later, both were sent north of the Black Sea to Crimea, lands first Christianized by the Apostles Philip and Andrew.

After returning to monastic life in Constantinople, they were sent to the Balkans to the Moravian kingdom, a confederation of Slavic peoples who resisted the Carolingian intrusion. The Slavs hoped that a connection with Constantinople would bring some needed military assistance. Before going, the brothers invented an alphabet for the Slavs so that the Scriptures and liturgical books could be given to them in their own language. Interestingly, these men took the alphabet with them and the Scriptures were translated in 863 (Cyril died in the midst of the work). Methodius continued the missionary work and, as the years passed, he preached among other Slavs, Czechs in Bohemia (the most famous duke and martyr was Saint Wenceslaus I), the Slovaks, the Poles, Serbs, and Croats.

Saints Cyril and Methodius holding the Cyrillic alphabet. A mural painting of Bulgarian icon-painter Zahari Zograf (1810–1853), Troyan Monastery, 1848. Courtesy of Mladifilozof.

The Rise of the Islamic Faith

The fortunes of Christianity in the seventh and eighth centuries appeared to have successfully repulsed the negative consequences of the demise of the Western Roman Empire. Missionary activity was flourishing, political stability was returning, parts of the empire were reconquered, and the Roman popes and eastern patriarchs were basking in Christian hegemony. However, a threat to the Christian movement was emerging from the deserts of Arabia. Muhammad (ca. 570–632), the "Apostle of God," was born to Abdallah and Amina and raised by an uncle, Abu Talib, after the death of his father. For several decades he lived the life of a **bedouin** shepherd traveling frequently with his uncle to Palestine and Syria. He later worked for a widow, Khadijah, whom he married. His marriage afforded him a degree of financial security.

Life of Muhammad. Muhammad, born in Mecca about AD 570 is considered by Muslims as a messenger, prophet, and founder of their religion. His early life as a merchant gave way to public preaching. He succeeded in uniting the warring tribes in Medina and subsequently conquered Mecca. His teachings, which he believed were revealed to him, are found in the Qur'an that forms the core of the religion of Islam. In his lifetime Islam spread throughout most of the Arabian Peninsula.

At some point, Muhammad made it a habit to meditate in a cave on Mount Hira near Mecca. About the year 610, he began receiving revelations from Gabriel, the angel of the Lord, that would latter be transmitted by oral tradition and enshrined in a holy book, the Qur'an. Encouraged by his wife, he began to proclaim his insights. Muhammad's message was a radical monotheism for bedouin animists with threats of punishment for negli-

A 1307 miniature illustration on vellum of Muhammad's first revelation from the angel Gabriel. At the Edinburgh University Library, Scotland. Courtesy of Mladifilozof.

gence and promises of heaven for submission (the term *Islam* means submission). According to Muhammad, the new revelations inaugurated the final world religion whose duty it was to purify, purge, correct, and complete all the others. It is an overwhelming monotheistic faith, but its emphases are more on practice than upon teaching. The faithful Muslim is expected to adhere faithfully to the "Five Pillars" (the profession of Allah as alone God, prayer five times daily, almsgiving, fasting during the month of Ramadan, and Holy Pilgrimage to Mecca).

> "The reward of the prayer offered in one's house or in the market (alone). And this is because if he performs absolution and does it perfectly and then proceeds to the mosque with the sole intention of praying, then for every step he takes toward the mosque, he is upgraded one degree in reward and one sin is taken off (crossed out) from his accounts (of deeds)" (*Hadith*, 10.30.620).

> "If there was a river at the door of any one of you and he took a bath in it five times a day would you notice any dirt on him? They said, 'Not a trace of dirt would be left.' The Prophet added, 'That is the example of the five prayers with which Allah annuls evil deeds" (*Hadith*, 10.6.506).

Persecution followed as Muhammad's followers increased (some fled to Ethiopia), though Muhammad was spared because of the prominence of his tribe, which was subsequently reversed after the death of his uncle and his wife in 619. Visions continued to but-

Jabal an-Nour, a mountain in Saudi Arabia that contains the Hira cave where Muhammad supposedly received his first revelation from God through the angel Gabriel. Courtesy of Ziad.

tress his religious claims, and he was invited by twelve clans in Medina to flee there for refuge, which he did in 622 (this is called the Hegira or "The Flight" and marks year one in the Muslim calendar). Muhammad was able to ward off attacks by Meccan forces, enlarge his army, and eliminate Jewish tribes in Medina that opposed him. In the year 630, he captured Mecca, the principal holy site, and most of the Meccans converted to Islam. Upon his death in 632, he was buried in Medina.

"Whoever observes fasts during the month of Ramadan out of sincere faith, and hoping to attain Allah's rewards, then all past sins will be forgiven" (*Hadith*, 2.29.37).

Within four years of the prophet's death, Muslim armies conquered Jerusalem and Damascus, and by the end of the century the construction of the Dome of the Rock on Mount Moriah in Jerusalem was commenced (the site marks a stop on the heavenly flight of the great prophet on a white stallion, as well as where he received the revelation to pray five times daily and the location where Abraham was about to sacrifice his son [Muslims claim the son was Ishmael]). By the beginning of the eighth cen-

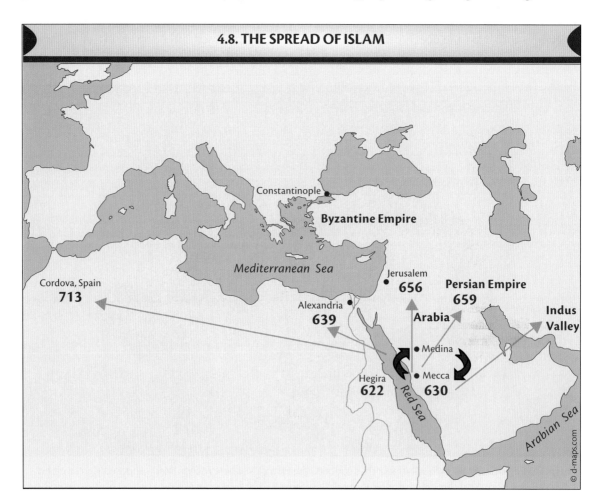

4.8. THE SPREAD OF ISLAM

4.9. THE HISTORY OF ISLAM

1453	Fall of Constantinople
1099	Capture of Jerusalem by the Crusaders
732	Battle of Tours
713	Conquest of Cordova, Spain, and the expansion into the Indus Valley
690	Construction of the Dome of the Rock, Jerusalem
636	Conquest of Jerusalem and Damascus
632	Death of Muhammad
630	Capture of Mecca
622	Hegira
570	Birth of Muhammad

tury, Muslims had pushed as far as the Indus Valley to the East, crossed the entirety of North Africa, and entered Europe, being stopped in central France at Tours in 732 by Charles Martel. In 758, a Muslim army burned and looted the city of Canton in China (in the defeat of a Chinese army on the Talas River in 751, Muslims found the secret to making paper!). Concerted attempts to overwhelm Constantinople, the first being in 669, failed.

There has been extensive discussion of the causes for the unparalleled Islamic military success (matched only later by the Mongolians under the Khan's for territorial expansion). The absence of a strong military establishment in Africa or the West was certainly a factor. The Islamic faith rose within a power vacuum. Another cause of Islamic effectiveness was the foreign policy of Byzantium toward the tribes between Medina and Syria (cutting off its subsidies) and its cruel treatment of the Copts of Egypt, Jacobites in Syria, and Jews in Palestine. This was in marked contrast to the Muslim conquerors who were often guardedly benevolent toward the subjected. However, they disallowed the repair or building of churches, exercised a nonconversion pact, and made it illegal for Christians to bear arms. They prohibited Christians from intermarrying, though Muslims could. Christians could not build houses over Muslim houses, and were deprived Christians of educational and job privileges, but Muslims gave them tax incentives for conversion. Further, the **Byzantine Empire** was fractured by theological disunity that prevented a unified resistance. The Orthodox, the Mono-

A seventh-century manuscript of the Quran at the University of Birmingham in England. Considered one the oldest in the world. Courtesy of Pigsonthewing.

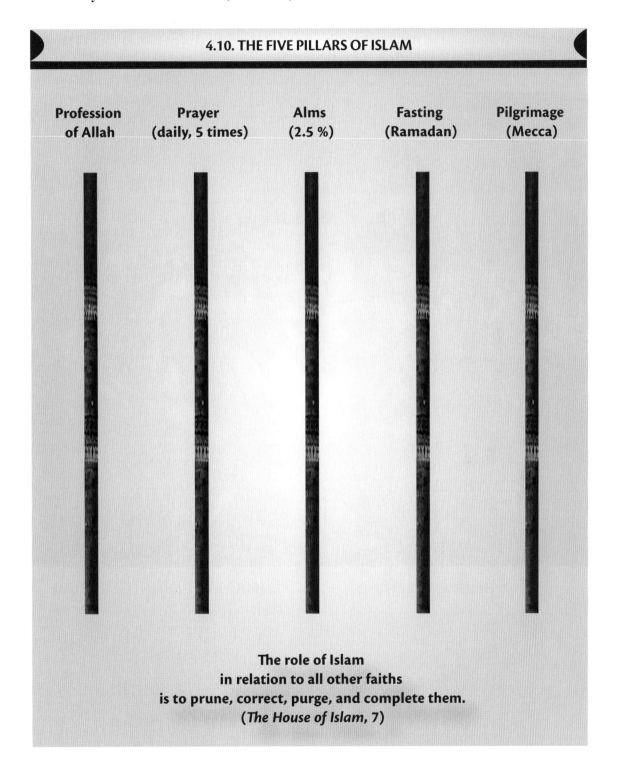

4.10. THE FIVE PILLARS OF ISLAM

| Profession of Allah | Prayer (daily, 5 times) | Alms (2.5 %) | Fasting (Ramadan) | Pilgrimage (Mecca) |

The role of Islam
in relation to all other faiths
is to prune, correct, purge, and complete them.
(*The House of Islam*, 7)

physites, the Nestorians, and the **Donatists** assumed adversarial roles toward each other. The harsh treatment of the Persian Empire to the east of Christian groups turned it into a Muslim ally.

A painting of the Battle of Tours by Charles de Steuben (1788-1856). At the Palace of Versailles. Courtesy of Frank Schulenburg.

GLOSSARY OF TERMS

Avars: a Turkish people-group that controlled portions of Central and Eastern Europe from the sixth through the ninth centuries.

Bedouin: the name given to several tribes of a nomadic, desert-dwelling Arabic ethnic group.

Byzantine Empire (Byzantines): the designation of the Roman Empire after the fall of the western portions to tribal intrusion after the fourth century. In late antiquity and the Middle Ages, its capital city was Byzantium (later changed to Constantinople when Constantine made the city his second capital in the fourth century). The Ottoman Turks destroyed the last visages of the Eastern or Byzantine Empire with the Islamic capture of Constantinople in 1453.

Carolingian Renaissance: an eighth- and ninth-century period of intellectual and cultural revival in Europe that reached its height during the reign of Charlemagne who sought to duplicate Augustine's model of the City of God. It reflected an intellectual and cultural advance from the era of the dissolution of the western portion of the Roman Empire before the Viking invasions that destroyed the remnants of Charlemagne's kingdom.

Chalcedonian Faith (Chalcedonian Convictions, Chalcedonianism): the creedal formulation of the Council of Chalcedon (451) that reaffirmed the christological statements of Nicaea (325) and Constantinople (381) declaring *Nestorianism* and *Eutychianism* to be heretical. The essence of the Chalcedon affirmation is that in Christ's incarnate state he was 100 percent God, 100 percent man, in one person, and without confusion of those two persons forever.

Cluny Reform Movement: a reforming movement within the Catholic Church of the eleventh century in the monastic community that emerged in Cluny, France. It proved a corrective to the church that had degenerated into a dark nadir of moral, political, and social confusion. The Cluny Movement became so influential that it was able to secure the highest office in the church for Hildebrand, Pope Gregory VII (1073–1085).

Danes: an ethnic group native to Denmark, part of the Scandinavian/Viking peoples who invaded Europe in the Middle Ages, bringing to an end the Carolingian Empire. Danish Vikings destroyed the famous monastery at Landisfarne and established a kingdom in Anglo-Saxon England called Daneslaw. The Danes embraced Christianity in the tenth century.

Dark Ages (Age of Darkness): a term that was applied by the Renaissance scholar, Erasmus, to the medieval period reflective of his opinion that the era was a time dominated by the darkness of imposed religious dogmatism. While there was the darkness of cultural and social decline as the Western empire crumbled at the beginning of the period and at the nadir of the Viking invasions that collapsed the remnants of the great Carolingian Empire, the millennium must not be thought of in such a negative light because of the cultural and intellectual achievements of the Charlemagnian era, the emergence of scholasticism with the rise of the universities, and the burst of learning that occasioned the rise of the Renaissance in the fourteenth and fifteenth centuries.

Donation of Pepin: a grant of land, the papal states, by Pepin (III) the Short, king of the

Franks, that subsequently became a basis for the Catholic claim to authority over civil governments. Facing threat from the Lombards in (now) northern Italy, Pope Stephen appealed for assistance from the Franks. In a gesture of gratitude, Pepin was granted the titles "King of the Franks" and later "Patrician of the Romans." In return Pepin granted territories taken from the Lombards to the church, territories over which it exercised civil authority for centuries.

Donatism: a North-African Christian schematic sect that emerged after the Diocletian persecutions over the issue of church readmission for those who recanted of their faith but subsequently sought reinstatement. The dispute was most importantly over the nature of the church. Donatists argued that the mark of the church was holiness and "traitors" forfeited membership privilege; Augustine argued that the redemptive nature of the church required readmission since the efficacy of the church's offices came from God and did not depend on the grace of its officers.

Double Predestinarianism (Double Predestination): the doctrinal position within the spectrum of the Calvinist tradition that God chooses both those who go to heaven as well as those who go to hell, a double election.

Frisians: a German ethnic group located along the coastal areas of present-day Netherlands and Germany. The Frisians came to the Christian faith through the work of Anglo-Irish missionaries as well as missionaries Boniface and Willibrod.

Greco-Roman Culture (Greco Roman tradition): a term used to express the influence of the "Mediterranean world" and the culture of ancient Greece assimilated into Roman culture that subsequently impacted later Western conceptions of religion, government, language, and culture.

Humanism: as used in the twelfth and thirteenth centuries in Europe, the term signified an interest in the study of the humanities, often within the rising universities. It focus was not so much a denial of the authority of the medieval church, but on understanding for oneself the truths taught by the church. While a leading contributor to the ethos of the sixteenth-century reformations, it is not to be identified with the secular humanism that arose out of the Enlightenment centuries later.

Hun (Huns): a nomadic, tribal people who came into the reaches of eastern Europe beginning in the later fourth century, contributing to the implosion of the western portion of the Roman Empire. The were unified under Attila the Hun who then penetrated into Gaul and Italy.

Iconoclastic Controversy: a series of debates in the Catholic church beginning in the eighth century that would drive a theological wedge between the Western Catholic churches and the eastern Catholic churches, contributing to the East-West Schism of 1054. The issue related to the second commandment, visual Christian art (largely woodcuts) in Christian worship, and the difference of meaning between "worship" and "veneration." Following the lead of John of Damascus, the Eastern churches' most prominent theologian, icons were considered wordless books to facilitate comprehension for the illiterate. Charlemagne took a more strident view, rejecting visual artistry of religious themes, particularly of the Christ.

Infralapsarianism: an attempt to understand the components of the eternal decree of God to redeem lost humanity by arguing a particular arrangement of the components of that decree. The explanation places the sequence in the following order: the creation decree of God; the decree of the fall of God's creation, particularly Adam; God's determination to save some out of fallen humanity; then the decree to provide the redeemer. See also *supralapsarianism.*

Lombards: a Germanic tribe that ruled portions of Italy from the sixth through the eighth centuries. Much of their territory was given to the church in the *Donation of Pepin,* and these lands became the Papal States.

Mass (Eucharist, Sacrament of the Eucharist): a term, though uncertain of origins, used within the Catholic Church from the early seventh century for what had been generally designated as the Eucharist or Thanksgiving Offering, the liturgical service centered around the Lord's Table (a Protestant term). Only at the Fourth Lateran Council (1215) did the Mass become an unbloodied reenactment of Christ's once-for-all bloodied sacrifice by mandate.

Middle Ages (Medieval Period): a term that suggests the second period of the four periods within what is now designated the Common Era (CE) in the scholarly, secular community. It is usually defined as the period of European history stretching from the fifth to the fifteenth centuries, bounded by the classical period and the modern period, the era between the collapse of the Roman Empire in the West and the rise of the Renaissance.

Monophysitism (Eutychianism): an attempt in the fifth-century Catholic Church to explain the relation of the deity of Christ to his humanity in the incarnate state by arguing for an amalgam of two characteristic sets into a third combination of the two. Condemned at the Council of Chalcedon (451), the view persisted in segments of the Christian churches in the East (Egypt, Ethiopia, Armenia, Lebanon), becoming known by this nomenclature. It, too, was condemned as heterodox at the Council of Constantinople in 553, leading to the first permanent schism in the professing church.

Nestorianism: a teaching in the fourth-century church concerning the relationship between Christ's two natures in the incarnation. Nestorius accepted the full humanity and deity of Christ, but seemed to reject the concept of his unity, disjoining the natures and giving Christ two joined natures, joined morally but not organically. The view was condemned at the third ecumenical council held at Ephesus (431). Advocates of this view continued in existence for several centuries, extending their teaching into the Far East.

Ostrogoths: the eastern branch of the Goths (the western branch being the Visigoths), a Germanic tribe, which established a kingdom in Italy and the Balkans in the fifth century. Justinian I attempted to reclaim Italy as part of the empire but was largely unsuccessful.

Penitential System (Penance): A practice that arose in Irish Christianity through the writing of pentitential books that designated outward acts reflective of inward contrition for wrongdoing. In the medieval period in the emerging Roman Catholic community, penitentialism became a sacrament of grace acquisition, the "second plank," or remedy for sin, taught in the writings of Lombard and Aquinas, creedally stated in the findings of the Council of Florence in the fifteenth century, and dogmatized in the church at the Councils of Trent in the following century.

Petrine Priority: a view of authority within the medieval Catholic church in the western portion of the former Roman Empire based on such passages as Matthew 16:18 and John 21, supposing that Peter acted as head of the college of the apostles as vicar of Christ on the earth and that through apostolic appointment a series of successors have been appointed to lead the church in the papal office.

Picts: a Celtic people-group who lived in

eastern and northern Scotland. They opposed the Roman conquest of their territories resulting in the protective barrier of the Hadrian Wall. Irish missionaries from the famous monastery at Iona christianized them in the seventh and eighth centuries.

Pope (Pontiff): a Latin term meaning "father." In the early church the term was generally used of the bishops by Marcellius, bishop of Rome, and Cyprian, bishop of Carthage in the third century. However, beginning in the seventh century bishops of Rome sought to make it a technical religious title of the office of the highest authority claiming Petrine apostolic succession.

Quartrodecians (Quartrodecian Controversy, Easter Controversy, Passover-Easter Controversy): a term, derived from a Latin word meaning "fourteenth," applied to those Christians in the early church who followed the Jewish festival calendar and celebrated the crucifixion of Christ on the fourteenth day of the first month (Nisan) in the Jewish calendar, the day of Passover. There is evidence that this was the pattern of the churches into the fourth century until the time of John Chrysostum, bishop of Constantinople. The ecumenical Council of Nicaea (325) declared that Sunday following the Passover should be the day of celebration.

Saracens: a people-group, bedouins, who lived in desert areas in and around the Roman province of Arabia. Eventually, by the crusader period, beginning in the late eleventh century, the term came to encompass the Arab population that embraced Islam and occupied the Holy Lands.

Saxons: a confederation of Germanic tribes who migrated into Britannia (Great Britain) during the early Middle Ages. Later, the tribes were forged into a single nation under Egbert and Alfred the Great in the eighth and ninth centuries to more effectively resist the Viking intrusions.

Second Plank (the Second Planck): a concept that seems to have been originally employed by Jerome, using a floating piece of wood as an illustration to describe the role of repentance as a restorative gift from God, the first plank being confession, the "planks" being a course of action after a "shipwreck" of baptismal innocence. In the development of sacerdotalism in the medieval church and the development of the sacramental system of grace, the first step to safety was baptism, which removed inherited Adamic inability and guilt, leaving the saint to cope with acts of disobedience, not a blighted constitution. The second step was the sacrament of penance or confessional contrition that caused a restoration to innocence and a new beginning in the journey to redemption.

Semi-Pelagianism (Cassianism): a view concerning the issues of sin and grace in the church often identified with the teachings of the fifth-century cleric/monastic John Cassian. Cassian struggled to explain the relationship between ability, responsibility, and culpability (as well as freedom and sovereignty) by arguing for a matrix of causative, cooperative factors. He suggested that when God detects religious sincerity, clearly deficient to cause redeeming mercies, God can act in grace to supply what human effort can conceive, but not accomplish. The view is a compromise of sorts between Augustinian inability—the necessity of uncaused, unmerited divine initiative in salvation—and the Pelagian view that humankind has the capacity to effect salvation by moral resolve and rectitude. The view was condemned at the Synod of Orange (529), but reemerges in the medieval church.

Single Predestinarianism: a view of the order of the component parts of the eternal and single decree of God to redeem humanity.

Advocates of this particular ordering suggest that God decreed human creation and the fall before the decree to redeem; that is, viewing the lostness of the race, God moved in compassion and love to avert the destiny of some in the context of having no obligation to any. It is the view that God did not predestine the reprobated to their state, but in choosing the elect out of the lostness passed over the others who would do as they please, evidencing the merit of condemnation.

Subordinationism: a view espoused in the early church by Origen, among others, prior to the Nicaea (325) and Constantinople (381) ecumenical councils, claiming that the Son is ontologically inferior to the Father, though not the view of Tertullian and Aristides. The latter spoke of a "triade of equal glories" and the former coined the term *Trinity*.

Supralapsarianism: an attempt to place in logical sequence the components of the eternal and single redemptive decree of God. Advocates of this perspective begin with the decree of divine election of some to life and others to eternal damnation followed by the creation decree of all people, the decree of the fall, and finally the decree to provide salvation for the elect.

Vandals: a Germanic people group that conquered portions of Africa in the fifth century and sacked Rome in 455. Portions of Vandal North Africa were reclaimed in the sixth century by Emperor Justinian I after the collapse of the empire in west.

Vikings (Norsemen): a Scandanavian people-group known for their longboats and seafaring exploration and conquest that reached North America, the Mediterranean, and Constantinople from the eighth through the eleventh centuries. The threat of Carolingian territorialism and increased population, but limited agricultural opportunities and resources, are frequently cited reasons for Viking expansion. The Vikings conquered much of England, establishing Danslaw, as well as kingdoms in Normandy and Sicily. They were hired mercenaries for the Slavic people who established the Varangian Kingdom with whom the Vikings blended. Numerous monasteries, including Iona and Landisfarne, were destroyed in the pillaging and looting and Europe was plunged into a nadir of darkness.

Visigoths: a branch of the Goths, a Germanic tribe that entered Europe after the defeat of a Roman army at the Battle of Adrianople (376), establishing rule on the Iberian Peninsula and in Italy in the fifth century. Though they initially were converts to Arian Christianity through the labors of Ulfilas (ca. 310–383), a missionary and Bible translator (*Silver Bible*), they accepted the Nicene faith in the sixth century.

Chapter 5 Outline

The Carolingian Collapse, the Vikings, and Political Renewal
  Vikings
  Henry the Fowler
  Otto
  Hugh Capet
The Renewal of Mission Activity
  The Danes
  The Norwegians
  The Swedes
  The Slavs
The Resurgence of the Papacy
  Clerical Immorality
  Monasteries
  Hildebrand, Gregory VII
  Series of Popes
  First Lateran Council
  Frederick I and Alexander III
  Innocent III
The Renewal of Monastic Spirituality
  Bernard of Clairvaux
  Victorines

  Mendicant Orders
  Franciscans
  Dominicans
  Carmelites
The Emerging Dispute: The Eastern and Western Catholic Churches
  Monophysite Controversy
  Icons
  Supremacy, Authority, and the Filoque
    Controversy
The Crusades
  First Crusade
  Second Crusade
  Third Crusade
  Fourth Crusade
  Fifth Crusade
  Sixth Crusade
  Seventh Crusade
  Other Crusades
  Effects of the Crusades

Chapter 5 Objectives

- That the reader will identify the causes for the collapse of the Carolingian kingdom

- That the reader will describe the influence of missionary activity in the middle medieval period

- That the reader will describe the increasing role of the papacy during the middle medieval period

- That the reader will identify the renewal and rise of monastic spirituality

- That the reader will identify the primary causes for the schism between the Orthodox and Western Catholic Churches

- That the reader will describe the causes for and the major events of the Crusades

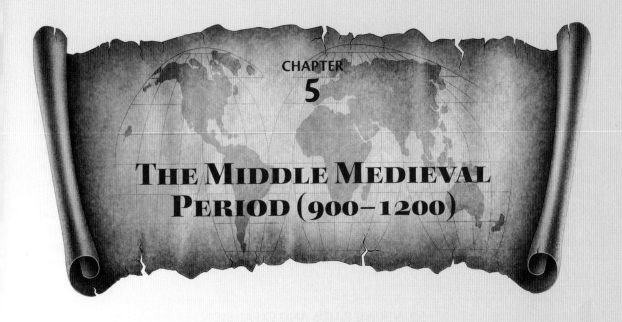

THE MIDDLE MEDIEVAL PERIOD (900–1200)

T HOUGH THE CAROLINGIAN KINGDOM was impressive, there was a fatal weakness, *gavelkind,* that is, the division of the kingdom among the king's heirs (it was providence that gained them a single heir from 751–830). When Louis the Pious, the most gifted ruler in over three hundred years, died, the kingdom was carefully partitioned to his three sons, with the title *king* granted to the eldest. Upon the death of all three, clerical and lay leaders would choose the successor. The birth of a son to a second wife divided the kingdom further. This led to the weakening of the empire and caused it to become easy prey for the Muslims to the south, the Scandinavians to the north, and the Magyars from the east. In effect, this left Europe without a centralized government. This meant that protection was a matter of landowners forming various alliances for regional preservation. In doing so, feudalism had its beginning.

The Carolingian Collapse, the Vikings, and Political Renewal

Scholars define the Viking Era as a period spanning three centuries, from the late eighth century to the Norman Conquest of England at the Battle of Hastings in 1066. The term *Viking* comes from an Old Norse word meaning "from the bay or inlet," suggesting they came into Europe from the sea. They occupied themselves with raiding, trading, and employment as mercenaries.

Vikings

The earliest Vikings, a group of Norwegians, raided on English soil in 787; in 793 the monastery at Landisfarne was attacked and subsequently abandoned. Norwegians generally invaded the island areas of England, Scotland, and Ireland. Danish Vikings invaded England from the east in the late ninth century and established a Viking state, Danelaw. Though most of the land was reduced to turmoil, Alfred of Wessex was able to prevent the taking of his realm. Danes also traversed the waterways of Western Europe. Swedish Vikings appeared to have raided in the eastern reaches along the Volga River, reaching Constantinople and Baghdad. Viking settlements were established in North America (Bjarni Herjolfsson, seeking Greenland but blown off course, came to Labrador and Newfoundland in 985; Leif Eriksson sailed there in 1001.) Vikings also invaded the Mediterranean (Sicily) and the northern coast of France (Normandy).

Out of the trauma and chaos occasioned by the collapse of a central government in Europe for the second time in the Christian era emerged the embryonic origins of modern nation-states.

Henry the Fowler

In central Europe, Henry the Fowler (876–936) founded a Saxon dynasty of kings in 912, though he did not take the title of emperor or king. In 918, the duchy of Franconia (a duchy was a defined territory ruled by a member of the aristocratic class, a duke) was added upon the death of its ruler Conrad I. This gave Henry two of the four major duchies. Because of military pressure from Henry, Bavaria and Swabia formed a confederation. When the **Magyars** invaded Germanic lands in 924, Henry secured

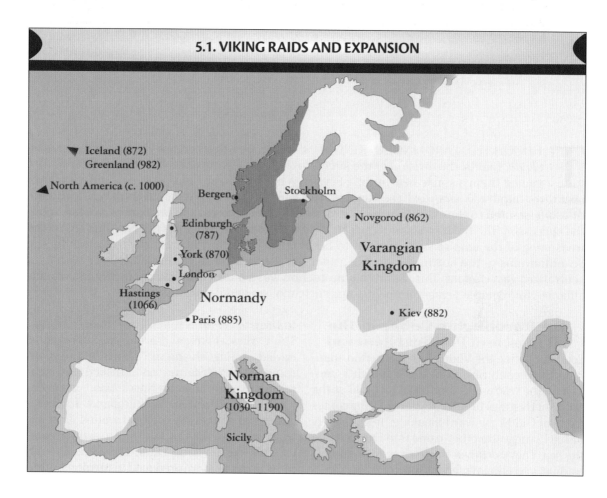

5.1. VIKING RAIDS AND EXPANSION

Iceland (872)
Greenland (982)
North America (c. 1000)
Bergen
Stockholm
Edinburgh (787)
Novgorod (862)
York (870)
Varangian Kingdom
London
Hastings (1066)
Normandy
Kiev (882)
Paris (885)
Norman Kingdom (1030–1190)
Sicily

Legend of the German crown offered to Henry I, by Hermann Vogel (1854–1921). Courtesy of Zigarettenbildche.

a truce in exchange for an annual tribute. Using the time to fortify his kingdom, he refused to pay the ransom and defeated the Magyar and Slavic invaders in 933. His last campaign was the invasion of Denmark and the adding of the territory of Schleswig to his kingdom. Henry refused to receive a crown from the church, beginning a controversy that would last for centuries (the theory being that he who crowns is greater that he who is crowned).

Otto I

Otto I (912–973) succeeded his father, Henry the Fowler, in 926 and was crowned in Charlemagne's capital, Aachen, by the Archbishop of Mainz as the emperor of the Holy Roman

Statue of the Magdeburg Rider, thought to be of Otto I. Courtesy of Ajepbah and Crisco 1492.

Empire, rightful successor of the great Carolingian king. In this power alliance of church and state, the former offered its wealth, its sway over the masses, and its intellectual hegemony of educational endeavors. The state offered the church its protection and wealth. Under Otto I, known as Otto the Great, and his successors an intellectual renaissance began anew.

Hugh Capet

When the last of the West Francia kings died in 987, Hugh Capet (940–996) (apparently he was fond of capes) became King of the Franks and established a dynasty, laying the foundation for the creation of a nation-state (the first to claim the title, "King of France," was Philip IV, called "the Fair" [1268–1314]). When his father, Hugh the Great, died in 956, he inherited numerous fiefs around Paris and Orleans, becoming a powerful feudal lord. Gradually, other feudal lords and **counts** recognized his leadership, and the Archbishop of Rheims crowned him (though he had to be rescued from rivals by the archbishop). Hugh Capet remained a loyal son of the church favoring clerical reform, especially the **Cluny Reform Movement**.

The Renewal of Mission Activity

Attempts to reach into Scandinavia during the robust days of the Carolingian Empire were largely futile because the efforts of Ansgar and others were often linked with the fear of political entanglements. An entry for the extension of the gospel to the Scandinavians occurred when the aggressive Vikings pummeled Europe beginning in the late eighth century. The settlement of the invaders in Danelaw, Normandy, and Sicily, as well as contact with Constantinople opened them to new religious ideas. Through Danelaw, for example, intermarriage between Celts, Saxons, Angles, and Scandinavians became the context for social and religious assimilation.

The Danes

The Danes were exposed to Christianity initially

during the Carolingian Empire. The first king to embrace Christianity was Harold Bluetooth (ca. 910–ca. 986). The hold of Christian faith appears, however, to have been nominal and syncretistic. (Harold's son, Sweyn Forkbeard, was also baptized). It was during the reign of Sweyn Forkbeard's son, Canute, that Christianity began to flourish. Canute (ca. 980–1035) completed the conquest of England and ruled the land for over thirty years. His territorial domain stretched from England to parts of Norway and Sweden. He was generous to the churches, restoring pillaged monasteries in England, replenishing church treasuries, and building churches throughout his kingdom. He also made a pilgrimage to Rome in 1027 and secured financial benefits from the pope for the churches.

The Norwegians

As with the Danes, contact with Christianity among Norwegians came largely through Viking raids on the British Isles and the Frankish kingdoms. The Norwegian king, Haakon the Good (ca. 920–960), was introduced to Christianity in England, but he failed in his attempts to bring it into his own country though he sought a bishop and priest from England. Later, Anglo-Saxon missionaries from England and Germany were successful in bringing Christianity to Olaf I (ca. 960–1000), and he is said to have built the first Christian churches in the land. Under his successor Olaf II (995–1030), Christianity was firmly established in the land.

The Swedes

Sweden received Christian missionaries from

Olaf II (later Saint Olaf) of Norway killed at the battle of Stiklestad in a painting by Peter Nicolai Arbo (1831-1892). Courtesy of Interpretix.

Invitation to Church History: World

the Frankish kingdoms in the ninth century. The first Swedish king to embrace the faith throughout his reign was Olof Skotkonung (ca. 980–1022) who was baptized in 1018. A later successor, Eric IX (ca. 1120–1160), consolidated Christian gains in his country and extended the church into Finland. In his attempt to support the Christian churches through mandated tithes, Swedish nobles rebelled, and he was attacked and beheaded upon leaving a church near Uppsala. For his efforts to promote Christianity, he was called Eric the Saint.

The Slavs

The coming of Christianity to the Slavic peoples appears to be connected to Swedish Vikings who plied the rivers eastward and southward in the ninth and tenth centuries into what is now Russia, Belarus, and the Ukraine, engaging in pillaging, trading, and mercenary activities, reaching the Caspian Sea and Constantinople. Seeking military protection from each other, four Slavic tribes invited Vikings, mostly Swedes called Varangians ("those who promise to protect"), to rule over them. Under the leadership of Rurik in the 800s, several cities were founded, including Novogorad and Kiev, and the Varangians dominated the emerging nation, Russia. Unlike other areas of Viking influence, the Vikings melted into the Slavic culture over subsequent centuries, losing their particular identity.

Rurik (ca. 830–ca. 879), the name means "famous ruler," founded a dynasty; successors moved the capital from Novogorad to Kiev and founded the state of Kiev Rus, which lasted until the Mongol invasions in the early thirteenth century. In 980, Vladimir (955–1015), called "the Great," came to the throne and greatly expanded and consolidated his empire. Included in his efforts to strengthen the empire was the establishment of a national religion. According to the *Primary Chronicle*, an ancient source document, Vladimir sent delegates to learn of Judaism, Islam, and Christianity

(German and Greek). He rejected Judaism for unknown reasons, Islam because there was "no happiness among them, but instead only sorrow and a dreadful stench," and German (Western) Catholicism because "in their many ceremonies . . . [he] beheld no glory there." His delegates, however, were impressed with the magnificence of worship in Greek (Eastern) Catholicism ("We knew not whether we were in heaven or on earth. . . . God dwells there among them").

In the same time frame, Valdimir felt that he received divine guidance in conquering a city and divine help in being miraculously cured of blindness. He, therefore, submitted to Christian baptism and called upon his nation to do so as well. Vladimir destroyed pagan

Vladimir on the Millennium of Russia Monument in Novgorod. Courtesy of Dar Beter.

Invitation to Church History: World

shrines throughout his nation in what appears to have been a genuine embrace of Christianity.

Churches were established with distinctive design—multicolored with onion shaped domes. St. Sophia Cathedral in Novogorad (989) had thirteen domes constructed of wood; St. Sophia in Kiev (1037–1043) had thirteen domes of stone construction. The onion-shape symbolized Christ, the flair at the top, the prayer of the saint through Christ, and the mounted cross above, the means of approach to heaven.

According to the *Primary Chronicle,* Vladimir ordered the most promising children in his realm to be religiously educated, recognizing the accomplishment as a fulfillment of Isa. 29:18 ("In that day, the deaf shall hear the words of a book, and out of their gloom and darkness the eyes of the blind shall see" [ESV]).

A vibrant Christianity flourished among the Slavic people for over two centuries. Subjugation followed in the thirteenth century

5.2. THE SPREAD OF THE CHURCH: THE WITNESS OF VERNACULAR TRANSLATIONS

with the invasion of over 35,000 Mongolians. Batu Khan crossed the Volga River in 1236 and destroyed Kiev in 1240. The only city to be spared was Novogorad. Christianity declined as the bond with Constantinople was severed.

The Resurgence of the Papacy

The decline of the Carolingian Empire in the ninth century witnessed a decline of religious vitality, much as had occurred in the sixth century with the decline of the western portion of the Roman Empire. In the midst of the fracturing of the empire and the waste laid to the land by the invasive Vikings, the church gradually found protection in whatever governments remained (**dukes**, counts, **margraves**). Scholars have called the circumstance that resulted the "feudalization of the church." In turning to secular powers, the church often surrendered its authority to the state, much as serfs surrendered their freedoms to lords. Churches gradually served the needs of rulers at the same time that most people looked to the church to save them from the horrors of hell. Dukes became bishops without religious qualifications or concerns. Dukes formed federations that eventually became nation states, and this was particularly the case in West Francia; kings ruled over the churches appointing favorites to significant offices.

Clerical Immorality

At the same time as political instability prevailed in Francia and Germany in the tenth century, clerical morals reached a spiritual nadir. As sad, as it is shocking, the first half of the tenth century [popes (904–963) from Sergius III to John XII] has been designated as the Pornocracy, or "rule of the harlots," a period when the papacy was dominated by powerful women in the Theolphylact family (it was widely believed Marozia was the concubine of Pope Sergius III and the mother of John XI who allegedly arranged the murder of John X to replace him with a favorite, Leo VI). Though later

Gregorian reformers may have exaggerated the details, the era reflects the nadir in the papal's lack of morals.

No contemporary exceeded Peter Damian (1007–1072) in providing the vivid details of moral, social, and spiritual disorder in the church. He was a monk and friend of Hildebrand, who wrote a scathing treatise, *Book of Gomorrha*, in 1050 during the pontificate of Leo IX (Leo thought Damian had exaggerated, but Damian did not withdraw his accusations). In the book, Damian claims to address the vices that are replete in the church, homosexuality, sodomy, and pedophilia among them, not to mention concubinage and wife swapping. Eventually Damian was appointed a cardinal in the Gregorian church and served as a papal legate under several popes as a leading voice for reform.

Italian stamp of Saint Peter Damian by Giovanni di Paoli. Courtesy of rook76-Fotolia.

Monasteries
In the south of East Francia, an area along the Loire River particularly susceptible to Viking forays and Magyar intrusion from northern Italy, the situation was acute. A pious nobleman, Gerald of Aurillac (ca. 855–907) established a monastery on his lands that would be free of lay and ecclesiastical control; according to his biographer, Odo (877–942), his motives were devoid of self-interest and nominally connected to the papacy that was particularly weak at the time. The monastic endeavor failed, but it served as a model for a monastic movement that became highly successful, the Cluny Reform Movement.

In 910 William the Pious, Duke of Acquitaine, founded a monastery in the region of Burgundy, central East Francia. The monastery was unique; it was founded to be a reforming institution, free of state and ecclesiastical control, though the pope was declared its protector. Abbots were to be chosen by the monks, not by a bishop. The abbey at Cluny became the central hub of numerous others. Each of the others was served by a prior, a second in command, chosen by the abbot. Thus, the Cluny

Movement was organizationally independent and internally hierarchical. It strictly adhered to the **Benedictine Rule** and quickly became a model of piety. Through the eminence of a succession of abbots, Bruno being the first, Cluny established monasteries throughout Europe, gained enormous wealth, and became politically powerful in matters of church and state. Cluny became the principal center of the Christian faith after Rome.

The first abbot of the monastery at Cluny was Bruno of Segni (ca. 1047–1123). The spirit of clunaic reform can be seen in a pamphlet that he wrote, *On the Simoniacs* (**simony** was the practice of buying and selling church offices for personal advantage). In part he complained, "The Church had been so corrupted that hardly anyone might be found who either was not a simoniac or had not been ordained by a simoniac (10)." Bruno was succeeded by Odo (ca. 878–942), who has been designated "the glory of the great abbey of Cluny" for his monastic and clerical reforms, as well as the role of piety in daily life.

Hildebrand, Gregory VII
Of all the reforming monks associated with Cluny, Hildebrand (ca. 1020–1085) is the most

celebrated. He rose to the office of the papacy and struggled to end lay investiture, political appointment to offices in the church against Henry IV of Germany. Hildebrand was born in Tuscany of humble origins and trained for service in the church at the Santa Maria monastery in Rome directed by an uncle. He initially served John Gratan, an archpriest, who became Gregory VI, a reformist pope (he came to the papal chair when three claimed the throne [one he bribed to step down, a twenty- year-old, and the other stepped aside]).

After Gregory's death, Hildebrand joined the Benedictine monastics at Cluny. A short time later Bruno, bishop of Toul, who was on his way to Rome to become Leo IX, asked Hildebrand to join him. Though the emperor at Worms had elected Bruno, he submitted to

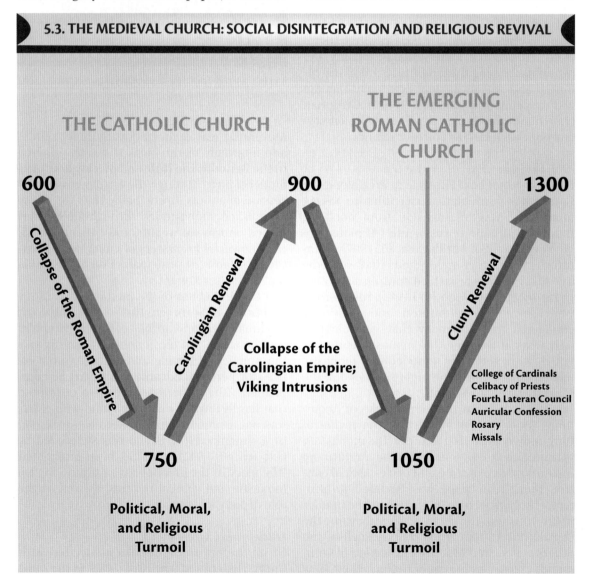

5.3. THE MEDIEVAL CHURCH: SOCIAL DISINTEGRATION AND RELIGIOUS REVIVAL

THE CATHOLIC CHURCH

THE EMERGING ROMAN CATHOLIC CHURCH

600

900

1300

Collapse of the Roman Empire

Carolingian Renewal

Cluny Renewal

Collapse of the Carolingian Empire; Viking Intrusions

College of Cardinals
Celibacy of Priests
Fourth Lateran Council
Auricular Confession
Rosary
Missals

750

1050

Political, Moral, and Religious Turmoil

Political, Moral, and Religious Turmoil

the Roman clergy before assuming the post. Leo IX opposed the practice of simony that had weakened the church spiritually and the practice of clerical matrimony in the tenth and eleventh centuries. He connected simony with clerical marriages, apparently because churchmen passed offices to their children as an inheritance. Accordingly, during his pontificate (1049–1054), Leo IX convened the reformist Easter Synod of 1049 that prohibited clerical marriages above the office of **subdeacon** (this became a major issue in the Gregorian reform strategy to eliminate simony). At a later synod held in Mainz, the issues of clerical marriage and simony were again addressed.

Popes after Leo IX were generally reformed-minded. However, it was Hildebrand who served them with masterful diplomatic skill and wise administration (in many ways he was the power behind the papal throne). An interesting interlude in the issue of lay investiture occurred during the pontificate of Victor II (1055–1057) when he was appointed guardian over the son of King Henry III of Germany. In effect, while Henry IV was a child, the papacy ruled the nation. During the pontificate of Nicholas II (1059–1061), the power to appoint popes was placed in the cardinals, the highest-ranking churchmen under the pope.

Upon the death of Alexander II in 1073, Hildebrand was elected to the church's highest post (1073–1085). He took the name Gregory in honor of Gregory VI, the reformed-minded pope that he admired as a godly man. Gregory VII became one of the most powerful popes of all time. In the Lenten Synod of 1074, he enacted several reforming decrees. For example, clerics who obtained office by purchase were required to desist from the ministry, clerical moral failure demanded a relinquishment of office, and sacramental functions by a priest who failed to conform to such mandates were to be considered as void. When clerics in Germany,

France, and Italy protested that they would rather give up their posts than their wives, Gregory sent legates to enforce his decrees and depose the rebellious.

The Dictates of Gregory VII:

"That the Roman pontiff alone can with right be called universal" (2).

"That a sentence passed by him may be retracted by no one; and that he himself, alone of all, may retract it" (18).

"That the Roman church has never erred; nor will it err to all eternity, the Scripture bearing witness" (22).

Controversy emerged over Gregory VII's legislative measures; a synod that gathered in Paris in 1074 protested the reforms, claiming that the benefits of the sacraments were not dependent on the moral virtues of the officiating priest. An antipope party emerged under the leadership of Guibert (ca. 1029–1100), archbishop of Ravenna, who opposed Gregory's sanctions. Henry IV, the German monarch, gathered a synod in 1080, had Gregory deposed, and then Guibert recognized as his successor (Clement III).

Though scholars dispute the date of the composition of *The Dictates of the Pope,* there is little doubt that the document is consistent with Gregory's principles and his understanding of his office. In the midst of Gregory's reforms and the hostilities they generated, the pontiff felt compelled to enumerate the authority and significance of his post. Beyond the immediate circumstances that called forth the *Dictates,* it is an important document because it demonstrates the growing perception of papal authority over the churches. Among the twenty-seven decrees are these:

That the Roman pontiff alone can with right be called universal (2), That he alone can depose or reinstate bishops (3), That of the pope alone all princes shall kiss the feet (9), That it may be permitted to him to depose emperors (12), That a sentence passed by him may be retracted by no one . . . (18), That he himself may be judged by no one (19), That the Roman church has never erred; nor will it err to all eternity, the Scripture bearing witness (22), That the Roman pontiff, if he has been canonically ordained, is undoubtedly made a saint by the merits of St. Peter . . . (23), That he may absolve subjects from their fealty [loyalty] to wicked men [kings] (27).

It was in this era that the *Isidorean Decretals*, forged documents from the ninth century, which included the fraudulent eighth-century *Donation of Constantine*, became popular. The use of the *Donation* makes evident the growing assertion of papal prerogatives:

> Constantine desires to promote the Chair of Peter over the Empire and its seat on earth by bestowing on it imperial power and honor (1), The Chair of Peter shall have supreme authority over all churches in the world (2), and Constantine gives up the remaining sovereignty over Rome, the provinces, cities and, towns of the whole of Italy or of the Western Regions to Pope Sylvester and his successors (9).

The decretals claimed historic precedence for papal authority from the early church era.

The controversy over Gregory's reforms and the rise of the antipope Clement III, who was a puppet of Henry IV, must be seen within the context of the investiture crisis. The issue concerned the appointment of bishops. Henry was convinced that, since bishops exercised considerable political influence, it was imperative for the safety of the empire that he select them. Gregorian reformers identified political interference as a source of ecclesial corruption.

In 1073, Gregory issued a decree forbidding lay investiture, threatening excommunication of any guilty parties. As the conflict deepened, Henry wrote Gregory claiming divine authority for his rule; argued that the pope had ascended to power through ignorant officials, bribery, and political intrigue; and that he should withdraw from the holy office to be replaced by a holy man ("thou who does not fear God, dost dishonor in me his appointed one"). Gregory responded quickly by excommunicating Henry and releasing his subjects from obeying him:

> I withdraw, through thy power and authority [the authority of St. Peter], from Henry the king, son of Henry the emperor, who has risen against thy church with unheard of insolence, the rule over the whole kingdom of the Germans and over Italy. And I absolve all Christians from the bonds of the oath which they have made or shall make to him; and I forbid any one to serve him as King (Letter, 22 February 1076).

Fearing the rebellion of his nobles, Henry felt he had no other choice but to secure the mercies of Gregory to rescind the powerful indictment of excommunication. Gregory became fearful of reprisal by Henry and came to a fortress in Tuscany at Canossa; Henry came from Speyer as a penitent to meet him. With Gregory refusing to hear Henry's confession, the king and his entourage waited outside the fortress gates begging admission into the pope's presence for three days. Though humiliated, Henry was spared the loss of his kingdom, and he was once again received into the communion of the church, though Gregory did not restore his right to the throne, causing civil conflict when Henry sought to regain it. At this point, the theory that the pope, through Christ to Peter, possessed two keys, the key of authority over the church and the key of authority over the state, seemed vindicated.

This issue was not resolved by the 28 January 1077 pardon granted by Gregory. Henry returned to Germany, reclaimed his throne by defeating his adversaries, and had a rival, puppet-pope elected, Clement III. Gregory responded with a second decree of excommunication in 1080, but this time Henry's subjects were unwilling to reject his leadership, which the rival pope, Clement III, affirmed.

Gregory's condemnation of Henry, the second time, was an indirect speech in the form of a prayer, calling on God to bring the judgment of death swiftly ("And, in the case of the said Henry, exercise such swift judgment that all may know him to fall not by chance but by your power").

The loss of support from Henry's subjects and Gregory's bishops, as well as the appearance of a large army moving toward Rome in the spring of 1081 caused panic in the city. Unable to secure aid from the Normans to the south or Constantinople, the city acquiesced, Gregory fled for his life to Monte Cassino, and Henry installed Clement III in the papal chair. Gregory died in exile in 1085 having appointed the abbot of Monte Casino, Victor III, his successor. The issue of investment remained unresolved.

> After excommunicating King Henry IV of Germany, Pope Gregory VII effectively consolidated papal power over political rule during his papacy, though at cost to his tenure. He was forced to withdraw from Rome and subsequently died in exile in Salerno.

Series of Popes

The papacy continued to suffer as Clement III adamantly claimed the prerogatives of Peter's successor and a series of popes (Victor III, Urban II, and Paschal II), having regained Rome, perpetuated the claim that they were in the true succession to Peter. Conrad, the son of Henry IV, with papal sanction, rebelled and claimed the throne from his father, only to be defeated, causing increased tensions between state and church.

When Clement III died (1100), Henry IV had a successor appointed, Theodoric, and the papal schism continued. Upon Henry IV's death (1106), Paschal II, who supported Henry V's right to the throne, hoped that the investiture struggle would end. In a 1111 letter to Henry V, Paschal restored the kingdom to Henry IV's successors, argued that the functions of state and church should be separate (the church handling issues of a spiritual nature only, ending lay investiture), and proposed that church royalties and possessions should be returned to the state. However, the bishops of the church felt the compromise would surrender too much power to the state and it failed. Henry then captured Paschal and took him to Germany. A subsequent letter from Paschal, a month later, reversed the decision granting the king the right to invest bishops. Paschal returned to Rome and sanctioned the excommunication of Henry. There was no effective resolution in sight.

With Paschall's death, Gelasius II was hastily appointed as his successor with hope that the curia could bring an end to the chaos. Marching armies, papal fights, and brief restorations became the plight of Gelasius's (d. 1119) pontificate until he eventually fled to France. By such an action, he shifted papal policy toward France, where, unlike Germany or Italy, he was warmly received.

Callixtus II (d.1124), being of the aristocratic class, came to the papal chair with strong family connections with the monarchy; he was related to the emperor. The former archbishop of Vienna sought to bring an end to the investiture controversy. An agreement was reached with Henry V in the Concordat of Worms in 1122. The king relinquished the right to invest, and episcopal elections would be held in the presence of the king. If an election was controverted, the king would decide it. Political privileges remained with the state, and church possessions would be restored to the church.

First Lateran Council

Shortly after the Concordat at Worms was consummated, Callixtus convened the First Lateran Council (1123) to confirm it. In addition, the council of over three hundred churchmen affirmed several canons. While many of the canons enumerated the limits of clerical authority, several others addressed the issues championed by the seemingly victorious Gregorian/Cluny reform movement (simony, concubinage, and clerical marriages). Canon 1 prohibited simony, the buying and selling of church offices ("we altogether forbid anyone to be ordained or promoted in the church of God for money"). Canon 21 prohibited the possession of a concubine or entering into marriage ("We absolutely forbid priests, deacons, subdeacons and monks to have concubines or to contract marriages"). While celibacy was generally the domain of the monastic, it was not required of priests and bishops until this time. Here was a case of the church striving to rid itself of an evil, simony, only to create potential for another.

> "No one shall be consecrated bishop who has not been canonically elected. If anyone dare do this, both the consecrator and the one consecrated shall be deposed without hope of reinstatement" (First Lateran Council, 1123, Canon 30).

An interesting canon was the tenth. It gives the church the authority to grant forgiveness of sin, in this instance for service to the church, most particularly for the hazardous endeavor of undertaking a crusade for the church ("To those who set out for Jerusalem and offer effective help towards the defense of the Christian people and overcoming the tyranny of the infidels, we grant the remission of their sins, and we place their houses and families and all their goods under the protection of blessed Peter and the Roman church . . ."). Though this canon was a repetition of a decree issued by Urban II at the inauguration of the first crusade against the Muslims in the

Near East in 1095, it had a significant influence on how people thought of the church and the extent to which the church controlled their lives.

Frederick I and Alexander III

The boundaries of authority between church and state in an era when the two were intricately interconnected continued into the thirteenth century, the church impinging on the state and the state upon the church. An illustration of this seesaw rumbling concerned the relationship of Frederick I, called Barbarossa or "Red Beard" (1122–1190), and Alexander III.

Frederick, a popular and politically aggressive monarch, became king in Germany in 1152 and was crowned emperor by Adrian III in 1155. Tensions between emperor and pope arose in 1157 when a papal legate came to Frederick's court at Besancon with letters asking that the wealth of the German churches, at least in part, be transferred to Rome ("the lord pope had conferred upon us the distinction of the imperial crown and that he would not regret it if our Highness were to receive from him even greater benefices"). Fredrick rejected the notion that kingship was granted by the papal prerogative and dismissed the legate in anger. This episode commenced a struggle that would last for seventeen years. Frederick opposed Adrian III and rejected his successor, Alexander III, favoring rival claimants: Victor

Frederick Barbarossa submits to the authority of Pope Alexander III. Fresco, Palazzo Pubblico, Siena, Italy. Courtesy of Aljodasch.

IV (1159–1164), Paschal III (1164–1168), and Calixtus III (1168–1178) in succession (all now recognized as antipopes). International tensions rose as England and France sided with Alexander III.

Peace was finally restored between pope and king at the Peace of Vienna in 1177. Alexander was recognized as the only legitimate successor of Saint. Peter. Frederick promised loyalty for himself and his subjects, and they mutually agreed to restore each other's possession taken during the dispute ("the Roman church also will restore in good faith, every possession and holding which it took away from him through itself or through others . . .").

The height of Alexander's pontificate was the calling of the Third Lateran Council in 1179. Seeking to avert the turmoil that so often accompanied papal succession, the council decreed that two-thirds of the cardinals would secure the appointment and anyone assuming the position with less would be disqualified.

Innocent III

The zenith of papal power came in the pontificate of Innocent III (1198–1216). He came to the highest post in the church the day after being ordained a priest at the relatively youthful age of thirty-seven. Innocent stridently asserted papal power; he clearly became the most singularly powerful person in Europe. He forced King John of England to subservience. This younger brother of Richard the Lionhearted was also known as John "Lackland" because he lost English claims to territory on the continent (France). This is the John whose noblemen subjects forced the curtailment of his powers in signing the Magna Carta in 1215.

John entered a dispute with Innocent over succession in the archbishopric of Canterbury. It became a clash of titans. Innocent placed an interdict on England (a decree that all priestly functions would be discontinued [masses, marriages, baptisms, last rites, and funerals]), and John responded by confiscating church lands.

Finally, John was threatened with excommunication and a crusade against his kingdom. The king repented and his penance was vassalship, the loss of his kingdom (thereafter he paid an annual fee for the right to rule). Part of John's confession read:

> We bind in perpetuity our successors and legitimate heirs that without question they must similarly render fealty and acknowledge homage to the Supreme Pontiff holding office at the time . . . in lieu of all service and payment which we should render for them [the fiefs], the Roman Church is to receive annually . . . one thousand marks sterling . . . .

Innocent placed an interdict on France to protest the unlawful divorce of the king, Philip Augustus, which forced him to dismiss his concubine (some years later he returned to his wife). Innocent also became involved in the politics of Sicily, Spain, Portugal, Poland, Bulgaria, and Sweden. The demarcations devised in the Concordat at Worms (1123) were violated by both church and state. In the pontificate of Innocent III, the church unquestionably gained ascendancy over the state.

In Germany, Innocent entered the controversy over kingly succession in 1201 when three claimed the throne, stating, "It is the business of the pope to look after the interests of the Roman Empire, since the empire derives its origin and its final authority from the papacy." His choice, though not without considerable intrigue, was Otto IV, and he gained the throne.

Arguably Innocent's greatest achievement was the gathering of the Fourth Lateran Council (1215), the greatest church gathering of the Middle Ages. This huge gathering of church officials, over thirteen hundred, was originally called to consider a crusade against the Seljuk Turks. However, it turned out to be a great reforming council. From the perspective of later reformers in the sixteenth century, Luther and Calvin, the council was a turning point in the orthodoxy of the Catholic Church; it is there, according to their judgment, that the church took on a Romish hue.

"There is one Universal Church of the faithful, outside of which there is absolutely no salvation. In which there is the same priest and sacrifice, Jesus Christ, whose body and blood are truly contained in the sacrament of the altar under the forms of bread and wine; the bread being changed by divine power into the body, and the wine into the blood, so that to realize the mystery of unity we may receive of Him what He has received of us. And this sacrament no one can effect except the priest who has been duly ordained in accordance with the keys of the Church, which Jesus Christ Himself gave to the Apostles and their successors" (The Fourth Lateran Council, 1215, Canon 1).

The first canon of the council affirmed the doctrine of the Trinity as a basis for affirming the orthodoxy of Peter Lombard who had been accused by Joachim of Flora (ca. 1135–1202) of teaching a plurality of four in the Godhead (Canon 2). In Canon 1, the council also delineated the meaning of three sacraments: the Eucharist or Lord's Supper, baptism, and penance. For the first time in the history of the church the Eucharist was defined using the term *transubstantiation* to explain specifically the manner of the Lord's real presence, though the concept can be observed in the church as early as the pontificate of Gregory I. Unlike the differences of opinion between Radbertus and Ratramnus in the eighth century on the subject of Christ's presence at Corbie century, no allowance for differing opinion would be tolerated any longer. (The council did not connect the Eucharist with progressive, sanctifying grace. The council argued that redeeming grace procured incrementally through sacramental obedience had the potential of

bringing final grace in the beatific vision of heavenly rest, a connection later reformers of the church rejected.)

"All the faithful of both sexes shall after they have reached the age of discretion faithfully confess all their sins at least once a year to their own (parish) priest and perform to the best of their ability the penance imposed, receiving reverently at least at Easter the sacrament of the Eucharist, unless perchance at the advice of their own priest they may for a good reason abstain for a time from its reception; otherwise they shall be cut off from the Church (excommunicated) during life and deprived of Christian burial in death" (The Fourth Lateran Council, 1215, Canon 21).

What appears clear is that between the eighth and eleventh centuries the church had come to embrace the view of Radbertus in such a way as not to countenance the view of Ratramnus. Berengar of Tours (ca. 999–1080), a canon and teacher in the cathedral school of his city, came to the conclusion that Radbertus's view of the divine presence was incorrect. Berengar was condemned by Leo IX in 1050 and was forced to confess his errors on several occasions, but he retracted his recantations upon reflection. He felt that the Scriptures were the supreme authority in the church, not the councils or even the popes.

Berengar was bitterly opposed by Lanfranc (ca. 1105–1089), a teacher in the monastery at Bec in Normandy and subsequently the archbishop of Canterbury, who defended the doctrine of a transforming presence of Christ in the Eucharist. In his work, *On the Body and Blood of the Lord*, Lanfranc, explaining the Eucharist, appears to be the first to argue for a Aristotelian distinction between substance and accidence, that is, what something appears to be and what it is actually.

The fifth canon asserted the supremacy of the Roman Church over all other churches, specifically Constantinople—"which by the will of God holds over all others preeminence of ordinary power as the mother and mistress of all the faithful"— Canon 21 mandated annual confession of all sins by the laity to their priest and the performance of appropriate penances where required. Many of the canons regulated clerical conduct such as mandating celibacy (14) and prohibitions against drunkenness, games of chance, hunting, and visiting taverns (15). In a series of canons, clerics were forbidden to accept money for services (63–66). Larger churches, the cathedrals, were required to provide education for clerics and the poor (11). Canon 62 curtailed the use and misuse of relics; they were not to be sold or exhibited without papal approval. Canon 67 regulated the interest Jews could charge for lending money, and Canon 68 required Jews and Muslims to wear distinctive dress to demarcate them from Christians and not to appear in public during the celebration of Easter.

The Renewal of Monastic Spirituality

The Cluny Reform Movement contributed significantly to the revitalization of the papacy after the turbulence that accompanied the decline of the Carolingian Empire. Gifted and godly administrator-abbots accelerated reform and positively influenced a renewalist direction in the church.

Pontius, the seventh abbot of Cluny, however, allowed the monastic system to decline. Pontius was a nobleman of secular interests and executed his duties as an abbot so poorly that the pope asked for his resignation in 1122. The simplicity and piety of the clunaic monks was undermined by the acquisition of wealth. The combination of religious exercise and manual labor was abandoned; serfs were hired to work the properties, and the monks often slipped into a life of ease. The Benedictine ideal of poverty became difficult to follow and maintain. The direction of Cluny greatly improved under Peter the Venerable (ca. 1092–1157), though

troubles continued when Pontius returned and imprisoned him. With the pope's intervention, Peter regained his post and during his tenure the cathedral at Cluny was completed (1138), the largest in Christendom until the later renovations of St. Peter's Basilica in Rome.

Voices of protest against Cluny, particularly from the hermit Peter Damian, accusing the order of departing from the Benedictine Rule, resulted in 1098 in the beginning of a new monastic order, the Cistercians, the "White Monks," by Robert of Molesme (ca. 1028–1111) in Citeaux, France. Robert's passion was to practice an austere piety pursuing the contemplative life, self-sufficiency, and simplicity. Though he did not anticipate that the monastery at Citeaux would multiply into an order of monks, the Cistercians were recognized as such by Calixtus II in 1119.

Bernard of Clairvaux

The greatest of the Cistercians was Bernard of Clairvaux (1090–1153). Born of nobility at Fontaines, near Dijon, France, he was afforded a fine education so that he could pursue the study of the Scriptures. At the age of twenty-three, he and thirty companions entered the monastery at Citeaux. Three years later, he was directed by Abbot Stephen Harding to establish another monastery; he chose the town of Clairvaux. He located in an isolated, primitive place because he thought it promoted spirituality more than an urban area. During his career as abbot, he was heavily involved in papal politics and the theological disputes of his day, promoted mariolatry as a part of Cistercian spirituality, and used the rosary to assist the memory in prayer. By the time of his death, his order had grown to over 350 abbeys. Above all else, Bernard was committed to the pursuit of the contemplative life, a life devoted to God according to the narrow definitions of the Benedictine Rule.

Bernard's writings are voluminous, and he had a rare gift of preaching and speaking eloquence. The essence of Bernard's piety can be seen in the short treatise *On Loving God*. Love begins for Bernard within God himself who is a "Trinity of love." It was revealed in the eternal Son who became a human and a savior. Bernard said that human beings made in God's image and likeness possess, with God's gracious help, the capacity to love. He perceived spiritual maturity in four stages using the analogy of the human growth. Infants think and love only themselves, children love those nearest to them because of the care they receive, young adult love others for whom and what they are, and the mature love others because they are loved. Bernard wrote:

> At first a man loves himself for his own sake; he is flesh and able only to know himself. But when he sees that he cannot subsist of himself, then he begins by faith to seek and love God as necessary for himself; and so in this second stage he loves God not for God's sake but for his own sake. . . . When he has tasted and seen how sweet the Lord actually is then he passes to the third stage. Here he loves God for God's sake and not his own. And there he remains, for I doubt whether the fourth stage has ever been fully reached in this life by any man—the stage, that is, wherein a man loves himself only for God's sake.

"Indeed, he loved us while as yet we did not exist; he did even more, for he loved us when we were opposed to, and resisting him" (St. Bernard, *Of the Three Ways in Which We Love God*, 67).

"In taking flesh he condescended to me; in separating it from all stain of sin he consulted his own dignity; in submitting to death he made satisfaction to his Father and thus showed himself the kindest of friends, a prudent counselor, and a powerful helper. . . . Furthermore, that he might reconcile us with his Father, he bravely underwent death and overcame it, pouring forth his blood as the price of our redemption. If, then, the sovereign Majesty had not tenderly loved me, he would not have sought for me in my prison. But to this affection he joined wisdom to circumvent our tyrant, and patience to placate the just wrath of his Father" (St. Bernard, *Of the Three Ways in Which We Love God*, 68).

Bernard's works and sermons on redemption made him a favorite of the later reformer John Calvin. Calvin saw him as an Augustinian untainted by the subtle subterfuges of medieval teachers. This is dramatically evident in Bernard's work, *Treatise on Grace and Free Will* (1128), a book that plumed the depths of Paul's letter to the Romans.

"Free will enables us to choose, but it is grace that enables us to choose the good. Because we are granted the faculty of will, we are able to choose. To fear is one thing, but to fear God is another thing. To love indicates that we have affections. But it is only when these affections are associated with God that they become virtues. Thus to will is one thing, but to choose the good is quite another matter" (St. Bernard, *Treatise on Grace and Free Will*, 37).

Like Augustine, Bernard defended the freedom of the will, though in religious matters he defended the priority of antecedent grace.

> Without the two bound together, the work of salvation cannot be done. It is necessary to have a cause that produces it as well as a subject in which it is produced. God is the author of salvation. The faculty of free choice is the unique subject of it. God alone can give this, and free choice can receive it.

His point is that freedom is not opposed to inability, responsibility, or reward; however, it must be rooted in uncaused grace from the human perspective. Freewill enables people to make choices; grace allows them to make good choices.

"Grace begins all, and grace finishes all, but in such a

Vision of Saint Bernard with Saints Benedict and John the Evangelist (1504) by Fra Bartolomeo (1472–1517).

way that free grace works simultaneously with grace. So it is not a question of grace doing half the work and free choice the rest. Each does its own function in grace. Grace then does it all, but so does free choice. But there is this one qualification: Whereas all is done in free choice, all is done of grace" (St. Bernard, *Treatise on Grace and Free Will*, 51).

Victorines

Reflective of the piety that emerged in the twelfth century were also the Victorines, though their bent was towards a philosophical and educational approach to mystic contemplation. In 1108 William of Champeaux (ca. 1070–1141) retired from teaching at the cathedral of Paris and taught at the Abbey of St. Victor. He gathered a group of students and out of his teaching grew a mystic movement, founded by Hugh of St Victor, that increasingly opposed the rationalism associated with the scholastic movement.

The works of Richard of St. Victor (d. 1173) reflects the piety of the movement. Richard, a native of Scotland, came to Paris and joined the Augustinian canons under the supervision of Hugh in the abbey of St. Victor. He became a subprior in 1159 and prior in 1162 (a prior was a monk ranked next to the abbot). Richard stressed the intellectual life (for example, unlike Aquinas he believed that it was possible to prove the Trinity by the processes of speculative reasoning) as the ground for the contemplative life. The contemplative side of Richard was seen in two books, *The Twelve Patriarchs* and *The Mystical Ark*. In the first, contemplation was the crown of the virtuous life. In the second, he developed six different modes of meditation, likened to six features of the Ark of the Covenant God revealed to Moses (the wood, pure imagination; the overlay of gold and the crown, imagination and reason; the golden mercy seat, pure reason; and the two golden cherubim, two stages of intellectual insight). He wrote:

> The mode of contemplation which takes place by enlarging of the mind is accustomed to increase according to three stages: by art, by exercise, and by attention. We truly acquire for ourselves an art for something when we learn by accurate instruction or from wide investigation how something ought to be done. Exercise is when we put into use what we have received by means of art and make ourselves ready and prepared for carrying out such a function. Attention is when we pursue with zeal what we have accomplished with the greatest care. . . . And so by these three stages the inner recess of the mind is enlarged and made more capable for any learning and skill.

Mendicant Orders

The twelfth century brought enormous changes to Europe. A measure of political security returned with the emergence of nation-states; commerce began to flourish that fostered the growth of cities and the emergence of a middle class. With the shift from an agrarian, feudal culture to one of commerce and the trade, population shifted to the cities causing urban growth and rural decline and creating the urban poor. Further, popular unrest toward the church was manifest in the growth of what was considered heretical groups, such as the **Albigenses** and **Waldensians**. These factors brought something of a crisis in the monastic movement because their centers were rural. To meet the new pressing needs, a new monastic system emerged, the mendicant orders. **Mendicants**, earning a living by begging, hence the term, were bound secular priests. They identified with a religious order, but did not reside in the traditionally isolated monastery practicing a life of mystic solitude. Mendicants practiced austerity of life, refused ownership of property, and labored in preaching and teaching among the masses, as well as doing works of charity.

In 1274, Gregory X convened the Second Council of Lyon. It constituted a huge conclave of several hundred churchmen from bishops to prelates (it also included a delegation of Mongols). The council purposed to consider another crusade in the Holy Lands (something the Mongols wanted) and to heal the schism between the Western Catholic and Eastern Orthodox churches. It was also a reforming council. The council recognized four mendicant orders (Constitution 23): Franciscans, Friar Minors or Greyfriars; Dominicans, Friar Preachers or Blackfriars; Carmelites, Whitefriars; and Augustinians, Hermits of St. Augustine or Austin Friars. Members of these orders were called friars, not monks, because they lived in communities, not monasteries, and were distinguished by the color of their dress.

Franciscans

The Franciscans traced their order to Saint Francis of Assisi, Giovanni di Bernardone (ca. 1181–226). Though raised with financial advantages as the son of a wealthy Italian merchant, he found peace in the church and direction for life after hearing a sermon taken from Matthew

Saint Francis of Assisi by José de Ribera (1591–1652).

10:5. His would be a life passionately devoted to a replication of the life of Jesus, even to the receiving of the stigmata, the wounds of Christ.

Accompanied by friends, Francis journeyed to Rome in 1209 where Innocent III granted preliminary approval for a new order of priests (Honorius III officially sanctioned it in 1223). Rules drafted by Francis originally in 1209 (the first extant copy exists from 1223) governed the order of popular preachers. The tenth of the twelve rules reads:

> I admonish and exhort the brothers in the Lord Jesus Christ to beware of all pride, vainglory, envy, avarice, worldly care and concern, criticism and complaint. And I admonish the illiterate not to worry about studying but to realize instead that above all they should wish to have the spirit of the Lord working within them, and that they should pray to him constantly with a

pure heart, be humble, be patient in persecution and infirmity, and love those who persecute, blame or accuse us.

"Later, let them concede clothing of probation to the new brothers: Two tunics with hoods, belt and trousers, and a chaperon reaching down to the belt, unless the minister decides according to God that something else should be done. When the year of probation is over, let them be received into obedience, promising to observe this life and rule always; and, according to the command of the lord pope, it will be absolutely forbidden to them to leave the order, for according the holy gospel 'no one who puts his hand to the plow and then looks back is fit for the kingdom of God'" (*The Rules of St. Francis*, 2).

In 1212 a female order of the Franciscans, the Poor Clares, was founded. Fleeing from an unwanted marriage contract, Francis found a refuge for Saint Clare of Assisi (1194–1253) initially in a Benedictine nunnery and then into a house for female penitents where Agnes of Assisi, her sister, joined her. As more women joined them, accepting the austere life style, they were called "Poor Ladies." In 1263 the order was officially recognized by the church and took the name of its founder. Unlike the Greyfriars, Poor Clares lived in enclosures, did not travel, and devoted themselves to prayer.

An example of Franciscan piety and achievement was the great scholastic, Bonaventura (ca. 1217–1274). He was Italian by birth, and while in the faculty of arts at the University of Paris, he joined the Franciscan order, studying theology under Alexander of Hales. He taught and studied for the doctor in theology (1253–1257) when he was elected minister general of his order. As a theologian, he was faithful to his Augustinian heritage as well as to that of Anselm though he had little sympathy for the new Aristotelian rationalism of the scholastics.

Bonaventura wrote three works that are considered masterpieces: *Life of St. Francis*, *The Soul's Journey into God*, and *The Tree of Life*. In the *Soul's Journey*, the stages of the soul's progress are first, contemplation upon the physical universe and the human soul as a mirror to revealing God and leading to God through the humanity of Jesus (an emphasis on the humanity of Jesus was distinctive of Franciscan spirituality). Second was the intellectual phase, which leads to the mystical ecstatic sphere and the third stage was where the soul was ravished in the contemplation of the love of God. Of this final stage he wrote:

But if you wish to know how these things come about, ask grace not instruction, desire not understanding, the groaning of prayer not diligent reading, the Spouse not the teacher, God not man, darkness not clarity, not light but fire that totally inflames and carries us into God by ecstatic unctions and burning affections (7.6).

The *Tree of Life*, typical of Francis of Assisi's stress on the imitation of Jesus, was a meditation in which the reader was invited to picture a tree whose roots are watered by four rivers. The tree and garden was the church whose nourishment was supplied by God. Twelve branches extend from the trunk with leaves and fruit. The leaves are medicine to prevent and cure illness; the fruit nourishes faithful souls. The twelve branches are segments of Christ's life: birth, ministry, passion, death, exaltation, and glorification. Each branch or facet of Christ's life calls for meditation.

Dominicans
Dominic (1170–1221), a Spaniard, who was on a journey into France, was shocked when he saw evidence of a proliferation of heretic sects, mostly Cathari, sometimes called Albigenses. Since many of the heretics seemed to be well educated, he saw the need for more educated preachers. Because of the famines that had devastated his homeland, Dominic had to forego his studies in deference to the poor, but

now he determined to improve the education of others.

> "In this way our holy father, standing erect, bowed his head and humbly considering Christ, his Head, compared his lowliness with the excellence of Christ. He then gave himself completely in showing his veneration. The brethren were taught to do this whenever they passed before the humiliation of the Crucified One in order that Christ, so greatly humbled for us, might see us humbled before his majesty (Saint Dominic, *Nine Ways of Prayer*, 1).

Dominic founded an order that emphasized educated preachers. In 1215, he and a few followers established the order in Toulouse and secured papal approval at the Fourth Lateran Council from Innocent III. Besides education, the rosary is often associated with Dominic. Some suggest Dominic received it from the Virgin Mary in a 1208 vision, but others dispute this and say that the origins are in the thirteenth century. Devotion to the rosary became a characteristic of Dominican piety (original rosaries had 150 beads and were used in the repeating of the 150 Psalms).

Carmelites

There is little available on the origins of the Carmelites or Augustinians. The Carmelites appear to have originated in Palestine in the twelfth century, though records are not available to verify the claim. Hermits living on Mount Carmel, after the manner of the prophet Elijah, founded the order, according to tradition. The order received papal approval in 1216 by Honorius III. It began as a contemplative order and became a mendicant order in 1245. The Augustinians trace their origins to Augustine of Hippo, but there are not direct linkages. They developed in 1256 from a merger of four hermitic groups under the approval of Alexander IV (the Hermits of Tuscany, 1244; Hermits of John Bonus,1217; Hermits of Brettino, 1227; and the Williamites, 1211).

The Emerging Dispute: The Eastern and Western Churches

The unity of the catholic churches, the one visible body of Christ, ended in the eleventh century, though the seeds of division permeated the churches from the fourth century. In a sense, the separation of the churches began even before Constantine moved his capital to Constantinople in 330. The prevalence of Latin in the West, but Greek in the East, at times, led to communication difficulties. The Eastern approach to the perception of realities through the lens of Platonic dualism versus the Western attachment to philosophical realism resulted in differences of scriptural interpretation and the priority of certain doctrinal issues.

An example of early tensions among the churches was the day for celebrating Easter, the Quartrodecian Controversy (the term indicates the number fourteen and specifically has to do with the issue of the day of the celebration of the events of the Jewish **Passover** as it relates to the Christian celebration of the Easter event). The general Eastern custom was to observe Easter according to the Julian calendar developed in the Roman era. The Western custom was to observe Easter according to the Gregorian calendar, and specifically on Sunday, not Friday, emphasizing the resurrection rather than the crucifixion. Between the two calendars is a discrepancy of several days. The tensions became so divisive that Victor I of Rome, acting as the head of all the churches, excommunicated the **Quartrodecians** in the final years of the second century. At the Council of Nicaea (325) the churches agreed formally that Easter would be celebrated on Sunday, the first Sunday after the spring equinox since the two calendars differed. However, this did not settle the issue and others developed, and the separation of churches was further perpetuated when Theodosius I placed the church under two administrative heads in 395, a bishop in the West and a patriarch in the East. This often led to bickering, particularly during the great ecumenical councils, as to priority among the churches.

5.4. THE HISTORY OF THE ORTHODOX CHURCH: AN EASTERN PERSPECTIVE

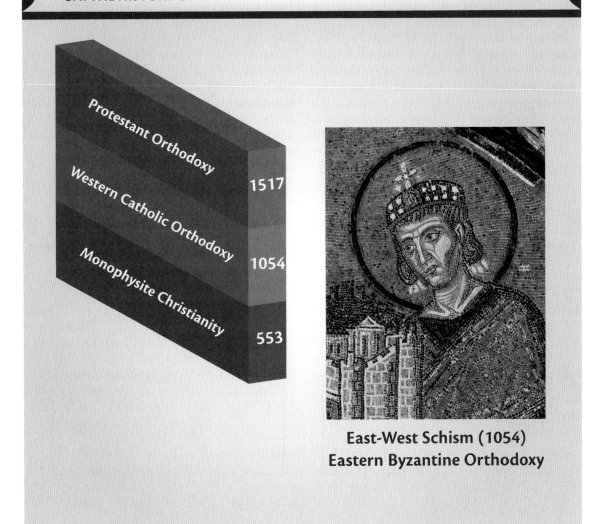

Protestant Orthodoxy 1517

Western Catholic Orthodoxy 1054

Monophysite Christianity 553

East-West Schism (1054)
Eastern Byzantine Orthodoxy

Monophysite Controversy

The earliest permanent division of the church was brought about over the **Eutychian** or **Monophysite** Controversy of the fifth and sixth centuries, causing dissolution of communion for thirty-five years (482–519). Felix III of Rome claimed that Acacius, patriarch of Constantinople, was soft on the Monophysites, sending a letter to Constantinople ordering him to appear in Rome. Acacius imprisoned the delegates and mutual ostracisms followed.

Icons

While the issue of the use of icons—representations of Christ, the Virgin Mary, and the apostles (not so much statuary)—caused considerable disruption in the Eastern churches,

Invitation to Church History: World

it did not have that effect in the West. The Second Nicaea Council in 787 resolved the conflict by making a distinction between veneration and worship. John of Damascus (ca. 676–749) argued, "What the Scripture is to those who can read, the icon is to the illiterate." Upon Charlemagne's insistence, the Western churches prohibited icons during his reign and adopted the council's finding after his death. The issue, however, did not provoke a schism; it was a case of the supremacy of state over the church.

Supremacy, Authority, and the Filoque Controversy

Tensions during the pontificate of Nicholas I (858–867) with patriarch Photius brought a second schism in 866–879. Nicholas, seeking to buttress papal supremacy, opposed the appointment of Photius and secured his excommunication in 863; Photius deposed Nicholas in 866. The primary issues seemed to be three: papal claims to supremacy; authority over churches in the Balkans, southern Italy, and Sicily; and the **Filioque Controversy**.

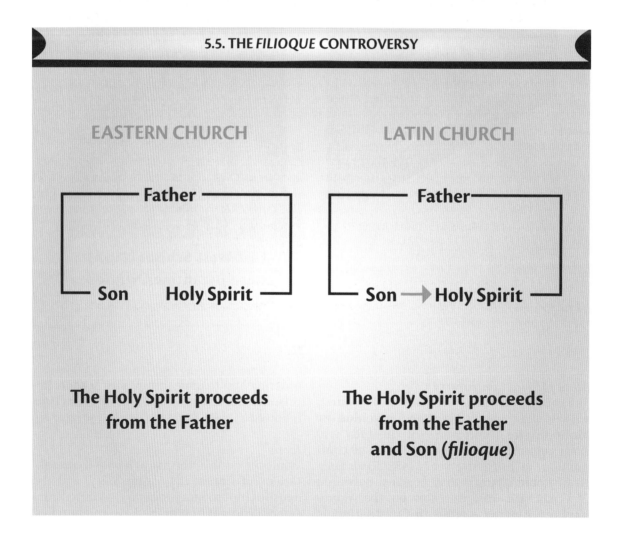

5.5. THE *FILIOQUE* CONTROVERSY

EASTERN CHURCH

Father
Son   Holy Spirit

The Holy Spirit proceeds from the Father

LATIN CHURCH

Father
Son → Holy Spirit

The Holy Spirit proceeds from the Father and Son (*filioque*)

The second of the issues involved a dispute over jurisdiction of churches, Constantinople basing its claim on Justinian's conquests in the sixth century. The third was more complicated in that it involved both a theological issue and the issue of the authority of creedal affirmation in the churches. The root of the later controversy was rooted in the findings of the Synod of Toledo in 589 that declared that the Holy Spirit was sent forth by the Father and the Son (the doctrine of double procession, the Spirit also precedes from the Son). Consequently, the synod amended the ecumenical Nicaea/Constantinople Creed of 381 by adding three words, "and the Son."

Photius centuries later denounced the West for desecrating the creed (obviously a reflection on the assertion of papal authority). The West argued that creeds are secondary sources of authority in the churches to the sacred writings; the East affirmed that all instruction given to the churches by the sacred Scriptures or other sources within the church, such as teachers or councils, was part of the authority of sacred tradition and inviolate. Tradition was the totality of authority-sources within the church and the church defined tradition.

The simmering, though often acrimonious, exchange of words reached a climax in the eleventh century. Leo IX (1002–1054), a Gregorian reform pope, sought to bring southern Italy and Sicily under his jurisdiction by military intervention. Having been crushed, and temporarily made a captive, he retaliated by sending legates to Patriarch Michael Cerularius (ca. 1000–1059), withdrawing the title of ecumenical bishop from him, and demanding that Roman supremacy be recognized. Mutual excommunications followed. Theoretically, union was achieved after the Crusaders sacked Constantinople in 1204 and again at the Second Lyon Council in 1274, but both were of short duration. In 1965 John Paul II and Patriarch Athenagorus of Constantinople nullified the mutual excommunications, paving the way for what may eventually be a healing of the schism.

The Eastern Orthodox churches, or, more accurately, the Orthodox Churches, claim that they collectively are the true heir of the ancient churches, not the Western (Roman) Catholic Church nor the Protestant churches. The Orthodox Church is actually composed of fourteen or so autonomous and self-governing churches, often defined along ethnic or na-

5.6. AUTHORITY DEBATE: SPLITTING OF THE CHALCEDONIAN CATHOLIC CHURCH

The Monophysite Catholic Church	The Eastern (Byzantine) Orthodox Church
553 ──────────────▶	1054
The Chalcedonian Catholic Church	The Western Catholic Church

tional lines (for example, the Syrian Orthodox Church, the Antiochean Orthodox Church, and the Greek Orthodox Church). Within the Orthodox community four churches rank first in honor (Constantinople, Alexandria, Antioch, and Jerusalem) with the Patriarch of Constantinople alone receiving the title of "Ecumenical" or universal, though he does not function in the authoritative role as the pope of Rome. The patriarch does not have the authority to impose his views on any of the churches (his authority is akin to that of the Archbishop of Canterbury within the Anglican community). The unity in the Orthodox Churches is a shared commonality of faith and the sacraments.

The Crusades

Though there have been many religious/military endeavors over the centuries to stamp out threats to the churches, the term *crusade* generally refers to those efforts between 1095 and 1291 to gain access for penitential pilgrims to holy sites in the Near East endangered by Muslim incursions. A crusader was one who took a vow, which was symbolized by a cross and confirmed by a military trip to Jerusalem.

Seljuk Turks, a Sunni Muslim dynasty that dominated the Middle East and Central Asia from the eleventh to the thirteenth centuries, controlled the Holy Land. They captured Baghdad in 1055, defeated a large Byzantine army in 1071, seized Jerusalem in 1076, and neared Constantinople, capturing Nicaea in 1092. The general peace that had allowed pilgrims to access holy sites, since the first Muslim conquest in the seventh century, came to an end. It was against this new, aggressive expression of Muslim faith that the first crusade was formed, not so much to establish a kingdom but to negotiate access to Christian pilgrimage sites. Later, the crusaders faced the **Mamelukes**, a slave class brought from the Caucasus to serve in the Seljuk armies. Over time, they came to power because of their prominence in the army. They gradually assimilated the Seljuks and ruled until the **Ottoman Turks** came to power in the sixteenth century.

At the same time, the church in the West was awakening from the disastrous consequences that accompanied the devolution of the Carolingian empire. The Cluny Reform Movement instilled new life and vitality to the papacy. The creation of new political alliances brought the birth of nation-states, the end of feudalism, the promise of economic growth through the trades, an emergent middle class, and a population shift to burgeoning cities. With new financial resources, a renewed papacy, and compliant European rulers, the distressful news about Jerusalem by Emperor Alexius Comnenus (1048–1118) could be addressed.

Urban II (1042–1099) aroused support for the first crusade with a speaking tour throughout France, hoping to reunite Christendom, eliminate the Seljuk threat, and establish papal supremacy. He was particularly successful with his stirring rhetoric at the Council of Clermont (1095) where he urged noblemen to lead the fight to reclaim Jerusalem for the penitential pilgrim. He promised a reward that the medievalist yearned to achieve. "All who die by the way, whether by land or by sea, or in battle against the pagans, shall have immediate remission of sins. . . Let those who have been serving as mercenaries for small pay now obtain the eternal reward." The same kind of affirmation occurs in the tenth canon of the First Lateran Council (1123).

"For effectively crushing the tyranny of the infidels, we grant to those who go to Jerusalem and also to those who give aid toward the defense of the Christians, the remission of their sins and we take under the protection of St. Peter and the Roman Church their homes, their families, and all their belongings, as was already ordained by Pope Urban II" (First Lateran Council, 1123, Canon 11).

First Crusade

The initial crusade had two phases. In the first, the Western army was composed of a large group of disorganized commoners, not military types, under the direction of Peter the Hermit and Walter the Pennyless. Upon entering Seljuk territory, this army was annihilated. A second army of trained soldiery followed and was able to capture important cities such as Nicaea, Antioch, and Jerusalem. The crusaders, "those who bear the cross," ruthlessly and indiscriminately put the inhabitants of Jerusalem to the sword and established a Latin kingdom composed of four subkingdoms governed by victorious dukes and princesses (the kingdoms of Antioch, Edessa, Jerusalem, and Tripoli).

Second Crusade

In the second crusade (1145–1149), the Turks recaptured Edessa, the outer perimeter of the Latin kingdom. The endeavor resulted in no gains in the East, though in the West crusaders captured the city of Lisbon. The great Cistercian, Bernard of Clairvaux, promoted this crusade, regretted its failure, and was appalled by the barbarous treatment accorded the Jews, just as in the prior crusade.

Third Crusade

The third crusade (1187–1192) was sparked by the annihilation of a massive crusader army at the Horns of Hittin near Tiberias and the recapture of Jerusalem by Saladin. The stunning report of these matters brought about the "Crusade of the Kings," a joint military adventure by Frederick Barbarossa of Germany, Richard the Lionhearted of England, and Phillip II of France. Again, the campaign met with little success and enormous brutality. Frederick drowned before engaging in a significant battle; Richard captured Cyprus and massacred the population; Richard and Phillip captured the fortress at Acre, but Philip then returned to Europe; and Richard assaulted Jaffa successfully, but he did not attack Jerusalem, fearing that he could neither capture it, or keep

A Crusader castle from the twelfth century in Byblos, Lenanon. Courtesy of Peripitus.

it. On his return to Europe he was captured by the king of Germany and held for ransom.

Fourth Crusade

Innocent III promoted the fourth crusade (1202–1204) with the intent of invading Egypt and then the Holy Lands. To do so, the Venetians were hired to transport the crusaders by sea, but they had their own agenda. The crusaders attacked the city of Zadar on the Adriatic coast instead and then proceeded to Constantinople where they devastated the city and established a Latin Kingdom (1204–1261).

Fifth Crusade

The fifth crusade (1217–1221) ended in defeat of an entire army in an attempt to capture Cairo.

Sixth Crusade

The sixth crusade (1228–1229) was more of a diplomatic mission than military conflict. Led by Frederick II of Germany, crusaders failed to conqueror Egypt; however, Frederick through negotiations gained control of Jerusalem, Bethlehem, and Nazareth (Muslims retaining dominion over the temple mount, the Dome of the Rock, and Al-Aqsa).

Seventh Crusade

When the Turks regained control of Jerusalem in 1244, the seventh crusade was launched (1248–1254), but it failed to accomplish any military objectives. The same fate befell crusaders in 1270 and 1271–1272. The crusader period ended in the Holy Lands when Acre fell to the Turks in 1291.

Other Crusades

In this era, there were numerous other **crusades** in Europe, as well as against invading Muslims in the Balkans and plundering Mongolians. The two most heralded of these crusades were the ill-fated "Children's Crusade" and the Albigenses crusade in France. The first

of these in 1212 was actually composed of wandering groups of poor peasants. None made it to the Holy Lands, and many either died along the way or were sold into slavery by greedy merchants. Only a few returned.

The second of these was a series of engagements (1209–1255) against a heretical, antiestablishmentarian sect that grew to significant numbers and influence in southern France, the Albigenses. Known also as the Cathari, "The Pure," this group appears to have adopted a dualistic concept of antimaterialism and spiritual perfectionism. The Council of Toulouse in 1119 sought the help of the state to quell them (the initial line of dealing with them was to send Cistercian and Dominican preachers to persuade them). Innocent III declared a crusade against them at the Fourth Lateran Council in 1215. The Albigenses were liquidated, and in the process thousands lost their lives, great fortifications were destroyed, and even the dead were exhumed and desecrated.

Effects of the Crusades

Though the crusades often revealed religious zeal at its worse, they had a profound influence. The crusaders became exposed to an intellectually and scientifically advanced culture and brought many of its advances back with them. Islamic culture had made superb accomplishments in mathematics (algebra), optics, architecture, and engineering in its great learning centers at Baghdad, Damascus, Cairo, and Cordova. Islamic scholars rediscovered the study of Aristotle (such as Averroes [1126–1198], called by some the father of secular thought in the West, as did the greatest Jewish scholar of the era, Moses Maimonides [1138–1204]). This rediscovery of Aristotle facilitated the development of Western universities and the Renaissance of the fourteenth and fifteenth centuries. The possibility of trade with distant places such as Asia brought a world of new commodities that changed the diet (spices) and redefined wealth (ivory, jade, and diamonds). Horizons were broadened and human potential greatly expanded. Sadly, the introduction of gunpowder would change how war was conducted.

The Crusades also gave rise to various organizations, such as the Knights Hospitallers or the Order of St. John founded in Jerusalem in 1080 to care for the needy. In the first crusade, the Order of St. John became a military organization charged with the care and protection of the Latin Kingdom. In facilitating their work, these knights constructed the great fortresses at Acre and Belvoir. The Knights Templar was founded in the first crusade as well and tasked with providing safety for pilgrims to Jerusalem. The large red cross they wore on their chests distinguished them. These knights proved to be a proficient military force. The vast majority of people in this order were noncombatants whose work was comprised of supporting the Latin Kingdom, including the building of fortresses (for example, Latrun and Ailit). A third order, the Teutonic Knights (1226) built the huge fortress at Montfort, though their presence in the Holy Lands was brief.

Other positive contributions that arose from the crusade era were the stalling of the Muslim and Mongolian threats to Europe and significant advances in the field of nursing and hospital care. The era inaugurated a time of the greatest expression of papal supremacy, though it came at the expense of alienating the Eastern churches after the conquests of Constantinople in 1204.

From a religious perspective, the crusades caused the proliferation of relics, with zealous crusaders bringing them back to enhance the prestige of the churches. Beginning in the fourth century, Christians prized relics (e.g., pieces of the cross, the swaddling clothes, the shroud that wrapped Jesus's body, the blood that he shed) that were often associated with miracles such as healings.

The indulgence system was elaborated and defined to promote the crusades. The system was justified in the thirteenth century this way: Christ's death obtained a treasury of merit for the forgiveness of sins; access to this abounding merit had been given to the church; and the church, given the care of souls, could dispense this grace through its official offices. The church promised the benefits of this additional grace to those who would venture out on a crusade, to parents and families of crusaders, and to anyone who offered support in any way. Sadly the crusades were the occasion for theological drift in the churches, a departure from the supremacy of unmerited grace to a belief that merit and grace were available on demand based on mere sincerity and a willingness to be culturally religious and outwardly conforming.

The darkest side of the crusades was the treatment of subjected peoples. Often the crusaders acted more like murderers, thugs, and robbers than those commissioned with the blessing of heaven to accomplish good. Their record of wanton destruction of fellow Christians in the sacking and looting of Constantinople, the brutalities extended to Christian heretics such as the Albigenses, and the massacres following military victories, such as the butchery at Antioch and Jerusalem, found a parallel in their treatment of the Jews who did not oppose them in Europe but sided with the Muslims in the defense of Jerusalem, fearing Christian mistreatment.

The councils of the church paint an **anti-Semitic** portrait that may have spawned mistreatment of the Jews. The Third Lateran Council (1179) prohibited Christians from working for Jews or Jews for Christians; in matters of court "the evidence of Christians is to be accepted against Jews in every case" (Canon 26). The Fourth Lateran Council (1215) required identifiable dress for Jews, contriteness at Easter, and punishment for those who would blaspheme Christ ("We command that such impudent fellows be checked by the secular princes by imposing them proper punishment so that they shall not at all presume to blaspheme Him who was crucified for us" [Canon 68]). In the first crusade, Jewish homes were ravaged, synagogues destroyed, and many killed. In Worms in 1096, for example, 800 Jews were taken from their homes and murdered; many in fear chose suicide. Similar atrocities occurred at Speyer, Mainz (Mayence), and in Cologne by Enrico, a German count, who was described in Jewish contemporary literature as "that Enrico the wicked, the enemy of the Jews." There were exceptions (the Jews would call them the "righteous Gentiles"), such as Bernard of Clairvaux who pled for their safety in the second and third crusades, as well as the Knights Templars. Bernard, for example, asked, "Is it not a far better triumph for the Church to convince and convert the Jews than to put them all to the sword?"

GLOSSARY OF TERMS

Albigenses: a neo-gnostic/Manichean sect of the twelfth and thirteenth centuries originating in Albi, France. Critical of the established church of the day, they were severely persecuted beginning in the reign of Innocent III and destroyed.

Anti-Semitism (Anti-Semitic): a prejudicialist view, expressed in hostility and hatred, against the Jewish race.

Benedictine Rule: a set of precepts developed by Benedict of Nursia in the sixth century to govern monastic communal life under the authority of an abbot.

Carolingian Kingdom: a large empire that emerged gradually out of the Frankish tribal kingdom consolidated by Clovis I reaching its apex of power and influence in the eighth and ninth centuries under the ruler of Charlemagne its capital was at Aachen.

Cluny Reform Movement: a reforming movement within the Catholic Church of the eleventh century in the monastic community that emerged in Clungy, France. It proved a corrective to the church that had degenerated into a dark nadir of moral, political, and social confusion. The Clungy Movement became so influential that it was able to secure the highest office in the church in Hildebrand, Pope Gregory VII (1073–1085).

Counts (Countess): a title indicating a person of aristocratic nobility. In the Middle Ages it generally designated a person under grant rule by a king of a territory with a kingdom. The term could also imply a military commander.

Crusades (Crusader): normally the term is used to identify a series of European military endeavors between 1095–1291 to interface with Muslim Arabs to recover access to the Holy Land to allow access for religious pilgrims and in the process secure a Latin kingdom. However, there were numerous religious military interventions in the later medieval period against not only Muslims, but supposed heretical groups such as Albigenses and Waldensians.

Dukes: a title of political rank only secondary to that of monarch. In the Middle Ages dukes were governors over provinces or territories.

Eutychianism: a fifth-century attempt to explain the relationship of the humanity and deity of Christ in the incarnate state. Eutychians argued that Christ was of two natures, human and divine, but they existed in a compound unity of a single nature. Condemned at the Council of Chalcedon (451), the persistence of the view in monophysitism led to the first permanent schism in the professing church.

Filioque Controversy (Filioque Clause): the term literally means "and the son." The dispute emerged between the church in the West and East over the authority of the creeds. Can a creed be amended? The catalytic issue was an addition to the Nicene Creed by the western church at the Synod of Toledo (589) stating that the Son, as well as the Father, sent the Spirit (called the doctrine of procession). The Eastern churches argued for a single procession, the western churches double. This was amount the issues that brought about the schism of 1054 creating a West Catholic Church and an Orthodox Church (Eastern).

Mamelukes: an Egyptian slave-class of Turkish background peoples that rose to political power and inaugurated a period of Muslim-Mameluke control over Palestine and Syria from 1250–1517. They successful opposed the Khan invasions from the East as well as the Catholic Crusaders from the West. Their political power declined with the emergence of the Ottoman Empire that control Palestine until the installation of the British Mandate in 1917.

Margraves: a medieval title for a hereditary office that involved military jurisdiction and protection of a region or province. In sixteenth-century Germany, it had lost its military nuance and became a title for a higher class of nobility or lords, higher than a count (*Graf*) and lower than a duke.

Magyars: a tribal people from the East, the Hungarians who settled in the fifth century settled south of the Caucasus Mountains on the Don River. In the ninth century they settled in the Danube River region, claiming land formerly in the Carolingian Empire.

Mendicants: the term means "begging," indicating those who sustain their living through the benevolence of others. In a religious context, it indicates religious groups or orders that exist through charity so that in the belief that such a lifestyle is deeply spiritual, they invest their energies in the service of others through care and preaching. The largest mendicant orders in the Roman Catholic community are the Dominicans and Franciscans.

Monophysitism (Eutychianism): an attempt in the fifth-century Catholic Church to explain the relation of the deity of Christ to his humanity in the incarnate state by arguing an amalgam of the two characteristic sets into a third combination of the two. Condemned at the Council of Chalcedon (451), the view persisted in segments of the Christian churches in the East (Egypt, Ethiopia, Armenia, Lebanon), becoming known by this nomenclature. It, too, was condemned as heterodox at the Council of Constantinople in 553 leading to the first permanent schism in the professing church.

Ottoman Turks: a Turkish-speaking people of Islamic faith that emerged as a ruling class gaining hegemony over the Seljuk Empire in the thirteenth century and governed the empire for over six hundred years. The Ottomans, expanding their lands captured Constantinople in 1453, destroying the last vestiges of the Roman Empire. They expanded the rule into the Holy Lands from 1517 until 1917.

Passover: The great Jewish festival that celebrates the deliverance through blood-covering and miracle from Egyptian bondage in the fourteenth century BC, the grandest of miracles described in the Old Testament and a shadow of the true Passover Lamb who was sacrificed to bring deliverance to his people by becoming the true sacrificial lamb.

Quartrodecians (Quartrodecian Controversy, Easter Controversy, Passover-Easter Controversy): a term, derived from a Latin word meaning "fourteenth," applied to those Christians in the early church who followed the Jewish festival calendar and celebrated the crucifixion of Christ on the fourteenth day of the first month (Nisan) in the Jewish calendar, the day of Passover. There is evidence that this was the pattern of the churches into the fourth century until the time of John Chrysostum, bishop of Constantinople. The ecumenical Council of Nicaea (325) declared that Sunday following the Passover should be the day of celebration.

Simony: the practice, all too frequent, on the late medieval church of the buying and selling of ecclesiastical, spiritual offices. The term is derived from the biblical account of Simon Magnus who sought to purchase religious privilege (Acts 8). This moral and religious abuse proved a precipitating cause for the Roman Catholic and Protestant reformations in the sixteenth century.

Subdeacon: an office within the Roman Catholic community, the lowest of the sacred ordinations. The function of a subdeacon is to carry the chalice of wine to the altar, make preparation for the Eucharistic ceremony, and read the Scriptures. The office appears to have emerged in the medieval period.

Waldensians: an early protest movement founded by Peter Waldo in the twelfth century in northern Italy that was heralded by later Protestants as a precursor to the Reformation because they criticized the morals and teachings of the medieval Catholic Church. The Waldensians stressed the importance of the Bible and preaching much in the tradition of Wycliffe of England and Huss of Bohemia, though Waldensians were much earlier. Condemned by the Fourth Lateran Council (1215) under Innocent III, they were subsequently severely persecuted. In the Reformation era, the Waldensians joined the Calvinist tradition of Protestant reform through the work of William Farel, Calvin's early coreformer in Geneva.

Chapter 6 Outline

Chapter 6 Objectives

- That the reader will identify the causes for the emergence of scholasticism

- That the reader will describe the influence of scholasticism on Christian thought

- That the reader will describe the institutional, spiritual, and doctrinal issues within the late medieval church

- That the reader will identify major forces for change within the late medieval church

- That the reader will describe the influence of Renaissance thinking on the approach to understanding Christian truth

CHAPTER
6

THE LATE MEDIEVAL PERIOD
(1200–1500)

T HE PRESENCE OF POLITICAL stability, the increase of economic prosperity, and the broadening world of Europeans through contact with the Muslim culture served as catalysts for change in Europe. Towns grew, trade flourished, guilds emerged, and a middle class sprang forth. In this context, particularly with the contact of churchmen with Islamic and Jewish scholars, European churchmen became aware of the deficiencies of monastic training as preparation for transcultural dialogue. Further, in the twelfth and thirteen centuries, Western Christians discovered the importance of the works of Aristotle. The contribution of the Greek philosopher was not so much in the realm of what can be known as in the arena of how one comes to know; that is, in method.

The Church, the Emergence of the Schools, and Scholasticism

The method of knowing in the monasteries emphasized the importance of faith and the spiritual disciplines. In short, monastic education prepared a priest to operate in the world of belief through simple faith and trust, a world where truth was assumed rather than argued. Monastic training involved an education that assumed what the truth looked like and perpetuated that knowledge in a monologic, discoursive fashion; it favored learning through hearing rather than discussion, questions, and contradictions. Monastic education in method was indebted to Plato. Truth came from above and from above it should be sought. This meant to the medievalist trust in the magisterial function of the church and abbot.

The methodological emphasis derived from **Aristotle** through contact with learned

Jewish and Islamic scholars, however, focused on process as well as outcomes. The scholastics sought to live in a world of profound religious beliefs, but teach and defend them through logic, grammar, and dialectics as opposed to decree.

Scholastic education generally took two forms. The first is called *questions*. Here a question would be posed, alternative answers set forth with arguments and counterarguments, and a solution proposed by a single teacher. The second is called a *summa*, or summary (e.g., Aquinas's *Summa Theologica*). The method

was the same as in the first approach, but the scope of it was broader; it covered the range of all possible questions and functioned as a summary of theological knowledge (it might be called "systematic theology" though the method would differ emphasizing the process as well as the conclusions. In this the scholastic employed the lecture method in proposing and resolving questions and the disputative method of engaging the student in the process).

Scholasticism may be defined as the educational approach adopted by churchmen between the high Middle Age and the emergence

A painting of a fourteenth-century university lecture by Laurentius de Voltolina. Courtesy of the Yorck Project.

of the **Renaissance**, between the twelfth and fifteenth centuries in western Europe.

First, it entailed a new environment for education, the school or classroom. In this instance, the focus shifted from education in the monasteries, the primary educational centers of the early medieval period, to schools that were attached to prominent churches, cathedral schools that became the seedbed for the universities.

Second, it involved the emergence of the professional classroom teacher or scholar (hence the term *scholasticism*). This teacher or scholar devoted himself to the preparation of questions,

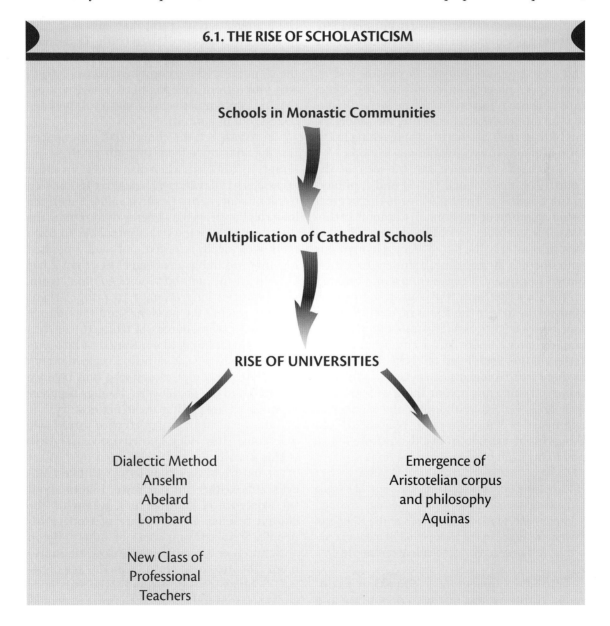

6.1. THE RISE OF SCHOLASTICISM

Schools in Monastic Communities

Multiplication of Cathedral Schools

RISE OF UNIVERSITIES

Dialectic Method
Anselm
Abelard
Lombard

New Class of
Professional
Teachers

Emergence of
Aristotelian corpus
and philosophy
Aquinas

executed learning through this new method, and assembled materials to facilitate learning.

Third, it gave rise to a restructuring of educational curriculum, the return of the ancient *trivium* (the study of grammar, logic, and rhetoric) that lead to the *quadrennium*, the arts (arithmetic, geometry, music, and astronomy).

Fourth, it brought about the textbook, summaries of what could be known to introduce students to a discipline (in this case theology). The earliest textbooks, Lombard's *Four Sentences* and later Aquinas's *Summa Theologica*, had an enormous influence in solidifying the structure of church doctrine, as these were the elemental introductions. In a sense, the scholastic era birthed the systematizing of teaching in the form of all-encompassing summarizations.

Lombard's influence can be seen in the Fourth Lateran Council (1215) and Aquinas's in the Council of Trent (1543–1564), the great defining moment of Roman Catholic orthodoxy. For example, to obtain degrees (bachelor's or master's [the latter being synonymous with doctor's at that time]), students were required to present a commentary or summary on the *Four Sentences* (the education from the study of the arts to the status of "doctor" was a fourteen-year process). Erasmus bitterly complained later, "There are as many commentaries on the 'Sentences' of Petrus Lombardus as there are theologians. There is no end of little *summas*, which mix up one thing with another over and over again and after the manner of apothecaries fabricate and refabricate old things from new, new from old, one from many, and many from one."

> "'Scholasticism,' if the term has any definable meaning, simply stands for the theology and philosophy and subsidiary disciplines of the schools of western Europe in the great period of medieval culture" (E. Fairweather, *A Scholastic Miscellany*, 18).

The development of a **Christian rationalist tradition** was met with opposition and concern from some within the church. The locus of the concern was the fear that the inadequacies of the fallen mind to perceive and comprehend divine truth would be used to diminish the voice of divine revelation, thus leading to a perversion of the faith. The "tradition of the mystics" argued that the injection of reason in the quest for truth could lead to the depreciation of truth; that faith and trust in authority was the path to truth. To Bernard of Clairvaux (1090–1153), it was the saint, not the disputant, who comprehended God. Truth was found from this perspective in the inner life, the contemplative life, not in rational discourse, but in humility.

In retrospect, the church had experienced the detrimental effects of both of these attempts to find truth when disjoined from either approach to knowledge. Each alone has proven to be of short-term, positive value, but in the long run has proven an enemy of the truth. The discovery of how the two approaches to truth methodologically worked out and operated together profitably has been easier than it has been to use the method to come to "final" truth. The centuries-long attempt to bring "Athens and Jerusalem," the academy and the church, together as twin sources of truth, to use Tertullian's metaphor, had continued to be a precarious balancing act, at best. Unquestionably, the greatest attempt at defining that balance was found in the medievalist Thomas Aquinas; however, we are getting ahead of the story.

The scholastics struggled with three basic questions: How does knowledge exist? How is this knowledge to be searched out? What is the nature of this knowledge? Unlike moderns, scholastics did not raise doubts about the existence of knowledge; it was what the church teaches as the legate of God to his people. Scholasticism was not inherently an antichurch or an antisupernaturalistic movement. The medieval period was the age of belief! Scholastics' approach to the existence and nature of universal truths reveals significant differences though the fact and shape of those truths was often consistent. The nature of the existence of truth and the proper methods of demonstrating them concerned the scholastic.

Three approaches were taken: Realism, Moderate Realism or Conceptualism, and Nominalism. The various approaches to truth reflect no minor issue; they deal with the nature of reality and authority. Realists, generally the earliest scholastics such as Anselm, argued that reality was in the perceived external object (the church is real and has authority, *ante rem [prior to objects]*). They were called dogmatists and their task was to demonstrate from the truth already revealed the rational coherency it.?

The Nominalist approach is more akin to modern rationalism and is reflective of the later scholastics. Truth, from this perspective, is not a matter of declaration and blind obedience; it is a matter of reason. Nominalists, such as Ockham and Biel, reversed the order of the Realists. Reality exists in the mind, in thought, prior to dogmatic statement. Reason or acts precede reality and define it, *post rem (after mental objects)*. For example, reason defines justice; justice does not precede reason. They were "proto-rationalists," yet in a world that affirmed the possibility of truth. Luther was trained in this tradition and that, in part, explains his detachment from the traditions of the church.

Conceptualists and Moderate Realists, such as Aquinas and Abelard, sought a position between the two (*in rem* [reflected in objects]). Reality exists in the finite because there is a concept that exists prior to it and behind it. Ideas are not beyond existence (Realism), nor are they in the mind (Nominalism); they are in the realm of experience, the realm of nature. Moderate Realists agreed with the Nominalist in method, not conclusion; they agreed with the Realist in conclusion, not method.

It could be argued that the "father of scho-

lasticism" is Aristotle, the root of the Western rationalist tradition as Plato is the root of the mystical, pietistic, or idealist tradition. Perhaps, as has been observed, the progress of Western thought is somehow footnoted on these two distinctly different approaches to the possibility of truth. This is true if the focus is upon metaphysics and epistemology, the quest to discover certain assumptions and the methods to be employed to find truth.

Anselm of Laon

The actual "father of scholasticism," as a medieval movement, is, most likely, Anselm of Laon (d. 1117). Anselm of Laon was a teacher and writer widely known for his biblical and exegetical studies. What makes him a scholastic is the employment of a particular method in his task of searching the Scriptures and in his teaching. Instead of taking the text at face value, he used rational analyses to resolve problems he discovered and that led him to systematizing his conclusions.

Anselm of Canterbury

Anselm of Canterbury (ca. 1033–1109), the archbishop of Canterbury, is often revered as the fountainhead of the movement because of the use of a rational approach to the defense of theology, principally the existence of God and substitutionary atonement. Anselm was born in Burgundy, northern France, and eventually entered the Benedictine monastery at Bec in Normandy where he later served as abbot. The acquisition of lands by the abbey in England following the Norman Conquest in 1066 brought him to England where he was well received. In 1093, he reluctantly accepted the pastoral office of the archbishopric of the oldest church in the country.

Anselm, a Benedictine monk born around AD 1033 in northern Italy, is considered the founder of scholasticism. As abbot of Bec in Normandy, he made the abbey a formidable center for learning across

Europe. As Archbishop of Canterbury, he came into conflict with Kings William II and Henry I of England regarding lay investiture and clerical homage to kings. Anselm was exiled by both kings. His writings constitute the first of the scholastic theologians recognizing the value of both faith and reason to absolute truth. He posited the satisfaction theory of the atonement whereby God's justice and man's debt was satisfied by the sacrifice of the God-man Jesus Christ by proposing the question, why the God-Man

Anselm believed that the duty of reason was to demonstrate the coherency of the faith; reason did not function to determine the faith (the Nominalist approach), nor was it the interplay of the perceiving mind and the objective truth (moderate realism). Once truth is found, it should be demonstrated through the second

Anselm of Canterbury as archbishop. Depiction in an English glass window of nineteenth century. Courtesy of Bocachete.

part of the *trivium*, logic. He wrote in the form of a prayer,

> I am not trying, O Lord, to penetrate thy loftiness, for I cannot begin to match my understanding with it, but I desire in some measure to understand thy truth, which my heart believes and loves. For I do not seek to understand in order to believe, but I believe in order to understand. For this too I believe, that "unless I believe," I shall not understand.

For Anselm, what appears to be true from a rational viewpoint should be held with speculative, though not necessarily skeptical, uncertainty, if it is not declared so by explicit statements of Holy Scripture.

Among his several works, two might be drawn out that reflect his theological interest and his methodological approach. The first is *Proslogion*, a work in which Anselm presented the ontological (Kant was the first to actually use the term) argument for the existence of God. Anselm made the point that humans have a perception of something greater than themselves, a sense of something beyond the limitations of their capacities (something more than an abstract, mental existence), and this universal perception can be used to demonstrate the biblical truth of the existence of God (the argument from being). Ideas must come from somewhere. If an idea of something beyond our smallness exists, then, it had to have an origination beyond finitude. Therefore, because we have this inherent thought, it had to come from beyond us. This alien beyondness for Anselm was the God of the Bible. The essence of his argument is better stated in his own words:

> Clearly than which a greater thing cannot be thought cannot exist in understanding alone. For if it is actually in the understanding alone, it can be thought of as

6.2. ANSELM AND THE MEANING OF THE ATONEMENT

Substitution

"A curse for us"
Galatians 3:13

existing also in reality, and this is greater. Therefore, if that than which a greater thing cannot be thought is in the understanding alone, this same thing than which a greater cannot be thought is that than which a greater can be thought. But obviously this is impossible. Without doubt, therefore, there certainly exists, both in the understanding and in reality, something than which a greater thing cannot be thought.

A theological work that illustrates his method is the much celebrated, *Why the God-Man*? The fact that he posed this treatise in the form of a question, rather than a statement, demonstrates his attachment to scholasticism.

The genre of the work is dialogical, a series of queries and answers, inquiries by an imaginary interlocutor and responses by the author.

Anselm explained that Jesus had to be both God and man, because the accomplishments of his death demanded it to be so logically. He argued that the place to begin in rationally understanding what the Bible clearly states about Jesus was with man's hopeless bondage to sin (he writes, "You do not know what an awful weight sin is."). Since God, being just and true, cannot remit the punishment due for humankind's dereliction having promised his wrath, justice must be forthcoming. The only solution was that a human should appease God, suffering the penalty of death for infraction, but none can render to God the infinite honor due him. Simply stated, man cannot appease God, and God is under no obligation to be appeased. Because all of this is true, Anselm believed that the divine and human Christ could be rationally demonstrated.

> "Therefore, consider it settled that, without satisfaction, that is, without voluntary payment of the debt, God can neither pass by the sin unpunished, nor can the sinner attain that happiness, or happiness like that, which he had before he sinned; for man cannot in this way be restored, or become such as he was before he sinned" (Anselm, *Why the God-Man?* Book 1.19).

> "If it be necessary, therefore, as it appears, that the heavenly kingdom be made up of men, and this cannot be effected unless the aforesaid satisfaction be made, which none but God can make and none but man ought to make, it is necessary for the God-man to make it" (Anselm, *Why the God-Man?* Book 2.6).

> "Moreover, if these two complete natures are said to be joined somehow, in such a way that one may be Divine while the other is human, and yet that which is God not be the same with that which is man, it is impossible for both to do the work necessary to be accomplished. For God will not do it, because he has no debt to pay; and man will not do it, because he cannot. Therefore, in order that the God-man may perform this, it is necessary that the same being should be perfect God and perfect man, in order to make this atonement. For he cannot and ought not to do it, unless he be very God and very man. Since, then, it is necessary that the God-man preserve the completeness of each nature, it is no less necessary that these two natures be united entire in one person, just as a body and a reasonable soul exist together in every human being; for otherwise it is impossible that the same being should be very God and very man" (Anselm, *Why the God-Man?* Book 2.7).

Peter Abelard

A second early scholastic, one who may serve as an example of monastic fears of rationalistic tendencies, is Peter Abelard (1079–1142). Born in France, he pursued the life of a student and was trained at the cathedral school of Notre Dame in Paris under Anselm of Laon. He was a brilliant academician and enjoyed immense popularity, though he entitled his autobiography, *History of My Calamities*. In the context of teaching, he met Heloise, the niece of canon Fulbert, and his affection for her grew into a secret relationship and a child. A secret marriage was arranged when the pregnancy was discovered so that his career in the church could continue. Uncle Fulbert made life so miserable for Heloise that the couple agreed that she should flee Paris. In rage, thinking that Abelard had sent his niece away to be rid of her, Fulbert and several accomplices attacked and castrated Abelard. Heloise subsequently became a nun and Abelard pursued a career as a scholarly monk. Their exchange of letters—over 113 have been discovered from the early years of their affair—is unique in the annals of that genre. They are buried beside each other at the Oratory of the Paraclete, the Benedictine monastery Abelard founded in Ferreux-Quincey, France.

Abelard's most celebrated work is *Sic et Non*, a collection of 158 questions with the divided opinions of the church fathers. It is a clear example of the dialectical method, questions that he may have prepared for student disputations. The premise of his work can be gathered from the following statement, "Doubtless the fathers might err; even Peter, the prince of the apostles, fell into error: what wonder that the saints do not always show themselves inspired? The fathers did not themselves believe that they, or their companions, were always right." Because he did not resolve the questions, he has been frequently charged with error, and his book has been placed on the church's index of prohibited books.

When Heloise entered the convent to pursue the life of a nun, Abelard entered the Abbey of St. Denise. Abelard, with an abrasive attitude, had conflicts with the monks, so he

Statue of Abelard at Louvre Palace in Paris by Jules Cavelier (1814–1894). Courtesy of Jastrow.

left and returned to teaching. In that capacity he wrote a work on the Trinity, *Theologia*. Bernard of Clairvaux was appalled that Abelard would seek to invade the realm of mystery and faith with the tools of logic and the dialectical method. Abelard's optimistic view that the proper use of logic could untangle mysteries, coupled with a demeaning stridency of attitude, led to the charge of **Sabellianism** (he failed to find satisfactory unity in the Godhead by confusing functions that distinguish the persons with inherent properties). At the Synod of Soissons (1121), Bernard pursued his condemnation, though Abelard likely was not at the synod, and Abelard was forced to consign his work to the flames. A second work on the Trinity increased Bernard's ire. Bernard was influential in the calling of the Synod of Sens (1141), where he secured Abelard's condemnation. When Abelard faced his opponent, he immediately appealed to Rome. Bernard then secured a papal condemnation. Abelard died at Cluny on his way to Rome to gain a hearing on the charges against him. He appears unquestionably a brilliant intellect, but flawed with a haughty character and rational arrogance.

Peter Lombard

Of the early scholastics, the influence of Peter Lombard (ca. 1095–ca. 1160) is unsurpassed in the development and systematizing of church doctrine, particularly as it relates to the nature of grace and function of the sacraments. Lombard, though from a poor Italian family, was afforded a good education that took him to Paris where, through the recommendation of Bernard of Clairvaux, he was introduced to the canons of Saint Victor and taught in the cathedral school of Notre Dame. It is likely that he heard Abelard lecture and mastered his techniques. He excelled as a master teacher of theology, and Paris became, with Oxford, the centers for academic, religious education. He was later ordained a priest in the church and rose through the ranks of the clergy to become the bishop of Paris shortly before his death.

Invitation to Church History: World

Born in Italy around AD 1095, Peter Lombard was a contemporary of Bernard of Clairvaux and following studies in France became a professor at the cathedral school of Notre Dame de Paris. A brilliant scholar, he wrote commentaries on the Psalms and Letters of Paul though his most renowned book was the theological textbook *The Four Sentences*, the most commented-upon book after the Bible in medieval Christian literature. He influenced Thomas Aquinas, Martin Luther, and John Calvin. Lombard became bishop of Paris shortly before his death in 1160.

Lombard was a voluminous commentator on the Holy Scriptures, particularly the Psalms and the epistles of Paul. However, his enduring legacy was the *Four Sentences* (ca. 1150), the

first major attempt to bring together the texts of Scripture and the insights of the fathers into a comprehensive arrangement of theological subjects in a systematic fashion. His masterpiece became a standard textbook in the universities until the sixteenth century, enjoying a popularity and influence second only to the Bible in those centuries. Lombard follows the divisions of John of Damascus's *Fount of Knowledge* and cites patristic passages largely from *Sic et Non* and the *Decretum* of Gratian. The volume begins with the doctrine of the Trinity (Book I) and proceeds to the doctrines of creation and fall (Book II), Christ and redemption (Book III), and the sacraments as means of acquiring the grace of Christ for salvation (Book

6.3. THE PETER LOMBARD—THE SEVEN SACRAMENTS EXPLAINED

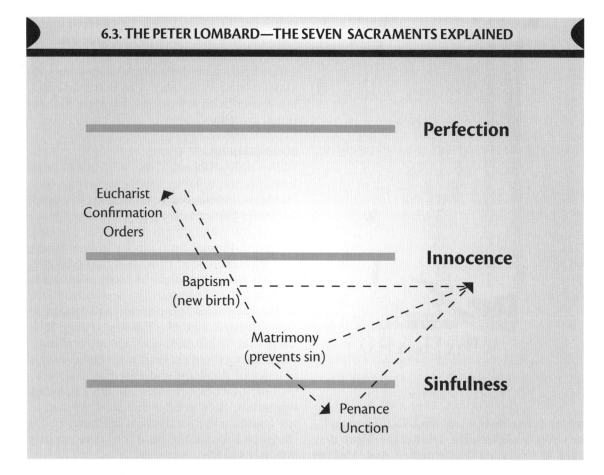

Invitation to Church History: World

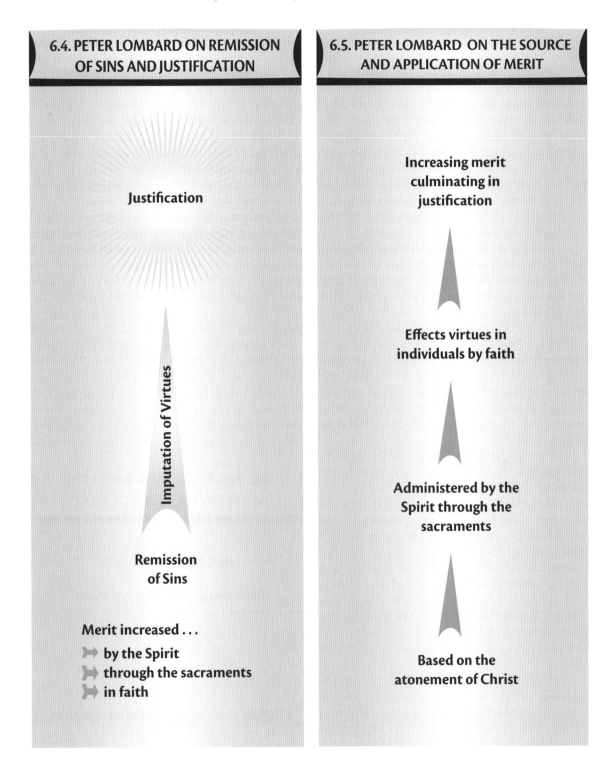

6.4. PETER LOMBARD ON REMISSION OF SINS AND JUSTIFICATION

Justification

Imputation of Virtues

Remission
of Sins

Merit increased . . .
- by the Spirit
- through the sacraments
- in faith

6.5. PETER LOMBARD ON THE SOURCE AND APPLICATION OF MERIT

Increasing merit
culminating in
justification

Effects virtues in
individuals by faith

Administered by the
Spirit through the
sacraments

Based on the
atonement of Christ

IV). Unlike Abelard in *Sic et Non*, Lombard answered many of the disputative questions that he posed. The shape of late medieval theology is a contribution of the *Sentences*. So important was this work that all the major scholastics that followed him felt compelled to write commentaries on the *Sentences*. In the emergent universities, students could obtain a bachelor's in Bible, as preparation for the priesthood, and then pursue a higher degree, Bachelor of the Sentences, by writing a commentary on Lombard's work, as preparation for teaching. Lombard made no claim to originality.

In Book I, the discussion of the existence of God, Lombard made extensive use of the cosmological argument, though he argued that the doctrine of the Trinity was dependent on divine revelation. His explanation of the Trinity brought the charge of quaternity (On this charge the Fourth Lateran Council [1215] exonerated him of all error [Canon 2]), perhaps an evidence of the influence of Abelard's over-extension of rationalism. Most importantly, Lombard argued that divine grace in predestination and election is antecedent to human merit.

In Book II, Lombard showed a dependence on Hugo of St. Victor (c. 1096–1141). He rejected the notion of the transmission of sin through procreation and asserted the will of humans was free to act, desire, or choose without any influences or necessity on the ground of reason, though he rejected Abelard's belief that true virtue was determined by purity of human motives rather than the criteria of the holiness of the character of God. Mankind is born into this world guilty because of the first Adam, but grace liberates the will enabling it to do well and merit the additional increment of divine grace.

In Book III, Lombard set forth his understanding of Christ (he was accused of the heresy of **Nestorianism** but exonerated) and the atonement of Christ. His view seemed influenced by Abelard though he did not as intricately connect Christ's death with a display of moral, melting love; further, he seemed not to have been influenced by Anselm in this regard. Christ's death was a triumph of divine love and grace. In Christ's death, a treasury, a storehouse, of redeeming grace was procured.

Book IV deals with the means of the acquisition of the purchased grace of Christ, the sacraments of the church. Underlying the discussion of the sacraments were several assumptions. First, and following Augustine, the path to heaven was the way of progressive justification, or gradual degrees for the sanctified that can lead to a final definitive justification, likely following some time in purgatory. Hence, the medievalist embraced the idea from Augustine that righteousness was infused as a gradual, experiential process, not imputed as a definitive, passive action by God. Second, Christ's death made salvation possible by providing the grace of salvation, but it did not procure it. Third, the saving merits of Christ could be increased and decreased depending on degrees of faithfulness and disobedience. And fourth, the church was the divine dispenser of the grace of Christ. Lombard's most significant contribution to

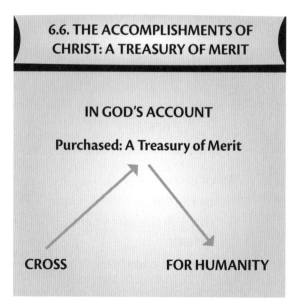

6.6. THE ACCOMPLISHMENTS OF CHRIST: A TREASURY OF MERIT

IN GOD'S ACCOUNT

Purchased: A Treasury of Merit

CROSS   FOR HUMANITY

the emergence of classic Roman Catholic theology is his articulation of soteriology. Lombard taught a salvation procured by the grace of God though he was not as clear that it was granted by grace apart from antecedent or simultaneous merit.

The means of the acquisition of incremental, justifying grace were the sacraments. Lombard limited the number of the sacraments to seven, which was affirmed at the Council of Florence in 1449, the first council in the church to do so, and at the great Council of Trent (1543–1563) that defined Roman Catholic dogmatic orthodoxy.]

Lombard taught that the guilt of Adam's first transgression was removed by the sacrament of baptism. The sacrament absolution did not redeem in itself, unless a person died before they committed personal sins. The baptized were rendered innocent and, given Lombard's definition of free will, had the ability to remain in that state or fall from it as all people do because of the force of uninfluenced voluntarism and/or uninfluencing bad examples.

Three sacraments functioned to acquire positive grace that could eventually merit final justification: confirmation, the Eucharist, and holy orders. Confirming the faith of the church was to be done once, holy orders were restricted to those who take up special function in the church as leaders, and the Eucharist was a daily repetitive sacrament of cleansing from venial sins. Lombard did not use the term *transubstantiation* to describe a miraculous change in the bread and wine (he used the term *conversion*). Lombard conceived the eucharistic ritual as a reenactment of Christ's once-for-all bloody sacrifice, obviously in some type of realistic, actual, symbolism meriting the distribution of a portion of the merit that Christ procured at Calvary. The sacrament of matrimony was viewed as preventative sacrament, a divine gift for those ungifted with chastity from falling into sin and losing grace.

Penance was often called the "second plank, to preclude the shipwreck of the soul. As baptism absolved the inherited guilt from Adam, penance restored righteousness to the soul caused by voluntary disobedience thereafter. Extreme unction, commonly called "last rites," was the distribution of grace through the abundance of grace at the church's disposal in the priestly office when confession and penance were impossible.

As Lombard explained about the mercies of God, redemption was rooted in the uncaused grace of God, though it came in the form of initial grace that must be increased in order to reach the justified and glorified state. Salvation was based on the atoning work of Christ and his grace. This grace was the gift of the Spirit supplied through the sacred offices of the church and led to works of charity. Acts of charity led to merit and merit, when accrued in sufficient proportion, obtained the state of justification. Lombard taught a mysterious, mutual, and causative **cooperationism** that began in grace, proceeded through grace-inspired obedience, and ended in the merited gift of eternal life.

Thomas Aquinas

The greatest of the scholastics, and one of the greatest of the churchmen through the centuries, is the Italian Dominican Thomas Aquinas (ca. 1225–1274). He was born into the aristocratic class, began his education at the age of five, and at sixteen entered the University of Naples. Above the protestations of his family, he joined the Dominican order at seventeen and trained under Albertus Magnus (ca. 1206–1280) in Cologne and Paris. He began his teaching career in Cologne as a lecturer in 1248, having obtained the status of bachelor of theology. There he began a literary career that would be vast and influential. After obtaining the status of master of theology, he became a doctor of theology and lectured in Paris, Rome, and elsewhere. Besides a prodigious writing and teaching career, he preached often and was a trusted counselor to several popes and numerous churchmen. His influence has been greater than Lombard's; his *Summa Theologiae* replaced the *Sentences* and has been accorded a place of sacred honor and trust in his order and the church. The "Angelic Doctor," along with Augustine, are the most influential churchmen in the Roman Catholic community. According to Pope Leo XIII (14 August 1879):

> St. Thomas Aquinas may be said to have been present at all the Ecumenical

Councils of the Church. After his time, presiding as it were, by his invisible presence and his living teachings over their deliberations and decrees; but that greatest and most special honor was given to the Angelic Doctor at the Council of Trent, when, during its sessions, together with the Bible and the formal decrees of the Sovereign Pontiffs, the Fathers of the Council had the open Summa placed upon the altar so that thence they might draw counsels, arguments, and oracles. This was a singular honor and praise accorded to St. Thomas which was not given to any of the Fathers or other Doctors of the Church.

Thomas's writings have produced schools or traditions of thought throughout Christendom; his influence is felt in metaphysics, epistemology, theology, philosophy, and ethics. Generally, his works have been divided into four categories. The first are his commentaries that include works on various biblical books, works on Aristotle's writings, and commentaries on various church fathers' works, such as Lombard's *Sentences*. The second is a series of short treatises called *Opsucula*. The third contains questions for disputation, thus *Quaestio*, with a variety of possible answers and arguments for and against each view, and conclusions. The fourth are his great syntheses, the *Summa Contra Gentiles* and the *Summa Theologiae*.

Thomas Aquinas. An altarpiece in Ascoli Piceno, Italy, by Carlo Crivelli (ca. 1435–1495). At the National Gallery, London. Courtesy of the Yorck Project.

Born in Aquino Italy around AD 1225, Thomas Aquinas was a Dominican priest renowned for his influential natural theology and scholastic philosophy. Influenced initially in his youth by Aristotle and Maimonides, Aquinas went on to study in Paris. Sent to be a professor in Cologne, his failure in his first theological disputation earned him the name "dumb ox." Nevertheless, he went on in his graduate studies to write commentaries on Lombard's Sentences. His commentaries on philosophy and theology culminated in his *Summa Theologica* which influenced Western philosophy.

The *Summa Contra Gentiles* (1258–1264) appears to have been written—though there is considerable dispute—as an apologetic summa designed as a handbook to help Dominican missionaries who were preaching in areas (especially Spain) where they were in contact with people educated in Aristotelian philosophy. The master of the dialectical method employed the same method to answer the churches critics. Stated Aquinas:

> . . . I have set myself the task of making known, as far as my limited powers will

allow, the truth that the Catholic faith professes, and of setting aside the errors that are opposed to it. To use the words of Hilary: I am aware that I owe this to God as the chief duty of my life, that my every word and sense may speak of Him.

The book has been generally described as having two major parts, though it is in four books. The first, Books I–III, concerns truths that he believed about the Christian faith also available through human reason. Book IV concerns those areas for which the church is revelation-dependent or those things beyond the grasp of the dialectical approach (e.g., the Trinity, the incarnation, the resurrection, the

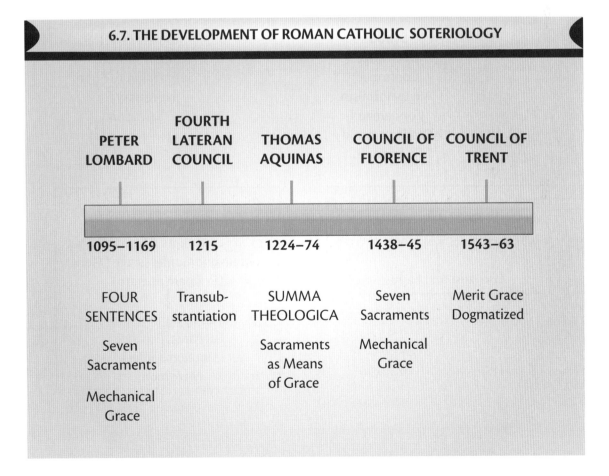

6.7. THE DEVELOPMENT OF ROMAN CATHOLIC SOTERIOLOGY

PETER LOMBARD	FOURTH LATERAN COUNCIL	THOMAS AQUINAS	COUNCIL OF FLORENCE	COUNCIL OF TRENT
1095–1169	1215	1224–74	1438–45	1543–63
FOUR SENTENCES	Transubstantiation	SUMMA THEOLOGICA	Seven Sacraments	Merit Grace Dogmatized
Seven Sacraments		Sacraments as Means of Grace	Mechanical Grace	
Mechanical Grace				

6.8. THE DOCTRINE OF SALVATION IN THE ANCIENT AND MEDIEVAL CHURCH

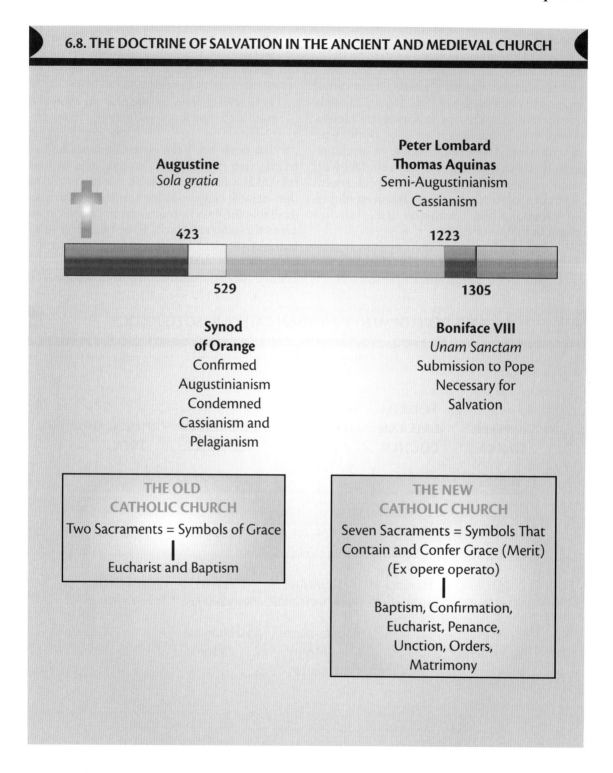

Augustine
Sola gratia

Peter Lombard
Thomas Aquinas
Semi-Augustinianism
Cassianism

423

1223

529

1305

**Synod
of Orange**
Confirmed
Augustinianism
Condemned
Cassianism and
Pelagianism

Boniface VIII
Unam Sanctam
Submission to Pope
Necessary for
Salvation

THE OLD
CATHOLIC CHURCH

Two Sacraments = Symbols of Grace

Eucharist and Baptism

THE NEW
CATHOLIC CHURCH

Seven Sacraments = Symbols That
Contain and Confer Grace (Merit)
(Ex opere operato)

Baptism, Confirmation,
Eucharist, Penance,
Unction, Orders,
Matrimony

sacraments). The two parts structurally divide in the same way: God as he is, God as revealed in action, and God as for his own glory. In the first part are Aquinas's celebrated proofs for the existence of God. It is clear that he was not a complete naturalist or rationalist. There were some Christian truths that we know only through revelation. In the *Summa Theologiae*, he wrote:

> The *Sacra Doctrina* (divinely inspired scripture) does not come within the philosophical disciplines that have been discovered according to human reason. Accordingly, there is needed another science divinely inspired beyond the philosophical disciplines . . . because man is ordained to God, to an end that surpasses the grasp of his reason (1–1.q.1.a1).

The role of reason was not to cause faith, but rather to put in order truths accepted on the basis of faith with a view to clarifying possible confusion. Since faith and reason were not antithetical or antagonistic, it was only when you had either false faith (incorrect religious claims) or false reason (illogical deductions or assumptions) that you had problems. Man lost the capacity to see enough sense in soteriological truths to properly follow the way of salvation. The fall did not destroy man's ability for rational thinking; sin did not reduce man to an animal. Nevertheless, the adamic effects of sin were significant enough to render it completely impossible for the human mind to, with sufficient certainty, appropriate the saving knowledge of God. Rational arguments were not able to overcome the effects of the fall. The theistic arguments for the existence of God, for example, created a general conception of God, but one not uniquely Christian. Christian theism was Trinitarian; Trinitarianism

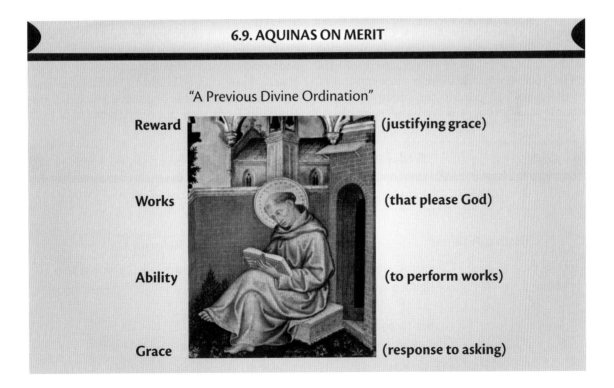

6.9. AQUINAS ON MERIT

"A Previous Divine Ordination"

Reward	(justifying grace)
Works	(that please God)
Ability	(to perform works)
Grace	(response to asking)

belonged to the category of the supra rational. Metaphysical truths could not be reduced to rational demonstration.

The *Summa Theologiae* was a huge work written with the intent of summarizing all of theology; Aquinas began the work in 1266 and it was incomplete at his death, though he seems to have discontinued the work a year prior and the speculative causes for the discontinuation are many. For those who have tried to work through it the purpose for writing is stunning.

> I have set myself the task of making known, as far as my limited powers will allow, the truth that the Catholic faith professes, and of setting aside the errors that are opposed to it. To use the words of Hilary: I am aware that I owe this to God as the chief duty of my life, that my every word and sense may speak of Him.

Of importance in tracing the theme of redemption through the history of our Lord's church, as well as history from its inception in the divine creation to its restoration in the divine recreation, was Thomas's understanding of the grace of God and the means of its attainment. Aquinas followed the same basic understanding of the redemptive process as Lombard, that is, sanctification preceded justification; however, Thomas was more elaborate and precise. Like Lombard before him, Thomas believed that humankind entered this world completely devastated by the inherited guilt of Adam. For the recovery of humankind, to save the soul, grace was required; grace could only find its origin in God, not humankind. The death of Christ and the mitigation of the just wrath of God were the actual causes of grace; Christ obtained grace through his sacrificial death for the human race. To participate in that grace, according to Thomas, the sacraments were important, for through them divine grace could be procured.

Sacraments, then, were spiritual remedies for the wounds inflicted on the soul by sinning. The first and principle cause of grace was God; however, the instrumental cause of grace was the sacraments. Says Thomas, "He cannot merit the first grace." A person could earn increments of divine grace though obtaining merit was not a work people could do without God's help. This was accomplished through cooperative grace. Divine grace led to charity, charity to merit, and merit to eternal life. "The meriting of eternal life depended principally on charity." Charity was not an increase of faith; it

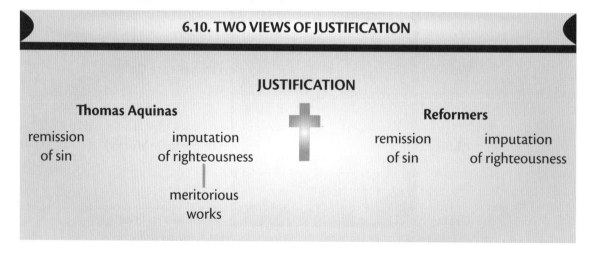

6.10. TWO VIEWS OF JUSTIFICATION

JUSTIFICATION

Thomas Aquinas			Reformers	
remission of sin	imputation of righteousness		remission of sin	imputation of righteousness
	meritorious works			

brought unformed faith to its true form. Faith was not the cause of charity for Thomas, it was the fruit of charity; charity caused unformed or implied faith to became a reality, though merit is always a secondary cause of grace ("a man merits an increase of grace by each and every meritorious action") Thomas, however, held to condign grace, grace based on divine justice, not congruous grace advocated by later scholastics, grace based on divine mercy. What made Thomas confusing was his adoption of Augustine's concept of justification as a process, a gradual infusion of saving grace: "Man is justified by faith, not in the sense that he merits justification by believing, but in the sense that he believes while he is being justified." This grace or merit was based on charity. Increased quantities of charity-based grace could be used to acquire greater degrees of merit.

The principal function of the sacraments was to effect greater degrees of union with Christ until union was realized in consummate justification. A way of viewing Thomas's understanding of the process of divine redemption is to see it in steps. The initial step is the unmerited infusion of divine grace at baptism that removes human guilt and renders one innocent though liable to voluntary misdeeds. The initial infusion of grace can be increased and decreased based on a willingness or unwillingness to seek the help of God through the means he has provided, the sacraments. This is the second step. The third step is eternal life cooperatively earned as a just due. Remission of sin through baptism, forgiveness without righteousness, leads to a life of the accumulation of grace, and a future justification in righteousness.

Albertus Magnus

There were other scholastics who held important teaching posts in the emerging universities throughout Europe. Albertus Magnus (ca. 1206–1280) has been recognized as the greatest German philosopher/theologian of the Middle Ages, the first to apply Aristotle's philosophy to Christian thought. He was recognized as one of thirty-three in Western catholic Christian histories to be accorded the title "Doctor of the Church." This Dominican scholar taught in several German cities before teaching in Paris where fellow Dominican Thomas Aquinas became his greatest student. Most of his works, which collectively encompassed thirty-eight volumes, were philosophical in nature, though he did write a summary of Lombard's *Sentences* and a *Summa Theologiae*.

Alexander of Hales

Like Albertus Magnus, Alexander of Hales (ca. 1183–1245), a Franciscan, was one of the first to grapple with the implication of Aristotle's work for Christian theology. In joining the faculty of the University of Paris in 1236, he formed a connection between his order and the school. He is credited with preparing the first substantive commentary on Lombard's *Sentences*, as well as a massive *summa theologiae*, called the *Summa of Friar Alexander*, that was unfinished at his death.

Roger Bacon

Roger Bacon (ca. 1214–ca1294), also a Franciscan, gained acclaim at the universities of Paris and Oxford (Franciscans were prohibited from the field of publications without the approval of the order, though papal approval could be secured at times). His interests focused on the sciences and linguistics, a major contribution being his attempt to articulate the scientific method.

Bonaventura

Bonaventura, John of Fidanza (ca. 1221–1274), was an Italian-born Franciscan who rose to the head of his order and was a cardinal in the church. After studies at the University of Paris, perhaps under Alexander of Hales, he became a lecturer on Lombard's *Sentences*. Philosophically, Bonaventura disagreed with Bacon and Aquinas and embraced a contemplative, platonic approach to knowledge more attuned to the Victorines and Bernard of Clairvaux. However, Bonaventura was a theologian, thought deeply, and employed reason in service of the faith. In his labors for the church, he was recognized for his effort at the Second Lyon Council in 1274 that effected a healing of the schism between Rome and Constantinople; at that council he died. His most heralded work, among the many, was his commentary on Lombard's *Sentences*.

John Duns Scotus

John Duns Scotus (ca.1266–1308), also a Franciscan, was born in England and pursued academic preparation at Oxford University. In 1302 he was a lecturer on Lombard's *Sentences* at the University of Paris from which he was dismissed for siding with Boniface VIII against Philip the Fair of France, but he later returned to continue his lectures. He died in Cologne where he was teaching. He is regarded as second only to Bonaventura in the Franciscan order, his metaphysical and philosophical thought exerting a deep influence on theological faculties across Europe until the French Revolution.

Scotus's unique contribution to theological development in the church was his defense of the Immaculate Conception of Mary. Most theologians, including Bonaventura, Bernard of Clairvaux, and Aquinas, did not embrace the sinlessness of the Virgin Mary because of the argument that the stain of original sin was universal and the death of Christ was viewed as the universal remedy. Since Mary was part of humankind, she could not have been born without sin. How could these be universal truths if one person was excluded? If sin was universal and the atonement was the universal remedy, Mary had to be born with original sin, or at least as the traditional argument was stated. Duns Scotus argued that the stain of original sin could be accounted as absent in Mary's case because the benefits of her son's death were applied to her in advance of her birth. Called the "marian doctor" for his defense of the Immaculate Conception of Mary and the "subtle doctor" for the intricacy of his argumentative abilities, Duns Scotus's view prevailed in 1854 when Pius IX, using his argument, declared as the dogma of the Roman Catholic Church that Mary was born without the stain of Adam's first sin.

William of Ockham

William of Ockham or Occam (ca. 1280–ca. 1348), a Franciscan, is considered among the most important scholastics. Born in England and trained at Oxford though he did not complete the master's degree, Ockham was one of the first medievalists to advocate a separation of church and state, as well as the development of the notion of property rights (Ockham argued that the church should not own property if they mean to follow Jesus and the apostles just as Saint Francis instilled in is followers. His views of these matters led to a clash with Pope John XXII, and he was later excommunicated from the church, though his nominalist approach to knowledge continued.

William spent the remainder of his days with a small band of Franciscan dissidents living in exile. He is generally known for the formulation of "Occam's (or Ockham's) Razor," the concept that if two postulations adequately defend a proposition, the simpler of them is to be preferred. Like the prominent scholastics, he produced significant works on logic, metaphysics, and theology.

It is in Ockham's understanding of grace and redemption that he greatly influenced the late medieval church (here you have a move away from Lombard and Aquinas), sometimes called "The Modern Way."

Ockham viewed divine grace through the lens of a reciprocal covenant between God and humankind. According to the covenant, God accepted our best human efforts, not because they were intrinsically worthy, but simply because he willed to do so. Justifying grace began by divinely

6.11. WILLIAM OF OCKHAM AND GABRIEL BIEL—THE STEPS OF SALAVATION

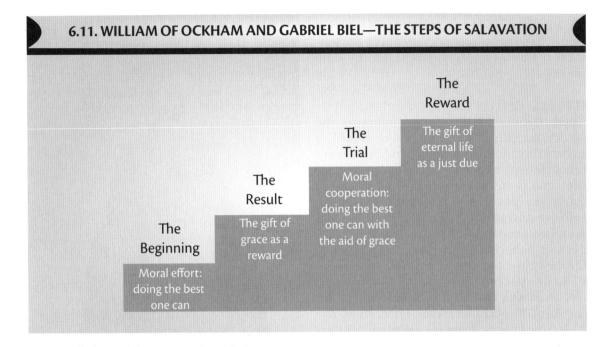

The Reward

The gift of eternal life as a just due

The Trial

Moral cooperation: doing the best one can with the aid of grace

The Result

The gift of grace as a reward

The Beginning

Moral effort: doing the best one can

ordained, unmerited self-assertion resulting in greater proportions of grace as a reward. The use of this grace, doing the best one could with it, led to the gift of eternal life as a just reward. Stated Ockham, "God will not deny grace to the man who does his best." Human works were not in themselves worthy of merit, but were so because God willed it so. According to Ockham, this approach to salvation preserved human freedom and responsibility. Acceptance by God was distinct from justification by God; the former could lead to the latter. It seems that the worst fears of Bernard of Clairvaux were incarnated in Ockham's defense of the biblical faith through a form of philosophizing that had more regard for the mind than the limitation Scripture imposes upon it. In Ockham was not the passive justification of Lombard and Aquinas; it was an active justification, which was part of the root thinking of Luther, Zwingli, Calvin, and many others in the sixteenth century.

Boniface VIII was the medieval pope who made the strongest ever claims to worldly and spiritual power

in his bull "Unam Sanctam" and was immortalized for his many feuds with Dante when the author in his inferno chapter in the book *Divine Comedy* portrays Boniface as destined for the eighth circle of hell where simony is punished.

The Late Medieval Church and Institutional Turmoil

The prominence and authority of the Catholic Church reached a zenith in the era of the great scholastics, the time of the crusading movements, and the political and ecclesiastical pontificate of Innocent III (1198–1216). After his pontificate the church began a precipitous decline that reached another nadir in the late fifteenth century. As scholars have analyzed the factors in this, one fact has been indisputable, the causes had come from mounting troubles within the church and disturbing events outside of it. The decline within the papacy can be illustrated by comparing the pontificates of two popes, Innocent III and Boniface VIII (1294–1303). Each claimed the highest prerogatives for the office, but only Innocent III could execute them. In Innocent there was a war of words, and the "sword" of church won. In Boniface, there was a war of words, but the state prevailed.

Boniface

Boniface came to the papacy following the abdication (1294) of the inept Celestine V, a hermit thrust into a world beyond his competence. Though qualified for the task of leading the church, he did not judge the changing times, the power of a growing nationalistic spirit or the strength of his opponents. His pontificate marked the beginning of a severe decline. Boniface, seeking to recoup prestige for the church, entered into political intrigue in Sicily, northern Italy, Denmark, Scotland, and France. In France, he clashed with Philip the Fair (IV) over two issues. First, Philip opposed the idea that the church should be exempt from French laws. He claimed that clergy should be tried in French courts for criminal behavior; the pope disagreed. Second, the king and pope clashed over the viability of taxing church property. Philip argued that the church had the benefits of public works endeavors such as roads, but did not contribute to the support of the state in such endeavors. Pursuant to the ongoing controversy, in 1296 Boniface issued *Clericis Laicos*, a papal bull denouncing the actions of the king. He accused the laity of high-handed treatment of the church and prohibited the exactions of Philip. The lack of revenues caused Boniface to inaugurate the Year of Jubilee in 1300, an event in which pilgrims could come to Rome to receive plenary forgiveness for sin and the canceling of punishments. Over 200,000 of the faithful descended on Rome bringing significant finances with them. Many surmised that it was more about greed than mercy! With the disagreements unresolved, Boniface issued *Unam Sanctam* in 1302, claiming sole supremacy in church and state:

Statue of Pope Boniface VIII at the Museo dell'Opera del Duomo in Florence, Italy. Courtesy of Sailko.

if the earthly power errs, it shall be judged by the spiritual power, if a lesser spiritual power errs it shall be judged by its superior, but if the supreme spiritual power errs it can be judged only by God not by man, as the apostle witnesses, "The spiritual man judgeth all things and he himself is judged of no man" (1 Cor. 2:15).... we declare, state, define and pronounce that it is altogether necessary to salvation for every human creature to be subject to the Roman Pontiff.

When tensions persisted, Boniface lost patience and excommunicated the king. Unlike Henry IV of Germany earlier, Philip was unaffected, except for the raising of his ire, and he had the pope imprisoned in 1303. After Boniface's death, Philip pressured his successor to bring

6.12. THE OLD CATHOLIC CHURCH AND THE ROMAN CATHOLIC CHURCH

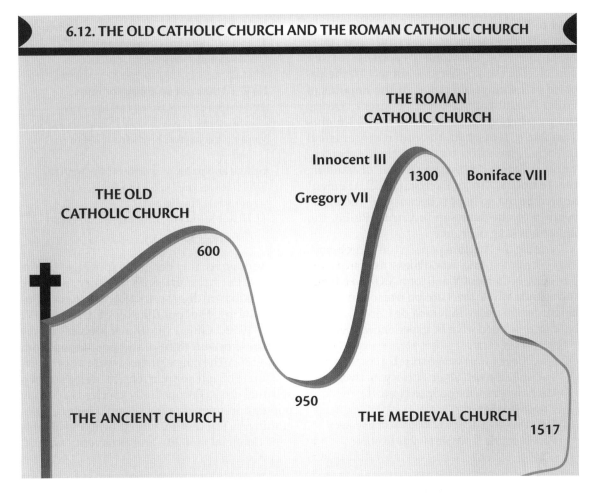

THE ROMAN
CATHOLIC CHURCH

Innocent III

THE OLD
CATHOLIC CHURCH

Gregory VII

1300   Boniface VIII

600

950

THE ANCIENT CHURCH

THE MEDIEVAL CHURCH

1517

heresy charges against him, but those were eventually dropped. (Dante would later place Boniface in hell as a result of various scandals.

> "That there is one holy, Catholic and apostolic church we are bound to believe and to hold, our faith urging us, and this we do firmly believe and simply confess; and that outside this church there is no salvation or remission of sins . . . we declare, state, define and pronounce that it is altogether necessary to salvation for every human creature to be subject to the Roman Pontiff" (Boniface VIII, *Unam Sanctam*).

Clement V

The tensions between pope and king of France had further ramifications. Not only had Philip secured a stunning victory over papal claims and aspirations, he dominated the church. Boniface's successor, Benedict XI (1303–1304), sought to continue his predecessor's claims in the issuance of *Unam Sanctam*, but his pontificate was brief and he was succeeded by Clement V (1305–1314), who capitulated his authority to Philip.

Clement, who was crowned pope in Lyon in 1305, moved the seat of the papacy from the Lateran Palace and Rome to Avignon in southern France, and it remained there with a momentary exception from 1309–1378. Reflective of the Jewish expulsion from the land to Babylon for seventy years, it has been dubbed "the Avignon captivity," and later by Luther "the Babylonian captivity" of the church. The papacy became subject to the caprice of the kings of France. At the impetus of Philip IV, and with Clement's consent, fearing the growing power and wealth of the Knights Templar of Jerusalem, the order was crushed in France, based on torture-extracted confessions of heresy. In the papal bull disbanding the Templars, *Vox in Excelso* (1312), Clement argued he did so in part because of "the intervention of our dear son in Christ, Philip, the illustrious king of France."

During the Avignon papacy, the church sank into corruption and worldliness as the popes, particularly Clement V and John XXII lived in extravagance while the Lateran Palace in Rome languished in decay. Raimond de Cornet, a troubadour, described what he experienced this way:

> I see the pope his sacred trust betray,
> For while the rich his grace can gain alway,
> His favors from the poor are aye
>   withholden.
> He strives to gather wealth as best he may,
> Forcing Christ's people blindly to obey,

> So that he may repose in garments golden.
> The vilest traffickers in souls are all
> His chapmen, and for gold a prebend's
>   stall
> He'll sell them, or an abbacy or miter.
> And to us he sends clowns and tramps
>   who crawl
> Vending his pardon briefs from cot to
>   hall—
> Letters and pardons worthy of the writer,
> Which leaves our pokes [pockets], if not
>   our souls, the lighter.
> (J. H. Robinson ed. , *Readings in European
> History*, 375)

Adding to the declining prestige of the papacy in the fourteenth century was the devastation of disease that swept across Europe during the pontificate of Clement VI (1342–1352). Called the **Black Death**, it may have destroyed a third of the population from 1347–1350. The consequences were a social catastrophe of epic proportions, as well as a deep spiritual crisis. Europe had experienced steady population increases for several centuries beginning in the tenth century, bringing significant financial stability and prosperity with it,

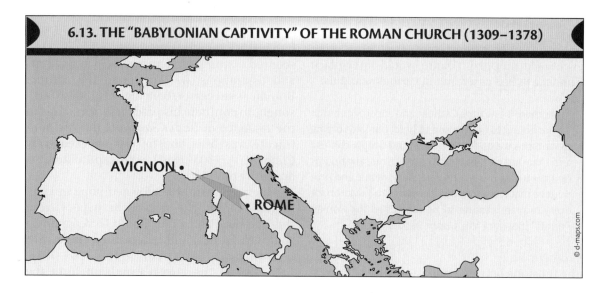

6.13. THE "BABYLONIAN CAPTIVITY" OF THE ROMAN CHURCH (1309–1378)

AVIGNON •

• ROME

© d-maps.com

but this ended in tragedy that some interpreted as having eschatological portent. It was a time when the church failed to fill the empty void of many seeking transcendental solace in a great era of despair.

Great Western Schism
The papacy was able to end its Avignon residence in the pontificate of Gregory XI (1370–1378), in part through the exhortations of Catharine of Siena (1347–1380), a mystic of the **Dominican tertiary**. Shortly after Gregory's return to Rome, he died and a dispute over succession plunged the church into a deeper crisis resulting from the loss of its moral and spiritual authority. With Gregory's death the **College of Cardinals**, largely composed of Frenchmen, elected an Italian to the highest office, Urban VI (1378–1389). The new pope proved noncompliant, as well as arrogant and imprudent. Before the Roman mobs could learn that the college had elected a non-Roman (he was from Naples), the College of Cardinals fled to Avignon for safety. In France, the college declared the election of Urban invalidated and chose Clement VII (1378–1394) as Gregory XI's successor (Clement was desig-

nated an antipope by the Roman Catholic establishment in Rome). In so doing the **Great Western Schism** divided the church, an era when two "vicars of Christ" emerged claiming singular authority.

The enormous lack of leadership in the church became tragically evident. The presence of two popes and two administrative centers became a huge burden in the mist of the growing penchant for elegance and grandeur in ceremony as well as a lavish lifestyle on the part of both pontiffs. With two popes, each excommunicating and thereby declaring the sacramental services of the other invalid, the question of who had possession of the keys to heaven and hell became uncertain. Further, national loyalties became strained without clear evidence of who was in control of the church. A lingering war between France and England, the **Hundred Years War**, only served to exasperate the issue.

Several solutions were envisioned to put an end to the problem. The theological faculty of the University of Paris was asked, but could not resolve the issue. A poll was taken of the revered and saintly in the church, but no majority vote could be achieved. Others felt that

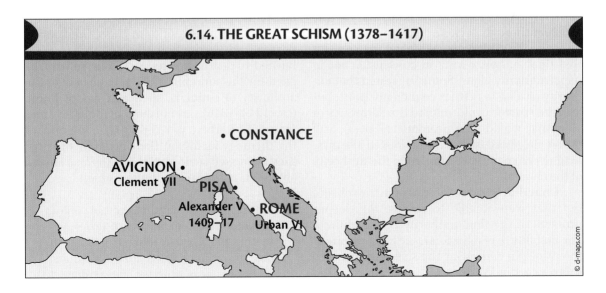

6.14. THE GREAT SCHISM (1378–1417)

CONSTANCE

AVIGNON
Clement VII

PISA
Alexander V
1409–17

ROME
Urban VI

© d-maps.com

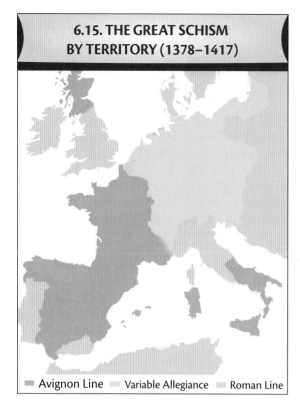

6.15. THE GREAT SCHISM BY TERRITORY (1378–1417)

■ Avignon Line ■ Variable Allegiance ■ Roman Line

initial attempt, however, made matters worse. Led by Jean Gerson (1363–1429), a member of the theological faculty at the University of Paris, and Pierre d'Ailly (1350–ca.1420), a teacher of Gerson, a bishop, and later a cardinal, a general council of the church was called to gather at Pisa in 1409. After the council convened, it promptly deposed the pontiffs, Gregory XII of Rome and Benedict XIII of Avignon, and elected Alexander V (1409–1410). However, neither of the deposed popes accepted the verdict of the council and continued in their offices, making three popes!

Conciliarists

Thinking that the failure at Pisa was rooted in a lack of political support, the Council of Constance convened in 1414–1418 to address the continuing schism. This time the council was called by Emperor Sigismund of the Holy Roman Empire and signaled the height of conciliar authority. The council deposed two of the popes and the third resigned leading the way for the appointment of Martin V as the singular head of an undivided church. Having ended the Great Schism, the council went on to matters of church reform. To radical voices that opposed the authority of council and the papal office, such as the now deceased John Wycliffe, Jerome of Prague, and John Huss, the council decreed condemnation (the latter two were burned to death as heretics). To those who argued for the supremacy of the papacy over the authority of councils, such as Giles of Rome (ca. 1243–1316), archbishop of Bourges, and James of Viterbo (ca. 1255–1307), a member of the theology faculty at the University of Paris, they expressed their sentiments in *Haec Sancta* (1415). In part, it reads that a council

both popes should resign and a new beginning made. Others suggested that the papacy should be abandoned entirely. The tack taken by most churchmen favored the working out of the problem through ecclesiastical councils. Such an approach inherently embraced the concept that final authority rests in consensus, not in papal authority alone. Some suggested that authority resided in neither council nor pope, but rather a stricter conformity to the Scriptures (a view that would gain prominence later). Still others suggested that authority rested in a mystical experience that transcends the authority of the church.

Conciliarists were able to heal the schism, but they were unable to resolve the deeper problem of the final authority in the church. The inability to resolve this issue became one of the principal causes for the sixteenth-century schism in the Western Catholic church. The

> legitimately assembled in the Holy Spirit, constituting a general council and representing the Catholic Church militant, it has power immediately from Christ; and that everyone of whatever state or dignity,

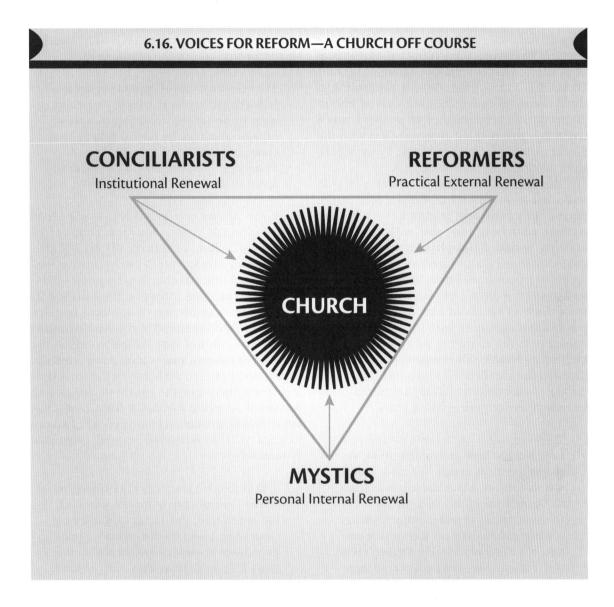

6.16. VOICES FOR REFORM—A CHURCH OFF COURSE

CONCILIARISTS
Institutional Renewal

REFORMERS
Practical External Renewal

CHURCH

MYSTICS
Personal Internal Renewal

even papal, is bound to obey it in those matters which pertain to the faith....

The outcomes of the council were not made public for some decades and not published until the sixteenth century. That coupled with the resurgence of papal supremacy made *Haec Sancta* inconclusive and ineffectual.

The Council of Constance mandated that the pontiffs call general councils periodically. Consequently, council convened at Pavia (1424), subsequently moved to Siena, and there disbanded for unknown reasons as it began to take up the subject of church reform. A second council was convened in Basel in 1431 by a legate of Martin V, and clearly forwarded its agenda of establishing conciliar supremacy in the church (for example, see session 18 dealing with the issue of councilor authority). Further, Basel was a triumph for the conciliarists from the viewpoint of its delineation of authority, though Eugenius IV, Martin's successor, stalled the ratification of the proceedings in an attempt to assert his supremacy. One accomplishment at Basel was a tentative agreement for reconciliation with the Eastern churches (session 19, 24); however, the agreement was rejected in the East.

The council was moved to Ferrara in 1438 and then to Florence in 1439 for fear of the plague. In continuing negotiations with the eastern churches, here also with the Armenian or **Verbal Monophysite** churches, the council defined its perspective on the sacraments of the church. This is the first "ecumenical" council to do so, though the conclusions were those of Lombard and Aquinas. Here it possessed much more authority than those of a teacher in the church; it was a decree of the highest leadership. The council not only enumerated the number and meaning of each sacrament, it clearly articulated their function in incrementally acquiring divine grace.

> There are seven sacraments of the new Law, namely baptism, confirmation, eucharist, penance, extreme unction, orders and matrimony, which differ greatly from the sacraments of the old Law. The latter were not causes of grace, but only prefigured the grace to be given through the passion of Christ; whereas the former, ours, both contain grace and bestow it on those who worthily receive them. The first five of these are directed to the spiritual perfection of each person in himself, the last two to the regulation and increase of the whole church (session 8.5).

The Late Medieval Church: Impiety, Spiritualism, and Doctrinal Error

Reflecting on the state of the church in his day, Calvin made a point that ecclesiastical and moral practices in the leadership stood in sharp contrast to previous centuries:

> There is scarcely a bishop, and not one in a hundred parish priests, who, if his conduct were to be judged according to ancient canons, would not be subject either to excommunication or at least to disposition from office (*The Institutes of Christian Religion*, 4.5.14).

Piety was at low ebb; greed and avarice took precedence over prayer and care. Simony (the buying and selling of church offices), the performance of sacramental absolutions for fees, the multiplication of churches by priests to increase their revenue without service to the parishes, clerical ignorance of spiritual matters, and condoned immorality reached daunting proportions. Luther was willing to argue that the church made a major shift away from apostolic and patristic authority in the early thirteenth century, and the purity of the church worsened over the centuries from that time. For example, the canons of the Fourth Lateran Council (1215) mandated annual provincial synods act

> with a genuine fear of God in correcting abuses and reforming morals, especially the morals of the clergy, familiarizing themselves anew with the canonical rules, particularly those that are enacted in this general council, that they may enforce their observance by imposing due punishment on transgressors (6).

The canons that followed dealt with clerical greed (7), the necessity of preaching Holy Scripture in the parishes (10), the necessity of an educated ministry (11), and numerous directives against immoral practices, including **concubinage** (14–16). The Third Lateran Council (1179) specifically prohibited simony (14) and condemned the selling of sacramental services as "utterly disgraceful" (7–8); the keeping of concubines was subject to excommunication (11); and the larger churches were to care for the educational needs of the churches (14).

The image of the church in the literature of the day was as unflattering as Erasmus's play about Julius II's disappointment with Peter at the gates of heaven in the sixteenth century. Dante Alighieri (1265–1321), in his imaginative vision of the Christian afterlife, the *Divine Comedy*, denounced the church for its corruption, consigning several popes to the inferno. Giovanni Boccaccio (1313–1375), an Italian Renaissance humanist, used satire to unleash an outpouring of criticism against the priesthood of the church in the *Decameron*. In his celebrated *Canterbury Tales*, Geoffrey Chaucer (ca. 1343–1400) portrays the cleric as an obese, jolly, self-absorbed person.

The neglect of the parish life reached serious proportions. Instruction in the Scriptures was infrequent and the laity turned to mysticism and the miraculous as substitutes. The Eucharist was enshrined with almost magical properties and people darted from church to church to see the host elevated, thinking that rich rewards would follow. Relics became an obsession as people flocked to see them. Fragments of the cross, a piece of the burning bush of Moses, drops of blood shed by the Savior, milk from the breast of the Virgin Mary, bones of various saints, and many other objects, could obtain years off purgatorial flames for parishioners and a fancy sum for church coffers.

The church, often depicted as a noahic ark in the troubled chaos of human existence, was drifting. Its message of redemption was increasingly becoming a sacramental Pelagianism, a salvation by human merit, the fruit of obedience. Some writer spoke of these ways of envisioning salvation as "the modern way."

Thomas Bradwardine

Thomas Bradwardine (ca. 1290–1349), the Oxford scholar and cleric, complained about this bitterly in his work against Pelagianism saying:

> Idle and a fool in God's wisdom, I was misled by an unorthodox error. . . . Sometimes I went to listen to the theologians discussing the matter [of grace and free will] and the school of Pelagius seemed to me nearest to the truth. . . . the text [Rom. 9:6] mentioned came to me as a beam of grace and, captured by a vision of the truth, it seemed I saw from afar how the grace of God precedes all good works with a temporal priority and natural precedence.

Thomas Bradwardine was an English scholar and briefly Archbishop of Canterbury born about AD 1290. He studied and was later a professor at Balliol College, Oxford. As chaplain and confessor to Edward III he became a diplomat to the king. While at Merton College he studied and taught mechanics, logic, and the mathematical theory of proportions, reinterpreting the teachings of Aristotle. In his work *On the Causes of God Against the Pelagians*, he emphasized the omnipotence of God regarding the past, present, and future.

Gregory of Rimini

The Augustinian friar, Gregory of Rimini (ca. 1300–1358), a trained scholastic at the University of Paris and a teacher in several Italian schools, believed that the churches were departing from the gospel:

> It is the opinion of many moderns that man, by his natural powers alone, with the general concurrence of God, can perform a morally good act in the present state of fallen nature, as for example to love God above all things, to be sorry for and to detest one's sins, etc. . . . They depart . . . from the definitions of the church and favor the condemned error of Pelagius . . . No one can merit the first grace . . . contrary to the opinions of the moderns.

Other Voices

The "modern way" of salvation gained a considerable hearing through William of Ockham (ca. 1285–1348), a Franciscan friar; Robert of Holcot (d. 1349), a Dominican friar and devotee of Ockham; and Gabriel Biel (ca. 1425–1495), a scholar in the Brethren of the Common Life, who systematized Ockham's teachings in the newly founded University of Tübingen. It was the writings of Biel that Luther read in the early years of his training, shaping his understanding of divine grace.

These scholars went beyond Lombard and Aquinas in the explanation of grace, merit, and salvation. Salvation did not begin in an expression of the unmerited, uncaused favor of God (and then increased by graced-caused activities); it began in an unrevealed covenant that God would grant grace if certain preconditions were met. The prerequisites had to do with sincerity of effort and doing the best one can possibly do without grace. Human works moved God to grant grace! This grace was by incremental infusion as a proper reward. The earnest recipient then entered a period of trial in this life by seeking to do his best with the help of God's grace. If the journey met with success, the individual was granted the gift of eternal life as a just reward. Thus, God had so arranged things that a person who rightly prepares himself/herself for grace would obtain it.

This view, though definitely scented with Pelagian thought, was different in at least one way. To Pelagius, human works had intrinsic moral value; to Biel, the value of obedience was derived from the covenant or compact made by God, not merely by doing good works. This was a distinction that the reformers rejected or missed. The consensus from the sixteenth-century perspective was that Biel and others were pelagian in their understanding of the means of grace.

Voices of Protest in the Late Medieval Church

The **Conciliar Movement** sought to reform the church from within, answering the perceived woes of the church through ecclesiastical legislation. Others expressed concern for the direction of the church as well, some from outside the establishment and others from within.

Albigenses

One of the earliest anti-establishment groups were the **Albigenses** (sometimes called the Cathar, "the pure"). The movement emerged in southern France in the twelfth century and gained considerable power and influence. The group appeared to have been a gnostic, ascetic sect professing a radical dualism between good, the spiritual, and evil, the material (for example, avoidance of certain foods and rejection of sexual contact in marriage). "Hell" was a physical entrapment to the attractions of the material world and redemption a spiritual, mystical journey to a separated state. The initial response by the church was to address their assertions through teaching and preaching. The Cistercians, later the Dominicans, were sent but had little success and a large measure of hostility. The Council of Rheims (1148) sought to remove the political protection of the sect with the threat of excommunication; the Council of Tours (1167) authorized the confiscation of Cathar property. The threats of excommunication became a formal canon (27) at the Third Lateran Council (1179). When the Albigenses proved recalcitrant, the Fourth Lateran Council (1215) authorized a religious crusade of extermination (Canon 3), offering a promise of soul-safety to those who would execute the tragedy. "Catholics who have girded themselves with the cross for the extermination of the heretics, shall enjoy the indulgences and privileges granted to those who go in defense of the Holy Land." The sect was completely eliminated by the end of the fourteenth century.

Waldensians

A less theologically aberrant movement was the **Waldensians** who emerged in the eleventh century. The group was early identified with Peter Waldo (d. 1218), though they were called the "Brethren in Christ," the "poor in christ," and the "poor in spirit." Peter was a well-to-do merchant in Lyon who felt called to preach to the poor. The group manifested ascetic tendencies, but were not dualistic; they were an orthodox, reformist group that sought to correct spiritual woes and neglects in the established church. For placing an emphasis on lay preaching and refusing to recognize the authority of the church in these matters, they were excommunicated at the Council of Verona in 1184.

For the Waldensians, the Bible was the authority for the priesthood of all believers—the warrant for lay ministry, not the councils or the pope. They rejected prayers for the dead; the veneration of saints and relics; the mass as a miraculous, material presence of Christ; purgatory; and the legitimacy of the sacramental function of unworthy clerics. The rapid growth of the movement in France, Switzerland, Italy, and Eastern Europe brought a repressive response from the church. With the requirement that the Waldensians be turned over to the secular authorities for punishment in 1184, the movement became the object of inquisition. Unlike the Albigenses, the Waldensians survived horrendous persecution and identified with the reformed wing of the sixteenth-century Protestantism. John Milton wrote a sonnet ("On the Late Massacre in Piedmont") commemorating their struggles:

> Avenge, O Lord, thy slaughter'd Saints,
>   whose bones
> Lie scatter'd on the Alpine mountains
>   cold,
> Ev'n them who kept thy truth so pure of
>   old
> When all our Fathers worship't Stocks and
>   Stones,
> Forget not: in thy book record their
>   groanes
> Who were thy Sheep and in their ancient
>   Fold
> Slayn by the bloody Piemontese that roll'd
> Mother with Infant down the Rocks. Their
>   moans
> The Vales redoubl'd to the Hills, and they
> To Heav'n. Their martyr'd blood and ashes
>   sow
> O're all th' Italian fields where still doth
>   sway
> The triple Tyrant [the pope]: that from
>   these may grow
> A hundred-fold, who having learnt thy way
> Early may fly the Babylonian woe.

Waldensians as witches (1451) in work by Martin Le France (1410–1461). Courtesy of W. Schild.

John Wycliffe

Clerics within the church raised the voice of protest, perhaps none so prolifically as John Wycliffe of England (ca. 1330–1384). Little is known of the early life of Wycliffe; his entire career was associated with Oxford University (Balliol College, Merton College, Queens College, and Canterbury Hall [now Christ Church College]), first as a scholar and then as a lecturer. During his time at Oxford, he was politically active in matters of court and represented the interests of his country to the papacy. He also served as parish priest, ending his career at Lutterworth. He lived through the era of the Avignon captivity, as well as the Black Death, and became increasingly a critic of ecclesiastical corruption. His political connections often spared him from trouble. His criticism of the church reached a crisis in 1381 over his rejection of the official understanding

of the Eucharist. Also there was the false claim of implication in the revolt of the peasantry called **Wat Tyler's Rebellion,** which seemed to be an application of his doctrine of grace into a form of liberation theology. He was forced to retire from the university in 1382 and spent the remainder of his days writing.

Wycliffe's earliest works were philosophical, and he influenced the university with his realism for a generation; but his religious writings had the most enduring influence on the church. In *On Civil Lordship* (1375–1376), he argued that rule should be based on grace and expressed moral integrity and that the corruption in the churches could be traced to the abandonment of the Benedictine vow of

John Wycliffe in stained glass at Wycliffe College Chapel, Toronto. Courtesy of Jphillips23.

Invitation to Church History: World

poverty. Violation of the grounds for leadership warranted disposition from office by the civil power.

A trilogy of works followed: *On the Church, On the Truth of Holy Scripture,* and *On the Power of the Pope* (1377–1378). In the first, he argued that the institutional church was not to be confused with the true Body of Christ. In the second, he declared that the Scriptures should take precedence over the decrees of councils, popes, and tradition. And in the third, he denied the divine institution of the papacy and attributed Peter's priority among the apostles to divine grace and his love for Christ. Further, he asserted that immorality disqualifies even the popes from holy office.

After Wycliffe published *On the Eucharist* (1382), a refutation of transubstantiation, the patience of the church came to an end, his political influence having waned. He was condemned in 1381 in a twenty-four-point summary of errors by Gregory XI that stated, in part:

> By the insinuation of many, if they are indeed worthy of belief, deploring it deeply, it has come to our ears that John de Wycliffe, rector of the church of Lutterworth, in the diocese of Lincoln, Professor of the Sacred Scriptures (would that he were not also Master of Errors), has fallen into such a detestable madness that he does not hesitate to dogmatize and publicly preach, or rather vomit forth from the recesses of his breast, certain propositions and conclusions which are erroneous and false.

Born around 1330, John Wycliffe was an English scholastic theologian and proto-reformer, bringing to bear the teachings of Scripture on the practices of the Roman church. Called "the Morning Star of the Reformation," he engaged in Bible translation whereby the first English version was produced. He believed Scripture was the sole authority for the believer. Decrees of the pope were not infallible except as based on Scripture. Ultimately he repudiated the entire papal system, attacking transubstantiation, a position that influenced Martin Luther over a century later. Wycliffe condemned the dogma of purgatory and the use of relics, pilgrimages, and indulgences. Though he developed many enemies in the Roman church, he died in peace.

Not only was Wycliffe a writer, popular preacher, and scholar, he made two other important contributions: the promotion of the **Lollards** and making the Bible available in his native tongue. The Lollards were lay preachers that Wycliffe trained and sent out to disseminate the gospel. A glimpse into the beliefs of the group can be gleamed from an anonymous document, the *Twelve Conclusions,* posted on the doors of Westminster Abbey and St. Paul's Cathedral in 1395. Some conclusions were the lack of moral integrity in the leadership of the church and the wrongness of auricular confession, relic veneration, pilgrimages, prayers for the dead, celibacy, and transubstantiation. The Lollards represented a protest movement that envisioned a better and purer time in the church's past. They seemed to have been ab-

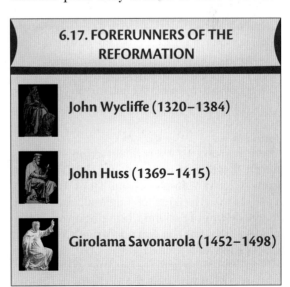

6.17. FORERUNNERS OF THE REFORMATION

John Wycliffe (1320–1384)

John Huss (1369–1415)

Girolama Savonarola (1452–1498)

sorbed into the sixteenth-century Protestant movement.

In addition, Wycliffe was concerned with the availability of the Bible and literacy. Though it is not certain how much of the New Testament Wycliffe actually translated into English from Latin, the entire Bible was completed before his death (the greater part likely by John Purvey [ca. 1354–1421], who subsequently died in prison).

The saga of Wycliffe's story did not end with his death in 1384. The work of the Lollards, the dissemination of the Bible, and the continued influence of his writings caused him to be a concern to the church. At the Council of Constance (1415), he was condemned, his writings burned, and he was disinterred, burned to ashes, and his remains scattered. His condemnation extended to forty-five accusations (Session 8:14, May 1415); later 260 charges were brought against him (Session 15:6, July 1415).

The Errors of John Wycliffe

"The Roman Church is the synagogue of Satan, and the pope is not the next and immediate vicar of Christ and His apostles" (37).

"It is not necessary for salvation to believe that the Roman Church is supreme among other churches" (41).

"It is foolish to believe in the indulgences of the pope and bishops" (42).

John Huss

There appears to be a direct connection between Wycliffe of England and the Bohemian (now Czech) reformer, John (Jan) Huss (ca. 1371–1415). The king of England, Richard II, married Anne of Bohemia, bringing an exchange of ideas between the two countries. Of peasant stock, Huss was trained in the Charles University in Prague, where he became a teacher as well as parish priest at the Bethlehem Chapel,

a church where the services were conducted in the native language. Wycliffe's ideas became a focal point in the university with the Czech students receptive to them, though the German students were resistant. The crisis in the university led to the exodus of the Germans as nations divided loyalties during the great schism. Further, Huss translated Wycliffe's *Trialogus*, three of his works, stridently preached against clerical abuses, and became rector of the university.

John Huss, dean of the faculty of philosophy at the University of Prague in the early 1400s, learned of Wycliffe's teachings when they reached Bohemia (Czechoslovakia) after Wycliffe's death. Huss translated Wycliffe's works into Czech. In 1411 after his sermons against abuses in the church, Huss was excommunicated and a year later placed under a strict ban. In 1414 the ban on Huss was lifted, and he was called (under the Emperor Sigismund's promise of safe conduct) to the Council at Constance in Switzerland to explain himself, the participants wanting to hear him defend his claim that the only true pontiff of the church was Jesus Christ. Sigismund, choosing the unity rather than the purity of the church, agreed to let the council decide the fate of Huss—despite his earlier guarantee of safe conduct. The council found him guilty of some 30 charges and turned him over to the secular authorities to be burned at the stake as a heretic. In July 1415 he was put to death as ordered and his ashes were scattered over the Rhine River.

The initial step against Huss was a papal bull issued in 1409 ordering the destruction of Wycliffe's writings, the condemnation of Huss's influence at Bethlehem Chapel, and a general prohibition against private preaching. When these measures proved ineffective, John XXIII (an antipope of the Pisa-papacy during the era of the Conciliar Movement) excommunicated him in 1411. Emperor Sigismund of Hungary called him, with the promise of safety, to the Council of Constance to answer for his views. Imprisonment followed, and he was subsequently burned to death as a heretic (6 July 1415). Huss was condemned on twenty-four charges (Session 15):

This holy synod therefore pronounces the said John Hus, on account of the aforesaid and many other matters, to have been a

Burning of Jan (John) Huss at the stake. Diebold Schilling the Older, *Spiezer Chronik* (1485). Courtesy of Fb78.

heretic and it judges him to be considered and condemned as a heretic, and it hereby condemns him.

Huss died singing, chained to a stake, with his books piled around him to perish in the flames.

Followers of Huss

The followers of Huss continued resistance to the church, splitting into two factions, a moderate party favoring a general, moral reform of the church but leaving major doctrinal differences unaddressed and a radical party following Wycliffe. The moderates followed the Four Articles of Prague (1420), seeking freedom to preach the Bible, celebrate the Eucharist with both the bread and wine (they were called Calixties [chalice] and Utraquists [both the bread and the wine]), and the relinquishment of secular authority by the church. The radicals were called Taborites, after a Hussite center in the town of Tabor. When the church organized crusades against the Hussites, they were able to defend themselves because they reflected a strident Czech nationalism. Largely based on the Four Articles of Prague, the moderates reached an agreement with the Catholic Church in 1432. The Taborites gradually lost power in the state and among the people. Nicholus Ludwig von Zinzendorf organized remnants of the Taborites in the seventeenth century and today their heirs are known as **Moravians** or United Brethren.

Jerome of Prague

Though overshadowed by his compatriot, John Huss, Jerome of Prague (ca. 1370–1416), another of those voices of dissent, was a portent of greater complaint to emerge in the church. Jerome was educated in Prague where he came under the influence of Huss and Wycliffe. He later studied in Oxford, focusing on Wycliffe's theological works, as well as Heidelberg, Cologne, and Paris. Returning to Prague in 1407, he became embroiled in the religious controversies of his day. He copied many of Wycliffe's works, bringing them back with him to Bohemia. He promised to assist Huss at the Council of Constance; however, having no promise of safety, he left Constance only to be returned in chains. Imprisoned and in ill health, he recanted his attachment to Huss and Wycliffe, but it did not spare him a trial. In the course of his trial, he boldly and eloquently recanted his recantation and was condemned to death by burning on 30 May 1416. His condemnation reads, in part:

> It is evident from the above that the said Jerome adhered to the condemned Wyclif and Huss and their errors, and that he was and is a supporter of them. This holy synod has therefore decreed and now declares that the said Jerome is to be cast away as a branch that is rotten, withered, and separated from the vine; and it pronounces, declares and condemns him as a heretic who has relapsed into heresy and as an excommunicated and anathematised person (Session 21).

The Errors of John Huss

"Ecclesiastical obedience is obedience according to the invention of the priest of the Church, without the expressed authority of Scripture" (Council of Constance, 15).

"If the Pope is wicked and especially if he is foreknown, then as Judas, the Apostle, he is of the devil, a thief, and a son of perdition, and he is not the head of the holy militant Church, since he is not a member of it" (20).

William Savanarola

An interesting voice of criticism was that of William Savonarola (1452–1498), a Dominican friar. His complaints were aimed at papal corruption, particularly Alexander VI, though he remained a loyal, late medievalist catholic with concerns that showed little interest in the potential theological decadence of the church. Born in Ferrara, where he took university studies prior to entering the priesthood in 1475, his fame largely derived from his second stay in the city of Florence between 1490 and his death by burning in 1498. Savanarola was a fiery apocalyptic preacher who had an ability to stir the masses. The appearance of a huge French army on the border in 1494 seemed to be the portent of an Armageddon, as did a simultaneous outbreak of syphilis in the city. The approach of a new century, as such circumstances seemed to suggest, lent further credibility to his preaching of the near-judgment coming of Christ and the beginning of a "golden age." People confused his passionate preaching with truth—suggesting that fear has short-term credibility as a motivating factor—and burned secular paintings, books, pornography, gambling equipment, and extravagant clothing (the "bonfire of vanities") in preparation for the "great day."

An eschatological extremist, Savonarola's message wore thin. When Florence was engulfed in rioting, Alexander VI had the oppor-

A 1498 painting of the hanging and burning of Savonarola in Museo di San Marco, Florence. Courtesy of Torvindus.

tunity to excommunicate his fiery preacher. After being tortured to extract a confession of error, he was burned to death in the city plaza in 1498. Whatever may be argued about the validity of his insights or the propriety of his methods, Savanarola was a lens into the state of the church in his day. His intense criticism of the church, coupled with moral earnestness, was attractive to sixteenth-century reformers as they sought to answer the criticism that their teachings were novel. Churchmen before Luther and Calvin shared similar views of the church in their time.

The Renaissance, an Intellectual Revolution

The term *renaissance*, as reflective of a movement, has no scholarly consensus to its duration or meaning, though the word strictly means a "rebirth." As such, it generally refers to a fourteenth-and-fifteenth-century movement, beginning in Tuscany, Italy, characterized by advancement in the arts and sciences; it was a cultural revolution, a revival of classical learning. **Renaissance humanists** felt that a return to an idealized past (*ad fontes*, "to the sources") was medicine for the woes of society and church. To northern Europeans, the quest for the roots of a usable heritage took many humanists to Christian sources. This caused the unanticipated realization that the church had changed over the centuries. Thus, this review of the past became another factor in the sixteenth–century reformations of the church. The Renaissance unleashed a movement in Western civilization that stretched to the twentieth century. While it represented a revival of classical learning, it can only distantly be conceived as a forerunner of modern democratic political theory; it was not an anticlerical movement, nor did it reject the assumption of ecclesiastical authority for either political or individualized sovereignty.

Motto of Renaissance: *ad fontes* ("back to the sources").

The Renaissance is more to be encountered in methodological advances in learning than in philosophical approaches to the nature of knowledge. The fall of the Roman (Byzantine) Empire, the capitulation of Constantinople to the Ottoman Turks in 1453, brought unexpected circumstances that lie at the root of the Renaissance. Scholars relocated to Italy in the fourteenth-and-fifteenth centuries as the Islamic threat became serious. Not only did they bring many ancient manuscripts with them, they opened academies that had a slightly different focus than the universities that were more tightly controlled by the church.

Many Roman Catholic and Protestant reformers were Renaissance humanists in training. The decline of scholasticism and emergence of **humanism**, an imprecise moment in history, set the stage for sixteenth-century developments because the orientations were distinct, feeding the growing distrust of the church (it was an indirect rejection of the church by pursuing other interests rather than frontally criticizing the establishment). The scholastics were preoccupied with religious and theological questions; the humanists (at this time, the term did not have the connotation that it would have in the twentieth cen-

tury.) were those scholars who showed an interest in the pursuit of the humanities, the study of man.

Humanists were not secularists but sought to broaden the scope of their investigations to science, medicine, the arts, and theology. To the scholastic the answers to questions were to be found in creeds, canons, and the Bible, while humanists did not express the urge to necessarily find solutions to perplexing issues. Further, the focus slightly shifted. To the humanist, truth was not necessarily church-based; truth was larger than merely church interests; it was nostalgic and expansive. To the scholastic, being rooted in a medieval worldview, the preoccupation was on reaching a world that was unseen and future; to the humanist, issues related to the immediate, daily, and practical predominated.

A fact of great importance is that the Renaissance was a seedbed of the sixteenth-century reformations of the church. What is common among the diverse groups that emerged (Roman Catholics, Protestant Catholics, rationalists, mystics, and those who sought political solutions to chaos) was disillusionment with the late medieval church—its ability to speak meaningfully, offer hope, and sustain loyalty. The reformers, for the most part, were children

6.18. SCHOLASTICISM AND RENAISSANCE HUMANISM COMPARED

	Scholasticism (1100–1300)	Humanism (1300–1500)
1. Major area of study	Theology	Science, Medicine, Theology
2. Questions	Answered in Theology	No Resolution Necessary
3. Truth	Church-based	Nostalgic, Free, Challenging
4. Focus	Otherworldly	Practical, Immediate

of the Renaissance in their education, view of the church, and outlook on life. Reformers such as Luther, Zwingli, and Calvin, adopted the Renaissance and nominalist approaches to truth, weakening the embrace of dogmatic, external views on ecclesiastical authority.

For example, humanists generally viewed the medieval period in stark contrast to how the church viewed it. Loyal churchmen viewed the period from the inception of Christianity as a continuous era of spiritual light and Christian civilization. Humanists saw the medieval period as retrogression from an era of light, a period of religious and cultural stagnation. The era prior to the rise of Christianity, and several centuries after, were viewed as a period of spiritual light and cultural advance, and, after a disappointing era, light was beginning to return.

Additionally, humanists were interested in understanding and returning to a past era as a means of revitalizing the present. For many humanists, particularly in southern Europe, the return-to-roots movement was engagement with Greco-Roman culture (the visual arts, poetry, literature, and architecture). However, the tendency in northern Europe was to locate origins in the earliest Christian period. It was characterized by a more religious concern than secular interests. It was an era where self-awareness emerged, where literary expression became as important as literary content. Culture and religion began to bifurcate in Italy, while it merged for several centuries in the northern European experience. These concerns, as a corollary, brought renewed interest in educational advance that often brought perspectives and freedoms that dogmatism and obscurantism could not provide, though sometimes detrimental to religion.

Lorenzo Valla

An example of the humanist impact on the church was the discovery of Lorenzo Valla (ca. 1401–1457), who concluded that the *Donation of Constantine*, a document supporting the claims of the Roman church over temporal priority (and used heavily from the eleventh century on), was an eighth-century fraud. The rise of the science of textual criticism also exposed the *Isidorean Decretals*, the basis for Roman spiritual claims, to the same judgment in the sixteenth century.

Guillaume Bude

Perhaps more pertinent to sixteenth-century Protestant reformers was the renewal of linguistic studies, particularly the study of the biblical languages. Guillaume Bude (ca. 1467–1540), a trained University of Paris humanist, published scholarly studies and critical analyses of Greek grammar and syntax, opening the way for a renewal of the study of the original languages behind the Latin Vulgate, a text with linguistic inadequacies and inaccuracies.

Johannes Reuchlin

In the field of Hebraic studies and to a lesser degree in Greek literature, Johannes Reuchlin (1455–1522), a German humanist, paved the way by producing a fairly reliable handbook of

6.19: THE MEANING OF THE RENAISSANCE

1. Revival of Classical Learning

2. Methodology (not Philosophy)

3. Not a Forerunner of Modern Democratic Liberalism

Hebrew grammar and championing the cause of such studies in the German universities.

Jacques Lefevre d'Etaples

Jacques Lefevre d'Etaples (ca. 1450–1536) was a prolific linguist as well as student of Aristotle. He completed a translation of the Old Testament in 1528 and the entire Protestant Bible in 1530, the first full translation into the French language. Though more interested in the broad reform of the church than specific Protestant ideas (though he had a significant influence on Calvin's development), he was renowned for his studies in the Psalms and the Pauline epistles.

John Colet

John Colet (ca. 1467–1519), a humanist scholar at Oxford and later dean of St. Paul's Cathedral in London, lectured on Paul's epistles (Romans and 1 Corinthians), taking a more literal approach to the interpretation of Scripture than was generally common at the time, and preached in English to huge crowds. At St. Paul's, he established a Latin and Greek school and endeavored to promote education. He was also a friend of Erasmus, whom he met at Oxford and with whom he exchanged correspondence on several occasions.

Desiderius Erasmus

The most significant of the Renaissance humanists was Desiderius Erasmus (ca. 1466–1536), the Dutch-born scholar, who was a critic of the church as well as an opponent of Luther in the defense of the church. Though likely a child born out of wedlock, his parents cared for him and he was afforded an education. In 1492, poverty forced him into monastic life, and he was ordained into the Augustinian order. He received formal academic training at the University of Paris and pursued the life of a scholar, teaching occasionally but mostly studying and writing.

In 1509 Erasmus wrote, and later published, a satire, *The Praise of Folly*. It had an enormous influence in its day and was important in the emergent criticism of the church leading to the reformations of the sixteenth century. Dedicated to a fellow critic, Sir Thomas More, Erasmus was spared the wrath of his church largely through his brilliance and institutional loyalty, the use of satire to make his points, and, at times, the veil of authorial anonymity. A case in point is *Julius Exclusis,* a popular play depicting Julius II before the gates of heaven that were closed to him. Written in 1513–1514, Erasmus depicted the great warrior pope as a moral derelict who brought wealth and splendor to the church, but with it debauchery of body and spirit.

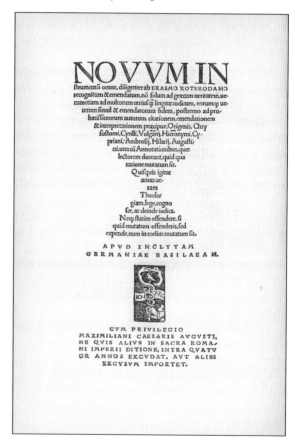

First page of Erasmus's 1516 edition of the New Testament. Courtesy of Pvasiliadis.

In 1516 he published the first Greek New Testament, commonly known at the *Textus Receptus* or "received text." His work was an immense success, a gift to a world hungry to have the sacred writings of the church. Luther used a subsequent edition of Erasmus's Greek text in the preparation of the German Bible of 1522; William Tyndale used a third edition for the first English New Testament (1526); and it made important contributions to the Geneva Bible (1557, 1560) and the King James Bible (1611).

Not only did Erasmus's Greek text place the Scriptures into the hands of teachers and priests, it shocked many to realize that Jerome's Latin Vulgate, a monumentally influential work of the fifth century, the Bible of a millennium, did not often accurately reflect the original meaning of the Greek text. With this insight came a second one. The Vulgate had unwittingly become a source of error in the church. Over the centuries, words had changed meanings or were twisted to support teachings that appeared to have no scriptural basis. For example, in Matthew 4:17, should we read, "do penance," an outward act, or "repent," an inward attitude? While the Greek text does not support the former reading, this reading was used to support the medieval sacrament of penance. Needless to say, as priests and scholars read Erasmus's text, comparing the church of the first century to that of their day, they discovered a contemporary church that stood in stark contrast to the Holy Scriptures.

Erasmus's *Handbook for the Militant Christian* (1503) stated his agenda for church renewal more positively. Later Protestant reformers might have agreed with him on many points—the emphasis on the centrality of Christ, the importance of the Scriptures, and the necessity of true piety. However, Luther would come to the opinion that Erasmus's criticism of the church and his description of true piety were flawed.

Desiderius Erasmus in 1523 as depicted by Hans Holbein the Younger (1497–1543). At National Gallery, London. Courtesy of Stw.

In Erasmus's understanding of human nature, human ability, the accomplishments of Christ, and the procurement of his benefits, he was far less a biblicist than he was a late medievalist. Erasmus's piety was built on the faulty foundation of human ability to causatively cooperate with grace in acquiring the benefits of grace. His notion of true Christianity made Christ a great exemplar and helper more than the absolute redeemer; it replaced justifying grace with progressive sanctifying grace; and it confused the essence of religion with its fruit, piety. A Protestant, sixteenth-century perspective on Erasmus would be that he was a conservative religious moralist, a critic, and child of his times, who missed, or refused to take up, the deeper issues and implications of human deformity, ability, and destiny.

Coming Changes
As the fourteenth century came to a conclusion, Western Europe was a world about to change dramatically. The Renaissance produced a world of new horizons, thought patterns, and discoveries. The fifteenth century was an era of discovery! The exploits of Columbus, Magellan, and Cortez are legendary. Copernicus argued that the sun was the center of the solar system, not the earth. Michelangelo painted the Sistine Chapel in the emerging new and extravagant papal residence in Rome. Beyond the advances in the sciences and the literary arts that so expanded the world of knowledge, a religious change was about to take place, change that would shape Western civilization for almost five hundred years. An intellectual renaissance was about to occur that would eventually birth the modern era.

6.20. FIFTEENTH CENTURY AND TODAY

	FIFTEENTH CENTURY	TWENTY-FIRST CENTURY
1. Lack of confidence in the Word of God	Papal pronouncements	Business know-how and psychological counseling
2. Sin's seriousness not understood	Flawed understanding	Sin trivialized, humanized, and made inoffensive
3. Minimized glory and efficacy of Christ's cross	The work of Christ not sufficient	Cross elminated from the felt need approach

GLOSSARY OF TERMS

Albigenses: a neo-gnostic/Manichean sect of the twelfth and thirteenth centuries originating in Albi, France. Critical of the established church of the day, they were severely persecuted beginning in the reign of Innocent III and destroyed.

Aristoteleian Method: an approach to knowing that emphasizes observation, analysis and conclusion, the study of particulars to arrive at universals. As many have indicated, it is a method that probes the specific to arrive at general principles.

Black Death: a disastrous plague carried by flea-infested rats that swept throughout Europe in the fourteenth century introduced. It was from China through the development of trade. Estimates of the enormity of the pandemic reached into the millions causing economic, social, and religious upheaval.

Christian Rationalist Tradition: an approach to the defense of the Christian faith in the tradition of Aristotle and Aquinas arguing for a place for mental reflection to demonstrate the truth-claims of Christianity and the compatibility of them with science and other disciplines that emerged through the academy of Christianity, implying that Christian truth is not irrational or non-rational but warranted.

College of Cardinals: a group of cardinals in the Roman Catholic Church who are tasked with service to the pope as counselors, governance of the church, and the election of the pontiff should that office become vacant.

Conciliar Movement: a movement in the four-teenth- and fifteenth-century church to restore the papacy after the duplicities and difficulties from the presence of rival claims to Saint Peter's chair. It raised the important issue of the origin of authority in the church unsuccessfully resisting the authority of a single person. The failure of the movement to resolve the issue of authority became one of the major causes of the disruption of the church in the Reformation era.

Concubinage: a practice in the medieval church that allowed priests to experience conjugal privilege without contractual marriage.

Cooperationism: a term normally employed to indicate divine/human effort in the attainment of salvation. While most Protestants are cooperationists, they would see the human act in salvation as a responsive, not causative, in contrast to the Roman Catholic teaching of divine/human causation.

Dominican Tertiary, Dominican Laity: the term "tertiary" means third of rank or order. St Dominic founded the monastic Dominican Order or Order of Preachers in the early thirteenth century to suppress heretical groups by persuasion rather than by militarism. The order was organized into ranks or levels: preaching priests, cloistered nuns, and seculars.

Great Western Schism (Great Schism, Papal Schism): a nadir in late medieval catholic church fortunes when rival popes, each appointed by the same College of Cardinals, claim to be the singular vicar of Christ (1378–1417). Not only was European political loyalties divided, exacerbated by the Hundred Years' War (1337–1453) between England and France, but this caused a questioning of the church's ancient claim to authority. The schism was brought to an end by the election of Martin V at the Council of Constance.

Humanism: as used in the twelfth and thirteenth centuries in Europe, the term signified an interest in the study of the humanities, often within the rising universities. Its focus was not so much on a denial of the authority of the medieval church, but to understand for oneself the truths taught by the church. While a leading contributor to the ethos of the sixteenth-century reformations, it is not to be identified with the secular humanism that arose out of the Enlightenment centuries later.

Hundred Years War: a series of military clashes between England and France (1337–1453) over the control of the disputed territories. Fought largely in northern France and the Low countries, the French secured the throne and England lost its territorial claims on the continent. The religious significance of the confrontation in the context of the Great Schism is that it was a contributing factor to the decline of the prestige and authority of the late medieval church.

Lollards: followers of the teaching of John Wycliffe of fourteenth century England, a professor at Balliol College and critic of the church. The Lollards were absorbed into the Protestant English Reformation of the sixteenth century.

Moravians (United Brethren): a Protestant religious group with roots in the fourteenth-century Hussite movement. In the eighteenth century, a group settled in the Moravian region of Germany where they were protected and led by German aristocrat, Nicholas Ludwig von Zinzendorff. The Moravians became leaders in the missionary movement of the church becoming the first church, as a singular church body, to send out missionaries.

Nestorianism: a teaching in the fourth-century church concerning the relationship between Christ's two natures in the incarnation. Nestorius accepted the full humanity and deity of Christ, but seemed to reject the concept of his unity, disjoining the natures and giving Christ two natures that were joined morally, not organically. The view was condemned at the third ecumenical council held at Ephesus (431). Advocates of this view continued in existence for several centuries, extending their teaching into the Far East.

Renaissance: a cultural and intellectual movement that emerged in fourteenth-century Italy and sustained discernible influence into the seventh through the seventeenth centuries in Europe. It proved to be a strong intellectual impetus for the sixteenth century reformations in that its focus on the humanities brought an emphasis on self-understanding. While it did not question medieval authority structures, it did question how they were embraced. Further, it was an impetus for the later Enlightenment period that stressed the importance of individual belief and search to find it, but divorced it from medieval assumptions of authority. Thus, scholars think of the modern period as having two parts: early modern and late modern; eras that shared the same approach to knowledge through the humanities, but embraced diverse theories of authority.

Renaissance Humanism: a cultural and educational reform emphasis that emerged in the fourteenth and fifteenth centuries in reaction to medieval scholasticism, emphasizing personal affirmation of truth through a study of the sources of belief-structures, as well as the engagement in civic life through speaking and writing with eloquence and clarity. Its focus was on the study of the humanities with the new curriculum of university education, a shift from the scholastic preoccupation with rational explanation of the medieval faith to the readoption and prominence of the Aristotelian method.

Sabellianism (Modalism, Patripassionism): the attempt to explain the Trinitarian existence of God by arguing for a strict singularity of God in person and attributes, but in a threefold manifestation. This explanation of the divine Trinity was consistently condemned in the fourth- and fifth-century ecumenical councils of the church.

Scholastic Movement (Scholasticism, the Scholastics): an intellectual movement that emerged in Europe following the intrusive Viking disruptions reflective of the economic philosophy in Europe. The context of its emergence was the realization that monastic education was outdated given philosophical advances in the Mediteranean world, specifically the dominance of the Aristotlean method in Spain and the East. The retooling brought about three phenomena: the emergence of the classroom as the center of the educational process, not the chapel; the writing of textbooks to synthesize vast sums of knowledge; the beginnings of systematic theology as later envisioned, called "summas"; and a new professional class, the scholar or teacher. The movement functioned as a servant of the church, not doubting its place or doctrine, seeking to show the rational coherency of it and, thus, providing a tool to explain and articulate the faith.

Taborites: with a designation derived from the fortress they established in 1420 a distance from Prague, this was a militant religious community that emerged in fourteenth-century Bohemia in sympathy with John Huss's complaints against the late medieval church. They were a Bible-based movement that insisted that the laity receive both the bread and the wine in the Eucharistic ritual and denied the Catholic view of its meaning, transubstantiation. The Taborites were crushed in 1452 when their fortress was captured by Catholic forces.

Verbal Monophysites (Severians): a view concerning the incarnate Christ. While the Monophysites rejected the dual nature Christology decreed at the Council of Chalcedon(451), arguing that a person is a single nature, that Christ was not two persons (Nestorianism), and, therefore, he possessed a single nature. Monophysites of this variety agreed in substance with the findings of Chalcedon, but disagreed with the language used in the Chalcedonian Creed.

Waldensians: an early protest movement founded by Peter Waldo in the twelfth century in northern Italy (and southern France) that was heralded by later Protestants as a precursor to the Reformation because it criticized the morals and teachings of the medieval Catholic Church. The Waldensians stressed the importance of the Bible and preaching much in the tradition of Wycliffe of England and Huss of Bohemia, though they predated them. Condemned by the Fourth Lateran Council (1215) under Innocent III, they were subsequently severely persecuted. In the Reformation era, the Waldensians joined the Calvinist tradition of Protestant reform through the work of William Farel, an early reformer in Geneva.

Wat Tyler's Rebellion (Peasant Rebellion of 1381): a serious insurrection of the lower working class in England who had been reduced to grinding poverty and slave-like conditions. In retrospect, this most prolific class struggle in English history proved the harbinger of the end of feudalism and serfdom in the country. The rebellion was short-lived, though the Tower of London was assaulted and some of the king's officials murdered, and leaders were summarily captured and executed.

Further Readings:
The Medieval Church (500–1500)

Primary Sources
for the Medieval Church

Abelard, Peter. *Sic et Non: A Critical Edition.* Blanche B. Boyer and Richard McKeon, eds. Chicago: University of Chicago Press, 1977.

Anselm, Saint. *The Major Works.* Brian Davies and G. R. Evans, eds. New York: Oxford University Press, 1998.

Aquinas, Thomas. *The Imitation of Christ: The First English Translation of the 'Imitatio Christi'.* Edited by B. J. H. Biggs. Oxford; New York: Oxford University Press, 1997.

_____. *Summa Theologiae: Latin Text and English Translation, Introductions, Notes, Appendices, and Glossaries.* New York: Blackfriars, McGraw-Hill, 1964.

Bernard of Clairvaux. *On Grace & Free Choice.* Trans. by Daniel O'Donovan. Kalamazoo, MI: Cistercian Publications, 1988.

Boethius. *The Consolation of Philosophy.* Rev ed. London: Penguin, 1999.

Fairweather, Eugene Rathbone. *A Scholastic Miscellany: Anselm to Ockham.* Ichthus, ed. Philadelphia: Westminster Press, 1981.

Francis of Assisi, Saint. *Francis of Assisi: Early Documents.* Regis J. Armstrong, J. Wayne Hellmann, and William J. Short, eds. Hyde Park, NY: New City Press, 2001.

Lombard, Peter. *The Sentences.* Trans. by Giulio Silano. Toronto: Pontifical Institute of Mediaeval Studies, 2007.

General Surveys
of the Medieval Church

Benedict XVI. *Church Fathers and Teachers: from Saint Leo the Great to Peter Lombard.* San Francisco: Ignatius Press, 2010.

Important Topics and People
of the Medieval Church

Aquinas, Thomas, and Anton Charles Pegis. *Introduction to Saint Thomas Aquinas.* New York: Modern Library, 1948.

Astell, Ann W. *Eating Beauty: The Eucharist and the Spiritual Arts of the Middle Ages.* Ithaca, NY: Cornell University Press, 2006.

Benedict, Anthony C. Meisel, and M. L. Del Mastro. *The Rule of St. Benedict.* Garden City, NY: Image Books, 1975.

Evans, G.R. *Bernard of Clairvaux.* New York: Oxford University Press, 2000.

Evans, G. R., ed. *The Medieval Theologians.* Malden, MA: Blackwell Publishers, 2001.

Fortini, Arnaldo. *Francis of Assisi.* New York: Crossroad Publishing Co., 1992.

Gobry, Ivan. *Saint Francis of Assisi.* Trans. by Michael J. Miller. San Francisco: Ignatius Press, 2006.

Hamburger, Jeffrey F. *The Mind's Eye: Art and Theological Argument in the Middle Ages.* Princeton, NJ: Princeton University Press, 2006.

Knell, Matthew. *The Immanent Person of the Holy Spirit from Anselm to Lombard: Divine Communion in the Spirit.* Colorado Springs, CO: Paternoster, 2009.

Kristeller, Paul Oskar, and Michael Mooney. *Renaissance Thought and Its Sources.* New York: Columbia University Press, 1979.

Lapsanski, Duane V. *Evangelical Perfection: An Historical Examination of the Concept in the Early Franciscan Sources.* St. Bonaventure, NY: Franciscan Institute, 1977.

Oberman, Heiko Augustinus. *Forerunners of the Reformation: The Shape of Late Medieval*

Thought. 1st ed. New York: Holt Rinehart and Winston, 1966.

Petry, Ray C. *Late Medieval Mysticism.* Philadelphia: Westminster Press, 1957.

Riatt, Jill, ed. *Christian Spirituality: High Middle Ages and Reformation.* New York: Crossroads, 1989.

Spinka, Matthew. *Advocates of Reform, from Wyclif to Erasmus.* Philadelphia: Westminster Press, 1953.

Spitz, Lewis William. *The Religious Renaissance of the German Humanists.* Cambridge, MA: Harvard University Press, 1963.

Tyerman, Christopher. *God's War: A New History of the Crusades.* Cambridge, MA: Belknap Press of Harvard University Press, 2006.

Weisheipl, James A. *Friar Thomas D'Aquino: His Life, Thought, & Work.* Washington, D.C.: Catholic University of America Press, 1983.

The Church, the Reformation, and Early Modern History (1500–1650)

Chapter 7 Outline

Chapter 7 Objectives

- That the reader will demarcate the two periods of the modern era chronologically and understand the basis of the division

- That the reader will identify the primary causes of the Protestant reformations

- That the reader will define the goals of the Protestant reformations

- That the reader will describe the life of Martin Luther

- That the reader will describe the defining characteristics of Lutheran thought

- That the reader will have some grasp of the history of sixteenth-century Lutheranism

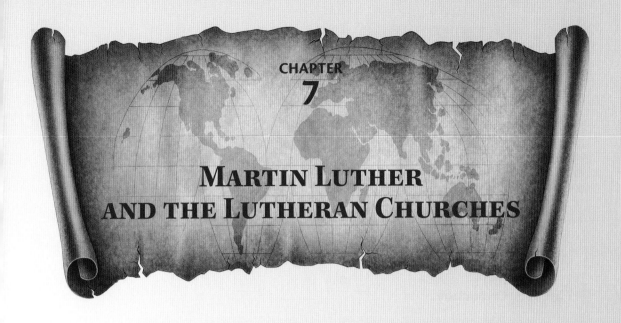

MARTIN LUTHER
AND THE LUTHERAN CHURCHES

THOUGH SCHOLARS HAVE WRITTEN as though the sixteenth century reform of the church was a single, monolithic event (perhaps attributable to a Protestant bias), the reformation of the late medieval church was a complex and variegated movement. In fact, while a common ingredient was the perception of a church that had spun into extravagance, impotence, and irrelevance, there was no unanimity as to the deliverance of the church from its morass. The solution of Luther was one option; that of Erasmus another; within these were differences and outside of them still more solutions.

In the larger perspective of centuries of reflection on the events of the sixteenth-century reformations, what is evident is that a collective part of a movement rejected medieval authority and ecclesiastical hegemony. The reformations were rooted in the intellectual impulse of the great Renaissance of the fourteenth and fifteenth centuries within Western Europe that resulted in what scholars have called the modern era, an era that stretched from 1500–1900. Within the modern era two periods are demarcated, the early modern period (1500–1650) and the late

modern period (1650–1900). The periods have in common the characteristics of the Renaissance revulsion to the imposition of external authority and an emphasis on the importance of the humanities. The early period did not reject external authorities entirely; it sought to replace one external authority (the hierarchical authority of the church) with another authority (the sacred writings as interpreted by pastors and scholars). The late modern period went a step further in rejecting all external authorities for internal authorities (the intellect and intuition, or feelings). The post

7.1. A PROTESTANT VIEW OF HISTORY

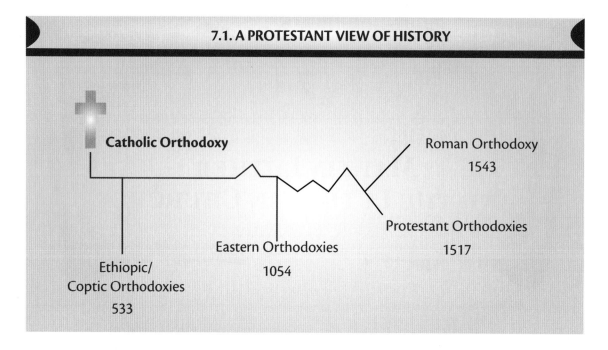

Catholic Orthodoxy

Roman Orthodoxy
1543

Protestant Orthodoxies
1517

Eastern Orthodoxies
1054

Ethiopic/
Coptic Orthodoxies
533

modern era bears witness to the folly of the entire endeavor (more of that later).

The Protestant Reformations

Among those broadly designated as Protestants, the term being coined in 1529 by Lutherans at the Diet of Speyer, scholars have divided into two segments: the magisterial reformers and the radical reformers. The former would designate those Protestant reformers such as Luther, Zwingli, Calvin, Knox, Cranmer, and others who sought to maintain the unity of church and state; the so-called radical reformers, though varying significantly in approaches to reforming the church and society (as well as in relationship to historic orthodoxy), maintained the necessity of the separation of church and state.

Renaissance	Reformation
Southern Europe	Northern Europe
Latin	German
Pre-Christian roots	Christian roots

Classical Humanism	Biblical
Arts & Sciences	Faith

The claim of the Protestant reformers was that the church was in need of significant correction; it had gradually become corrupt, deviating from a pristine purity in doctrine and practice. Luther made the point that significant deviation from orthodoxy came in the twelfth century, evidenced by the corrupting conclusions and redirections of the fourth of the Lateran Councils (1215). Calvin saw a progressive degeneration in the church from the time of Gregory the Great in the seventh century that reached an apex at the time of Bernard of Clairvaux in the eleventh century and again in his own day:

> Of old, Rome was indeed the mother of all churches, but after it began to become the see of Antichrist, it ceased to be what it once was (*Institutes of the Christian Religion*, 4.7.24).

7.2. THE REDEMPTION DEBATE: THE READING OF THE WESTERN CATHOLIC CHURCH

THE CATHOLIC
CHURCH

The
(Monophysite)
Catholic Church

553

The
(Chalcedonian)
Catholic Church

The Eastern
(Byzantine)
Orthodox Church

1054

The Western
Catholic Church

The Roman
Catholic Church

1517

The Protestant
Churches

7.3. THE REFORMERS ON JUSTIFICATION

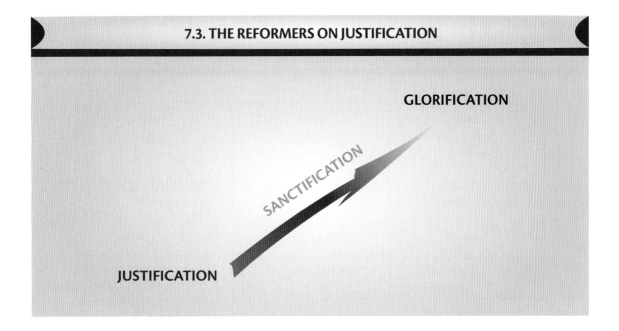

GLORIFICATION

SANCTIFICATION

JUSTIFICATION

In another place, Calvin's vitriol seemed unprecedented when he spoke of the papal corruption of the church, saying, "they put a foul harlot in the place of Christ's sacred bride" (4.2.3).

However, the Protestant reform movement was more than a negative reaction to institutional abuses through clerical ignorance, greed, and purposeful error; it was a rediscovery of the gospel that had been encrusted and distorted by errors that accumulated for centuries. It was the recovery and discovery of the ancient truths of a divine action in redeeming humankind without the necessity of human merit to do so. It was the insight that salvation was free in that it had been procured by Christ in his satisfaction of justice—divine wrath through divine intervention. This graciously divine substitution for the sinner and the procurement of a divine righteousness, was not granted by a gradual infusion (the reward of human obedience) but through a divine reckoning called imputed righteousness. It was the realization that divine salvation was procured in Christ on the cross, the divine instrument of divine wrath and mercy. This

salvation from sin was complete and forever, not as a theoretical possibility that had to be somehow grasped with the help of the church. With this insight came the rejection of late medieval conceptions of sin as merely a non-debilitating distraction or disease that could be overcome with the help of the church in dispensing divine grace in return for human obedience and compliance. The church's weak view of sin, clearly evident in Erasmus's complaints, and observed by the reformers, was the basis of all its misconceptions about redemption as brought about through sacramental obedience.

Reformation Questions

How is a person saved?
Where does religious authority lie?
What is the church?
What is the essence of Christian living?

From a Protestant perspective, the discovery of the reformers has been commonly encapsulated in the so-called five "alones," and, in a sense, the Protestants embraced a word that does not specifically appear in the sacred

7.4. THE THREE FUNDAMENTALS OF PROTESTANT REFORMATION TEACHING

Sola Scriptura	Sola Gratia	Sola Fide
The Content of Salvation	The Means of Salvation	The Appropriation of Salvation
Authority on in the Bible, not Pope or church	Gift from God, not from human effort to please God	Salvation from sin by faith alone, not by human works

writings, though Luther added it in his German translation of Romans 3:23–26. For this he received considerable criticism from his opponents for adding to the Scriptures, but his use of *alone* pinpointed the issues with late medieval theology and practice.

By arguing for the "Scriptures alone," Protestants made the point that the sacred text was the supreme arbiter of faith, not church councils or ecclesiastical authorities. In "Christ alone," the reformers asserted that the death of Christ as sin bearer completely procured redemption. It did not secure the possibility or potential for a divine requiting of divine wrath; it actually and completely provided it. By this assertion, Protestants were rejecting a redeeming function in the sacraments. In "grace alone," the claim was made that all human merit was excluded from salvation, that no criteria existed whereby humans could obligate God to act in mercy. Hence, this complete salvation was received from a gracious God through "faith alone," since human endeavor could not be the ground of salvation unless the Scriptures were incorrect and the

creature could accomplish salvation. Finally, because of the implications of the four "alones," the duty of the recipient of grace was a lifestyle reflective of gratitude that resulted in obedience; that is, a life lived for God's interests, a life of appreciative conformity out of love and gratitude for the inscrutable wonder of a free forgiveness in Christ.

Though the Protestant Reformation was a recovery of the teachings of the apostles and an attempt to bring the church and her offices into conformity with the Bible, it was more than that. It was an attempt to renovate society through the creation of a distinctively Christian approach to life and its institutions. The reformers experienced a world in which the sacred and the secular were not dichotomized, unlike the late modern era, In this sense, the sixteenth century inherited a medieval and Christian perspective.

In rejecting papal episcopacy as the form for church governance, the reformers were forced to think through the issue of church authority, as well as the meaning of the sacraments. The varied answers given by the re-

7.5. THE FIVE "SOLAS" OF PROTESTANT REFORMATION TEACHING

	Sola Scriptura	Sola Christus	Sola Gratia	Sola Fide	Sola Deo Gloria
The Meaning	Authority and sufficiency of the Bible	Exclusivity of the Provider	Totality of the provision	Means of appropriation	The purpose of it all
Relative to Salvation	Content	Basis	"Objective" (external) cause	"Subjective" (personal) agency	Reason for living a godly life
Its Origin	From God	From God's Son	From God's pleasure	Through the gift of faith	For God's glory

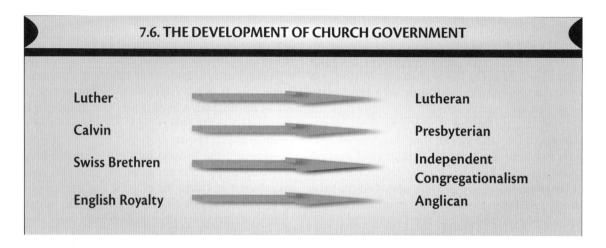

7.6. THE DEVELOPMENT OF CHURCH GOVERNMENT

Luther	Lutheran
Calvin	Presbyterian
Swiss Brethren	Independent Congregationalism
English Royalty	Anglican

formers created what subsequently became the great Protestant denominations. Generally, as developed in the sixteenth- and seventeenth-century Europe and England, the ecclesiastical options can be divided into two categories: those that maintained an interconnectedness of church and state and those less comfortable with the possibility of state interference or those that simply existed without the possibility of state assistance. Examples of the former would be the polity in the Church of England, the Lutheran churches, the Presbyterian and Reformed churches, and the English Congregational churches. Most prominent of the latter are the Baptists and perhaps the Quakers. It is the general practice of scholars to view the complex Protestant reform movement through the lens of the various church polities that emerged in the reform centers: Wittenberg, Zurich, Geneva, Strasbourg, Edinburgh, and London.

Martin Luther (1483–1546) and the Lutheran Churches

If there was a catalyst, a voice of protest, that rallied weary, empty souls and inspired them with hope for change, this was the person. Voices of disenchantment with the direction and fidelity of the church had been noticeable since the eleventh century, and even before,

reaching a shrilled pitch in the **Waldensians**, John Wycliffe, John Huss, John of Prague, Cardinal Rimini, and William Savonarola. However, the winds of culture and ecclesiastical might muffled their protests and the eyes and

7.7. MARTIN LUTHER

Born: November 10, 1483
Place of Birth: Eisleben, Germany
Died: February 18, 1546
Education: University of Erfurt
Place of Ministry: Wittenberg, Germany
Position: Professor of Bible and Theology
Contribution: "Justification by Faith Alone"
Major Works:
   Address to the German Nobility
   Freedom of the Christian Man
   German Translation of the Bible
   The Babylonian Captivity of the Church

ears of the masses were blinded and stuffed respectively.

The deafening winds gradually coalesced into a soft, pleasant breeze and people stopped to listen. They stopped because an obscure, troubled Augustinian monk from Wittenberg on the Elbe River was making sense. Someone was finally lifting his voice, and pen, to complain of a decadent church in great need of reform. In the eyes of papal authorities, he was a "wolf in clerical garb," a demon incarnate, a troubler of "Zion." To others, Luther was a forceful man who brought needed corrections. While interpretations of the man are myriad, all agreed that the Augustinian monk touched off a movement that changed the course of the late medieval church and western civilization for over five hundred years.

Luther and the Early Years (1483–1517)

Like most people who later make the headlines, Luther's beginning veiled any suggestion that his life would be unusual. He was born in Eisleben, the territory of Saxony (now Germany), to Hans and Margaret Luther. Hans worked in the copper mines and ap-

pears to have had little, if any, formal education; his mother possessed a better heritage than her husband and may have had some education. Baptized the day after his birth on St. Martin's Day in the nearby Church of St. Peter and Paul, he was raised in a traditionally Catholic family. He was accorded a fine education, initially in Latin schools at Mansfield, Magdeburg, and Eisenach, followed by matriculation at Erfurt University (1501–1505). The first of several religious crises changed his career on 2 July 1505 when, returning from a visit to his parents, he was caught in a thunderstorm. Fearing for his life, he prayed to Saint Anne for help (traditionally said to be the mother of Mary, a family saint, and the protector of miners). To the disappointment of his father, who had hoped his son would become a lawyer, Luther kept his promise and sought a career in the church.

Not far from the University in Erfurt was a monastery belonging to the Augustinian order; Luther sought admission and there trained for two years to become a priest. The monastery was under the direction of Johannes Staupitz (ca. 1460–1524), vicar-general of the Augus-

A 1527 portrait of Hans Luther (Luther's father) and Margaret Luther (Luther's mother) by Lucas Cranach the Elder (1472–1553). At the German National Museum. Courtesy of Qp10qp.

Posthumous portrait of Martin Luther as an Augustinian monk by Lucas Cranach the Elder (1472–1553). At the German National Museum. Courtesy of Jan Arkesteijn.

tinian Order in Germany, who became Luther's father-confessor.

Ordained a priest in 1507, Luther experienced religious uncertainties and dreadful fears. If peace of soul was a fruit of obedience and penance, why could he not find it? How could a holy and just God forgive sinners? If it required righteousness, how could he ever be righteous enough? Reflecting on those years in the monastery, he confided, "I was a good monk, and I kept the rule of my order so strictly that I may say that if ever a monk got to heaven by his monkery it was I."

To assuage Luther's unrest, Staupitz sent him to lecture at the University of Wittenberg, a school founded by Frederick the Elector, of Saxony, in 1502 (there Staupitz held a lectureship in the Bible).

Evidence of Luther's growing respect within the Augustinian order came in 1510 when he was chosen to carry letters to Rome for his order. A journey of nine months ensued as he witnessed firsthand the decadent state of the church in Rome. This was another turning point in his life. For his endeavor, Luther was granted a dispensation of ten thousand years off purgatory for a deceased member of his family; he applied it to his grandparents! On his return to Erfurt, he was permanently transferred to the University of Wittenberg where he became a doctor of theology and professor of Bible, a post he held until his death. Additionally, in 1515 he was appointed a district vicar in charge of eleven monasteries throughout Saxony and Thuringia.

Settling into his new post, he prepared lectures on various books of the Bible, principally Galatians, Psalms, and Romans. Each seemed to bring another religious crisis in his life; each seemed to open new vistas of religious truth. In what has been termed "the tower experience," Luther came to see that the righteousness that God required of the sinner was an alien righteousness; it was the righteousness of Christ freely and fully credited through faith.

The circumstance that thrust him into the limelight from obscurity was the controversy over the sale of indulgences in Germany. Sadly, Luther came to realize that God's grace was for sale in Rome! Begun by Julius II in 1506 and continued by Leo X, his successor, the Basilica of St. Peter replaced an earlier church on the site, as well as the somewhat distant Lateran Palace, as the site of the papal residence. The cost of the project was astronomical, and it would take over one hundred years to complete.

To finance the building, Leo granted the sale of indulgences throughout Europe; indulgences were church sanctioned forgiveness from the temporal punishment for sin. Leo, as did the popes since the Crusades, assumed that the church possessed a treasury of merit that had been purchased through Christ, which it could dispense on the basis of contrition (in this case money). Not only was the practice a lucrative source of revenue for the church, it was financed in Germany by Jacob Fugger of Augsburg, one of the wealthiest men in Europe, who underwrote papal interests as well as the election of emperors.

> "His misgivings began with the indulgence controversy in 1518–19, when he had to recognize that God's grace was for sale in Rome" (Oberman, *Luther*, 149).

The coming of an indulgence seller, John Tetzel, a Dominican priest, into towns near Wittenberg brought Luther's ire. Luther summarized Tetzel's claim in a typical Lutheresque fashion. "He had grace and power from the Pope to offer forgiveness even if someone slept with the Holy Virgin Mary, the Mother of God, as long as a contribution would be put into the coffer."

> "Therefore those preachers of indulgences are in error, who say that by the pope's indulgences a man is freed from every penalty, and saved" (Thesis 21).

> It is certain that when the penny jingles into

the money-box, gain and avarice can be increased, but the result of the intercession of the Church is in the power of God alone" (Thesis 28)." "The treasures of the indulgences are nets with which they now fish for the riches of men" (Thesis 66).

Luther and the Break from Rome (1517–1521)

Luther's response to indulgences, according to Philip Melanchthon, was expressed in the posting of the Ninety-Five Theses on the Castle Church door in Wittenberg, 31 October 1517. The intent of the theses was to raise the issue of indulgence abuse; it was not a rejection of the notion of indulgences or the papacy. The translation of them, however, from Latin into German caused a sensation through Europe; someone was finally lifting a voice of protest.

> "For the righteousness of God is the cause of salvation. Here, too, 'the righteousness of God' must not be understood as that righteousness by which he is righteous in himself, but as that righteousness by which we are made righteous (justified) by Him, and this happens through faith in the gospel" (Luther on Romans 1:17).

What Luther was attempting to do was to incite debates on the issue within his monastic order. The result was the Indulgence Controversy of 1518–1519. Tensions between the church hierarchy and Luther escalated. A debate at Heidelberg over the issues in 1518 won for Luther an ever-enlarging circle of friends. To stop the feisty monk, the church called Luther to Augsburg. Meeting in Jacob Fugger's bank before Cardinal Thomas Cajetan (1469–1534), Luther refused to repent of his actions.

In the presence of John Eck (1486–1543), a professor of theology, at Leipzig in 1519, Luther rejected the primacy of the pope and the infallibility of church councils. At a crucial juncture in the discussions, Luther confessed alliance with the ideas of John Huss, likely sealing his own doom. It was John Eck who was largely

A woodcut depicting the meeting of Martin Luther (right) and Cardinal Cajetan (left, before the book). Courtesy of Torsten Schleese.

responsible for the issuance of *Exsurge Domine*, Luther's bull of ecclesiastical excommunication (15 June 1520), and proved a tireless opponent of Luther and Lutheranism throughout his life.

> "At thy ascension into heaven thou has commanded the care, rule and administration of this vineyard to Peter as head and to thy representatives, his successors, as the Church triumphant. A roaring sow of the woods has undertaken to destroy this vineyard, a wild beast wants to devour it. . . . We prohibit this Martin from now on and henceforth to contrive any preaching or the office of preaching ("The Excommunication of Luther," *Exsurge Domine*, 15 July 1520).

Knowing the torrent of criticism that would follow his failure to repent (he was officially excommunicated on 3 January 1521), Luther busied himself producing three works in rapid succession, taking his views and rebuttals of the church public. In *Address to the German Nobility*, Luther attacked the validity of the "three walls" of church authority: the authority of church over the state, the authority of the church to interpret Scripture, and the authority of church councils called by the church.

Luther nailed his Ninety-Five Theses to the door of All Saints' Church (Castle Church) in Wittenberg on 31 October 1517, sparking the Reformation. The Latin inscription above informs the reader that the original door was destroyed by a fire, and that in 1858, King Frederick William IV of Prussia ordered the replacement be made. Luther's theses were engraved into today's bronze gate. Courtesy of Jost Tauchen.

In *The Babylonian Captivity of the Church*, Luther attacked the sacraments of the church, rejecting four as unwarranted and retaining three (baptism, Eucharist, and confession or contrition [there is considerable dispute on this issue by the scholars, but it was incorporated into Luther's *Small Catechism* of 1529]), each redefined. He adopted Augustine's definition of the sacraments as outward symbols of internal spiritual realities, the validity of them in the possession of the things symbolized. In this most strident treatise, he accused the papacy of being an antichrist.

In the last of the trilogy, *Freedom of the Christian*, Luther presents a brief synopsis of his understanding of the gospel. The inner is not the same as the outward person; that which is outward cannot affect the inward (this being among the errors of Rome). The inward person is only affected by faith alone in the Word of God alone.

Influenced by the church's condemnation of Luther, the emperor, Charles V summoned the recalcitrant monk to appear before him at the Diet of Worms in April 1521. Prince Frederick the Elector, who used his influence to prevent the hearing from being in Rome, secured a guarantee of Luther's safety. The journey of some three hundred miles took over a week as Luther encountered large supportive crowds and preached in several churches. At the appointed time, Luther appeared before the emperor, and his interrogation was led by John Eck (1486–1543), perhaps the foremost defender of the Roman Church and whom Luther had debated at the Leipzig Disputation in 1519.

"Unless I am convinced by the testimony of the Scriptures or by clear reason (for I do not trust either in the pope or in councils alone, since it is well known that they have often erred and contradicted themselves), I am bound by the Scriptures I have quoted and my conscience is captive to the Word of God. I cannot and will not recant anything, since it is neither safe nor right to go against conscience. May God help me. Amen" (Luther at the Diet of Worms, 18 April 1521).

Eck posed questions to Luther: first, with his

A 1877 painting of Luther before the Diet of Worms by Anton von Werner (1843–1915). Courtesy of Ckan Kartinb1.

Invitation to Church History: World

writings displayed on a table in the great hall, he was asked if he would repent of all the errors they contained. He replied that he would rescind any errors in them found contrary to the Holy Scriptures. Second, Eck asked Luther how he could be so arrogant as to teach contrary to 1500 years of the history of the church, an assertion that his ideas were novel and contrary to what had "always, everywhere, been taught in the church."

Shaken, Luther asked for time to think through an answer that he gave upon returning the following day. Luther doubted the assumption behind the charge of novelty, saying that there was not unsullied centuries-old teaching in the church, its teachers having never been unanimous in their instruction; they had contradicted themselves as Abelard demonstrated in *Sic et Non* centuries earlier. At that point, Luther appealed to the authority of the Scriptures, conscience, and reason. A month later, the emperor issued the Edict of Worm condemning Luther as a "reviver of old and condemned heresies and inventor of new ones." His books were to be destroyed, his movement suppressed, and he was declared to be a criminal charged with treason ("to kill this moral pestilence") against the state.

Several days after the diet, Luther left Worms, but on the return to Wittenberg he was whisked away for protective seclusion to the Wartburg Castle near Eisenach, which was instigated by Frederick the Elector, his prince. He remained there for ten months under an assumed name, Junker Georg (Knight George), allowing his hair to grow as well as a beard, as the currents of religious change gained momentum across Europe. In what Luther described as a "lonely tenement of the bats," he achieved in less than two months his greatest literary achievement, the translation of the New Testament into the German language. Printed in 1522, the translation not only brought the Bible to the German people, but it contributed remarkably to the standardization of the German language, since Luther carefully selected words to best communicate across

the various German dialects). By 1534 he completed the translation of the Hebrew Scriptures, which proved immensely popular.

The reform movement in Germany evidenced radical tendencies that disturbed Luther. Reports came to Wartburg that Andreas Karlstadt (1486–1541), the highly educated chair of the department of theology at the University of Wittenberg, the man who awarded Luther a doctorate in 1512 and who was excommunicated with Luther at the Diet of Worms, was creating such religious chaos that state intervention was a possibility.

Karlstad replaced the Catholic Eucharist with a reformed liturgy and destroyed statuary and religious art in the churches that he deemed iconoclastic. Luther returned to Wittenberg in March 1522 to quell the riotous spirit of the religious reform movement. Karlstad left the city for a pastorate elsewhere, propagating his various views.

Luther's return to Wittenberg marked a new phase in the growing movement, the establishment of the identity of reform of the churches in Germany under his watchful care. Luther's tools were the preaching and teaching of the Scriptures, a growing literary productivity, and pastoral oversight of the spiritual health of the churches. An example of his pastoral concerns is evidenced in the publication of both the *Small Catechism* and *Large Catechism* (1529). Having witnessed firsthand "the deplorable, miserable condition" of biblical knowledge in the churches, he prepared the catechisms and addressed them to the pastors, urging them to instruct their congregations.

Luther and the Formation of a Movement (1522–1530)

The Peasants' War (1524–1526)
The Lutheran movement was shaped in the 1520s by conflict in many ways. For example, Luther's foreboding fears that radical elements would bring the wrath of the state on

A circa 1521 portrait of Martin Luther as Junker Georg by Lucas Cranach the Elder (1472–1553). At the Museum of Fine Arts in Leipzig, Germany. Courtesy of nevsepic.com.ua.

The Wartburg room where Luther translated the New Testament into German. An original first edition is kept in the case on the desk. Courtesy of Jan Arkesteijn.

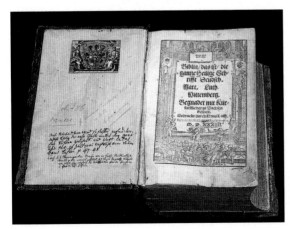

Luther's translation of the Bible, 1534. Courtesy of Torsten Schleese.

the embryonic movement caused him to resist Karlstadt and later Thomas Müntzer (1488–1525), who considered violence a part of reform.

Müntzer, who pastored for some time in Zwickau (hence the term "Zwickau Prophets"), combined rising social unrest due to mounting class consciousness with religious fervor and apocalyptic preaching, creating what became known in 1524 as the **Peasants' War**. The peasants attempted to abolish class distinctions, establish a commonwealth, and practice absolute social equality. For some in the peasants' movement," communalism and pacifism were also practiced. They are generally identified within the broad Anabaptist movement because of their rejection of infant baptism and church/state union.

Luther's response to this movement was a flurry of pamphlets. In *Treatise on Secular Authority* (1523), he showed himself a supporter of the state, arguing that the state is the minister of God and its function is to make and administer just laws and punish lawlessness, maintaining a stable society (his view reflects those of Augustine). *Against the Murderous Thieving Mobs of Peasants* (1525) was an extremely harsh attack on the peasant movement. His advice was blunt. "Therefore, let everyone who can, smite, slay, and stab, secretly or openly, remembering that nothing can be more poisonous, hurtful, or devilish than a rebel."

The revolt against establishmentarianism was crushed with an enormous loss of life. The net effect was that peasants who poorly understood Luther's message of liberation as an embrace of social equalitarianism felt the sting of his rebuke. Consequently, many areas of Germany, particularly in the south and central regions, rejected Lutheranism and returned to the Roman Church.

The Separation from the Humanists

Another way in which the Lutheran movement was shaped was by the controversy with Erasmus. Though Erasmus and Luther shared a perception of the need for church reform, they differed profoundly on the issues of the role of human endeavor in salvation. In 1524, Erasmus published *The Freedom of the Will,* arguing that the human will retains the power to cooperate with God in the accomplishment of redemption. Though the human will was not sufficient of itself to obtain salvation, contrary to **Pelagianism**, it was not so blighted that it had no causative agency. Grace and human response together could obtain what neither alone was capable of. Erasmus stood opposed to Augustine's teachings on human sin and the necessity of grace and in opposition to Luther (actually

Erasmus was urged by princes and pope to engage Luther at this point).

> "Erasmus pinned his hopes on the progress of time and the educated man, the best defender of the loftiest interests, whose innate, ineradicable striving for self-actualization is purified by God and then finds consummation in true piety. From Erasmus's perspective Luther was impatience personified, a monk who would listen to no one, who had not learned from history and threatened the cause of piety and education by casting doubt on man's moral disposition and perfectibility" (Oberman, *Luther,* 216).

Luther recognized Erasmus brilliance and felt compelled to prepare a formal rebuttal, *The Bondage of the Will* (1525). While Luther did not see Erasmus's arguments as insurmountable, he did recognize that his opponent was one of the few who actually grasped the central issue in the dispute; the root of the controversy concerned the nature and capacities of humankind for good. Erasmus embraced a view of humankind that allowed for educability and progressive perfectibility. Luther viewed humankind as completely fallen and unable to do anything that would necessitate anything but God's wrath. The human will is not a power that could affect good in any way; it is enslaved to base motives and corrupting influences with no ability to alter its condition.

Luther and Erasmus stood on differing sides of a great anthropological divide, the figurehead of two traditions. For Luther, this issue was the heart of the matter; for Erasmus, though he differed from Luther, it was an obscure and ancillary issue. The one, however, flattered human potential, exalted in the hope of human progress through programmatic orderings, education, and progress in the sciences. It was the reemergence of an ancient tradition, the harbinger of an optimist view of human potential that would become somewhat later a foundational assumption of the Enlightenment and now post modernity. The

Enlightenment was the celebration of the unfallen self and the adoration of human potential; it was Erasmian rationalism disjoined from the authority of the late medieval church, a revisitation of the Greeks in religious dress.

Luther's view of human potential being impotent to bring substantive change, at first sounded demeaning, but it lifted the burdened sinner and opened the vista of hope through free grace and unmerited pardon through a divine substitute. Jesus, according to Luther, was alone sufficient to end the bondage of sin and death without the necessity of human merit in attitude or action.

Luther and the Institution of Marriage

When Luther reflected in 1532 on the reform movement in church and society that was so much a part of his life, he numbered among the most significant accomplishments the restitution of marriage to its rightful place in culture. Though the roles and perception of women within most reformation circles would be viewed as archaic by later standards, it contrasted remarkably with the standards of the late medieval church and sixteenth-century society in general. In many German cities, brothels were sanctioned, clerics treated sex outside of marriage as a lesser of possible evils, and sexual license was a right of passage into adulthood.

A 1528 portrait of Katharina von Bora on canvas by Lucas Cranach the Elder (1472–1553). At the Lower Saxony State Museum. Courtesy of Hajotthu.

"It was only four hundred years ago that the priests of Germany were compelled by force to take the vows of celibacy" (The Augsburg Confession, Article 23).

The medieval church often portrayed women as dangerously seductive beings and matrimony as a way to avoid lust, but little more. Clearly the monastic rule was elevated over the marital state. Though modern feminists would deplore Luther's stance that the woman's role was restricted to the home and care of children, he was adamant that the bordello was not their place. Marriage was an honorable state in which a man and woman vowed to live together in a state of holy wedlock, raising children for the glory of God, nurturing them in the faith of true religion and as worthy citizens of the state.

Katharina von Bora was fifteen years younger than her husband Martin Luther: poor, not remarkable for beauty or culture—but healthy, strong, frank, intelligent, and high-minded. She was called the "morning star of Wittenberg" and rose at 4 AM. Katharina took over the household, particularly the household expenses; it is said that Dr. Luther did not have a clue how to run a household. She also proved herself to be a good housewife, swineherder, and gardener. She was locally famous as an herbalist and brewer of beer, and massage therapist. She was a model housewife and accomplished business woman. She handled Luther's finances since he was always giving away his money. As Luther said, "God divided the hand into fingers so that money would slip through." She remodeled the old monastery to take in thirty students and guests. Luther hadn't made his bed for a year . . . it was "foul from sweat."

Luther, as well as the reformers in general, opposed the celibacy of the priesthood, encouraging former nuns and priests to marry, holding up clerical marriage as the model of the home in society. For Luther marriage, expressed in *The Estate of Marriage* in 1522, was a gift from God that created and sustained human life. While marriage lost its sacramental function to Luther, it nonetheless remained a sacred gift. He once noted, "Next to God's Word there is no more precious treasure than holy matrimony."

On 13 June 1525, Luther and Katharina von Bora (1499–1552), a former nun, were married in a civil ceremony in Wittenberg. Sent to a Benedictine convent school at the age of five, Katharina or Katie subsequently was sent to the Cistercian convent at Nimbschen and became a nun at sixteen. With several nuns, and Luther's help, Katie left the convent in 1523 and resided in Wittenberg with the Cranach family (Lucas Cranach the Elder [1472–1553] was a former mayor and councilman who operated a pharmacy, a print shop, and taught art; Cranach was a great painter in his own right).

After several failed attempts to secure a marriage for her, Luther showed interest in her as did Katie in him. Martin and Katie had six children: Hans or Johannes, Elizabeth, Magdelena, Martin, Paul, and Margaret. Elizabeth died in infancy; Magdalena or Lenchen at thirteen. Luther wanted of his sons a soldier, a

scholar, and a peasant. He got a lawyer, a private citizen, and a doctor.

Luther, Lutheranism, and the Holy Roman Empire

The relationship of the state to the Lutheran movement changed in 1526. The emperor, Charles V, had strained relationships with the papacy and Clement VII, but the Turkish threat in the East functioned to lessen hostilities. The emperor called the Diet of Speyer and, though the Edict of Worms was not annulled, its effect was temporarily suspended; the princes were granted the right to determine the religion of their regencies. In exchange for needed military assistance against the Turks that were pushing into Hungary, Lutheran Protestants gained the benefit of religious toleration, though it divided the nation along religious lines.

When the threat had lessened by 1529 and the Turkish push through Hungary toward Vienna had been repulsed, Charles called a second Diet at Speyer to promote further reconciliation within his fractured empire. However, when Charles's motive for the diet was not made clear to his presiding legate in time, Ferdinand and other Roman Catholics sought to reverse the policy of religious tolerance invoked three years earlier. The protestation of the diet's attempt to suppress the Lutheran movement by six German princes and fourteen cities with the signing a formal document on 15 April 1529 caused the coining of a new term, Protestantism. Some Lutherans resisted verbally the revocation of the first Edict of Speyer (1526). Thus the term **Protestant** in its original context was associated with protest, though it has now attained a wider significance.

The mounting politico/religious crisis with its threat of war between the emperor and the Lutherans caused Martin Bucer, the reformer at Strasbourg, and Philip of Hesse, among others, to consider rapprochement between Luther and the German Swiss reformer Ulrich Zwingli of Zurich. The hope was that a theological agreement would lead to a political alliance. Several reformers representing both the Lutheran and Swiss viewpoints met at Marburg Castle in Germany in October 1529, though the principal leaders were Luther and Zwingli. Each had prepared their opinions on fifteen doctrinal points and, surprisingly, agreed on fourteen of them. The last was the Eucharist. There formidable disagreement ended any hope of unity among them. More than theology caused the lack of resolution; political and social differences contributed to the outcome. This was one of the darkest moments in the history of the Reformation—the fracturing of the Protestant movement.

The emperor found it difficult to deal with the Lutheran menace due to the Turkish threat in the East and hostilities with France in the West. Conflict with France ended in 1529. The conflict with Clement VII seemed ameliorated when he crowned Charles emperor of the Holy Roman Empire in Bologna, but the Turkish threat was mounting in intensity. Charles felt it was time to address the religious tensions among the Germans and prepare for war if he proved unsuccessful in halting the Lutheran movement. The Lutherans were instructed to present their claims.

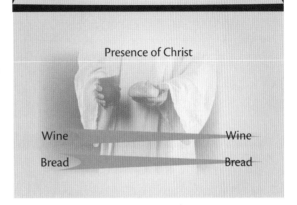

7.8. CONSUBSTANTIATION: LUTHERAN CONCEPT OF THE LORD'S TABLE

Presence of Christ

Wine — Wine
Bread — Bread

In March 1530, Elector John of Saxony instructed Luther, Philip Melanchthon, Justin Jonas, and Johannes Bugenhagen to prepare a document (the Torgau Articles). After revision, the document was presented to the diet, becoming the Augsburg Confession of Faith, the greatest statement of Lutheran orthodoxy. Charles was unmoved by the document and determined to unite Germany under one religious faith, Roman Catholicism.

For the Lutherans the failure at Augsburg was a portent of dark days of religious strife. Accordingly, several Lutheran cities and free cities formed the **Schmalkaldic League** in 1531, a mutual defense pact. Charles's preoccupation with France and the Turks prevented his action against the Lutherans until the 1540s. He defeated the league in 1547 in the **Schmalkaldic War** (1546–1547), capturing significant Lutheran leaders. The emperor imposed the Augsburg Interim in 1548 that called for the reestablishment of Roman Catholic practices in Lutheran territories. The interim proved unenforceable (as was the later Leipzig Interim). Lutherans resisted it and Charles was too war-weary to press its claims. As a result, Charles granted toleration to the Lutherans in 1555 with the Peace of Augsburg. Religious af-

A 1557 woodcut of the Marburg Colloquium. Courtesy of Torsten Schleese.

7.9. THE HISTORICAL DEVELOPMENT OF LUTHERANISM

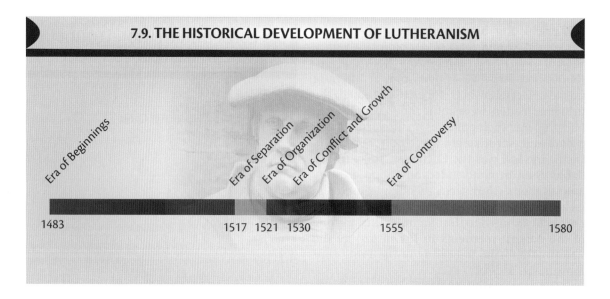

Era of Beginnings   Era of Separation   Era of Organization   Era of Conflict and Growth   Era of Controversy

1483   1517   1521   1530   1555   1580

filiation was to be determined by the devotion of the princes!

Luther's Later Years (1530–1546)

Luther did not enjoy robust health after 1531, the years of controversy gave rise to various ailments. The long struggle with Rome took a heavy toll, as did his own vigorous and volatile personality. In the 1530s the scandal of Philip of Hesse's marital intrigue in which Luther counseled bigamy caused significant acrimony and turmoil. He suffered with kidney and bladder stones, arthritis, digestive problems, hearing loss, and heart problems. Further, the death of his daughter Magdalena (Lenchen) in 1542 brought on a bout of severe depression. He grew so weary of the Wittenbergers that he despaired, told Katie to sell their possessions. He planned to leave the city, only to be dissuaded by Melanchthon and others.

> "I gobble up food like a Bohemian and guzzle like a German; God be thanked for it. Amen" (Letter to Katie, 2 July 1540).

As Luther's health deteriorated, he appeared to be short-tempered and harsh. His declining health may have been a factor in a profoundly anti-Semitic pamphlet, *The Jews and Their Lies* (1543). Though short of urging their conversion, he seems never to have arisen above the general Christian attitude of the time on this matter. He appears to have been a person who gained monumental successes in life, but he could not pause to enjoy them and rest in his accomplishments. His last pamphlet was aimed at his old nemesis, Rome, and was entitled *Against the Papacy of Rome Founded by the Devil!* (1545).

> "I prefer the books of Master Philippus [Melanchthon] to my own. I am rough, stormy, and altogether warlike. I am here to fight innumerable monsters and devils. I must remove all stumps and stones, cut away thistles and thorns, and clear the wild forests, but Master Philippus comes along softly and gently, sowing and watering with joy, according to the gifts which God has abundantly bestowed upon him" (Luther).

In extremely poor health, Luther left Wittenberg in January 1546 only to return for interment in the Castle Church. He was called to Eisleben, the city of his birth some sixty-three years before, to settle a dispute among Mansfield counts. He was successful, but he became gravely ill. He languished for several weeks, preaching at St. Andreas Church when he could, but he died of pulmonary arrest on 18 February 1546 in a physician's home near the church.

Lutheranism after Luther

The death of Luther brought a crisis to the evangelical churches in Germany, as Luther had called them. Gone was their leader, the glue that had brought cohesion to the movement. Philip Melanchthon (1497–1560) became the recognized leader within the movement, though this was severely contested at times.

Melanchthon was a well-trained humanist scholar; he was quiet in spirit, a conciliator by nature, a lover of peace in the churches, and cautious. Some considered him weak in leadership qualities, lacking entirely the forcefulness of Luther. His genius was not so much in the realm of creative powers or a gripping leadership style as it was in the realm of the organization, systematization, and defense of the thoughts of others, especially Luther's.

Philipp Melanchthon's house in Wittenberg, Germany. Courtesy of A. Savin.

In 1521, he published the first defense of reformational theology in a systematic format, the *Loci Communes* (*Common Thoughts on Theology*), a work that went through one-hundred editions in his lifetime. Luther was so inspired by it that he felt it should be placed among the church's most cherished writings. Though not the only contributor to the composition of the Augsburg Confession (1530), Melanchthon was the most important one. The confession remains the primary expression of Lutheran faith.

Though Melanchthon's contribution to Lutheranism is unquestioned, many came to feel that his conciliatory mood was causing doctrinal drift from Luther's convictions. For example, Lutherans debated the function of the Old Testament law. Luther viewed the Mosaic

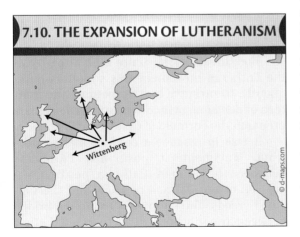

7.10. THE EXPANSION OF LUTHERANISM

Wittenberg

© d-maps.com

EFFIGIES PHIL: MELANCHTHONIS · ANN · AET · XXX CZ LVCA CRONACHIO PICTORE · · M · D · XXXVII ·

A 1537 portrait of Philip Melanchthon by Lucas Cranach the Elder (1472–1553). At the State Art Gallery in Karlsruhe, Germany. Courtesy of Oursana.

Andreas Osiander (1498–1552) caused a controversy by suggesting that a believer was not justified by the imputed righteousness of Christ but by the indwelling of the righteous Christ. Justification then, in his view, was progressive through union with Christ. His emphasis was on Christ *in* the believer, more fully recognized by the believer, rather than *for* the believer. Osiander's view of justification implied a participational model.

Georg Major (1502–1574), a student of Melanchthon's and professor at Wittenberg, following the Leipzig Interim (1548) argued that good works were necessary for salvation, a view that seemed to be too conciliatory to the Roman Catholic view, though not in any meritorious sense. Nicholas von Amsdorf (1483–1565) strenuously opposed Major. Melanchthon rejected the notion of good work as necessary for salvation, but was willing to say the good works were simply "necessary" without further elaboration or connection to salvation.

The issue of the place of human volition in the matter of salvation—man's freedom and converting grace—exposed the degree that Melanchthon's humanist training influenced his theology. Called the synergistic controversy, Melanchthon, and other prominent Lutherans, were willing to soften Luther's understanding of the bondage of the will, advocating a weakened form of cooperative grace. Amsdorf opposed the synergism and the corollary of it, the rejection of divine predestination.

The threat to the unity and integrity of the Lutheran movement was serious. Consequently, to preserve and perpetuate the heritage of doctrinal orthodoxy, Lutheran scholars prepared the Formula of Concord (1577).

It was in essence a confessional or doctrinal statement; it positioned Lutherans between the Roman Catholic position expressed at the Council of Trent and the Calvinist creeds. The intent was to build a bridge between those who strictly followed Luther

code as functioning to bring a person to Christ through threats of punishment, but not as a rule for the Christian since its basic motive was fear, not grace. For others the law had a continuing function in the believer's sanctification, causing some to see an intrusion of the reformed perspective. Another phase of the discussion of the use of the law had to do with gospel presentation, though such a discussion spilled over into the relation of the law to the believer. John Agricola (ca.1494–1566), a Latin educator in Eisleben, argued that the law should not be preached because it was the gospel that produced repentance; Melanchthon opposed his view.

("the True Lutherites") and the moderates (the Philipites). It was an attempt to interpret the Augsburg Confession in a manner conciliatory to both parties.

The formula affirms the bondage of the human will (imputed righteousness as opposed to infused righteousness in salvation), the importance of the law for Christians (good works are important in sanctification), the physical presence of Christ in the Eucharist, freedom in matters of indifference, and divine predestination to life. This was followed in 1580 with the Book of Concord, a compilation of ten creeds and apologies. These include the Formula of Concord, the Augsburg Confession, Luther's two catechisms, the Smalkaldic Articles, and three ancient creeds (the Apostles Creed, the Nicene Creed, and the **Athanasian Creed**). The Book of Concord remains the confessional standard of the Lutheran churches.

Title page from the 1580 Book of Concord. Courtesy of Finn B. Andersen.

GLOSSARY OF TERMS

Athanasian Creed: a sixth century Trinitarian doctrinal confession. It differs from the Apostles' Creed and the Nicene-Constantinople creeds of an earlier time by its inclusion of condemnatory statements or anathemas of what the creed specifically rejects. Its designation is derived from the now-discredited assumption that it was composed by the bishop of Alexandria in the fourth century.

Pelagianism (Pelagians): a teaching promulgated in the fifth-century church concerning the nature of humankind and the human factor in salvation. Pelagius taught that Adam's first sin affected only himself and not the race except by setting a precedent that has been subsequently and voluntarily pursued universally. Rejecting original sin and inherent birth depravity, sin was defined as moral selfishness, remedied by resolve. Further, Pelagius rejected the divine initiatives of predestination, election, and foreknowledge, redefining the terms as predicated on human action. The view was condemned in the Catholic Church through the writings of Augustine and at the Synod of Orange (529).

Peasants' War (Peasants' Revolt): an uprising of the economically strapped lower class in Germany, mostly in the southern and central regions, between 1524–25. Applying the religious upheaval of the day against authority structures the peasants envisioned a form of proto-liberationism. While Luther recognized the social inequities of the day and the plight of the poor, he greatly feared the consequences of anarchy and stridently opposed it. The rebellion ended in a disaster with thousands of peasants killed; it was the largest popular uprising in Europe prior to the French Revolution.

Protestant (Protestantism): the term suggests a movement of resistance. In this instance, it was a rejection of the pelagian direction observable in the late medieval church, and a condemnation of the decline of moral integrity and pastoral compassion. The term was coined at the Second Diet of Speyer (1529) when it became apparent that Charles V's toleration of the Protestant movement in 1526 was about to be revoked. A conclave of cities that embraced Luther's teachings uttered a protest. Hence, the reforming movement came to be known as Protestantism.

Schmalkaldic League: an alliance of Lutheran princes and cities for the purpose of mutual defense from the threat of Charles V, the emperor of the "Roman Empire" who was motivated by Roman Catholic sympathies, given the revocation of religious toleration following the Diet of Speyer in 1529. Named for the city in which the alliance was created in 1531, the league did not formally accept the creed, the doctrines most essential to the Protestant Reformation, in which Luther envisioned orthodoxy being the primary voice in its construction. However, named the Schmalkaldic Articles, it did become one of the several Lutheran confessions incorporated into the Book of Concord (1580).

Schmalkaldic Wars: A series of clashes in 1546 and 1547 between the forces of Charles V, emperor of the Holy Roman Empire, and the Lutheran Schmalkaldic League. The result of the struggle was the defeat of the Lutheran forces at the Battle of Muhlberg. Though Lutherans faced defeat, their ideas continued to gain ever-wider audiences, so Charles V was compelled to grant their legal right to exist.

Waldensians: an early protest movement founded by Peter Waldo in the twelfth century in northern Italy that was heralded by later Protestants as a precursor to the Reformation because it criticized the morals and teachings of the medieval Catholic church. The Waldensians stressed the importance of the Bible and preaching much in the tradition of Wycliffe of England and Huss of Bohemia, though Waldensians were much earlier. Condemned by the Fourth Lateran Council (1215) under Innocent III, they were subsequently severely persecuted. In the Reformation era, the Waldensians joined the Calvinist tradition of Protestant reform through the work of William Farel, a leading voice for reform in Geneva prior to Calvin's prominence.

Chapter 8 Outline

Chapter 8 Objectives

- That the reader will identify the two broad categories of the Protestant Reformations

- That the reader will distinguish the Reformed tradition from Lutheran theology

- That the reader will describe the lives and contributions of Zwingli, Bullinger, Calvin, and Beza

- That the reader will describe the spread of Reformed thought

- That the reader will understand the meaning, interests, and history of the Arminian tradition within Protestant faith

- That the reader will come to an awareness of the differences between the great Protestant traditions: Lutheran, Calvinist, and Arminian

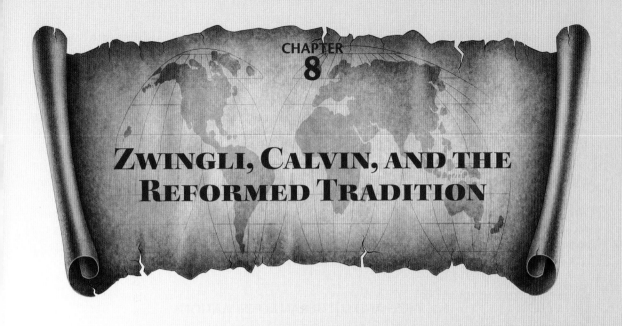

ZWINGLI, CALVIN, AND THE REFORMED TRADITION

THOUGH NOT ATTAINING THE stature of Luther or Calvin in the annuals of reformation history, Zwingli was none-the-less important. He was born into a prominent middle class family in Wildhaus, where his father served as a district official, in the canton or county of St. Gallen to the southeast of Zurich. An uncle served as the parish priest in the small town at the time of his birth and another relative was the abbot of the Benedictine monastery in Fischingen in Thurgau. His initial training was received under his uncle, the parish priest, who by that time had moved to Wesen. He received further training at Bern before entering the universities of Vienna (1498–1502) and Basle (1502–1506). His education was in classical studies (philosophy, poetry, music, astronomy, physics, and literature) in contrast to Luther's that was largely biblical in content.

Ulrich Zwingli (1484–1531) and the German Swiss Churches

The Making of the Reformer
In 1506 Zwingli was appointed parish priest in Glarus where he continued his humanistic studies that included the study of the biblical languages and the earliest Christian writers. Further, he became an admirer of Erasmus. Through Erasmus, he became a student of the Scriptures, a critic of the church, and a defender of Swiss nationalistic interests. Between 1513–1516, he served as a chaplain to Swiss mercenaries in the service of the papacy. His service to the church brought the recognition of Julius II that included an annual stipend. The defeat of the Swiss mercenaries by the French caused the loss of his parish appointment in Glarus as the city developed pro-French attachments and sympathies. Subsequently,

Zwingli found employment in Einsiedeln in 1516 and continued his nationalistic fervor, but he became a critic of Swiss mercenary involvement. Einsiedeln, a pilgrimage site to the **Shrine of the Black Virgin**, brought to Zwingli an awareness of the abuses of indulgences within the church. At the same time, likely attributable to Erasmus's influence, Zwingli's preaching intensified as he riled again church abuses and Swiss mercenary service.

The Reformation in Zurich

Zwingli's notoriety as a preacher brought about his appointment to the cathedral in Zurich, the Grossmünster, in 1519. He preached his first sermon on his thirty-fifth birthday beginning in the Gospel of Matthew and proceeding through the book, followed by the book of the Acts and the Pauline epistles. In his preaching, Zwingli attacked the moral degradations common among monks and priests, denied the papal authority to excommunicate, and rejected the veneration of saints, the authority of the church to exact tithes, and the damnation of unbaptized infants. In January of 1519, Bernhardin Samson, a Francisican monk from Milan, a counterpart to John Tetzel, came to Zurich to sell indulgences for the building of St. Peter's in Rome. The city refused his entrance.

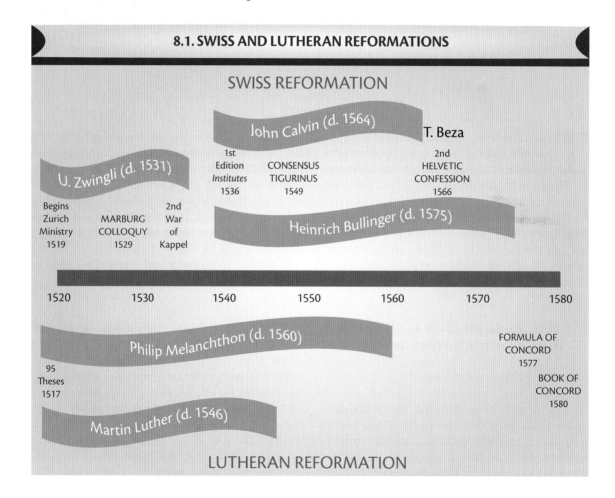

8.1. SWISS AND LUTHERAN REFORMATIONS

SWISS REFORMATION

John Calvin (d. 1564)   T. Beza

U. Zwingli (d. 1531)

| 1st Edition *Institutes* 1536 | CONSENSUS TIGURINUS 1549 | 2nd HELVETIC CONFESSION 1566 |

Begins Zurich Ministry 1519   MARBURG COLLOQUY 1529   2nd War of Kappel

Heinrich Bullinger (d. 1575)

1520   1530   1540   1550   1560   1570   1580

Philip Melanchthon (d. 1560)

FORMULA OF CONCORD 1577

95 Theses 1517

BOOK OF CONCORD 1580

Martin Luther (d. 1546)

LUTHERAN REFORMATION

Invitation to Church History: World

In 1520 the city experienced a devastating plague that swept one in four of the population. Zwingli refused to depart from his people, caring for the sick until he was stricken to the point of death. It appears that this experience, along with several other factors, most assuredly, caused a significant change in Zwingli's ministry. He began to stress more rigorously that the Bible should be interpreted in a literal fashion and adhered to exclusively.

> "That Christ, having sacrificed himself once, is to eternity a certain and valid sacrifice for the sins of all faithful, where from it follows that the mass is not a sacrifice, but is a remembrance of the sacrifice and assurance of the salvation which Christ has given us" (Article 18 of the sixty-seven Articles by Ulrich Zwingli).

In the spring of 1522 during the Lenten season, Zwingli inspired controversy when he opposed traditional religious dietary restrictions by advocating the eating of pork. The city council accepted the admonition of the bishop of Constance, but reserved the right to deal with religious matters in their city. In the summer, Zwingli and others petitioned the bishop to discontinue the requirement of celi-

Grossmünster (great cathedral), built between 1100–1220, and where Zwingli ministered. Courtesy of TTstudio-Fotolia.

A 1549 painting of Anna Reinhard (1487–ca. 1538), wife of Ulrich Zwingli, by Hans Asper (1499–1571). Courtesy of Sanblatt.

bacy for clerical office. Zwingli had apparently secretly married Anna Reinhard, a widow with three children, earlier in 1522. Until a public marriage ceremony in 1524, his relationship to her was considered that of **concubinage**. The couple had four children of their own subsequently.

> "That Christ is our justice, from which follows that our works in so far as they are of Christ are good" (Article 22 of the sixty-seven Articles by Ulrich Zwingli).

Religious unrest continued unresolved in the city with the result that the city council met with the various factions to address the tensions. The bishop of Constance sent Vicar-General Faber as an observer, but without authority to act since the bishop did not view the meeting as officially sanctioned by ecclesiastical authorities. Zwingli prepared a document, the "Sixty-Seven Articles," setting forth his position. The conclusion of the First Zurich Disputation, January 1523, was that the preachers in the city were mandated to conduct their services only in conformity to Holy Scripture, clearly a triumph for Zwingli.

> "Christ has borne all our pains and labor. Therefore whoever assigns to works of penance what belongs to Christ errs and slanders God" (Article 54 of the sixty-seven Articles of Ulrich Zwingli).

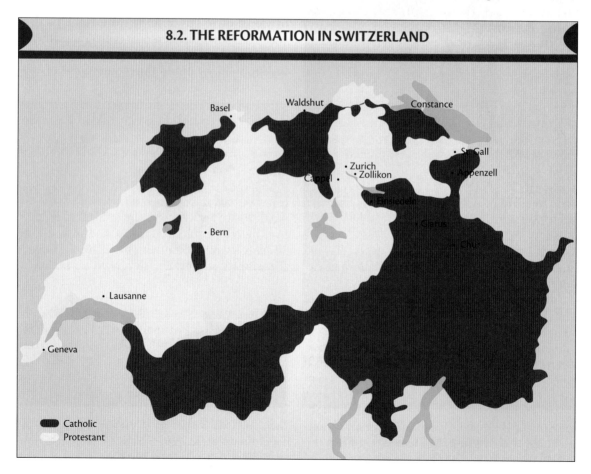

8.2. THE REFORMATION IN SWITZERLAND

Basel · Waldshut · Constance

· St. Gall
· Zurich
· Zollikon
Cappel · · Appenzell

· Einsiedeln

· Bern · Glarus

· Chur

· Lausanne

· Geneva

■ Catholic
□ Protestant

The impetus toward reform in Zurich gained further momentum in October 1523 with the calling of a second disputation in the city. The issues centered on the use of religious images in worship and the meaning of the Eucharist. With an attendance of about nine hundred, the council heard arguments from various viewpoints. The council adopted a moderate stance; unwilling to condemn the use of images or abolish the mass outright, they adopted a gradualist approach to reform. Zwingli and the other ministers were instructed to provide more insight on these issues through their preaching. A deadline was set for May 1524 to resolve the issues. While images were removed from the churches, the issue of the mass was unresolved. On **Maundy Thursday** of 1525, Zwingli instituted a new order of the Lord's Table observance; parishioners sat at tables to emphasize the communal significance of the sacrament. Church properties were seized and used for the needs of the city's poor; Zwingli proposed the creation of the Prophets School to train former priests and the translation of Bible at the school and its printing in the city. The reformation had fully come to the Zurichers.

The Spread of the Reformation in the Swiss Cantons

In 1524 five Swiss cantons (the "Five States") formed an alliance to resist the new religious ideas. The initial form of opposition was exhibited in a debate of the issues. Calling on prominent Roman Catholic scholars, such as John Eck, to help them, the alliance called the canons to gather at Baden for a formal disputation. Though Zurich sent representatives, Zwingli did not attend; Johannes Oecolampadius (1482–1531) of Basel defended the Protestant viewpoint. The consequence of the Baden Disputation was a divided confederation, thirteen cantons standing firm in Roman Catholicism and five embracing the need to reform the churches.

8.3. ULRICH ZWINGLI

Born—January 1, 1484
Place—Weilpaus, Switzerland
Died—October 11, 1531
Educated—University of Bern
Ministry—Zurich, Switzerland
Position—People's Priest in the Grossmünster
Contribution—Father of the Reformed tradition
Major Work—*Sixty-Seven Theses*

A 1549 painting of Ulrich Zwingli by Hans Asper (1499–1571). Courtesy of Kurt Spillmann.

The city of Bern formally adopted reformation in 1528. Berchtold Haller (1492–1536), the priest at St. Vincent's church, had introduced reformist ideas into the city in the early 1520s and saw the mass abolished in 1525. He attended the Baden Disputation in 1526 and the Berne Disputation of 1528. Haller, among others, composed the Ten Theses of Bern, insisting on the supremacy of the Bible and the abolition of contrary religious practices. Zwingli led the Bernese in the confrontation, and the city aligned with the Zurichers. In Basle, the mass was formally abolished in 1529 and the city embraced the Protestant cause under Oswald Myconius (1488–1552), Oecolampadius's successor. Myconius compiled a confessional standard for the churches, the Confession of Basle (1534).

The intense religious controversy portended that a military solution to the disputes. In 1529 Zwingli was successful in forming an alliance of reformed cities, the Christian Civic Union, throughout several German-Swiss cantons. Sensing military intervention, the Five States cemented a tenuous political agreement with Austria. When a reformed preacher was executed in an alliance canton in 1529, Zurich under Zwingli mobilized for war; Bern, fearing reprisal from Roman Catholic canons to the West, refused to assist the Zurichers. War was averted when Austria refused to aid the alliance, leaving the Catholic cantons severely outnumbered with superior numbers on the battlefield and compelled to accept an armistice. Since Berne did not agree with Zwingli's armistice agreement, settling only for the alliance's disengagement with Austria, Zwingli was sorely disappointed and lost considerable influence in the reformed cantons.

A 1557 wood carving of the Marburg Colloquy. Courtesy of Torsten.

The German and Swiss Reformations remained divided over the Lord's Supper. At the Colloquy of Marburg in 1529 though agreeing on fourteen points of discussion, Luther held fast to Christ's literal presence through consubstantiation, Zwingli said that it was symbolic. Luther said "I would rather have pure blood with the Pope, than drink mere wine with the Enthusiasts (Zwinglians)." Zwingli ultimately tired of Luther treating him "like an ass."

Zwingli experienced further disappointment following the Marburg Colloquy (1529). Though Luther and Zwingli disputed the meaning of the Eucharist (Zwingli embracing the view of Andreas Karlstadt, an issue among several that caused Luther unease), it remained the hope of Martin Bucer of Strasbourg, among others, that the two could find rapprochement on the issue. Philip of Hesse viewed a potential agreement as effecting a political alliance between the Saxons and Swiss. Though Zwingli and Luther found substantial agreement of fourteen doctrinal points, the fifteenth, the Eucharist, proved insurmountable. The result was that the reforming movement would divide into at least two traditions. Luther saw the

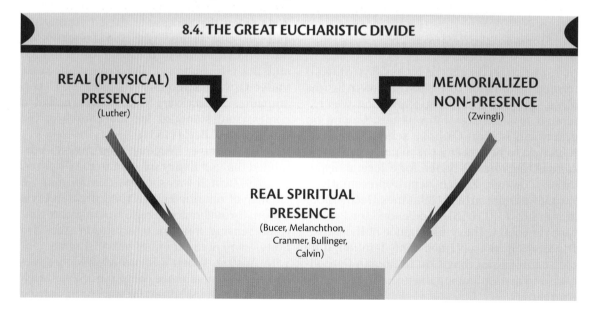

8.4. THE GREAT EUCHARISTIC DIVIDE

REAL (PHYSICAL) PRESENCE
(Luther)

MEMORIALIZED NON-PRESENCE
(Zwingli)

REAL SPIRITUAL PRESENCE
(Bucer, Melanchthon, Cranmer, Bullinger, Calvin)

meetings of 1–4 October 1529 as fruitless and was not disappointed; Zwingli thought he was successful and that misperception proved disappointing.

> "Thus Marburg marked a profound painful turning point in Reformation history, as joy of having discovered the Bible to be the exclusive foundation of Evangelical faith could not remain undiminished when the reformers came to disagree over the 'clear' text of Scripture" (Oberman, *Luther*, 244).

The Death of Zwingli and the Rise of Johannes Henry Bullinger

The disappointment at Marburg to secure a military alliance through Luther failed to forestall Zwingli's attempts in that regard. Efforts proved successful in 1530 when Zurich, Basle, Strasbourg, and Philip of Hesse formed a military alliance. The alliance was short-lived when Philip became offended by Zwingli's uncompromising view of the Eucharist and subsequently formed the **Schmalkaldic League**, leaving the Swiss reform cities vulnerable to military incursion.

Tensions between the Five States, the Roman Catholic alliance, and the reform cantons escalated over the allowance of reform preachers to enter Catholic cantons,

a concession in Zwingli's view granted by the treaty that ended the conflict of 1529. The means of forcing the Five States to allow preaching in their cantons divided the reforming alliance; Zwingli favored war, the others less dramatic measures. The alliance collapsed leaving Zurich alone as the Five States declared war on Zurich. The **Second Kappel War** resulted in Zwingli's death on the battlefield, 11 October 1531.

One of the disastrous consequences following the defeat of the Zurichers at Kappel was a Roman Catholic resurgence; Catholics regained the city of Bremgarten, for example, expelling Henry Bullinger (1504–1575). Bullinger came to Zurich when the city council invited him to the Grossmünster on the condition that he avoid political issues. Bullinger refused the stipulation because he wanted freedom to preach the content of the Bible; the council hired him because of his pulpit eloquence nonetheless.

Bullinger was born into the family of a priest at Bremgarten (the bishop of Constance allowed priests to maintain women in a concubinage status, having excused the penalties in exchange for an annual fee). During his training at the University of Cologne, he was exposed to Luther's ideas, though he came to his conviction

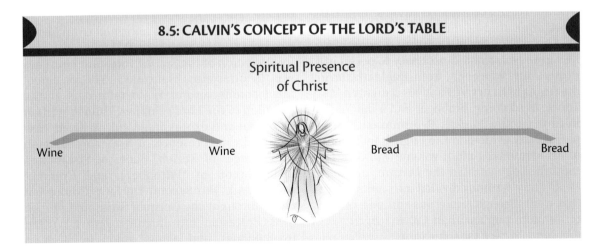

8.5: CALVIN'S CONCEPT OF THE LORD'S TABLE

Spiritual Presence of Christ

Wine   Wine   Bread   Bread

through the study of the church fathers and the scholastics. In 1522 he directed a cloister school at Kappel and had frequent contacts with Zwingli, even studying for several months at the Prophets School in Zurich. When his father was deposed from the church in Bremgarten, his son replaced him! In 1531 he arrived in Zurich to assume Zwingli's post with his wife and two children (they eventually had eleven in all with his six sons following him into the ministry).

Bullinger's *Decades* were a series of fifty theological sermons divided into five groups of ten sermons each. Though they were detailed in their exposition of doctrine, they were quite readable by the layman of his day. In the mid-sixteenth century they were more popular than Calvin's *Institutes* at least in England, numbering 214 editions in Latin and the vernacular, compared to only 2 English editions of Calvin. The influence of Bullinger's correspondence was wide, even reaching to the crown of England, and his work on the Helvetic Confession and his revisions of the Consensus Tigurinus helped bring Zwingli's Zurich theology with Calvin's Geneva theology into a unified Reformed tradition.

He was a spellbinding preacher; some thought of him as Zwingli returned from the dead. His nonpolemical, conciliatory demeanor made him, in Calvin's estimation, "the common shepherd of the Christian churches," one of the most influential of the Protestant reformers. This accolade was not without a basis. First, he showed enormous hospitality to persecuted Protestants, especially from England, during the reigns of Henry VIII and his daughter, Mary Tudor. In so doing, Bullinger had a marked influence on the English Reformation. This is particularly evident in the English publication of his sermons, a multi-volume work on pastoral theology entitled the *Decades* or *"House Book"* (fifty sermons divided into units of ten), that went through numerous editions, proving to be more popular than Calvin's *Institutes of Christian Religion* for some time.

A 1550 painting of Heinrich (Henry) Bullinger by Hans Asper (1499–1571). Courtesy of Magnus and Sidonius.

Second, he sustained a large correspondence with reformers and statesmen throughout Europe. Third, Bullinger was a theological diplomat. In 1536 Bullinger and other Swiss reformers, produced the First Helvetic Confession; the intent of the confession, which was Bullinger's personal statement of faith, was to provide a uniform statement of beliefs among the Swiss reformed churches (it was rejected in Strasbourg). Paving the way for the union of the Swiss Protestant churches was the Consensus Tigurinus (1549), an agreement among several major reformers on the meaning of the Lord's Supper. Though written by Calvin and expressing a spiritualized view of the divine presence, it was agreed upon by Bullinger of Zurich, Bucer of Strasbourg, Melanchthon of Wittenberg, and Cranmer of England. The Second Helvetic Confession (1566) brought the German Swiss and French Swiss Protestant movements together. Written by Bullinger, and agreed upon by Beza, it became a standard in defining the European reformed tradition.

John Calvin (1509–1564) and the French Swiss Reformation

The City of Geneva and Initial Reform
At the beginning of the sixteenth century the city of Geneva was ruled by bishops of the church closely affiliated with the **House of Savoy**, a dynasty of dukes that had ruled from the twelfth century, exercising authority over territories that today span southern France, much of Italy, and parts of western Switzerland. Geneva, the principal city of the canton of Geneva, gradually gained independent status in the 1520s from the House of Savoy, forming a military alliance with Fribourg and Bern. In the early 1530s, Geneva freed itself from the church through the influence of Bern, which had accepted reformation ideals. Two councils ruled the city: the Little Council and the Council of Two Hundred. These embraced the reformation by declaring that the Bible was to be preached from the city's pulpits, though the city was not secure, being divided into dangerous, competing factions.

Reform was introduced to the city through work of William Farel (1489–1565), who was introduced to reformist ideas by Jacques Le-

A painting of William Farel at the Public University in Neuchâtel, Switzerland. Courtesy of Torsten.

fevre (ca.1455–1536) through his studies in Paris and who labored in Meaux until he was forced out of the country for his intense, fiery, disruptive preaching. He then labored in Strasbourg, Basle, Bern, and Zurich where he made acquaintances with Bucer, Haller, Oecolampadius, Myconius, and Zwingli.

8.6. THE CONSENSUS TIGURINUS

Article 7: The Ends of the Sacraments

The ends of the sacraments are to be marks and badges of Christian profession and fellowship or fraternity, to be incitements to gratitude and exercises of faith and a godly life; in short, to be contracts binding us to this.

But among other ends the principal one is, that God may, by means of them, testify, represent, and seal his grace to us. For although they signify nothing else than is announced to us by the Word itself, yet it is a great matter, first, that there is submitted to our eye a kind of living image which makes a deeper impression on the senses, by bringing the object in a manner directly before them, while they bring the death of Christ and all his benefits to our remembrance, that faith may be the better exercised; and, secondly, that what the mouth of God had announced is, as it were, confirmed and ratified by seals.

Farel came to Geneva for the first time in 1532 when the city was in religious and political turmoil and preached in private homes until the city council forced him to leave. He returned the next year and labored tirelessly; the city formally embraced his views on 28 August 1535. In the interim between his visits, Pierre Robert Olivetan (1506–1538) carried on the work, producing a French translation of the Scriptures in 1535. John Calvin, his cousin, wrote a Latin preface for the volume.

The Emergence of John Calvin (1534–1536)

Undoubtedly the most influential Protestant thinker, writer of the sixteenth century, Calvin was born in Noyon, Picardy, France, on 10 July 1509 into a staunch Roman Catholic family. His father, Gerard, was a lawyer. Influential in the church, his father secured offices for his four sons, each receiving a salary without the need of qualification or duty. In 1523, Calvin entered the College de la Marche in Paris, where he commenced his training for the ministry. There he appears to have been influenced toward the church reform movement by five people: Jacques Lefevre, who had definite Protestant leanings and was a mentor in the faith to many; Corderius or Mathurin Cordier (ca.1480–1564), a Latin scholar who later moved to Geneva; Nicholas Cop, the reform-minded rector of the university and son of the king's physician; Pierre Robert Olivetan, who translated the Bible into French; and Melchior Woldmar, who taught Calvin the biblical languages and introduced him to the writings of Luther, then sweeping across Europe.

> "First, when I was too firmly addicted to the papal superstitions to be drawn easily out of such a deep mire, by a sudden conversion He brought my mind (already more rigid than suited my age) to submission [to Him]. I was so inspired by a taste of true religion and I burned with such a desire to carry my study further, that although I did not drop other subjects, I had no zeal for them" (Calvin, *Commentary on the Psalms*).

After his father had a falling out with the church in 1528, leading to his excommunication in 1531, he encouraged his son to discontinue his studies for the priesthood and pursue law, transferring from Paris to Orleans and later to Bourges. Calvin found himself increasingly involved in the religious issues that gripped Europe at the time. In 1531, the year of his father's death, he returned once more to study in Paris, devoting himself almost entirely to the study of theology; later he added the early church fathers to his reading. It seems likely that Calvin experienced conversion to Christ at this time, though he only indicates that his awakening came suddenly.

A definitive break for Calvin came on **All Saints' Day**, 1 November 1533, when Nicholas Cop delivered an address at the commencement of the fall term at the University of Paris. Calvin was implicated in the preparation of the stridently reformist message and was forced to flee the university and subsequently left France in 1534 for Basel. During his stay in that city, he completed the first edition of the immensely influential *Institutes of Christian Religion* (1536). The work in its first edition was composed of

8.7. JOHN CALVIN

Born—July 10, 1509
Place—Nyon, Picardy, France
Died—May 27, 1564
Educated—University of Paris
Ministry—Geneva, Switzerland
Position—Pastor
Contribution—"Savior of
   the Reformation"
Major Works—
   The Institutes of the
     Christian Religion
   Commentary on the Scriptures
   Reply to Sadoleto's Letter
     to the Genevans

Anonymous portrait of John Calvin (1509–64) (oil on panel) by Swiss School (16th century). Courtesy of Bibliotheque Publique, Geneva, Held Collection.

six chapters dedicated to Francis I. Arguably one of the few books that have shaped subsequent history, it became a lifelong project for Calvin; he added materials and shifted content around as he reflected upon it through four later editions, the final completed in 1559. The earliest edition reflects what scholars call his "Lutheran" emphasis, by which they generally mean his choice and arrangement of topics (the priority of the law, creed, and prayer).

> Twenty years older than John Calvin, William Farel the thunderous French evangelist, had been working in Geneva for four years before he met Calvin. Having read Calvin's *Institutes*, he implored the twenty-seven-year old scholar to help him with the reformation in Geneva, saying to Calvin that the wrath of God would fall upon him and his reforming activities would come to naught because of his selfishness. Calvin heard the word of God in what Farel said and stayed. The city fathers two years later sent the two away; three years later Calvin was invited back. He refused to return to Geneva until he got a visit from Farel.

In this era as a wandering student, forcibly exiled from his homeland, Calvin traveled as far south as Ferrara, Italy, returned to France to settle family affairs, and then left the country for Strasbourg, a free imperial city, impelled by the king's threat that heretics had six months to recant or face persecution.

The Initial Stay in Geneva (1536–1538)
Intending to stay one night in the city, Calvin remained longer because a man who subsequently returned to the Roman Church informed William Farel of his presence. Farel, the fiery evangelist, witnessed the city's embrace of reform, but the issue was by no means settled as divisive factions threaten to plunge the city into chaos. Though Calvin was desirous of pursuing private scholarly activities, not at all confident of his abilities as an activist, Farel's insistence convinced him to forego Strasbourg.

Calvin attempted to quell the factiousness in the city by creating rules for society and church life that strictly conformed to his understanding of the Scriptures. He asked that the openly immoral be excluded from the Eucharist, that church discipline be established, including the rule of excommunication. Within the city, he sought to prohibit commerce on Sunday, establish compulsory education, create a system of charity for the poor, promote fair business practices, and reform the city's governmental structure.

Calvin and Farel met with staunch opposition from the city's council. The council refused the ministers the practice of a weekly Eucharist and the right of excommunication. When the reformers refused to serve the Eucharist on Easter Sunday 1538 (the issues concerned Bern's attempt to create uniformity of worship in the churches by insisting that unleavened bread be used in the sacrament, Calvin and Farel wanted a synod to decide the manner), the council ordered their expulsion from the city.

8.8. THE LIFE OF JOHN CALVIN

CALVIN: The Student		CALVIN: The Reformer		
France	Europe	Geneva	Strasbourg	Geneva
1509	1534	1536	1538	1541 1564

The Years in Strasbourg (1538–1541)

A synod followed in Zurich. Calvin was criticized for his unsympathetic and inflexible attitude in the Genevan crisis, and attempts by Bern and Zurich to have the reformers reinstated failed. Martin Bucer (1491–1551) and Wolfgang Capito (1478–1541) invited Calvin to Strasbourg to serve a congregation of French refugees; he was subsequently granted citizenship in the city, suggesting that the wandering scholar had the prospect of a permanent residence. Engulfed in his work, Calvin preached or lectured daily.

In addition to the preparation of a commentary on Paul's *Letter to the Romans*, Calvin prepared a second edition of the *Institutes of Christian Religion* (1539). The second edition demonstrates the influence of Bucer on Calvin in that such doctrines as predestination and providence assumes greater prominence in his developing understanding. The third edition, completed in Geneva (1543), indicates that during his pastorate of the French congregation in Strasbourg, he devoted considerable time to the study of ecclesiology. In addition, Calvin took up the study of Augustine and Chrysostom.

Encouraged by friends, Calvin considered marriage. In August 1540, he married a widow with two children, Idelette de Bure (John and Idelette Stroders had Anabaptist connections, but joined Calvin's French congregation in Strasbourg, where a warm relationship between the Stroders and Calvin ensued). After John Stroders died suddenly, Calvin continued the friendship with the widow and her family. Though considering marriage to another for some time, he was encouraged to become engaged to John's widow. From their union came three children, but none survived infancy. Idelette, though increasingly of poor health, appears to have been a caring wife and mother, and their relationship was warm and productive. She died March 1549; Calvin remained a widower thereafter.

John Calvin's wife Idelette in a 1909 copy painting by Xavier Wurth (1869–1933). Courtesy of SusanLesch.

That the reform measures of Calvin and Farel did not gain the sanction of the Genevan Council, thus prompting the removal of the city's most vocal reformers, did not imply that the city had rejected the Protestant movement entirely. Sensing a weakening of Protestant sympathies in the city, Cardinal Jacopo Sadoleto, bishop of Carpentras and a prominent scholar, wrote a letter to the city suggesting its return to the Roman Catholic fold. Unable to compose a suitable reply, the city council turned to Calvin. The consequences were significant. Not only did the council change their minds about Calvin's reform efforts, eventually inviting him to return, but Sadoleto's letter and Calvin's answer are monumental statements of the two sides of the mounting ecclesiastical schism in Europe.

The letter and the reply are worthy of a pause in the narrative. Sadoleto made several points in his letter. First, he began his letter with the assertion that the authority to judge truth from error resided in the Roman Catholic Church, and its decisions, reflected in its decrees and councils, being safeguarded by the Holy Spirit. From this postulate, the claim was made that to reject the teachings of the church was to reject the Spirit of God, thereby imperiling deluded souls and threatening access into heaven.

Second, Sadoleto took up a discussion of justification, making the point that "we obtain this blessing of complete and perpetual salvation by faith alone in God and in Jesus Christ." He then explained what he meant by a faith-alone justification. Christ's atoning death, he said, had made salvation possible. Grace had been procured through Christ's death, but it was not granted without the sanction of the church. The church had been granted the means of pardon, becoming the sacred repository of divine grace and could dispense that grace as a reward for sacramental obedience. Human sincerity of heart expressed in ecclesiastical conformity, merited forgiveness and grace.

Third, the bishop then argued that salvation resided in this centuries-old church and the reformers were soul-threatening usurpers.

The reply composed by Calvin was a defense of the character and motives of his and Farel's work in Geneva as well as a rebuttal. He began his reply by agreeing with Sadoleto that the promotion of piety and obedience to God is vital; in fact, Calvin claimed that his opponent's insistence in these matters was one of the roots of the Reformation. Calvin rejected the historical argument of Sadoleto as spurious stating that his own teaching was closer to the ancient church than to the late medieval church. He argued that the church had departed from its earliest teaching in order to support its own selfish interests and lifestyles. Calvin followed with a defense of reformation teaching, demonstrating that in doctrine, sacraments, and discipline, the reformers represented the Bible accurately and Sadoleto did not.

Taking up the doctrine of justification, a doctrine rooted in the recognition of absolute human incapacity to merit God's gratuity, Calvin said that human endeavor played no causative part in the acquisition of a right standing before God. However, while justification and sanctification must be distinguished, they must not be separated, according to Calvin (thus responding to the charge that Protestants are antinomians and a threat to Christian piety). The gift of eternal life, the life of God the Holy Spirit in the soul, necessitated godly living because the indwelling Spirit was holy. Works, including the sacraments, did not commend the favor of God to humans, but it flowed out of God's favor to them!

A painting of Jacopo Sadoleto (1477–1547). Jacopino del Conte (1515–1598) has been suggested by some as the artist. Courtesy of Adam.

"I, O Lord, as I had been educated from a boy, always professed the Christian faith. But at first I had no other reason for my faith than that which then everywhere prevailed. Thy Word, which ought to have shone on all thy people like a lamp, was taken away, or at least suppressed as to us. . . . I believed, as I had been taught, that I was redeemed from death by the death of thy Son from liability to eternal death, but the redemption I thought of was one whose virtue could never reach me. I anticipated a future resurrection, but I hated to think of it, as being an event most dreadful. . . . They [teachers], moreover placed this desert in the righteousness of works, so that he only was received into thy favor who reconciled himself to thee by works. . . . The method of obtaining it, which they pointed out, was by making satisfaction to Thee for offenses . . . by good to efface from thy remembrance of our bad actions. . . . I was still far-off . . . had all my life long been in ignorance and error" (Calvin, *The Saldoleto Calvin Letters*, 87–89).

From the doctrine of justification, Calvin turned to the question of authority, the-church-as-never-erring claim. According to Calvin, the Catholic Church had been devoured and blighted over the centuries, departing from apostolic faith for human inventions. Had not a remnant risen in protest, the church would have become completely corrupted.

The Return to Geneva (1541–1564)

Calvin's return to the city is best encapsulated in his own words. "Afterwards the Lord had pity on the City of Geneva and quieted the deadly conflicts there. . . . I was compelled against my own will, to take again my former position. The safety of that church was far too important in my mind for me to refuse to meet even death for its sake. But my timidity kept suggesting to me excuses of every color for refusing to put my shoulder again under so heavy a burden. However, the demand of duty and faith at length conquered and I went back to the flock from which I had been driven away." (Calvin, *Commentary on the Psalms*). Farel, though invited to return, refused to leave his reforming work in Neuchâtel.

The reforms that the city council were reluctant to invoke during Calvin's initial stay were readily embraced at this time, at least officially. In 1541 the city accepted Calvin's *Ecclesiastical Ordinances* as the organizational definition of the churches; it was revised in 1561 to reflect Calvin's understanding of the Scriptures more strongly. The churches were to have four offices: pastors charged with preaching the Scriptures and offering the sacraments (denominated the consistory), doctors appointed as instructors with teaching duties, elders chosen by the city council charged with maintaining moral order, and deacons charged with caring for the poor. Calvin's concept of government was based on the separation of powers, civil and religious, the pastors forming one legislative body and the city with the elders, a composite of laity, the other. The power of excommunication resided in the magistracy initially; only later did Calvin's desire that it reside in the consistory prevail. The civil magistracy had jurisdiction in the selection of pastors with the consistory and the congregation.

Though Calvin faced continued opposition to his reforming policies, the council gradually conceded to his wishes. Citizenship was granted the Frenchman in 1559. Remnants of medieval popery were abolished. Though a realist in his understanding of the human condition, Calvin did not allow the impossibility of ultimate success to blight the endeavor to make Geneva a model of biblical piety. Attendance for the sermon was mandatory for all, the theatre and tavern were closed; pious social gatherings were promoted.

"God's grace is tasteless to men until the Holy Spirit brings its savor" (Calvin, *Institutes*, 3.24.14).

In 1553 the tide of opposition from the city council began to ebb. Earlier he contended with Jerome Bolsec (d. 1584) who rejected the doctrine of predestination and was banished from the city in 1551 (for Calvin the "breach" of truth merited execution; the city council did not agree). Bolsec attempted to identify with the reformed movement, but his views were unacceptable. He later sought revenge upon Calvin and Beza by writing acrimonious biographies about them and returned to the Roman Catholic Church.

Sebastian Castellio (1515–1563), repulsed by the Roman Catholic inquisition in Lyons, came to Protestant and reformed sympathies by listening to Calvin in Strasbourg. Later he became a preacher with Calvin in Geneva, but did not share Calvin's adversity to doctrinal variance, advocating toleration. Nor did he embrace Calvin's church/state theory advocating a stronger separation of powers (he appears to be a man of opinions before they became acceptable). He left Geneva and became a professor of Greek at the University of Basel, incurring the literary wrath of both Calvin and Beza for his writings on toleration.

> "Far be it from us to say that judgment belongs to the clay, not to the potter" (Calvin, *Institutes*, 3.23.14).

The issues surrounding Servetus were not considered a matter of tolerable indifference by either Roman Catholics or Protestants. Servetus, a Spanish scholar interested in Muslim/Christian dialogue, concluded from his studies that the doctrine of the absolute deity of Jesus was not biblical; thus, he explicitly denounced the Holy Trinity of God. Pausing in Geneva on his way to Italy in 1553, he was recognized and Calvin had him arrested. Without the privilege of counsel, Servetus was condemned to death at the stake; Calvin supported Servetus's demise, though he argued for the sword (a more merciful tool of extinction). Opposition to the burning of Servetus brought strident comments from the pen of Castellio and a firm rebuttal and defense of the action by Calvin. In this age of tolerance, the action of the city council and Calvin appear extreme. However, the sixteenth century shared neither the insightful benefits nor baneful curses of the **Enlightenment**.

A Spanish theologian, Michael Servetus had been condemned by the Catholic church for his unorthodox teachings. Even Protestant Europe opposed his vehement denial of the Trinity. When Servetus unexpectedly arrived in Geneva in 1553, having escaped a Catholic prison, both sides felt the need to demonstrate their zeal for orthodoxy. Servetus boldly took a seat at the Cathedral of St. Pierre while Calvin was preaching and was immediately recognized

8.9. SERVETUS ON THE TRINITY

On the Errors of the Trinity
Book 1, Argument

Any discussion of the Trinity should start with the man. That Jesus, surnamed Christ, was not a hypostasis but a human being . . . In short, all the Scriptures speak of Christ as a man.

The doctrine of the Holy Spirit as a third separate being lauds us in practical tritheism no better than atheism, even though the unity of God is insisted on . . . the Holy Spirit as a third person of the Godhead is unknown in Scripture . . . The doctrine of the Trinity can be neither established by logic nor proved from Scripture, and is in fact inconceivable. . . .

Numerous heresies have sprung from this philosophy, and fruitless questions have arise out of it. Worst of all, the doctrine of the Trinity incurs the ridicule of the Mohademans and the Jews. It arose out of Greek philosophy rather than from the belife that Jesus Christ is the Son of God.

and arrested. Calvin was responsible for Servetus's arrest and conviction, though he had preferred a less brutal form of execution and even visited him in jail trying earnestly to persuade him of his errors. Servetus dismissed Calvin with a laugh. Servetus was burned at the stake on 27 October 1553.

The execution of Servetus marked the harbinger of triumph for Calvin and the reform movement in Geneva. As persecuted Protestants from Europe, most particularly exiles from the intolerant Mary Tudor of England, swelled, the population of Geneva outnumbering the native citizenry. Calvin enjoyed a virtual hegemony. Given the right to excommunicate by the city council, the consistory moved quickly to handle dissidence. Thousands came to find refuge in the city; hundreds were forced to leave.

Other than the institution of reform measures in Geneva with council approval, Calvin's great achievement was the establishment of the Academy of Geneva in 1559. Among the teachers brought to the school was Theodore Beza, the man that would succeed Calvin in 1564. The school began with 162 students and within ten years had over 900 students from all over Europe.

The Importance of the Institutes of Christian Religion

It may not be too much to assert that the *Institutes of Christian Religion* is one of the greatest books ever written, at least if judged by its continued influence in shaping Christian thought for over five hundred years. It has galvanized a tradition that has been singularly effective in presenting a coherent demonstration of Christian truth with a profound piety and missionary passion.

"not all the articles of true doctrine are of the same sort. Some are so necessary to know that they should be certain and unquestioned by all men as the proper principles of religion. . . . Among the churches there are other articles of doctrine disputed which still do not break the unity of faith" (Calvin, *Institutes*, 4.1.12).

The first edition of the *Institutes* was published in Basel in 1536. It was composed of six chapters. The book became a life-long project for Calvin; he added materials and shifted content around as he reflected upon it. The earliest edition reflects what scholars call his "Lutheran" emphasis. By this they mean his choice

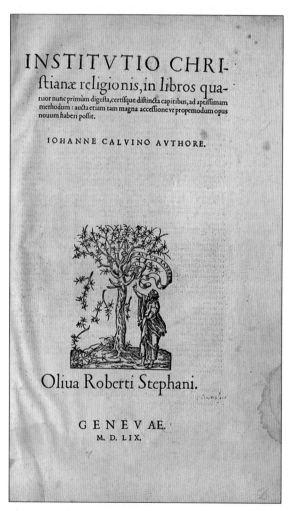

The 1559 title page to Calvin's *Institutes of Christian Religion*. Courtesy of Awadewit.

of topics and their arrangement (the priority of law, creed, and prayer). The volume through every edition, enlargement, and rearrangement contains the prefatory letter to Francis I of France. Calvin says that he wrote it so that the king might have a fair understanding of the "new" Protestant. The impetus in writing the work initially may have come from Calvin's friendship with one of the king's sister who shared his Protestantism and persecution.

By the definitive fifth edition, the work had expanded to four books and eighty chapters. This reflects Calvin's own studies, his contact with Bucer in Strasbourg, a deepening awareness of the Fathers, and the theological struggles that he encountered with Lutherans, Socinians, and others. The volume is a biblical, exegetical theology, not a systematic theology; it is almost a church history text reflecting Calvin's grasp of the history of the church. It does not, however, reflect an attempt to organize divinity into the seven branches of theological knowledge or to write a summa or encyclopedia of knowledge. There are some topics entirely absent, such as eschatology or the later—developed covenantal over-structure shaping the organization of the biblical data.

> "it is foolish and rash to inquire concerning unknown matters more deeply than God permits us to know" (Calvin, *Institutes*, 3.15.6).

Four features of Calvin's theology book strike a reader while reflecting on his work in light of the tradition's development. First, Calvin discussed providence in Book 1 but never used the term "sovereignty"; his term for the discussion is the omnipotence of God. Second, the discussion of predestination is in Book 3, as is the discussion of the external means of salvation, not in the Trinitarian discussion of Book 1. This places the doctrine of election in a different light than that of most Reformed discussions. Third, the book begins with a letter to a king and ends with a discussion of civil govern-

ment. Calvin was concerned with life in a fallen, troubled world, not in the creation of a utopian theocracy. Fourth, Calvin took into account the inadequacy of human rational ability, the reality of an incomplete disclosure of God, and the incomprehensibility of God. He was willing to say, "I don't know" (something later Calvin seems less willing to confess in a world challenged from within and without).

> "Meanwhile, since Scripture everywhere bids us wait in expectation for Christ's coming, and defers until then the crown of glory, let us be content with the limits divinely set for us" (Calvin, *Institutes*, 3:25.6).

There has been considerable discussion of about how the book is to be approached. According to at least one Calvin scholar the central theme of the book is that "God is King." If approached and read from this perspective, it could be understood through the grid of personal and experiential knowledge; it is a handbook on piety. Further, approached from a divine perspective, it is an attempt to crown God as "Lord of the nations."

> "Why do you, then, accuse him because he does not temper the greatness of his works to your ignorance" (Calvin, *Institutes*, 3:23.5).

The Spread of the Reformed Tradition

The organizational genius of Calvin, the centralization of Protestant thought in the production of literature (Calvin's commentaries as well as the *Institutes*), the emphasis on divine grace through a transcendently powerful God, and the stress on education through catechism and creed provided the Calvinists a forward momentum. Unlike the failed attempt to bring a consensus and union between the German Swiss and Lutherans at the Marburg Colloquy in 1529, the Protestants were able to secure a unified front through the union of several Swiss canons.

In 1549, the theological issue that became the insurmountable chasm between Zwingli and Luther was broached in a document called the *Consensus Tigurinus,* an agreement between Bullinger of Zurich and Calvin of Geneva concerning the meaning of the Lord's Supper or Eucharist. The sacrament of God's presence was not to be interpreted with Luther's stark realism nor Zwingli's empty realism; the manner of God's presence was spiritual. This agreement paved the way for a later formal merger of the two movements on the basis of the 1562 Second Helvetic Confession composed by Bullinger (he revised it in 1564).

Unlike the First Helvetic Confession (1536), composed by reformers from several Swiss cantons as well as Bucer of Strassburg, which was criticized for being too brief and far too Lutheran, the second became widely accepted by reformed churches from Scotland, Hungary, Poland, and Switzerland. Perhaps second to the Heidelberg Catechism, the Second Helvetic Confession was the most widely recognized expression of the reformed faith in the sixteenth century. Geneva, most particularly the Academy of Geneva under Theodore Beza (1519–1605) and later Francois Turretin (1623–1687), became the recognized center of the Reformed tradition.

The Spread of Calvinism into the Palatinate of Germany

The **Palatinate** was that portion of the German states defined by the Rhine River in southeastern Germany with Heidelberg as its geographic center, the city being the center of the German Renaissance and the Reformation. Luther was influential in the region following the Heidelberg Disputation (1518) and his views were embraced by Frederick II and Otto Henry, the latter allowing a diverse faculty at the university. During the reign of Frederick III (1559–1576), Protestant fortunes turned toward reformed sympathies with the promulgation of the Second Helvetic Confession by the

elector and the publication of the Heidelberg Catechism (1563). Under Frederick's successor, Louis VI, Lutheranism revived in the Palatinate and the Reformed tradition declined only to resurge by the century's end.

The Heidelberg Catechism
"Q. What is your only comfort in life and in death? A. That I am not my own, but belong body and soul, in life and in death to my faithful Savior, Jesus Christ. He has fully paid for all my sins with his precious blood, and has set me free from the tyranny of the devil. He also watches over me in such a way that not a hair can fall from my head without the will of my Father in heaven; in fact, all things must work together for my salvation."

To settle the conflict between Lutherans and Calvinists in the Palatinate, Frederick III called upon Zacharias Ursinus (1534–1583), a former student of Philip Melanchthon and a teacher in the university, who had accepted reformed insights, to prepare a catechism with the assistance of Caspar Olevianus (1536–1587), a professor and later court preacher. It

8.10. THE CENTER OF CALVINISM IN GERMANY

proved to be a most congenial statement of Reformed Protestantism. The catechism was composed of 129 questions divided into three parts: the depth of human misery, the redemption provided through Christ, and the need for grateful obedience to Christ.

In reaction to the Heidelberg Catechism, the Lutheran Joachim Westphal (1510–1574), pastor in Hamburg, appears to have coined the term "Calvinism" as a pejorative term, suggesting an alien, unsanctioned movement in Germany. Tension between the Lutheran and Reformed traditions generally revolved around different interpretations of the Eucharist, the third function of the law, and the relationship of church and state, though other issues were involved as well.

A significant difference between the two traditions of Protestant faith concerned the *ordo salutis*, the sequence of the decrees within the decree of God. The fact of distinct approaches to the content of the Bible defined the tone and priorities of each tradition. The Reformed tradition found its redemptive starting point in heaven, while the Lutherans tended to approach theology with a more human interest, the cross of Christ. Lutherans saw redeeming grace as resistible and grace subject to loss while the Reformed viewed grace as divinely irresistible, God causing the will to be made willing.

To Lutherans repentance led to faith, while to Calvinists it followed from faith. Again, to Luther, though not the case with all Lutherans, the Mosaic Code had the singular function of alerting the lost to the hopeless condition; Calvinist viewed the law as a guide to Christian conduct. It seems that the Lutheran emphasis on the free grace of God in Christ caused them

8.11. THEOLOGICAL DIFFERENCES BETWEEN THE LUTHERAN AND CALVINIST REFORMATIONS

Issue	Lutheran	Reformed
Ordo Salutis	Calling, illumination, conversion, regeneration, justification, sanctification, glorification	Election, predesination, union with Christ, calling, regeneration, faith, repentance, justification, sanctification, glorification
Grace of God	Grace received through baptism or preaching enables one to avoid resisting the regenerating grace of God	Irresistible
Repentance	Leads to faith	Flows from faith
Baptism	Causes regeneration, removing guilt and power of sin	Incorporation into the Covenant of Grace
The Law	To reveal God's holiness and drive the sinner to Christ	To reveal God's holiness, to drive the sinner to Christ, and to show the believer how to please God (sanctification)
Lord's Supper	Christ present in the sacrament objectively	Sign and seal of the Covenant of Grace to believers; Christ present by faith
Church and State	The church to tutor in the faith the rulers who support Protestantism	Holy commonwealth in which church and state both Christian yet perform their separate functions
Regulative Principles	Whatever is not forbidden in Scripture is permissible	Whatever is not commanded in Scripture is forbidden

to be alert to the threat of mixing law with grace; the Calvinists perceived the Lutherans to be protecting grace by obscuring the place and necessity of works.

Regarding the relationship of the church to the state, Luther conceived of two distinct, though not entirely separated spheres, as did the Calvinists. However, Luther viewed the state as a necessary nuisance whose purpose was to curb anarchy by promoting civil order. Calvinists viewed the state as ordained of God to preserve civil order and to punish moral and religious aberration. Both argued that the state has been given the duty of bearing the sword. Calvin envisioned the possibility of a society governed by the dictates of the Holy Scriptures; Luther was not as optimistic.

Finally, Lutherans and Calvinists differed on what has been called the regulative principle or "things in difference." The issues were those matters neither approved nor prohibited by the Holy Scriptures. Lutherans took the view that, since God had not spoken on the matter, it was a matter of prudence; Calvinists took the position that the silences of God should be viewed as a prohibition since one could not discern the mind of God in the midst of silence.

The Spread of Calvinism into France

Unlike Germany, the reformed tradition of Protestantism in France did not have to contend for a place with another potent form of Protestantism; the clash was with a strongly embedded Roman Catholic interpretation of Christian orthodoxy. During the reign of Francis I (1515–1547), France embraced the cultural renaissance that was sweeping across Europe. The king was open to the new intellectual currents, at least to the degree that he understood their implication (history suggests that his knowledge was minimal). However, as a portent of future conflict, Luther's works were condemned in Paris in 1521.

Nonetheless, the intellectual climate across Europe was changing. For example, during Calvin's studies in Paris (1523–1527), he was influenced by four people: first, Jacques Lefevre, also from Picardy, who had Protestant sympathies; second, Corderius (a Latinist) who later came to Geneva; third, Nicholas Cop who was a physician to Francis I; and fourth, Pierre Robert d'Olivet (also of Noyon, a nephew, and translator of the Scriptures (he produced the first French Protestant Bible [1535]; Calvin wrote the preface). Calvin found what others, such as Farel, discovered in their studies, evangelical faith.

"And in order to leave no occasion for troubles or differences between our subjects, we have permitted, and herewith permit, those of the religion called Reformed to live and abide in all the cities and places of this our kingdom and countries of our sway, without being annoyed, molested, or compelled to do anything in the matter of religion contrary to their consciences . . . upon condition that they comport themselves in other respects according to that which is contained in this our present edict" (*The Edict of Nantes*, Article 6).

Francis I had a change of view in 1534 when agitation over Protestantism became too much

8.12. THE REFORMATION IN FRANCE

Beginnings	Calvin	Religious War	Toleration	
1507	1536	1560	1598	1685

for his tolerant humanist leanings. The specific occasion of religious conflict was the "affair of the placards," the public rejection of the Catholic mass. Persecutions of Protestants caused many to flee, among them Calvin and Farel. In spite of increased persecution under Henry II (1547–1559), Protestantism continued to grow. Calvin, though residing in Geneva, cast a continuing influence in shaping the Protestant faith in France through the enormously popular *Institutes of Christian Religion*. In 1559 with over 2000 Protestant churches, suggesting

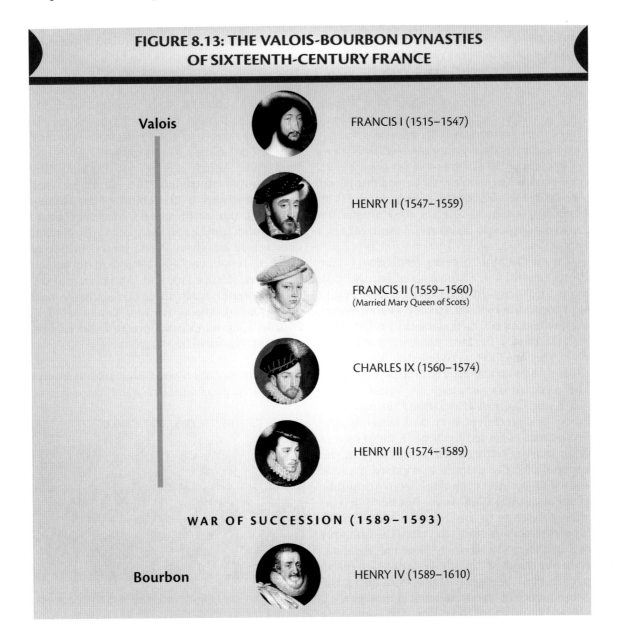

FIGURE 8.13: THE VALOIS-BOURBON DYNASTIES OF SIXTEENTH-CENTURY FRANCE

Valois

FRANCIS I (1515–1547)

HENRY II (1547–1559)

FRANCIS II (1559–1560)
(Married Mary Queen of Scots)

CHARLES IX (1560–1574)

HENRY III (1574–1589)

WAR OF SUCCESSION (1589–1593)

Bourbon   HENRY IV (1589–1610)

thousands of adherents, a national reformed church was organized around the Gallican or La Rochelle Confession of Faith with presbyterial church polity in Paris (Calvin composed the initial draft).

> "We forbid our subjects of the R(eformed) P(rotestant) R(eligion) to meet any more for the exercise of the said religion in any place or private house, under any pretext whatever, . . . "(Louis XIV, *Revocation of the Edict of Nantes*, Article 2).

> "We enjoin all ministers of the said R.P.R., who do not choose to become converts and to embrace the Catholic, apostolic, and Roman religion, to leave our kingdom and the territories subject to us within a fortnight of the publication of our present edict, without leave to reside therein beyond that period, or, during the said fortnight, to engage in any (290) preaching, exhortation, or any other function, on pain of being sent to the galleys . . ." (Article 4).

In an attempt to bring resolution to the Protestant/Roman Catholic conflict, the Colloquy of Poissy in 1561, was called under state authority by Catherine de Medici, queen mother and regent, during the early reign of her son, Charles IX. The focal point was the Eucharist. Catherine, hoping to forestall further tensions, sought conciliation with the Protestants. The attempt was opposed by James Laynez (1512–1565), a Jesuit, insisting that papal decrees took precedent over civil councils. The Protestants were led by Beza of Geneva and Peter Martyr Vermigli of Zurich. Later in the negotiations, the Catholics proposed a vague statement on the Eucharist reflective generally of the Augsburg Confession. Neither side was willing to agree to the diluted statement; the hope of conciliation failed, as had the Colloquy of Regensberg (1541) where Beza and Melanchthon represented the Protestants. Extensive persecution throughout Europe came as the consequence of failed ecumenical dialogue.

Thousands lost their lives for confessing Protestantism. The controversy became so strident that religious war gripped the nation for several decades (1562–1598). The wars were a dynastic conflict of succession with profound religious overtones between the Bourbons (Protestant) and the Guises (Roman Catholic); it also had international implications between Philip of Spain and Elizabeth of England.

The darkest moment for the Protestant cause was what has come to be known as the St. Bartholomew's Day massacre, August 1572. Fearing the implications of a possible Protestant alliance with England and the Dutch, the Roman Catholics turned to violence. The leader of the Protestants, Admiral Gaspard de Coligny, was murdered in Paris and thousands killed across the nation. The Protestants controlled the southern and eastern portions of the country; the Roman Catholics, the northern and western. To end the conflict, and knowing that no Protestant king would be given Paris, Henry, prince of Navarre, renounced Protestantism to accept the crown (Henry IV), end the strife, and declare toleration for Protestants, hoping to heal his shattered nation. He was assassinated in 1610 by a Roman Catholic who believed that Henry had failed in his religious duty.

> Gaspard II de Coligny was a Burgundian nobleman who rose to the rank of admiral and colonel-general

A painting of the Saint Bartholomew's Day massacre by François Dubois (1529–1584).

in the French military. He became a Huguenot (a French Calvinist) under the influence of his brother and exchanged correspondence with John Calvin. He established Huguenot colonies in Brazil and Florida. Though initially friends with the royal family, years later religious and political hostilities between them led to conflict, leading to Coligny's death in the St. Bartholomew's Day massacre in 1572.

The **Huguenots**, as French Protestants were called, suffered setbacks throughout most of the seventeenth century with their center at La Rochelle besieged. Roman Catholicism became the official religion of the state once again with the revocation of the Edict of Nantes in 1685 under Louis XIV. Vast numbers of Huguenots fled to Prussia in the East, England, and the British North American colonies. Unlike other religious and ethnic groups, the Huguenots blended into their new cultural environs eventually losing their distinct identity.

"And in order to leave no occasion for troubles or differences between our subjects, we have permitted, and herewith permit, those of the said religion called Reformed to live and abide in all the cities and places of this our kingdom and countries of our sway, without being annoyed, molested, or compelled to do anything in the matter of religion contrary to their consciences, . . . upon condition that they comport themselves in other respects according to that which is contained in this our present edict" (*The Edict of Nantes*, Article 6).

The Spread of Calvinism into the Spanish Netherlands

The story of the reformation in the Netherlands is interlaced with political and social issues that gripped Spain and her empire in the sixteenth century and spilled over into religion. Spain's rise to world domination was not without financial problems as the nation faced monetary collapse. Philip II, seeking to economically stabilize his nation, imposed heavy taxes on the Spanish Netherlands. This harsh treatment encouraged the Dutch and Flemish to resist the crown though they had reached an agreement that called for the removal of Spanish troops in 1561. Largely under William

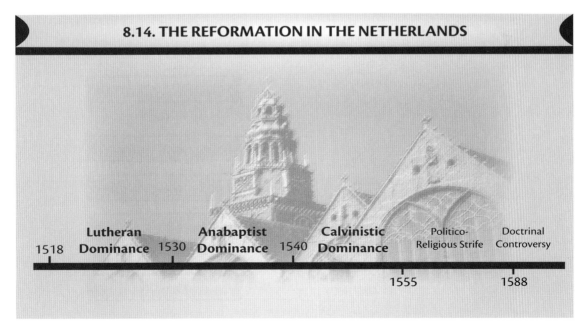

8.14. THE REFORMATION IN THE NETHERLANDS

1518 | Lutheran Dominance | 1530 | Anabaptist Dominance | 1540 | Calvinistic Dominance | Politico-Religious Strife | Doctrinal Controversy | 1555 | 1588

of Orange (or the Silent (1533–1584]), resistance, essentially Protestant in the region, led to strife generally viewed by Protestants as the government's attempt to impose Roman Catholicism to quell growing unrest that was augmented by poor harvests. Philip II determined to suppress dissonance through military might. He sent the Duke of Alva, the newly appointed governor of the Netherlands, with 9,000 troops to end the uprising and enforce religious conformity. The result was a Spanish reign of terror that included the devastation of Antwerp and the loss of thousands of lives. In effect, Alva's military presence in the Spanish Netherlands divided the country, the southern provinces remaining staunchly Roman Catholic and the seven northern provinces, called the United Provinces, Protestant and staunchly Calvinist. A twelve-year truce of hostilities between the northern and southern provinces was agreed upon in 1609. By 1621, when the agreement expired, the Dutch had become a world power and Spain had declined militarily and economically. A new nation had been born from the ashes of political, social, and religious controversy—Holland or the Dutch Republic.

Unlike Charles V, who allowed a degree of self-government in the Spanish Netherlands, his successor, Philip II, tightened his allegorical fist. His strident suppression of Protestants, as well as political freedoms, played into the hands of the growing Calvinist faction. In 1568 the first assembly of the Reformed Churches of the Netherlands at Wesel met under a cloak of secrecy. Three years later the churches' first manual of church order was written. In 1561 Guy de Bres (1522–1567), a Calvinist preacher and later martyr, composed the Belgic Confession of Faith (*Belgic* then a term meaning the Netherlands) to show Philip II that the emerging Calvinist party was not rebellious, but loyal. The confession became the standard of church doctrine almost from its inception; in 1581 the Heidelberg Catechism was added also. It was formally adopted at the Synod of Dordt (1618–1619) as one of the expressions of Dutch Calvinism. In spite of Philip's sinister attempt to crush the Calvinists, a sizable and potent church gradually emerged.

8.15. THE DIVISION IN THE PROTESTANT CHURCHES

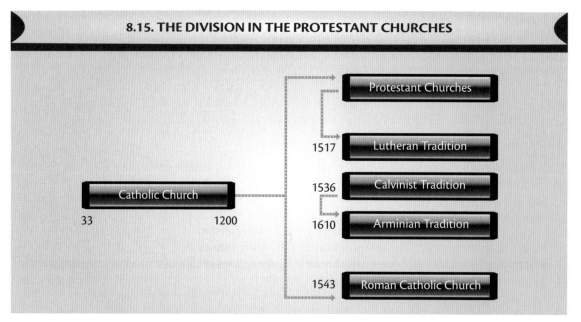

"We believe that Jesus Christ is ordained with an oath to be an everlasting High Priest, after the order of Melchisedec; and that he has presented himself in our behalf before the Father, to appease his wrath by his full satisfaction, by offering himself on the tree of the cross, and pouring out his precious blood to purge away our sins. . . . Therefore: he restored that which he took not away, and suffered, the just for the unjust, as well in his body as in his soul, feeling the terrible punishment which our sins had merited. . . . Wherefore we justly say with the apostle Paul: that we know nothing, but Jesus Christ, and him crucified; we count all things but loss and dung for the excellency of the knowledge of Christ Jesus our Lord, in whose wounds we find all manner of consolation. Neither is it necessary to seek or invent any other means of being reconciled to God, than this only sacrifice, once offered. . . . (*The Belgic Confession of Faith*, Article 21).

It was in the context of the conflict with Spain, having political and religious overtones, that Jacob Arminius rose to prominence in the churches. Born near Utrecht in 1560, he suffered the loss of his father in his infancy and his mother through martyrdom as a teenager. Through the kindness of patrons, he was able to attend school in Utrecht and later study theology at the University of Leiden. Subsequently, he studied under Beza in Geneva before taking a pastorate in Amsterdam. From the pastorate, he took a teaching post in the University of Leiden. However, it was during the pastorate

8.16. THE ORIGINS OF ARMINIANISM

CALVINISM   COORNHERTIANISM

ARMINIANISM (1610)
"The Five Remonstrants"

that questions were raised concerning his allegiance to the Belgic Confession, but complaints went uninvestigated. When a vacancy came in the university, Arminius secured state appointment over the uncertainties of church officials (an important unresolved issue was the spheres of authority of state and church. Arminius favored more state control of appointments than many church officials).

A professor of theology at the University of Leiden, Jacob Arminius had studied in Geneva under Theodore Beza, successor of John Calvin. While Calvin was careful to be silent when the Bible ceased to speak, this was not always true with Beza. Arminius took exception to Beza's teachings and was concerned that Calvinist doctrines made God the author of sin while he wanted to stress the importance of faith and holiness in the Christian life, as

A ca. 1620 painting of Jacobus Arminius (1560–1609) by David Bailly (1584–1657). Courtesy of ClassArm.

8.17. THE FORMATION OF THEOLOGY IN THE REFORMATION ERA

	ROMAN CATHOLICISM	REACTION 16th Century	CALVINISM (Reformed Tradition)	REACTION 17th Century	ARMINIANISM
Salvation	Cooperation (Church, Man, and God)		Grace		Gracious Cooperation (Church, Man, and God)
Man	Moral and Spiritual Ability		Moral and Spiritual Inability		Spiritual Ability

well as upholding the goodness and mercy of God. But Arminius was accused of being Pelagian, and the matter escalated. His followers, the Remonstrants, fomented a debate that resulted in the Synod of Dordt in 1618 where the five points (actually four articles that were later restructured into the now popular five statements) of Calvinism were developed in refutation of Arminius's teachings.

Upon the affirmation of conformity to the church's standard before Franciscus Gomarus (1563–1641), a strict Calvinist on the university faculty, Arminius joined the faculty, but the suspicions of nonconformity continued. Arminius appears to have kept his pledge to abide in the church's doctrinal standards in his lectures, but not so privately in tutoring his students. When former students applied for church positions, they failed the doctrinal test, asserting to have been influenced in their views by their mentor.

Franciscus Gomarus graduated from Cambridge, pastored a Dutch Reformed Church in Frankfort, and was a professor at the Leiden University. He held to supralapsarianism and differed with Jacob Arminius. The opposing views came to debate in 1604 in a disputation. Anonymous articles accused Arminius of heresy, and in 1608 Gomarus and Arminius debated before the Supreme Court in The Hague. They separately argued their positions before the national assembly where their speeches were ordered banned

from publication. This ban was ignored. Gomarus and his followers took a leading part as Contra-Remonstrants at the Synod of Dordt.

It appears that tensions with Arminius's adherence to Calvinism took a distinct turn when the Leiden professor attempted to refute an opponent of the church, Dirck Coornhert (1522–1590). Coornhert took part in the struggle against Spanish rule, enduring imprisonment and exile, but rejected the concept of a state church and was critical of the Heidelberg Catechism, rejecting the doctrine of predestination. The popularity of Arminius as a pastor, preacher, and teacher led to a substantial following. Among them was Simon Episcopus (1583–1643), who developed his teachings after his mentor's death in 1609; Arminius did not systematize his thought.

"That, accordingly, Jesus Christ the Savior of the world, died for all men and for every man, so that he has obtained for them all, by his death on the cross, redemption and the forgiveness of sins; yet that no one actually enjoys this forgiveness of sins except the believer" (Article 2, *Remonstrances*).

The essence of Arminius's insights was that traditional Calvinism, at least as expressed in the confessions, offered a flawed explanation of the Christian faith, in that Calvinists provided an inadequate explanation of Christian doc-

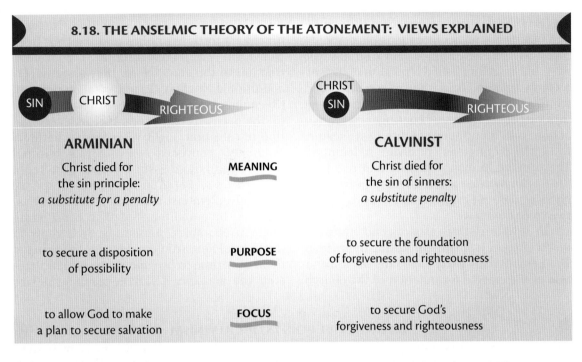

8.18. THE ANSELMIC THEORY OF THE ATONEMENT: VIEWS EXPLAINED

ARMINIAN		CALVINIST
Christ died for the sin principle: *a substitute for a penalty*	**MEANING**	Christ died for the sin of sinners: *a substitute penalty*
to secure a disposition of possibility	**PURPOSE**	to secure the foundation of forgiveness and righteousness
to allow God to make a plan to secure salvation	**FOCUS**	to secure God's forgiveness and righteousness

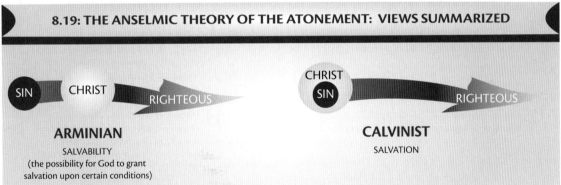

8.19: THE ANSELMIC THEORY OF THE ATONEMENT: VIEWS SUMMARIZED

ARMINIAN
SALVABILITY
(the possibility for God to grant salvation upon certain conditions)

CALVINIST
SALVATION

trine because it was based on the unwarranted assumption that human inability and human culpability are compatible. A doctrine of human responsibility could not be erected on the doctrine of absolute moral and spiritual incompetence. To the Arminians, neither Scripture nor reason supported such a position. Instead they erected a system that purported to bring the two truths into alignment, particularly as reflected in the work of Episcopus and,

for a short time, in the work of Phillip van Limborch (1633–1712), leader of the **Remonstrant Party**.

To clarify their position, the Arminian Party, perhaps more properly the Remonstrant Party, looked at the Christian truth of redemption from the perspective of the recipient, rather than starting from the perspective of the giver. Their concerns were salvation from the grass-roots, not the heavenlies, though this is not to suggest they rejected the wonder and beauty of the incomprehensible deity. The Remonstrant Party argued that God is sovereign, but he relinquished a portion of his sovereignty to man. Thus, they rejected the doctrines of particular election and atonement, injecting the concept of contingency. Human action and continued faithfulness seemed to be the requirement of divine redemption. They limited human depravity and redefined the foreknowledge of God, deemphasizing the passive voice of Scripture and making the active voice dominate.

In 1610 forty-three pastors and educators met to prepare a document stating their views. The Remonstrant Party called for the affirmation of the creedal formulation of the church, but with refinement or redefinition. The document set forth five points and thus has been called the "Five Remonstrants." In contradistinction to the confessions, they asserted: (1) conditional election, (2) universal atonement, (3) cooperative ability, (4) resistible grace, and (5) the necessity of perseverance as the condition of salvation. Eight years later a national synod was convened at Dordt that rejected the proposals and issued a four-part reply, *The Articles of Dordt*. In the synod's response to the Five Remonstrances, they combined assertions three and four together, considering them inseparables, presenting their reply in the form of four articles. Calvinists rearranged them over time to five and centuries later created the acrostic, TULIP, a teaching device

8.20. THE FIVE POINTS OF CALVINISM

FIVE ARTICLES OF THE REMONSTRANTS	FIVE POINTS OF CALVINISM
1 Human nature is corrupt and cannot think, will, or do anything good. However God, through Christ, has restored some ability in these areas which allows individuals to have saving faith. (3)	**T** **Total Depravity**. Due to Adam's sin, man's human nature is corrupt, and every person stands condemned in God's sight. If God does not act directly on an individual, that person has no hope of ever being saved.
2 God has determined that those who through the grace of the Holy Spirit believe, persevere, and obey shall be saved by the work of Christ. (1)	**U** **Unconditional Election**. God elects certain persons to be saved, based solely upon his determination, utterly apart from anything a person may or may not do.
3 Christ has died for all so that all men can through faith be saved (2)	**L** **Limited Atonement**. The atonement is limited in that Christ died only for the elect.
4 No aspect of salvation is accomplished without grace; however, this grace can be resisted (4)	**I** **Irresistible Grace**. God's election also involves his acting in grace on the elect toward their salvation; they cannot resist the power of his Spirit to save.
5 Once someone has been saved, they have full power to persevere through God's grace inasmuch as they desire his help. (5)	**P** **Perseverance of the Saints**. Once someone has been saved by God, they remain forever in that condition. They will persevere until the very end of their lives.

to articulate their antithesis to Remonstrant Party claims.

> "For it was the entirely free plan and very gracious will and intention of God the Father that the enlivening and saving effectiveness of his Son's costly death should work itself out in all the elect, in order that God might grant justifying faith to them only and thereby lead them without fail to salvation. In other words, it was God's will that Christ through the blood of the cross (by which he confirmed the new covenant) should effectively redeem from every people, tribe, nation, and language all those and only those who were chosen from eternity to salvation and given to him by the Father; that Christ should grant them faith (which, like the Holy Spirit's other saving gifts, he acquired for them by his death)" (Point 2, Article 8 of the Synod of Dordt).

Regardless of one's perspective on the Calvinist/Arminian dispute of the seventeenth century, the issues created a viable and vivacious new tradition within Protestantism, the Arminian Tradition.

The Spread of Calvinism into Scotland

The gradual disgruntlement with the late medieval church, as well as the positive influences of the Renaissance to entertain new ideas, was the background for the spread of Luther's ideas across Europe, including Scotland. Not only were Luther's books banned, but Patrick Hamilton, who received training in Wittenberg, was martyred at St. Andrews under the direction of Archbishop James Beaton in 1528, the first of many. Though evidence exists that the church attempted to curb moral and religious excesses, the momentum for reform escalated.

In addition, Scotland had become the center of international political intrigue. Henry VIII of England sought an alliance with the Scots by marrying his infant son, Edward, to Mary Stuart (1542–1567), the infant Queen of the Scots. Military invasion followed the plan's failure, but the English were repulsed. Catholic sympathies, led by Cardinal David Beaton, sought a French alignment with Mary Stuart later marrying the king of France. Under the impetus of Beaton, George Wishart (ca. 1513–1546), a former student in Geneva and translator of the First Helvetic Confession into English, was martyred in 1546. Sometime later, Cardinal Beaton, the last Catholic cardinal of Scotland, was assassinated in reprisal. With Beaton's murder, St. Andrews castle became a center of Protestantism.

The marriage of Mary Stuart to Francis II in 1558 pushed the nation to a religious crisis. Protestant lords, "the Lords of the Congregation," bound themselves to a covenant to preserve the Protestant cause, inspired by the ascension of Elizabeth I to the English throne in 1558. Mary, the nation's monarch, was forced to accept Protestantism as Edinburgh embraced the new faith. Meeting in Edinburgh in 1560, the parliament declared the church Protestant, adopting as its creed the Scottish Confession of Faith. This confession was replaced in 1644 by the Westminster Confession of Faith.

John Knox (ca. 1510–1572) was the central figure in this sixteenth century reformation. Trained at St. Andrews, he was influenced by George Wishart, among others, toward Protestantism. Implicated in the murder plot of Cardinal Beaton, and chaplain to the Protestant garrison at St. Andrews castle, Knox was taken prisoner after the fall of the city to a French fleet in 1547. After nineteen months as a galley slave, Knox somehow gained his release to England. He then supported the Protestant resurgence in the reign of Edward VI as a preacher at Newcastle upon Tyne and as one of six chaplains in the service of the King of England. The repercussions of Mary Tudor's strident pro-catholic policies forced Knox to the continent where he lived in Geneva, meeting Calvin, and then in Frankfurt where he led an English-refugee congregation. A dispute over liturgy in the church led to his disconnection and the development of presbyterial polity that was later embraced in Scotland. He returned to Geneva and from there back to Scotland. The convening of the Reformation Parliament of 1560 found Knox and the nobles adamant to push forward reforms. A committee of five was charged to prepare a new confession of faith and a directory of discipline defining the doctrine and polity of the church.

> "John Knox was a strange and rather frightening character. He was narrow-minded and intolerant. He lacked generosity of spirit and loved to hate. But he possessed immense courage and feared no one. In the pulpit, he was at his most powerful. He mesmerized thousands of Scots, who were prepared to lay their lives down for Protestantism at his behest. By his preaching, he molded both nobility and ordinary folk into a formidable fighting force and thus left his stamp on the Protestantism of Scotland for centuries to come" (R. Tudur Jones, "Preacher of Revolution," *Christian History* 46 [1995], 8).

The stormy relationship of the preacher of St. Giles Church and the queen was legendary, Knox scornful of her Catholic affiliations and Mary of his vitriolic outbursts. He was summoned to Holyrood, the queen's palace on several occasions to answer for his conduct and, in the process, vented his own opinions of the monarchy.

The Spread of Calvinism into Hungary

The devastating defeat of the Hungarians by the Turks under Suleiman I at the battle of Mohacs in 1526 divided the nation into three. The defiantly Roman Catholic Hapsburgs ruled western Hungry from Vienna—central Hungary, including the capital, Buda, and Transylvania, a independent state under the sway of Turkish influence. Initially influenced toward reformation ideals by the writings of Luther, the potential of German imperialism and Roman Catholic countermeasures aborted a lasting influence. The threat of Turkish invasion did, however, have a positive effect; the Hapsburgs were reluctant to persecute Protestants for fear of the lost of political influence, thus allowing reforming preachers in their territory. Transylvania openly embraced reformation ideals. By virtue of a slow attrition, Roman Catholic influence waned in the sixteenth century.

Though trained in Wittenberg under Luther and called the "Luther of Hungary," Matthias Devay (d. 1547) embraced a reformed definition of the Lord's Supper. He was a vocal pastor in Buda and elsewhere, established a printing press, published the first books in the Hungarian language, and wrote several trea-

A statue of John Knox by Kim Traynor at the former John Knox Memorial Institute in Haddington, Scotland. Courtesy of Martin York.

8.21. THE STUART DYNASTY OF SIXTEENTH-CENTURY SCOTLAND

	JAMES IV	1485–1513	Married Margaret Tudo, Henry VIII's sister
	JAMES V	1513–1542	Married Madeleine of Valois (1537) Mary of Guise (1538–42)
	MARY STUART	1542–1567	Married Francis II of France
	JAMES VI	1567–1625	Also James I of England (1603–1625)

tises and confessions. Among other significant reformers were Martin Kalmancsehi Santa (1500–1557) of Debrecen, Stephen Szegedi Kis (1505–1572), Gregory Szegedi (d. 1569), and Peter Melius Juhasz (1536–1572). By the century's end, Calvinism prevailed as the dominate expression of Protestant thought. In 1567 under the leadership of Peter Juhasz, a national church was formed, adopting the Second Helvetic Confession; in 1590 the Bible was published in Hungarian, the work of Gaspar Karoli (ca. 1529–1591), a Calvinist pastor.

As also true among the Calvinists in Holland, the Hungarian Calvinists experienced harsh persecution by the Roman Catholic Hapsburgs and so armed themselves for protection. The leader of the Hungarian Protestant faction was Stephen Bocskay (1557–1606), later honored by being placed on the Reformation monument in Geneva. His efforts led to religious toleration in 1606 in the Peace of Vienna. The peace agreement was short-lived; the Hapsburg king favored the inquisition as a tool to suppress the reform movement. Hungarian Protestants faced horrendous persecution in the seventeenth century, causing many to flee the country.

Born in Hungary in 1557, Stephen Bocskay was a Protestant nobleman who was the chief councilor

A statue of Stephen Bocskay (1557–1606) at the Memorial Park of National Memory in Ópusztaszer, Hungary. Courtesy of Váradi Zsolt.

the south. During the reign of King Sigismund I (1506–1548), Protestant influences were actively suppressed though the new ideas came into the country through students who studied in such universities as Wittenberg, Geneva, and Zurich. His successor, Sigismund Augustus II (1548–1572) was more sympathetic to the movement, perhaps more from a scholarly and cultural viewpoint than a narrowly religious one, even conducting some correspondence with Calvin.

John à Lasco (1499–1560) emerged as the most distinguished reformer in the country. Though educated as a priest, à Lasco was influenced by the reform movements in Basel and Zurich toward reformed Protestant opinions. His convictions took him initially to England where he pastored a "strangers church" in London until the reign of Mary Tudor. Subsequently, he took his threatened flock to Germany, but in 1556 he was recalled to Poland by the king and the higher nobility to become his secretary and an advocate of reform. Among his contributions were the translation of the Scriptures, the organization of the churches, and a striving to bridge the hostilities between

of Prince Sigismund Bathory. Advising his prince to first ally with the Hapsburg Holy Roman Emperor and then the Ottoman Turks, he helped avoid the imposition of Roman Catholicism on Hungary and insure independent Protestant religious liberties. He negotiated the Peace of Vienna in 1606 to secure a peace among the Hapsburgs, the sultan, and the prince of Transylvania for both Hungary and Transylvania, after which he was acknowledged as Prince of Transylvania.

The Spread of Calvinism into Poland
Luther's writings had an impact of the Kingdom of Poland and the Duchy of Lithuania, designated as the Poland-Lithuanian Commonwealth, as well as influences from Bohemia to

A painting of Edward VI giving permission for John à Lasco to set up a congregation for European Protestants in London in 1550. Attributed to Johann Valentin Haidt (1700–1780). Courtesy of Jfhutson.

Calvinists and Lutherans in the spirit of Martin Bucer of Strasbourg.

The tolerant policy of Sigismund II toward Protestantism was reversed in Poland through the influence of Stanislas Hosius (1504–1579), a Jesuit bishop and participant at the Council of Trent. Through these influences, the **Jesuits** were sanctioned in 1564 to establish schools and as a consequence made rapid progress in reversing Protestant gains. Protestantism continued to exist, but experienced marginalization as did the Orthodox Church.

GLOSSARY OF TERMS

All Saints' Day: originating in the early medieval period and celebrated from the pontificate of Gregory IV on November 1st, the day honors the church's saints and martyrs. It was on this day in 1533 that Nicholas Cop delivered an address, perhaps written by Calvin, creating open conflict between Catholic humanists and Protestant sympathizers.

Arminianism: a tradition of theological interpretation that emerged in sixteenth-century Holland in opposition to the prevailing Calvinism of the day. Arminians argued that the best defense of the faith was in modifying Calvinism in the areas of anthropology, soteriology, and the nature of the atonement as expressed in the Five Remonstrances of 1610, believing that human inability and responsibility were incompatible and so surrendered human inability.

Concubinage: a practice in the medieval church that allowed priests to experience conjugal privilege without contractual marriage.

Enlightenment (Age of Reason): a movement begun in eighteenth-century Europe that emphasized the inner capacities of man (rational reflection, intuition) as opposed to external authority sources such as the church or the Bible to improve social and society performance. Strenuously opposed by the religious community as well as secular materialists, the Enlightenment spawned the modern era, a three-century experiment in the redemptive values of science and technology. Though highly successful in the technical realms, the venture collapsed under the weight of holocausts and wars, suggesting that the blight of human discord could not be remedied by social advances

alone. The movement filled life with opportunities but emptied it of meaning, creating Postmodernism.

First Kappel War: a confrontation in 1529 between Protestant and Roman Catholic cantons in Switzerland. The "war" ended without a battle, but divided loyalties and alliances.

House of Savoy: In the sixteenth century the House of Savoy was a ruling party that exercised authority over a region that encompassed parts of southern France and western Italy. In the sixteenth century, the Duchy of Savoy, largely under French Roman Catholic influence, threatened the Swiss Canton city of Geneva, Calvin, and the Protestant Reformation.

Huguenots: though the term is of disputed origins, it is the name given to French Protestants in the sixteenth century. It may be that the term is reflective of a Genevan political party. The French Protestant community emerged in 1559 through the Gallican Confession. Huguenots had a turbulent history in the sixteenth century, gained toleration in 1598 under Henry VI, and lost it in 1685 under Louis XIV, many leaving France for Prussia, England, and British America.

Jesuits (Society of Jesus): a Roman Catholic religious order founded by Ignatius Loyola in 1540 and officially sanctioned by Paul III in 1543. The order was composed of priests who committed themselves to poverty (mendicants), the strident preservation and extension of Roman doctrine, and the dictates of the church. Militantly aggressive as an arm of the church, it opposed Protestant gains and, being missionary-minded, spread the faith globally in the sixteenth century and beyond.

Maundy Thursday (Holy Thursday, Covenant Thursday): a celebration during Holy Week recognizing the events in Jesus's day prior to his crucifixion, emphasizing the Passover meal with the disciples and the institution of the New Covenant Lord's Supper, the episode of the Lord's garden agonies, his arrest by the Romans, and his confrontations with the Jewish leadership.

Palatinate: a region in southwestern Germany bounded by the Neckar and Rhine rivers. In this area, with a center at Heidelberg, the Calvinist tradition became prominent in the sixteenth century as expressed in the Heidelberg Catechism.

Presbyterianism (Presbyterial Polity): A term that designates the polity of those churches in the Calvinist tradition that was crafted by Thomas Cartwright, the Puritan Cambridge University scholar in Elizabethan England, and enshrined in the Westminister Confession of Faith (1646). The governance of the church is in what is called the presbytery, a regional gathering of the sessions, the ruling elders and teachers, of the local churches.

Remonstrant Party (Arminian Party): a group of religious scholars in Calvinist Holland in the early seventeenth century, following the lead of Jacob Arminius, that believed that the better defense of Calvinist faith against the invasive religious Enlightenment was in a revision of the Belgic Confession of Faith, the creedal standard of the churches. Struggling with the age-old dilemma of explaining the relationship between inability, responsibility, and culpability, the group prepared the "Five Remonstrances" in 1610 and appealed to the state to revise its confession. An assembly of divines from across Europe convened the Synod of Dordt in 1618 and rejected all five revisions and issued a four-point statement in reply. Out of the rejection came the Arminian tradition of Protestant interpretation.

Schmalkaldic League: an alliance of Lutheran princes and cities for the purpose of mutual defense from the threat of Charles V, the emperor of the "Roman Empire" who was motivated by Roman Catholic sympathies, given the revocation of religious toleration following the Diet of Speyer in 1529. Named for the city in which the alliance was created in 1531, the league did not formally accept the creed, the doctrines most essential to the Protestant Reformation, in which Luther envisioned orthodoxy being the primary voice in its construction. However, named the Schmalkaldic Articles, it did become one of the several Lutheran confessions incorporated into the Book of Concord (1580).

Shrine of the Black Virgin (Shrine of the Holy Lady, the Black Madonna): while there are many such shrines to the Virgin Mary, the particular one within the context of the sixteenth-century division of the Western Catholic Church into Roman Catholic and Protestant factions is the pilgrimage site in Einsiedeln, Switzerland, the second parish of the then Ulrich Zwingli. Housed in the Benedictine monastery, the shrine raised doubts about the authenticity of late medieval catholic truth claims, becoming a source of reformational dissent.

Second Kappel War (Second Battle of Kappel): a military engagement between Protestant Zurichers and nearby Roman Catholic cantons that proved a temporary setback for the Protestant cause in Switzerland with the death of Ulrich Zwingli on the battlefield (1531).

Chapter 9 Outline

Chapter 9 Objectives

- That the reader will distinguish the Radical Reformations from the Magisterial Reformations

- That the reader will describe the foundations and development of the Anabaptist movement in Europe and the Baptist emergence in England

- That the reader will identify the content, meaning, and development of the Church of England

- That the reader will describe the reasons for the emergence of the Puritan movement within the Church of England

- That the reader will identify other significant attempts to reform the late medieval church

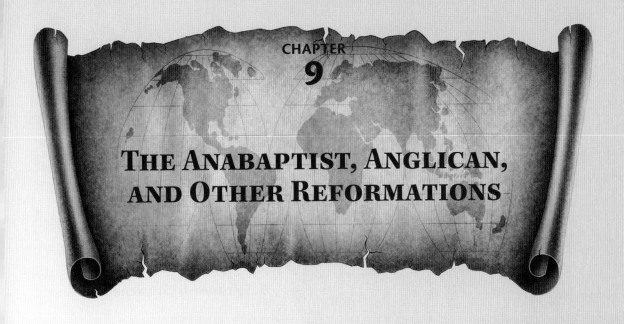

CHAPTER
9

THE ANABAPTIST, ANGLICAN, AND OTHER REFORMATIONS

S CHOLARS HAVE GENERALLY FOUND it helpful to separate the Protestant Reformation into two broad categories: the **Magisterial Reformation**s and the **Radical Reformation**s (the latter is sometimes called the **Free Church Tradition** within Protestantism). The criteria for distinguishing the two groups largely rests on the issue of the relationship of church to state and their respective spheres of authority. The magisterial reformers envisioned an interdependency between the church and state, though there was not uniformity of explanation among them. Luther, for example, viewed the state as a necessary nuisance to curb the tendencies of anarchy in society; Calvin viewed the state far more positively, advocating the possibility of a commonwealth. By far, the majority of the reformers did not question the role of the state in the church; the complete separation of powers was not envisioned. Such a concept would be a child of the Enlightenment with its secularizing tendencies.

The Anabaptists or the Free Church Tradition

However, some reform-minded movements on the continent and in England advocated the complete separation of state and church. Though often quite diverse in perspectives, these movements have been seen collectively because of certain commonalities, principally the complete rejection of any role of the state in ecclesiastical affairs. This hostile attitude has brought to their movement the label of the Radical Reformation.

While many of the various groups are within the Protestant family, they represent a very diverse spectrum of theological views. Some, like the **Münsterites** and **Hoffmanites**, embraced bizarre apocalyptic overtones with militant political and cultish teachings. Others reflected

9.1. ANTIPEDOBAPTIST GROUPS

ANABAPTIST

Melchior Hoffman (1495–1543), an Anabaptist prophet, in an engraving by Christoffel van Sichem (1581–1658). Courtesy of Finnrind and Temadchopper.

1. Radicals: Zwickau Prophets

2. Rationalists: Anti-Trinitarians

3. Spiritualists: Schwenkfelders

4. Orthodox: Swiss Brethren

heterodox views of Protestant theology outside of the mainstream of historic orthodoxy. Some, however, expressed views well within the reformation perspective, but they did diverge on such matters as the church's relationship to the state and the meaning of baptism.

Sorting out the Radical Tradition is complicated. First, the advocates of the movement, at least as expressed on the continent, did not possess educational and intellectual prowess over their Protestant opponents, drawing their leadership and constituency from the lower classes.

Second, because the movement often manifested a popular orientation, there was little literary productivity, the exceptions being the Michael Sattler, Andreas Karlstadt, Balthasar Hubmaier, and Menno Simons on the continent in the sixteenth century, who could defend their claims with persuasive, biblical argumentation. The lack of literary output was caused, in part, by the hostility toward the movement

and the martyrdom that often was experienced by advocates of the movement. The church and government leaders in the sixteenth century saw little else than the threat of anarchy in the social and political views of the Radical Tradition. Since the "radicals" found it hard to get a serious audience for their opinions, having left fewer literary documents, historians have had a more difficult time understanding them in light of mountains of prejudice, appropriate and otherwise.

Third, the magisterial reformers viewed the radical reformers as a threat. The Protestant reformers taught a doctrine of freedom from medieval conventions that some took to an extreme of justification for political insurrectionism. The Peasants' War in Germany is a formidable example. Luther feared that in that and the Zwickau prophets movement a crushing political reaction by the state that could threaten his entire reformation. This was certainly the perspective of Zwingli and Calvin as well.

An oil painting of Anabaptist leader Michael Sattler preaching in the woods by Mike Antip. Courtesy of Magnus Manske.

A tangential issue in the discussion of the Radical Reformation is the relationship of the continental movement to the rise of English Baptists in the seventeenth century. Until recent decades, Baptist historiography tended to minimize continental origins, largely, it seems, to distance themselves from an unwillingness to be identified with unceremonious beliefs and actions by their continental cousins. It will be argued subsequently that the Baptist tradition has roots from certain manifestations of the continental movement, however it may have profited from its English heritage.

The Anabaptist Movement and Its Beginnings in Zurich
Though the Radical Reformation was a spectrum of theological opinions and diverse leaders, there was a strand that, at least in part, represented a centrist and conservative perspective on reform—the Zwinglian reform movement in Zurich. When Zwingli approached the daunting task of introducing reformation teaching in Zurich, he gathered around himself a number of promising young men, attracting them through his humanist literary interests. He was successful in gaining several to his efforts.

At the First Zurich Disputation in January 1523, the city council embraced the cause, largely due to Roman Catholic miscues. Though the council embraced reform, it was more in theory than practice. However, it served as a mandate for Zwingli to define the movement and push it forward. He started a school with two of his prominent converts, Conrad Grebel (1498–1526) and Felix Manz (ca.1498–1527), teaching the biblical languages.

Often called the "father of Anabaptists," Conrad Grebel was initially a follower of Ulrich Zwingli but differed with him on a variety of issues including how quickly to progress on Reformed practice. They ultimately broke on the topic of infant baptism. The city council sided with Zwingli and the continuation of infant baptism, while Grebel refused to baptize anyone without a prior experience of salvation. The council insisted on exile from the canton of Zurich, but Grebel was asked to baptize George Blaurock, an adult in 1525. The Anabaptists, or Swiss Brethren, as they are often designated, and the beliefs of Grebel had a lasting impact on the Amish, Mennonite, and Baptist churches.

The slow pace of progress, as well as a growing discontent with Zwingli pressed the city to immediate reforms that caused a growing division. In the Second Zurich Disputation, October 1523, the all-important issue of the interpretation of the Eucharist brought a crisis; Zwingli failed to demand its immediate abolition as an unbloodied reenactment of the crucifixion of Christ resulting in divine merit in the forgiveness of sins. Yet in Zwingli's view, reform had to progress within the dictates of the city council and, therefore, he cautioned against precipitous action. The wedge between the polarized reformists reached a climax when the city threatened Zwingli's followers with punishment in January 1525 if they did not desist.

The issues that separated Zwingli from his followers were political and theological. Zwingli felt that the hope of reforming the church was through cooperating with the city fathers, even if his plans had to be deferred (the city became Protestant in 1525 following the Third Zurich Disputation, but it was unacceptable to some who envisioned a more thorough reformation). Grebel and others wanted to

press for reform with or without the approbation of the city council.

Grebel, the son of a Zurich merchant-councilman, appears to have been converted through contact with Zwingli in 1522 after studying at the University of Vienna for three years and two years at the University of Paris (finishing without a degree due, perhaps, to a wayward lifestyle). He, and about fifteen others, separated initially over the Eucharistic Controversy. The division became irrevocable on 17 January 1525 when the city council affirmed baptism in contradistinction to Grebel's and the group's embrace of believer's baptism (baptism being an outward sign of a previous event, not a sign of a future reality).

This emerging party accepted believer's baptism, but with radical implications politi-

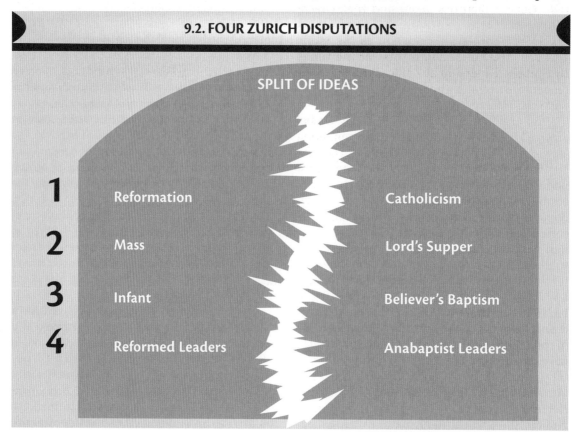

9.2. FOUR ZURICH DISPUTATIONS

SPLIT OF IDEAS

1	Reformation	Catholicism
2	Mass	Lord's Supper
3	Infant	Believer's Baptism
4	Reformed Leaders	Anabaptist Leaders

cally and ecclesiastically. Such a view of church membership, separating it from civil citizenship, threatened to dissolve the medieval synthesis of church and state, constructing a dichotomy, a disunion in society. In the Anabaptist view advocated at that time, the state was a deterrent to the kingdom (not even Luther's necessary-evil view). The church was not composed of the citizenry of Zurich, but only those with a reliance on the profession of their conversion; the church was gathered out of the world through preaching, not state/church baptism.

Seven days after the council's mandate to have all unbaptized children baptized within eight days, Grebel and others gathered in the home of Felix Manz to determine a course of action. In the Manz home in Zollicon, near Zurich, George Blaurock requested that Grebel baptize him and he in turn baptized others (likely by pouring or sprinkling as the mode was not an issue of controversy at the time). By Grebel's leadership at Zollicon, he has been recognized as the "father of the Swiss Brethren" and the "father of the Anabaptists."

Reprisal from the state came swiftly. Grebel engaged in an itinerant ministry disseminating his views, but was imprisoned in 1525, where he appears to have written a defense of believer's baptism, before dying the following year. Felix Manz was arrested several times for illegal preaching and drowned on 5 January 1527, becoming the first Anabaptist martyr. George Blaurock (ca. 1491–1529), educated at the University of Leipzig and a former priest, was severely beaten in a Zurich prison in the context of Manz's demise and later burned at the stake. Balthasar Hubmaier (ca. 1480–1528), educated at the University of Freiburg and a literary figure in the early movement, was burned to death and his wife drowned by Roman Catholic authorities. His works not only included a defense of believer's baptism and freedom of religious exercise, but a scholarly response to Luther's affirmation of the bondage of the will and

The German Anabaptist Balthasar Hubmaier (ca. 1480–1528). Gravure by Christoffel van Sichem (seventeenth century). Courtesy of Leos vän.

predestination. Unlike early Anabaptists generally, he advocated participation in government including bearing the sword. Michael Sattler (ca. 1490–1527), executed by Roman Catholic authorities, was prominent in the construct of the Schleitheim Confession. At the Second Diet of Speyer in 1529, the death decree was issued against all Anabaptists throughout the Holy Roman Empire.

"Those that until now have followed the Edict of Worms [1521, the condemnation of Luther] should continue to do so. In the areas where this has been deviated from, there shall be no further new developments and no-one shall be refused Mass. Finally, the sects which contradict the sacrament of the true body and blood, shall absolutely not be tolerated, no more than the Anabaptists" (The Second Diet of Speyer).

Though the Anabaptists were not monolithic in theological expression, often a prominent leader defined the beliefs of the group that rallied around him. The Schleitheim Confession of 1527 was an important lens into early Anabaptist beliefs. Composed of seven articles, the first spelled out believer's baptism defining it with a death/resurrection motif, an outward symbol of the conversion experience, being the almost universal insight among the Anabaptist. The other articles included the exercise of excommunication (the ban) of disobedient members before the service of the Lord's Table; the interpretation of the Lord's Table as a remembrance ceremony for the baptized; physical separation for worldliness; the pastor as the church leader; governmental non-participation, including pacifism; and a prohibition against oath-taking.

"Baptism shall be given to all those who have learned repentance and amendment of life, and who believe truly that their sins are taken away by Christ, and to all those who walk in the resurrection of Jesus Christ, and wish to be buried with Him in death, so that they may be resurrected with Him and to all those who

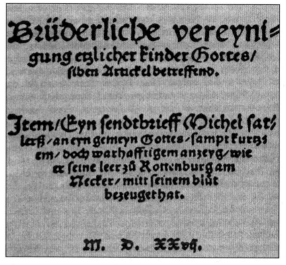

The title page of the *Schleitheim Confession.* Courtesy of Magadan.

with this significance request it (baptism) of us and demand it for themselves. This excludes all infant baptism, the highest and chief abomination of the Pope" (The Schleitheim Confession of Faith [1527], Article 1).

The Anabaptist Movement and the Spread into Germany and Holland

Lacking in strong, stable leadership, the movement often wobbled. Melchior Hoffman (ca. 1495–1543) appears to have been the embodi-

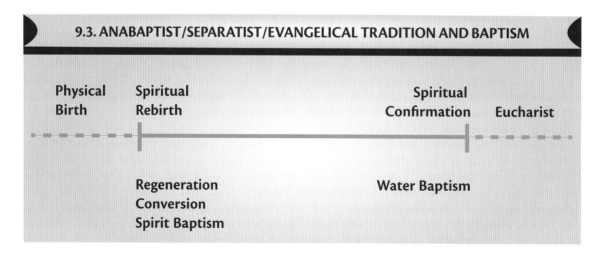

9.3. ANABAPTIST/SEPARATIST/EVANGELICAL TRADITION AND BAPTISM

Physical Birth — Spiritual Rebirth — Spiritual Confirmation — Eucharist

Regeneration / Conversion / Spirit Baptism

Water Baptism

ment of Luther's worst fears that the Evangelical Movement, the name he used for the Reformation churches in Germany, would spiral into anarchy and libertinism. Hoffman added apocalyptic visions to buttress his claims that the Lord would return in 1533 and establish the "New Jerusalem" in Strasbourg. Though he spent the last decade of his life in prison, his influence is evident in the larger Anabaptist movement, particularly in Menno Simons, who accepted his view that Christ's flesh was not earthly.

The tragedy of Münster cast a negative shadow over the entire European movement. Arriving in Münster from the Spanish Neth-

9.4. ANABAPTIST CONCENTRATIONS AND MOVEMENTS

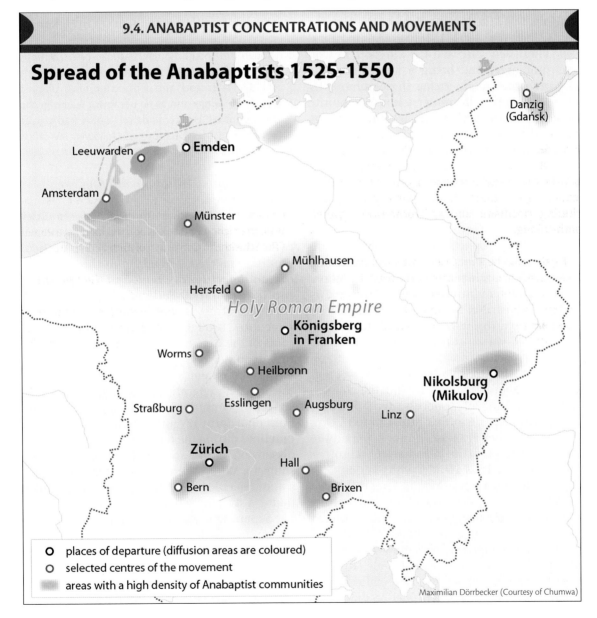

Spread of the Anabaptists 1525-1550

Danzig (Gdańsk)

Leeuwarden

Emden

Amsterdam

Münster

Mühlhausen

Hersfeld

Holy Roman Empire

Königsberg in Franken

Worms

Heilbronn

Nikolsburg (Mikulov)

Straßburg Esslingen Augsburg

Linz

Zürich

Hall

Bern

Brixen

o places of departure (diffusion areas are coloured)
o selected centres of the movement
   areas with a high density of Anabaptist communities

Maximilian Dörrbecker (Courtesy of Chumwa)

Invitation to Church History: World

erlands in 1534, the Anabaptist Jan Matthijs (ca. 1500–1534), a Melchiorite and visionary prophet, with a coterie of followers and sympathizers in the city, gained control hoping to create a theocratic kingdom (they did not embrace a pacifistic spirit evident in Conrad Grebel or Menno Simons). Roman Catholics and Lutherans were summarily expelled. When Matthijs was killed in the siege of the city, Jan van Leiden (ca. 1509–1536) proclaimed himself "king." Believing that the kingdom of God was imminent, and being a Münsterite, the city prepared by practicing the commonality of goods, baptism by immersion (a Melchiorite distinctive), and, strangely, polygamy. The siege of the city eventually proved successful, actually an Anabaptist opponent in the city opened the gates, and the Münsterites were crushed. It marked the end of the viability of the Anabaptist cause as a political movement.

It could be argued, and most likely should, that the Melchiorites and Münsterites represent the Zwickau Prophets and the political radicalism of the Peasants' Revolt, more so than the mainstream continental Anabaptist tradition. Though Hoffman introduced Anabaptist views in the Spanish Netherlands, his influence on brothers Obbe (ca. 1500–1568) and Dirk Philips (1504–1568) was a turning point in the emergence of a pacifist, non-political manifestation of Anabaptism. Obbe Philips led the movement until he withdrew from it in 1540; the connection to later Anabaptist success was his baptism of Menno Simons, a former priest, in 1537. Dirk Philips, a former Franciscan monk, joined the movement through the influence of his brother in 1534, emerging as a leader with Simons.

The significance of Menno Simons (1496–1561) in the stabilization of the Anabaptist movement is incalculable. Though an ordained priest, Simons joined the Anabaptists in 1537 to singularly shape the movement in the dark aftermath of the Münsterite episode. To clear the movement of negative associations and theological misconceptions, Menno published

The Foundation of Christian Doctrine in 1539. His theology reflects reformational insights from the perspective of Anabaptists, with the exception of his adoption of Hoffman's belief that Jesus's flesh was not derived from Mary, fearing that it would impugn his absolute perfections, suggesting that Jesus's flesh was "celestial" in nature. His name eventually became synonymous with the Anabaptists in Holland.

> Though ordained a Roman Catholic priest, Simons first became a follower of the Anabaptist movement in 1537. He escaped the persecution of Anabaptist leaders in Switzerland as he became a leader in the Low Countries. He is considered to have had a great influence on English Baptists. His followers are called Mennonites.

The Anabaptist Tradition and English Baptists

Though it is not uncommon, at least in older historiography, to look askance at continental roots, it seems now to be firmly established. Baptists emerged in England in the early seventeenth century in two forms, General Baptists in 1612 and the Particular Baptists in 1638. Each appeared to have been influenced in that direction through Mennonite contact. The roots of the General Baptists, so designated by their embrace of a universal view of the intent of the atonement, originated with the rise of the English separatist movement in the late sixteenth century. The establishment of an Episcopal form of government and liturgical practices during the reign of Elizabeth I caused dissension among some of her reform-minded subjects. While the avenue of dissent varied, some rejected any thought of compromise taking a strongly separatist stance.

Separatists found it disadvantageous to remain in England, particularly with James Stuart's ascendancy after 1603. Led by Thomas Helwys (ca. 1575–ca.1616) and John Smyth (ca. 1554–1612), groups of separatists resettled in Holland where they were influenced by Rhinelander Mennonites to embrace believer's baptism by immersion. Smyth sought to identify with the Mennonites in Holland, and was successful in doing so. Helwys and John Morton returned a group to England and established a General Baptist church in London in 1612.

The Particular Baptists, like the General Baptists, found their ecclesiastical roots in resistance to the episcopacy of the Elizabethan church in the late sixteenth century. However, unlike their counterparts, the Particularists, did not assume a strong separatist stance, but was part of an attempt to work within the established church to alter its ecclesiology through qualified participation in the political process. To abolish episcopacy entailed the creation of an alternative government for the

churches. Thus in the later decades of the century, both a presbyterial and a congregational state-church ecclesiology emerged, the former

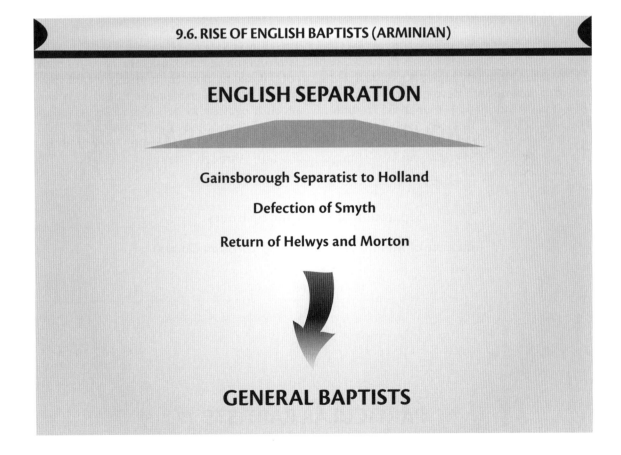

crafted by Thomas Cartwright's lectures at Cambridge University in the 1570s and the latter by Henry Jacobs (1563–1624). Jacobs was initially of separatist persuasion and fled to Holland. However, influenced by John Robinson, he adopted congregational polity and returned to England in 1616 to establish the first Congregational church in England.

Though the church established by Henry Jacobs, along with John Lathrop and Henry Jessey, was not Baptist, the Particular Baptists did spring from this church. In 1638 a group separated from the congregational church embracing distinctive baptistic doctrine led by John Spilsbury. The contact with a baptistic orientation, in this case the Mennonite conception of baptism, appears to have emerged through the influence of Menno's *Foundation Book of Christian Doctrine* in England. In

addition to an emphasis on believer's baptism and the death-resurrection meaning of the sacrament (a view that distinguished them from the Congregationalist emphasis of an outward sign of an invisible reality), the group embraced a particularist understanding of the extent of the atonement.

Henry Jacob, a graduate of Oxford, after joining the English Dissenters known as Brownists, went into exile in Holland in 1593 where he formed a group of former Anglicans into a semi-separatist faction referred to as Independents. Calvinistic in theology but independent in church government, he is considered to have formed in Southwark the first Congregational church in England. He traveled to Virginia and founded "Jacobopolis" in 1622.

Taking advantage of the religious tolerance

9.7. RISE OF ENGLISH BAPTISTS (CALVINISTIC)

ENGLISH CONGREGATIONALISM

Separation of Eaton and Spilsbury

Influence of Menno's *Foundation of Christian Doctrine*

PARTICULAR BAPTISTS

practiced in the Puritan commonwealth era (1640–1660), the Baptists spread throughout the land. In 1644, under the lead of William Kiffin (1616–1771) and Hanserd Knollys (1599–1691), the Baptists crafted the First London Confession of Faith as their doctrinal standard. Most prominent of Baptists in the seventeenth century were John Bunyan (1628–1688) and John Gill (1697–1771), in the eighteenth century William Carey (1761–1834), and in the nineteenth century Charles Haddon Spurgeon (1834–1892).

A wealthy wool merchant with connections in Holland, William Kiffin came to faith in his teens as a result of Puritan preaching. He later became pastor of one of seven Calvinist Baptist churches in England, known as Particular Baptists. He played a major role in drafting the First London Confession of Faith in 1644 and signed the Second in 1677. He served in Parliament under Cromwell, and was well connected with King Charles II, under whom he was appointed to several governmental offices. He helped persecuted Baptists in Ireland, France, and Germany.

The Anglican Community or the Church of England

The winds of change that were sweeping across the continent simultaneously reached into England in the early sixteenth century. The popularity of Luther's writings certainly bore its influence among the priests and other intellectuals of the day. At the popular level of the society, the lingering influence of the Wycliffites was discernible in the preaching of his followers, the **Lollards**. **Renaissance Humanism** was felt in the major university centers such as Oxford and Cambridge with its reinterpretation of medieval history and the church's role, the rise of a quest to recover the past, and an elevated interest in the study of man. The influence of the teaching of John Colet (1467–1519), dean of St. Paul's Cathedral, London, who became an advocate of Bible teaching, though he was clearly outshone in England by Erasmus,

expressed the new concerns for biblical awareness. Perhaps the greatest precondition of reform in England, at least as it relates to making the Bible available to the masses, was William Tyndale (ca.1494–1536). His Bible had the advantage of his knowledge of the original languages and the good fortune of the popularity of the print medium.

The catalytic impetus toward religious reform came from an unwitting source, King Henry VIII, a devout Roman Catholic monarch (he wrote a criticism of Luther's views entitled "Assertion of the Seven Sacraments against Luther" and was declared "Defender of the Faith" in 1521 by the pope). Scholars have observed that the reformation in England had an unanticipated beginning as compared with the continental reformation. In the latter it became within the church and manifested political implications; in the former it began as a political issue and grew to serious religious ramifications.

King Henry's father, Henry VII, claimed the throne after his victory over Richard III in a conflict over succession, the **War of the Roses** in 1485, and established the Tudor dynasty. Henry groomed his son Arthur to succeed him and solidified his rule through a series of marriages of his children. Arthur was married to Catharine of Aragon, the daughter of King Ferdinand and Queen Isabella of Spain; Margaret to James IV, king of Scotland (largely to establish a political alliance). However, Arthur died before ascending the throne and his brother, Henry, who had been educated for service in the church, was catapulted to assume the highest office in the land and married his brother's widow, Catherine. When the marriage failed to issue a male heir, Henry, fearing the political chaos experienced by his father over succession rights, felt that God had not favored the marriage to his brother's widow and sent **Cardinal** Wolsey (also appointed Lord Chancellor of England) to France to enlist the king in pressuring the pope to secure an annulment. The endeavor failed and the marriage was subsequently annulled in the English courts.

Disappointment with papal reticence caused Henry and the church to come into conflict. In 1533 Henry secretly married Anne Boleyn, who had previously resisted his attempts to have her as a mistress. The separation of the English church from the papacy became a subsequent reality. Wolsey was dismissed (perhaps at the insistence of Anne Boleyn though he retained the archbishopric of York), and Anne's chaplain, Thomas Cranmer, was appointed Henry's new **archbishop** of Canterbury. Cranmer declared Henry's marriage void. Henry became the head of the Church of England, though he still considered himself a Roman Catholic. Thus, the monarch of England defined the church, a situation that caused English religious history to be turbulent in the sixteenth century.

The young man, Henry VIII, 1509. At the Denver Art Museum. Courtesy of Phaedriel.

> Desiring a male heir and unable to get one from his first wife, Henry broke from the Roman Catholic church which would not grant him a divorce. As Supreme Head of the Church of England, he dissolved the monasteries and took Catholic land for the crown, remaining Catholic in his theology, though excommunicated by the Pope. Ultimately married six times, each of his first three wives gave him an heir and later monarch to succeed him (Mary and Elizabeth), though it was the third, Jane Seymour who gave him a son, Edward VI.

Henry remained a Roman Catholic in faith, though he rejected the authority of Rome over the church in his realm. Protestantism emerged in the land, but Henry attempted to suppress it forcing many to flee their homes for the continent, becoming "Henrician exiles." Henry's aim was clearly to shift authority from the church, from pope to king, not the theological reform of the church.

Though Henry seemed initially open to Lutheran dialogue in the aftermath of the issuance of the Act of Supremacy (1534), perhaps through the influence of the new **archbishop**, his excommunication by the Church of Rome in 1538 seemed to push the monarch to express his conservative religious views. In 1539 the king sanctioned the "whip with the six strings" against the Protestants. The document made clear the king's religious sentiments by affirming such essential Roman doctrine as justification by faith and works, the sacrament of penance for absolution, corporeal presence in the Eucharist, purgatory, and prayers for the dead. In addition, it declared religious aberrancy a crime against the state. The *Six Articles* became the strict definition of the Church of England until Henry's death.

9.8. THE WIVES OF HENRY VIII

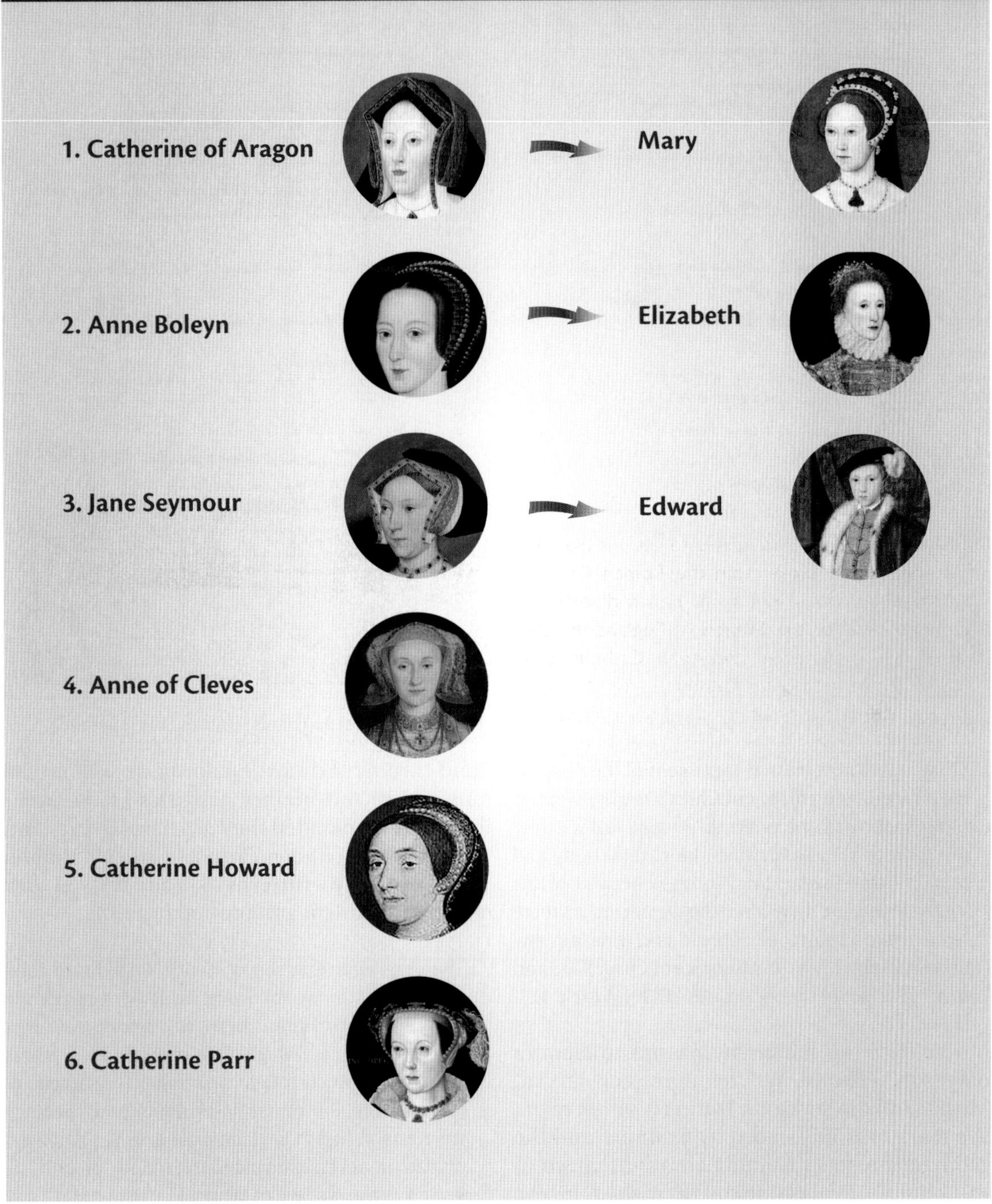

1. Catherine of Aragon → Mary

2. Anne Boleyn → Elizabeth

3. Jane Seymour → Edward

4. Anne of Cleves

5. Catherine Howard

6. Catherine Parr

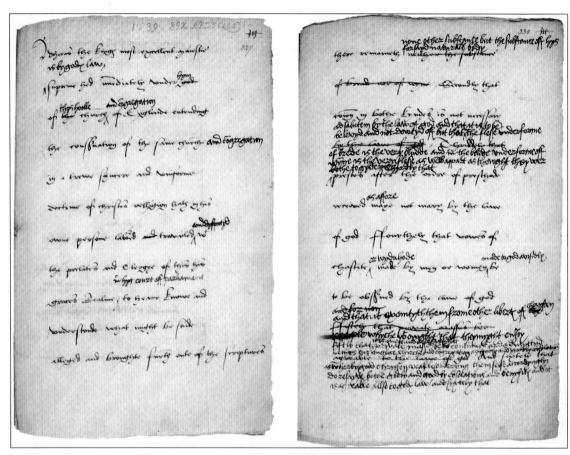

One of the final drafts of the Six articles (1539), amended in King Henry VIII's own hand. Courtesy of Feuerrabe.

"That in the most blessed Sacrament of the Altar, by the strength and efficacy of Christ's mighty word, it being spoken by the priest, is present really, under the form of bread and wine, the natural body and blood of Our Saviour Jesu Christ, conceived of the Virgin Mary, and that after the consecration there remaineth no substance of bread and wine, nor any other substance but the substance of Christ, God and man" (The Act of the Six Articles [1539], Article 1).

In 1547 the monarchy passed to Henry's only son, Edward VI, the nine-year-old lad birthed by Jane Seymour. During his brief reign, the realm was influenced by Cranmer and the monarch's regents to pursue a reformation in the church. Protestantism flourished in the

land through Edward's policies, as well as the organizing and literary activities of the archbishop that included the *Forty-Two Articles* and the *Book of Common Prayer* (a work detailing church **liturgy** written in 1549 and revised with a more Calvinistic orientation in 1552).

The only legitimate son of Henry VIII, Edward took the English throne following his father's death. He was tutored by Henry Bullinger, successor of Swiss Reformer Ulrich Zwingli. One of his chaplains was John Knox, Scottish Reformer and later student of John Calvin. Protestant institutions and theology were established in England during his reign in ways his father never anticipated. He ruled for only six years dying at the age of fifteen. His first cousin, Lady

9.9. RULERS OF ENGLAND

Henry VIII
(1509–1547)

Charles I
(1625–1649)

Edward VI
(1547–1553)

"Long Parliament"
(1640–1660)

Mary
(1553–1558)

Charles II
(1660–1685)

Elizabeth
(1558–1603)

James II
(1685–1688)

James I
(1603–1625)

"Glorious Revolution"
(1688–1689)

William (1689–1702)
and Mary (1689–1694)

9.10. NONCONFORMITY IN ENGLAND

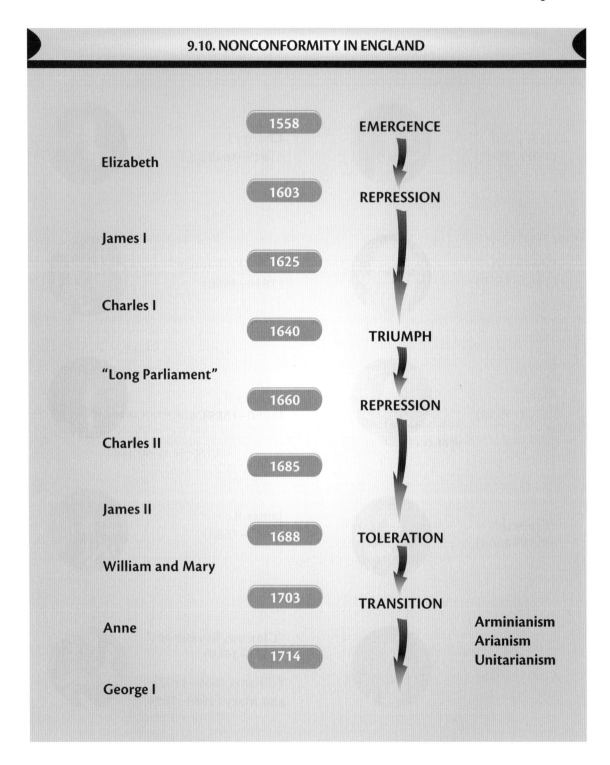

	1558	EMERGENCE
Elizabeth		
	1603	REPRESSION
James I		
	1625	
Charles I		
	1640	TRIUMPH
"Long Parliament"		
	1660	REPRESSION
Charles II		
	1685	
James II		
	1688	TOLERATION
William and Mary		
	1703	TRANSITION
Anne		Arminianism
	1714	Arianism
George I		Unitarianism

Jane Grey, to whom he gave his throne, ruled for nine days.

The swing toward Protestantism came to an abrupt reversal with the ascension of Mary Tudor, the daughter of the spurned Catharine of Aragon, who redefined the church and embraced Rome. Her marriage to Prince Philip of Spain (later Philip II) was not favored by the ma-jority of her subjects and later became the basis for the claim of Philip to the English throne under Elizabeth I, Mary's successor, as well as the Spanish Armada episode. Mary's repression garnered her the title of "Bloody Mary," though her father brought more to the stake than she. However, prominent bishops were killed in her reign, such as Nicholas Ridley, Hugh Latimer,

9.11. COMPARISON OF ANGLICANISM AND PURITANISM

	ANGLICANISM	PURITANISM
PREACHING AND RITUAL	Liturgy, ceremony, rituals, etc. directs minds to God	Proclamation of Word brings individuals to encounter Christ, strip away rituals
POLITY	Episcopacy, 1500 year-tradition	Episcopacy not biblical (Presbyterian, Congregational, and some Episcopal)
SCRIPTURE TRADITION AND REASON	Must use Bible, tradition, and reason because Scriptures are not explicit on church polity and practice	Cut away tradition—anything seeming Romish—Bible only
CONVERSION AND NURTURE	Communal understanding of religion, Christians seek nurture in church	Emphasis on personal struggle with sin and freedom of conscience in doing so. Conversion as direct from God with means.

and John Hooper, and even extended to her archbishop, Thomas Cranmer.

The only remaining child of Henry came to the throne in 1558, Elizabeth I, the daughter of Anne Boleyn. Her religious convictions were not clearly evident because a spirit of pragmatism seemed to govern her choices more than religious resolve. Elizabeth's embrace of Protestantism appears to have been rooted in the establishment of throne rights, having been declared illegitimate in the eyes of Rome, and the fear of a Roman Catholic crusade to challenge her right to govern England.

The church that emerged under Elizabeth was structured to placate her Protestant subjects, who had favor in the House of Commons, and her Roman Catholic subjects, who were powerful in the House of Lords. By the Act of Supremacy, Elizabeth was declared the Supreme Governor, not head, of the church. The church became known as the *via media*, the church of the middle way, because of the attempt to balance more than one vision of the church. For example, the new Book of Common Prayer, the liturgical ordering of the church, reverted back to a blend of the 1549 and 1552 books. The *Forty-Two Articles* were reduced to thirty nine, but remained Calvinistic. The formulators of the Anglican Church were Thomas Cranmer, who crafted the Prayer Books and the original Protestant creed, and Richard Hooker (1554–1600) who was the architect and defender of the Church of England in his *Of the Laws of Ecclesiastical Polity*.

> "Works done before the grace of Christ and the inspiration of His Spirit, are not pleasant to God, forasmuch as they spring not of faith in Jesus Christ, neither do they make men meet to receive grace, or (as the School authors say) deserve grace of congruity: yea, rather for that they are not done as God hath willed and commanded them to be done, we doubt not but they have the nature of sin" (The *Thirty-Nine Articles*, Article 13).

As one would surmise the presence of power factions within a church that was structured to be tolerant and inclusive caused dissension. The most strident of these parties were the Puritans, a group of influential preachers and prolific writers who believed that the **Elizabethan Settlement** (1559) was a move in the right direction, but it was incomplete. The liturgy of the church contained frightful remnants of popish religion, not the simplicity and purity of worship available on the continent. For the many in the movement who had fled England during the reign of Mary Tudor to the continent, the worship styles they experienced in Geneva, Zurich, Frankfurt, and Strasbourg seemed far more biblical than what they would encounter upon their return to their native soil.

The Puritan movement, as it emerged in Elizabethan England, was not entirely cohesive in its opposition to an Episcopalian structuring of the church. Some within the broad movement returned to accept the Elizabethan Settlement and took offices with some reluctance (these sometimes have been called Episcopalian Puritans). Some others found the church so objectionable that any parley with it was out of the question.

> William Perkins was considered one of the most prominent leaders of the Puritan movement during the reign of Elizabeth I. A fellow and rector in Cambridge, he was opposed to conformists in the Church of England and disagreed with the separatists. He was thus considered a "moderate Puritan," denouncing kneeling to take Communion while defending Presbyterian forms of church government. He is renowned for promoting Theodore Beza's views on "double predestination" in England.

These separatist Puritans settled in northern England in Scrooby and Gainsborough, but they later fled to Holland where some joined the Mennonites. Others returned to England to establish the first Baptist churches, and still others sojourned to the New World where they adopted congregational church government and are popularly known as the Pilgrims of Massachusetts. Yet another faction, and likely the largest, was willing to enter the church, but refused to practice what they felt were unbiblical forms of worship. Their strategy was at least twofold: first, to work for change in the church through proper political avenues and, second, to create alternatives to episcopacy, hoping that it would be adopted as the official definition of the church.

An example of the political activism of the Puritans was the vestments controversy (1563–1569). With roots in the refusal of John Hooper to wear vestments at his installation as bishop of Gloucester during the reign of Edward VI (he later rescinded on the issue), the vestments controversy can be capsulated in the Puritan petitions at the Convocation of English Clergy in 1563. The Puritan party petitioned for the elimination of saint's days, the wearing of priestly garments, kneeling at Eucharistic services, and of organs in the churches. Such remonstrations proved of no avail as Archbishop Matthew Parker refused to concede to Puritan demands. This was followed in the 1570s by the admonitions controversy that called for the replacement of episcopacy with a presbyterian form of government in the church, a view rebuffed by Archbishop John Whitgift (ca. 1530–1604). Whitgift responded to Thomas Cartwright's development of presbyterianism through a series of lectures on the book of Acts and by removing him from his teaching post at Cambridge. Cartwright (ca. 1535–1603) later fled to the continent.

Considered the father of English Presbyterianism, Thomas Cartwright was Puritan in his theology and worship, coming into disagreement first with Mary I, for which he was ejected from Cambridge, and later Elizabeth I, with whom he disagreed on church government. He favored elder rule rather than the crown-approved control by bishops. Though he pastored in Antwerp for a decade, his return to England resulted in his imprisonment. Nevertheless, five-hundred pastors embraced Cartwright's Presbyterian ideas by 1590.

Within the Puritan movement diversity emerged as to the way to reform the state church. As indicated above, Thomas Cartwright formulated a presbyterian structure of church governance that figured into the Admonitions Controversy. It appears that Henry Jacobs (1562–1624), a separatist, though he embraced the notion that the Church of England was the true church needing reform, developed a congregational form of governance that was embraced by the English Pilgrims that settled in North America in 1620. Jacobs established the first congregational or independent church in London in 1616.

THOS. CARTWRIGHT. B.D.

A painting of Thomas Cartwright by Gustavus Ellinthorpe (1821–1892). At Mansfield College, University of Oxford. Courtesy of Jfhutson.

A painting of James I of England attributed to both Jon de Critz the Elder and Paul van Someren. At Prado Museum in Madrid, Spain. Courtesy of Muriel Gottrop.

The passing of the Tudor dynasty in 1603 and the emergence of the Stuarts of Scotland brought a degree of optimism among the Puritans that the Church of England might shift away from episcopacy. James VI, the Scottish king, now James I of England, reigned over a land that was definitely Presbyterian in church order. When presented with the **Millenary Petition** upon his arrival at **Hampton Court**, a document signed by a thousand Puritans asking for church reform, it became apparent that his sympathies were to retain episcopacy in the English church.

James enforced his supremacy over the church demanding clerical conformity to the Thirty-Nine Articles and the Prayer Book liturgy. Of the positive effects of the conference from a Puritan perspective was the allowance by the king of a new translation of the Scriptures, the King James Bible (1611). Roman Catholics might have faired well under James, given the religious orientation of his parents, but the infamous Gunpowder Plot (1605), a plan orchestrated by Guy Fawkes to blowup parliament and kill the king in reprisal for his anti-Catholic measures proved detrimental for such hopes.

James seemed favorable to Calvinistic emphases in the church, though he advocated toleration and moderation generally. His ecumenical spirit caused him to seek ecclesiastical unity with religious factions on the continent, as well as with the Orthodox community. In this context, he embraced the calling of the **Synod of Dordt** (1618–1619), sending an official delegation. His moderate spirit did not sit well with the Puritan faction that strongly opposed concession with the Remonstrant or Arminian Party of Holland. Initially accepting the conclusions of the synod, James reversed his position prohibiting the public preaching of its findings.

The deeper issues appear to have been the political implications of the Calvinistic orientation as it related to the doctrine of predestination and Presbyterian ecclesiology. James concluded that Calvinism/Presbyterian governance was incompatible with the divine right theory of kingly rule, granted too much privilege to parliament, strengthened individualism, and was exclusive in the distribution of divine favors. At the same time, the strongly **sabbatarian** Puritans felt his scourge with the publication of the *Book of Sports* (1618), a work advocating lawful recreational activities on Sunday.

Puritan frustrations continued to mount with the succession to the throne of Charles I in 1625 because he linked divine right, royal supremacy, and Anglican governance of the church together. A portent of frustrations to follow was the king's 1625 marriage to Princess Henrietta Maria of France, a Roman Catholic. In 1628 the king appointed William Laud (1573–1645) the bishop of London and in 1633 archbishop of Canterbury, becoming in the process the king's chief ecclesiastical advisor. Laud was no friend of Calvinistic Puritans and struck a policy that was pro-Arminian and pro-Catholic. In the face of resistance to his policies that included decorating the churches and stone altars, Laud imprisoned opponents, exercised branding for the publication of errant ideas, and effectively stifled Puritan influence at Oxford University. Many Puritans in the 1630s found a refuge in migration to the New World, principally Massachusetts.

Religious reversals occurred simultaneously with political frustrations. In 1629 Charles dismissed parliament to rule the nation as an absolute monarch. Laudian influence and Charles's penchant for power had reached an apex only to plunge the king into a path that would lead to civil rebellion. Having no Parliament to supply the financial needs of the nation, he imposed a series of heavy taxes, principally what were called "ship taxes"— taxes for coastal defense in times of war—that made him increasingly disliked.

Stuart policies brought the nation to war with continental powers in the 1630s leading to defeat by Spain and France. Voices of protest emerged claiming that Parliament had not sanctioned the ship tax, nor a later tax to raise an army to suppress unrest in Scotland caused by the Laudian insistence in 1637 that the northern nation accept the *Prayer Book* in the churches. Charles's army was defeated by the Scots in northern England, the Scots occupying parts of the country and the king forced to pay a huge ransom to forestall further penetration. The rebellious mood spread to Ireland where staunchly Catholic elements protested the relinquishing of territories to Protestants by James I. Protestants thought that the Irish unrest was another ploy of the king to impose his pro-Catholic policies, as thousand of Protestants were rumored to have been killed. The king was forced to recall Parliament in 1640 to seek legitimate revenues to stifle the fires of rebellion that were flaming across his kingdoms.

The King and Parliament came into conflict, resulting in a precipitous descent into civil war. In 1641 Parliament presented the king with the Grand Remonstrance, a document that narrowly gained a majority vote calling for the reduction of the power of bishops. In January 1642 Charles stormed Parliament with an army demanding the arrest of leading parliamentarians, but they had fled. In the same month parliament reacted with the *Nineteen Articles* calling for a diminution of the king's authority. Parliament was split over the measure; royal and anti-royal factions within Parliament began to assemble armies for a showdown. War became the inevitable consequence.

Parliament effectively took control of the reins of government as the nation was plunged into a series of civil clashes that led to the defeat of the royalist factions and the rule of the nation by Parliament, the Long Parliament era, from 1640–1660. Parliament secured an agreement with the Scots, the Solemn League and Covenant (1643), for support in their cause against the royalists in return for the abolition of episcopacy. Parliament accused William Laud of treason and imprisoned him in the Tower of London. Following a trial in 1644, he was beheaded for crimes against the state.

In 1643 the Parliament called for an assembly of divines to advise them in the matter of the restructuring of the state church. The Westminster Assembly was composed of a minority of laymen and 121 clergymen from four religious viewpoints: an Episcopalian minority that included James Ussher (1581–1656), primate of Ireland, archbishop of Armagh, and biblical chronologist; a Presbyterian majority led by Samuel Rutherford (ca. 1600–1661), among others; a Congregationalist faction lead by Thomas Goodwin (1600–1680); and a few Erastians, politically loyal royalists. Amidst considerable discussion and conflict over opposing perspectives, the Presbyterian Puritans prevailed. In the ensuing years, the **Directory of Worship**, the **Westminster Confession of Faith**, and the longer and shorter catechisms were composed. With episcopacy formally abolished in 1645, it appeared that the documents of the Westminster divines would predominate, but the congregational or independent faction gained ascendancy in national affairs.

> Q. 1. "What is the chief end of man? A. Man's chief end is to glorify God, and to enjoy him forever."

> Q. 2. "What rule hath God given to direct us how we may glorify and enjoy him? A. The Word of God, which is contained in the Scriptures of the Old and New Testaments is the only rule to direct us how we may glorify and enjoy him" (*The Westminster Shorter Catechism*, Questions 1 and 2).

Independents, Puritans who advocated local church autonomy in the direction of its decision-making, were not comfortable with the bent of the Westminster Assembly and they had the advantage of the emergence of Oliver Cromwell (1599–1658) as the head of the **New Model Army**, or parliamentary forces as they were called. Matters seemed to reach a climax

Portrait of King Charles I in his robes of state by Anthony van Dyck (1599–1644). In the Royal Collection at Windsor Castle. Courtesy of Hohum.

A painting of Oliver Cromwell by Robert Walker (1599–1658). At the National Portrait Gallery in London. Courtesy of Dcoetzee.

when the parliament was too divided to reach a conclusion about the fate of the king. Some favored the continuation of the monarchy; others that he should be tried for treason. Resolution came in the parliamentary impasse when Colonel Thomas Pride of the New Model Army removed the non-Congregationalists from parliament, creating what has been called the Rump Parliament in 1648. With the roadblock cleared by "Pride's Purge," the way was open for the trial of the king and his subsequent beheading in 1649.

The nation was ruled by a Congregationalist controlled parliament that proved ineffective. In frustration over parliament's ineptitude, Oliver Cromwell purged it once more, creating the "Barebones Parliament" that empowered

A painting of Cromwell dissolving the Parliament by Andrew Carrick Gow (1848–1920). Courtesy of Adamsk.

him as the "Lord High Protector" of the nation; the Rump Parliament had chosen Cromwell as its supreme army commander in 1649. Under the leadership of Cromwell, the parliamentary army crushed a Scottish attempt to restore Charles in return for the reestablishment of Presbyterians in their land as well as the Irish, the latter a dark episode of cruelty on the part of Cromwell and the New Model Army.

> "I was by birth a gentleman, living neither in any considerable height, nor yet in obscurity. I have been called to several employments in the nation—to serve in parliaments—and (because I would not be over tedious) I did endeavour to discharge the duty of an honest man in those services, to God, and his people's interest, and of the commonwealth; having, when time was, a competent acceptation in the hearts of men, and some evidence thereof" (Oliver Cromwell, speech to the First Protectorate Parliament,1654).

With the death of Cromwell in 1658, his son, Richard, succeeded him. Because of his supposed Presbyterian leanings, the leaders in the army, as well as a division in Parliament, made it difficult to rule. Some favored the return of the monarchy while others desired an army-controlled protectorate. The power of the army crumbled and with it the hope of a protectorate; the monarchy was restored in 1660.

The return of the monarchy in Charles II, the son of Charles I, brought not only the restoration of episcopacy, but a repression of Puritanism. The passage of the Act of Uniformity in 1662 required conformity to the laws and liturgy of the Anglican Church. Puritans lost political influence and were labeled nonconformists. The Conventicle Act of 1664 prohibited nonconformists from holding religious services; the Five Mile Act (1665) barred dispossessed clergy from visiting their former parishes. In effect, the **"Great Persecution,"** as it was caused, marginalized the Puritan in England.

A painting of a Conventicle preacher before the justices by Robert Inerarity Herdman. At Royal Scottish Academy of Art & Architecture. Courtesy of Jfhutson.

"Wherefore, unto him we give our affections unto whom we give our all, ourselves and all we have; and to whom we give them not, whatever we give nothing at all" (John Owen, *Grace and Duty of Being Spiritually Minded*, 7:396).

Charles II was Roman Catholic in persuasion, but he did not allow that to be made known to his subjects who were overwhelmingly Protestant. His successor and brother, James II, was openly so. Roman Catholics occupied high offices in James's administration; he had a Jesuit priest as his private confessor; and he entertained a papal nuncio (the first monarch to do so since Mary Tudor). James's tolerant religious attitudes and his growing political power alarmed the Anglican clerics who were forced to concede to his measures as the Anglican grip on religious privilege was being dissolved. To complicate matters, James's wife, Mary, bore him a son in 1688 who was clearly heir apparent.

The threat of a Roman Catholic dynasty pushed the Anglicans to action. Influential Anglicans invited William of Orange (1650–1702) to bring an army to England and depose the king. When William III landed his large Dutch army, the English confessed loyalty to him. James fled, abdicating his rule, symbolized by casting the Great Seal of State into the Thames River. Consequently, the daughter of James, Mary, a mild Anglican, was declared queen by parliament, and she ruled the land with her husband William of Orange.

Called the **Glorious Revolution**, the ascension of William and Mary, James's son-in-law and sister, in 1688 brought a check to the absolutist monarchy of James II. The new king accepted a constitutional monarchy in which parliament ruled with the king through a cabinet. Additionally, the Declaration of Rights later called a Bill of Rights, guaranteed fundamental privileges to the English people (e.g., freedom of speech).

The ascension of William III and Mary II brought to an end the religious struggles within the nation. Episcopacy would define English church government, Protestant dissenters were granted toleration (effectively ending the era of Puritan backlash that came with the restoration of the monarchy), and Roman Catholics were excluded from religious and political privilege. In Scotland, Presbyterianism became the recognized religion of the state. In Ireland, William crushed Roman Catholic opposition at the Battle of Boyne in 1690, stripping them of the basic rights and privileges of others in the nation.

Other Protestant Reformations

Though it is common to focus upon the emergence of Protestantism and Roman Catholicism in the sixteenth century, speaking of them as encompassing Reformation history, this perspective is somewhat distorted. There was general agreement that the late medieval church was in need of reform, but there were more than one or two approaches to the problem. At least three significant alternative solutions are discernible as well: a political solution, a mystical path, and a rationalistic approach. What seems to be a common thread is that they find their roots in a partial acceptance of the Protestant Reformation, though they are generally conceived as aberrations.

A Political Approach to Reformation

An example of a militant, political approach to reform was Ulrich von Hutten (1488–1523). Though vaguely aligned with Luther in the spirit of reform, he did not seem to grasp the deeper insights of the man. He saw what he believed were the ravages of despotism and greed rampant in the churches. Von Hutten joined Franz von Sickingen (1481–1523) in what was dubbed the Knights' Revolt of 1522. Sickengen gathered a large army to attack Trier, seeking to diminish the power of the archbishop and elevate the power of the knights. The defeat of von Hutten and von Sickingen symbolized the collapse of the power of the feudal knight to shape reform.

The Peasants' War of 1524–1525 offers another example of an attempt to be relieved of social and political oppression through a military solution wrapped in religious rhetoric. It was, as Luther so greatly feared, a misapplication of his doctrines of religious freedom to lower nobles and peasants plunged into debt and poverty. Though Luther sympathized with many of the arguments of the peasants, he strenuously opposed their militaristic solution. While Luther was at the Wartburg Castle following the Diet of Worms, Andreas Carlstadt (1586–1541) brought the reform movement to the radical edge and was joined by Nicholas Storch (d. 1525), and other Zwickau Prophets, calling for even more radical measures.

> The man who awarded Martin Luther his doctorate at the University of Wittenberg, Andreas Carlstadt was an iconoclastic and occasionally radical German Reformer, bringing the first reformed service to Wittenberg while Luther was in hiding at Wartburg Castle following the Diet of Worms. During the mass he delivered it in German rather than Latin and allowed communicants to take both the bread and the cup. He presaged what would become some of the hallmarks of the later Swiss Reformation—lack of church music, marriage of priests, emphasis on the spiritual and not physical presence of Christ in the communion—and even some views of the Swiss Brethren, like rejection of infant baptism. He argued with and ultimately broke with Luther.

The peasantry in Saxony and Thuringia were excited to political revolt. In that context Thomas Münster (1488–1525) came to Wittenberg briefly combining an eschatological mysticism with aggressive militarism as a means to accomplish reform. The resultant Peasants' War led to a tragic decimation of the peasant class in Germany, over 100,000 were lost. The cause was lost and so was Luther's attachment to many who came to realize that they had misunderstood his intentions.

While the hope of social reform combined with political militancy can be seen in the Zwickau Prophets and the followers of Thomas Münster, reform took a radical eschatological bend in others, though religion found its way into the rhetoric of all these movements. It can be seen in the followers of John of Leiden (ca. 1509–1536), who claimed that he was the reincarnation of the biblical King David. In the sixteenth century with his followers he took over the city of Münster, Germany, claiming it to be the New Jerusalem and its leaders prophets.

A movement emerged in the turbulent period of the Long Parliament or Interregnum of seventeenth-century England called the Fifth Monarchy Men. Believing that the books of Revelation and Daniel predicted that, after four kingdoms emerged and declined, a fifth would come to end all kingdoms. It would be made up of religious Puritan dissidents who would create the final kingdom of God on the earth. With 1666 approaching, and the number 666 having eschatological value, monarchists believed that they would defeat the antichrist and inaugurate the kingdom. The movement dissolved in the restoration of the monarchy after 1660, many of its proponents having lost credibility following the death of Charles I in 1649. They opposed Cromwell's Protectorate and

A colored drawing of the burning of Little Jack (Jacklein) Rohrbach, a leader of the peasants during the war. Courtesy of Schmelzle. Artist unknown.

the disbanding of the Rump Parliament for the Barebones Parliament because it did not recognize the rule of King Jesus. This brought them into disfavor in the 1650s after assassination plots were discovered.

A Mystical or Spiritualist Approach to Reformation

Though not uniform in expression, mystical spirituality in the reformation era, whether Roman Catholic or Protestant, envisioned a relationship with God that was direct, personal, and intimate. Expressed in negative terms, mystics viewed the forms and structures of established religious authority as prohibitive of religious maturity. Sometimes this approach denigrated the role of the sacraments as well as the authority of Scripture, but certainly always prominent was the role of the human mediator in genuine religious experience.

An example of this general approach was Caspar Schwenkfeld (1490–1561), who early embraced Luther's cause, but later had a falling out with him over the meaning of the Eucharist and the two natures in the one Christ. He rejected both the sacramentalism of the Roman community and what he felt was an inordinate attachment to the letter of the Scriptures among Protestants, believing that God communicates authoritatively beyond the Bible to his collective people by means of the Spirit. Among his teachings were a mystical presence of the Lord in the Eucharist, a rejection of infant baptism, opposition to war, and government intervention over one's conscience. The followers of Schwenckfeld, who refused to be designated as a church were in the middle of the religious spectrum between the magisterial reformers and the continental Anabaptists.

Influenced by Martin Luther, Andreas Carlstadt and Thomas Müntzer, Caspar Schwenckfeld was a leader of the Reformation in Silesia. In turn he influenced Swiss Anabaptism, Continental Pietism and English Puritanism. He disagreed with Luther on the communion and taught against war, oaths, and infant baptism. His followers, Schwenkfelders, formed a community on the property of Count Zinzendorf in Herrnhut, Germany, some later migrating to Philadelphia, Pennsylvania.

Sebastian Franck (1499–1543), a former priest and later an advocate of Luther's reform, came to reject the mainstream of Protestant beliefs for a mystical Protestant faith. He believed that out of the Protestant traditions, which he denounced as delusory and anti-Christ, would emerge an invisible spiritual church that would be governed by neither liturgical ritual, sacramental forms, or sermons. In essence, he denounced ecclesiastical establishmentarianism of any sort for a individualized spiritual mysticism, the inner illumination of the Spirit being the believer's only guide. Unlike Schwenckfeld, who seems to have been a considerable influence on his mature thought, he left behind no movement, suggesting the consequences of his non-theological, ecumenical, and non-institutional idealization of religion.

The most celebrated example of Protestant mysticism were the Quakers. **Quakerism** emerged from within the Puritan movement during the Interregnum or Puritan Common-

Caspar Schwenckfeld (1489–1561) by Theodorus de Bry (1528 –1598). Courtesy of Torsten.

wealth era between 1652–1656. In essence, the movement's founder, George Fox (1624–1691), viewed the Puritans as spiritually stagnate and so envisioned a restoration of first-century primitivism and piety, viewing themselves as the "people of God," "children of the Light," and the "Society of Friends." The term *Quaker* came from an English judge who Fox exhorted to tremble before them and the judge replied by using this epithet in 1650. After concluding that the organized church was hopelessly absorbed in trivialities, Fox gathered followers in 1652 and began the movement.

Among several distinguishing features of this Protestant sect was an emphasis upon inner light or the direct leading of God in a person's life that rendered the Bible as an indirect, secondary guide (Robert Barclay [1648–1690], the Quaker apologist, spoke of the Scriptures as a "secondary rule, subordinate to the Spirit," the Spirit and the Word of God being separated). Quaker services or "tarrying meetings" were egalitarian in that people gathered to wait upon the Spirit or for another member of the gathering to bring a message from God. Historically, Quakers rejected the notion of an ordained ministry, as well as the sacraments. At least in Barclay, the earliest Quakers taught a divine, universal presence of God in all humankind sufficient to redeem if acknowledged, though the same person could remain ignorant of the sacrifice of Christ.

A Rationalistic Approach to Reformation
Another significant approach to reform in the sixteenth century, one rooted in neither outward medieval sources of authority or the inward illumination of the human spirit, was one that placed authority for religious belief in the rational faculties. In essence, the faculty of reason was judged to be the divine guide in religious belief. Inherent in this approach is the assumption, contrary to traditional Protestant conceptions, that the mind alone is an objective arbiter of truth. The rational spirit came to religion to judge its assertions on the anvil of reasonability, a theory of truth that suggested that the natural standards of reasonability were the exclusive criteria to determine what is true. What is true is what is repeatable and subject to verifiability exclusively. Consequently, the rational approach to truth was to be cautious about statements that defied the laws of logic as we know them commonly.

The teaching of Michael Servetus (ca. 1511–1553), a Spanish physician/scholar, is embryonic of this tendency toward reform. Servetus approached religion with the assumption that its present form had been corrupted over the centuries and the way of true reform was to

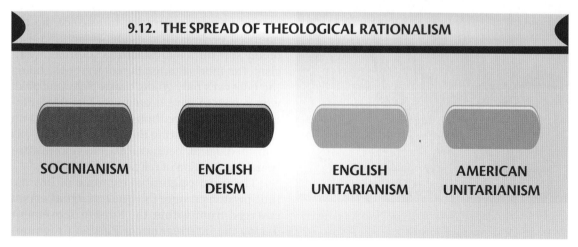

9.12. THE SPREAD OF THEOLOGICAL RATIONALISM

SOCINIANISM   ENGLISH DEISM   ENGLISH UNITARIANISM   AMERICAN UNITARIANISM return to the original doctrines of the Christian faith. He believed that the doctrine of the Trinity was a corrupt intrusion imported from Greek philosophy. The method that Servetus employed has had an enduring legacy through the centuries much to the detriment of the Christian faith.

"But as in our day have arisen certain frantic men, such as Servetus and others, who, by new devices, have thrown everything into confusion, it may be worthwhile briefly to discuss their fallacies. The name of Trinity was so much disliked, nay, detested, by Servetus, that he charged all whom he called Trinitarians with being Atheists. I say nothing of the insulting terms in which he thought proper to make his charges. The sum of his speculations was, that a threefold Deity is introduced wherever three Persons are said to exist in his essence, and that this Triad was imaginary. . . ." (Calvin, *Institutes*, 1.13.22).

Servetus's life ended at the stake in Calvin's Geneva, evidencing the fact that his views were judged destructive of the faith. However, he reflected the rationalistic spirit of men like Bernadino Ochino (1487–1564), a convert to Protestantism, but one who came to anti-Trinitarian views after pastorates in England and on the continent. Because of his views, he fled Zurich, where he had pastored an Italian refugee church, to Poland. The influence of Ochino and Servetus on Lelio Socinus (1525–1562) and his nephew, Faustus Socinus (1539–1604), made them significant in

9.13. THREE PERSPECTIVES OF THE PROTESTANT REFORMATION

POLITICAL	MYSTICAL	RATIONALISTIC
Munsterites	Sebastian Franck	Socinians
German Peasant Revolt	Caspar Schwenckfeld	Unitarians
Fifth Monarchy Men	Quakers	Deists
Muggletonians	Shakers	

the rise of **Socinianism**, later known as **Unitarianism**. The actual movement coalesced in Racow, Poland, from advocates who fled there in the 1570s and became somewhat popular among the upper classes. The first significant development of the emergent movement was the protest of Peter Gonesius, a Polish student at a gathering of the Reformed Churches in 1556 at Secemin, who spoke against the doctrine of Holy Trinity. Gonesius became a leader among the Polish Brethren. A schism from the Calvinist church happened formally in 1565 and became known as the Minor Reformed Church of Poland. By 1579, the year Faustus Socinus arrived in the country, there were about a hundred congregations. Suppressed in Poland, Socinians found refuge and influence in Prussia, Holland, and England.

The theological platform of the movement, attributed to the influence of Socinus, is the **Racovian Catechism**, published in the city of Racow, the center of Polish Socinian influence in the seventeenth century. In answering a question about the integrity of a denial of Trinitarian orthodoxy, the catechism argued from a rationalist point of view. A person is a single unity of characteristics; if God is a person, he must be a single unity of characteristics. Such a belief about God has no parallels in rational thought and is, therefore, nonsensical.

"Prove to me that in the one essence of God, there is but one Person?

"This indeed may be seen from hence, that the essence of God is one, not in kind but in number. Wherefore it cannot, in any way, contain a plurality of persons, since a person is nothing else than an individual intelligent essence. Wherever, then, there exist three numerical persons, there must necessarily, in like manner, be reckoned three individual essences; for in the same sense in which it is affirmed that there is one numerical essence, it must be held that there is also one numerical person" (*The Racovian Catechism* [1574], 33–34).

More important than the movement in itself is that Socinianism reflects roots in the **Renaissance** distinctively adverse to the Renaissance heritage of the magisterial reformers. It is a movement not so much rooted in an earlier Christian tradition, but in a Greco-Roman tradition that predates the Christian era and became dominant after the seventeenth through the twentieth centuries in the West. It is part of a greater movement that valued the freedom of inquiry as opposed to imposed authority. It witnessed the decline of the hegemony of external authority sources (the church, tradition, Scripture) and the rise of the importance of the rational faculties as arbiter of truth. It is the pathway to the "Age of Reason," later denominated as the **Enlightenment**, that has brought significant advances in learning and science, but also an emptying of the soul, a denial of the possibility of the supernatural as a reality.

GLOSSARY OF TERMS

Anabaptist Movement: a tradition within Protestantism that emphasized believer's baptism, congregational authority, and the separation of church and state. Though a general term for a variety of anti-magisterial groups, a conservative element emerged among them in Zurich that is the origin of Baptists.

Archbishop: an ecclesiastical term indicating an administrator who is in charge of a diocese over several bishops, as well as religious orders within their jurisdiction.

Cardinal: a high ecclesiastical office in the Roman Catholic community. Among one's duties as a member of the Sacred College of Cardinals is the election of the next successor to Saint Peter should the pontificate be unoccupied, acting as the pope's official counselors, and dealing with matters of church governance. Cardinals were often advisors to monarchs.

Directory of Worship: a manual or pastoral handbook, written by the Assembly of Divines at Westminster (1645), as the replacement of the Book of Common Prayer in the Anglican service. It defined the nature and course of ministerial functions including preaching restricting its sources to scriptural warrant, eliminated much traditional church liturgy

Elizabethan Settlement (Elizabethian Church): a set of parliamentary decisions concerning the structure of the English state-church in 1558/9 following the Roman Catholic direction imposed by Elizabeth's predecessor, Mary Tudor. The Act of Supremacy separated the church from papal rule and made the monarch the head of the English Church; the Act of Conformity established the ecclesiastical

structure of the church along the lines of the Book of Common Prayer and the doctrinal confession of the church in the Thirty-Nine Articles.

Enlightenment (Age of Reason): a movement begun in eighteenth-century Europe that emphasized the inner capacities of man (rational reflection, intuition) as opposed to external authority sources such as the church or the Bible to improve social and society performance. Strenuously opposed by the religious community as well as secular materialists, the Enlightenment spawned the modern era, a three-century experiment in the redemptive values of science and technology. Though highly successful in the technical realms, the venture collapsed under the weight of holocausts and wars suggesting that the blight of human discord could not be remedied by social advances alone. It filled life with opportunities but emptied it of meaning, creating postmodernism.

Free Church Tradition: a general designation for those churches that reject any role of the state in the affairs of the church. Accompanying the rejection of the state is the rejection of infant baptism, a nonliturgical approach to worship, a memorialist view of the Eucharist, and the embrace of believer's baptism.

Glorious Revolution: a change of dynasty in England in 1688 from the Stuart monarchs to the House of Orange, William and Mary, monarchs from Holland. It has been so called because the change of authority was without a violent revolution to install it. The English parliament invited the daughter of James II and her husband (William III) to ascend to the throne after her father's abdication.

Great Persecution: a term used for the period after the restoration of the English monarchy after the Long Parliament era. It was a time, the 1660s and 1670s, when the Anglican establishment and the king imposed restrictive laws and imprisonments repressing the Puritan movement once in transcendence.

Hampton Court (Hampton Court Conference): the residence of the English monarchs beginning with Henry VIII, who departed from the traditional residence of monarchs in the Tower of London. It was there that the Puritans petitioned James I that he allow the same ecclesiastical structure in England as under the Scots (the Millenary Petition). James refused the request, promoting the continuation of the Anglican form of government, but did grant authority to publish a new English Bible, the King James Bible (1611).

Hoffmanites (Melchior Hoffman): followers of the Dutch Anabaptist Melchior Hoffman (ca. 1495–1543). Hoffman advocated the soon return of Christ and with it a destruction of the ungodly, but his prophetic prediction proved false. His eschatological/political radicalism contributed to the Münster Episode of millennialist frenzy and a questionable origin of Baptists. Hoffman influenced Menno Simons in his denial of the full humanity of Jesus Christ, saying that in the incarnation Jesus possessed only "heavenly flesh."

Liturgy (Liturgical Practices): a form of religious worship prescribed by structure, authored forms including written prayers, sacramental wordings, and homilies or sermons. Litugurical worship is found in the Orthodox, Protestant, and Roman Catholics communities though generally shunned in the Free Church tradition.

Lollards: followers of the teaching of John Wycliffe of fourteenth-century England, a professor at Balliol College and critic of the church. The Lollards were absorbed into the Protestant English Reformation of the sixteenth century.

Magisterial Reformation: a general division within the sixteenth-century Protestant movement over the issue of the relationship or inter-relationship of the state and the church. Magisterial reformers viewed that state and church were integrally connected, each fulfilling necessary functions in the maintenance of societal cohesiveness, though differences can be observed. Luther saw the state as evil but necessary, Calvin the state as godly and the union of church and state a religious commonwealth.

Melchiorites: see *Hoffmannites*

Millenary Petition: a document of signatures by one thousand English Puritans requesting that their new monarch, James I (James VI of Scotland) abolish the episcopal governance of the Church of England and replace it with the presbyterial form of authority practiced in his native Scotland (1603). The king rejected the proposal saying, "No bishop, no king."

Münsterites (Münster Episode): a politically and religiously radical sect of Anabaptists in the sixteenth century aligned with the Zwickau Prophets in demeanor. Led by Jan Matthijs and John of Leiden, the group attempted to establish a sectarian, communal government in the city of Münster, Germany, 1534–1535, claiming it to be the "New Jerusalem." Leiden, who claimed to be the successor of the biblical David, assumed dictatorial prerogatives in the short-lived experiment. The political radicalism of the Münsterites was a turning point in Anabaptist history in that it thereafter sought to avoid political extremism.

New Model Army: a term given to the military

established by the English Parliament in 1645 that lasted through the Commonwealth period. The organization of the army was "new" in that it was mobile, not being restricted to one geographical region, and its soldiery was composed of full-time professionals, not local militia. Led by Oliver Cromwell, the army was composed of Puritan sympathizers and various religious sectaries.

Peasants' War (Peasants' Revolt): an uprising of the economically strapped lower class in Germany, mostly in the southern and central regions, between 1524–25. Applying the religious upheaval of the day against authority structures the peasants envisioned a form of proto-liberationism. While Luther recognized the social inequities of the day and the plight of the poor, he greatly feared the consequences of anarchy and stridently opposed it. It ended in a disaster with thousands of peasants killed; it was the largest popular uprising in Europe prior to the French Revolution.

Pragmatism: a theory for the establishment of human virtue and moral decision-making arguing that functional utility or favorable outcomes are the ground of choice making. It asks the question, "Will it produce a good or favorable outcome is a particular action is pursued?"

Quakerism (Friends): a Protestant religious group that arose in England in the 1650s, the Long Parliament era, founded by George Fox, that in contrast to the Puritan tradition advocated "inner light," that God often spoke to his people directly, not through the Holy Scriptures exclusively, in the context of "tarrying meetings" when the congregation sat in silence, the sexes segregated, awaiting a divine word to someone who then would relay it. Quakers rejected the professional minster, advocating lay ministry; called their places of worship "meeting houses," not churches; stressed equality of gender in ministry; embraced

pacifism; and were aggressive in the dissemination of their religious ideals.

Racovian Catechism: a statement of the theological convictions of the emergent Socinian movement in Poland in 1605. The movement derives its name from its most prominent early advocates Lelio and Faustus Socinus who stepped aside from Christian orthodoxy to embrace an Arian conception of Christ and thus deny the Trinity of God. In retrospect, the Socinian Movement was a harbinger of the Enlightenment with its subjection of religious faith to reasonability and verifiability.

Radical Reformation: it is a general practice among scholars of the Protestant reforming movements of the sixteenth century to see two broad categories: what has been designated as the Magisterial Reformation and the Radical Reformation. The latter, quite variegated in goals and theology, rejected the concept of a state-church harmony and interconnectedness and was sometime called "free church movements." Those called the Anabaptists in the movement rejected the notion of a folk church entered through infant baptism and practiced the gathered church concept expressed by believer's baptism. The implication of such a theory was a denial of the role of the state and thus came the charge of treason that was declared at the Diet of Speyer in 1529.

Remonstrant Party (Arminian Party): a group of religious scholars in Calvinist Holland in the early seventeenth century, following the lead of Jacob Arminius, that believed the better defense of Calvinist faith against the invasive religious Enlightenment was in a revision of the Belgic Confession of Faith, the creedal standard of the churches. Struggling with the age-old dilemma of explaining the relationship between inability, responsibility, and culpability, the group prepared the "Five Remonstrances" in 1610 and appealed to the state to revise its confession. An assembly of divines from across Europe convened at the Synod of Dordt in 1618 and rejected all five revisions and issued a four-point statement in reply. Out of the rejection came a third tradition of Protestant interpretation, the Arminian one.

(The) Renaissance: a cultural and intellectual movement that emerged in the fourteenth century in Italy and spread throughout seventeenth-century Europe, it celebrated a resurgence of classical learning. It proved to be a strong intellectual impetus for the sixteenth-century reformations in that its focus on the humanities carried an emphasis on self-understanding, that while it did not question Medieval authority structures, it did question how they were embraced. Further, it was an impetus for the later Enlightenment period that stressed the importance of individual belief, the search to find it, and the rejection of medieval assumptions of authority. Thus scholar think of the modern period as having two parts: early modern and late modern—eras that shared the same approach to the humanities but embraced diverse theories of authority.

Renaissance Humanism: a cultural and educational reform emphasis that emerged in the fourteenth and fifteenth centuries in reaction to medieval scholasticism, emphasizing personal affirmation of truth through a study of the sources of belief-structures, as well as the engagement in civic life through speaking and writing with eloquence and clarity. Its focus was on the study of the humanities with a new curriculum for university education, a shift from the scholastic preoccupation with rational explanation of the medieval faith to the readoption and prominence of the Aristotelian method.

Sabbatarianism (Sabbatarian): a view developed among sixteenth-century Calvinist Protestants beginning with Henry Bullinger of Zurich and becoming a common emphasis within the Puritan tradition in England and North America. It is the perception and practice that Sunday is the new Sabbath-rest, a shadow fulfilled of the seventh-day rest from God's creative activities in Gen. 2:1–4. While the day was not to be spent passively, being a day for worship, catechism in the family, and the doing of deeds of love and mercy, it was a day set aside in trust of God's provision by refraining from wage earning.

Socinianism (see also the Racovian Catechism): a teaching concerning the Trinity of God and the person of Christ that emerged in the sixteenth century and was encapsulated in the Racovian Catechism of 1605. Socinians denied the divine Trinity asserting that Jesus was less than God; it reflected a revival of Arianism and was the harbinger of the religious Enlightenment. This teaching brought fruit in the rise of both Unitarianism and Deism in England and in North America.

Synod of Dordt: a gathering of church scholars in 1618 from across Europe under the authority of the Dutch government to reevaluate the Belgic Confession of Faith, the creedal statement of the state-church, in light of the "Five Remonstrances" proposed by the Arminian Party. The synod rejected each of the proposed amendments and issued a four-point reply in affirmation of its Calvinist approach and interpretation of theology.

Unitarianism: a religious movement that appeared near the end of the eighteenth century in the United States, though a century earlier in England. Influenced by the Enlightenment assumption of the nature of truth and knowability, it rejected the orthodox doctrine of the Trinity, viewed Christ as an example of humanity at its best, and explained salvation was the fruit of moral rectitude achievable through watchful care and the pursuit of passionate duty. In 1819 William Ellery Channing, pastor of

Federal Street, Boston, delivered an address at the ordination of Jared Spark, then a Baltimore pastor and later president of Harvard College entitled "Unitarian Christianity," defining the movement with clarity and precision.

War of the Roses: a conflagration over dynastic succession to the throne of England between two rival branches of the Plantagenets, the House of Lancaster and the House of York, between 1455 and 1485. Henry Tudor (Henry VII) defeated Richard III of the House of York, married into the Yorks, and united the two houses. The Tudor dynasty of monarchs ruled England from 1485–1603, during the early Reformation of the church through the reign of Queen Elizabeth I. The War of the Roses derived its name from the flowers that adorned the rival houses: the York white rose and the Lancaster red rose.

Westminster Assembly (Westminster Assembly of Divines): a gathering of divines from across Europe tasked with the restructuring of the Church of England after the collapse of the monarchy under Charles I in the Puritan Commonwealth era. Called by the Long Parliament from 1643–1649, and directed by William Twisse, the assembly produced a presbyterial church governance through the composition of the Westminster Confession of Faith, the Longer and Shorter Catechisms, a revision of the Thirty-Nine Articles, and the Directory of Worship. However, differences within the Puritan majority (variance of ecclesiastical understanding) and the presence of a strong Congregationalist Puritan faction in the military prevented the installation of the Presbyterian ecclesiology as the state religion. Nevertheless, the work of the assembly of divines has been deeply influential in the Calvinist communities worldwide.

Westminster Confession of Faith: a statement of the religious convictions held by the Reformed Tradition of the Protestant movement, as well as the high watermark in reformed confessionalism. Completed by the Westminster Assembly of Divines in 1646, the document was not accepted in England due to Congregational Puritan pressure, but it replaced the Scottish Confession of Faith written in the previous century by John Knox and remains the standard of Orthodoxy in most conservative reformed communities in the United States, even worldwide.

Chapter 10 Outline

Chapter 10 Objectives

- That the reader will distinguish between the Protestant Reformations and the Roman Catholic Reformation

- That the reader will identify the major decisions of the Council of Trent

- That the reader will describe the causes of the Thirty Years' War

- That the reader will describe the effects of the Thirty Years' War

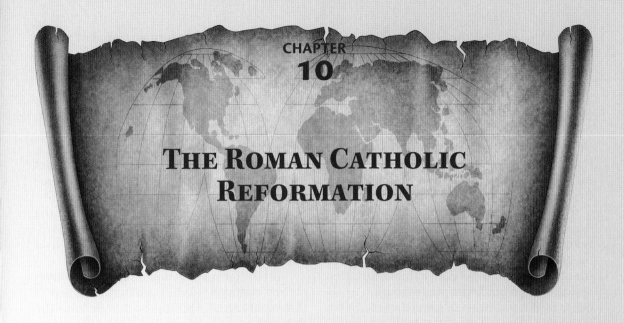

THE ROMAN CATHOLIC REFORMATION

T HE ARGUMENT ADVANCED IN the discussion of the Protestant and Roman Catholic churches is that they distinctly emerged in the sixteenth century in the context of perceived weaknesses in the late medieval church needing reform and correction. Churchmen and laity alike saw the need to correct the church, but they did not agree on the nature of the needed reform. Roman Catholics, perhaps represented by Disiderius Erasmus, viewed the church in need of the educational and moral reform of its spiritual life and clergy. Others, such as Luther, applauded the emphasis on a renewal of piety rooted in the Scriptures, the importance of the reestablishment of biblical studies that took the sacred text with a greater degree of literalism, and the grounding of the teachings of the church in the Bible. However, in their judgment the much-needed reforms proposed by an Erasmus simply did not reach to the heart of the matter. To them, the reforms proposed by the Roman Church were important, though ancillary, and did not address the deepest issues. These differences in the perception of the problem and the corrective for it brought about two distinct traditions within the professing Christian church.

Another assumption in the study of both Romanism and Protestantism is that neither are the distinct and sole claimants to the centuries of teaching that preceded them. Both traditions selectively borrowed from the witness of the past, neither faithfully imbibing the teachings of all her teachers (a given since there is a lack of unanimity in the witness of the past). If either or both would claim a historical advantage, it would be precarious. Roman Catholic scholars argued that its teachings coincided with what the church "has everywhere and always taught," but this was a difficult argument to sustain. When Charles V asked Luther how he could be so arrogant as to go against fifteen hundred years of the teaching of the church, Luther denied the possibility of the assumption. Both traditions selectively used the past to argue their claims; however, there were significant differences. Roman Catholics assumed a continuity, making tradition and the Holy Scriptures equal in authority; Protestants saw the problem with history and made the historical witness secondary to the divine. Each shared the same centuries of the past, but each found support for their opinions selectively.

A significant example of this is their use of Augustine of Hippo, the great fifth-century scholar, in their truth claims. Protestants found his emphasis on the absolute necessity of grace, the absolute inability of man to merit salvation, and the stress on divine predestination as the cause of grace (as least in some Protestant traditions) as supportive of the biblical witness. However, this same exalted bishop taught that baptism removed the stain of original sin; sin was the absence of good, not guilt; and that justification was a process of progressive righteousness.

In the context of a church disturbed by moral, ecclesiastical, and spiritual decadence in the late medieval period, both Roman Catholics and Protestants addressed the chaos in church, state, and the human soul. Both claimed to be the historical original in a new context, asserted the other harmful, and expressed their views in formal, complete creeds in the sixteenth century.

The Beginnings of the Roman Catholic Reformation

It is important to understand that Roman Catholicism is more than a reaction to the emergence of Protestantism; it is a movement that, like Protestantism, sought to remedy the ills of the late medieval church. That the church was in need of restoration was questioned by few at the end of the fifteenth century. In fact the origins of the Roman Catholic reformist movement predates the Protestant movement by a half century.

The reform movement in the Roman church commenced in Spain in the context of the expulsion of Muslims and Jews from the Iberian Peninsula, the unification of the nation under Ferdinand and Isabella, and the labors of Francisco Ximenes de Cisneros (1436–1517), a Franciscan. In 1469 the kingdoms of Castile and Aragon centralized royal power at the same time that Muslims fractured into competing factions, leading the way for the final reclaiming of the peninsula in 1492, which ended nearly eight centuries of Moorish influence.

In the nationalistic zeal that would lift Spain to world dominance in the sixteenth century, religious fervency gripped the land

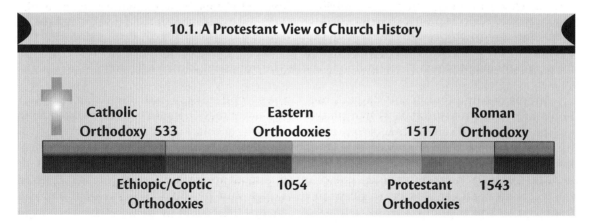

10.1. A Protestant View of Church History

| Catholic Orthodoxy 533 | Eastern Orthodoxies | 1517 | Roman Orthodoxy |

| Ethiopic/Coptic Orthodoxies | 1054 | Protestant Orthodoxies | 1543 |

and the Inquisition ensued, resulting in the forcible expulsion of both Muslims and Jews. In this context, a priest, who would later become the archbishop of Toledo (a 1495 appointment secured by Isabella) and cardinal (1507) in the church, Francisco Ximines, the private confessor of Isabella and advisor on state affairs, rose to dominance seeking the improvement of the church.

> Francisco Ximenes de Cisneros was a Franciscan confessor of Queen Isabella of Spain and became Archbishop of Toledo and later cardinal. Though the Inquisition was initiated ten years before he took the role, he became Grand Inquisitor of Castile and Lyon. He vehemently opposed the Moors, turning their captured mosques into Christian churches. He reformed the Franciscan order, eliminating concubinage and obligating friars to confession and preaching. Upon the death of Ferdinand and Isabella, he was appointed regent of Spain until the arrival in Spain of Charles V from Flanders, who would become the Holy Roman Emperor.

A man of strict discipline and ascetic piety, he devoted himself to the interests of the state and church. Monasteries under his domain were reformed with the instigation of strict discipline. He forbade clerics of his order to possess property, causing many to leave Spain. In addition, he spared no effort in the relief of the poor. One of his most remarkable contributions to the life of the church was in the realm of the education of priests. In 1499 he founded the University of Complutense at Alcala, a center of the Spanish Renaissance, that would have at its height some 7,000 students.

His interest in theological studies led to various treatises and concern for biblical knowledge, as in his sponsorship of the Complutensian Polyglot, six different versions of the Bible in parallel columns (including the Hebrew, Greek, Aramaic, and Latin). The New Testament was completed in 1514 and the Old Testament in 1517. It was the first printed poly-

Francisco Jiménez de Cisneros by Matias Moreno (1840–1906) at Prado National Museum. Courtesy of Lancastermerrin88.

glot of the Scriptures. Consistent with his ecclesiastical convictions, he embraced traditional Roman Catholic theology and was responsible for a great deal of moral and intellectual progress in the church.

In addition to de Cisneros of Spain, and the humanist scholar Erasmus, many others saw the need for reform from within the Roman Catholic perspective. Among these was Gasparo Contarini (1483–1542) of Venice who as ambassador of his republic and member of its senate represented his nation at the Diet of Worms in 1521, though he did not meet Luther there. In 1535 this diplomat-statesman accepted the cardinal's hat and served in Rome where he labored to correct abuses in the government of the church. He was also instrumental in the papal sanction of the Jesuits in 1540 founded by Ignatius, a reforming order in the church.

Contarini took part in the conciliatory conference called by Emperor Charles V at Ratisbon (now Regensburg, Germany) in 1541, a colloquy established in the hope of reconciling Lutheran and Roman Catholic differences. At Ratisbon, he drafted the Roman Catholic statement on the crucial doctrine of justification that some felt conceded too much to Protestants (overstating the role of faith), but he remained unwavering in his commitment to Roman orthodoxy.

An Italian diplomat, ambassador and cardinal, Gasparo Contarini after studying at the University of Padua served as Venetian ambassador to the court of Charles V at the same time Venice was in alliance with Charles's enemy Francis I of France. He served as Pope Paul III's papal legate to the Conference of Regensburg, opening a dialog between the Roman church and Protestants in Germany. Ignatius Loyola attributed the papal acceptance of the Jesuits to the work of Contarini.

The most significant apologist of the Roman Catholic position in the sixteenth century was Robert Bellarmine (1542–1621), who was beatified, gaining the status of sainthood

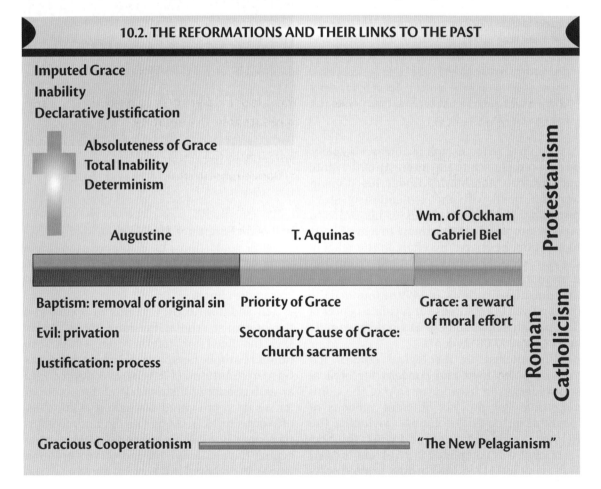

10.2. THE REFORMATIONS AND THEIR LINKS TO THE PAST

Imputed Grace
Inability
Declarative Justification

Absoluteness of Grace
Total Inability
Determinism

Augustine   T. Aquinas   Wm. of Ockham
                                                            Gabriel Biel

Baptism: removal of original sin   Priority of Grace   Grace: a reward of moral effort

Evil: privation   Secondary Cause of Grace:
                             church sacraments

Justification: process

Gracious Cooperationism   "The New Pelagianism"

Protestanism

Roman Catholicism

in 1930. While Cardinal Bellarmine, a Jesuit scholar and papal advisor, did not believe that the papacy possessed the key of temporal power, he was nonetheless the most eloquent and prolific defender of the church against the reformers. He participated in the trial of Galileo in 1616 for his support of the Copernican theory of the universe as opposed to the Ptolemaic theory embraced by the church and Luther. Bellarmine's most significant work in Roman Catholic polemics was *Disputation on the Controversies of the Christian Faith on the Heresies of this Time* (3 vols, 1586–1593). Unlike

many cardinals of the day who lived their lives in splendor, Bellarmine conducted his life with ascetic simplicity and devotion to his church and his people.

Italian Jesuit and Cardinal, Robert Bellarmine held an important role in the Counter-reformation—arguing against the Protestant King James I of England—and effected the reforms of the Council of Trent. Known for his preaching and polemical teaching, he was ordered by Pope V to notify Galileo Galilei of the Congregation of the Index condemning Copernican teachings on a stationary sun and orbiting earth.

10.3. THE EMERGENCE OF THE ROMAN CATHOLIC CHURCH

Latin used in prayer and worship, imposed by Pope Gregory I	600	Rosary, repetitious praying with beads, invented by Peter the Hermit	1090
Prayers directed to Mary, dead saints, and angels	600	The sale of indulgences established to reduce time in purgatory	1190
Kissing pope's feet began with Pope Constantine	709	Transubstantiation, proclaimed by Pope Innocent III	1215
Veneration of cross, images, and relics authorized	786	Confession of sins to priests, instituted by Pope Innocent III	1215
College of Cardinals established	927	The doctrine of seven sacraments affirmed	1439
Canonization of dead people as saints initiated	995	Tradition claimed equal in authority with the Bible, Council of Trent	1545
Attendance at Mass made mandatory	1000	Apocryphal books declared canon by Council of Trent	1546
Celibacy of priesthood, decreed by Pope Gregory VII	1079		

The Emergence of New Orders in the Church

As indicated above, the centrality of the church in the life of late medieval society was eclipsed largely due to internal troubles within the church. The moral character of the church became blemished as the pursuit of power and privilege appeared to take precedence over the practical issues of pastoral care, concern for the disadvantaged, and piety. Many who experienced dissatisfaction and alienation from the church did not include those who saw issues at a deeper level such as theological deviation. For people of these concerns, the discomfort was allayed through the creation of greater benevolence and concern on the part of the church, hence, the rise of new reforming orders.

The earliest of these was the Roman Oratory of Divine Love (1517), inspired by the work of Catherine of Genoa (1447–1510) and modeled after the Genoa Oratory of Divine Love founded by Ettore Vernazza (1470–1524). This order of devoted clerics and laity focused on the plight of the poor and sick, as well as personal spiritual renewal; its work became a significant contribution to the recovery of the church.

The Theatine Order (1524) was founded by Gaetano dei Conti di Tiene and Giovanni Caraffa, a bishop and later pope (Paul IV), among others. The goal of the organization was to improve the moral and religious life of the clergy, as well as laity, and to respond to the Protestants. Priests were encouraged to follow the ascetic discipline of the Benedictine vow of poverty, chastity, and obedience. Not only were hospitals and churches established, but the order was the first to promote foreign missions with notable work in the Near and Far East.

The Order of Friars Minor Capuchin, or Capuchins, was founded in 1525 by Matteo de Bascio (ca.1495–1552), a Franciscan, who believed that his order was no longer following the rules of Saint Francis, the order's founder. As strict Franciscans, the Capuchins pursued a life of poverty, austerity, and simplicity, gathering their living by begging. They accomplished remarkable work among the poor and proved often to be heralded preachers. Members were forbidden to even touch money or wear shoes. The Capuchines, an order of nuns, was founded in 1538.

The Ursuline Order (1535) was established with the singular purpose of educating young girls. Founded by Angela de Merici (1474–1540), the Ursulines were the first teaching order of women established within the church. In addition, the Ursulines cared for the sick.

Of the numerous reforming orders to arise within the sixteenth-century church, the Society of Jesus, or Jesuits, was the most prolific. The order was founded by Ignatius Loyola (1491–1556), a truly remarkable historic personage. Like Calvin, he was afforded church

Saint Ignatius of Loyola, depicted in armour with a Christogram on his breastplate. A sixteenth-century painting by the French school of artists. Courtesy of Thomas Gun.

appointment while yet a youth, though, unlike Calvin, his later years were marked by dissipation. A change of direction occurred subsequent to Spanish military service in which he was severely wounded. Reading the lives of the saints and of Jesus during his convalescence, as well as experiencing a dream, brought a radical change in his life. Retiring to a cave to practice the disciplines of piety, as well as record what became the *Spiritual Exercises*, a series of meditations, Ignatius was brought through suffering to greater degrees of devotion.

After unsuccessful attempts to complete university training in Spain, Loyola entered the University of Paris in 1528, completing the MA degree in 1535. In the midst of willing privation and suffering at the hands of others, Ignatius made his way to Rome in 1537 to offer his services to the pope, and the "Company of Jesus" was informally constituted and formally sanctioned in 1540. Ignatius prepared the directives of the society. The order was directly subservient to papal bidding and purposed to become active in foreign missions, the education of youth, and pastoral care of the disadvantaged. The successes of the Jesuits in the sixteenth century were not only significant in turning the tide of Protestant advance, but in foreign missions.

The missionary endeavor of the Jesuits, as well as their use of inquisition to quell heresy, is most exemplified in Francis Xavier (1506–1552). Loyola and Xavier met as students at the University of Paris; Xavier joined others led by Ignatius to found the Company of Jesus in 1540. Most of Xavier's missionary activities were under Portuguese auspices, the monarch requesting Jesuits to serve in his distant colonies. Arriving initially in the Portuguese colony of Goa (India) in 1542, he would travel as far as Japan. It can be argued that the era of the sixteenth and seventeenth centuries was a time of great Roman Catholic missions, paralleling the international dominance of Spain and Portugal.

Xavier's death came on a journey with the Portuguese embassy to China.

> Student and friend of Ignatius Loyola, Francis Xavier, the Spanish Basque religious leader of the Roman Catholic Reformation was one of the first seven members of the Society of Jesus, known as the Jesuits. He was a missionary in India, Borneo, Japan, and China.

Body of Saint Francis Xavier in a silver casket at Basilica of Bom Jésus in Goa, India. Courtesy of Evrik.

The Tools of Suppression: Index and Inquisition

One tool for the suppression of undesired ideas by the church was censorship. Promoted by Paul IV in 1559, the index was a list of prohibited books the church officially forbade the faithful to read on threat of torture and death.

As a tool to suppress religious dissidence, the use of torture and death was instigated in the medieval era against the **Albigenses** in southern France and the **Waldensians** of France and Northern Italy beginning in the fourteenth century. The ground for suppression of heresy was a papal declaration by Innocent IV issued in 1252. The church granted the state authority to create tribunals for this purpose and these were reinstated in 1478 at the behest of Ferdinand and Isabella of Spain by Sixtus IV. Though the Inquisition functioned throughout the empire, it principally targeted Muslims and Jews in Spain whose forced conversions were suspect. It was later instituted in Portugal after many Jews fled there. The Inquisition was not extended to Protestants until Paul III created the Congregation of the Holy Office of the Inquisition in 1542 (currently it is denominated as the Congregation for the Doctrine of the Faith).

> Pope Paul III, in the midst of the Protestant Reformation, convened the Council of Trent in 1545. Michelangelo's "Last Judgment" in the Sistine Chapel was finished during Pope Paul's reign, and Michelangelo also worked on his palace in Rome and was appointed supervisor of the building of St. Peter's Basilica.

The Council of Trent (1545–1563)

The significance of the Council of Trent in the dogmatic formulation of Roman Catholic doctrine can hardly be overstated. Protestantism and Roman Catholicism were formulated in the sixteenth century; both religious systems selectively used the data of the previous centuries. The doctrinal formulation of Roman theology can be found in the Fourth Lateran Council of 1215 under Innocent III, the Council of Florence of 1439 under Eugenius IV, and, most magnificently, at Trent under Paul III, Julius III, and Pius IV. Paul III called for such a council as early as 1537 to gather in Mantua, Italy; however, conflicts forestalled the beginning of the council, which convened in December 1545 in Trent, Italy.

That the council met in twenty-five sessions over a period of eighteen years witnesses to the fact that differences between Roman Catholics and Protestants were irreconcilable.

Hopeful rapprochement was a thing of the past for the two parties. Under Paul III, Cardinal Caraffa organized the Inquisition to find a solution in terror rather than talk. In 1555, Caraffa succeeded Paul III as Paul IV, though no sessions convened under his aggressive leadership. Before the calling of the great council, one final attempt was made at conciliation by the emperor. The session held at Hagenau in 1540 proved fruitless, but reconvened the following year at Worms with Melanchthon, John Eck, and Gasparo Contarini. The emperor ordered the talks to be moved to Ratisbon (now Regensburg), and there the talks failed once more. The teachings of the two parties were simply incompatible! This set the stage for the greatest of the Roman Catholic formative councils in history.

The council had twofold intent. First, it sought to address the Protestant issue by creating a document that would become an authority once the Inquisition was unleashed (in this sense the council sought to deal with the intrusive menace of Protestantism).

A 1588 painting of the Council of Trent by Pasquale Cati da Jesi (1550–1620). Courtesy of Victuallers.

Second, it was a reforming council intent on addressing the problems in the church. The doctrinal formulation of the council, the Dogmatic Decrees, was Roman polemics. The council addressed beliefs put at risk by Protestantism, issuing both positive explanations of Roman Catholic views and condemnatory diatribes of Protestant errors. In addition, the church council composed the Tridentine Profession of Faith (1564), sometimes called the Creed of the Council of Trent and the Creed of Pius IV, as a positive statement of Roman creedalism.

The twenty-five sessions were conducted under three popes with significant time intervals: eight under Paul III (1545–1547), six under Julius III (1551–1552), and eleven under Pius IV (1562–1563). Of these sessions, several are crucial in understanding the theological heritage of Roman Catholicism as it is juxtaposed against Protestant opponents.

The fourth session, 8 March 1546, took up the issue of authority and made three crucial points: first, the canonical books were declared to be seventy-three in number; the difference with the Protestant position was the admission of seven books attributed to the intertestamental period; second, the witness of tradition was declared to have equal authority with Scripture; and, third, the church alone was declared to have the correct interpretation of the Bible through her teachers.

"But if any one receive not, as sacred and canonical, the said books entire with all their parts, as they have been used to be read in the Catholic Church, and as they are contained in the old Latin vulgate edition; and knowingly and deliberately contemn [sic] the traditions aforesaid; let him be anathema" (*The Canons and Decrees of the Council of Trent*, Session 4).

The fifth session, 4 April 1546, stated their official position on human frailty. The council decreed that adamic unity was such that all are born without holiness and justice though sin was defined as privation, the absence of debilitating guilt. Further, that inherited sin was transmitted through parental propagation, but was removed through the sacrament of infant baptism. Baptism removed the stain of original sin leaving a person only to cope with their voluntary acts of sin. Thus, the creedal statements of Trent made it clear that the Roman Church rejected the Protestant notion of human inability.

"If any one denies, that, by the grace of our Lord Jesus Christ, which is conferred in baptism, the guilt of original sin is remitted; or even asserts that the whole of that which has the true and proper nature of sin is not taken away; but says that it is only erased, or not imputed; let him be anathema" (*The Canons and Decrees of the Council of Trent*, Session 5.5).

The sixth session, 13 January 1547, spoke to the doctrine that Luther considered the one "upon which the church stands or falls," justification. The participants concluded that salvation was realized through cooperative grace, a causative infusion from God coupled with consequent human action. It was the act of being progressively made morally righteousness. Justifying grace was infused, not imputed; it was allotted incrementally, not declared instantaneously. Justification was the reward of a faith that was caused by works (at least in a secondary sense), not by faith alone. The creed stated that hope of life with God came only at the end of an arduous journey of faith and faith-works. However, since grace could be lost though moral failure, it could be regained through penance, the so-called "second plank" of forgiveness, if a person had the strength to do so. Should a person be unable due to infirmity to perform acts suggestive of repentance, the gift of grace could be gratuitously granted by the church through the sacrament of Extreme Unction since it is the repository and dispenser of the grace purchased by Christ through his sacrificial death.

"If any one saith, that by faith alone the impious is justified; in such wise as to mean, that nothing else is required to cooperate in order to the obtaining the grace of Justification, and that it is not in any way necessary, that he be prepared and disposed by the movement of his own will; let him be anathema" (*The Canons and Decrees of the Council of Trent*, Session 6, Canon 9).

"If any one saith, that men are just without the justice of Christ, whereby He merited for us to be justified; or that it is by that justice itself that they are formally just; let him be anathema" (*The Canons and Decrees of the Council of Trent*, Session 6, Canon 10).

Sessions 7, 13, and 21–24 deal with the subject of the church. The sacraments, seven in number, are defined as means of grace. That is, the grace procured through Christ's sacrifice has been given to the church to distribute; the grounds are sacramental obedience. Unlike the Protestant position in which the sacraments, two in number, nourish or strengthen the grace received at the moment of redemption commencing the Christian life, here the sacraments function to convey increments of grace that when amassed in sufficient quantity can merit eternal life. The sacrament of the Eucharist, for example, is

10.4. JUSTIFICATION AND THE COUNCIL OF TRENT

Canon 30

If any one saith, that, after the grace of Justification has been received, to every penitent sinner the guilt is remitted, and the debt of eternal punishment is blotted out in such wise that there remains not any debt of temporal punishment to be discharged either in this world, or in the next in Purgatory, before the entrance to the kingdom of heaven can be opened [to him]: let him be anathema.

Canon 32

If any one saith, that the good works of one that is justified are in such manner the gifts of God, as that they are not also in the good merits of him that is justified; or, that the said justified, by the good works which he performs through the grace of God and the merit of Jesus Christ, whose living member he is, does not truly merit increase of grace, eternal life, and the attainment of that eternal life,—if so be, however, that he depart in grace,—and also an increase of glory: let him be anathema.

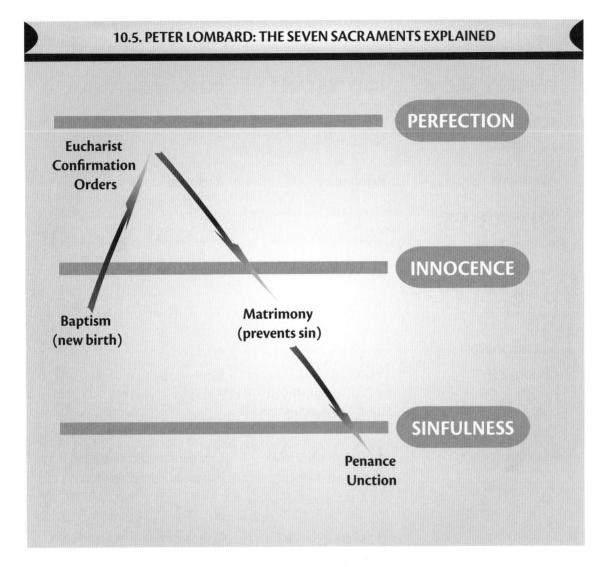

10.5. PETER LOMBARD: THE SEVEN SACRAMENTS EXPLAINED

PERFECTION

Eucharist
Confirmation
Orders

INNOCENCE

Baptism
(new birth)

Matrimony
(prevents sin)

SINFULNESS

Penance
Unction

an "antidote" for daily faults; its fruit is the forgiveness of sins since the repetition or reenactment of the first crucifixion is "truly propitiatory." Penance restores the grace lost through disobedience that was originally obtained through baptism.

"If any one saith, that baptism is free, that is, not necessary unto salvation; let him be anathema" (*The Canons and Decrees of the Council of Trent*, Session 7, Canon 5).

The Tridentine Profession of Faith (1564) is a twelve-point creed; it is what all Roman Catholics are called upon to embrace, a confession without which salvation is impossible (Article 12). The idea of creating a creed following the dogmatic decrees of the Council of Trent was first expressed in the twenty-fourth session by Pius IV. (The term "Tridentine" is a Latin term that refers to Trent, Italy.) The creed begins with an affirmation of the Nicene Creed and then mandates in succession a belief that

10.6. THE DIFFERENCES BETWEEN ROMAN CATHOLICISM AND PROTESTANTISM

FIVE KEY AREAS	PROTESTANT	ROMAN CATHOLIC
SCRIPTURE		
Sufficiency	*Sola Scriptura*	Tradition of equal authority with Scripture
Apocrypha	Rejected	Accepted
ANTHROPOLOGY		
Original Sin	Total depravity and guilt inherited from Adam	Corruption and predisposition to do evil inherited from Adam
Human Will	In bondage to sin	Free to do spiritual good
SOTERIOLOGY		
Good Works	Produced by the grace of God, unworthy of merit of any kind	Meritorious
Regeneration	A work of the Holy Spirit in the elect	Grace infused at baptism, increased by sacrament
Justification	An objective, final, judicial act of God	Forgiveness of sins received at baptism, may be lost by commiting sin, regained by penance
Predestination	Rooted in God's decrees	Rooted in God's foreknowledge. Christ's death as the merit for blessings of salvation: blessings passed on to sinners through sacraments

10.7. THE DIFFERENCES BETWEEN ROMAN CATHOLICISM AND PROTESTANTISM

FIVE KEY AREAS	PROTESTANT	ROMAN CATHOLIC
SOTERIOLOGY		
Atonement	Christ's death a substitutionary penal sacrifice	Christ's death the merit for blessings of salvation: blessings passed on to sinners through sacraments
Grace of God	Common grace given to all, saving grace given to elect	Prevenient grace, given at baptism, enabling one to believe; efficacious grace cooperating with the will, enabling one to obey
ECCLESIOLOGY		
Church and Salvation	Distinctions between visible and invisible church	Outside the (visible) church there is no salvation
Sacraments	A means of grace only as received by faith	Conveys justifying and sanctifying grace *ex opere operato* (by works)
Priesthood	All believers are priests	Priestly office mediates between God and man
Transubstantiation	Rejected	Affirmed
ESCHATOLOGY		
Purgatory	Denied	Affirmed

Scripture and tradition are of equal authority, the church's singular role in interpreting the Scriptures correctly, seven sacraments as salvation-grace mediums, sin and justification as defined by Trent, the Eucharist as propitiatory in conveying Christ's purchased grace, purgatory, venerations of images, and recognition of Rome as the mother of all churches. The eleventh article mandates an affirmation of all the findings expressed in the Council of Trent.

> "I embrace and receive all and every one of the things which have been defined and declared in the holy Council of Trent concerning original sin and justification" (*The Tridentine Profession of Faith*, Article 4).

The Thirty Years' War and the Peace of Westphalia.

The implications of the Thirty Years' War (1618–1648), a multinational conflict with devastating effects, fought largely on German soil, had important religious as well as political consequences in shaping the map of Europe. The religious root of the conflict was the uneasiness over the Peace of Augsburg (1555), an agreement that formally recognized both Roman Catholicism and Lutheranism in Germany. Thereby, the religious perspective of each German prince determined the religious affiliation tolerated within his territory. In consequence, the German states became a patch-work quilt, the patches often changing with princely succession (some willing to trade religion for political advantage), creating enormous tensions religiously, socially, and politically.

As the seventeenth century approached, the German states experienced a degree of equilibrium between Roman Catholic and Lutheran enclaves; the Calvinists, though significant, were excluded from the Peace of Augsburg. The emperor was elected by three electors of each religious party with the king having a seventh vote. In this volatile context, the **Roman Catholic Church** pressed the In-

quisition, largely through the Jesuits, to reclaim religious territory; all sides armed for a potential military solution to the tensions.

The war began in **Bohemia** over the issue of succession, a Catholic monarch over a largely Protestant population. Bohemian nobles rejected the king's advisors, treating them with impunity (an episode called the "Defenestration of Prague" in which the advisors were cast out of a castle window into a moat). Transylvania and Hungary joined the Bohemians and Frederic V, ruler in the Calvinist Palatinate, claimed the Bohemian throne. Not gaining the support of England and Holland, the Catholic Ferdinand II struck back with Spanish support, and the Protestant coalition was defeated at White Mountain, near Prague, in 1620 ending the Bohemian phase of the war. Subsequently Frederic was unable to remove Catholic armies that occupied the upper and lower Rhine Valley.

To arrest the advance of the Spanish Hapsburgs, the Dutch, English, and French (secretly) formed an alliance led by the king of Denmark, Christian IV, who had holdings within the German states. Under Danish leadership, conflict commenced in 1626 and eventuated in the defeat of the poorly supported Danes. With Catholic forces in triumph, the emperor issued the Edict of Restitution requiring that lands protestantized after the Peace of Augsburg of 1555 had to be returned; the religious map of the German states was reversed.

Fearing Roman Catholic imperial power in the northern region after the defeat of the Danes, Sweden entered the conflict, inaugurating another phase in 1630 under Gustavus Adolphus. After initial gains, particularly the victories over Catholic armies at Breitenfeld (1631) and Lutzen (1632), the fortunes of war gradually turned. Gustavus Adolphus lost his life in the victory at Lutzen, and the Swedes experienced a constant diminution of troop strength in months of campaigning, leading to a disastrous defeat at Nordlingen in 1634.

As a result the Protestants signed the Peace of Prague with the Hapsburg emperor ending the conflict; lands in Protestant hands in 1627 were allowed to remain so.

With Protestants generally willing to end the struggle in the German states, the French took up arms in defense of what they considered national interests against the threat of Hapsburg domination of Europe. The Dutch crippled the imperial empire with Spanish defeats at sea; Portugal declared its sovereignty from Spain in 1640; the Swedes invaded the northern German states; and the French inflicted a stunning defeat on the Spanish in 1643. The war continued for several years though mutuality of exhaustion made it increasingly evident that there would be no singular victor and all sides would suffer deepening negative consequences if peace could not be negotiated.

Several peace agreements between belligerents consummated in the Peace of Westphalia in 1648. The devastation of the German states was horrific. Illustrative of the cost of the conflict was the sacking of Magdeburg by Roman Catholic forces under Count Tilly in

The Peace of Westphalia treaty at Münster depicted in The Ratification of the Treaty of Münster, a painting by Gerard ter Borch (1617–1681). Courtesy of Jan Arkesteijn.

May 1631 following a siege that began in November of the previous year. Mayhem followed the fall of the city with a massacre that reduced the town of 30,000 to some 5,000 (estimates suggests that the total carnage reached 5 million for the entire war).

As a consequence of the treaty, Holland secured its sovereignty from the Spanish; Switzerland was recognized as a sovereign state; Sweden obtained territories on the southern shores of the Baltic, and France gained territory to the east (Alsace). A fruit of the peace was the effectual dissolution of the Holy Roman Empire (within the borders on what is generally recognized as Germany today), thereafter existing in name only, as territories within the empire were granted sovereignty. The empire began with Otto I in 962 and technically ended in the era of the Napoleonic Wars in 1806 with the abdication of Francis II.

From a religious viewpoint, the peace brought an end to the era of the reformation in the sense that the territories claimed by Prot-estants and Roman Catholics stabilized with mutual recognition. The Peace of Augsburg was recognized; the religion embraced in the patchwork quilt of various states within the empire was to be determined by the faith of the ruling prince, Lutheran or Roman Catholic. If a prince chose to change religious attachment, the forfeiture of the crown was the consequence. Territorial religious affirmation became static. Also, Calvinists gained legitimacy in the empire, if a territory was ruled by a prince of that persuasion, such as portions of the Palatinate. Lands gained by Protestants after 1624 generally remained as such. The territories ruled by the Habsburgs (Bohemia, Austria, and Hungary) reverted to Roman Catholicism. The Reformations in Europe were brought to an end, giving the continent new features of acceptable religious affirmation, tolerance, and religious tranquility. Religious pluralism became an accepted, though qualified reality, in Europe in the seventeenth century.

GLOSSARY OF TERMS

Albigenses: a neo-gnostic/Manichean sect of the twelfth and thirteenth centuries originating in Albi, France. Critical of the established church of the day, they were severely persecuted beginning in the reign of Innocent III and destroyed.

Bohemia: a region of what today is in a portion of the Czech Republic with its capital being Prague, as in the fifteenth century, the era of the reformer John Huss.

Roman Catholic Church: a movement that gradually emerged out of the increasingly moral, social, and theological divergences and controversies within the late medieval church. Like its counterpart the Protestant movement, proponents claim historic verification for its teaching ("that which has always and everywhere been taught in the church"), though seriously flawed and lacking demonstrable consistency through the centuries. It seems that the defining moments of the church were the Fourth Lateran Council, the Council of Florence (1439), and the enormously important formal creedalization and dogmatization of its teaching at the Council of Trent in the sixteenth century.

Waldensians: an early protest movement founded by Peter Waldo in the twelfth century in northern Italy that was heralded by later Protestants as a precursor to the Reformation because they criticized the morals and teachings of the medieval Catholic church. The Waldensians stressed the importance of the Bible and preaching much in the tradition of Wycliffe of England and Huss of Bohemia, though Waldensians were much earlier. Condemned by the Fourth Lateran Council (1215) under Innocent III, they were subsequently severely persecuted. In the Reformation era, the Waldensians joined the Calvinist tradition of Protestant reform through the work of William Farel.

Further Readings:
The Early Modern Church (1500–1650)

Primary Sources from the Early Modern Church

Arminius, Jacobus. *Arminius Speaks: Essential Writings on Predestination, Free Will, and the Nature of God*. John D. Wagner, ed. Eugene, OR: Wipf & Stock, 2011.

Calvin, Jean. *Commentaries*. Grand Rapids: William B. Eerdmans Publishing Co., 1960.

_____. *Institutes of the Christian Religion*. Philadelphia: Westminster Press, 1960.

Erasmus, Desiderius, Beatus Rhenanus, and John C. Olin. *Christian Humanism and the Reformation: Selected Writings of Erasmus, with 'The Life of Erasmus'* by Beatus Rhenanus. New York: Fordham University Press, 1975.

Klaassen, Walter. *Anabaptism in Outline: Selected Primary Sources*. Scottdale, PA.: Herald Press, 1981.

Luther, Martin, *Works*. Jaroslav Jan Pelikan and Helmut T. Lehmann, eds. St. Louis, MO: Concordia Publishing House, 1958.

Noll, Mark A. *Confessions and Catechisms of the Reformation*. Grand Rapids: Baker Book House, 1991.

Owen, John. *Works*. 15 vols. Reprint.1850–1853. Carlisle, PA: Banner of Truth Trust, 1965–1966.

Rickaby, Joseph. *The Spiritual Exercises of St. Ignatius Loyola*. London: Burns & Oates, 1915.

Schroeder, Henry Joseph. *Canons and Decrees of the Council of Trent*. Rockford, IL: Tan Books and Publishers, 1978.

Tappert, Theodore G. *The Book of Concord: The Confessions of the Evangelical Lutheran Church*. Philadelphia: Fortress Press, 1981.

Zwingli, Ulrich, Samuel Macauley Jackson, and Clarence Nevin Heller. *Commentary on True and False Religion*. Durham, NC: Labyrinth, 1981.

General Surveys of the Early Modern Church

Bainton, Roland Herbert. *The Reformation of the Sixteenth Century*. Boston, MA: Beacon Press, 1952.

Grimm, Harold John. *The Reformation Era, 1500–1650*. New York: Macmillan, 1954.

Hillerbrand, Hans Joachim. *The Reformation: A Narrative History Related by Contemporary Observers and Participants*. New York: Harper & Row, 1964.

Spitz, Lewis W. *The Protestant Reformation, 1517–1559*. St Louis, MO: Concordia Publishing House, 1985.

Important Topics and People of the Early Modern Church

Bainton, Roland Herbert. *Erasmus of Christendom*. New York: Scribner, 1969.

_____. *Hunted Heretic: the Life and Death of Michael Servetus, 1511–1553*. rev. ed. Providence, RI: Blackstone Editions, 2005.

Baker, J. Wayne. *Heinrich Bullinger and the Covenant: The Other Reformed Tradition*. Athens, OH: Ohio University Press, 1980.

Delumeau, Jean. *Catholicism Between Luther and Voltaire: A New View of the Counter-Reformation*. Philadelphia: Westminster Press, 1977.

Dickens, A. G. *The Counter Reformation*. New York: Harcourt Brace & World, 1969.

_____. *The English Reformation*. London: B.T. Batsford, 1989.

Estep, William Roscoe. *The Anabaptist Story: An Introduction to Sixteenth-Century

Anabaptism. Grand Rapids: William B. Eerdmans Publishing Co., 1996.

Kendall, R. T. *Calvin and English Calvinism to 1649.* Oxford: Oxford University Press, 1979.

Knappen, M. M. *Tudor Puritanism: A Chapter in the History of Idealism.* Chicago: University of Chicago Press, 1939.

Leith, John H. *Assembly at Westminster: Reformed Theology in the Making.* Richmond, VA: John Knox Press, 1973.

Marty, Martin. *Martin Luther.* New York: Viking Penguin, 2004.

McNeill, *John Thomas. The History and Character of Calvinism.* New York: Oxford University Press, 1954.

Muslow, Martin. *Socianianism and Arminianism: Antitrinitarians, Calvinists, and Cultural Exchange in Seventeenth-Century Europe.* Boston, MA: Brill, 2005.

Oberman, Heiko A., *Luther: Between God and the Devil.* New York: Image Books, 1989.

Potter, G. R. *Zwingli.* New York: Cambridge University Press, 1976.

Selderhuis, Herman J. *John Calvin: A Pilgrim's Life.* Downers Grove, IL: IVP Academic, 2009.

Shaw, Robert. *The Reformed Faith: Exposition of the Westminster Confession of Faith.* Fearn, Ross-shire, Scotland: Christian Focus Publications, 2008.

Steinmetz, David Curtis. *Calvin in Context.* Oxford: Oxford University Press, 2010.

Weir, Alison. *The Six Wives of Henry VIII.* New York: Grove Press, 1991.

Williams, George Huntston. *The Radical Reformation.* 3rd ed. Kirksville, MO: Sixteenth Century Journal Publishers, 1992.

PART 4

THE ENLIGHTENMENT AND LATE MODERN HISTORY (1650–1900)

Chapter 11 Outline

Chapter 11 Objectives

- That the reader will identify the religious causes for the rise of Enlightenment thought

- That the reader will describe how pietism attempted to revitalize churches in light of the encroachment of the Enlightenment approaches to knowledge

- That the reader will describe the main features of Enlightenment thought

- That the reader will identify the major thinkers in the development of Enlightenment epistemology

- That the reader will describe the development of liberal theology in light of the encroachment of the Enlightenment approaches to knowledge

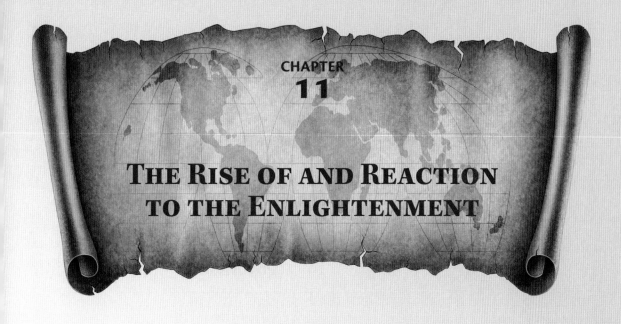

CHAPTER
11

THE RISE OF AND REACTION TO THE ENLIGHTENMENT

T HE TERRITORIAL DESIGNS OF the dissenting parties in the Reformation era ended with the tragedy of the Thirty Years' War. The parties, principally Roman Catholic and Protestant, begrudgingly acquiesced to the legitimate existence of their opponents; the map of Europe was drawn along rigid religious and political lines. Nations affirmed their religious allegiances and the various German states became a patchwork quilt of regional affiliations. Roman Catholics and Protestants felt a degree of repose and confidence that religion, though bruised, possessed an unchallenged status in the Western world.

Pietism and Religious Liberalism

However, a movement, though hardly discernible and consequently not perceived as an threat, would emerge that eventually questioned the viability of the Reformation's two great polarities, Protestantism and Roman Catholicism, at least as traditionally interpreted. In the world created by the assumptions of the **Enlightenment**, which held center stage in determining values for three centuries, new ideas and important truths that could safely guide and guard societies from the ravages of war and destitution posed potent opposition to authoritarian conceptions of religion. The net result was that religion's defenders were often forced to seek security in some form of retreat or segregation from the world of intellectual discourse. They had to formulate some kind of accommodation to the emergent ideas that seemed to speak with more surety than the once widely accepted, but increasingly discredited, ideas of external authorities whether they be in the church, Bible, or state.

In many ways, one of the most salient sto-

399

11.1. THE ROOTS OF MODERNITY

RENAISSANCE	REFORMATION	ENLIGHTENMENT/MODERN	POSTMODERN ERA
	1517	1650 1900	
	Locus of Reality	Rational	Nonrational
	Authority	Reason	Self
	Worldview	Progressive Positivistic	Anxiety Despair

ries of the last three centuries, which has functioned as an interpretative grid since the Reformations, has been an attempt of religionists to come to grips with the emergence of the Enlightenment, its assumptions and consequences. In the end, it could be argued that the Enlightenment has triumphed over its religious opponents only to suffer a cataclysmic demise brought on by its own successes. The ultimate difficulty with the Enlightenment was that it spawned a materialistic quest that revealed the shallowness and poverty of its approach to the meaning of life, which emptied the soul, destroyed interpersonal relationships, and took away a sense of security.

The Meaning of the Enlightenment: The Foundation of a New Social Experiment

The movement, later called the Enlightenment, emerged in the seventeenth and eighteenth centuries. One could argue that its roots are in the **Renaissance** of the fourteenth and fifteenth centuries as Western Europe emerged from what Erasmus suggested were the "Dark Ages." The intellectual accomplishments of the rebirth of learning, expressed in the rise of **Humanism**, an interest in man as a focus of study, was a not-so benign reaction to late medieval authoritarianism. The Enlightenment did not question the fact of truth as much as the method for acquiring truth. The Renaissance spirit was a profound element in the rise of the sixteenth-century reforming movements since the cry *ad fontes* ("to the sources") resulted in some harsh criticism of the church. Indeed, one result of the movement was the attempted reform of the churches along more historic lines; many Roman Catholics and all Protestants argued that the church had veered from the past. This facet of the Reformation movement sought authority in the past, but within the teachings of the Bible and the church's traditional doctrinal expressions. It was a movement that viewed the first-century origins of the church as definitive for authority, disparaging other authority sources such as reason, conscience, or natural revelation.

"The theology of the Enlightenment did not begin, as it is often shown to begin, with a criticism of Trinitarian and christological teaching, or of the miracles of the

Bible, or of the biblical picture of the world, or of the supranaturalism of the redeeming event attested in the Bible. Its starting-point in the 'rational orthodoxy' which was conservative in all these matters was a re-adoption of the humanistic, Arminian, Socinian, and finally the acknowledged Roman Catholic rejection of what were supposed to be the too stringent assertions of the Reformers concerning the fall of man—the indissolubility of human guilt, the radical enslavement of man to sin, the *servum arbitrium*" (Barth, *Church Dogmatics*, 4.1.479).

However, another segment of the Renaissance, in its quest to address the disruptions in culture and society, suggested that the solution was in *ad fontes,* but not in the first century; the model for a better social experience might be in emulating the Greeks and Romans. The emphasis shifted from a pursuit of authorities that impose jurisdiction from without to authority, normally reason, from within. In a sense, then, the Reformation represented a conservative break or readjustment within a medieval view of truth. A simultaneous movement, being more radical, questioned truth that would be solely based on the values of others, whether it be church, state, or the Bible. This lesser view of the nature of truth came to the forefront after the Reformation era, overshadowed it, and supplanted it.

The Enlightenment, which came after the Reformation era, generally viewed the previous era as a good start in its rejection of medieval authoritarianism, but one that did not go far enough, hence the tragic ending in a devastating war to a century of religious upheaval. In essence, the Enlightenment sought to replace theology with philosophy, making the search for truth inward rather than outward. The fundamental assertion of the movement was the affirmation of the reliability of the rational faculties to arrive at a safer truth than other methods. It is not too much to say that it represented a faith in the omnipotence of human reason and a belief in redemption through education, and thus the rise of the sciences and

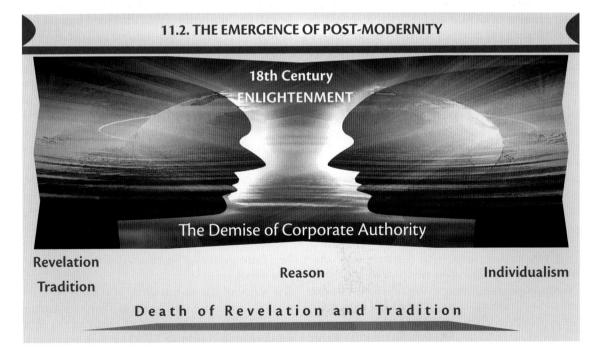

11.2. THE EMERGENCE OF POST-MODERNITY

18th Century
ENLIGHTENMENT

The Demise of Corporate Authority

Revelation

Tradition

Reason

Individualism

Death of Revelation and Tradition

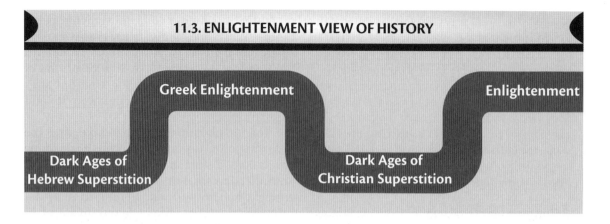

11.3. ENLIGHTENMENT VIEW OF HISTORY

Greek Enlightenment

Enlightenment

Dark Ages of
Hebrew Superstition

Dark Ages of
Christian Superstition

technology. The seventeenth and eighteenth centuries have been called the "Age of Reason."

There have been no more perceptive critics of the Enlightenment than Karl Barth, the Swiss theologian, or Hans Kung, the Roman Catholic scholar, in the last century. For the former, the Enlightenment's most salient feature was its affirmation of the positive function of human reason, which was a denial of the reformational belief in human deformity and the blightedness of all human faculties. A corollary to faith in human potential was the denial, or at least the redefinition, of the need and nature of divine revelation, the potential of human nature, and the meaning of salvation.

Kung persuasively argued that the shift from the medieval consensus of truth led to faith in autonomous reason and the sovereignty of the state as the mechanism of its execution. The natural sciences, natural law, and natural religion replaced divine grace as essential to the definition of religion. The "Marseillaise" replaced the "Te Deum," uplifting statecraft over church craft, the capital building and legislative functions over the steeple. It seemed that rationalism, linked to the sciences, evidenced by a plethora of new inventions and discoveries, could unlock the mysteries of the universe; God was being squeezed out of it as an explanatory cause and comfort.

Humankind, according to Immanuel Kant, was finally being lifted out of the servile stage and was now capable of thinking and acting on his own; the portent for the liberation of humankind seemed promising through technology and science. Humans could reach an exalted status of accomplishments, not possible when the church held sway over souls! In the mind of Kant, humanity was on the verge of a great day, a deliverance from an immature stage of development, which was a period in human history dominated by external authorities that curtailed human potential.

Foundational to the emergence of philosophy and its ascendancy over theology was the question of how people come to know things; the science of epistemology (the question of "what can be known" is a consequence of this question). Christian antiquity answered the question by assuming the inadequacy of the human quest for knowledge, hence a dependence on divine revelation. The rise of the mathematical sciences with the emphasis on logic seemed to hold great hope for answering the most perplexing questions of life.

The Emergence of Secular Approaches to Knowledge

The story of the dominance of reason is often placed in the life and work of René Descartes (1596–1650), frequently referred to as the first modern man because his approach to knowledge made him one of the central figures in the Scientific Revolution. His quest for objective truth, the search for "clear and distinct ideas," led him to rational reflection, not ancient texts. What Descartes believed was that the mind contained the sources of knowledge, sources of truth discernible through reflection. He came to the realization that his own existence could not be challenged because of his own mental conclusions in that regard (*cogito ergo sum*, "I think, therefore, I am"). "Because thought exists, I exist," he argued. Truth was to be found in the mind, not a book, by learned reflection, not revelation. What is important is not so much Descartes's conclusions, but his method of knowing. The starting point of philosophy is the mind and the method is deductive reflection. Beginning at this point, Descartes

Portrait of René Descartes (1596–1650) by Frans Franchoisz Hals (1582/1583–1666) at the Louvre Museum. Courtesy of Dedden.

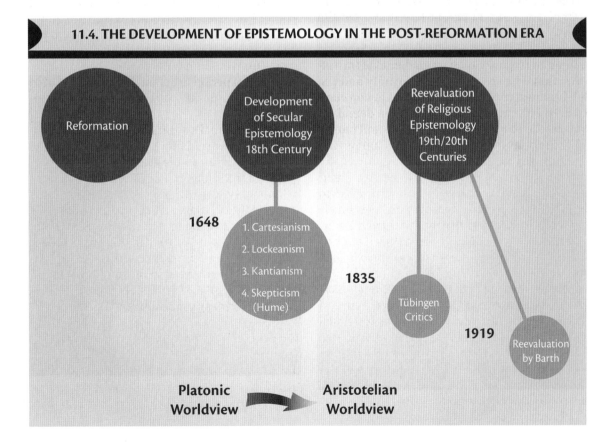

11.4. THE DEVELOPMENT OF EPISTEMOLOGY IN THE POST-REFORMATION ERA

Reformation

Development of Secular Epistemology 18th Century

Reevaluation of Religious Epistemology 19th/20th Centuries

1648

1. Cartesianism
2. Lockeanism
3. Kantianism
4. Skepticism (Hume)

1835

Tübingen Critics

1919

Reevaluation by Barth

Platonic Worldview → **Aristotelian Worldview**

excluded the possibility of supernatural revelation that was not filtered through human experience. Suddenly, the realm of knowledge was reduced to natural revelation! The error of the Enlightenment was not in the elevation of the rational faculties; it was in the conclusion that such avenues of knowledge were the only ones.

Though the approach of John Locke, Thomas Hobbes, and George Berkeley, among others, represented a reaction to Descartes, their approach still limited the possibility of knowledge to the finite, revealing their roots in the ancient Greeks and the Enlightenment.

Locke (1632–1704) argued that the reliance on the mind to the denigration of the senses was a mistake. The "father of British empiricism" or the "Sensationalist school" suggested that the mind is a blank slate; that information, gathered through the operation of the senses, can be etched on the mind; and that through reflection truth can be derived. In contrast to Descartes, knowledge was an inductive, not deductive, science; knowledge was a function of experience.

David Hume (1711–1776) had a devastating critique of both **Cartesians** and **Lockeans**. Though frequently identified with Empiricism, the Scot raised the issue of the validity of inductive reasoning since it is based on the assumption of uniformity of sense perception rooted in the past, the past being non-repeatable and unknowable. Instead, he argued that knowledge is based on natural instincts, somewhat in the tradition of **Scottish Common Sense Realism** propounded by Francis Hutcheson. Thus, Hume denied the certainty of cause-effect relations. Most devastating in *An Inquiry into Human Understanding* (1748) was his argument against

Portrait of John Locke by Godfrey Kneller, National Portrait Gallery, London. Courtesy of Stephencdickson.

A painting of David Hume by Allan Ramsay (1713–1784) at the Scottish National Gallery. Courtesy of Dcoetzee-Bot.

Invitation to Church History: World

the possibility of miracles and the criticism of the argument of design for the existence of God. His criticism of the rationalist approaches to the acquisition of finite knowledge was as troubling as his attack on the credibility of divine revelation.

The exact relationship between the ideas of David Hume and Scottish common sense moral philosophy, as reflected in the work of Francis Hutcheson, is disputed. Hume and the Common Sense School rooted knowledge in the subjective or moral faculties as intuitive and innate. However, Hume's general goal in rejecting the rationalizing tendencies of the empiricists was to use reason to disprove its reasonability and found an alternative approach to knowledge in the inner self; Hutcheson's attraction to moral philosophy was a way to preserve truth, not question its possibility. Thomas Reid (1710–1796), the founder of the common sense school, argued that the world was not a mental creation, but possessed reality based upon an innate intuition that it is so. Knowledge was instinct-based and intuitive, not reflective in nature.

The importance of Immanuel Kant (1724–1804) can hardly be overstated in the emergence of the modern era or in his contribution in the history of philosophy. The Konigsberg professor of logic and mathematics was shaken by the protestation of the Scot David Hume that rationalism leads to skepticism about the nature of truth, not truth. To counteract Hume's extremes in this regard, Kant developed what has generally been known as "the critical philosophy." Generally, it is valid to assert that nineteenth century German theologians embraced Kant's understanding of epistemology, its meaning and limitations, so that later theology or religious understanding was thereby shaped in its assertions.

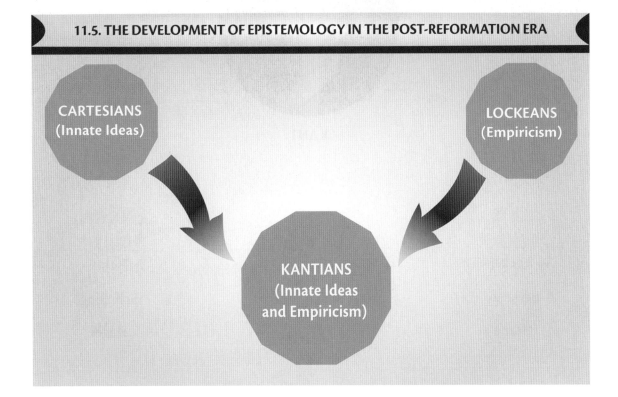

11.5. THE DEVELOPMENT OF EPISTEMOLOGY IN THE POST-REFORMATION ERA

CARTESIANS
(Innate Ideas)

LOCKEANS
(Empiricism)

KANTIANS
(Innate Ideas
and Empiricism)

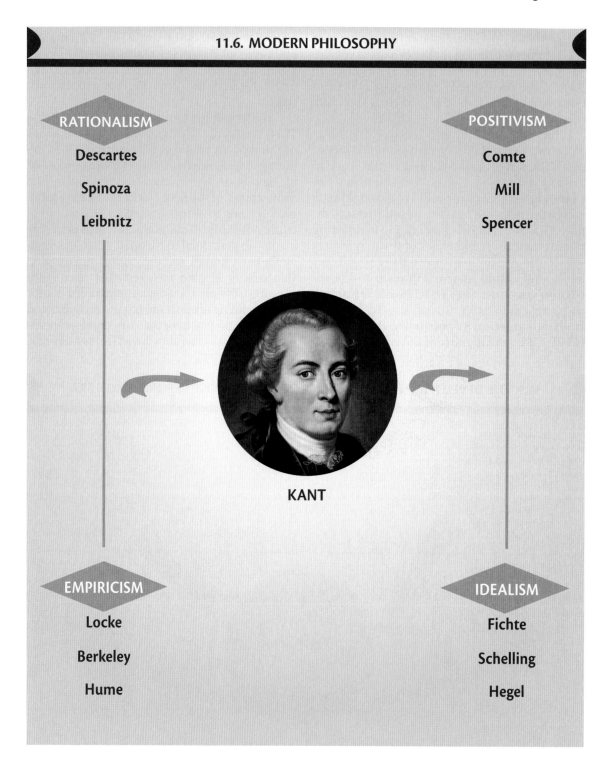

11.6. MODERN PHILOSOPHY

RATIONALISM

Descartes

Spinoza

Leibnitz

POSITIVISM

Comte

Mill

Spencer

KANT

EMPIRICISM

Locke

Berkeley

Hume

IDEALISM

Fichte

Schelling

Hegel

11.7. POSITIVISM AND IDEALISM

POSITIVISM

Comte   Logical Positivism (A. J. Ayer)

Mill   Anaytical Philosophy (B. Russell)

Spencer   Linguistic Analysis (L. Wittgenstein)

KANT

IDEALISM

Fichte   Phenomenology (Husserl; Heidegger)

Schelling   Existentialism

Hegel

Theistic   Atheistic
(Kierkegaared)   (Sarte)

Though Kant was born to pietistic parents and educated as such, his writings set Western philosophy on a new path that it still follows today. Kant's view that knowledge of the world is dependent upon certain innate categories or ideas in the human mind is known as **idealism**. Ultimately it denied the uniqueness of Bible and Christianity.

In his *Critique of Pure Reason* (1781), Kant argued that rationalism alone could not establish validity, because equally impressive arguments can be marshaled to the contrary. Kant placed religion (i.e., the existence of God, freedom of the will, and immortality of the soul) in a sphere outside of reason's grasp. Since these assertions were beyond experience, rational argument cannot establish them one way or the other, knowledge being the fruit of experience and mental reflection. Hence, the mind and experience were safe and accurate guides in the world; however, in the spiritual world where knowledge was unavailable to our minds and experience, there could be no knowledge.

If religious knowledge was unavailable because the Bible was, at best, little more than a subjective witness to the invisible (to Kant the Bible was not a communication from God), the existence of religion was threatened. Kant answered this problem in the *Critique of Practical Reason* (1788) and *Religion within the Limits of Reason Alone* (1791). He postulated that the existence of God was warranted by an innate sense of moral duty, the categorical imperative, based on the existence of moral law in the universe. Christian religion was not about the redemptive revelation of God in Christ as it was the subjective perception of how we should live to be worthy of God's kindness. Thus, Kant reduced religion to morality, a morality innately found in all humankind, morality being the life of God in the soul. Revelation was not to be conceived as a communication from God to humankind, a medieval delusion formulated to hold minds captive to church and cleric. Instead, religion was a moral faculty within all.

The Early Struggles to Readjust Religion to the Rationalistic Spirit

The rejection of revelation as paramount to the establishment of true religion inaugurated a quest to redefine the ancient faith so that it would be retained as important and viable, but clearly one that required reconfiguring. The net result of clever attempts to maintain religion without the "irrational" truth claims of traditional Christian faith (i.e., the Trinity of God, the incarnation of Jesus Christ, divine redemption through the shedding of his blood) resulted in a vague embrace of little more than a "great, distant being" that somehow governed the universe because design without designer was inconceivable, at least until the nineteenth century.

The great French playwright, Voltaire (1694–1778), spoke against a religion based on revelation, but he argued the existence of God like a "watch presupposes a watchmaker." This God was a transcendent architect, largely impersonal (one to gaze upon from a distance, but not personally knowable).

Jean-Jacques Rousseau (1712–1778), a French novelist, embraced Voltaire's distant god that was accessible only by stargazing. Despising the possibility of special revelation, or of human corruption, his faith for human progress was in the arts and sciences. Sounding like the later Thomas Jefferson, Rousseau suggested that the blight of human behavior was rooted in the lack of educational advancement that had corrupting influences on society (sin being rooted in knowledge deficiency and environmental influences).

The moderation of the English, as opposed to the more critical French thinkers, was evident in John Locke (1632–1704). It would be difficult to call Locke a deist (perhaps it is better to suggest that he was a transitional figure) since he believed that revelation was a legitimate source of knowledge, that revelation must come to us and is not within us (as Kant would later assert), that God's existence is ra-

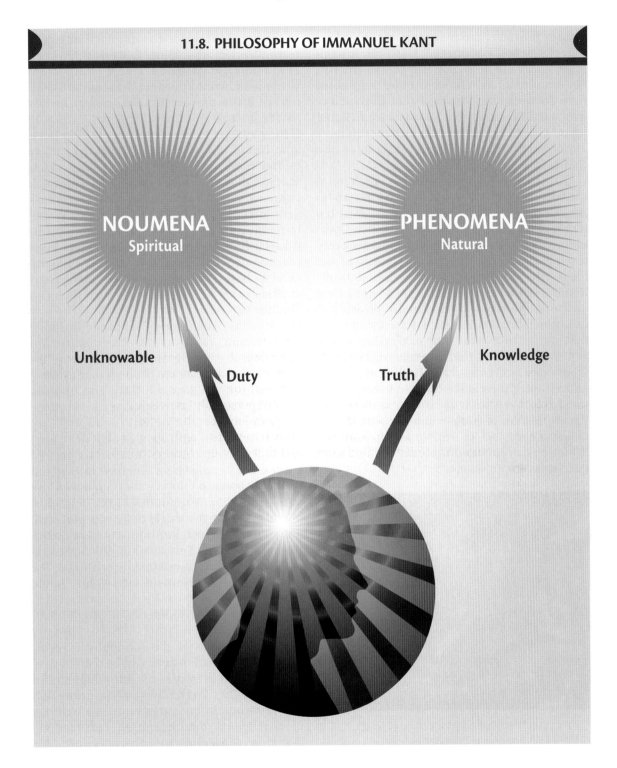

11.8. PHILOSOPHY OF IMMANUEL KANT

NOUMENA
Spiritual

PHENOMENA
Natural

Unknowable

Knowledge

Duty

Truth

tionally provable, and that some of the biblical miracles actually happened. However, his tolerant spirit both in religion and political theory, his stress that morals were more important than doctrine, and his stress that Christianity was simple suggests that he was a transitional figure between the world that unquestionably embraced religious authority and a later one that questioned its viability.

The roots of English **deism** are largely associated with Herbert of Cherbury (1583–1648) though the political turmoil, and religious triumph of the Puritan, during the British Commonwealth era (1640–1660) momentarily brought an end to the initial inroads of his ideas. This English diplomat rejected traditional religion, anticipating Kant's later views on the nature of religion. His credo consisted of five principles: the existence of God (but a denial of the Trinity), the duty of worship of this God by humankind, that the essence of religion is morality and virtue, that sin is real and requires repentance, and a future personal judgment based on behavior. Divine religion was the expression of proper morals without the necessary embrace of traditional Christian affirmations. It confused the fruit of the Christian faith with its essence!

A painting of Herbert of Cherbury by Isaac Oliver (1556–1617). Courtesy of Lotsofissues.

Deism experienced resurgence after the restoration of the king, flowering between 1690 and 1730. Matthew Tindal (1657–1733) wrote what would become the standard definition of the movement, *Christianity as Old as Creation or the Gospel a Republication of Nature* (1730). Unlike Herbert of Cherbury, who based his conclusions on innate ideas in the mind, perhaps reflecting Descartes, Tindal followed Locke's empiricist approach to knowledge. An interesting facet of Tindal's demonstration of the validity of deism was the assertion of the corruption of the primitive faith in the early church, a view later championed by Thomas Chubb of England as well as Joseph Priestley (*The Corruptions of Christianity* [1782]) who deeply influenced Thomas Jefferson.

Other influential English deists included John Toland (1670–1722), *Christianity Not Mysterious . . .* (1696); Anthony Collins (1676–1729), *A Discourse on the Grounds and Reasons of the Christian Religion* (1724); and Thomas Woolston (1670–1733), *Discourses on the Miracles of Our Savior* (1727–1730).

Unlike deism with its absentee deity governing the world through the maintenance of natural law, a movement emerged in England in the eighteenth century that embraced the anti-Trinitarian assumptions of the deists but postulated that the single deity was personal. The roots of the religious movement are often traced to Michael Severtus and the Socinians of the sixteenth and seventeenth centuries. The founder of **Unitarianism** was John Biddle (1615–1662), whose *Twelve Arguments*, a tract, led to several imprisonments in Cromwellian England.

The influence of the rationalistic revolt against the Christian faith can be seen in Germany through the works of Gotthold Ephraim Lessing (1729–1781), philosopher, dramatist, and librarian. In his latter years, his writings of a religious nature caused considerable alarm in conservative Lutheran circles. He

published *Fragments* (1774–1778), supposedly by an unknown author, though actually
the work of H. S. Reimarus (it appeared that it
was safer to publish anonymous writers than
make his own opinions available to scrutiny).
Reimarus, a deist and biblical critic, rejected
the supernatural claims of the Bible claiming
that the writers of the Bible perpetuated
frauds. He argued, as Lessing propounded in
his "ugly ditch" metaphor, that the passing of
time makes historical accuracy impossible.
In suggesting that any belief system that argues primitive continuity is at best uncertain,
Lessing became influential in the German
movement to reclaim the historical Jesus that
has, as a beginning assumption, that the Bible
had become human production.

In *Nathan the Wise* (1779), Lessing made

A painting of Gotthold Ephraim Lessing by Anton Graff (1736–1813). Courtesy of Maksim.

11.9. ORTHODOXY AND UNITARIANISM COMPARED

	ORTHODOXY	UNITARIANISM
SOURCE OF TRUTH	Reformation Empiricism Rationalism	Reformation Empiricism Rationalism
GOD	Theistic; plural, personal	Theistic; single, personal
MEDIUM OF REVELATION	Supernatural; natural	Natural
PERSON OF CHRIST	God/man	Archetypal Man
NATURE OF SIN	Derived and personal depravity Moral inability	Personal depravity Moral inability
ATONEMENT	Penal	Exemplary

the point that truth was not a matter of historic accuracy; it was a function of faith that acts morally as certain truths are valid. Thus, Christianity was valid because of its ability to sustain moral power; the accuracy of its historic judgments was unimportant.

Critical assumptions about the integrity of the biblical witness were propagated by Johann Semler (1725–1791) and Julius Wellhausen (1844–1918) in Old Testament studies and in New Testament studies by David Strauss (1808–1874), Ludwig Feuerbach (1804–1872) and Ferdinand Christian Baur (1792–1860), the so-called Tübingen School of Higher Criticism.

The Rise of Eighteenth-Century Pietism: A Reaction to the Enlightenment

The rationalistic trends in the universities would have an inevitable effect upon the churches in the seventeenth and eighteenth centuries since these great centers of learning trained generations of pastors and priests. Since God reveals his Son by the Spirit and chooses his citizens personally in mysterious ways and humans must believe through faith in Christ, it is not surprising that Christian faith, at least from a human perspective, is but

a single generation from decline. The grand success of an era of gospel explosion, such as the Reformation, does not offer the portent of utopian days in subsequent generations. The fortunes of the great gospel enterprise seem in retrospect to be built more on an undulating landscape than on a firm base that allows the steady march of unbroken, observable progress. Good days follow not-so-good ones, but the reverse is also true.

Given the fact that the best of human souls are blighted with error born of ignorance, rebellion, and prejudice, the church is in a constant state of renewal because it is in a constant state of flux. Just as the seeds of hope emerge from tragic times, so the downward progress of fortunes descend from great times of success and progress. Every generation has to be reintroduced to "Joseph"; every generation supposes that the dislikes brought forward from the previous generation justify improvements by the new generation. As such, life seems to simply go on from crisis to triumph and triumph to crisis.

It may be stretching the boundaries of historic causation to blame exclusively the turning away from historic orthodoxy on the inroads of the Enlightenment; humans, constantly rebellious and unwilling to be instructed and humbled of pride and prejudice, find in the

11.10. THE ENLIGHTENMENT AND THE HISTORY OF MAN

INFANCY   PROGRESSIVISM   ADULTHOOD

Past   Present

Irrationality (Myth Makers)   Reason

Traditional Religion (Superstition)   Rational Religion

Primitive Passion and Feeling (Hume)
Projections of Human Needs (d'Holbach)

currents of the day apparent intellectual and emotional legitimacy for their actions. The Enlightenment, however, was a huge factor in the creation of a world of ideas and consequent conclusions vastly different from those ever experienced in the Christian era. The intellectual forces marshaled against the church, fueled by advances in the sciences (e.g., Newtonian science), posed a dramatic threat to the penetration of Christianity in Western cultures.

The omnibus clouds that appeared on the horizon for the churches brought a discernible darkness over the spiritual vitality of Christianity; this was addressed on the continent and in England with a multi-faceted response, led by **pietism**, a movement that sought to revitalize the churches. It could be argued, depending on how the term is defined, that the evangelical movement was the net result. That is, the evangelical movement made certain features of historic orthodoxy (such as the centrality of the personal conversion experience, a stress on spiritual cultivation through small

groups, an embrace of Christian orthodoxy but not doctrinal or creedal hair splitting, a spirit of transdenominationalism, and an emphasis on the need to spread the gospel) as the central focus of true faith.

German pietism was expressed as a protest to the perception of declining spiritual values and vitality in the Lutheran community. The pietists' complaint was that the seventeenth-century churches were overly rationalistic, stressing the content of faith to the neglect of the experience of it. They emphasized the practical fruit of faith as manifest in outward conduct, the essence of the sermon as practical rather than intellectual, the necessity of pastoral activity in nurturing the flocks of God, and the importance of an individual conversion experience.

The embryonic roots of the pietist movement can be observed in the emphasis of small group meetings for spiritual nurturing in the ministry of Henry Bullinger of Zurich that became a stable in the Puritan practice of piety.

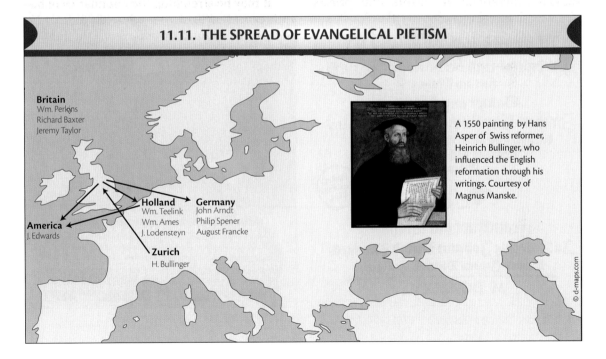

11.11. THE SPREAD OF EVANGELICAL PIETISM

Britain
Wm. Perkins
Richard Baxter
Jeremy Taylor

Holland
Wm. Teelink
Wm. Ames
J. Lodensteyn

Germany
John Arndt
Philip Spener
August Francke

America
J. Edwards

Zurich
H. Bullinger

A 1550 painting by Hans Asper of Swiss reformer, Heinrich Bullinger, who influenced the English reformation through his writings. Courtesy of Magnus Manske.

© d-maps.com

The pietistic movement can formally be traced to Philipp Jakob Spener (1635–1705) in Frankfort; later when he became a court preacher in Dresden, Saxony, he joined his efforts with August H. Francke. The publication of *Pia Desideria* or *Heartfelt Desire for a God-Pleasing Reform of the True Evangelical Church* (1675) was a manifesto for revitalization. Spener called for Christians to gather in small groups for prayer, mutual edification, and Bible study and organized conventicles with regularity.

Further, the laity should be encouraged to exercise the spiritual gifts in service to others. As to the training of pastors, Spener argued for higher spiritual standards and that clergy should use their pulpits for edification and inspiration rather than learned discourses on obscure topics. Opposition to his proposals led to his retreat from controversy, and he spent the latter years of his life in pastoral work.

Crucial to establishing the University of Halle as a center for the pietist movement, August H. Francke (1663–1727) was an educator who was influenced by Spener. Converted in 1687, Francke was appointed a professor of Greek and oriental languages at the newly established University of Halle in 1692. There he taught languages and theology for the remainder of his career.

The title page from *Pia Desideria* (1676) by Philipp Jacob Spener. Courtesy of Esilerey.

August Hermann Francke (1663–1727) by unknown artist. Courtesy of Torsten Schleese.

In the late 17th century, as professor at the Martin Luther University in Halle, August Hermann Francke was also pastor at Glauca, a village suburb of Halle. Following the destruction of the Thirty–Years' War, Francke collected orphan children from the streets and opened a school for them and another for the poor. These two schools were the beginning of the Francke Foundation in Halle.

Under Francke's influence the university, and the church he served nearby, became a center of the pietist movement. He founded an orphanage that later became a model for George Muller's famous Bristol, England, work in the nineteenth century. He also established a home for unmarried women, a school for disadvantaged children, and a dispensary.

He contributed significantly to the emerging Protestant missions' movement. The King of Denmark and Norway, Frederick IV, contacted Francke in 1705 with a desire to send missionaries to Danish territories in what is now India. The result was the Danish-financed Danish-Halle mission, the first Protestant mission to India. The first two missionaries sent to the Tamil people were Bartholomew Ziegenbalg (1683–1719) and Henry Plutschau (1678–1747). They learned the language of the Hindu people, translated the Scriptures (also Luther's catechism), and established educational centers. The record of the work of this mission provided a strong impetus for the growing mission enterprise.

Spener and the pietist movement influenced the German aristocrat Nicolaus Ludwig von Zinzendorf (1700–1760). Receiving his earliest education in Halle, he followed his family's preference of politician and landowner; yet his interest in the revitalization of the Lutheran churches along pietistic lines became his passion. His life took a decisive turn in 1722 when he offered asylum to a group of persecuted Christians from Bohemia, allowing them to reside on his estate in Moravia and build a town, Heernhut. Zinzendorf not only assumed the economic care of these people; he assumed pastoral duties and leadership. Following a prayer meeting at Herrnhut in 1732, the group, now called **Moravians**, committed themselves to missionary work on a broad scale.

By the time of Zinzendorf's death in 1760, Moravian missionaries (226 in number) had

Zinzendorf's waistcoat at Lititz Moravian Archive and Museum in Lititz, Pennsylvania. Courtesy of Bohemian-roots.

Invitation to Church History: World

been sent to the West Indies (Leonard Dober and David Nitschmann were sent out in 1732 to St. Thomas), Greenland, the native populations of North America, slaves in British America and South America, the East Indies, Africa, and Egypt.

There were examples of significant mission work under state-church sponsorships such as the Dutch Reformed to the Walloons (1644) and the Lutherans in Denmark to India through the Danish-Halle Mission (1706) under Frederick IV. There were also outreaches such as those by the Church of England through the Society for the Propagation of the Gospel in Foreign Parts (1701) and one by the Dutch East India Company to serve their laborers and the native populations. However, the Moravians reflect the first missionary sponsorship of Protestant missions by a local gathering of believers.

The pietist movement emerged in England in the eighteenth century through the labors of a host of prominent voices such as George Whitfield and John Wesley. Like their German counterparts, the passion of these men was to revitalize what was considered to be a state-church that had drifted into dry orthodoxy, was ravished by the inroads of religious liberalism, and lacked evangelical, gospel passion. The upper classes in England were attracted to the easygoing progressivism of the rationalists whose pulpit fare tended to be more moralistic than bibliocentristic while moral standards declined and illiteracy mushroomed. The religion of England, many perceived, stood in need of repair!

In a century dominated by profound and prolific preachers, perhaps no eighteenth-century figure cast such a lengthy shadow over English religious life and fortunes as John Benjamin Wesley (1703–1791). A man of great courage and fortitude, though small of stature, he sought to renew a church and unwittingly established a new one. He was born the fifteenth child of a parish priest, Samuel, of Epworth, England and his wife Susanna Annesley. Prepared for college in the Epworth parsonage

by his parents and at Charterhouse School, London, he entered Christ Church College, Oxford, in 1720 and obtained Episcopal ordination in 1728. Prior to this, he was appointed a teaching fellow at Lincoln College, Oxford, where he remained for several years though he assisted his aging father periodically in the Epworth parish.

Returning to Oxford in 1728, he joined with several others, George Whitfield (1714–1770) and Charles Wesley (1707–1788), his brother, among them, to meet for spiritual development and edification. These gatherings were popularly known as the Holy Club, but those who were judged overly preoccupied with issues of personal piety were dubbed "Bible moths," "Sacramentarians," and "Methodists," a term later lifted from dishonor for the movement. At that time, the group, meeting for the reading of pietistic literature, prayer, and the reading of Scripture, deeply influenced by the writings of William Law (*A Serious Call to the Devout and Holy Life* [1728]), Jeremy Taylor (*The Rule and Exercises of Holy Living* [1650] and *Dying* [1651]), Thomas à Kempis, and Henry More, the Cambridge mystic. The spark that ignited John Wesley's later endeavors had apparently not been struck at this time.

> "Give me one hundred men who fear nothing but sin and desire nothing but God, and I care not whether they be clergyman or laymen, they alone will shake the gates of Hell and set up the kingdom of Heaven upon the earth" (John Wesley).

> "Hark! the herald angels sing, / Glory to the newborn King" (Charles Wesley, hymn writer, leader of the Methodist movement).

> "It is well known that more people are drawn to the tabernacles of Methodists by their attractive harmony, than by the doctrine of their preachers. . . . Where the Methodists have drawn one person from our communion by their preaching, they have drawn ten by their music" (Robin A. Leaver, quoting Edward

A painting of John Wesley by English artist George Romney (1734–1802) at the National Portrait Gallery, London. Courtesy of Dcoetzee.

Miller in "The Hymn Explosion," *Christian History* 10 [1991], 17).

Unrest of soul seems to have been at least one of the motives for the missionary hiatus to Georgia under the auspices of the Society for the Propagation of the Gospel in Foreign Parts (1735–1738), an embryonic colonization effort under the direction of James Oglethorpe, a parliamentarian and social reformer. Accompanied by his brother Charles, John Wesley was sent to undertake pastoral duties among the English settlers in Savannah, as well as missionary work among the Indians. The British saw the colony as a buffer against Spanish aggression to the South and a relief for the nation's overcrowded debtors' prisons.

While the time in Georgia proved disappointing, marked by soul-searching, personality clashes, and moral intrigue, several contacts with pietistic Moravian missionaries, such as August Spangenberg (1704–1792), proved a portent of better things to come. Fleeing the possibility of legal proceedings in Savannah and largely discredited in the eyes of many Savannah citizens, Wesley returned to England where he met another influential Moravian, Peter Bohler (1712–1775). Bohler and Wesley had conversations over the latter's spiritual state, which he confessed was poor (the way of religious vibrancy through asceticism proved unfulfilling to him). He later recorded in one of his journals, "I who went to America to convert the Indians was myself never converted to God." Gathering with a group of Moravians in Aldersgate Street, London on 24 May 1738, while listening to someone reading the preface to Luther's commentary on the Romans, Wesley indicated that his "heart was strangely warmed. I felt I did trust in Christ, Christ alone for salvation."

"In the evening I went very unwillingly to a society in Aldersgate Street, where one was reading Luther's

preface to the Epistle to the Romans. About a quarter before nine, while he was describing the change which God works in the heart through faith in Christ, I felt my heart strangely warmed. I felt that I did trust in Christ, Christ alone, for salvation; an assurance was given me that He had taken away my sins, even mine, and saved me from the law of sin and death" (*The Diary of John Wesley*, 24 May 1738).

While scholars have debated the exact nature of Wesley's Aldersgate experience, it was truly life-transforming. Only two weeks later

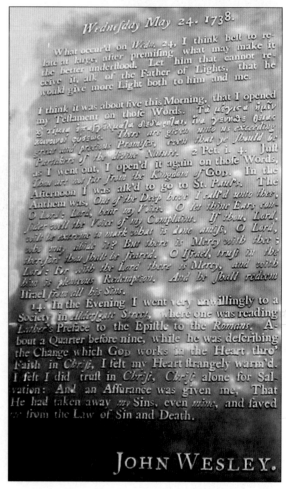

Monument in London to John Wesley's Aldersgate experience. Courtesy of Man vyi.

Wesley was in an Oxford pulpit proclaiming the necessity of being "born again." Wesley's new message proved too much for many in his own religious community; gradually he found himself excluded from Anglican pulpits. By 1739, he joined George Whitefield in open-air preaching. When he found that he could not renew the Church of England from within, he sought to create a grassroots movement from without to accomplish it. Wesley, the tireless worker, organized small gatherings of believers interconnected by circuit preachers who laced the country. Unwittingly, Wesley and others laid the groundwork for the organization of **Methodism** (North America in 1784, England in 1795), as well as the transdenominational, theologically reductionistic evangelical movement.

The theological perspectives of Wesley, as they differed from the main currents of his day, were instructive because they proved foundational not only in later movements such as the British and North American holiness movements and the Pentecostal/charismatic movements, but also in Methodism. Wesley fashioned an interpretation of theology reflective, in part, on his Oxford studies in early **patristics**, his rejection of ascetic/mystic piety and the perceived intolerable extremes of Calvinism. His passion was to preach a Christianity that was immediately practical, understandable,

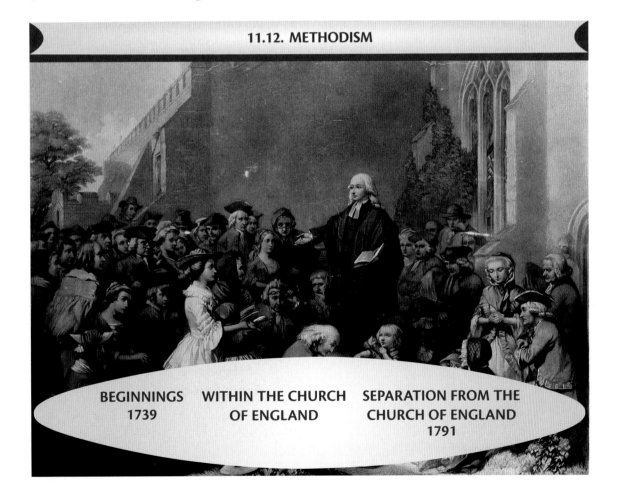

11.12. METHODISM

BEGINNINGS 1739   WITHIN THE CHURCH OF ENGLAND   SEPARATION FROM THE CHURCH OF ENGLAND 1791

heart-felt, full of missionary zeal, and devoid of high churchmanship. His was a theology of the imperative mood and the active voice, not the passive voice of Scripture.

Seeking to ground duty in moral responsibility, Wesley was adamant in his rejection of the Calvinistic notion of inability. He found in the concept of preparatory grace a universal diffusion of ability based on Christ's universal atonement that dissolved inherited guilt and inability, though it was not sufficient to do any more than render a person salvable, a way to resolve the dilemma of inability and responsibility. Placing the necessity of repentance before saving faith, he argued that conditions must be met for the latter to happen. Not only must repentance be in evidence, but it must also be maintained lest the redeeming grace of Christ be lost. Wesley urged his hearers to pursue holiness into a state of "perfect love" where the struggle against sin was greatly diminished.

In his concepts of sin, grace, and salvation, Wesley rejected the Calvinistic doctrines of human inability, divine election and predestination, and limited atonement as contrary to the gospel. Wesley feared antinomianism and thus sought a refuge for obedience in the possibility of loss of privilege. In the process of preaching a "practical, experiential" gospel, his opponents argued that he made the justification of the sinner tentative at best.

The Rise of Nineteenth Century Liberalism: An Embrace of the Enlightenment and an Attempt to Preserve the Faith

The Enlightenment tradition that merged in the eighteenth century disparaged the medieval notion of extrinsic sources of authority whether they be tradition or Scripture. The quest for authentic data upon which to make

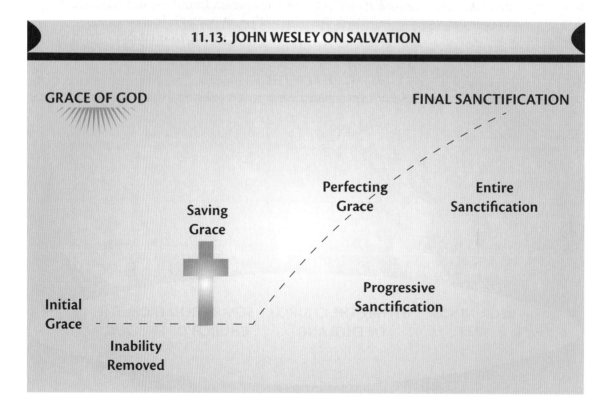

11.13. JOHN WESLEY ON SALVATION

GRACE OF GOD

FINAL SANCTIFICATION

Perfecting
Grace

Entire
Sanctification

Saving
Grace

Progressive
Sanctification

Initial
Grace

Inability
Removed

life's decisions turned inward. The time-honored place accorded the Bible was denigrated and inner faculties, such as the mind or intuition, gained a prominence not recognized since the pre-Christian dominance of Greco-Roman culture.

The epistemological form that the Enlightenment scholars early embraced was either the deductive approach to truth postulated by Descartes or the inductive theory of the British empiricist John Locke. The weakness of both approaches became apparent in the work of David Hume, who was able to demonstrate logically the irrationality of rationalism, threatening the entire endeavor of truth-searching. Seeking to deliver truth from the perils of skepticism and materialism, Immanuel Kant postulated a theory of knowledge that seemed effective. Truth was a matter of mental reflection and empirical fact-gathering. Kant's theory of knowledge dominated the nineteenth century. However, it raised serious problems within the religious community.

If religious scholarship embraced the philosophical insights of **Kantianism**—that truth was intrinsic in nature, rather than a divine disclosure from outside human experience—the issue of the shape and content of religious verities had to be revisited. The quest for a viable replacement for supposed archaic, outmoded conceptions in the midst of a concerted endeavor to provide an explanation of truth that would support the important role of religion, avoiding the perils of skepticism, became the task of serious religious scholars in the eighteenth century. Though socinianism, deism, and unitarianism are rightly conceived as attempts to define Christian faith in light of an emergent Enlightenment rationalism, there were some important differences in the religious revolt of the eighteenth and subsequent centuries; generally, the eighteenth century revolt held the Bible in high regard, perceiving it as a revelation from God, but reinterpreting it through a rationalistic lens.

The enterprise to establish Christian reli-

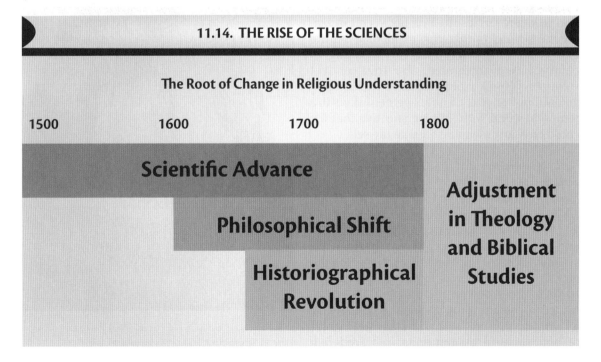

11.14. THE RISE OF THE SCIENCES

The Root of Change in Religious Understanding

1500   1600   1700   1800

Scientific Advance

Philosophical Shift

Historiographical Revolution

Adjustment in Theology and Biblical Studies

gion within a new theory about the nature of truth emerged in the late eighteenth century and created a new, significant tradition within Christendom. While the endeavor in itself was remarkable, and the motive for adjustment of Christian content commendable from the perspective that it was enjoined to defend the faith, it proved to be a failed attempt. And even worse, its redefinition of faith, at least in the view of antagonists, abetted the decline of religion throughout the West. What began with hopeful promise, the defense of the Christian faith, led to such truncated revisionism and distortion that it managed to lose the essence of religious truth, reducing it to mere morals, the fruit of the faith, not its essence. In reducing religion to moral codes and priorities,

Christian religion became little more than common grace dispensed through programmatic kindness. As a result, in more recent decades, Christianity has been confused with minority rights, international aide, self-help management techniques, and political activism. Religion's essence has become so redefined that in many circles the line between governmental self-help programs, religiously neutral benevolence agencies, and the meaning of church has disintegrated. The transcendent value of religion has been replaced with the singular importance of life management skills in a temporal world with little perspective that life could have any meaning outside the self.

Schleiermacher and the Discovery of the Subjective

The struggle to preserve Christian faith within a Kantian truth theory that rejected the Bible as the supreme authority in matters of faith and made it a subjective witness, became the serious task of nineteenth-century theologians. If the Bible was largely a discredited truth source, how could religion be maintained and what would it look like? The first to attempt to defend the faith in this new world of philosophical assumptions was Frederich Schleiermacher (1768–1834), often recognized as the "father of modern Protestant theology." Schleiermacher's concern was the preservation of Christian truth in light of the discrediting of traditional conceptions and the dangerous encroachment upon it by the secularizing tendencies of the Enlightenment. His blended heritages seemed to hold promise for the endeavor. He was influenced in his training at the University of Halle by Moravian piety and Kantianism. As a Reformed pastor, he was deeply influenced by the emerging Romantic Movement, itself a reaction to rationalism. After a short pastorate at Stolp, he became a preacher and professor at Halle. With the es-

A statue of Friedrich Schleiermacher at Palais Universitaire in Strasbourg, France. Courtesy of Ji-Elle.

tablishment of the University of Berlin in 1810, he obtained a chair in the theology department. It was Karl Barth who suggested the immense importance of Schleiermacher when he argued that he established a new era in the history of Christian thought, not merely a school of thought.

"The authority of Holy Scripture cannot be the foundation of faith in Christ; rather must the latter be presupposed before a peculiar authority can be granted to the Holy Scriptures" (Schleiermacher, *The Christian Faith*. 2.519).

Schleiermacher accepted the Kantian premise that knowledge was experienced-based as to origin and conceptualization; that is, religious consciousness took the place traditionally accorded to Scripture. Religion was the psychological awareness of divine existence with a resultant dependence; Scripture was secondary, an a-historical witness to truth, not truth encrypted into human language by divine fiat. Truth was community-oriented in nature; it came apart from the Bible; in fact, the religious community created its validity by dependence upon it. Human consciousness, church consciousness, determines what truth is.

"The beginning of His life [the life of Jesus] was also a new implanting of the God-consciousness which creates receptivity in human nature; hence this content

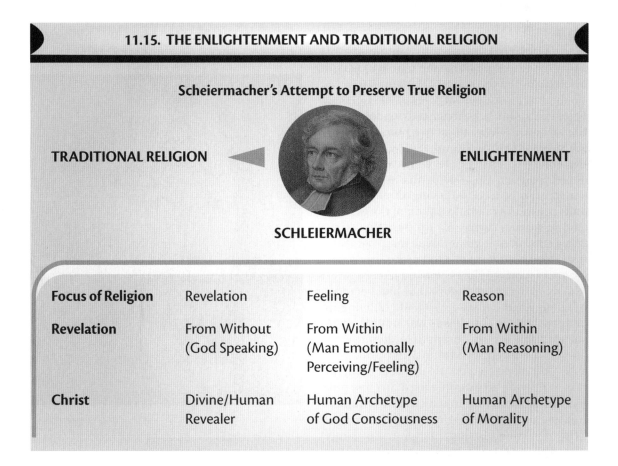

11.15. THE ENLIGHTENMENT AND TRADITIONAL RELIGION

Scheiermacher's Attempt to Preserve True Religion

TRADITIONAL RELIGION ◄ SCHLEIERMACHER ► ENLIGHTENMENT

Focus of Religion	Revelation	Feeling	Reason
Revelation	From Without (God Speaking)	From Within (Man Emotionally Perceiving/Feeling)	From Within (Man Reasoning)
Christ	Divine/Human Revealer	Human Archetype of God Consciousness	Human Archetype of Morality

and that manner of origin are in such a close relation that they mutually condition and explain each other. That new implanting came to be through the beginning of His life, and therefore that beginning must have transcended every detrimental influence of His immediate circle; and because it was such an original and sin-free act of nature, a filling of His nature with God-consciousness became possible as its result" (Schleiermacher, *The Christian Faith*, 2. 389).

Though Schleiermacher's system of defending religious truth began with a set of unprovable assertions, as all systems of explanation do, the issue of viability was determined rationally by consequences. Defining traditional religion as "fairy tales" (that is miracles, revelation, and inspiration), he believed that placing its truth claims in the realm of the subjective could preserve religion. While Schleiermacher provided the religious community with a way of preserving the realm of religious faith, he also planted the seeds of destruction.

In his monumental work, *The Christian Faith* (1821–1822), Schleiermacher defined the Christian faith as a subjective perception, not a historical reality, the value of religion being the ability to create a romanticist feeling of dependence on God. He denied a Trinitarian conception of God, believing that Jesus was an expression or manifestation of the one true God in human form only (at best the Trinity was a triad of a singular divine manifestation). Jesus was not so much God as he was a caricature of what godliness looked like. He was a Jewish, first-century figure that had become a religious ideal because of his life of living dependently upon God. Jesus was not the divine substitution for sin to appease divine wrath and obtain a reprieve from a just God. What this God-inspired person did for humanity was to provide an example for living in a cruel world frightened by injustice and inhumane treatment. The theologian could accord the title of "divine" to him, but he was simply one who revealed God in an extraordinary manner. While Schleiermacher's definition of the Christian faith was so a-historical that it could not be invalidated, it also could not be validated and was clearly a radical departure from ancient truth sources and interpretations.

"If we are to express ourselves with any accuracy we cannot say, either, that Christ fulfilled the divine will in our place or for our advantage. This is to say, He cannot have done so in our place in the sense that we are thereby relieved from the necessity of fulfilling it. No Christian mind could possibly desire this, nor has sound doctrine ever asserted it" (Schleiermacher, *The Christian Faith*, 456).

Georg Hegel and the Concept of Cosmic Progress

Philosophic advances indelibly influenced Christian religion in the nineteenth century,

A 1831 painting of Georg Wilhelm Friedrich Hegel by Jakob Schlesinger (1792–1855) at the Old National Gallery in Berlin. Courtesy of FreeArt1.

particularly in Europe. The increasing inadmissibility of another world, the personal existence of God, and communication from God to humankind caused truth searchers to find alternative paths to explain the world as it was and to offer hope. In the realm of a rational approach to knowledge, no one exceeded the influence of Georg Wilhelm Friederich Hegel (1770–1831). Hegel, attracted to philosophical idealism as reflected in **historicism**, introduced the idea of progress into world events. To Hegel the world was progressing toward a kind of philosophical triumph through an impersonal force, or spirit (the *Geist*), in developmental stages. This nonstatic but evolutionary theory of change through conflict, and this idealistic yet materialistic approach brought a crisis in the quest for objectivity, disparaged any help from the past, and offered new ways to explain religion in non-traditional venues.

In Hegel, the argument of history was rendered inconsequential, an understanding essential to the defense of traditional concepts of Christianity. The centrality of God was displaced by the quest for human consciousness through an impersonal power native to all that has consistently progressed through various stages of development Christianity being one of them in man's upward climb, but a surpassed stage in human development. Hegel's theory of the nature of truth as emergent became a very usable commodity that led to various directions: British; historicism; radical materialism in Marx, Engels, and Nietzsche; and existentialism in Kierkegaard, Sartre, and Camus.

The influence of **Hegelianism** can be seen in the work of Ferdinand Christian Baur (1792–1860), the founder of the **Tübingen School of Higher Criticism** (the term meaning an approach to the biblical writings that assumed the texts were untrustworthy due to overt error or unintentional confusion). Baur explained early Christianity as a conflict of Peter and James, reflecting the Jewishness of primitive Christianity, with Paul or Paulism, reflecting Greek Christianity as a later interpretation. These viewpoints coalesced through a variety of tensions into Catholic Christianity in the second

11.16. HEGEL AND THE HISTORY OF CIVILIZATION

Key to Change	The *Geist* (Spirit)
Motive of Change	Quest for Self-Consciousness
Process of Change	Nationalistic/Historicist
Method of Change	Dialecticalism (harmonization of opposites) Oriental Despotism vs. Freedom = Greek World Greek World vs. Freedom = Roman World Roman Despotism vs. Freedom = Christianity Christianity vs. Freedom = Secularism (Industrial Age)

and third centuries when most of the New Testament books were supposedly written. Hence, a Hegelian explanation of revisionism and synthesis through confrontation and conflict offered an interpretation of the Bible with naturalist assumptions undergirding it. The presupposition of early dating of the Gospels by later **Ritchlians** brought the decline of the Tübingen approach after the 1840s.

David Strauss and the "New" Jesus

The increasingly open ridicule of the Bible as a reliable truth source can be seen in the Tübingen scholar, David Strauss (1808–1874). Strauss received his early education for entrance into at the University of Tübingen under Ferdinand Christian Bauer at Ulm, where he was introduced to a critical approach to biblical studies. He was early a devotee of Schleiermacher's approach to reading the Bible, served a curate for some time, and taught in a seminary. However, he resigned from

pastoral duties to study under Schleiermacher at Berlin where he was somewhat attracted to Hegel's understanding of the dynamics of history. Resigning a lectureship at Tübingen allowed him to devote greater time to writing his controversial work *The Life of Jesus Critically Examined* (1835); thereafter, he became a private scholar publishing a two-volume work, On *Christian Doctrine*, in 1840. Whereas Strauss saw retrogression through the centuries of Christian orthodoxy, Hegelians, such as Bruno Bauer, envisioned progressive development.

"The more the disciples became convinced of this necessity, the more they made themselves believe that Jesus must have performed miracles . . . And so in their enthusiastic *fancy* [italics mine] without intending to deceive, they began to adorn the simple picture of Christ with a rich garland of miraculous tales, especially applying to him all the characteristics

A portrait of Ferdinand Christian Baur by Christoph Friedrich Dörr (1782–1841). Courtesy of Mewa767.

A portrait of David Friedrich Strauss. Creator unknown. Courtesy of Axel.Mauruszat.

Invitation to Church History: World

of the Messiah . . . till at length the real history was entirely covered, and in fact, destroyed by the 'parasitic plants'" (Strauss, *The Life of Jesus*, 3:383).

In Strauss's view, the life of Jesus recorded by the New Testament writers was not a reliable historical account of his life or claims; they were fabricated myths by overzealous devotees or acts of unconscious misperception. Strauss set in motion the quest to recover the historical Jesus, a portrait obtainable through the application of scientific assumptions. The effect of Strauss's work in the Gospels and Baur's work in the New Testament corpus as a whole brought ethical and existential categories into prominence, rejecting the role previously established by revelation and tradition. Strauss was remarkably influential in Old Testament studies as well as Wilhelm Vatke (1806–1882) who was critically important in the development of Julius Wellhausen's **JEDP** theory of the origin or collection of various source documents used later to create the books traditionally ascribed to Moses and the Israelites.

Ludwig Feuerbach and Religion
One of the trends in the redefinition of Christianity through the dominance of Kantian epistemology can be seen in Feuerbach, who moved entirely into the realm of the psychological, viewing religion as a human invention devised to bring stability to an unstable existence. Ludwig Andreas Feuerbach (1804–1872) received his education at Heidelberg and Berlin where he became a devotee of Georg Hegel. He accepted Hegel's concept of progress but later broke from his mentor. Instead of a progression toward an idealized form of religion, Feuerbach concluded that religion was a steppingstone in the drama of human progress that had become obsolete. He finished his educational career studying the natural sciences and gave up his early quest to serve the church.

Feuerbach expressed his views in three major works: *The Essence of Christianity* (1841),

Engraving of Ludwig Andreas Feuerbach in the 1872 edition of *Die Gartenlaube*. Courtesy of P. S. Burton.

The Philosophy of the Future (1843), and *The Essence of Religion (*1846). Taking a major theme from Hegel that history is the march toward the complete manifestation of the Spirit, an impersonal force relentlessly pressing forward in human affairs, Feuerbach identified the emerging force as man himself seeking his own individuality with religion as a passing stage on the road of progress. Religion then was simply man seeking to objectify his own existence; the existence of God was actually the existence of human consciousness. He argued, "Theology is nothing else than anthropology—the knowledge of God nothing else than a knowledge of man." If man could break the shackles of primitive religious thoughts, as well as philosophy, turning instead to the natural or social sciences, he would find in the study of himself the redemption long anticipated by humanity.

The influence of Feuerbach's approach to knowledge was a monumental influence in the dominance of secularism and materialistic theories of problem solving. For centuries humankind had sought solutions in otherness, now he was being invited to make the startling discovery that the real redeemer was within all the time. While the early Enlightenment thinkers did not doubt that God still had an important place and role in the universe, some of the later thinkers found no place for him in any objective sense. God did continue to exist, but he did so as man. Trust was replaced with management techniques and searching the inner labyrinth of the human psyche was salvific.

The influence of Feuerbach can be seen in the moderate existentialist thought of Søren Kierkegaard, though he transmuted it into a defense of his Christian views (here the method of accessing truth is the issue, not all his conclusions). His influence can certainly be seen in the more radical existentialism of Heidegger, Sartre, and Camus. In the realm of the development of the psychological sciences, Feuerbach's teaching is replete in the assumptions of Sigmund Freud (1856–1939) who postulated a behavior theory based on the inner self.

In terms of Feuerbach's contribution to the thought of Karl Marx (1818–1883) alone, his significance would be established as one of the most prominent shapers of opinion in the last two centuries. Religion was the mere projection of human appetites to Feuerbach, but it was a needless, damaging burden to Marx; it was "the opiate of the people." The key to understanding human aberrancy was the recognition of the social disintegration caused by class struggle; at the root of dysfunction was a socio-political problem, not the depravity of the human soul. Redemption could be achieved through the equalization of wealth in a classless society. At the root of all problems was social discontinuity, a tragedy that had come about through religion. Religion was the cry of humankind for help, but help was not found in religion; it was found in the dissolution of it.

The tendency in recent centuries to find within man the solutions to life's perplexities, with the complementary and progressive relegation of religion to archaic irrelevance or the reinvestment of religion with new perspectives and goals, is a fruit of the Enlightenment's pursuit of importance and relevancy with its redefinition of meaning and hope. Just as David Hume employed reason to demonstrate that reason without qualifications leads to ignorance and skepticism, Feuerbach and his followers, demonstrated the enormous destructive consequences of confusing theology with anthropology. Man has not learned the lesson that it is not our duty to aspire to replace God with ourselves, but to humble ourselves before he who alone is God.

Albrecht Ritschl and the Ritschlian School

Albrecht Ritschl (1822–1889) received most of his academic training at the University

A photograph of Albrecht Ritschl (1822–1889). Courtesy of Adam sk.

of Tübingen where F. C. Baur introduced him favorably to Hegelianism and personally shaped his early views as to the origin of early Christianity. Later, as professor of evangelical theology at Bonn, he rejected his mentor's views and the Tübingen approach to New Testament criticism, finding the sharp antithesis between Peter and Paul untenable.

"The origin of the Person of Christ—how His Person attained the form in which it presents itself to our ethical and religious apprehension—is not a subject of theological inquiry, because the problem transcends all inquiry. What ecclesiastical tradition offers us in this connection is obscure in itself, and therefore is not fitted to make anything clear. As Bearer of the perfect revelation, Christ is given us that we may believe on Him. When we do believe on Him, we find Him to be the Revealer of God. But the correlation of Christ with God His Father is not a scientific explanation. And as a theologian one ought to know that the fruitless clutching after such explanations only serves to obscure the recognition of Christ as the perfect revelation of God" (Ritschl, *The Christian Doctrine of Justification and Reconciliation*, 451–52).

The approach adopted by Ritschl, and subsequent advocates of his view, was to view the Bible as containing the revelation of God, not as myth or fabrication by jaundiced devotees (Ritschlians recognized the need for objectivity, recognized the weakness of a subjective approach to truth, and sought to establish religion on an objective basis by taking a higher view of the Bible). However, the Bible was not an entirely trustworthy guide to religious knowledge because the original message of the Bible was trampled with accretions of errant Hellenisms and Babylonian mythology. Adopting a scientific approach, Ritschlians sought to extract from the Bible, from the layers of misrepresentation engrafted into it, the original and true message of God, that is, to peel away the barnacles that attached to the hull of the allegorical ship until the original was uncovered. Ritschl's attempt to recover in the revelation of God, the authentic Jesus, shows his attachment to Schleiermacher's subjectivity and Kantian's epistemology. He followed his mentor in identifying humankind's need of redemption by Jesus.

11.17. ALBRECHT RITSCHL

Liberalism and the Reduction of Christianity to Ethics

"Christianity . . . resembles not a circle described from a single center, but an elipse which is determined by two foci."

The Christian Doctrine of Justification and Reconciliation

Redemption

Ethics

"It is unbiblical, then, to assume that between God's grace or love and His righteousness there is an opposition, which in its bearing upon the sinful race of men would lead to a contradiction, only to be solved through the interference of Christ" (Ritschl, *Reconciliation*, 473).

The key to separating the unauthentic from the truth within the Bible was the person of Jesus, a christocentric approach. That which was found in the Bible consistent with Jesus in demeanor and teaching was reliable. However, the endeavor floundered on the anti-supernaturalist assumption that the real Jesus was merely a Jewish peasant who possessed remarkable insight into the intentions of God, intentions not understood by his followers, at least until recently. Jesus's message, real Chris-

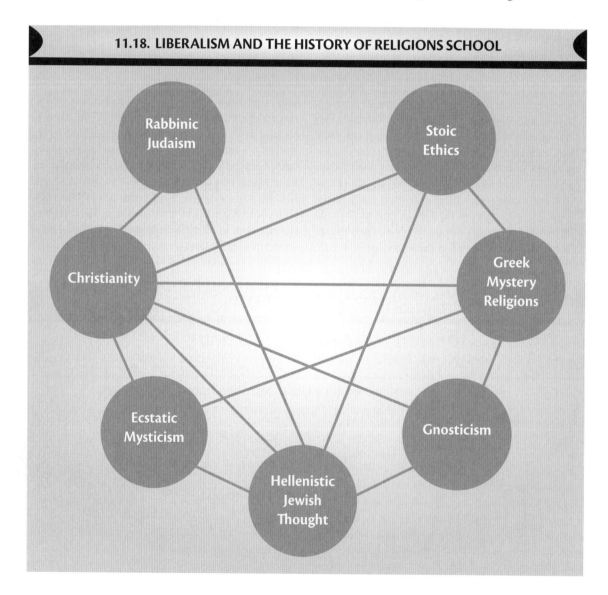

11.18. LIBERALISM AND THE HISTORY OF RELIGIONS SCHOOL

11.19. LIBERALISM AND THE HISTORY OF RELIGIONS

	ORTHODOXY	UNITARIANISM
Source of Truth	Reformation Empiricism Rationalism	Reformation Empiricism Rationalism
God	Theistic; plural, personal	Theistic; single, personal
Medium of Revelation	Supernatural Natural	Natural Supernatural
Person of Christ	God/Man	Archetypal Man
Nature of Sin	Derived and personal depravity Moral inability	Derived and personal depravity Moral inability
Atonement	Penal	Exemplary

tianity, was about community, the redeeming ethical efficacy of the kingdom of God in the hearts of humankind. God was love, all his attributes were subsumed under this singularity; concepts like divine wrath were simply "sub-Christian" to him. The Christian faith in the teachings of Ritschl and his followers, such as Adolf von Harnack (1851–1930) and Wilhelm von Herrmann (1846–1922) were merely moralities.

Hermann Gunkel and the History of Religions School

From 1880–1920 a group of German biblical scholars, given the availability of extensive knowledge of various religions and cultures, formulated an approach through comparative analysis. The view had echoes of seventeenth-

A photograph of German theologian Hermann Gunkel.
Courtesy of Jvarhaug.

century deism and unitarianism in that true religion was defined as the commonalities between religions and the discontinuities as unimportant and ancillary. This coterie of scholars reacted against the Ritchlians who sought to build theology from the firm ground of historical analysis, but whose conclusions seemed arbitrary and historically indefensible.

The work of Old Testament scholars such as Hermann Gunkel (1862–1932), Ernst Troeltsch (1865–1923), and Wilhelm Bousset (1865–1920) identified the fact that Israel's religion was shaped by its surrounding cultures. This insight, coupled with the knowledge of non-Christian religions, the assumption of **developmentalism**, and a Hegelian embrace of progress through struggle, became the gird for the definition of the true essence of religion. The general conclusions drawn by these scholars were that all religions, including Christianity, was context-situated and, therefore, not absolutely truthful assertions, since the content of Christian faith was shaped by other Near Eastern religions. Jesus was a historical figure, but not as depicted in the New Testament writings, and Paul borrowed heavily from **Gnosticism** and pagan **mystery religions** and restructured (i.e., perverted) primitive Christianity.

GLOSSARY OF TERMS

Cartesians: The term assigned to the approach to knowledge acquisition advocated by René Descartes, the seventeenth-century mathematician/philosopher. Those who embrace his method of knowing would argue that there are three realms of knowledge: the mental, the material, and the supernatural. The material can be known through mental deduction based upon divine postulates in the mind and through reflection.

Categorical Imperative: the moral assumption advocated by Immanuel Kant that God has placed into humankind a sense of moral duty that functions as the way to know God. Kant's assumptions were that the Bible is not at all divine and cannot be known apart from human existence and that human morality is the standard of redemption required of God. Kant sought to preserve a place for religious life, but turned theology into morality alone, which proved destructive of it.

Deism: a form of religious philosophy between traditional orthodoxy and naturalism that rejected the immanence of God for a deity that was a distant watchmaker. God made the universe to operate by natural law, separated himself from it, and restricted knowledge of himself, limiting it to rational and empirical discoveries of the intricacies of his creation. Deists such as Herbert of Cherbury, John Biddle, and Benjamin Franklin viewed the essence of religion to be found in moral conduct. It is a form of the rationalist Enlightenment of the seventeenth and eighteenth centuries in religious dress.

Developmentalism (Evolution): a branch of the biological sciences that focuses on advances in the natural growth of the species. Based on the assumption of epigenesis, that all life sprang from a common source and progressed from simplicity to complexity, developmentalism was naturalistic in its explanation of animal and human life.

Enlightenment (Age of Reason): a movement begun in eighteenth-century Europe that emphasized the inner capacities of man (rational reflection, intuition) as opposed to external authority sources such as the church or the Bible to improve social and society performance. Strenuously opposed by the religious community as well as secular materialists, the Enlightenment spawned the modern era, a three-century experiment in the redemptive values of science and technology. Though highly successful in the technical realms, the venture collapsed under the weight of holocausts and wars, suggesting that the blight of human discord could not be remedied by social advances alone. The movement filled life with opportunities but emptied it of meaning, creating postmodernism.

Evangelicalism (Evangelical Movement): though the term has become difficult if not impossible to define, it generally has been a designation for Protestants conservatives who share a set of common attitudes and interests such as the importance of a religious conversion, the necessity of gospel proclamation, missionary passion, and transdenominational cooperative efforts. The roots of this ecumemical conservative enterprise were typically identified with the eighteenth-century Wesleyan and Whitefieldian religious awakenings in England or in North American revivalism either in the eighteenth or nineteenth centuries.

German Idealism: a philosophical/theological movement that emerged in the late eighteenth and early nineteenth centuries in reaction to the Kantian rationalism/empiricist approach to knowledge, arguing that truth is internal and personal. The mental or mind took precedence over the senses in knowledge acquisition and theology was reduced to the realm of natural theology. Representatives of German Idealism are Fichte, Schelling, and Hegel.

German Pietism: a religious movement that emerged in the eighteenth century as a reaction to the rationalistic tendencies in Germany within the Lutheran tradition. Pietists such as Jacob Spener and August Franke insisted that faith without subjective experience was dangerous, that a spiritual conversion was integral to biblical faith, that missionary activity was not an optional activity and that Christians should meet in small groups to encourage each other in Christian duties.

Gnosticism: a second-century heresy that elevated obscure and mystical knowledge over faith. A potent threat to the church, Gnostics promoted a radical dualism of spirit from matter, emanationism, a belief there is a plurality of gods with one semi-god creating the material world. Salvation came through secret knowledge involving asceticism, a denial of the incarnation of Christ.

Hegelianism: a philosophical approach to the nature of history proposed by G. W. F. Hegel. Of great significance to the Christian Faith, Hegel suggested that there is a linear, progressive, evolutionary development in human existence. Combining rationalism with a theory of opposites clashing (a thesis and antithesis, despotism and freedom), civilization is propelled ever-improvingly forward through an impersonal force (the *Geist*) toward a peaceful era of human freedom. This naturalistic theory of history challenged the Christian theory of human devolution and the value of the collective past.

Higher Criticism (Historical Criticism, Historical-Critical Method): an approach to reading the biblical writings that sought to understand their original meaning through the study of the historical context of their composition. Emerging in the seventeenth and eighteenth centuries, its attempt to discern the content of the Bible rested on questionable epistemological, philosophical, and theological assumptions that frequently led to a denial of the orthodox, historic Christian understanding of the message of the Bible.

Historicism: a view of history that emphasizes the role of context, largely cultural forces, in the understanding of events. Prominently proposed by Hegel and later borrowed by Karl Marx, who used the theory in a materialistic direction, the theory argues, opposed to rationalist theories of progress, that cultural forces shape and determine the direction of the history of nations and peoples.

Humanism: as used in the twelfth and thirteenth centuries in Europe, the term signified an interest in the study of the humanities, often within the rising universities. It focus was not so much a denial of the authority of the medieval church, but an attempt to understand the truths taught by the church. While a leading contributor to the ethos of the sixteenth century reformations, it is not to be identified with the secular humanism that arose out of the Enlightenment centuries later.

Idealism (see German Idealism): a philosophical approach to the nature of knowledge, arguing that the structure of reality is immaterial or mentally constructed.

JEDP Theory (Documentary Hypothesis): an approach to reading the Pentateuch, the five books traditionally ascribed to Mosaic authorship, suggesting that the books were assembled from a variety of accounts, some parallel and some distinct, over several centuries and formatted in the present form by unknown redactors or editors. Julius Wellhausen postulated that five sources made up the Pentateuch: Jehovah emphases (J), Elohistic sources (E), deuteronomic sources (D), and priestly sources (P). Building on Enlightenment assumptions of knowledge imposed on the biblical texts, the theory was a potent threat to Mosaic authorship and biblical integrity. The theory has been largely discredited in the scholarly community of late.

Kantianism: an approach to the nature of knowing that is an amalgam of Descartes's rational, reflective deductionism and Lockean empiricist inductionism. Kant argued that knowledge of objects is obtained by an interplay caused by the acquisition of knowledge through the senses and reflection within the mind.

Lockeans: an approach to the nature or means of knowing postulated by John Locke in contrast to the Cartesian deductive method. Locke argued that the mind was a blank page and that knowledge was acquired through the five senses. His approach was called "sensationalism," and he is generally recognized as the "father of English empiricism."

Marxism (Marxist Materialism): a philosophy developed by Karl Marx that centers around a materialist interpretation of history and the Hegelian dialectic model of social change. Marx and Lenin argued that the blight of the human condition is attributable to social and economic disparity, clearly the antithesis of the capitalistic, free enterprise approach to societal organization.

Methodism (The Methodist Church): A major Protestant tradition that emerged in the context of the eighteenth-century revivals in England under John Wesley and others. The founders desired to reform the Anglican community that they served in view of the detrimental inroads of religious rationalism, but the reformist societies separated from the Church of England in 1784 in the United States and in 1795 in England to form a separate denomination that now claims over seventy-million members worldwide.

Moravians (United Brethren): a Protestant religious group with roots in the fourteenth-century Hussite movement. In the eighteenth century, a group settled in the Moravian region of Germany where they were protected and led by German aristocrat, Nicholaus Ludwig von Zinzendorff. The Moravians became leaders in the missionary movement of the church, becoming the first church, as a singular church body, to send out missionaries.

Mystery Religions: religious cults that flourished in the Greco-Roman era and in the early Christian period, each having its own sacred rites and rituals. Secrecy characterized these religious expression with disclosure made available only to the "enlightened." Many of these were eventually persecuted when the Roman Empire under Theodosius I made Christianity the sole religion.

Patristics (Patrology): generally the term indicated the study of the earliest church fathers from the post-apostolic era to Augustine.

Pietism: a movement that arose in Germany in the seventeenth and eighteenth centuries that opposed the rationalistic treads in the Protestant churches. Pietists, such as Spener and Francke, argued that true conversion was more than creedal assent; it was a change of heart, the affectional faculty of the invisible soul that integrally would lead to an interest in spiritual growth and missionary passion both nearby and abroad. The pietist movement became one of the sources of the modern Protestant missionary enterprise as well as the nineteenth century emerging evangelical movement rooted in the prior century's religious awakenings.

Renaissance: a cultural and intellectual movement that emerged in the fourteenth century in Italy and spread throughout seventeenth-century Europe, it celebrated a resurgence of classical learning. It proved to be a strong intellectual impetus for the sixteenth-century reformations in that its focus on the humanities carried an emphasis on self-understanding. While it did not question medieval authority structures, it did question how they were embraced. Further, it was an impetus for the later Enlightenment period that stressed the importance of individual belief, the search to find it, and the rejection of medieval assumptions of authority. Thus scholars think of the modern period as having two parts: early modern and late modern—eras that shared the same approach to the humanities but embraced diverse theories of authority.

Renaissance Humanism: a cultural and educational reform emphasis that emerged in the fourteenth and fifteenth centuries in reaction to medieval scholasticism, emphasizing personal affirmation of truth through a study of the sources of belief-structures, as well as the engagement of civic life through speaking and writing with eloquence and clarity. Its focus was on the study of the humanities with the new curriculum of university education, a shift from the scholastic preoccupation with rational explanation of medieval faith to the readoption and prominence of the Aristotelian method.

Ritschlianism: an approach to reading the Bible championed by Albrecht Ritschl who believed that the Bible contained revelational material though encrusted with errant concepts engrafted into the text over centuries of transmission, even misperception by its writers. The Ritschlians proposed a method for recovering the essential message of the Bible that became popular in classic American liberalism with its christocentric approach. Simply put, all that was found in the Bible in accord with what Jesus would have said or done was valid; however Ritschlians, German or American, viewed Jesus as merely an inspired and inspiring person.

Scottish Common Sense Realism (Scottish Common Sense Moral Philosophy, Scottish Common Sense Political Philosophy): a product of the Enlightenment quest to establish a foundation for ethics and virtue in the context of the general disparaging of the traditional source of authority, the Scriptures, as the Enlightenment approach as a whole turned away from external authority to internal sources. In common sense realism, guidance was not derived from the cognitive faculties, but from the assumption of an innate, instinctual capacity not attainable by education or practice, instantaneously and inherently placed in all humans by nature or the God of nature. The fact that some truths were intuitive appeared to be evidence that moral truths were also. This school of thought was predominant in the early nineteenth century of the United States with its cultural embrace of equalitarianism and individualism. It become the glue for corporate moral values so necessary in a democratic view of popular self-government, thus replacing the role of religion, even though some saw it as a support and buttress of Protestant religion in the context of unwitting pluralism.

Socinianism (see also the Racovian Catechism in complete glossary): a teaching concerning the Trinity of God and the person of Christ that emerged in the sixteenth century and was capsulated in the Racovian Catechism of 1605. Socinians denied the divine trinity asserting that Jesus was less than God; it reflected a revival of Arianism and was the harbinger of the religious Enlightenment. This teaching was behind the rise of both Unitarianism and Deism in England and in North America.

Tübingen School of Higher Criticism (Historical Criticism): a movement centered in a coterie of German scholars at Tübingen University in the nineteenth century that pioneered work in literary criticism, particularly in the field of higher criticism, which was devoted to the study of the origin of the biblical texts to understand the background of their origins. Presuppositionally freighted with the assumption that the Bible was a product of a natural history and human writers, at best inspiring but not inspired, the German scholars of this school did not believe the Bible to be the eternal word of God.

Unitarianism: a religious movement that appeared near the end of the eighteenth century in the United States, though a century earlier in England. Influenced by the Enlightenment assumption about the nature of truth and knowability, it rejected the orthodox doctrine of the Trinity, viewed Christ as an example of humanity at its best, and concluded that salvation was the fruit of moral rectitude achievable through watchful care and the pursuit of passionate duty. In 1819 William Ellery Channing,, pastor of Federal Street, Boston, delivered an address at the ordination of Jared Spark, then a Baltimore pastor and later president of Harvard College, entitled "Unitarian Christianity," defining the movement with clarity and precision.

Chapter 12 Outline

The Conservative Reaction to the Rise of Liberalism and Secularism in Europe
Søren Kierkegaard and True Religion
The Emergence of Conservative Scholarship
  German Conservative Scholarship
  English Conservative Scholarship
  Dutch Conservative Scholarship

The Nineteenth-Century Religious Situation in England
The Broad Church Movement
The Oxford or Tractarian Movement
The Anglican Low Church
Religious Nonconformity

Chapter 12 Objectives

- That the reader will describe the emergence of conservative Christian scholarship

- That the reader will define the Broad Church movement in the Church of England

- That the reader will distinguish between High Church and Low Church practices

- That the reader will describe the major evangelical contributions of Low Church Anglicanism

- That the reader will understand the contributions of conservative Non-conformists in nineteenth-century England and their influence in North America

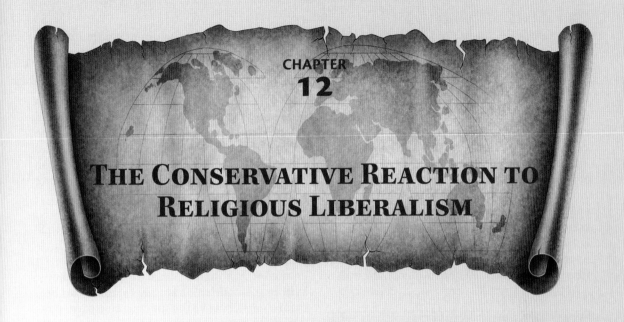

THE CONSERVATIVE REACTION TO RELIGIOUS LIBERALISM

T HOUGH SØREN KIERKEGAARD (1813–1855) was not recognized generally in his century as a significant writer and thinker; this would be accorded him in the subsequent century. The Dane made a significant contribution to the defense of traditional Christian views in the context of European engagement with **Kantian rationalism** and Hegelian progressivism. Kierkegaard was born, educated, and lived in Copenhagen, rarely leaving his native city. Financial security afforded him the life of a private scholar. He remained a devout Lutheran Christian throughout his life, though a critic of Danish state-church religion, fearing rational tendencies that might result in the loss of Lutheran piety and an upsurge of pseudo-intellectualism. Reflective in some degree of his melancholic disposition, he was influenced by his family's attachment to piety and the Lutheran concepts of sin, death, and judgment. His negative perspective on life sharply contrasted with Georg Hegel, his opponent who had an optimistic view of human progress.

The Conservative Reaction to the Rise of Liberalism and Secularism in Europe

Søren Kierkegaard and True Religion
Kierkegaard must be understood within the religious context of his day, particularly the methodology and nomenclature of his Hegelian opponents, though he may have read them only at a secondary level. Contrary to the anthropocentric and pantheistic tendencies of his day, Kierkegaard saw an infinite, qualitative difference between God and humans. Humans were infinite inferiors who had to recognize

their status. He postulated stages in human maturity, a semblance of a Hegelian structure of progress, but ethics was the initial stage and religion, separate from ethics, the final stage (the gist of *Fear and Trembling*). These insights led him to argue that true religion was not the embrace of certain ideas as emotionally detached truths; true faith included a heartfelt embrace that was emotional, personal, and subjective.

In fact, religious truth was subjectivity. It was the ascent to truths that were personally meaningful, but beyond the grasp of the intellect alone. In the personal apprehension of religious truths as true, one could find the true meaning of the self. Truth simply could not be

The Søren Kierkegaard statue in the Royal Library Garden in Copenhagen, Denmark. Courtesy of Jean-Pierre Dalbéra and Ramblersen.

obtained through detachment, mere intellectual rigor; it entailed the deepest experience of the subjective. Reason alone could not recover the loss of self, which was the discovery of the true self, it required a suspension of reason and a leap of faith that was beyond rational verity. True religion was the realization that the human pursuit of God needed the existential element. The absurdity of the Christian faith, and the focal point of it, was that the infinite God came to humankind through the incarnation.

In many respects, Kierkegaard writings must be seen as a defense of historic Christian truth stated in a contemporary, often confusing manner, at least to non-Hegelians. Within his context, it is easy to condemn him from a conservative perspective sensitive to rationalists and subjective approaches to truth. It is interesting that many of his twentieth-century critics, among them John Paul Sartre and Martin Heidegger, detached his philosophical views from his religious convictions, advocating the former while rejecting the latter.

The Emergence of Conservative Scholarship
Though the revisionist wing of Protestantism dominated European intellectual life in the universities, it would be incorrect to suggest that the rising assault against traditional interpretations of the Christian faith met with little significant resistance. **Enlightenment** assumptions would increasingly dominate the academy; but, the Christian enterprise was not at a loss for defenders with significant intellectual alacrity and literary output. However, the era's "winners" with their triumphant bias sometimes denigrated their opponents as intellectual pygmies who clung to a fading, discredited past.

History is frequently the story of the triumphant, but there is another side of the story, though a caveat is sometimes necessary. It is not always wisdom that defends a cherished truth by adopting an indefensible epistemology. This can be illustrated in the conservative mediating scholars in nineteenth-century Germany who embraced Schleiermacher's notion of verification, but not his theological conclusions.

German Conservative Scholarship

For example, Johann August Wilhelm Neander (1789–1850), a theologian and church historian, held a professorship at the University of Berlin after 1813. Influenced by Schleiermacher while studying at Halle, he experienced a religious conversion in 1806 and subsequently changed his name from Mendel to Neander ("born again one"). Unlike Schleiermacher, Neander embraced traditional expressions of the Christian faith and possessed an irenic spirit that did not see a conflict between reason and faith. Among his several literary accomplishments was a multi-volume history of the church and a reply to David Strauss's critical *Life of Jesus*.

Like Neander, August Tholuck (1799–1877) can be classed a mediating theologian within the university system of Germany because he adopted a conservative pietism but also embraced some higher critical tendencies; he did not see Christianity threatened by a critical approach to the Scriptures because, like Schleiermacher and Neander before him, he believed that true religion was a matter of the heart.

While Tholuck was orthodox, he argued that experience was more important than dogmatic belief. His teaching career began at the University of Berlin, but in 1826 he gained an appointment at Halle where through his teaching, preaching, and personal character he brought his views to prominence. His commentaries on Romans, Hebrews, and the Gospel of John established him as a conservative scholar; in addition, he also published a reply to Strauss's *Life of Jesus*.

One of the most prolific biblical scholars of the century was Ernst Wilhelm Hengstenberg (1802–1869). Initially educated in the rationalist tradition, he was influenced by Neander and

A photograph of August Tholuck sometime before 1877. Courtesy of JuTa.

Tholuck and through them embraced conservative Lutheran orthodoxy. His teaching career was spent at the University of Berlin where he strenuously defeated traditional views, edited a major theological journal, protested the theological views of Schleiermacher, and published numerous commentaries on the books of the Bible.

A student of Hengstenberg, Johann Keil (1807–1888), excelled as an Old Testament, conservative biblical scholar. With Franz Delitzsch (1813–1890), Keil coproduced a commentary series on the Old Testament. In addition to his scholarly activity, Delitzsch established a school for the training of missionaries to work among the Jewish population and translated Greek Scriptures into Hebrew.

In New Testament and patristic studies, Theodor Zahn (1838–1933) distinguished himself as a conservative scholar, teaching at Erlangen and Leipzig. Thrice nominated for the Nobel Prize in Literature, he wrote numerous commentaries and cooperated with Adolf von Harnack on an edition of the works of the church fathers.

English Conservative Scholarship
Educated at Trinity College, Cambridge, Brooke Foss Wescott (1825–1901) emerged as a scholar, obtaining the Regius Professorship

A photograph of Ernst Wilhelm Hengstenberg. Courtesy of Yorg.

of Divinity at Cambridge, excelling as a lecturer. He was renown for his New Testament textual studies that included a critical Greek text edited with Fenton Hort, and his several commentaries and theological works. In later years he often preached at Westminster Abbey. In 1890, he was appointed Bishop of Durham succeeding the scholarly J. B. Lightfoot.

Wescott met Joseph Barber Lightfoot (1828–1889) at Cambridge where a friendship was formed for life. Lightfoot was a New Testament scholar who sought to employ his scholarly propensities in the defense of the conservative faith at Cambridge and in the church. His literary productions were many, including several commentaries; he concluded his career as Bishop of Durham.

Fenton Hort (1828–1892), Irish by birth, was trained at Cambridge where he formed a triumvirate friendship with Wescott and Lightfoot. He concluded his career as the Lady Margaret's Professor of Divinity at Cambridge. Among his literary accomplishments were a critical edition of the New Testament in conjunction with Wescott, commentaries, and works on early Christian history.

It is clear that the defense of traditional Christian faith required an understanding of the early church; this triumvirate of Westcott, Lightfoot, and Hort spoke persuasively for the credibility of historic Christianity.

Two additional English scholars merit mentioning for their scholarly defense of the faith: Henry Barclay Swete (1835–1917) and W. H. Griffith Thomas (1861–1924). Swete followed Wescott as Regius Professor at Cambridge in 1890 until his retirement in 1915. Among his numerous works were a Greek text of the Old Testament and a commentary on the Revelation. Griffith Thomas received the majority of his education at Oxford, Christ Church College and, after two pastorates, became the principal of Wycliffe Hall, Oxford (1905–1910), an Anglican training center. Subsequently, he served as a professor at Wycliffe College, To-

A photograph of Fenton Hort. Courtesy of Billinghurst.

A photograph of Abraham Kuyper. Courtesy of ATX-NL.

ronto, Canada (1910–1920). Among his publications were numerous biblical commentaries and related works and *The Principles of Theology* (1930), a widely received doctrinal survey based on the *Thirty-Nine Articles* of the Church of England. His contribution to the periodical literature of his day was staggering.

Dutch Conservative Scholarship

An immensely influential conservative scholar/ statesman was Abraham Kuyper (1837–1920); at the turn of the century he rose to the status of his nation's prime minister. Kuyper became a minister in the Dutch Reformed Church, identifying with its conservative wing that eventually brought his suspension from the church and the formation of the Doleantie ("grieving

ones") movement. In 1892 Kuyper's Doleantie, then consisting of over 200 churches, merged with the Christian Reformed Church, an 1834 succession from the Dutch Reformed Church. Among his many accomplishments, he founded the Free University of Amsterdam in 1880 and served as a teacher of theology. As a leader of the Calvinist resurgence in Holland, as well as in the United States, his major writings included *Lectures on Calvinism* (1898), *Encyclopedia of Sacred Theology: Its Principles* (1898), and *The Work of the Holy Spirit* (1900).

Herman Bavinck (1854–1921), a colleague of Kuyper, was trained in the liberal tradition, completing his doctorate in 1880. After a brief pastorate, he accepted a teaching post at the Theological School at Kampen. When Kuyper became prime minister, Bavinck assumed his post at the Free University of Amsterdam. Among his writings that carried his influence abroad were *The Doctrine of God* (4 vols., 1906–1911), *Our Reasonable Faith* (1909), and *Philosophy of Revelation* (1909).

The Nineteenth-Century Religious Situation in England

The unique beginnings of the Church of England within the sixteenth-century Protestant Reformation in general, and the social/political context of the reign of Elizabeth I (1558–1603) in particular, caused the church to be unusually diverse, with polarized factions forming from its inception. Elizabeth's religious policy was to define the church in such a way that a degree of Protestant latitude prevailed. The church, as defined by its creedal instruments, was Calvinist in theological orientation, but did not embrace the narrowism of Genevan polity that would have disallowed ecclesiastical forms that included written prayers, kneeling at the **Eucharist** observance, and religious **iconography**.

Though the matters that polarized the Church of England traditionally concerned the issues of ecclesiastical polity, the nineteenth century witnessed the serious inroads of Enlightenment philosophical and social perspec-tives on religion. In effect, the Church of England experienced new tensions as it sought to maintain the unity of the visible church in the context of an increasingly potent liberal element. Generally, the church segmented or polarized without division into a High Church, which tended to embrace varying degrees of liturgical worship, and the Low Church, which eschewed a liturgical approach to worship and embraced the centrality of the Bible expressed in sermons of a plain, practical nature, with a conservative theology. The former was pulled toward two directions throughout the century—Anglo-Catholicism and German **liberalism**; the latter maintained traditionally conservative, often evangelical, attitudes and practices.

The Broad Church Movement

The distinguishing characteristic of the movement, largely though not exclusively in the High Church wing, was a willingness to embrace tolerance of theological perspectives (hence, also called the "latitudinarian movement." The perspective embraced the function of language in the Romantic philosophy of Samuel Coleridge (1772–1834), who had been heralded as the originator of this particular approach to defining religious significance. **Romanticism** arose as a response to the inadequacies

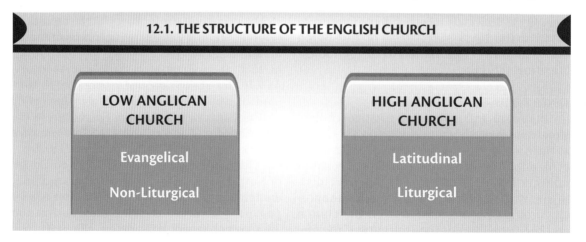

12.1. THE STRUCTURE OF THE ENGLISH CHURCH

LOW ANGLICAN CHURCH	HIGH ANGLICAN CHURCH
Evangelical	Latitudinal
Non-Liturgical	Liturgical

of Enlightenment rationalism that elevated the mind, but emptied the soul. In the place of the mind and scientific verification, romantics elevated the private and intuitive, the emotional and instinctual.

The leading spokesman for the movement was Arthur P. Stanley (1815–1881), who received his early education under Thomas Arnold (1795–1842), an early advocate of the liberal tradition in the church. Stanley later was appointed as professor of ecclesiastical history at Oxford and canon of Christ Church; in 1863 he became the Dean of Westminster. He thought that the rise of rationalism betokened either a decline or renewal of Christianity. However, fashioning himself in the tradition of renewal, he believed that to succeed the Christian faith required redefining, believing that he was standing at the dawn of the final evolutive stage of Christian development. Sounding like past expressions of the liberal tradition and Hegel, Stanley argued that the essence of religion was not to be found in its dogmatic teachings; its central truths had to do with morals, especially those exemplified in Jesus.

A painting of Arthur Penrhyn Stanley by Lowes Cato Dickinson (1819–1908) in National Portrait Gallery, London. Courtesy of Dcoetzee.

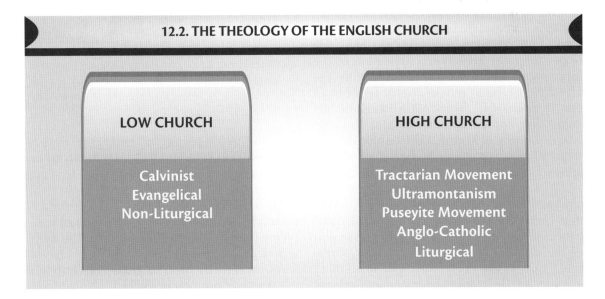

12.2. THE THEOLOGY OF THE ENGLISH CHURCH

LOW CHURCH	HIGH CHURCH
Calvinist Evangelical Non-Liturgical	Tractarian Movement Ultramontanism Puseyite Movement Anglo-Catholic Liturgical

The Oxford or Tractarian Movement

The movement emerged in the first half of the nineteenth century as a response to the decline of authority structures and rising secular trends in the church and state. It was called the Oxford movement because its intellectual center was in Oxford, the **tractarian movement** because of the prominence of its literary organ, *Tracts for Our Times* (1833–1841), and the Anglo-Catholic movement because of its tendency to embrace some Catholic emphases. Its adherents were pejoratively dubbed Puseyites and Newmanites.

Unlike the Broad Church movement, the Oxford advocates elevated patristic Christianity as the non-schismatic ideal. The movement's proponents viewed the "Catholic Church" as composed inherently of two branches within a singularity: Roman and Anglican. This allowed for some degree of latitude of beliefs, selectively choosing from variegated panoply of teachings to formulate creedal affirmation and liturgical practices. In some ways, obviously without the historical rootedness and doctrinal fidelity, it had affinity with the twentieth-century ecumenical unionism.

The most prominent early advocate of tractarianism was John Henry Newman (1801–1890), an Anglican priest attracted to the movement through John Keble (1792–1866). He began the most influential publication of the movement, *Tracts for Our Times*. With the "Tract 90," Newman announced the rejection of the "three-branch" theory of Christendom, arguing that Roman Catholicism was the only true expression of historic Christianity. He subsequently converted to Roman Catholicism and eventually became a cardinal in the church.

With scholarly acuity, Newman became an apologist for his church with his prolific writings. He articulated a theory of historical/theological development that allowed for expansion of the church's teaching beyond Holy Scripture, such as the decree of papal infallibility at Vatican I. He justified later Roman Catholic

A chromolithograph of John Henry Newman, published in *Vanity Fair*, January 20, 1877. Men of the Day, No. 145. "Tracts for the Times." Caricature by Sir Leslie Ward. Courtesy of Schoenstater.

teaching by suggesting an emergent, explanatory model of doctrinal development. In his view, the church was warranted in teaching beyond the limitations of Scripture as long as the newer teaching followed the criteria of principles that were consistent with and complementary to (but not in antithesis) the Bible, as well as a universality principle ("what has always, everywhere been taught in the church.")

Another prominent Oxford advocate was

Henry Edward Manning (1808–1892). Of a Low Church upbringing, he became a friend of Newman, leaving the Anglican community in 1851 for Rome and eventually obtaining the status of cardinal.

When John Henry Newman left the movement, Edward Bouverie Pusey (1800–1882) became the recognized leader of Anglo-Catholicism. Pusey was for many years a professor of Hebrew at Oxford University and canon at Christ Church. Unlike so many who left the An-

glican community, Pusey remained in the Anglican community throughout his life.

The Anglican Low Church

Though firmly within the Anglican community, a comparatively small group of churches embraced a less liturgical worship style while manifesting both Puritan and pietistic emphases. The doctrine and attitudes, though not the exclusivistic and separatist mindset, expressed within the Low Church took on the hue of a broader evangelical movement that emerged through the religious revivals of the eighteenth century in England, Scotland, and British North America.

The Anglican Low Church were in the minority numerically; however, they sustained a remarkable and enduring influence that has provided insights and motivations that has enriched the Christian cause throughout the world. Among the professional clergy a few examples are worth noting.

Perhaps no parish priest is more celebrated in the Low Church tradition than John Newton (1725–1807), whose later years were as positively remarkable as his early tragic ones. Born to a sea captain in a London suburb and enduring the loss of his mother at age seven, he was taken to sea by his father at

An 1882 caricature of Cardinal Manning from Punch, December 9, 1882. Courtesy of Malcolm Farmer and Magnus Manske.

An 1879 engraving of the vicarage at Olney where John Newton spent his first years as a minister and probably wrote "Amazing Grace." Courtesy of Lucien leGrey.

age eleven. After some years participating in the African slave trade as a seaman, including a stint of involuntary servitude in Africa, he became a ship captain, purchasing slaves and conveying them to the America's for sale. He was converted as a slave trader in 1748, but he continued in the trade without signs of remorse over it until 1755. Afterward, he obtained secular employment as a customs agent, but he felt a distinct call to the ministry. In 1764 he applied for ordination without university training by having three recommendations and a knowledge of the Bible and Latin. The wealthy Lord Dartmouth appointed him to his parish, Olney, the Church of St. Peter and St. Paul, as a priest. He ended his ministerial career at St. Mary Woolnoth, London (1780–1807).

Newton was a passionate preacher of the gospel and letter writer, never tiring of rehearsing the wonder of his redemption from the dregs of human depredation. Newton enjoyed the writing of hymns for his parishioners, composing the *Olney Hymnal* (1779) along with Thomas Cowper (1731–1800). Among his most recognized hymns are "Glorious Things of Thee Are Spoken," "How Sweet the Name of Jesus Sounds," and "Amazing Grace." Cowper, who struggled with depression and insanity throughout his life, gave the church, among others, "There is a Fountain Filled with Blood" and "Light Shining Out in Darkness" (now known for its opening lines, "God moves in mysterious ways, his wonders to perform; he plants His footsteps in the sea, and rides upon the storm").

A critic of the latitudinal and ritualistic tendencies within the Anglican community was John Charles Ryle (1816–1900). A parish vicar for thirty-eight years, he was appointed the Anglican bishop of Liverpool in 1880 with the recommendation of the Prime Minister Benjamin Disraeli. With a deep interest in the Puritan tradition, Ryle became the leader of the evangelical wing of his church. Ryle's emphasis

on biblical content in his preaching, the establishment and support of local parishes, and voluminous literary output left an enduring impact on the shape of evangelicalism in England and North America. Among his books are commentaries on the four gospels, historical biographies, and practical works (none exceeding *Holiness: Its Nature, Hindrances, Difficulties, and Roots* [1879]).

An evangelical cleric who had an influential ministry was Charles Simeon (1759–1836). Trained at Eton College and King's College, Cambridge, Simeon labored as vicar of Holy Trinity Church, Cambridge, sustaining a strong influence on university students, among them Henry Martyn (1781–1812), whose service in India included the translation of the New Testament into Hindi, Persian, and Arabic. Simeon's interest in foreign missions was expressed in the founding of the Church Missionary Society (1799), the Society for Promoting Christianity among the Jews (1809), and in advising the East India Company in the appointment of chaplains. Among a litany of missionaries sponsored by the Church Missionary Society were Robert Moffat (1795–1883) and David Livingstone (1813–1873), the latter being a national hero in Victorian England for his African

12.3. CHARLES SIMEON (1759–1836)

THE REV. CHARLES SIMEON, M.A.
Senior Fellow of King's College

And fifty-four years vicar of this parish; who whether as the ground of his own hopes, or as the subject of all his ministrations, determined to know nothing but
JESUS CHRIST AND HIM CRUCIFIED.
1 Cor.11.2.
"He being dead yet speaketh"

exploration. Simeon's most prestigious literary contribution was *Horae Homileticae*, a commentary on the whole of the Scriptures. His personal diary is a treasure in the pietist tradition.

A cofounder of the Church Missionary Society with Simeon was Thomas Scott (1747–1821). Scott became a cleric without the embrace of a living relationship with the Savior, but was influenced in the direction by the nearby parish priest, John Newton. When Newton moved to St. Mary Woolnoth, Scott replaced him at Olney before becoming a hospital chaplain in London. In London, he began a commentary on the entirety of the Scriptures in serial fashion that went through numerous editions and proved quite popular in England and America in the nineteenth century.

Though the Low Church was always a minority within the Anglican community, it did not lack in social interest, which proved an impetus for evangelical endeavor, instigated among the laity and supported by an active clergy. Quite exemplary in this regard was the Clapham Sect, a group of evangelical Christians (generally meeting in the London suburb of Clapham), which gathered to encourage one another in the use of their privilege for the promotion of the public weal.

Most prominent within Clapham Sect was William Wilberforce (1759–1833), a parliamentarian, who after his conversion in 1785 became a spokesman against the various forms of social injustice, principally vice and the African slave industry. His twenty-year campaign effort witnessed the official end of the trade in the British Empire in the year of his death. Additionally, Wilberforce aided in the creation of Sierra Leone, a nation for freed slaves, and a mission, the Church Mission Society (1799).

Anthony Ashley-Cooper (1801–1885), Earl of Shaftesbury, entered parliament in 1826 and immediately distinguished himself in the promotion of philanthropic endeavors. Among his interests was securing legislation for the

---

12.4. HENRY MARTYN (1781–1812)

"O God of the nations, you gave your faithful servant Henry Martyn a brilliant mind, a loving heart, and a gift for languages, that he might translate the Scriptures and other holy writings for the peoples of India and Persia: Inspire in us a love like his, eager to commit both life and talents to you who gave them; through Jesus Christ our Lord, who lives and reigns with you and the Holy Spirit, one God, for ever and ever. Amen."

Lectionary
Feast of Henry Martyn
19 October

A 1794 portrait of William Wilberforce (1759–1833) by Anton Hickel (1745–98) at Hull Museum in Kingston upon Hull, England. Courtesy of WonRyong.

better treatment of the mentally impaired and improving the labor conditions of mill, factory, and mine workers. Other concerns were the plight of children in the rising industrial complex (fictionalized in Charles Dickens's *Oliver Twist* [1838]), including their welfare, education, and health care. Alongside these issues were religious concerns, which the British and Foreign Bible Society, the Church Missionary Society, and the non-conformist Young Men's Christian Association addressed.

A remarkable lady who later identified with the evangelical party was Hannah More (1745–1833), a poet, novelist, and playwright. After some time in the literary circles of London, More gradually experienced a deepening religious awakening and was subsequently influenced by John Newton and William Wilber-

force. Her poem, *Slavery* (1788) was published at the time of the initial parliamentary debates on the slave trade. In addition to social commentary, she became distinguished for her philanthropic endeavors such as the creation of schools for the poor, and the founding of the Cheap Repository Tracts that continued after her initial work in the Religious Tract Society. She wrote best-selling works expressing evangelical convictions, supported the British and Foreign Bible Society, and became an icon of the evangelical women of her day.

Robert Raikes (1736–1811) founded the Sunday School Movement, recognized by some

An 1821 painting of Hannah More by Henry William Pickersgill at the National Portrait Gallery, London.

A statue of Robert Raikes at Victoria Embankment Gardens, London. Courtesy of Ham II.

Invitation to Church History: World

as the greatest lay movement in the history of the church. As editor of a reform-oriented journal in Gloucester, Raikes came to the conviction that the way to help the poor in the city's slums, particularly exploited and vulnerable children, was through education. On Sundays beginning in 1780, with the support of Thomas Stock, a Gloucester cleric, Raikes and others gathered boys, later also girls, for instruction in reading, with the Bible at the core of the curriculum. By 1833, directed by principally laity, the Sunday School Movement was ministering to over a million and a quarter children weekly, approximately 25 percent of the entire population of children.

Religious Nonconformity
While Anglicanism continued to be the official

state-sanctioned form of Protestantism in England, other Protestant religious bodies experienced religious freedoms though without the financial support of the state. Thus, outside the Church of England, various Protestant groups flourished and also Roman Catholicism re-emerged.

Following the Protestant triumph in seventeenth-century England, Roman Catholics were forced to retreat from public office into secluded enclaves. It was not until 1778 that Catholics were granted the legal right to own property and join the military (the context of these changes being the incorporation of largely Roman Catholic Canada following the Seven Years' War in Europe, the French and Indian War in British America, and the tolerant spirit of the Enlightenment). Additionally,

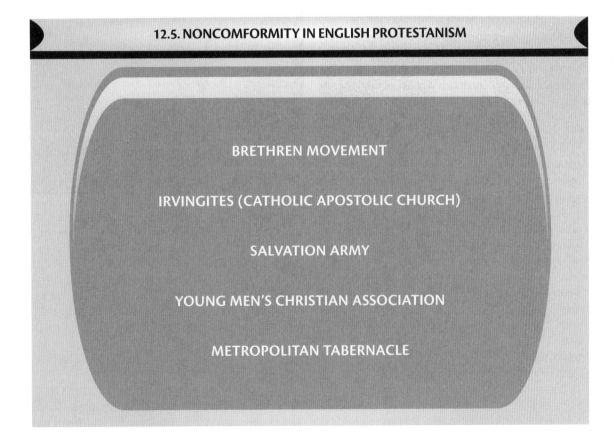

12.5. NONCOMFORMITY IN ENGLISH PROTESTANISM

BRETHREN MOVEMENT

IRVINGITES (CATHOLIC APOSTOLIC CHURCH)

SALVATION ARMY

YOUNG MEN'S CHRISTIAN ASSOCIATION

METROPOLITAN TABERNACLE

during the French Revolution, many Catholics fled to England fearing English repression less than the Jacobin revolutionaries, and in 1801 the United Kingdom of Great Britain and Ireland was formed, greatly increasing the presence of Catholics in the nation. In 1829 the Catholic Emancipation Act extended to Catholics franchise privileges as well as the right to hold public office. The Irish Potato Famine of the 1840s and 1850s witnessed the large immigration of Irish Catholics to the United States and also the migration of many into the large industrial cities of England, altering the social fabric of both nations.

An excellent example of the flourishing of English nonconformity was the emergence of the Brethren, or Plymouth Brethren. While John Nelson Darby (1800–1882) was not technically the founder of the anti-establishmentarian movement, he marked its history in a singular manner through his writings, leadership, and extensive travels. Born into financial security and social standing in his Anglo-Irish heritage, Darby completed his education at Trinity College, Dublin. In 1819 in preparation for a career in law, he also won the highest accolades for his study of Greek. Eschewing the legal profession, and in light of a spiritual renewal while at Trinity College, he chose to seek ordination in the Church of Ireland with a view to Catholic missions.

As a curate in County Wicklow, Darby became successful in his evangelistic endeavors. However, he experienced disillusionment with the state church when Irish Catholic converts were required by the archbishop of Dublin to swear allegiance to the monarch, halting his work. Resigning his post in protest, and at the same time recovering from an accident, he began to meet informally with a group of men, including Anthony Norris Groves (1795–1853), in 1827. Out of these meetings, and similar ones in Plymouth, England, the movement emerged in the 1830s.

Groves is frequently recognized as the "fa-

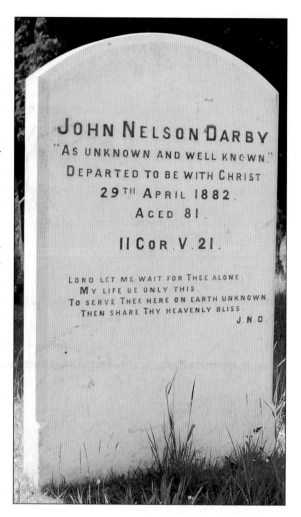

Gravestone of John Nelson Darby in Bournemouth, Dorset, England. Courtesy of Stöffu.

ther of the faith missions movement" in that without denominational backing and emphasizing a life of trusting God for resources, he became a missionary to Muslims in Baghdad, now Iraq, and later served in India. Groves's pamphlet, "Christian Devotedness," had a significant impact on George Muller and Hudson Taylor.

The emerging movement revealed many of the characteristics of reactionary protest, in this case against state-church authoritarianism, but also a positive desire to restore the church to primitive patterns and orthodoxy, an early emphasis of Groves. As a restoration movement, a quest to return to a New Testament ecclesiastical purity, Brethren eschewed the role of a single, pastoral leadership model for a plurality of lay elders; called churches, chapels, or assemblies, and made the "preaching of the Word" and the "breaking of bread" (the Eucharist or Lord's Table, observed weekly), the central foci of their meetings. Additionally, adherents worshiped in unadorned buildings, operated without a salaried staff, did not take offerings formally in the worship services, often sang without instrumentation, and required women to wear head coverings and remain silent.

This spiritually and Bible-centered lay movement can be found throughout the world. It has been marked by gifted teachers such as Darby, whose extensive travels, voluminous commentaries, letters, and Bible translations greatly popularized the movement, as did those of William Kelly (1821–1906), C. H. Mackintosh (1820–1896), and Samuel Tregelles (1813–1875). George Muller (1805–1898), who married Groves's sister Mary, became something of an iconic figure of the faith life through his work with orphans in Bristol, England.

The **Brethren movement**, emphasizing the right of all Christians to independently study the Scriptures and reach conclusions for themselves, experienced divisions from its inception. Darby, an avid Bible student, developed an understanding of the structure of the Bible known as modern **dispensationalism**,

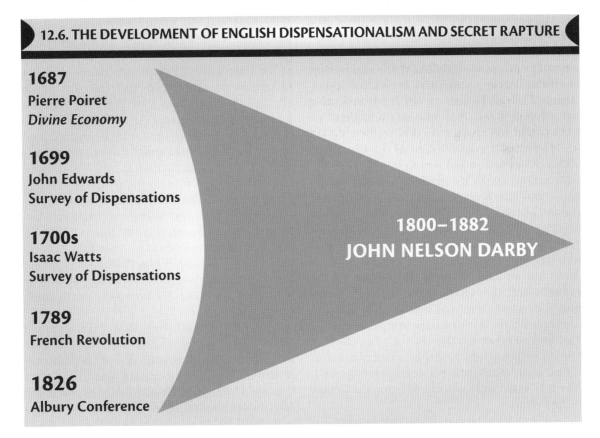

12.6. THE DEVELOPMENT OF ENGLISH DISPENSATIONALISM AND SECRET RAPTURE

1687
Pierre Poiret
Divine Economy

1699
John Edwards
Survey of Dispensations

1700s
Isaac Watts
Survey of Dispensations

1789
French Revolution

1826
Albury Conference

1800–1882
JOHN NELSON DARBY

The concept was to read the Bible correctly is to drive a wedge between the Old and New Testaments, separating Israel and the church, creating two distinct peoples of God, an earthly and heavenly; with two distinct programs, an earthly and heavenly; and with two distinct prophetic destinies, entailing earthly fulfillments of promises for the one and spiritual heavenly fulfillments for the other.

Darby went further than others in the 1840s and proposed the "church age" as a parenthesis in God's program, the doctrine of the **pretribulational** rapture of the church prior to an earthly millennium and a thousand-year reign of Christ on earth in fulfillment of God's promises to Abraham, the nation's patriarch. The church in the interim would experience bliss in heaven before it returned with Christ at the close of time.

Disputes arose within the movement over the limitations for participation in the Lord's Table. Darby took the view that only those who were properly separated from groups that would not agree to the unique views of a particular fellowship, but yet remained orthodox in faith and practice, should be excluded. This led to a division among the Brethren.

Exclusive Brethren followed the separatist views of Darby and William Kelly (1821–1906), who edited Darby's collected writings, while the Open Brethren followed a more relaxed policy advocated by Benjamin W. Newton (1807–1899). Newton, who had invited Darby's participation in the Plymouth assembly, disagreed further with him over church government, the validity of the secret rapture of the church, and the distinctions between Israel and the church implying that Darby's scheme embraced two ways of salvation, one for Israel and another for the church. The conflict between Darby and Newton became acrimonious, each manifesting a domineering spirit. Newton eventually withdrew from the Plymouth assembly.

Darby influenced the broader evangelical movement, the separatist branch, particularly in the field of dispensationalism and **premillennial**, pretribulational eschatology (and to a lesser degree in ecclesiology). His numerous travels, including seven trips to North America, the simplicity and piety of Brethren teachers in general, and the sense of declining cultural influence of Christianity created a fertile field for the propagation of Brethren distinctions, particularly in eschatology and in their theological organization of Scripture-content. Out of his influence in North America, the late nineteenth-century Bible conference movement emerged that in turned spawned the Bible institute movement.

Another nineteen-century nonconformist movement that has had a significant impact on the shape of Christianity, actually a forerunner of the pentecostal/charismatic branch of evangelicalism, was the Catholic Apostolic Church founded by Edward Irving (1792–1834). A Scotsman, Irving was trained for the ministry at the University of Edinburgh, licensed by the Kirkcaldy presbytery, served initially under Thomas Chalmers at St. John parish in Glasgow, and was appointed in 1821 to the Caledonian (Presbyterian) Chapel in London. Irving's popularity rose rapidly (a much larger church was erected for his audiences in 1827 at Regent Square) through his eloquent oratory in the London area. Given complaints about some heterodox views, he withdrew from the authority of the Church of Scotland in 1833 and founded an independent church that eventually embraced sign-gift practices, believing that the first-century functions could and should be a part of the church's function, particularly prophecy.

In 1824 Irving met Henry Drummond (1786–1860), a wealthy aristocrat and missions enthusiast; Irving interested him in prophetic studies and the result was the Albury Conferences held at Drummond's estate south of London beginning in 1826. Irving became convinced that an outpouring of the Spirit was near as a portent of the end of times that would include the renewal in the churches of "signs and wonders." From the meetings Drummond financed *The Morning Watch* (1829–1833) to

Edward Irving by Hamilton MacCarthy, 1867. Courtesy of Stephencdickson.

propagate prophetic themes. In addition to the Albury meetings, there were also the Powerscourt Conferences in County Wicklow near Dublin beginning in 1831. Hosted by Lady Theodosia Powerscourt (a wealthy widow) these conferences were dominated by early Brethren, including Darby, who shared Irving's prophetic interests, but not his attachment to a renewal of the extraordinary gifts of the spirit.

An added impetus to the credibility of the combination of end-time prophecy and spirit-gift renewal was the report of divine visitations in western Scotland in 1828. Of particular note was Mary Campbell, who heard Irving during a dramatic preaching tour and his assistant A. J. Scott. She became convinced that regeneration and the baptism of the Spirit were distinct, separate events with the latter evidence by tongues. She later moved to London and was an influence in Irving's church. Because of the prominence of spiritual gifts of prophecy and tongues at Regent Square, Irving was pressured to leave and gather a new church in 1832, himself now enabled to speak in tongues.

From Irving's Newman Street Church a movement emerged that became known in 1849 as the Holy Catholic Apostolic Church combining charismatic emphases, revivalist themes, and premillennial end-times teaching. The **Irvingite** movement was a significant forerunner of the pentecostal/charismatic movements of today.

One of the most prolific nonconformist humanitarian/missions agencies in the late nineteenth century, and one of the largest today, is the Salvation Army. Born into substantial wealth, William Booth (1829–1912) experienced the consequences of his family's bankruptcy and his father's alcoholism. His formal education ended at thirteen, and he served an apprenticeship as a pawnbroker. His religious conversion through Methodist auspices at fifteen altered his plans, and eight years later he became a full-time Methodist evangelist. His

THE

Christian Mission,

UNDER THE SUPERINTENDENCE OF THE

REV. WILLIAM BOOTH,

IS A

SALVATION ARMY

RECRUITED from amongst the multitudes who are without God and without hope in the world, devoting their leisure time to all sorts of laborious efforts for the salvation of others from unbelief, drunkenness, vice, and crime.

"I believe that is the only way we shall be able, in the enormous population of this ever-growing country, to maintain the cause of our Lord and Master—to welcome every volunteer who is willing to assist the regular forces; and to arm, so far as we can, the whole population in the cause of Jesus Christ."—ARCHBISHOP OF CANTERBURY.

"The working classes will never be reached but by an agency provided from among themselves."—THE EARL OF SHAFTESBURY.

Manifesto of The Salvation Army, May 1878. Courtesy of Jack1956.

William Booth and his granddaughter Catherine Bramwell-Booth during the 1904 motorcade. Courtesy of Magnus Manske.

success then led to the founding of the Christian Revival Society in 1865, later renamed The Christian Mission, working in East London among the destitute.

The designation of this paraecclesiastical ministry as the Salvation Army came in 1878, and the movement was organized along strident military lines with its own flag and officers (William Booth became General William Booth). Though initially received with hostility by the state church, the movement entered the global scene in the 1880s; in Booth's lifetime the ministry of gospel-heralding and social compassion reached into fifty-eight countries. In addition to a magazine that he edited and songs he composed for the army, Booth wrote a number of books. Among them was a social manifesto that became a best seller, *In Darkest England and the Way Out* (1890). He argued that the industrial revolution left England impoverished with a quality of life not superior to the underdeveloped nations.

The other prominent parachurch ministry that emerged in the late nineteenth century was the Young Men's Christian Association or the YMCA. Like the Salvation Army, it was created to address the negative implications of the industrial revolution from a Christian perspective and combined religious fervor with social concern. Like many thousands who came into the cities seeking employment, George Wil-

Sir George Williams, founder of the YMCA, by John Collier, given to the National Portrait Gallery, London. Courtesy of Dcoetzee.

volumes as the New Park Street Pulpit sermon series, *John Ploughman's Talks*, *Lectures to My Students*, *The Treasury of David*, *The Soul Winner*, *Spurgeon's Morning and Evening*, and numerous commentaries; and established Spurgeon's College to train pastors, as well as orphanages and colportage societies.

Spurgeon was reared in a Christian home though he did not experience redemption until the age of fifteen when he visited a sparsely attended Primitive Methodist chapel on a snowy evening in Colchester. Within the year (1850), he preached his first sermon and was called as the pastor of a small Baptist church at Waterbeach in Cambridgeshire. Four years later he was called to New Park Street Chapel, Southwark, London, to a church previously led by such Baptist greats as Benjamin Keach (1640–1704), John Gill (1697–1771), and John Rippon (1751–1836). His extraordinary giftedness quickly gave him name recognition though only nineteen years of age.

Within a year the first of his sermons was published and thereafter published weekly

liams came to London to work in a draper's shop. Appalled by the working conditions and the oft-degenerate social environment, Williams, who rose to become a financially secure department store owner, with eleven friends, collaborated to found the first YMCA in 1844 to promote a healthy culture for young, single men. In recognition of the enormous contribution that the YMCA movement made to English life, Williams was knighted by Queen Victoria in 1894 and was interred at St. Paul's Cathedral in 1905.

The contribution of nineteenth-century English nonconformity would not be complete without mention of Charles Haddon Spurgeon (1834–1892), heralded yet as the "prince of preachers," though he was a strict and vocal Calvinist Baptist. It has been argued that he spoke to over ten million people in his lifetime. He became a prolific author of such timeless

Tomb of Charles H. Spurgeon, West Norwood Cemetery, London. Courtesy of Perseus1984.

An 1885 painting of Charles Haddon Spurgeon by Andrew Melville in National Portrait Gallery, London. Courtesy of Dcoetzee.

with an enormous circulation; his sermons would become the "New Park Street Pulpit" series for the duration of his ministry. His popularity outgrew the chapel, so services were moved to Exeter Hall and later Surrey Music Hall where he preached to audiences in excess of ten thousand. By the age of twenty-two, he was the most heard pulpiteer of his day. In 1861 the congregation moved to permanent buildings, Metropolitan Tabernacle in Southwark, the largest church structure of the day, seating five thousand with standing room for another thousand. There he preached the remaining thirty-one years of his ministry.

In the later years of his life, Spurgeon became involved in what has been called the "downgrade controversy." In the 1880s he believed that the Baptist faith was being weakened by the intrusion of progressive, liberal religious ideas and withdrew from the Baptist Union in 1887 in protest. After his death, his wife compiled an autobiography from his letters and other literary remains in four volumes (1897–1900), a classic in its own right. Of England's greatest preachers (among them John Wesley [1703–1791] and George Whitefield [1714–1770] of the eighteenth century and Martin Lloyd-Jones [1899–1981] of the twentieth century), Spurgeon, frequently recognized as the "prince of preachers," was without peer in the nineteenth century.

GLOSSARY OF TERMS

Brethren (Plymouth) Movement: a movement born in early nineteenth-century Ireland and England that rejected the paralyzing effect of state-controlled ecclesiastical life and the formal ordination of leadership, preferring plural elder-directed chapels and assemblies, (not to be designated churches), emphasizing the centrality of the Lord's Supper in weekly worship, the importance of Bible explanation, a premillennialism/dispensationalist approach to reading the Bible, and the right of every Christian to independently study the Scriptures.

Dispensationalism: a way of understanding the Bible as a whole that developed in the nineteenth century. While the term is not easily defined, its advocates make a sharp, discontinuity or distinction between the biblical testaments: each having a distinct people (Israel and the church), each possessing distinct promises and programs (earthly and heavenly), and each having distinct destinies (fulfillment in an earthly kingdom, a millennium, and heaven). In contrast to a covenantal approach to biblical content and organization, dispensationalists reject the notion of a single people of God with a single destiny.

Enlightenment (Age of Reason): a movement begun in eighteenth-century Europe that emphasized the inner capacities of man (rational reflection, intuition) as opposed to external authority sources such as the church or the Bible to improve social and society performance. Strenuously opposed by the religious community as well as secular materialists, the Enlightenment spawned the modern era, a three-century experiment in the redemptive values of science and technology. Though highly successful in the technical realms, the venture

collapsed under the weight of holocausts and wars, suggesting that the blight of human discord could not be remedied by social advances alone, filling life with opportunities but emptied it of meaning, creating postmodernism.

Eucharist (the Lord's Supper, the Table of the Lord, Holy Communion, the Thanksgiving): a sacrament (sacred mystery) or ordinance in the various traditions of professing Christendom that Christ instituted to supersede the Passover ritual in remembrance of him who became for the church the final Passover, the final covering for human guilt and sin. The professing churches have been divided over the meaning of Christ's presence in the Eucharist and the fruit of its observance.

Hegelianism (Hegelianism Progressivism, Hegelian Dialectic): a philosophical approach to the nature of history proposed by G. W. F. Hegel. Of great significance to the Christian faith, Hegel suggested that there is lineal, progressive, evolutionary development in human existence. Combining rationalism with a theory of opposites clashing (a thesis and antithesis, despotism and freedom), civilization is propelled, ever-improvingly forward through an impersonal force (the *Geist*) toward a peaceful era of human freedom. This naturalistic theory of history challenged the Christian theory of human devolution and the value of the collective past.

Iconography: the use of religious art, statuary, depicting and representing religious figures used in liturgical worship.

Irvingite Movement: a nineteenth-century manifestation of the Pentecostal embrace of the extraordinary spiritual gifts that emerged in London in the 1830s under Edward Irving, who established the Apostolic Christian Church. The Irvingites played a significant role as forerunners of the modern pentecostal/charismatic movements, as well as an important part in the development of premillennial eschatology through participation in the early English Bible conference movements.

Kantianism (Kantian Rationalism): an approach to the nature of knowing that is an amalgam of Descartes's rational, reflective deductionism and Lockean empiricist inductionism. Kant argued that knowledge of objects is obtained by an interplay caused by the acquisition of knowledge through the senses and reflection within the mind.

Liberalism (Religious): a departure from traditional orthodoxy motivated by an attempt to preserve, defend, and perpetuate the viability and acceptability of Christian adherence in light of formidable philosophical, epistemological, and scientific evidence that brought into question the way the Bible was to be understood and the Christian faith explained.

Premillennialism: a view of the end times that argues that Christ will return in two phases: initially to fulfill promises made through the ancient prophets to literally rule over his people, and will do so for a thousand years in an era of unprecedented spiritual, cultural, and social advance; and subsequently to judge the earth and its inhabitants, inaugurating the eternal, spiritual state. Some, though not all, premillennialists interpret their view through the overarching grid of dispensationalism, making the millennium a time of fulfillment of divine promises to God's ancient people Israel, based on the assumption that the Bible presents two distinct peoples of God (Israel and the Church), separate programs for each, and two destinies relative to promise fulfillment

(the earth and heaven, one in time and one out of time).

Pretribulationalism: a view of end-time events that is associated with some forms of dispensationalist premillennialism. For advocates of this approach to futuristic events, those who embrace the concept of a literal reign of Christ on the earth for a thousand years, the issue is that of the seventieth week of Daniel 9, a seven-year period of precursory judgments on the earth. The question is: When will Christ return relative to this period? Pretribulationalists believe the Christ will return in the clouds to remove the church from the earth prior to an era of judgmental terror.

Romanticism (Romantic Movement, Romantic Philosophy): a movement in the latter half of the eighteenth century in reaction to the dangers of Enlightenment rationalism and the Scientific Revolution with their quest for truth primarily in the cognitive faculties at the denigration or diminution of the affective and emotional faculties of the human makeup. Like its counterpart, the Romantic movement, expressed religiously in transcendentalism and mysticism, finds the quest for meaning in humankind, the emotive and the intuitional, the balance or harmony with nature.

Tractarian Movement (Anglo-Catholic Movement, Oxford Movement, Puseyite Movement, Ultramontanism): a movement within the nineteenth-century English church enamored with the medieval church as an ideal and the return to the authority structures of the Catholic Church. Some questioned the validity of traditional authorities and some such as John Henry Newman returned to the Roman Catholic fold where he reached the status of cardinal. Called the tractarian movement because of a manifesto-type series of publications, "Tracts of Our Times;" Anglo-Catholic because of its High Church and Catholic orientations;

Oxford movement because its intellectual center in Oxford, England; Puseyite movement because Edward Pusey was a prominent advocate; and ultramontonism (meaning literally, "beyond the mountains") because it found the solution to the ecclesiastical issues of the day in Rome.

Further Readings:
Enlightenment and the Late Modern Period (1650–1900)

Beck, Lewis White. *Eighteenth-Century Philosophy*. New York: Free Press, 1966.

Barth, Karl. *Evangelical Theology: An Introduction*. Grand Rapids: MI: Eerdmans, 1979.

_____. *Protestant Theology in the Nineteenth Century: Its Background and History*. New ed. Grand Rapids: William B. Eerdmans, 2002.

Breghier, Emile. *The Seventeenth Century*. Trans. Wade Baskin. Chicago: The University of Chicago Press, 1966.

Brehier, Emile. *The Eighteenth Century*. Trans. Wade Baskin. Chicago: The University of Chicago Press. 1967.

Bromiley, Geoffrey William. *An Introduction to the Theology of Karl Barth*. Grand Rapids: William B. Eerdmans, 1979.

Brown, Colin. *Christianity & Western Thought*. Downers Grove, IL: InterVarsity Press, 1990.

Busch, Eberhard. *Karl Barth: His Life from Letters and Autobiographical Texts*. Philadelphia: Fortress Press, 1976.

Cassirer, Ernst. *The Philosophy of the Enlightenment*. Princeton: Princeton University Press, 1951.

Cragg, Gerald R. *The Church and the Age of Reason, 1648–1789*. Grand Rapids: William B. The Eerdmans, 1960.

Erb, Peter C. *Pietists: Selected Writings*. New York: Paulist Press, 1983.

Gay, Peter. *The Enlightenment: An Interpretation; the Science of Freedom*. New York: Knopf, 1978.

Hampton. Norman. *The Enlightenment*. New York: Penguin Books, 1981.

Halâevy, Elie. *A History of the English People in the Nineteenth Century*. 2d rev. ed. London: E. Benn, 1949.

Hampton. Norman. *The Enlightenment*. New York: Penguin Books, 1981.

Halâevy, Elie. *A History of the English People in the Nineteenth Century*. 2d rev. ed. London: E. Benn, 1949.

Hazard, Paul. *European Thought in the Eighteenth Century, from Montesquieu to Lessing*. Gloucester: Peter Smith, 1973.

Russell, Bertrand. *A History of Western Philosophy*. New York: Simon and Schuster, 1945.

Smart, Ninian. *Nineteenth Century Religious Thought in the West*. Cambridge New York: Cambridge University Press, 1985.

Welch, Claude. *Protestant Thought in the Nineteenth Century*. New Haven: Yale University Press, 1972.

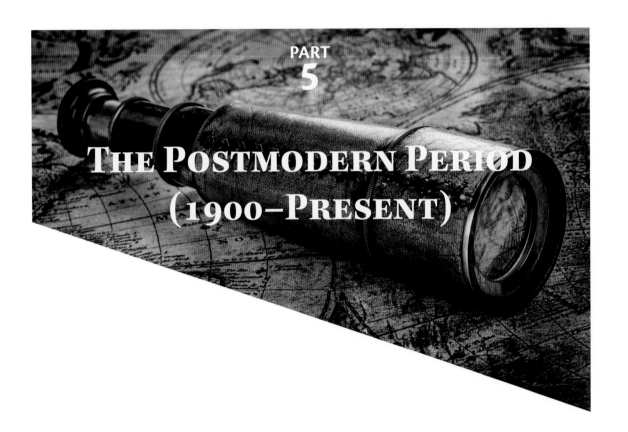

PART
5

THE POSTMODERN PERIOD (1900–PRESENT)

Chapter 13 Outline

Barth and Theological Revisionism

The Rise of Neoliberalism

The Fracturing of the Liberal Tradition

Roman Catholicism

The Modern Ecumenical Movement

The Charismatic Movement Worldwide
Within Roman Catholicism
Within Protestantism

Chapter 13 Objectives

- That the reader will grasp the important contribution of Karl Barth to the redirection of European theology in the twentieth century

- That the reader will understand the impact of Rudolph Bultmann on the twentieth-century liberal tradition

- That the reader will understand the struggles in the Roman Catholic Church to maintain its traditional orthodoxy in the midst of modernism and postmodernism

- That the reader will describe the intent and development of the Ecumenical Movement worldwide

- That the reader will understand the development, impact, and contribution of the Charismatic movements in Europe and beyond

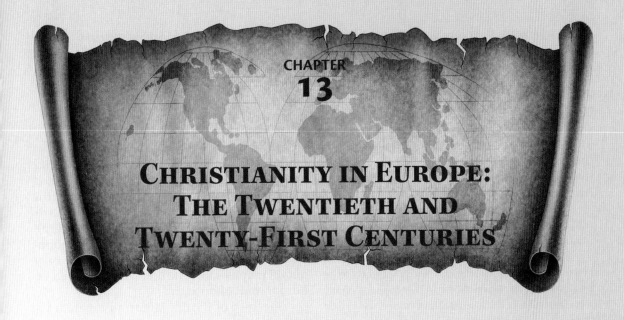

CHRISTIANITY IN EUROPE: THE TWENTIETH AND TWENTY-FIRST CENTURIES

T HEOLOGY IN THE TWENTIETH century, in a significant sense, was born in 1919 in the study of a church in Safenwil, Switzerland. Karl Barth (1886–1968), through the study of the book of Romans juxtaposed against the rhetoric of progress through science and technology while Europe was torn apart by war, became dissatisfied with the direction of his university religious studies under Wilhelm Herrmann and Adolph von Harnack, among others, as well as the direction of German theology inaugurated by Friedrich Schleiermacher at the beginning of the previous century. He was also troubled politically and socially by the identification of German theology with German militarism. Out of his work came *Der Romerbrief*, a commentary on Romans, which brought him to the lectern of several prestigious European universities and changed the direction of theological thought away from **classic liberalism** to what has been denominated as **neo-orthodoxy** or **dialectical theology**.

Barth and Theological Revisionism

Barth's theology was a reaction to the perceived inadequacy of the nineteenth-century revision of the Christian faith with its stress on the immanency of God, philosophical rationalism, and contextualized moralism. At one point Barth described nineteenth-century German theology as a human monologue with its own divinity, thus erecting a system in which God could not be found. Barth reversed the order of religious conversation. Religion was not a dialogue of man with God; it was a revelation of the transcendent God to man through the divine intermediary Jesus Christ! Unlike the liberalism of his training, he viewed humankind hopelessly and profoundly flawed. Barth then constructed a system with a transcendent God ("wholly other"), a system in which God must take the initiative to break through (reaching down) to humanity (the theology of the Word) in the Christ event (**theology of crisis**).

"Of this essence of God it must now be said that the unity of it is not only not removed by the threeness of the 'Persons,' but that it is rather in the threeness of the 'Persons' that its unity consists. Whatever is to be said about this threeness, it can by no means signify the threeness of the essence. Three-in-oneness in God does not mean a threefold deity, either in the sense of a plurality of deities or in the sense of the existence of a plurality of individuals or parts within the one deity. The name of Father, Son, and Spirit means that God is the one God in a threefold repetition; and that in such a way, that this repetition itself is grounded in His Godhead; hence in such a way that it signifies no alteration in His Godhead; but also in such a way that only in this repetition is He the one God; in such a way that His Godhead stands or falls with the fact that in this repetition He is God; but also precisely for the reason that in each repetition He is the one God" (Karl Barth, *Church Dogmatics*, 1.1.402).

"If we paraphrase the statement 'the Word became flesh by 'the Word assumed flesh,' we guard against the misinterpretation already mentioned, that in the incarnation the Word ceases to be entirely Himself and equal to Himself, i.e., in the full sense of Word of God. God cannot cease to be God. The incarnation is inconceivable, but it is not absurd, and it must not be explained as an absurdity. The inconceivable fact in it is that without ceasing to be God the Word of God is among us in such a way that He takes over human being, which is His creature, into His own being and to that extent makes it His own being" (Karl Barth, *Church Dogmatics*, 1.2.160).

"For me the Word of God is a happening, not a thing. Therefore the Bible must become the Word of God, and it does this through the word of the Spirit. Inspiration is not an attribute of Scripture but an event in which God uses the Scripture to communicate revelation" (Godsey, ed. Karl Barth's *Table Talk*, 26).

Barth was criticized by the liberal tradition for his conservative theological maneuvering and by the conservative tradition for his lack of absolutism in authority and theological content. It may be accurate to say that Barth viewed the dike of liberalism, holding back the waters of secularism and atheism, as hopelessly cracking, but his alternative at best only put off momentarily the breaking of the dike in Europe and America.

The root of Barth's failure to create a viable alternative to liberalism (except for himself, as well Dietrich Bonhoeffer [1906–1945], and Thomas Torrance [1913–2007], among

An image from a 1986 stamp honoring Karl Barth (1886–1968). Courtesy of Paulae.

others) lay in his theory of the authentication of faith. Being no **inerrantist**, Barth believed that the Bible only became the Word of God in an existential encounter with Jesus Christ, and, at a particular moment, with a text of the Bible. Perhaps, without meaning to do so, he caused the message of the Bible to vary depending on what portion or portions did or

Sculpture of Dietrich Bonhoeffer (1906–1945) by Fritz Fleer in front of St. Peter's Church, Hamburg. Courtesy of Parexus.

did not become the Word of God to the observer.

Through a piecemeal theory of authentication, he discovered the content of theology, at times unsurpassed and unheralded by his conservative critics. Barth, shaken by the trauma of World War I, opened the door for a revisionist approach to theology in general, which is reflected in the role of natural revelation in the work of his disciple Emil Brunner of Zurich, Switzerland, and more radically in the work of Rudolph Bultmann. with whom he maintained a lively correspondence.

The Rise of Neoliberalism

While Barth cried for the return of Christian faith to the authority of the Holy Scriptures, his work proved to be only a temporal detour in the course of revisionism within the liberal tradition in Europe and North America. Barth sought to reinstate deity into theology and replace a moral Jesus with the incarnate Son of God (he believed John 1:14 was the guiding text in the rediscovery of the real Jesus). He also affirmed a social redemption and moral kingdom, a confused nationalism with a God-inspired, spiritual-in-essence salvation.

While conservative critics have, and rightly so, denounced some of his religious conclusions, such as his moral-triumphalist view of the atonement of Christ, his existential verificationalism, hues of universalism, and a redefinition of faith, Barth succeeded in redirecting the path of Christian faith. The flaw in his theology was in his theory of authenticating religious truth, leaving the possibility, which became a reality, that a variety of conceptions of the Christian faith could be derived. His insights proved him an advocate of divine revelation from a reformed theological perspective, but his methodology left Christianity with more subjective, less objective, moorings.

Barth saw the damage that the nineteenth-century theologians from Schleiermacher to Ritschl and Gunkel, among others, had caused in the "dike" that was holding back the vast lake of secularism that threated to overwhelm Europe in a sea of materialism. Despite Barth's best efforts, the "dike" burst and Europe was deluged with a flood of secularity and religious apathy. European cathedrals, once a symbol of the vitality of faith, became increasingly museums and relics with lessening attendance and marginal influence, fit only for tourists who could marvel at their architecture and appreciate the sanctity of quietude they offered for meditation.

The liberal tradition in Europe, refashioned in the 1930s and 1940s, was dubbed **Neoliberalism**, and sometimes **"realistic theology."** Leaders in this tradition attempted to come to grips with a theology that questions the notion of material, social, and spiritual progress, as well as the methodological insights emanating from Europeans scholars such as Karl Barth and Emil Brunner (1889–1966). European theology never regained a hearing in the public square, even with the nebulous revision of lib-

eralism that Barth outlined, undoubtedly because of the world war, the avalanche of secularity, and various post-war crises.

European post-Barth religious scholars had little influence in creating a coherent, cohesive intellectual movement in Europe to reshape and revitalize Christian faith, probably because of no agreed-upon criteria for the recovery of the essential content of the Bible; nevertheless, their influence recast the liberal tradition in North America.

A number of religious scholars have shaped the emerging new faces of liberalism in America. For example, Walter Marshall Hort (1895–1966), theology professor at Oberlin College, became a spokesman for the revisionist movement with the publication of *Realistic Theology* (1934), as well as H. P. Van Dusen and John C. Bennett at Union Theological Seminary, New York. Perhaps the most outspoken critic of old liberalism from within Neoliberalism was Reinhold Niebuhr (1892–1971), a Detroit, Michigan, pastor and later professor at Union

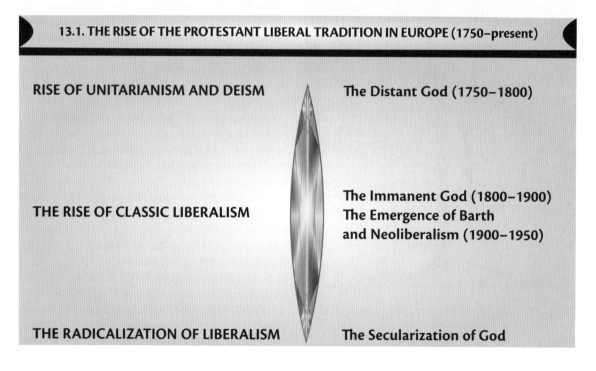

13.1. THE RISE OF THE PROTESTANT LIBERAL TRADITION IN EUROPE (1750–present)

RISE OF UNITARIANISM AND DEISM   **The Distant God (1750–1800)**

THE RISE OF CLASSIC LIBERALISM   **The Immanent God (1800–1900)**
                                            The Emergence of Barth
                                            and Neoliberalism (1900–1950)

THE RADICALIZATION OF LIBERALISM   **The Secularization of God**

Theological Seminary, New York (1928–1960). Niebuhr's criticism of classic liberalism, expressed in North America in Ritschlian terms, focused on its naïve **idealism** and progressive utopianism.

Disillusioned with the promises of the liberalism of his heritage, Niebuhr found an alternative to the weak anthropology of liberalism in the American Puritan Jonathan Edwards and the methodological insights and theology of Karl Barth. In so doing, he became a champion of "theological realism," generally known as neoliberalism or American **neo-orthodoxy**. In one of his most influential works, *Moral Man and Immoral Society* (1932), he recoiled against the concept of individualistic moral progress through self-love and self-resolution, taking a corporate, environmental definition of the human dilemma.

While cultural and religious realism may have been preferable to cultural and religious idealism, Neoliberal churchmen only slightly revised the liberal tradition of progress and overt optimism relative to the human condition. While Barth provided liberalism with a more serious approach and respect for the Bible, it was still a revelation of God through the lens of the rational and anti-supernatural. The Christ-figure was seen more than a better flowering of humanity, but the accordance of deity still proved unwarranted and anti-cultural. Jesus was the ultimate teacher, but more than an example of personal progress. Sin was the blighting reality of inordinate self-love, but its manifestation was corporate and individual, the former influencing the latter. Redemptive hopes largely found expression in an improved world and a blissful tomorrow.

> "Contemporary Christian proclamation is faced with the question whether, when it demands faith from men and women, it expects them to acknowledge this mythical world picture of then the past. If this is impossible, it has to face the question whether the New Testament proclamation has a truth that is independent of the mythical world picture, in which case it would be the task of theology to demythologize the Christian proclamation" (Bultmann, *New Testament and Mythology*, 3).

The Fracturing of the Liberal Tradition

In the late 1950s and 1960s the influence of Barth and Brunner upon theology waned with the growing prominence of Rudolph Bultmann (1884–1976), a New Testament professor at Marburg University for most of his career. Bultmann's approach to religion was a step back into the nineteenth century and was a blend of various methodological attempts, largely existential in nature, to discover the essential message, the **kerygma**, within the Bible. Barth broke from Bultmann in the late 1920s fearing his interpretative naturalism. Like Barth, Bultmann separated history into two categories, facts ("*historie*") and the story of the facts ("*ges-*

Reinhold Niebuhr(1892–1971). Courtesy of Vdjj1960.

chichte"). Assuming that the Bible was encased in cultural irrelevancies and myths, Bultmann proposed that the Bible must be demythologized.

The demythologizing of the Bible was accomplished through form criticism, a method of determining the type of literature and thereby establishing boundaries of how it was to be read. The subjective, existential nature of this way of reading the Bible might result in any number of determinations of the essential "myth" or message within the Bible; in effect, for Bultmann, the Bible seemed to have had little, if any, historical timelessness. In Bultmann, you have echoes of the nineteenth-century quest for the historical Jesus, which has resurfaced more recently in contemporary liberal circles.

The adoption of the Bultmannian approach to recovering the "authentic myths" that compose the revelation of God in the Bible led to the move in the 1960s and after in the passing popularity of radical theologies, mostly in North America. In retrospect, the liberal tradition lost its cohesiveness and fractured into competing theories and "kerygmas" not unlike the fracturing of its counterpart, evangelicalism.

In April 1966 *Time* magazine called atten-

Rudolf Karl Bultmann (1884–1976), a German Lutheran theologian and professor of New Testament at the University of Marburg. Courtesy of Jü.

tion to a theological development in America, the **God Is Dead Movement**. Rooted in Nietzsche's philosophical pessimism and Heidegger's existentialism, Thomas J. J. Altizer, a professor of religion at Emory University, Atlanta, Georgia, in *The Gospel of Christian Atheism* (1966) and Paul van Buren (1924–1998), then a professor of religion at Temple University, Philadelphia, Pennsylvania, in *The Secular Meaning of the Gospel* (1966); announced the end of the possibility of metaphysics in the wash of

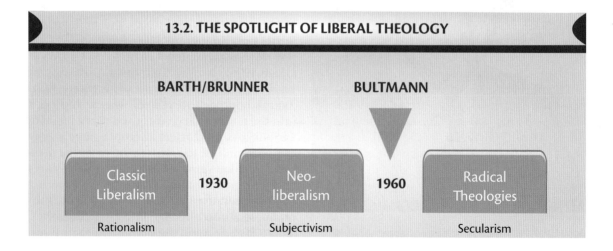

13.2. THE SPOTLIGHT OF LIBERAL THEOLOGY

BARTH/BRUNNER   **BULTMANN**

Classic Liberalism	1930	Neo-liberalism	1960	Radical Theologies
Rationalism		Subjectivism		Secularism

Western secularism. To such anti-theologians the "kernel" of God's relevance had been lost and God had been found to be meaningless and unnecessary. What was left from this de-mythologizing was a Jesus-figure who urged freedom from self-concern. Christianity was then linked with social change. Since God had been banished, the sense of guilt and despair need no longer bother humans; they were now free to live to their potential.

John Robinson (1919–1983), an Anglican bishop and Cambridge professor, in *Honest to God* (1963), argued that a transcendent God was invalid, but the notion of an innate principle of love was viable (this he derived from Paul Tillich's idea of the "ground of all being"), as well as the concept of religion-less Christianity. Harvey Cox, then professor of Harvard Divinity School, Cambridge, Massachusetts, in *The Secular City* (1965) argued that the church was not an institution, but individualized social otherness.

The quest for the authentic within the in-authentic Scripture resulted in quite a variety of theologies. Jurgen Moltmann (b. 1926), a professor at Tübingen University, combined elements of **liberation theology** and environmental concerns into a "**theology of hope**," (the title of his initial major publication [1967]), a gospel of reconciliation for the poor and the oppressors of the poor through the cross (*God in Creation* [1985]).

While Moltmann correctly identified the woes of culture seen largely in Enlightenment science, his solution to the human dilemma was far from orthodox Christian faith. Sin was rooted in science and the destruction of creation; the cross was a **panentheistic** mystical intrusion without any objective reality, creating an ongoing possibility of human expansiveness of potential, and salvation was to be found in the hope of unending conversations with any number of conflicting belief systems.

Wolfhart Pannenberg (1928–2014), a professor at Mainz University, found the au-

Harvey Cox (1929–) examining a Honeywell fragmentation device at the time of Vietnam bombardment (1973). Courtesy of Jan Arkesteijn.

thentic in the resurrection of Christ, in Christ as God-man, and promoted the "**theology of history** or resurrection." While Pannenberg rejected Barth's dismissal of natural theology, he believed in the reality of the resurrection of Christ as an inspiring hope for the church. In his most celebrated work, *Jesus: God and Man* (1968), he denied the Chalcedonian view that Jesus Christ in the incarnation was both God and man, preferring to think of Jesus through the renovating, revivifying effect of the resurrection, not the fact of the empty tomb as an accomplishment of Christ's atoning mission.

Both Moltmann and Pannenberg sought to invest in the credibility of the historical record of the Christian faith, but they have only succeeded in providing religious meaning that

Invitation to Church History: World

Wolfhart Pannenberg (1928–2014) in 1983. From the German Federal Archives. Courtesy of BArchBot.

cannot be called historic orthodoxy except in a vague sense.

Paul Tillich (1886–1965), a professor at Union Theological Seminary, New York, presented a psychological/existential interpretation of Christianity expressed in the "**theology of being**." Pierre Teilhard de Chardin (1881–1955), a paleontologist who sought to bridge evolutionary theory with religion, in the posthumously published *The Phenomenon of Man* (1959) argued that the spirituality of humankind developed, as the material being, through an evolutionary process to an "omega point," the assumption of human into divinity. His views have been called the "**theology of evolution**."

"Man's predicament, out of which the existential question arises, must be characterized by three concepts: finitude with respect to man's essential being as a creature, estrangement with respect to man's existential being in time and space, ambiguity with respect to man's participation in life universal. The questions arising out of man's finitude are answered by the doctrine of the Christ and the symbols applied to it. The questions arising out of the ambiguities of life are answered by the doctrine of the Spirit and its symbols. Each of these answers expresses that which

is a matter of ultimate concern in symbols derived from particular revelatory experiences" (Paul Tillich, *Systematic Theology* 3, 285–86).

""'Personal God' does not mean that God is a person. It means that God is the ground of everything personal and that he carries within himself the ontological power of personality. He is not a person, but he is no less than personal. . . . classical theology employed the term *persona* for the Trinitarian hypostases but not for God himself. God became 'a person' only in the nineteenth century, in connection with the Kantian separation of nature ruled by physical law

Bust of Paul Johannes Tillich (1886–1965) by James Rosati in New Harmony, Indiana. Courtesy of Musickna.

from personality ruled by moral law" (Paul Tillich, *Systematic Theology* I, 245).

Though various other kerygmatic theologies find expression in the liberal tradition (e.g., **feminist theology**, **political liberation theology**, and **black power theology**), one that influenced the evangelical spectrum of theology was **process theology** (sometimes called "Openness Theology" or "Process Theism"). Advocates of this form of theology, who were critical of secular, materialistic approaches to life as well as classic theism, combined evolutionary concepts in an attempt to understand God.

Process theology questioned the omniscience and sovereign power of God's action in the universe as traditionally interpreted. God was both being (static) and becoming, absolute and temporal. He did not know the future or control future events, but entered into them as they transpired through the process of "luring action," not persuasive control. The role of humanity in affecting social justice was that he/she actualized the presence of God.

Among the most prominent advocates of this attempt at conceptualizing God were John Cobb, Jr. (b. 1925), of the Claremont School of Theology, Claremont, California; Schubert Odgen (b. 1928) of the Southern Methodist University, Dallas, Texas; and Norman Pittenger (1905–1997), a professor at the General Theological Seminary, New York.

"The greatest single factor in determining that specialty is the way in which, with a high degree of awareness of what was going on, the man Jesus as the center of the event accepted his vocation, made his decision and his subsequent decision, and set about fulfilling the aim which was his own" (Norman Pittenger, *The Last Things*, 124).

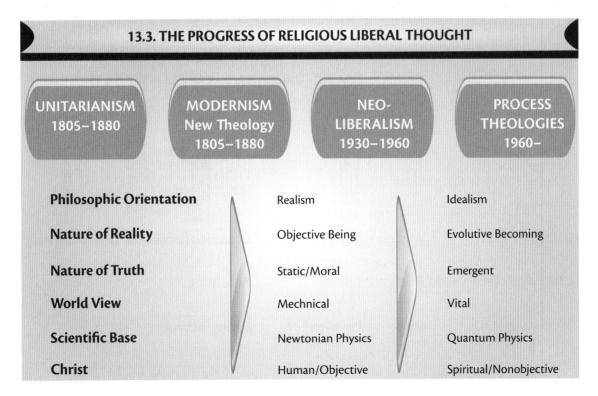

13.3. THE PROGRESS OF RELIGIOUS LIBERAL THOUGHT

UNITARIANISM 1805–1880	MODERNISM New Theology 1805–1880	NEO-LIBERALISM 1930–1960	PROCESS THEOLOGIES 1960–

Philosophic Orientation	Realism	Idealism
Nature of Reality	Objective Being	Evolutive Becoming
Nature of Truth	Static/Moral	Emergent
World View	Mechnical	Vital
Scientific Base	Newtonian Physics	Quantum Physics
Christ	Human/Objective	Spiritual/Nonobjective

Once enamored by the development of the sciences (intellectual, social, and technological), the liberal tradition found a justifiable basis for the rejection of traditional interpretations of Christian orthodoxy. Sciences no longer offered any hope for human redemption; in fact, science was now blamed for the precarious plight of the earth threatened by the advances of technology and the human race replete with social injustice, exploitation, and capitalistic greed. The solution for human redemption within the liberal tradition was to reinvent the sciences by enveloping them within a baseless set of assumptions about humanity, the earth, and redemption. This solution would be acquired by capitulation to pluralist values and incessant dialogue (now called "conversant") with a firm faith that the solution to humankind's emptiness was a matter of discovery, not divine disclosure within the perimeters of an ancient book, the Bible, and ancient traditions.

> "The primordial nature and the consequent nature of God are not two individual elements which, as joined together, form the deity. We cannot, at this point, make any meaningful analogies either to the union of the three persons in God . . . or the two natures in Christ. . . . We are speaking here simply of one God, who is represented as an actual entity and who manifests at least two ways in which his divinity is related to the world" (Robert Mellert, "What is Process Theology?", 45).

While the liberal tradition remains an influential, though waning, force in North American religious and cultural life, it has lost a great measure of its coherency on the shoals of **Bultmannian existentialism**. The liberal tradition lacks an agreed upon set of values, a

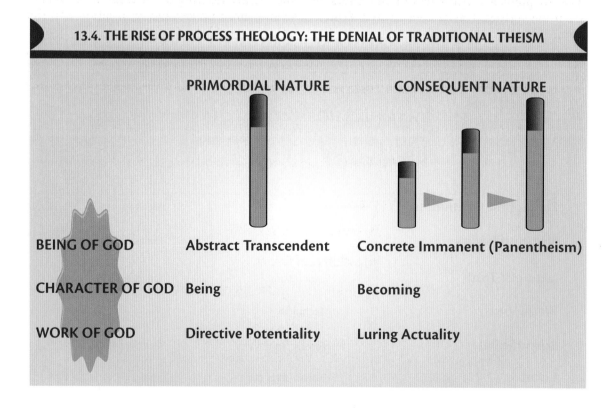

13.4. THE RISE OF PROCESS THEOLOGY: THE DENIAL OF TRADITIONAL THEISM

PRIMORDIAL NATURE   CONSEQUENT NATURE

BEING OF GOD	Abstract Transcendent	Concrete Immanent (Panentheism)
CHARACTER OF GOD	Being	Becoming
WORK OF GOD	Directive Potentiality	Luring Actuality

prescribed set of goals, and a clearly delineated program for their accomplishment. As such, it has many of the characteristics of its historical nemesis—traditional orthodoxy—as expressed in American evangelicalism. Perhaps like early evangelicalism/fundamentalism, the American liberal tradition was unified in its belligerency or antipathy to its counterpart. Neither the conservative tradition of Protestant faith nor the liberal tradition of it has been successful in Europe or North America in making religion integrally important in the values of its people.

Roman Catholicism

The **Roman Catholic Church**, being an authoritarian community of faith based on ancient creeds and conciliar decrees, had struggled, like its Protestant counterpart, with the inroads of the Enlightenment and its willingness to predicate truth within the limits of scientific verities. Unlike conservative Protestants, who claimed that their sole source for authority was the Bible, the Roman Church had additional authority structures that served as bulwarks against intrusive novelty. These included the tradition of the church, the magisterium, the conciliar decisions of the church over the centuries, and the ability of the head of the church under Christ to make definitive judgments. Thus, the stability of the Roman Catholic Church in Europe had been significantly augmented by the conservative reaction of the Roman pontificate to the anti-religious direction of forces emerging throughout Europe in the nineteenth and twentieth centuries.

During the pontificate of Pius IX (1846–1878), the church buttressed its theological defenses in 1854 by dogmatizing the Immaculate Conception of Mary, the idea that Mary, Jesus's mother, was conceived without the stain of Adam's sin. Such a mandate was an attempt to protect the uniqueness of Jesus in his person and claims, reacting to the trend in university scholarship to reject the incarnation and the uniqueness of Jesus Christ.

13.5. THE ROMAN CATHOLIC CHURCH IN THE NINETEENTH CENTURY

THE INITIAL STRUGGLE TO MAINTAIN ORTHODOXY

1854   The Immaculate Conception of Mary Dogmatized

1869–70   Vatican I

   (a) Defense against Liberalism

   (b) Syllabus of Errors

   (c) Dogmatizing of Papal Infallability

"When he speaks *ex cathedra*, that is, when in discharge of the office of pastor and doctor of all Christians . . . he . . . is possessed of that infallibility with which the divine Redeemer willed" (Vatican I, Session 4:4).

To further preserve the orthodoxy of the church, Pius IX announced an ecumenical gathering of the church, the first such enclave of church leaders since the Protestant disruption of the sixteenth century mandated the calling of the Council of Trent. Called Vatican I (1869–1870) because it was the first council to meet in the Vatican Basilica, the enclave considered the dangers of the intrusion of rationalism, socialism, and atheistic materialism and sought to formulate a response. One response was to enlarge the authority sources of the church by adding to Scripture and tradition the dogmatic authority of papal decrees or papal infallibility (the idea that when the pontiff speaks in his official capacity, *ex cathedra*, he sets forth binding regulations, stipulations, and definitions for the church). It is the idea that the papal office can contravene the findings of any council of the church; the issue of conciliar authority versus papal authority had remained unresolved since the medieval era and was a major issue that precipitated the Roman Catholic/Protestant schism in the sixteenth century. An additional element in the church's reactions to liberalizing intrusions was the *Syllabus of Errors* (1864), a list of viewpoints that were prohibited from being sanctioned and taught in the church.

The approach of Leo XIII (1878–1903) to the swirl of intellectual challenges in the church was less regressive than his predecessor. Known for his intellectual interests, he exhibited progressive tendencies, being particularly interested in a renewal within the church of the theology/philosophy of Thomas Aquinas, known as Thomism (actually it seems to have been more of a methodological approach to the acquisition of knowledge than Thomas's particular religious views in some cases).

The progressive turn of Leo XIII came to an end in the pontificate of Pius X (1903–1914), who returned the church to the ways of Pius IX as evidenced by the issuance of a *New Syllabus of Errors* in 1907. In retrospect the *Syllabus* was

An 1871 painting of Pope Pius IX by George Peter Alexander Healy (1813 –1894). Courtesy of Green Bonsai.

not so much the occasion for the exclusion of error in church teaching as it was the suppression of it; error went underground, finding safety behind lecterns and pulpits, but not in being published.

The pontificates of Benedict XV (1914–1922) and Pius XI (1922–1939) were overshadowed by the tragedies of the Great War and the global economic depression that followed. Pius XII (1939–1958) was a traditionalist in the ilk of Pius IX and Pius X. In 1950, he exercised his papal authority by stating dogmatically the doctrine of the **Immaculate Assumption of Mary**, the mother of Jesus, that is. Mary, having completed the course of her earthly life, merely slept, being not subject to mortal decay, and was taken to heaven, there to reign with her son near his very heart (while Mary is sometimes spoken of in the church as a coredeemer with Christ, it is not officially sanctioned in the church).

> "We pronounce, declare, and define it to be a divinely revealed dogma that the immaculate Mother of God, the ever Virgin Mary, having completed the course of her earthly life, was assumed body and soul to heavenly glory" (Pius XII, The Immaculate Assumption of Mary, 1950).

The growing influence and participation of Roman Catholics on the North American scene became evident in the 1928 presidential cam-

Inmaculada Concepción (ca. 1630) by Francisco de Zurbarán (1598–1664). Courtesy of Escarlati.

paign pitting Alfred Smith, the Roman Catholic governor of New York, against his Republican opponent, the Quaker Herbert Hoover. Though Smith met defeat and religious animosity characterized the election, he became the first Roman Catholic American to run for the nation's highest office. Americans did elect their first Roman Catholic president in November 1960, John F. Kennedy.

In the tradition of Leo XIII, John XXIII (1958–1963), a progressive, sought to reform the church. The dissent in the church, suppressed by the *Syllabus of Errors* and other pontifical maneuvers, began to lose its grip. John XXIII acknowledged past moral failures in the church and sought to build bridges with other religious groups. For further reform, he called the Second Vatican Council (1962–1965) and presided over its initial session, but died shortly thereafter.

The election of a successor brought Paul VI (1963–1978) to the church's highest office, inheriting a reforming council that, as a traditionalist, he saw of little need. As a result, the issue of doctrinal change was not substantively addressed, though the language of the documents published by the council was ambiguous at some points to placate the progressive in the church. For example, the documents of Vatican II announced truth in other religious expressions, but connected it in origin to its source in the Roman Church. The hostility often expressed by the church to Protestantism was noticeably nullified by the winds of ecumenicity so prevalent in that decade; Protestant were "separated brethren," yet "brethren" nonetheless.

Paul VI avoided any attempt at theological reform by asserting the right of papal review of all conciliar decisions. In retrospect, it was in a sense a reforming council because there was the enlargement of lay participation in the church, a change in the language of the liturgy of the church to the vernacular, an access of the laity to the Eucharistic cup, the end of meatless

Friday, and the removal of Saint Christopher, the patron saint of protection in travel, from automobiles.

Paul VI condemned artificial means of conception as an option for the faithful (as had Pius XI in 1930 in the encyclical *Casti Connubii*) and strongly opposed abortion by the encyclical *Humanae Vitae* (1968), arguing for the sanctity of life. In addition, Paul VI affirmed the celibate requirements for the priesthood in *Sacerdotalitis Caelibatus* (1967).

After the very brief pontificate of John Paul I (1978), John Paul II (1978–2005) enjoyed the second longest pontificate on record (only Pius IX's was longer) and was the first non-Italian pontiff since the second decade of the sixteenth century. John Paul II, a non-progressive pope,

echoed the opinions of Pius XII. Reflective of his strong conservative stance on theology and his passion that the church remain so, John Paul II, under the direction of Cardinal Joseph Ratzinger, published a new catechism for the church, *The Catechism of the Catholic Church* (1994).

"So how does the new Catechism of the Catholic Church handle the issues of justification and believers' assurance? Unfortunately, they are not legitimately addressed at all. In fact, justification is treated as something of a nonproblem, which leads me to confess a real degree of concern. The Roman Catholic reader of this catechism will learn little, if anything, of the Reformation debates over this matter or of Protestant sensitivities over Roman

Pope Paul VI during Second Vatican Council by Lothar Wolleh (1930–1979). Courtesy of Photini13.

Pope John Paul II during a visit to Germany, 1980. Courtesy of TharonXX.

Catholic teaching" (McGrath, "Do We Still Need The Reformation?" *Christianity Today* 38 [12 December 1994]: 31).

The Catechism of the Catholic Church (1994) states of Adam's first sin, "It is a deprivation of original holiness and justice, but human nature has not been totally corrupted: it is wounded in the natural powers proper to it; subject to ignorance, suffering, and the dominion of death; and inclined to sin—an inclination to evil that is called 'concupiscence.' Baptism, by imparting the life of Christ's grace, erases original sin and turns a man back towards God, but the consequences for nature, weakened and inclined to evil, persist in man and summon him to spiritual battle" (405).

The catechism did not address the weighty issues that have divided Protestants from traditional Roman Catholics. For example, the doctrine of justification was not addressed in so as to salve conservative Protestants; in fact, the doctrine was explained in such a way as to give the impression that it was not a divisive and contentious concern. On issues like the function of indulgences, the second great plank of sin's remedy; the existence of an interim state of purgation after death (purgatory); the authority of the canonical of Scriptures and its relationship to the function of tradition, not to mention the authority of papal pronouncements; the redemptive nature of the sacraments, as well as the number of them; the nature of human blight by birth-inheritance; the extent of sin's debilitation; the function of the priesthood as dispenser of divine, redemptive grace; the advocacy of progressive justification, as opposed to declarative justification through the imputation, not infusion, of merit; and the role of Mary, there has been no substantive change.

13.6. THE POPES SINCE VATICAN I

Pius IX (845–78)	———	Vatican I, "Syllabus of Errors," Infallibility
Leo III (1878–1903) Pius X (1903–14)	———	Return to Pius IX's ways, "New Syllabus of Errors"
Benedict XV (1914–22)	———	World War I
Pius XI (1922–39)	———	Encyclical against birth control
Pius XII (1939–58)	———	Anti-modernist, anti-Semitic, pronounced the dogma of Mary's assumption
John XXIII I (1958–63)	———	A progressive pope, called Vatican II to reform the church
Paul VI (1963–78)	———	Traditional pope, anti-modernist
John Paul I (1978) John Paul II (1978–2005) Benedict XVI (2005–2013)	———	Anti-modernist, traditionalist, sainted Pius IX (2000)
Francis (2013–present)	———	Rule still being evaluated

"During the 1980s, the Vatican, especially under Pope John Paul and Cardinal Ratzinger, has placed great emphasis on the importance of confession and has disciplined some teachers who have appeared to be undercutting Vatican interests. But polls of the Catholic laity indicate that these actions of the pope and his guardians of Catholic doctrine amount to little more than sticking fingers in a dike through which torrents of relativity are now pouring. The American Catholic church is awash with such amazing confessional diversity that its members are frequently indistinguishable from a variety of Protestants and even non-Christians" (David Wells, *No Place For Truth*, 121).

John Paul II robed himself with the public demeanor and statecraft of a progressive, but in reality he was not. An illustration of theological posturing is his beatification of Pius IX in 2000 in whose pontificate the church promulgated the **Immaculate Conception of Mary** (1854), published the *Syllabus of Errors* (1864), and called Vatican I (1869–1870) where the church added papal infallibility as a third bulwark against the intrusion of nontraditional beliefs.

With the death of John Paul II in 2005, Joseph Ratzinger was appointed to the highest office in the church as Benedict XVI. Ratzinger, the lead figure in the 1994 *Catechism of the Catholic Church*, was as firm a conservative as his predecessor. At the same time that the church appeared to be fortifying its traditional stances on theological and social issues, the church was struggling to maintain hegemony

13.7. STRUGGLE TO PRESERVE OTHODOXY IN THE ROMAN CATHOLIC CHURCH

1963–65	Vatican II
	(An openness to Protestant ecumenicism)
	Protestants = "errant brethren"
	Dialogue with other faiths encouraged Bible translation and reading permitted Mass in vernacular and lay participation
1967	The Duquene weekend and the beginning of charismatic renewalism
1968	*Humanae Vitae* (The condemnation of artificial means of contraception)
1978	John Paul II
	Personal charm
	Theological traditionalism
	Selective pragmatism
1994	*The Catechism of the Catholic Church* (a restatement of traditional theology)

over the minds of the faithful in an increasingly secular and materialistic culture. Its ability to attract youth was in steep decline, and many of the laity could not longer fully support the church's view on marriage and divorce, as well as its prohibition against the use of contraceptives and the practice of abortion. It was increasingly difficult to fill the clerical ranks, and a significant number in the church favored the dropping of the celibacy mandate. There was a rising voice for the ordination of women to the priesthood; in addition, many did not believe that the divorced should be excluded from the ranks of the faithful, and an enlarging constituency believed one could contradict church teaching and remain a faithful Catholic.

> "The Eucharist is thus a sacrifice because it re-presents (makes present) the sacrifice of the cross . . . it applies its fruit" (*The Catechism of the Catholic Church* [1994], 1366).

The Modern Ecumenical Movement

The essence of the Ecumenical Movement was that Christ placed importance on the unity of those who professed to be his followers. The practical effect of unity within Christendom would be the more effectively harnessing of enormous potential for the extension of the gospel. However, the difficulty arose with the lost of a cohesive affirmation of a theological core of beliefs that defined the meaning of the Christian faith, a set of goals to be obtained, and methodology to accomplish them.

The failure from a conservative perspective was not in the worthiness of the goal of Christian unity, but the loss of theological integrity by consenting members through unwarranted toleration and diversity. With the rise of liberalism within denominationalism, the meaning of the gospel became a subject of disagreement. The liberal tradition embraced the notion that sin was a function of social discontinuity, and the way to alleviate societal disintegration was

through programs to improve the social condition (e.g., elevating the education levels, and supplying health reform, anti-war activism, and human rights).

While these were issues that the Christian churches were called upon to address, the liberal rejection of the deity of Christ, blood atonement, and the necessity of regeneration through the Spirit had left it without the most important message in the world, at least according to conservatives. The liberal tradition, in rejecting historic Christian faith, was left with an emphasis on the fruit of faith, though at times they rejected the faith itself. The social work done by the participants of the liberal tradition was frequently excellent and highly commendable; yet the religious essence of its teachings was wanting.

The **World Council of Churches** was formed in 1948 in Amsterdam, Holland. It was a fellowship of religious groups with a deep interest in expressing the Christian faith through unity of endeavor; the WCC became an international agency with headquarters in Geneva, Switzerland. It is currently composed of nearly 350 religious bodies from some 150 countries, claiming to be a unifying voice for 590 million people. Membership is derived from most of the Orthodox Churches; the Anglican community; significant numbers of mainline denominations such as Baptist, Presbyterian, and Methodists; some Pentecostal bodies; and various independent groups. The Roman Catholic Church is not a member of the WCC, though it sends recognized delegates to many of its official meetings.

While gaining its impetus from nineteenth-century interdenominational cooperative missional endeavors, the roots of the World Council of Churches were in the **Edinburgh Missionary Conference** of 1910, chaired by the missionary statesman John R. Mott (1865–1955), a Methodist layman who led the Student Volunteer Movement for Foreign Missions and the World Student Christian Federation. Con-

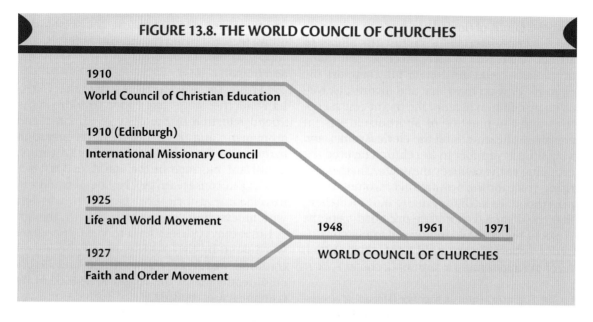

FIGURE 13.8. THE WORLD COUNCIL OF CHURCHES

1910
World Council of Christian Education

1910 (Edinburgh)
International Missionary Council

1925
Life and World Movement

1948   1961   1971

1927
WORLD COUNCIL OF CHURCHES

Faith and Order Movement

John Raleigh Mott (1865–1955). Courtesy of Materialscientist.

sisting almost entirely of European and North American delegates, the motto of the conference was "The Evangelization of the World in this Generation." This led to the creation of the International Missionary Council in 1921.

The actual formation of the WCC (1948) came in the wake of the tragedies of World War II as many awoke to the serious crises facing the global community. The WCC brought together two existing organizations, the Faith and Order Movement and the Life and Work Movement. The former, an organization committed to seeking religious unity through ecumenical dialogue, grew out of a conference held in Geneva, Switzerland, in 1920, a gathering of some eighty churches. Under the leadership of Charles Brent (1862–1929), an American Episcopal bishop, 400 delegates assembled in Lausanne, Switzerland, in 1927 to formally organize.

The Life and Work Movement focused on practical, social issues as extensions of the gospel and grew out of meetings in Stockholm, Sweden, in 1925 under Nathan Soderblom (1866–1931), the primate of Sweden.

The vision for the merger of the two organizations, creating the WCC, was cast as early as 1937, but the global crisis made it impossible until after World War II. The WCC was formally created in Amsterdam, Holland, and gathers in corporate sessions about every six to eight years. At the third such gathering, this one held in New Delhi, India, the International Missionary Council formally affiliated, as did the World Sunday School Association (now the World Council of Christian Education) at a WCC assembly held in Lima, Peru, in 1971. The latest of the international enclaves of the WCC, the tenth, took place in Busan, South Korea, in the fall of 2013; Agnes Abuom of the Anglican Church, Nairobi, Kenya, was chosen to be the first female moderator of its central committee.

Conservatives, while not opposed to the spirit of ecumenical unity, disparage the endeavors of the WCC, suggesting that the kind of unity embraced in these organizations has come at the expense of a denial of historic Christian orthodoxy. Also, the neglect of the traditional definitions of orthodoxy has led in their judgment to redefining the Christian faith and the consequent loss of the historic gospel. Conservatives believe that often the social agenda of the WCC is politically leftist in spirit with naïve underlying presuppositions about effecting change in the world. While the WCC does commendable social work, conservatives argue that without a firm, cognitive embrace of the historic gospel, simple social care alone is not the true gospel. At best, it is helping people in the improvement of their immediate social circumstance while confusing the immediate with the eternal.

The more theologically conservative, global counterpart to the WCC is the World Evangelical Alliance, a British evangelical cooperative organization dating to the mid-nineteenth century. The WEC works in some 129 countries and claims a constituency of some 600 million evangelicals.

The roots of cooperative religious endeavor emerged in the nineteenth century organizationally as early as the **Plan of Union** (1801) in North America, an agreement between the

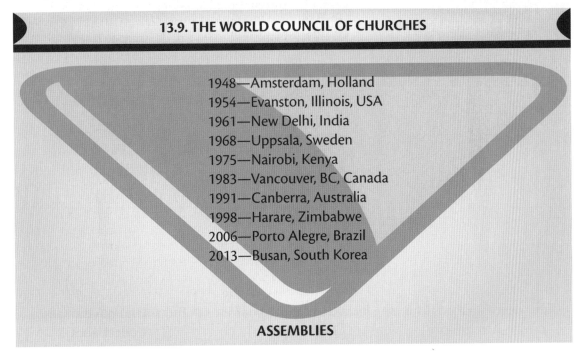

13.9. THE WORLD COUNCIL OF CHURCHES

1948—Amsterdam, Holland
1954—Evanston, Illinois, USA
1961—New Delhi, India
1968—Uppsala, Sweden
1975—Nairobi, Kenya
1983—Vancouver, BC, Canada
1991—Canberra, Australia
1998—Harare, Zimbabwe
2006—Porto Alegre, Brazil
2013—Busan, South Korea

ASSEMBLIES

Presbyterians and Congregationalists to extend the outreach of home missions in the establishment of schools and churches. The **American Board of Commissioners for Foreign Missions** (1810), the first American sending society, was a transdenominational effort of three reformed bodies. Agencies that garnered a broader denominational spectrum of participants were, for example, were the American Sunday School Union (1824), the American Tract Society (1825), the YMCA (1851), and the Evangelical Alliance (1867). Though denominational distinctives were suppressed, there was essential agreement among the participants as to the centrality of the Bible, the meaning of the gospel, and the importance of gospel proclamation.

Two members of the American branch of the Evangelical Alliance (the alliance is a child of the British Evangelical Union, now the World Evangelical Alliance [1846]), Samuel Schmucker and Philip Schaff proposed the reunion of the Christian churches in the nineteenth century. Schmucker (1799–1873) was a professor at the Lutheran Gettysburg Theological Seminary, Gettysburg, Pennsylvania. In 1858 he issued "A Fraternal Appeal to the American Churches, with a Plan for Catholic Union on Apostolic Principles" calling for the Apostolic Protestant Church of America. He organized the soon-to-fizzle Society for the Promotion of Christian Union, but continued to prepare the soil for a later breakthrough. In 1870, the American branch proposed union in "The True Unity of Christ's Church." Philip Schaff (1819–1893), a professor of theology and

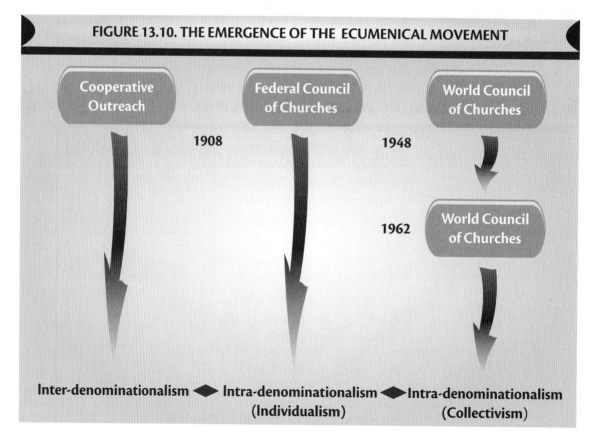

FIGURE 13.10. THE EMERGENCE OF THE ECUMENICAL MOVEMENT

Cooperative Outreach — 1908 — Federal Council of Churches — 1948 — World Council of Churches — 1962 — World Council of Churches

Inter-denominationalism ◆ Intra-denominationalism (Individualism) ◆ Intra-denominationalism (Collectivism)

Invitation to Church History: World

church history at Union Theological Seminary, New York, became a strong advocate as well, proposing a "Reunion of Christendom" in 1893. Although these, and other, early proposals for unity did not meet with a favorable response, they prepared the climate and set the stage for the creation of the North American Federal Council of Churches in 1908.

The theological culture of the last quarter of the nineteenth century (for example, the development of the **social gospel movement** within the liberal tradition) set the stage for the emergence of the ecumenical movement. The initial stage for the rise of ecumenical consciousness was a series of meetings in the 1890s in several major cities to develop an impetus for the creation of a national organization. In 1901 a conference in Philadelphia led to the forming of the National Federation of Churches and Christian Workers that aimed to address the interests of disadvantaged workers. The

NFCCW became the seedbed out of which the Federal Council of Churches emerged in 1908. The agenda of the emergent organization became evident in 1905 when the federation became exercised over human rights violations in the Belgian Congo; as an ecclesiastical pressure group, they sought to address social, political and economic issues as a means of procuring social justice which, in turn, was understood to be the fulfillment of the Great Commission.

The Charismatic Movement Worldwide

One of the truly prolific movements that emerged in the twentieth century, becoming an international entity, was the Pentecostal/charismatic or renewalist movement. Actually, this major, rapidly growing expression of Christian faith was composed of a variety of movements; it was clearly not monolithic in its teachings or practices.

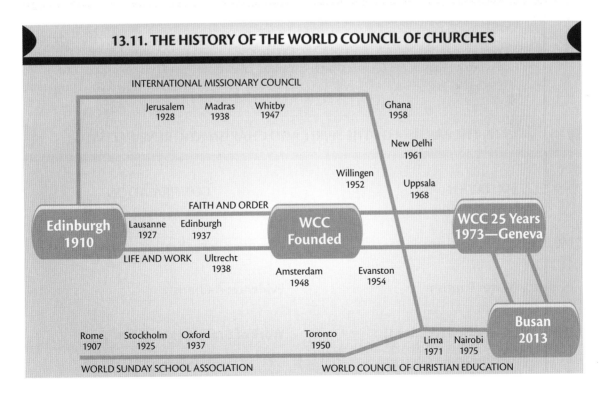

13.11. THE HISTORY OF THE WORLD COUNCIL OF CHURCHES

Within Roman Catholicism

The context for the charismatic emphases within the Roman Catholic Church was the spiritual renewal that formed the backdrop for the calling of Vatican II (1962), a reforming council. John XXIII urged faithful Catholics to pray for a "new Pentecost" through the promotion of reform and unity, linking renewal in the church to the charismatic gifts.

As the Council proceeded amidst large press coverage and numerous international observers, Catholics were daily asked to pray this prayer (*Documents of Vatican II*, 793): "O Holy Spirit, sent by the Father in the name of Jesus, who art present in the Church and dost infallibly guide it, pour forth, we pray, the fullness of Thy gifts upon the Ecumenical Council. . . . Renew Thy wonders in this our day, as by a new Pentecost. Grant to Thy Church that, being of one mind and steadfast in prayer with Mary, the Mother of Jesus, and following the lead of blessed Peter, it may advance the reign of our Divine Savior, the reign of truth and justice, the reign of love and peace. Amen."

"May there be repeated thus in the Christian families the spectacle of the apostles gathered together in Jerusalem after the Ascension of Jesus to heaven, when the newborn Church was completely united in communion of thought and prayer with Peter and around Peter, the shepherd of the lambs and of the sheep. And may the Divine Spirit deign to answer in a most comforting manner the prayer that rises daily to Him from every corner of the earth: Renew your wonders in our time, as though for a new Pentecost, and grant that the holy Church, preserving unanimous and continuous prayer, together with Mary, the mother of Jesus, and also under the guidance of St. Peter, may increase the reign of the Divine Saviour, the reign of truth and justice, the reign of love and peace. Amen" (*Documents of Vatican II*, 709).

The council causatively linked, "renewal" with the charismatic gifts and ministries of the Holy Spirit (*Documents of Vatican II*, (21–22): "In order that we may be unceasingly renewed in Him, He has shared with us His Spirit, who, existing as one and the same being in the head and in the members, vivifies, unifies, and moves the whole body."

In 1966 a group of faculty members at Duquesne University, Pittsburgh, Pennsylvania, began to read charismatic literature and at a weekend retreat, called the Duquesne

13.12. THE BAPTISM OF THE SPIRIT AND CHARISMATIC RENEWALISM

INITIATION	CONFIRMATION
Meaning: Spirit Baptism	Meaning: Actualization of Spirit Baptism
Evidence: Water Baptism	Evidence: A Charism
Work of Grace: Given (the Seed)	Work of Grace: Released (the Fruit)

A portrait of Pope John XXIII (1881–1963) who encouraged renewal in the Roman Catholic Church. Courtesy of Gedoughty02.

Weekend, in February 1967, several participants received spiritual renewal, accompanied by the manifestation of tongues. Within a few months, the interest in renewal was felt at Notre Dame University, South Bend, Indiana, as well as other campuses.

By 1969 growing interest led to the establishment of an annual Catholic Charismatic

Conference at Notre Dame University, Indiana. This conference attracted 450 participants, which included some 25 priests. By 1971 the annual conference was renamed the International Conference on Charismatic Renewal with an attendance of over five thousand. In 1974 the conference drew over 30,000 participants including over 700 priests. In 1975 the international conference was held in Rome; Paul VI performed a pontifical mass for the throngs that had gathered.

As in the Protestant **charismatic movement**, the locus of the Catholic charismatic movement was in the care-group or small prayer meeting. The centers of the Catholic Charismatic Renewal (CCR) became two: Ann Arbor, Michigan (the Word of God community) and South Bend, Indiana (the People of Praise community).

Catholics, believing in the importance of the unity of Christendom, embraced ecumenical mission of the Protestants, envisioning through it a merger under Roman Catholic auspices. In recent years publicity of the Roman Catholic charismatics has waned, suggestive that the movement, as a renewing impetus, is no longer at the forefront of the church's agenda. Many Roman Catholics have found and continue to find new spiritual resources through it. Though difficult to assess accurately, Roman Catholic charismatics make up a significant proportion of the overall movement.

Within Protestantism

Though there is no agreement on the origins of the Pentecostal and subsequent charismatic movement, most find the beginnings in the North American Protestant movement.

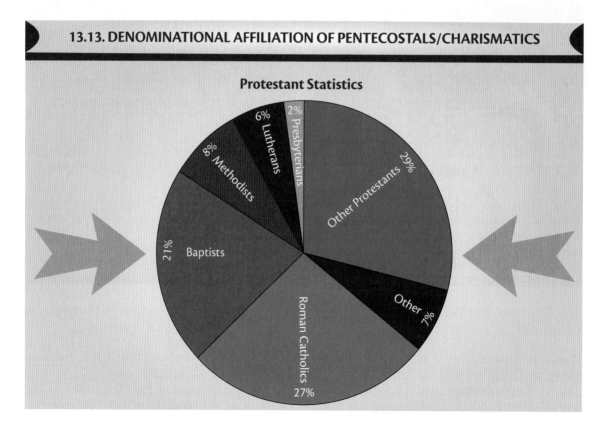

13.13. DENOMINATIONAL AFFILIATION OF PENTECOSTALS/CHARISMATICS

Protestant Statistics

- Presbyterians 2%
- Lutherans 6%
- Methodists 8%
- Baptists 21%
- Roman Catholics 27%
- Other 7%
- Other Protestants 29%

The spread of the movement seems to pivot on the life and ministry of Thomas Ball Barratt (1862–1940), called "the apostle of the Pentecostalism in Europe." An Englishman, trained at Wesleyan College, Taunton, England, he worked in the mining industry in Norway and was licensed by the Methodist Church of Norway. He pastored the First Church, Oslo. In 1902 Barratt left the church to become the superintendent and founder of the Oslo City Mission and in 1904 editor of the *City Post*. In 1905 he went to the United States to collect funds for the interdenominational city mission. While living in the mission house of the Christian and Missionary Alliance in New York, he read of the Pentecostal movement in Los Angeles and embraced its teachings. The

movement spread rapidly throughout Norway and across Europe.

On 7 January 1907 Barratt wrote from the Olso Mission (Frodsham, *With Signs Following*, 81): "Over twenty have now received their Pentecost, God be praised! The papers are stirred up, some against, but others are very civil and merely state facts as they are. Crowds throng the places where meetings are held. Souls are being saved and God's name is honored. Hallelujah."

In Sweden the major person in the early Pentecostal movement was Lewi Pethrus (b. 1884). Pethrus was born and raised in the Baptist heritage; first he labored as an evangelist (1902–1904), and then after Bethel Seminary in Stockholm, he went to pastor a small Baptist church in Lidkoping. Subsequently Pethrus pa-

Thomas Ball Barratt (1862–1940) at sixteen years old. Courtesy of Halvard.

Lewi Pethrus (1884–1974). Courtesy of Raphael Saulus.

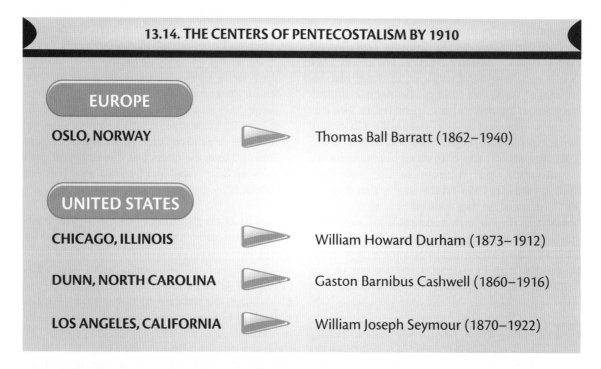

13.14. THE CENTERS OF PENTECOSTALISM BY 1910

EUROPE

OSLO, NORWAY — Thomas Ball Barratt (1862–1940)

UNITED STATES

CHICAGO, ILLINOIS — William Howard Durham (1873–1912)

DUNN, NORTH CAROLINA — Gaston Barnibus Cashwell (1860–1916)

LOS ANGELES, CALIFORNIA — William Joseph Seymour (1870–1922)

stored a small Baptist church in Stockholm that became entirely Pentecostal. When Pethrus was removed from the church and the denomination, he founded the Filadelfia Church.

Lewi Pethrus wrote of his longing for a deeper spiritual experience (Frodsham, *With Signs Following*, 87): "I had a wonderful experience in the year 1905. The Lord cleansed my heart and then I had a great desire to be filled with God. The biography of Charles Finney showed me that there was a blessing I could receive. I read a book by Dr. A. J. Gordon, which told of being filled with the Spirit. No one ever preached on the Baptism of the Spirit at that time, and I had never seen anyone receive the fullness of the Spirit, but I understood there must be something in it. I was holding revival meetings and a few souls, from ten to twenty, were coming to the cross in the meetings; but when I saw them coming, weeping, I also saw the emptiness of my own soul and heart. I got away from the revival meetings, threw myself on the floor in

my room, and cried to God that He might fill me. I felt I was empty; I was clean, but I was the first experience of thousands of others at the same time. There were thousands of others with the same experience, crying to God, 'Give us a revival and fill us with the Holy Spirit.'"

The principal figure in the introduction of Pentecostalism to England was the Episcopalian vicar A. A. Boddy, pastor in Sunderland in the north of the country. Boddy, rector of All Saints Church, labored with Evan Roberts in Wales during the Welsh Revivals out of the Low Anglican Church. The context for the reception of Pentecostalism was the Keswick Conferences of the late nineteenth century. The Keswick movement, a counterpart to the National Holiness movement, in North America was officially organized in 1875 by Canon Hartford-Battersby in his parish at Keswick. Prominent American Holiness advocates such as the Smiths (Hannah and Robert), Boardman, Finney, and Asa Mahan were the teachers of sanctification, and such evange-lists as D. L. Moody and R. A. Torrey were its popularizers. Keswick sanctification made large inroads through F. B. Meyer and other Englishmen who traveled internationally. In addition to annual Keswick Conventions, the Pentecostal League (not charismatic, but Ho-liness) stressed a deeper spiritual experience (a cleansing from sin) through "a Baptism."

"In the year 1906, the Lord laid it upon the hearts of a number of children of God in Sunderland in the north of England to meet together for prayer. They met in the vestry of an Episcopal church and were frequently joined by the godly vicar of this church, Pastor Alexander A. Boddy. They were tarrying for enduement with power from on high and praying for God to give a gracious revival. News came to them of the revival that the Lord was giving in Los Angeles and they read with great joy the first papers that came from Azusa Street. The news came that the revival had crossed the Atlantic and the Lord was pouring out His Spirit in Norway in the meet-ings of Pastor Barratt, who had received the Baptism in the Spirit in New York. Pastor Boddy made a visit to Norway and was convinced that the work he saw there was truly of the Lord" (Frodsham, *With Signs Following*, 73).

Jonathan Paul and Emil Meyer, native Ger-mans, probably spread Pentecostalism into Germany. Jonathon Paul, a Berlin pastor, read about the events in Oslo and went to investi-gate the matter. He actively participated with Barratt in Fredrickstad, Norway. Emil Meyer of Hamburg also visited Barratt in Oslo in 1907.

In the 1960s a new mood emerged within Pentecostalism, calling for change; the result was the emergence of the charismatic move-ment. As its parent, the neo-Pentecostal or char-ismatic movement is largely of North American roots. As Pentecostalism progressively became both affluent and theologically stable, wit-nessed by participation in various national and international organizations, a stress was placed on mass, cooperative evangelism. Convictions

arose that the "latter rain" had become but in-frequent showers; indeed, some troubled, older Pentecostals wondered if the days of revival were over. However, with a new face, refined tastes, and brighter surroundings Pentecostalism de-veloped further in North America.

The connecting link from North Amer-ican into European Protestantism seems to have been the influence of Michael Harper (1931–2010). Unlike Dennis Bennett, another Anglican, Michael Harper came out of a strong evangelical rather than Anglo-Catholic tradi-tion. In 1950 he began study at Emmanuel Col-lege, Cambridge, as a law student and in the same year experienced an evangelical conver-sion at King's College Chapel. He then became quite active in the Cambridge Inter-Collegiate Christian Union. In 1952 he changed his course of study from law to theology and entered Ridley Hall Theological College in Cambridge. He was ordained in 1956 and was assigned as a curate of All Souls Church, Langham Place, London, in 1958 under its rector John Stott. While preparing for a weekend parish confer-ence at St. Luke's Church, Hampstead, in Sep-tember 1962, Harper experienced something that changed his life dramatically; at first he and his wife equated it with a "second blessing" or entire sanctification made popular by the Holiness movement.

In 1964 Harper resigned from All Souls Church in the midst of controversy with Rector Stott who did not share his views. He then be-came the leading impetus for Fountain Trust and *Renewal* magazine (1966). Harper be-came an international advocate of neo-Pente-costalism and eventually was regarded as the movement's most articulate British spokesman and theoretician.

In 1975 Harper resigned as director of Fountain Trust and editor of *Renewal* in order to travel and lecture. Under Thomas Smail the Fountain Trust moved from London to East Molesey, Surrey, where it hoped to establish a research center and "fellowship house." Harper has subsequently been active in the Anglican renewal movement as canon of Chichester after 1984. In 1995 he left the Anglican community to join the Antiochene Orthodox Church over the issue of the ordination of women to Anglican parishes and served through it promoting his charismatic interests.

The charismatic movement in Europe became an international movement. particularly under the influence of Full Gospel Businessmen's Fellowship and the ecumenical broadness of David J. du Plessis (1905–1987), a South African Pentecostal. As the sectarian traits of classical Pentecostalism began slowly to abate in the post-war era, du Plessis emerged. He took an active part in the organizational meetings of the World Pentecostal Fellowship (a leader of the 1948 Paris Conference) and also took up residence in the United States in 1948, joining the Assemblies of God in 1955. He began to attend and was warmly received in meetings of the World Council of Churches in the 1950s.

During the remainder of his life, du Plessis continued his ecumenical posture. He was an observer at Vatican II and was cochairman of a five-year "dialogue" between the Roman Church and the charismatic renewalists. His affiliations brought defrocking in 1962 from the Assemblies of God, but he continued to bring the renewalist movement together worldwide.

The mainline churches, facing declining membership and resources, embraced the charismatic movement as a hopeful source of their own spiritual renewal. The movement did that in some instances, but as a whole did not move to the forefront of mainline churches. Generally the liberal tradition's hopes for success in organizational conformity and social definitions of the gospel made the ethos and theological interests of charismatics difficult to embrace.

Despite a mixed reception from some Christians, the charismatic movement has found a place in the major denominations worldwide and offered a place of refuge and strength for many.

GLOSSARY OF TERMS

American Board of Commissioners for Foreign Missions: the first foreign mission board (1810), a transdenominational effort of three reformed bodies, was created in the United States following the famous Haystack Prayer Meeting at Williams College in 1806. The first missionaries under its auspices were Adoniram Judson and Luther Rice who joined William Carey in India, the former moving to Burma a year latter.

Barthianism: see *Neo-Orthodoxy*.

Black Power Movement (Black Power Theology): a manifestation of Liberation Theology that originally emerged in South America in the 1950s, focusing upon social justice and equity, using Christian terms and symbols though often reinterpreting them for polemical value. *See Political Liberation Theology.*

Bultmannian Existentialism: a radical, subjective approach to reading the Bible based on the assumption that the Bible is mythology, a disjunction of faith and history, though Rudolf Bultmann did embrace the notion that there was some authenticity in the biblical texts about the Christ.

Charismatic Movement (Pentecostalism, Charismatic Renewalism): the term generally indicates a person, movement, or church that embraces the notion that the extraordinary spiritual gifts have not ceased, that they remain vital to the church's faith and task, and that they evidence a spiritual vitality when consistently practiced. It is a difficult term in the sense that non-charismatics embrace the reality and importance of spiritual giftedness, but do not regularly practice the extraordinary gifts in church life.

Classic Liberalism: a term that generally refers to the attempt in North American Protestantism to preserve and protect the Christian faith from the inroads and implications of the sciences and philosophy by redefining it. Classic liberals follow the path of Albrecht Ritschl who argued that the Bible only contained the revelation of God, that Jesus was a merely inspiring person, that sin is strictly moral in nature, and that Christ's death was simply a grand moral example.

Dialectical Theology (Neo-Orthodoxy, Crisis Theology): an orientation to theology that developed in reaction to rationalistic tendencies in nineteenth-century liberalism arising in the post World War I decades emphasizing the tensions and paradoxes in Christian faith without the need or possibility of resolution, the transcendent unknowableness of God as opposed to divine immanence that characterized the previous century's quest for God.

Edinburgh Missionary Conference (1910): A major gathering of over 1,200 missionary leaders from Europe and North America (only 5 percent from outside those areas) to promote world missions. Under the leadership of John R. Mott, a continuing agency was created, the International Missionary Council (1921), that became one of the major consolidating organizations to form the World Council of Churches in 1948.

Feminist Theology: while difficult to define because of its variegated nature, the concept has to do with feminist inquiry and perspectives about gender discrimination and power inequities. It uses the term *theology* in a very broad sense, detaching it from the historical meaning of the term. It is more accurately a rights movement concerned with issues of discrimination in sexual preferences, in language with reference to God, in hiring practices, and in financial remuneration.

German Idealism: a philosophical/theological movement that emerged in the late eighteenth and early nineteenth centuries in reaction to the Kantian rationalism/empiricist approach to knowledge, arguing that truth is internal and personal. The mental or mind took precedence over the senses in knowledge acquisition, and theology was reduced to the realm of natural theology. Representatives of German idealism are Fichte, Schelling, and Hegel.

God Is Dead Movement: an American Protestant liberalism that arose in the 1960s arguing that the modern, increasingly secularist culture has rendered the existence of God irrelevant. In retrospect, the movement bore witness to the failed attempt of the Enlightenment to secure a meaningful place for God in human existence and was a harbinger of postmodernism. Among its advocats were Thomas J. J. Altizer, William Hamilton, Paul Van Buren, and John A. T. Robinson.

Idealism (see German Idealism): a philosophical approach to the nature of knowledge, arguing that the structure of reality is immaterial or mentally constructed.

Immaculate Assumption of Mary: the teaching dogmatically embraced in the Roman Catholic Church during the pontificate of Pius XII (1950) that Mary, having completed the course of her earthly life, merely slept at her death, not being subject to mortal decay, and was taken to heaven there to reign with her son near his very heart. It is an attempt to solidify Catholic devotionalism and piety.

Immaculate Conception of Mary: the

teaching dogmatically embraced in the Roman Catholic Church during the pontificate of Pius IX (1854) that Mary, the mother of Jesus, was preserved from original sin from the moment of her conception. The doctrine appears to have been brought forth, at least in part, to protect the deity and true humanity of Christ in view of the inroads of theological liberalism in the nineteenth-century church.

Inerrancy (Inerrrantism): an approach to explaining the Protestant churches' historic belief in the absolute truthfulness of the biblical writings by arguing that, being of divine origin and a product emanating from the divine character, they are without error in both words and message. Though containing anthropomorphic language, nonliteral figures of speech, and scribal discrepancies, the Bible came from God through human sources and was perfectly preserved in the original manuscripts.

Kerygma: a transliterated Greek word meaning "message." In the realm of religious studies, it is used in relation to the teaching or proclamation of Jesus, and others, as revealed in the Bible.

Liberation Theology: a general term for reading the Bible and constructing its central message based on the issues of social injustice, gender discrimination, and racial inequality. Dealing with such issues through political, social, and even military intervention may be a justifiable expression of the redemptive message of the Bible.

Neoliberalism (Realistic Theology): a theological movement that emerged in the United States in the 1930s within the liberal tradition that is critical of classic liberalism, particularly the component of triumphal, optimistic progressivism. The clarion call for this movement was the 1938 sermon by Harry Emerson Fosdick entitled "The Church Must Go Beyond

Liberalism." Sometimes called Realistic Theology, its advocates, such as Walter Horton, John C. Bennett, and H. P. Van Dusen, interpreted the human condition in darker terms than their predecessors, yet remained solidly within the liberal tradition of understanding the person of Christ and human salvation.

Neo-Orthodoxy: an approach to theology in reaction to nineteenth-century religious Liberalism argued in methodology by Karl Barth of Germany. The movement generally viewed the Scriptures with greater confidence than did earlier movements, yet did not accord them with infallibility. Barth argued that the Scriptures become the Word of God at the intersection of the Spirit, the individual text, and the living Christ, meaning that his verification theory was subjective and piecemeal. Consequently, advocates of Barth's approach to revelation lack cohesiveness in understanding, and he proved to be only a temporary conservative reaction to progressive liberalism.

Panentheism (Panentheistic Mystical Intrusion): a belief that God exists by interpenetrating nature. Thus, the natural realm is the habitation of God who is the animating force behind everything. Such a belief is found in Baha'i, Buddhism, Hinduism, and Sikhism, as well as in several Christian groups.

Plan of Union: a cooperative missions effort (1801) inaugurated by the Congregationalists and Presbyterians to combine finances and energy to establish schools and churches in the area north of the Ohio River to western New York. The plan was to build seminaries to be staffed by both denominations and that graduates by virtue of their ordination would be qualified to serve in either community. Through the endeavor, however, a schism developed in the Presbyterian community, and its beliefs became categorized as New England Congregational theology, a modification of historic Calvinist teachings.

Political Liberation Theology: the application of the Christian gospel of spiritual deliverances to social, cultural, and political injustices and moral inequities. Often radically socialist in tenor, advocates envisioned the root of injustice in the capitalistic enterprise and fomented popular pressure, even violence, to create a leveling of societal authority.

Process Theology: a recent development within the Protestant liberal tradition predicated on the scientific shift away from Newtonian physics to quantum physics discovered by Max Planck and deriving implications from Heisenberg's indeterminacy principle relative to subatomic particles and Einstein's relativity theory. In rejecting classic theism, advocates argue that there are two polarities in God, one sovereign and unchanging, and the other, evolutive and becoming, making it impossible for God to know nonrealities, meaning the future. God is grounded in the past but actively involved in the future by hoping or luring it into existence. When the future becomes the present, God can know it. This, it is proposed, makes God more compassionate and caring, thus less distant and detached. Grasping the reality of the past, God is fixed and determined; ignorant of the future God who is responsive to human needs.

Roman Catholic Church: a movement that gradually emerged out of the increasingly moral, social, and theological divergences and controversies within the late medieval church. Like its counterpart the Protestant movement, proponents claim historic verification for its teaching ("that which has always and everywhere been taught in the church"), though that claim is seriously flawed, lacking demonstrable consistency through the centuries. It seems that the defining moments of the church were the Fourth Lateran Council, the Council of Florence (1439), and the enormously important formal creedalization and dogmatization of its teaching at the Council of Trent in the sixteenth century.

Realistic Theology: see *Neoliberalism.*

Social Gospel Movement: an emphasis within the broader liberal tradition in the United States parallel to the progressive era (1890–1917) that sought to ameliorate social inequities through legislation. Advocates, such as Washington Gladden and Walter Rauschenbusch, suggested that sin was environmental and social in nature and propagation. The movement culminated in the Rauschenbusch's *A Theology for the Social Gospel* (1917).

Theology of Being: an approach to Christian theology within the liberal tradition espoused by Paul Tillich (1886–1965) as a psychological mystical analysis of human self-understanding. According to Tillich, God is not a person, the concept being symbolic, but is the ground of our ultimate concerns (the concept of the Trinity being an ecclesiastical tool to suppress inquiring minds). The "persons" of the Trinity should be interpreted in the framework of human need. The "Father" is a symbol of care in the midst of human alienation; the "Son," of human inadequacy, finitude, and self-sacrifice; and the "Spirit," a synthesis of the two. The Trinity is a psychological human invention to secure stability in view of life's torments and exigencies.

Theology of Crisis (Theology of the Word, Barthianism): an approach to Christian theology expressed by perhaps the greatest theologian, if one is to use the criteria of influence rather than traditional orthodox conceptions in the twentieth century. Reacting against the anthrotheistic trajectory of nineteenth-century theology beginning with Schleiermacher, Barth strove to defend the transcendence of

God. Barth reversed the previous century's attempts to discover God, arguing that God cannot be found by human contrivances; he is the God who can only be known by his prerogative of self-disclosure. This he does through an encounter with the living Word, the Christ, and in the written word, a portion of the Bible, by the Spirit in a moment of spiritual, revelatory crisis. In that remarkable instance, repeated numerous times, the Bible becomes the very words of God. The difficulty was not so much his conclusions at times, but his theory of verification of biblical truth.

Theology of Evolution: an approach to Christian theology within the liberal tradition that became popular in the 1960s and 1970s in the United States that fractured theology into a variety of individualized kerygmas, or messages. Teilhard de Chardin (1881–1955) combined evolutionary biology, paleontology, and Hegelianism to construct a theology. According to de Chardin, humankind has progressed over time toward a higher consciousness, the omega point, a collective, mystical unity in the body of Christ. God is the energizing power, a force, behind the evolutionary development of humans as spiritual beings.

Theology of History (Theology of Resurrection): an approach to Christian theology within the liberal tradition postulated by Hans Urs von Balthasar (1905–88). Adopting a Hegelian approach to the progress of history, his solution to the struggles within the human existence was the person of Christ; and thus Balthasar's approach to combining history, solution, and meaning into Christology. Christ is seen as the Lord and apex of history as Creator and Redeemer. Sympathetic echoes of Barth's approach to theology (his interests, starting points, and conservatism) can be detected in Balthasar.

Theology of Hope (Theology of Resurrection): an approach to Christian theology expressed by Jurgen Moltmann within the liberal tradition that focuses on the resurrection of Christ within a future *eschaton*. The ambiguities and tragedies of the human experience are to be understood in the Christian's embrace of a bright future based on the resurrection of Jesus Christ. Sin is living without hope; despair is a premature failure to find surety in hope. Ultimately, this creation will be transformed into a new creation. However, Moltmann understood the Trinity as modes of the expression of human freedom, hence his tendencies to liberationist and ecological interpretations of theology. The "Father" corresponds to political freedom, the "Son" to communal freedom, and the "Spirit" to spiritual freedom.

World Council of Churches: Formed officially in 1948 in Amsterdam, Holland, the WCC is an organization of 349 Protestant churches worldwide claiming a constituency of over 560-million people. Theologically latitudinal and socially oriented in its mission, the WCC serves through a variety of agencies that are concerned with global issues of hunger, racial and social inequity, and peace to name a few. Conservative Protestants have looked askance at the movement because of its theological latitude and largely social agendas that, while worthy, overshadow the central message of the gospel and the claims of Jesus Christ.

Chapter 14 Outline

The Premodern Worldview

The Modern Worldview

The Postmodern Worldview

The Reaction to Modernity:
A Pattern Emerges

The Liberal Tradition
and Postmodernity

Religious Conservativism
and Postmodernity

Chapter 14 Objectives

- That the student will understand the meaning of the various ways truth has been sought, capsulized, and embraced through the centuries since the advent of Christianity

- That the student will gain some insight into the structure of values and decision-making that characterize the public arena and how it is often anti-thetical to the Christian faith

- That the student will grasp the reality that the modern period was as detri-mental to Christian affirmations as the postmodern period

- That the student will come to appreciate the struggles of Christian clerics and scholars to defend and propagate authentic Christian faith in a world of flux and change, reflecting on the notion that accommodation is re-quired to maintain cultural relevancy but culture concession is dangerous

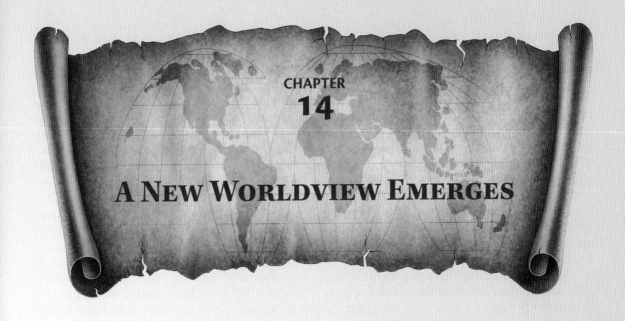

CHAPTER
14

A NEW WORLDVIEW EMERGES

A S WRITERS AND SCHOLARS have thought about the centuries between the advent of the Christ and today, they offer different perspectives on the interpretative grid or lens through which centuries are to be viewed and the information organized, valued, and selectively presented. From at least one point of view, twenty centuries could be seen through the light of dominant religious opinions. If so, it could be argued that in the initial four centuries of the existence of the post-Pentecost (Acts 2) people of God, the church emerged in a hostile world dominated religiously by pagan and neopagan beliefs and practices. The religious views of Christians appeared to the Roman authorities as a threat to the empire because, at least in part, they did not accord proper respect to the gods who had to be appeased and cajoled lest they respond in judgmental ways. This changed in the fourth century with the Christian alliances of Constantine and Theodosius I, inaugurating an era that spanned for nearly a millennium and half (300–1750), revealing Christianity's acceptance and expansion, largely without external threats, particularly in Western Europe.

Since 1750, due to the rise of philosophical and theological **rationalism**, Christianity has gradually been eclipsed as the primary source for meaning, values, and direction. It can be argued that Christianity has ceased to be the most important factor in shaping life and worldview, at least in the northern hemisphere, and Christians in the West must realize that they live within cultures that no long embrace Christian opinions or values (this is only a Western perspective, as will be denoted subsequently).

One way of viewing the history of Christianity is this: The pre-Christian era (from Christ to the fourth century), the Christian era (from the fourth century to the eighteenth century), and the emergence and dominance of the post-Christian era (since the eighteenth century to the present).

Another perspective on the last twenty centuries is to think in terms of the relationship between what is available for humans to know and how humans come to perceive and understand what is available to know, that is, to think through the relationship of metaphysics and epistemology. The former is generally understood to be a branch of philosophy concerned with the question of what exists; the latter as a branch of philosophy that focuses upon methods of accessing what can be known and its justifiability.

Both branches of philosophy are freighted with an abundance of assumptions and appear in numerous varieties. However, with that caveat stated, an outline of the centuries under consideration can be constructed through the lens of these two seminal branches of philosophy as they relate to the realm of knowability, and we can know something, particularly in respect to the knowledge of God, commonly designated as theology (constructed from the barest etymology of the word, the study of God).

In the broadest sense, the past twenty centuries can be seen in two parts: those centuries in which metaphysics and epistemology were conceived as a unity with the starting point being metaphysics, not epistemology (from Christ to the eighteenth century) and those centuries, the eighteenth and nineteenth, in which a unity is maintained but epistemology took precedence over metaphysics, determining the meaning and extent of the latter. The twentieth century witnessed the destruction of the idea of metaphysics and the relativity of epistemology, at least in the West and in the northern hemisphere: the industrialized, enlightened, prosperous nations.

If this perspective determines the way we should view the past twenties centuries, it is understandable that recent writers operating within twentieth-century assumptions and prejudices have sought new nomenclature for characterizing the eras before and after Christ, the Christian way of describing the structure of history that was once dominant. The more generally accepted way of separating the centuries is no longer BC (Before Christ) or AD (After Christ), but BCE (Before the Common Era) and CE (the Common Era). The new perspective, reflective of the domination of epistemology over metaphysics, rejects the primacy of metaphysics or reduces metaphysics to **deconstructionist** individualism wherein corporate metaphysics and epistemology are no longer possible. Religious concepts, including the significance of the Christ, have become private, individualized value judgments; Christ is no longer viewed as the interpretative grid for understanding life and establishing values. A catastrophic reconfiguration in perspective has taken place in recent centuries.

If this general perspective of the past twenty centuries has validity, it is possible to view the history of the Christian faith as a theme in the development of the Common Era, seeing it through the lens of the relationship of metaphysics and epistemology. Those who pursue this approach suggest that three distinct worldviews have dominated the centuries: the **prescientific** or **precritical worldview**, the **Enlightenment** or rationalist worldview, and the postmodern or deconstructionist worldview.

The Premodern Worldview

To argue that the premodern worldview is anti-intellectual assumes that rationalism is the only correct approach to knowledge and all others are inferior. It is the failure to understand that the rational, empiricist approach to knowledge is adorned with non-demonstrable presuppositions. The prescientific view which dominated the quest for religious knowledge for seventeen centuries argued that metaphysics determined epistemology, that what is known leads to how we know. Belief is prior and shapes reasons; it is not that reason determine the nature of faith.

The starting point in this approach was a matrix of revelatory truths about God, faith, and the church. Premodernists assumed that the way to know themselves, actually the only way, was through the self-revelation of God mediated through the offices of the church. The precritical worldview would not countenance the notion that the mind could arrive at ultimate, final truths. That was a matter of beginning with faith in the God revealed through the pages of the Bible.

In that world of conceptualizing reality, all branches of philosophy were handmaids of theology, the two being inseparable. In the skillful hands of philosopher/theologians such as Thomas Aquinas the faith was shown to be consistent with reason, but there were some realities that could only be grasped through revelation. Christianity to the premodern was neither irrational (contrary to reason) nor a-rational (without reasons of embrace), but dependent in part on source-truth beyond the acquisition of mere reason alone.

The Modern Worldview

By the early seventeenth century a new perspective gradually emerged, a child of the **Renaissance** and the Reformation. Called by a variety of names (the Age of Reason, the Enlightenment, the Age of Science) and emerging to predominance in the eighteenth and nineteenth centuries, its definers and defenders juxtaposed the relationship of metaphysics and epistemology. Epistemology determined metaphysics; reasonability determined the limits of knowledge. A finite faculty, the mind, became the arbiter of what can be known. It manifested a willingness to reject traditional approaches to truth by prioritizing reason, while simultaneously subordinating the other two sources, the Bible and tradition, to it. Thus, the possibility of knowledge beyond the

grasp of reason was rejected as nonscientific and anti-intellectual.

All the knowledge available to humankind was within the sphere of reason alone. Thus begins an experiment in the preoccupied West for three hundred years. With the assumption that reason determines knowledge, not that it is a perceiving/evaluative faculty, modernity demanded a revision of the relationship of God to the universe, of the nature and capacities of humanity, and clearly of the role and nature of the Bible.

Modernity placed great hope and trust, expressing it in terms of blatant optimism, that time, research, and intellectual scrutiny could achieve a better world free from tyrannies political, moral, and religious. It is with modernity that the church struggled for three centuries so as to continue to make a contribution and maintain a place of importance in shaping moral values. The outcome of the struggle was the gradual loss of the centrality of religion in the lives of many people.

The liberal Protestant tradition turned to accommodation and concession in the face of the Enlightenment challenge, gradually defining religion not by revelation, but by the sciences. The role that religion played in society would become that of social science, an emphasis on life management techniques and perspective, with the loss of the transcendent role of faith and hope.

The achievements of the Enlightenment were outstanding, effecting major advances of the frontiers of knowledge. However, it brought an emptiness of the soul that could not be filled through leisure exploitation and materialist pursuits, a secular value system that the churches, even conservatives ones, embraced.

In the nineteenth century, the assumptions of Enlightenment rationalism to deliver on its optimistic promises came under severe scrutiny by those who employed the rationalistic method; it seemed to burst apart in the following century with its mass human waste and wantonness. The blighted dimensions of the human psyche seemed unable to be ameliorated by educational and scientific advances. In fact, and contrary to the Enlightenment thought, such advances only heightened the capacity of humanity to exploit its devious propensities. Reason could just as readily demonstrate one or another opposing principle, just as a David Hume had argued (he made the point that on the basis of reason that reason could not bring certitude). Reason might lead to some obscure, distant place for God; locate him within human existence; or grant him no existence at all. It might lead to moral postulates, but it may just as possibly destroy the possibility of any moral verities.

The weaknesses of a strictly rationalist approach to knowledge were sounded by philologist-turned-philosopher at the University of Basel, Friedrich Nietzsche (1844–1900). He questioned the progressive optimism of the Enlightenment, arguing that this is all the world that will ever be, that in this world humankind are left only to their own reflections and devices, that there is no help outside ourselves. Borrowing from the Enlightenment that either so stressed divine transcendence that immanence was lost or immanence was so emphasized that transcendence was lost, Nietzsche took rationalism a step further, arguing that God does not exist, and truth was only perspectival, non-objective, and personal affirmations, with no ultimate values. Through Nietzsche the viewpoint was argued that the greatest human quest is not for preservation, but for power.

"What then is truth? A movable host of metaphors, metonymies. . . : in short, a sum of human relations which have been poetically and rhetorically intensified, transferred, and embellished, and which, after long usage, seem to a people to be fixed, canonical, and binding. Truths are illusions which we have forgotten are illusions—they are metaphors that have become worn out and have been drained of sensuous force, coins which have lost their embossing and are now considered as metal and no longer as coins" (Frederick Wilhelm Nietzsche, "On Truth and Lies in a Nonmoral Sense," 84).

The extensive influence of Nietzsche's ideas was manifested in the emergence of **pragmatism** and **existentialism**. Both are responses to what was perceived as the failure of the Enlightenment to explain human significance; both are attempts to establish significance in other than the faculty of the mind; and both attempted to establish the criteria of value, making unacceptable the insights of the Enlightenment that the premodern worldview was intellectually invalid.

Existentialists, such as Jean-Paul Sartre

Portrait of Friedrich Nietzsche by photographer Gustav Schultze, Naumburg, taken early September 1882. Courtesy of Anton.

Jean-Paul Sartre in Venice; August of 1967. Courtesy of CyberXRef.

William James in Brazil in 1865. Houghton Library, Harvard University. Courtesy of Rob at Houghton.

(1905–1980) and Albert Camus (1913–1960), followed Nietzsche in asserting that truth does not possess an objective stature or quality; in fact, objective truth does not and cannot exist. All that is true is the private self and truth is a personal, private determination. Truth lacks objectivity. It is not to be found in religious affirmations of a reality external and beyond humans; it is not to be found in the world in which human existence is found through observation and reflection; it is within the self and the self-alone.

To establish the ground for morals in a valueless vacuum, Nietzsche's enormous influence bore fruit in the development of philosophical pragmatism and utilitarianism. Again, the advocates of this orientation accepted the destructive Enlightenment criticism of premodern approaches to truth, as well as the intellectual weaknesses of rationalism.

A foremost proponent of pragmatism was William James (1842–1910), a professor at Harvard University in the field of psychology. Truth was not objective; it was subjective and relative; it was what was valued for its residual benefits. Truth was situation-based; it was what leads to what the observer determines are good ends of any particular action.

The Postmodern Worldview

The assertion that truth is ultimately not objective, but merely perspectival (in the view of the observer only) brought the denouement of the Enlightenment experiment. While this did not occur at one particular moment in time, it became evident in the early twentieth century in Western Europe as expressed in the changes in mood and values disseminated in the visual and literary arts, the emergence of the impressionists in art, and deconstructionists in literature. In North America the decline of Enlightenment values and assertions did not surface at the popular level of society and culture until the post-World War II era. Worldview changes could be observed as reflected in the visual arts (impressionism and ashcan art, for example) as well as in the literary arts. However, the tragedy of two world wars and a global depression fore-

stalled manifestation of the significant philosophical changes that were taking place.

By the 1960s and 1970s, the social dislocations following the assassination of John F. Kennedy in the context of the Cuban missile crisis, the torrid and violent student reaction to U.S. involvement in the Vietnam War (including the tragic consequences as witnessed at Kent State University), the hippie movement that flaunted traditional morals, and the Watergate episode leading to the resignation of Richard Nixon and prison terms for his top advisors), seemed to have been the last straw for faith in external authority structures, trust in societal progress, and belief in corporate ethics and moral responsibility. Disillusion replaced trust; faith turned inward; and right and wrong became personal and private in determination.

It is not easy to define postmodernity and perhaps it is more insightful to speak of it in terms of attitudes or moods. What is clear is that postmoderns have rejected the world that the Enlightenment and modernism sought to

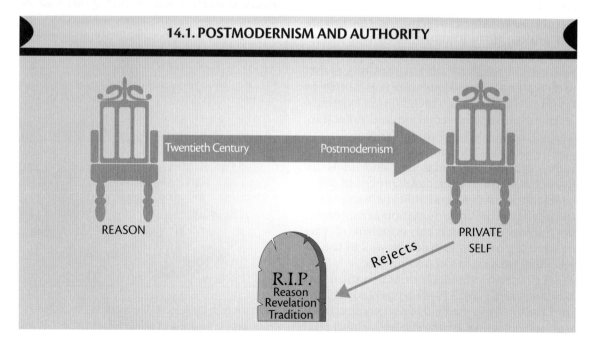

14.1. POSTMODERNISM AND AUTHORITY

Twentieth Century   Postmodernism

REASON

PRIVATE SELF

Rejects

R.I.P.
Reason
Revelation
Tradition

erect; it is the recognition of the failure of the modernist project three hundred years in the making. Some have preferred to call it "ultra-modernism," recognizing that in a very real sense it was a child of modernity, resulting in pessimism about discovering absolute truth. There are only "truths," though often found in conflict with other "truths"; solace is discovered in the private, personal realm of one's existence.

Postmoderns prefer to enter into dialogue about "truths," what they call "conversation," that should lead to mutual tolerance of diversity, not resolution. Unlike moderns who believed in an overarching meaning and theme in life, what is called a metanarrative, whether it be progress through national consciousness, capitalist materialism and free markets, or socialism, postmoderns are skeptical that there is a metanarrative, a higher meaning than simply daily existence. It is the belief that every individual should make something beautiful of his/her self. It is John Lennon's great line, "Everything is beautiful; everything is fine."

From a historical perspective, Christian orthodoxy embraces the philosophical priority of metaphysics, that the existence of truth is neither exclusively dependent on the human faculties of perception nor limited to source-acquisition through the mind or the senses. The grand Christian assumption has been that there is what has been called a "sixth sense" or source of knowledge and that is the self-revelation of God accessible through the senses but that is dependent on a regenerating and subsequently illuminating work of the Spirit of God—that Christian faith begins with the self-revealing God who has spoken through a divine disclosure.

Without the presupposition of revelation, the Christian faith is merely the thought-structure of another disposable and fleeting attempt to explain behavior in the human sphere and offer some kind of solution to human emptiness and blight. For Christian orthodoxy, epistemology follows first principles; it does not and cannot lead to them. It is what secular and some religious philosophers and historians have dubbed with a pejorative bias "precritical" or "prescientific."

"What is the relation between Christianity and modern culture; may Christianity be maintained in a scientific age? It is this problem which modern liberalism attempts to solve. Admitting that scientific objections may arise against the particularities of the Christian religion—against the Christian doctrines of the person of Christ, and of redemption through His death and resurrection—the liberal theologian seeks to rescue certain of the general principles of religion, of which these particularities are thought to be mere

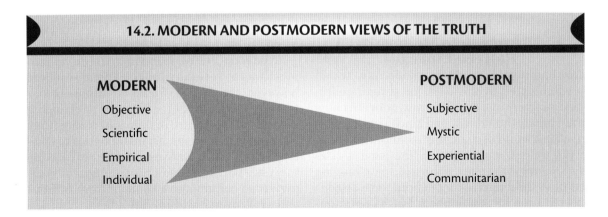

14.2. MODERN AND POSTMODERN VIEWS OF THE TRUTH

MODERN	POSTMODERN
Objective	Subjective
Scientific	Mystic
Empirical	Experiential
Individual	Communitarian

temporary symbols, and these general principles he regards as constituting 'the essence of Christianity'" (J. Gresham Machen, *Christianity and Liberalism*, 5).

If the critics are correct in their assumption that only reason or personal values only lead to what can be known, the criticism of anti-intellectualism and intellectual incoherence charged against Christian orthodoxy is valid. However, are not the critics liable to the charge of unsustainable presuppositions that are treated as axiomatic as Nietzsche and Sartre, among others, have argued?

The Christian orthodox response to modernity and postmodernity is that in basic assumptions the two are not far apart. While they are separable when it comes to the nature of truth (Is truth objective, being verifiable through argument based on repeatability and observability? Or is truth not subject to arguments, but merely personal and relative?), they share the same incomplete starting point. Each rejects, without question, that there is any truth available that is beyond the scientific method or personal experience. Christian faith fundamentally asserts that there is an immense world of reality that is only accessible through divine disclosure. Both make the fatal mistake of being with the great "I," the self, rather than the Great Being. Consequently, from a Christian perspective, they can only arrive at incomplete, inadequate truth, missing far more truth than can be obtained.

The Reaction to Modernity: A Pattern Emerges

The questioned posed by modernity, which predominated in the West for several centuries, and now by postmodernity, concerns how the church should respond since it has found itself in a world of changing assumptions about truth, values, and priorities. The issue is relevancy: how is the church to speak in a changing culture. The church cannot afford to be disconnected from its parishioners. Since communi-cation is within a shared context, the church must be aware of context to speak meaningfully and relevantly. With change comes the necessity of change. It is vital to ask the question: What can be given away or discarded and what must be kept at all costs? This is the dilemma that all churches encounter if they want to have a sustaining voice.

Generally speaking, the churches responded to the impact of modernity in one of two ways. The liberal tradition reacted to the emerging rational movement by adopting the approach to knowledge and assumptions of the Enlightenment. The knowledge of God, which they rigorously sought to preserve, was allowed only to the extent of what information was available through the scientific, **Baconian method**. The knowledge of God became an extension of self-knowledge. This required the liberal tradition to change their view of the authority of the Bible and, consequently, how the Bible is to be read. From a conservative and orthodox vantage point, accommodation degenerated into concession with the result that the essence of the Christian faith was abandoned. What the Christian faith became in that tradition was often worthy of acclaim, but what remained of vital truth was grotesque, anorexic, and skeletal. Liberalism responded to modernity by redefining the faith. It emphasized the fruit of Christian faith, social care and compassion, without the core of the faith. Morals became the faith and Christianity, a religion not of theological verities, but social and moral truths.

The conservative reaction to the Enlightenment was as variegated as the liberal reaction; however, the former found it impossible to surrender historic Christian faith to changing theories of the nature of time and reality (they were not willing to subject metaphysics to epistemology). Conservatives refused to redefine the Christian message and consequently experienced cultural estrangement from without and controversy within. The liberal tradition overwhelmed the churches and conservatives found themselves required to restructure outside the traditional denominations. Conservatives have struggled, as have their liberal counterparts, to maintain a religious influence in the prevailing culture.

The Liberal Tradition and Postmodernity

The same question that modernity posed to the churches in the twentieth century is now proposed by postmodernity in the twenty-first century. How are churches to remain vital sustaining their role, if there is any, in the health and future of the culture? At same time the question is being asked, when does accommodation, the attempt to speak in an understanding and relevant way, end and the tragedy of concession, giving away too much, begin?

The liberal tradition seems to have allowed orthodox theology to be lost in the struggle with modernity and absolutist moral standards to postmodernity. Pluralism, relativism, and tolerance seem to be by far the cardinal virtues in this tradition. Liberalism today has stepped beyond the morals proscribed in the Bible. Often religious liberalism's perception of morality is quite contrary to the Bible, executed in the context that is more informed by cultural trends that have relativized freedom and tolerance.

The liberal tradition, which succumbed to modernity, is now devastated by postmodernity. The liberal tradition with the rise of modernity rejected the theology of the Bible and lived off the fumes of its morals; the liberal tradition in postmodernity has jettisoned the moral absolutes of the Bible and now have nothing to offer but pragmatic self-help schemes and the call for governmental intervention.

Religious Conservativism and Postmodernity

The conservative reactions to the changes that have entered culture over the most recent decades are far too variegated and complex to admit to generalization. Further, the historian has been greatly hindered in discerning meaningful trends and rendering decisive statements, without the perspective of decades. Now less than two decades into the twenty-first century, it is too early for conservative scholars to speak with clarity.

A new trend within the complex maze of Protestant Christendom is offering a distinctly different lens to make some sense of the myriad of pieces of what appears to be an unassembled jigsaw puzzle. A premodern would say that the mystery of the unassembled parts is found in the yet undisclosed, incomprehensible wisdom of God who has revealed himself in the Bible truly, but not completely.

Modernists would say that with greater research, planning, applied technology, and graceful effort they could figure out a way to assemble the pieces. Simply wait, time will bring with it greater insight. Polio was conquered, was it not? A man walked on the moon, did he not? Postmodernists would say that you can assemble the pieces any way because there is no single objective. Any puzzle order will work, and all attempts are valid.

The distinctives hammered out in the **Protestant Reformation** along doctrinal lines (**Arminianism**, **Calvinism**, **Lutheranism**) and ecclesiastical lines are no longer the best way to describe contemporary Protestant religion, particularly evangelical/conservative branches. In a very real and disturbing, yet undeniable sense, the Reformation influence of the sixteenth century has declined in Western culture and the churches (witness the current trend to separate from denominational titles, for example). Instead, it is suggested that it would be clearer to think of how conservatives access the truth. Though most evangelicals would argue for a premodern understanding of what can be known, the sum of knowledge being greater than what can be acquired by experience and experimentation, there is no consensus among evangelicals as to the quest for objectivity in reading the Bible. The great divide is, therefore, between postconservative evangelicals and traditionalist evangelicals.

Postconservative evangelicals have argued that traditional evangelicalism unwittingly has embraced the rationalist approach to knowledge; that, as much as religious conservatives struggled against the inroads of the Enlightenment, they have adopted a theory of knowledge that has led to the endangerment of the Christian faith. The accusation by postconservative scholars is that the traditionalists have reduced the Bible to self-evident truths that can be collected into a series of timeless, logical propositions that dismiss the historical context of the Bible, resulting in a nonliterary reading of the text.

Some evangelicals believe that Scottish common sense and rationalist theories of knowledge acquisition have been allowed far too much sway in reading the Scriptures. While these insights may have some legitimacy, traditionalists have criticized the postconservative scholar for embracing the recognition of the role of context and literary genre but also confusing epistemology with metaphysics. Critics have also asserted that some are too dependent on the creedal formulations of the past. To use the past as the measure of orthodoxy, whether it is the ecumenical creeds of the late patristic era or the confessional and catechetical formulations of the sixteenth century, is to deny the progressive and contextual nature of truth.

In postconservative thought, the words of the Bible are not as authoritative as the writers of the Bible; what is authoritative is not the teachings or doctrine but the "story" the writer is seeking to convey. The experience of the reader has greater interpretative potential than the actual words of the writer. The locus of revelation is not so much in the text as it is in the observer's consequent religious impressions and experience. Such an approach seems reflective of the early liberal approach to the Bible in the late nineteenth century. The Bible is not so much the Word of God as it is an oc-

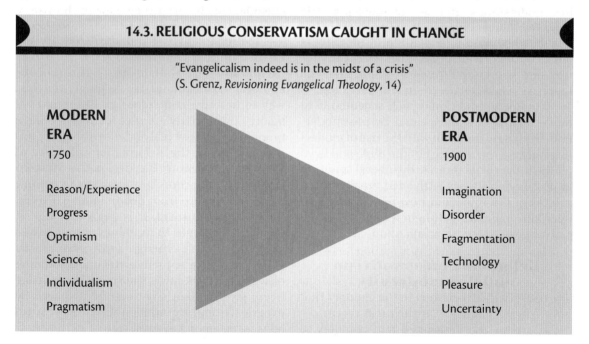

14.3. RELIGIOUS CONSERVATISM CAUGHT IN CHANGE

"Evangelicalism indeed is in the midst of a crisis"
(S. Grenz, *Revisioning Evangelical Theology*, 14)

MODERN ERA 1750	POSTMODERN ERA 1900
Reason/Experience	Imagination
Progress	Disorder
Optimism	Fragmentation
Science	Technology
Individualism	Pleasure
Pragmatism	Uncertainty

casion for the Word of God to break forth in the experience of the reader.

William Newton Clarke (1840–1912), a prominent proponent of early American Protestant liberalism through the insights of a Ritchlian approach to the Bible, appeared to resonate with the postconservative understanding of the Bible (admittedly there are differences in their respective approaches to the Bible in that Clarke saw non-revelatory data in the Bible while the postconservative takes an entirely different and personalized approach). Clarke recognized that there were two distinct approaches to the Bible; one that he called a historic, "scholarly view" and the other a "popular view " each an "appalling distance apart."

In *The Use of the Scriptures in Theology* (1905), Clarke claimed that "every intelligent student of the Bible knows that the ancient method is wrong." An understanding the Bible is seen though the lens of personal experience. He wrote in the work cited above, "Is it a matter of common experience that every lover of the Bible analyzes the book into the elements he best understands, and has for himself a little Bible of his own making within the Bible. . . ."

In the somewhat biographical *Sixty Years with the Bible* (1909), the rehearsal of his interpretative sojourn, Clarke explained how he changed from believing that the words of the Bible had meaning to discerning the spiritual meaning of the Bible, the essence of the Bible not being in the words but in thoughts and concepts, in "the ethical and spiritual principles." The Bible became for Clarke not so much a message as an inspiration. As a result, Clarke disparaged the previous accomplishments of the church and its progress in understanding theology, having said, "I belong to a generation that has outlived the necessity of such theories."

"I was beginning to know also, in slight degree, how much it means that the Bible is a genuinely historical book, having its rise and habitat in the human world, recording vital dealings between God and men, and to be understood in the light of its historical origins, intentions, and development. No longer an unrelieved level of equal authority, it was beginning to have its hills and dales, its lights and shades, as a book of real life, the life of God in man and of man with God" (William Newton Clark, *Sixty Years with the Bible*, 68).

Among traditionalist evangelicals, which is a very wide constituency, several trends are discernible as they have sought to react to the emergence of post modernity, which has brought with it a decline in historic Protestant allegiances and affirmations, particularly discernible in the Baby Busters, children born between 1960 and 1980, and Generation X or the Millennials, children born after 1980 and reaching adult status in the twenty-first century.

In growing up, Baby Busters, the children of the postwar Baby Boomers, experienced the Cold War, the energy crises of the 1970s, economic recession, the AIDS tragedy, the Challenger disaster, and the Iranian hostage episode, which was a precursor of the rise of militant Islam. It was the first generation of Americans to experience the home computer, cable television, and the Internet.

The Millennials, Generation Y, Generation Next, or the Trophy Generation (so called because of quest for success and recognition) has been deeply influenced by the massive increase and availability of knowledge through media and digital technology that has created the uncertainty of truth, morals, and purpose. American youth have been educated on the virtues of values clarification (the insight that there are no absolute verities, only private choices) and tolerance (though intolerance has become an evil). Religious faith has declined in importance among American youth, a recent survey suggesting that 20 percent did not believe in God and another 32 percent were unsure. Church attendance among young adults has diminished significantly as well.

While traditional evangelicals differ significantly in theological starting points and the prioritization of various doctrinal perspectives, they appear to be bound together by a prescientific or premodern perspective—the assumption that metaphysics precede epistemology. The fullest degree of religious knowledge must begin with the assumptions that God exists, that God has chosen to reveal himself to humankind, that the vehicle that God chose was Christ, that Christ revealed the Father to his apostles and other followers, that the central message that Christ delivered was spiritual union with God through his own debt-paying sacrifice to appease the just wrath of a holy God toward sinners, and that some of Christ's disciples left literary remains that God so supervised in the composition and preserved in his providence that they are accurate and true reflections of the revelation through Christ.

While God reveals himself in and through nature, it is inadequate to reveal what God has done for his people to make them his children and what he expects of them, a life of gratitude expressed in obedience. Traditional evangelicals believe that the assumptions about the existence and revelation of God in Christ and the Bible are the starting points simply because the wisdom of God can never be accessed by finite beings; it must be revealed to them. They also believe that such beginning assumptions are entitled, being neither a-rational nor irrational, because with them the Christian faith offers an explanation of what is observable in human behavior and offers hope that the human tragedy will end. Traditionalists do not believe as they do because the faith can be proven, lest there be not room for faith, but that it is reasonable and they have a right to embrace it.

Traditionalists are found in many faith groups that seem to be defying the general trend of numerical decline from the numerous varieties of Pentecostal and charismatic churches to a plethora of denominational bodies, such the Southern Baptist Convention, the Presbyterian Church in America, and the Evangelical Free Church, to the independent church movement. This is not to say that the traditional churches have been without internal turmoil—such as style of worship (the traditional versus contemporary or the blended services), the seeker-friendly philosophy of attracting attendees, and the role of women. The enormous breadth and variety of traditionalist proclamation of the gospel is impossible to completely describe.

In the twenty-first century religious conservatism appears to be in the same torturous maelstrom of indecision and redefinition as was the American liberal tradition at the end of the nineteenth century. In some quarters, certainly reflective of segments of the emergent/emerging conversation, buttressed and shaped by the epistemological insights of postmodernity, historic Christian faith is being ridiculed with the same rhetoric and arguments that began to appear in the 1890s. The old liberalism is making a renaissance in the guise of a new evangelicalism: postconservative, postreformational, and postpatristic Christianity. With a modified understanding of the human blight of the soul, a redefining of the accomplishments of Christ, the restructuring of the gospel, and the elimination of divine justice and infinite wrath (hell), the new evangelicalism is little more than the rebirth of a tried and failed explanation of human improvement.

The liberal tradition and the "new evangelical conversants" have firmly rejected traditional confessions of the Christian faith and threaten to reduce Christianity to the morals of do-goodism without any objective basis other than the amorphous rhetoric of moral tolerance. Elements of "evangelicalism" are liberalism revisited in the dress of a new epistemology of knowing and the result is a new way of reading the timeless book.

"This is part of the problem with continually insisting that one of the absolutes of the Christian Faith must be a belief that 'Scripture alone' is our guide. It sounds nice but is it not true?" (Rob Bell, *Velvet Elvis*, 67).

This, however, is not to suggest that Christianity is imperiled by the actions of well meaning, pseudo-friends; it is not. What merely delights the mind cannot assuage the conscience, though it can weaken and delude it. If the term *evangelicalism* can be used of those who profess the "old" gospel in a new set of cultural values, it will endure with many finding the "old, old story" of heaven gained and hell disdained, abounding in endless joy and comfort in spite of a culture that has lost every semblance of an anchor except the frail self, materialism, and entertainment. This is not the time for the prophets of God to preach the soothing gospel of "I'm ok, you're ok."

Though there is much to cause consternation and disappointment in the religious kaleidescope of Christianity, there is much cause for great delight. The true gospel has the potential through advances in the technological sciences to reach vast numbers of people in unprecedented ways. The historic mission fields of the world are becoming missionary sending centers and a generation is quietly and surprisingly emerging that will form the next waves of servants to carry the gospel around the world, across the street, and down dark ghettos. However, American Christianity appears on the brink of struggling with a new liberalism, evangelical liberalism, which threatens to bring a new potential for weakening the visible church. While it is a serious moment for those who embrace the old faith as ever new, it will fade like sad memories because the Lord has promised that the "gates of hell" will not prevail against his church.

GLOSSARY OF TERMS

Arminianism: a tradition of theological interpretation that emerged in sixteenth-century Holland in opposition to the prevailing Calvinism of the day. Arminians argued that the best defense of the faith was in modifying Calvinism in the areas of anthropology, soteriology, and the nature of the atonement as expressed in the Five Remonstrances of 1610, believing that human inability and responsibility were incompatible and so surrendered human inability.

Baconian Method: a means of the acquisition of knowledge through observation, inductive reasoning, and rational reflection espoused by Sir Francis Bacon in 1620.

Calvinism: an approach to the understanding of Holy Scripture that emphasizes the divine omnipotence of the triune God and the perspectives of eternity as the starting points of the divine disclosure of revealed truth that are relentlessly followed in understanding the content and metanarrative of the Bible. Correctly attributed in seminal structure with Calvin's *Institutes of the Christian Religion*, commentaries, and creedal formulation, the movement has evolved in varying contents and is reflective of a variegated set of organizational perspectives.

Deconstructionism: see *Postmodernism/ Deconstructionism/Ultramodernism*.

Enlightenment (Age of Reason): a movement begun in eighteenth-century Europe that emphasized the inner capacities of man (rational reflection, intuition) as opposed to external authority sources such as the church or the Bible to improve social and society performance. Strenuously opposed by the religious community as well as secular materialists, the Enlightenment spawned the modern era, a three-century experiment in the redemptive values of science and technology. Though highly successful in the technical realms, the venture collapsed under the weight of holocausts and wars, suggesting that the blight of human discord could not be remedied by social advances alone. The movement filled life with opportunities but emptying it of meaning, creating postmodernism.

Existentialism: an approach to the concept of knowing that was a reaction to Enlightenment rationalism, particularly Kantian rationalism. It insists that the starting point must be the individual self and experience, not reflection or empiricism; truth is subjective and personal. Theistic existentialism is reflected in the writings of Søren Kierkegaard, who adopted Hegel's idealist approach to dispel it; atheistic existentialism can be seen in Paul Sartre.

Lutheranism (Lutheran): a major tradition of Protestant orthodoxy that emerged in the sixteenth century, largely associated with the insights of Martin Luther. The tradition finds as its starting point in the personal accomplishments of Jesus Christ (therefore, sometimes referred to as the Theology of the Cross) and is reflective in its liturgy, including a strongly literal nonsacramental interpretation of the Eucharist.

Postmodernism (Deconstructionism/Ultramodernism): a view of reality expressed as a way of understanding values that rejected the assumptions of modernity, the three-hundred-year experiment and exploitation of the advances in the scientific and technology realms to secure a level of improved human condition through rationalistic devotion to the powers of the mind with its emphasis on human potential, optimism of success, and progressivism. Having lost faith in the Enlightenment agenda, as evidenced early in the writings of Nietzsche, this approach turned away from the mind, corporate consensus, and faith in progress to find solace in the inner self, private values, and individualistic tribalism.

Pragmatism: a theory for the establishment of human virtue and moral decisionmaking arguing that functional utility or favorable outcomes are the ground of choice making. It asks the question, "Will it produce a good or favorable outcome if a particular action is pursued?"

Prescientific/Precritical Worldview: an approach to life, value, and meaning that deposits authority outside human dimensions of knowledge acquisition; it is adherence to the notion that metaphysics (what is ultimately valid and true) precedes epistemology (how one knows those things). The first priority is faith as a foundation that leads to understanding, not understanding (epistemology) seeking the structure of faith and truth. It is a worldview that asserts human frailty and incompetence and at the same time recognizes that knowledge must first be revealed before it is discovered. Often ridiculed as anti-intellectual and archaic, if not demeaning to the human self, it prevailed in the church from its inception until the inroads of the Enlightenment, with its optimistic assumption of human potential sustained an indelible influence.

Protestant Reformation: an attempt to reform the late medieval Catholic church. Contrary to its Roman Catholic nemesis, itself also a reforming endeavor, the Protestant reformers believed that moral correction and educational enhancement were only the superficial issues, though certainly important. The heart of the Protestant passion was the recovery of the gospel of the absolute grace of God expressed in the insight that divine righteous is reckoned solely because of the provision of Christ, not incrementally infused through sacramental obedience; that Christ's substitutionary death did not secure a possibility or chance of salvation (a chance being no chance at all) but that it accomplished all that is required for God in justice to declare the sinner justified and acquitted.

Rationalism (Rational Worldview): an approach to the acquisition of knowledge that emerged in the Enlightenment that rejected medieval notions of external authority, whether it be the Scriptures, the institutional church, or both. Rationalists argued that all that can be known must meet the criteria of repeatability, verifiability, and worthiness of belief that would seem to reject the unseen and the possibility of the supernatural. As a method of knowing, rationalism is often appropriate; as a method of knowledge of all things it is deficient because it excludes the possibility that the existence of what the approach disqualifies is possible.

Renaissance: a cultural and intellectual movement that emerged in fourteenth-century Italy and sustained a discernible influence into the seventh century in Europe and spread throughout the seventeenth-century Europe that celebrated a resurgence of classical learning. It proved to be a strong intellectual impetus for the sixteenth-century reformations in that its focus on the humanities brought an emphasis on self-understanding. While it did not question medieval authority structures, it did question how they are embraced. Further, it was an impetus for the later Enlightenment Period that stressed the importance of individual belief and search to find it, but divorced it from medieval assumptions of authority. Thus, scholars think of the Modern Period as having two parts: early modern and late modern; eras that shared the same approach to knowledge through the humanities, but embraced diverse theories of authority.

Renaissance Humanism: a cultural and educational reform emphasis that emerged in the fourteenth and fifteenth centuries in reaction to medieval scholasticism, emphasizing personal affirmation of truth through a study of the sources of belief-structures, as well as the engagement of civic life through speaking and writing with eloquence and clarity. Its focus was upon the study of the humanities with the new curriculum of university education, a shift from the scholastic preoccupation with rational explanation of the medieval faith to the readoption and prominence of the Aristotelian method.

Ritschlianism: an approach to reading the Bible championed by Albrecht Ritschl who believed that the Bible contained revelational material though encrusted with errant concepts engrafted into the text over centuries of transmission, even misperception by its writers. The Ritchlians proposed a method for recovering the essential message of the Bible that became popular in classic American liberalism with its christocentric approach. Simply put, all that was found in the Bible in accord with what Jesus would have said or done was valid; however Ritchlians, German or American, viewed Jesus as merely an inspired and inspiring person.

Roman Catholic Church: a movement that gradually emerged out of the increasingly moral, social, and theological divergences and controversies within the late medieval church. Like its counterpart the Protestant movement,

proponents claim historic verification for its teaching ("that which has always and everywhere been taught in the church), though seriously flawed and lacking demonstrable consistency through the centuries. It seems that the defining definitional moments of the church were the Fourth Lateran Council, the Council of Florence (1439), and the enormously important formal creedalization and dogmatization of its teaching at the Council of Trent in the sixteenth century.

Romanticism (Romantic Movement, Romantic Philosophy): a movement in the latter half of the eighteenth century in reaction to the dangers of Enlightenment rationalism and the scientific revolution with its quest for truth primarily in the cognitive faculties with the consequential denigration or diminution of the affective and emotional faculties of the human makeup. The Romantic Movement, expressed religiously in transcendentalism and mysticism, finds the quest for meaning in humankind, though in a different faculty, the emotive and the intuitional, the balance or harmony with nature.

Secularism (Secularity): a term coined in the early nineteenth century to postulate a division between church and state, suggestive that the two spheres are separate and independent. The term has come to define a system of beliefs and consequent practices that are not informed by the traditions and conceptions of the place and value of religion. Clearly, it is not a synonym for inappropriate behavioral patterns; it embraces the assumption that values can be sustained in society without the necessity of religious values.

Further Readings:
Postmodernism Period (1900–Present)

Brown, Colin. *Philosophy and the Christian Faith*. London: Inter-Varsity Press, 1973.

Kuhn, Thomas S. The Structure of Scientific Revolution. Chicago, The University of Chicago Press. 1970.

Neill, Stephen, and Tom Wright. *The Interpretation of the New Testament, 1861-1986*. New ed. New York: Oxford University Press, 1988.

Johnson, Paul. *Intellectuals*. New York" Harper&Rowe publishers, 1988.

Grenz, Stanley J. and Olson, Roger E. *20th Century Theology: God and the World in a Transitional Age*. Downers Grove, IL: IntyerVarsity Press, 1992.

Harris, Horton. *The Tübingen School: A Historical and Theological Investigation of the School of F.C. Baur*. Grand Rapids, MI: Baker Book Houe, 1990.

Ramm, Bernard L. *After Fundamentalism: The Future of Evangelical Theology*. 1st ed. San Francisco: Harper & Row, 1983.P

Reardon, Bernard M. G. *Religious Thought in the Nineteenth Century*. London: Cambridge University Press, 1966.

Robinson, Marilynne. *The Death of Adam: Essays on Modern Thought*. Boston: Houghton Mifflin, 1998.

Tarnas, Richard. The Passion of the Western Mind. New York;: Ballantine Books, 1991.

POSTCRIPT: WHAT IS REALLY HAPPENING?

ON 24 AUGUST 410, Alaric the Visigoth ravished the ancient capital of the Roman Empire, the city of Rome. Aside from the display of barbarism and the toll of human suffering, the psychological shock that the great city had been devastated and the empire in the West rapidly imploding sent inquisitive minds into a state of consternation. Why did the great city fall to the barbarians? The city had not experienced such destruction in nearly 800 years, the last being by the Gauls in 387 BC. Perhaps more importantly, the great empire embraced the Christian faith under Constantine and had become the sole religion of the empire under Theodosius I in AD 380. How could this have happened? Could it be that the God of the Christians was weak and ineffectual? To many of the educated classes, as well as many that were not, the question demanded an answer. What is happening? How does one makes sense of all this?

Augustine, bishop of Hippo, in the fifth century wrote a response to such inquires that has been recognized as unsurpassed in influence, *The City of God*. It is a defense of God and his ways among the nations; and, at the same time, it is a theodicy, an answer to the problem of evil, an explanation of divine providence, a defense of God's goodness in the affairs of humankind, and an eschatology (an explanation of the course of human events and their culmination). What he presented was a theory of history from a divine perspective that, though modified subsequently over the centuries, has remained intact.

The question that Augustine focused his intellectual and literary abilities to answer is relevant as this study of the history of the Christian church draws to a conclusion. The great leader in the church made the point that nations rise and fall subject to the inscrutable and omnipotent will of God; nations are as the prophet Isaiah described them, dust in a scale and a drop of water in a bucket, though they display the appearance of permanence. In reality nations find their origin in the purposes of an infinite God who lifts them up and dashes them to pieces when the intent of their existence spins its course. All nations find their beginning and end in the divine purposes of God.

There is another story of divine intent that weaves its way through the nations and time; it is the grand invisible metanarrative that rises above the nations of the world, past and present; it transcends temporalities and will triumph over them. All nations, and their many peoples, will end with time, but with their demise the greatest story ever told will come to fruition.

The greater story is so complex and dazzling that it seems preposterous, insane, and simply unbelievable. In this world of such massive contortions and convolutions are actually two people groups. Each group is characterized by love, one a love for self and the other a love for God and people, the latter being the supporting cast of the great redemptive drama and those who are the objects of it. It is only at the end of times that the two groups will be definitively separated. In the meantime, what Augustine called the "two cities" continue to function together, though they do so with a degree of constant conflict, sometimes overt and destructive and at other times subtle.

If the grand metanarrative of human history is a redemptive drama in which God is gathering a people to dwell in his presence forever, how is that explained? The answer is found in the sacred writings of the Christian faith, the Bible. The Bible unfolds a redemptive story, but the unfolding of that story is through the creation of time and nations. The Bible begins with the story of a divine creation, a garden in which God dwelt in the presence of humankind. The dwelling of God was defaced through the introduction of human sin, leading to expulsion from the garden, its destruction, and the advent of violence and death. However, that is not the end of the story since the Bible ends with the reappearance of a garden par-

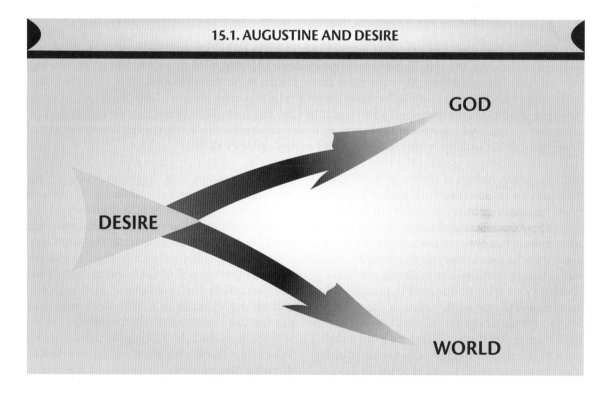

15.1. AUGUSTINE AND DESIRE

GOD

DESIRE

WORLD

adise, a gathered people from all the nations of the earth, with God once more and forever dwelling in the midst of his people.

While human history has been punctuated by more years of international conflict than it has of peace, the world from a Christian viewpoint will culminate in the reestablishment of a durative peace and tranquility. What God is doing is gathering the participants of the new garden from the defaced garden, the pseudo realm of existence marked by conflicts and strife (though also temporal joys and delights). After centuries of anticipating the one who would make the garden possible, Jesus Christ came and through his death as the world's redeemer conquered death, as evidenced by his resurrection. Based on the payment that Jesus offered in himself to appease and placate the just wrath of God, God is both just and the one who justifies those who place their faith in the provisions of his Son at Calvary. Based on the

provisions of Christ, the gathering of a new people in a new garden became possible.

The spiritual story, the invisible story, is that of a divine redemption being played out among the nations. The history of the Christian church is the story of the agency that God ordained for the proclamation of the story of his Son's epic-changing death on a cross. The instructions to the church are plain, "Therefore go and make disciples of all nations . . ." (Matt. 28:20); ". . . as the Father has sent me I am sending you" (John 20:21). The history of the church is the story of the extension of divine grace through the instrumentation of human efforts, often at the high cost of enormous personal sacrifice, in the gathering of the constituents of the new garden. The story goes on daily and will do so until the kingdom of the Lord Jesus, all the true people of God from the first Adam to the very last to be called, who have been redeemed through the second Adam (1 Cor. 15:50–57). At

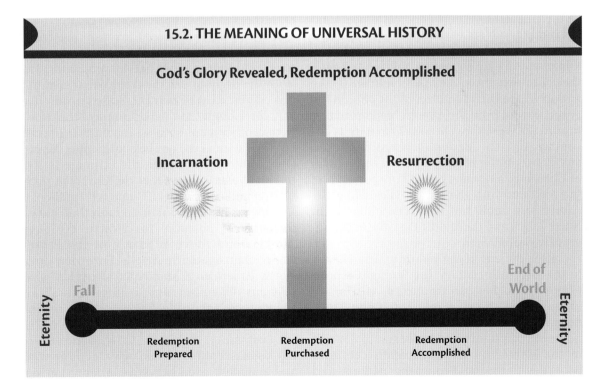

15.2. THE MEANING OF UNIVERSAL HISTORY

God's Glory Revealed, Redemption Accomplished

Incarnation

Resurrection

Eternity

Fall

End of World

Eternity

Redemption Prepared

Redemption Purchased

Redemption Accomplished

Christ's second coming and the end of time, the kingdom of Christ, the people that he purchased, will be given to God the Father who shall reign forever and ever (15:20–28).

That is how this world will end and that is how things will be understood from the vantage point of eternity. However, what appears to be the immediate prospects of the Christian faith should the end of times be decades, even centuries away? What is clear, looking at the history of centuries of the proclamation of the story of God's mercy through his people, is that different geographical regions of our world have had the benefit of gospel witness and that the shadow of intensity has moved with the centuries. The gospel was given to an ethnic people, the ancient Israelites, in covenants, symbols, ceremonies, and feasts. They were to be a light to the nations around them, but they often fell victim to their religious habits and dispositions. What ancient Israel failed to be, the true Israel, Jesus Christ (John 8:12) became as the true light of the world. With his ascension and the advent of the Spirit of God, a new age began in the expansion of the gospel. Certainly and deeply rooted in ancient Judaism, the church was given the task unfulfilled by the nation. In the early centuries of the church the gospel spread from the eastern Mediterranean toward the West, the centers of Christianity becoming Antioch, Alexandria, Constantinople, and Rome. In the medieval period the centers of Christian faith emerged in Europe north of the Alps and into the British Isles while the church lost significant territorial influence in North Africa and the Middle East due to the aggressive Islamic faith.

After the era of the reform of the church in the sixteenth century, the Roman Catholic Church launched an extensive missionary program that stretched into South and North America, as well as India and the Pacific rim nations. Protestant missions began to flourish in the eighteenth and nineteenth centuries with the European Protestant nations and

North America becoming the hub of Christian influence into the twentieth century. The locus of Christian faith appears to be shifting once more. Northern European nations, once a center for Protestant missionary extension, have become a missionary field. While North America remains the center of Christian faith, significant signs suggest that it will not long be the case as the current century takes its course. There is, for example, a growing biblical illiteracy in the churches in the West. At the same time that Christianity appears to be declining in the West, new centers of Christian faith are emerging in Africa, China, the Pacific Rim nations, and South America. The color of Christian faith is turning brown, black, and oriental. It has been argued that by the middle of the century the strength of Christianity will be located south of the equator in the southern hemisphere.

A sense of the shift in Christian population centers can be grasped by the realization that at the beginning of the nineteenth century only 1 percent of all Protestant Christians lived outside of Europe and North America. By the century's end that number had increased to 10%. With the beginning of the twenty-first century, it is estimated at 66 percent. Stated in another way, for example, at the beginning of the twentieth century it has been estimated that 10-million Christians lived on the continent of Africa. One hundred years later, the estimate is 360 million. Some suggest that the Christian population in the Republic of China is 80 million.

The segment of Christian faith that shows the greatest potential for growth in South America and Africa is clearly of the Pentecostal/charismatic heritage. European and North American Christianity struggles with religious liberalism and cultural pluralism, showing evidence of declining numbers and increased biblical illiteracy while churches in the Far East, Africa, and South America are generally less susceptible to theological compromise and manifest a conservative orientation on social and moral issues that have caused disruption and dissension in the churches in the West. It seems clear that the focus of Christian strength is shifting away from North America to other global regions. Regions that have been the object of European and North American missionary endeavor for nearly two-hundred years are rapidly becoming missionary-sending centers to the West, especially in light of vast population migrations into the West.

The shape of the future of our Lord's church will continue to be the subject of a vast volume of literature. No scholar fully grasps the meaning of the events that transpire before her or him. The church waits in hope, the immediate future yet to unfold, when the Lord of the church will come to gather his purchased people into a new realm of existence on a renovated earth with sin and death conquered, to dwell in the presence of his people, and to receive their praise and delight forever. No one knows when that will occur, but the church actively rests knowing that the kingdom will someday be given by Jesus Christ to God the Father and time shall be no more!

In 1867 Walter C. Smith composed a poem based on 1 Timothy 1:17, ironically the very text that Jonathan Edwards encountered that removed his doubts concerning the doctrine of divine sovereignty and proved the gateway into his conversion. It is a fitting capstone to the far-from-completed story of the grand redemptive metanarrative that is being realized on the stage of global history. The past is the cradle that contains the story of the infinite, all-wise, incomprehensible God who has con-

descended to a broken humanity to restore to them his eternal presence through Christ that all his people might behold his glory forever. That story is yet to be completed. Have you joined as a participant in that great redemptive story?

> Immortal, invisible, God only wise,
> In light inaccessible hid from our eyes,
> Most blessed, most glorious, the Ancient
>   of Days,
> Almighty, victorious, Thy great name we
>   praise.
>
> Unresting, unhasting, and silent as light,
> Nor wanting, nor wasting, Thou rulest in
>   might;
> Thy justice, like mountains, high soaring
>   above
> Thy clouds, which are fountains of good-
>   ness and love.
>
> To all, life Thou givest, to both great and small;
> In all life Thou livest, the true life of all;
> We blossom and flourish as leaves on the
>   tree,
> And wither and perish—but naught chan-
>   geth Thee.
>
> Great Father of glory, pure Father of light,
> Thine angels adore Thee, all veiling their
>   sight;
> All laud we would render; O help us to see
> 'Tis only the splendor of light hideth Thee.

EPILOGUE

John 1:4

In him was life, and that life was the light of all mankind.

Colossians 1:13

For he has rescued us from the dominion of darkness and brought us into the kingdom of the Son he loves.

Revelation 21:1-6

[1]Then I saw "a new heaven and a new earth," for the first heaven and the first earth had passed away, and there was no longer any sea. [2]I saw the Holy City, the new Jerusalem, coming down out of heaven from God, prepared as a bride beautifully dressed for her husband. [3]And I heard a loud voice from the throne saying, "Look! God's dwelling place is now among the people, and he will dwell with them. They will be his people, and God himself will be with them and be their God. [4]'He will wipe every tear from their eyes. There will be no more death' or mourning or crying or pain, for the old order of things has passed away."

[5]He who was seated on the throne said, "I am making everything new!" Then he said, "Write this down, for these words are trustworthy and true."

[6]He said to me: "It is done. I am the Alpha and the Omega, the Beginning and the End. To the thirsty I will give water without cost from the spring of the water of life.

COMPLETE GLOSSARY OF TERMS

Adoptionism: a second-century heresy that believed that Jesus was adopted as God's son at his baptism.

Albigenses: a neo-gnostic/Manichean sect of the twelfth and thirteenth centuries originating in Albi, France. Critical of the established church of the day, they were severely persecuted beginning in the reign of Innocent III and destroyed.

All Saints' Day: originating in the early medieval period and celebrated from the pontificate of Gregory IV on November 1st, the day honors the church's saints and martyrs. It was on this day in 1533 that Nicholas Cop delivered an address, perhaps written by Calvin, creating open conflict between Catholic humanists and Protestant sympathizers.

American Board of Commissioners for Foreign Missions: the first foreign mission board (1810), a transdenominational effort of three reformed bodies, was created in the United States following the famous Haystack Prayer Meeting at Williams College in 1806. The first missionaries under its auspices were Adoniram Judson and Luther Rice who joined William Carey in India, the former moving to Burma a year latter.

Anabaptist Movement: a tradition within Protestantism that emphasized believer's baptism, congregational authority, and the separation of church and state. Though a general term for a variety of anti-magisterial groups, a conservative element emerged among them in Zurich that is the origin of Baptists.

Anti-Semitism (Anti-Semitic): a prejudicialist view, expressed in hostility and hatred, against the Jewish race.

Apollinarianism: a fourth-century heresy that believed that Jesus had a human body and lower soul but did not possess a human mind. The view was condemned at the second ecumenical council (Constantinople, 381) under the direction of Theodosius I.

Apostolic Fathers (Church Fathers, Earliest Fathers): the small group of writers or anonymous writing that came within two generations or less of the era of the canonical writers, giving the first glimpses of church life outside the New Testament writings.

Archbishop: an ecclesiastical term indicating an administrator who is in charge of a diocese over several bishops, as well as religious orders within their jurisdiction.

Arianism: the late third-century heresy that Jesus is inferior to God the Father and was not eternally preexistent. Such an understanding of the incarnate Christ was condemned at the ecumenical councils held at Nicaea (325) and Constantinople (381) only to reemerge in the church in the sixteenth century as Socinianism and in the eighteenth century as Deism and Unitarianism.

Aristoteleian Method: an approach to knowing that emphasizes observation, analysis and conclusion, the study of particulars to arrive at universals. As many have indicated, it is a method that probes the specific to arrive at general principles.

Arminianism: a tradition of theological interpretation that emerged in sixteenth-century Holland in opposition to the prevailing Calvinism of the day. Arminians argued that the best defense of the faith was in modifying Calvinism in the areas of anthropology, soteriology, and the nature of the atonement as expressed in the Five Remonstrances of 1610, believing that human inability and responsibility were incompatible and so surrendered human inability.

Athanasian Creed: a sixth century Trinitarian doctrinal confession. It differs from the Apostles' Creed and the Nicene-Constantinople creeds of an earlier time by its inclusion of condemnatory statements or anathemas of what the creed specifically rejects. Its designation is derived from the now-discredited assumption that it was composed by the bishop of Alexandria in the fourth century.

Avars: a Turkish people group that controlled portions of Central and Eastern Europe from the sixth through the ninth centuries.

Baconian Method: a means of the acquisition of knowledge through observation, inductive reasoning, and rational reflection espoused by Sir Francis Bacon in 1620.

Barthianism: see *Neo-Orthodoxy*.

Bedouin: the name given to several tribes of a nomadic, desert-dwelling Arabic ethnic group.

Benedictine Rule: a set of precepts developed by Benedict of Nursia in the sixth century to govern monastic communal life under the authority of an abbot.

Black Death: a disastrous plague carried by flea-infested rats that swept throughout Europe in the fourteenth century introduced. It was from China through the development of trade. Estimates of the enormity of the pandemic reached into the millions causing economic, social, and religious upheaval.

Black Power Movement (Black Power Theology: a manifestation of Liberation Theology that originally emerged in South America in the 1950s, focusing upon social justice and equity, using Christian terms and symbols though often reinterpreting them for polemical value. See *Political Liberation Theology*

Bohemia: a region of what today is in a portion of the Czech Republic with its capital being Prague, as in the fifteenth century, the era of the reformer John Huss.

Brethren (Plymouth) Movement: a movement born in early nineteenth-century Ireland and England that rejected the paralyzing effect of state-controlled ecclesiastical life and the formal ordination of leadership, preferring plural elder-directed chapels and assemblies, (not to be designated churches), emphasizing the centrality of the Lord's Supper in weekly worship, the importance of Bible explanation, a premillennialism/dispensationalist approach to reading the Bible, and the right of every Christian to independently study the Scriptures.

Bultmannian Existentialism: a radical, subjective approach to reading the Bible based on the assumption that the Bible is mythology, a disjunction of faith and history, though Rudolf Bultmann did embrace the notion that there was some authenticity in the biblical texts about the Christ.

Byzantine Empire (Byzantines): the designation of the Roman Empire after the fall of the western portions to tribal intrusion after the fourth century. In late antiquity and the Middle Ages, its capital city was Byzantium (later changed to Constantinople when Constantine made the city his second capital in the fourth century). The Ottoman Turks destroyed the last visages of the Eastern or Byzantine Empire with the Islamic capture of Constantinople in 1453.

Caesaropapism: a view of the relationship of the church and the state that combined secular government with spiritual authority into a single power structure under the bishop of Rome. It has commonly been designated as the theory of the "two Swords," initially proposed by Gelasius I in the late fifth century and frequently supported by the use of Matthew 16:18. Both Roman Catholics and some Protestants embraced the concept in various forms.

Calvinism: an approach to the understanding of Holy Scripture that emphasizes the divine omnipotence of the triune God and the perspectives of eternity as the starting points of the divine disclosure of revealed truth that are relentlessly followed in understanding the content and metanarrative of the Bible. Correctly attributed in seminal structure with Calvin's *Institutes of the Christian Religion*, commentaries, and creedal formulation, the movement has evolved in varying contents and is reflective of a variegated set of organizational perspectives.

Cardinal: a high ecclesiastical office in the Roman Catholic community. Among one's duties as a member of the Sacred College of Cardinals is the election of the next successor to Saint Peter should the pontificate be unoccupied, acting as the pope's official counselors, and dealing with matters of church governance. Cardinals were often advisors to monarchs.

Carolingian Kingdom: a large empire that emerged gradually out of the Frankish tribal kingdom consolidated by Clovis I reaching its apex of power and influence in the eighth and ninth centuries under the ruler of Charlemagne its capital was at Aachen.

Carolingian Renaissance: an eighth- and ninth-century period of intellectual and cultural revival in Europe that reached its height during the reign of Charlemagne who sought to duplicate Augustine's model of the City of God. It reflected an intellectual and cultural advance from the era of the dissolution of the western portion of the Roman Empire before the Viking invasions that destroyed the remnants of Charlemagne's kingdom.

Cartesians: The term assigned to the approach to knowledge acquisition advocated by René Descartes, the seventeenth-century mathematician/philosopher. Those who embrace his method of knowing would argue that there are three realms of knowledge: the mental, the material, and the supernatural. The material can be known through mental deduction based upon divine postulates in the mind and through reflection.

Cassianism: also known as semi-Pelagianism, is frequently understood as a mediating anthropological and soteriological position between the views espoused by Augustine and

Pelagius. John Cassian, from whom the term is derived, argued that divine grace can begin in human sincerity and be finalized by causative cooperativeness between human efforts and divine ones. The Roman Catholic Church is often defined as Cassian by Protestant critics, but the church officially advocates the primacy of grace, though mandating human obedience in cooperation with God to obtain heaven.

Catechumen: in early Christianity the term meant a person who was willing to receive instruction in the faith with the eventual possibility of baptism, the symbol of true Christian profession.

Categorical Imperative: the moral assumption advocated by Immanuel Kant that God has placed into humankind a sense of moral duty that functions as the way to know God. Kant's assumptions were that the Bible is not at all divine and cannot be known apart from human existence and that human morality is the standard of redemption required of God. Kant sought to preserve a place for religious life, but turned theology into morality alone, which proved destructive of it.

Cenobitism: a monastic tradition that emphasizes life in community, as opposed to living as a hermit in solitude. This form of isolated spiritual experience became predominant eclipsing an earlier form, the single hermit living alone in a cave, on a pole, or in some other barren environment.

Chalcedonian Faith (Chalcedonian Convictions, Chalcedonianism): the creedal formulation of the Council of Chalcedon (451) that reaffirmed the christological statements of Nicaea (325) and Constantinople (381) declaring *Nestorianism* and *Eutychianism* to be heretical. The essence of the Chalcedon affirmation is that in Christ's incarnate state he was 100 percent

God, 100 percent man, in one person, and without confusion of those two persons forever.

Charismatic Movement (Pentecostalism, Charismatic Renewalism): the term generally indicates a person, movement, or church that embraces the notion that the extraordinary spiritual gifts have not ceased, that they remain vital to the church's faith and task, and that they evidence a spiritual vitality when consistently practiced. It is a difficult term in the sense that non-charismatics embrace the reality and importance of spiritual giftedness, but do not regularly practice the extraordinary gifts in church life.

Christian Rationalist Tradition: an approach to the defense of the Christian faith in the tradition of Aristotle and Aquinas arguing for a place for mental reflection to demonstrate the truth-claims of Christianity and the compatibility of them with science and other disciplines that emerged through the academy of Christianity, implying that Christian truth is not irrational or non-rational but warranted.

Classic Liberalism: a term that generally refers to the attempt in North American Protestantism to preserve and protect the Christian faith from the inroads and implications of the sciences and philosophy by redefining it. Classic liberals follow the path of Albrecht Ritschl who argued that the Bible only contained the revelation of God, that Jesus was a merely inspiring person, that sin is strictly moral in nature, and that Christ's death was simply a grand moral example.

Cluny Reform Movement: a reforming movement within the Catholic Church of the eleventh century in the monastic community that emerged in Clungy, France. It proved a corrective to the church that had degenerated into a dark nadir of moral, political, and social confusion. The Clungy Movement became so influential that it was able to secure the highest office in the church in Hildebrand, Pope Gregory VII (1073–1085).

College of Cardinals: a group of cardinals in the Roman Catholic Church who are tasked with service to the pope as counselors, governance of the church, and the election of the pontiff should that office become vacant.

Conciliar Movement: a movement in the fourteenth- and fifteenth-century church to restore the papacy after the duplicities and difficulties from the presence of rival claims to Saint Peter's chair. It raised the important issue of the origin of authority in the church unsuccessfully resisting the authority of a single person. The failure of the movement to resolve the issue of authority became one of the major causes of the disruption of the church in the Reformation era.

Concubinage: a practice in the medieval church that allowed priests to experience conjugal privilege without contractual marriage

Cooperationism: a term normally employed to indicate divine/human effort in the attainment of salvation. While most Protestants are cooperationists, they would see the human act in salvation as a responsive, not causative, in contrast to the Roman Catholic teaching of divine/human causation.

Counts (Countess): a title indicating a person of aristocratic nobility. In the Middle Ages it generally designated a person under grant rule by a king of a territory with a kingdom. The term could also imply a military commander.

Crusades (Crusader): normally the term is used to identify a series of European military endeavors between 1095–1291 to interface with Muslim Arabs to recover access to the Holy Land to allow access for religious pilgrims and in the process secure a Latin kingdom. However, there were numerous religious military interventions in the later medieval period against not only Muslims, but supposed heretical groups such as Albigenses and Waldensians.

Danes: an ethnic group native to Denmark, part of the Scandinavian/Viking peoples who invaded Europe in the Middle Ages, bringing to an end the Carolingian Empire. Danish Vikings destroyed the famous monastery at Landisfarne and established a kingdom in Anglo-Saxon England called Daneslaw. The Danes embraced Christianity in the tenth century.

Dark Ages (Age of Darkness): a term that was applied by the Renaissance scholar, Erasmus, to the medieval period reflective of his opinion that the era was a time dominated by the darkness of imposed religious dogmatism. While there was the darkness of cultural and social decline as the Western empire crumbled at the beginning of the period and the nadir of the Viking invasions that collapsed the remnants of the great Carolingian Empire, the millennium must not be thought of in such a negative light because of the cultural and intellectual achievement of the Charlemagnian era, the emergence of scholasticism with the rise of the universities, and the burst of learning that occasioned the rise of the Renaissance in the fourteenth and fifteenth centuries.

Deconstructionism: see *Postmodernism/ Deconstructionism/Ultramodernism.*

Deism: a form of religious philosophy between traditional orthodoxy and naturalism that rejected the immanence of God for a deity that was a distant watchmaker. God made the universe to operate by natural law, separated himself from it, and restricted knowledge of himself, limiting it to rational and empirical discoveries of the intricacies of his creation. Deists such as Herbert of Cherbury, John Biddle, and Benjamin Franklin viewed the essence of religion to be found in moral conduct. It is a form of the rationalist Enlightenment of the seventeenth and eighteenth centuries in religious dress.

Desert Fathers: hermits, ascetics, and monks who retreated to isolated, unpopulated areas beginning in the third century in Egypt. In so doing, they provided a model for the later development of Christian monasticism.

Developmentalism (Evolution): a branch of the biological sciences that focuses on advances in the natural growth of the species. Based on the assumption of epigenesis, that all life sprang from a common source and progressed from simplicity to complexity, developmentalism was naturalistic in its explanation of animal and human life.

Dialectical Theology (Neo-Orthodoxy, Crisis Theology): an orientation to theology that developed in reaction to rationalistic tendencies in nineteenth-century liberalism arising in the post World War I decades emphasizing the tensions and paradoxes in Christian faith without the need or possibility of resolution, the transcendent unknowableness of God as opposed to divine immanence that characterized the previous century's quest for God.

Diaspora: a word that generally means "scattering." In reference to the Bible, and most particularly to the Jewish people, it refers to the dispersal of the Jews into the nations of the world by the Assyrians, Babylonians, and Romans.

Directory of Worship: a manual or pastoral handbook, written by the Assembly of Divines at Westminster (1645), as the replacement of the Book of Common Prayer in the Anglican service. It defined the nature and course of

ministerial functions including preaching restricting its sources to scriptural warrant, eliminated much traditional church liturgy

Dispensationalism: a way of understanding the Bible as a whole that developed in the nineteenth century. While the term is not easily defined, its advocates make a sharp, discontinuity or distinction between the biblical testaments: each having a distinct people (Israel and the church), each possessing distinct promises and programs (earthly and heavenly), and each having distinct destinies (fulfillment in an earthly kingdom, a millennium, and heaven). In contrast to a covenantal approach to biblical content and organization, dispensationalists reject the notion of a single people of God with a single destiny.

Dominican Tertiary, Dominican Laity: the term "tertiary" means third of rank or order. St Dominic founded the monastic Dominican Order or Order of Preachers in the early thirteenth century to suppress heretical groups by persuasion rather than by militarism. The order was organized into ranks or levels: preaching priests, cloistered nuns, and seculars.

Donation of Pepin: a grant of land, the papal states, by Pepin (III) the Short, king of the Franks, that subsequently became a basis for the Catholic claim to authority over civil governments. Facing threat from the Lombards in (now) northern Italy Pope Stephen appealed for assistance from the Franks. In a gesture of gratitude Pepin was granted the titles "King of the Franks" and later "Patrician of the Romans." In return Pepin granted territories taken from the Lombards to the church, territories over which it exercised civil authority for centuries.

Donatism: a North African Christian schematic sect that emerged after the Diocletian persecutions over the issue of church readmission for those who recanted of their faith but subsequently sought reinstatement. The dispute was most importantly over the nature of the church. Donatists argued that the mark of the church was holiness and "traitors" forfeited membership privilege; Augustine argued that the redemptive nature of the church required readmission since the efficacy of the church's offices came from God and did not depend on the grace of its officers.

Double Predestinarianism (Double Predestination): the doctrinal position within the spectrum of the Calvinist tradition that God chooses both those who go to heaven as well as those who go to hell, a double election.

Dukes: a title of political rank only secondary to that of monarch. In the Middle Ages dukes were governors over provinces or territories.

Edinburgh Missionary Conference (1910): A major gathering of over 1,200 missionary leaders from Europe and North America (only 5 percent from outside those areas) to promote world missions. Under the leadership of John R. Mott, a continuing agency was created, the International Missionary Council (1921), that became one of the major consolidating organizations to form the World Council of Churches in 1948.

Elizabethan Settlement (Elizabethian Church): a set of parliamentary decisions concerning the structure of the English state-church in 1558/9 following the Roman Catholic direction imposed by Elizabeth's predecessor, Mary Tudor. The Act of Supremacy separated the church from papal rule and made the monarch the head of the English Church; the Act of Conformity established the ecclesiastical structure of the church along the lines of the Book of Common Prayer and the doctrinal confession of the church in the Thirty-Nine Articles.

Enlightenment (Age of Reason): a movement begun in eighteenth-century Europe that emphasized the inner capacities of man (rational reflection, intuition) as opposed to external authority sources such as the church or the Bible to improve social and society performance. Strenuously opposed by the religious community as well as secular materialists, the Enlightenment spawned the modern era, a three-century experiment in the redemptive values of science and technology. Though highly successful in the technical realms, the venture collapsed under the weight of holocausts and wars suggesting that the blight of human discord could not be remedied by social advances alone. It filled life with opportunities but emptied it of meaning, creating postmodernism.

Eucharist (the Lord's Supper, the Table of the Lord, Holy Communion, the Thanksgiving): a sacrament (sacred mystery) or ordinance in the various traditions of professing Christendom that Christ instituted to supersede the Passover ritual in remembrance of him who became for the church the final Passover, the final covering for human guilt and sin. The professing churches have been divided over the meaning of Christ's presence in the Eucharist and the fruit of its observance.

Eutychianism: a fifth-century attempt to explain the relationship of the humanity and deity of Christ in the incarnate state. Eutychians argued that Christ was of two natures, human and divine, but they existed in a compound unity of a single nature. Condemned at the Council of Chalcedon (451), the persistence of the view in monophysitism led to the first permanent schism in the professing church.

Evangelicalism (Evangelical Movement): though the term has become difficult if not impossible to define, it generally has been a designation for Protestants conservatives who share a set of common attitudes and interests such as the importance of a religious conversion, the necessity of gospel proclamation, missionary passion, and transdenominational cooperative efforts. The roots of this ecumemical conservative enterprise were typically identified with the eighteenth-century Wesleyan and Whitefieldian religious awakenings in England or in North American revivalism either in the eighteenth or nineteenth centuries.

Existentialism: an approach to the concept of knowing that was a reaction to Enlightenment rationalism, particularly Kantian rationalism. It insists that the starting point must be the individual self and experience, not reflection or empiricism; truth is subjective and personal. Theistic existentialism is reflected in the writings of Søren Kierkegaard, who adopted Hegel's idealist approach to dispel it; atheistic existentialism can be seen in Paul Sartre.

Feminist Theology: while difficult to define because of its variegated nature, the concept has to do with feminist inquiry and perspectives about gender discrimination and power inequities. It uses the ter*m theolog*y in a very broad sense, detaching it from the historical meaning of the term. It is more accurately a rights movement concerned with issues of discrimination in sexual preferences, in language with reference to God, in hiring practices, and in financial remuneratio**n**.

Filioque Controversy (Filioque Clause): the term literally means "and the son." The dispute emerged between the church in the West and East over the authority of the creeds. Can a creed be amended? The catalytic issue was an addition to the Nicene Creed by the western church at the Synod of Toledo (589) stating that the Son, as well as the Father, sent the Spirit (called the doctrine of procession). The Eastern churches argued for a single procession, the

western churches double. This was amount the issues that brought about the schism of 1054 creating a West Catholic Church and an Orthodox Church (Eastern).

First Kappel War: a confrontation in 1529 between Protestant and Roman Catholic cantons in Switzerland. The "war" ended without a battle, but divided loyalties and alliances.

Free Church Tradition: a general designation for those churches that reject any role of the state in the affairs of the church. Accompanying the rejection of the state is the rejection of infant baptism, a nonliturgical approach to worship, a memorialist view of the Eucharist, and the embrace of believer's baptism.

Frisians: a German ethnic group located along the coastal areas of present-day Netherlands and Germany. The Frisians came to the Christian faith through the work of Anglo-Irish missionaries as well as missionaries Boniface and Willibrod.

German Idealism: a philosophical/theological movement that emerged in the late eighteenth and early nineteenth centuries in reaction to the Kantian rationalism/empiricist approach to knowledge, arguing that truth is internal and personal. The mental or mind took precedence over the senses in knowledge acquisition, and theology was reduced to the realm of natural theology. Representatives of German idealism are Fichte, Schelling, and Hegel.

German Pietism: a religious movement that emerged in the eighteenth century as a reaction to the rationalistic tendencies in Germany within the Lutheran tradition. Pietists such as Jacob Spener and August Franke insisted that faith without subjective experience was dangerous, that a spiritual conversion was integral to biblical faith, that missionary activity was not an optional activity and that Christians should meet in small groups to encourage each other in Christian duties.

Glorious Revolution: a change of dynasty in England in 1688 from the Stuart monarchs to the House of Orange, William and Mary, monarchs from Holland. It has been so called because the change of authority was without a violent revolution to install it. The English parliament invited the daughter of James II and her husband (William III) to ascend to the throne after her father's abdication.

Gnosticism: a second century heresy that elevated obscure and mystical knowledge over faith. A potent threat to the church, Gnostic faith reflects each teacher though common characteristics can be discerned: a radical dualism of spirit from matter; emanationism, a belief in a plurality of gods with one semigod creating the material world; salvation through secret knowledge, involving asceticism; and a denial of the incarnation of Christ.

God Is Dead Movement: an American Protestant liberalism that arose in the 1960s arguing that the modern, increasingly secularist culture has rendered the existence of God irrelevant. In retrospect, the movement bore witness to the failed attempt of the Enlightenment to secure a meaningful place for God in human existence and was a harbinger of postmodernism. Among its advocats were Thomas J. J. Altizer, William Hamilton, Paul Van Buren, and John A. T. Robinson.

Great Persecution: a term used for the period after the restoration of the English monarchy after the Long Parliament era. It was a time, the 1660s and 1670s, when the Anglican establishment and the king imposed restrictive laws and imprisonments repressing the Puritan movement once in transcendence.

Great Western Schism (Great Schism, Papal Schism): a nadir in late medieval catholic church fortunes when rival popes, each appointed by the same College of Cardinals, claim to be the singular vicar of Christ (1378–1417). Not only was European political loyalties divided, exacerbated by the Hundred Years' War (1337–1453) between England and France, but this caused a questioning of the church's ancient claim to authority. The schism was brought to an end by the election of Martin V at the Council of Constance.

Greco-Roman Culture (Greco Roman Tradition): a term used to express the influence of the "Mediterranean world" and the culture of ancient Greece assimilated into Roman culture that subsequently impacted later Western conceptions of religion, government, language, and culture.

Hampton Court (Hampton Court Conference): the residence of the English monarchs beginning with Henry VIII, who departed from the traditional residence of monarchs in the Tower of London. It was there that the Puritans petitioned James I that he allow the same ecclesiastical structure in England as under the Scots (the Millenary Petition). James refused the request, promoting the continuation of the Anglican form of government, but did grant authority to publish a new English Bible, the King James Bible (1611).

Hegelianism (Hegelianism Progressivism, Hegelian Dialectic): a philosophical approach to the nature of history proposed by G. W. F. Hegel. Of great significance to the Christian faith, Hegel suggested that there is lineal, progressive, evolutionary development in human existence. Combining rationalism with a theory of opposites clashing (a thesis and antithesis, despotism and freedom), civilization is propelled, ever-improvingly forward through an impersonal force (the *Geist*) toward a peaceful era of human freedom. This naturalistic theory of history challenged the Christian theory of human devolution and the value of the collective past.

Higher Criticism (Historical Criticism, Historical-Critical Method): an approach to reading the biblical writings that sought to understand their original meaning through the study of the historical context of their composition. Emerging in the seventeenth and eighteenth centuries, its attempt to discern the content of the Bible rested on questionable epistemological, philosophical, and theological assumptions that frequently led to a denial of the orthodox, historic Christian understanding of the message of the Bible.

Historicism: a view of history that emphasizes the role of context, largely cultural forces, in the understanding of events. Prominently proposed by Hegel and later borrowed by Karl Marx, who used the theory in a materialistic direction, the theory argues, opposed to rationalist theories of progress, that cultural forces shape and determine the direction of the history of nations and peoples.

Hoffmanites (Melchior Hoffman): followers of the Dutch Anabaptist Melchior Hoffman (ca. 1495–1543). Hoffman advocated the soon return of Christ and with it a destruction of the ungodly, but his prophetic prediction proved false. His eschatological/political radicalism contributed to the Münster Episode of millennialist frenzy and a questionable origin of Baptists. Hoffman influenced Menno Simons in his denial of the full humanity of Jesus Christ, saying that in the incarnation Jesus possessed only "heavenly flesh."

House of Savoy: In the sixteenth century the House of Savoy was a ruling party that exercised authority over a region that encompassed parts of southern France and western Italy. In the sixteenth century, the Duchy of Savoy, largely under French Roman Catholic influence, threatened the Swiss Canton city of Geneva, Calvin, and the Protestant Reformation.

Huguenots: though the term is of disputed origins, it is the name given to French Protestants in the sixteenth century. It may be that the term is reflective of a Genevan political party. The French Protestant community emerged in 1559 through the Gallican Confession. Huguenots had a turbulent history in the sixteenth century, gained toleration in 1598 under Henry VI, and lost it in 1685 under Louis XIV, many leaving France for Prussia, England, and British America.

Humanism: as used in the twelfth and thirteenth centuries in Europe, the term signified an interest in the study of the humanities, often within the rising universities. Its focus was not so much on a denial of the authority of the medieval church, but on understanding for oneself the truths taught by the church. While a leading contributor to the ethos of the sixteenth-century reformations, it is not to be identified with the secular humanism that arose out of the Enlightenment centuries later.

Hun (Huns): a nomadic, tribal people that came into the reaches of eastern Europe beginning in the later fourth century, contributing to the implosion of the western portion of the Roman Empire. The Huns were unified under Attila the Hun who then penetrated into Gaul and Italy.

Hundred Years War: a series of military clashes between England and France (1337–1453) over the control of the disputed territories. Fought largely in northern France and the Low countries, the French secured the throne and England lost its territorial claims on the continent. The religious significance of the confrontation in the context of the Great Schism is that it was a contributing factor to the decline of the prestige and authority of the late medieval church.

Iconoclastic Controversy: a series of debates in the Catholic church beginning in the eighth century that would drive a theological wedge between the western Catholic churches and the Eastern Catholic churches, contributing to the East-West Schism of 1054. The issue related to the second commandment, visual Christian art (largely wood cuts) in Christian worship, and the difference of meaning between "worship" and "veneration." Following the lead of John of Damascus, the Eastern churches' most prominent theologian, icons were considered wordless books to facilitate comprehension for the illiterate. Charlemagne took a more strident view, rejecting visual artistry of religious themes, particularly of the Christ.

Iconography: the use of religious art, statuary, depicting and representing religious figures used in liturgical worship.

Idealism (see German Idealism): a philosophical approach to the nature of knowledge, arguing that the structure of reality is immaterial or mentally constructed.

Immaculate Assumption of Mary: the teaching dogmatically embraced in the Roman Catholic Church during the pontificate of Pius XII (1950) that Mary, having completed the course of her earthly life, merely slept at her death, not being subject to mortal decay, and was taken to heaven there to reign with her son near his very heart. It is an attempt to solidify Catholic devotionalism and piety.

Immaculate Conception of Mary: the teaching dogmatically embraced in the Roman Catholic Church during the pontificate of Pius IX (1854) that Mary, the mother of Jesus, was preserved from original sin from the moment of her conception. The doctrine appears to have been brought forth, at least in part, to protect the deity and true humanity of Christ in view of the inroads of theological liberalism in the nineteenth-century church.

Inerrancy (Inerrrantism): an approach to explaining the Protestant churches' historic belief in the absolute truthfulness of the biblical writings by arguing that, being of divine origin and a product emanating from the divine character, they are without error in both words and message. Though containing anthropomorphic language, nonliteral figures of speech, and scribal discrepancies, the Bible came from God through human sources and was perfectly preserved in the original manuscripts.

Infralapsarianism: an attempt to understand the components of the eternal decree of God to redeem lost humanity by arguing a particular arrangement of the components of that decree. The explanation places the sequence in the following order: the creation decree of God; the decree of the fall of God's creation, particularly Adam; God's determination to save some out of fallen humanity; then the decree to provide the redeemer. See also *supralapsarianism*.

Irvingite Movement: a nineteenth-century manifestation of the Pentecostal embrace of the extraordinary spiritual gifts that emerged in London in the 1830s under Edward Irving, who established the Apostolic Christian Church. The Irvingites played a significant role as forerunners of the modern pentecostal/charismatic movements, as well as an important part in the development of premillennial eschatology through participation in the early English Bible conference movements.

JEDP Theory (Documentary Hypothesis): an approach to reading the Pentateuch, the five books traditionally ascribed to Mosaic authorship, suggesting that the books were assembled from a variety of accounts, some parallel and some distinct, over several centuries and formatted in the present form by unknown redactors or editors. Julius Wellhausen postulated that five sources made up the Pentateuch: Jehovah emphases (J), Elohistic sources (E), deuteronomic sources (D), and priestly sources (P). Building on Enlightenment assumptions of knowledge imposed on the biblical texts, the theory was a potent threat to Mosaic authorship and biblical integrity. The theory has been largely discredited in the scholarly community of late.

Jesuits (Society of Jesus): a Roman Catholic religious order founded by Ignatius Loyola in 1540 and officially sanctioned by Paul III in 1543. The order was composed of priests who committed themselves to poverty (mendicants), the strident preservation and extension of Roman doctrine, and the dictates of the church. Militantly aggressive as an arm of the church, it opposed Protestant gains and, being missionary-minded, spread the faith globally in the sixteenth century and beyond.

Kantianism (Kantian Rationalism): an approach to the nature of knowing that is an amalgam of Descartes's rational, reflective deductionism and Lockean empiricist inductionism. Kant argued that knowledge of objects is obtained by an interplay caused by the acquisition of knowledge through the senses and reflection within the mind.

Kerygma: a transliterated Greek word meaning "message." In the realm of religious studies, it is used in relation to the teaching or proclamation of Jesus, and others, as revealed in the Bible.

Liberalism (Religious): a departure from traditional orthodoxy motivated by an attempt to preserve, defend, and perpetuate the viability and acceptability of Christian adherence in light of formidable philosophical, epistemological, and scientific evidence that brought into question the way the Bible was to be understood and the Christian faith explained.

Liberation Theology: a general term for reading the Bible and constructing its central message based on the issues of social injustice, gender discrimination, and racial inequality. Dealing with such issues through political, social, and even military intervention may be a justifiable expression of the redemptive message of the Bible.

Liturgy (Liturgical Practices): a form of religious worship prescribed by structure, authored forms including written prayers, sacramental wordings, and homilies or sermons. Litugurical worship is found in the Orthodox, Protestant, and Roman Catholics communities though generally shunned in the Free Church tradition.

Lockeans: an approach to the nature or means of knowing postulated by John Locke in contrast to the Cartesian deductive method. Locke argued that the mind was a blank page and that knowledge was acquired through the five senses. His approach was called "sensationalism," and he is generally recognized as the "father of English empiricism."

Lollards: followers of the teaching of John Wycliffe of fourteenth-century England, a professor at Balliol College and critic of the church. The Lollards were absorbed into the Protestant English Reformation of the sixteenth century.

Lombards: a Germanic tribe that ruled portions of Italy from the sixth through the eighth centuries. Much of their territory was given to the church in the *Donation of Pepin*, and these lands became the Papal States.

Lutheranism (Lutheran): a major tradition of

Protestant orthodoxy that emerged in the sixteenth century, largely associated with the insights of Martin Luther. The tradition finds as its starting point in the personal accomplishments of Jesus Christ (therefore, sometimes referred to as the Theology of the Cross) and is reflective in its liturgy, including a strongly literal nonsacramental interpretation of the Eucharist.

Macedonianism: an interpretation of the relationship of the Holy Spirit to God the Father that did not recognize ontological equality, much as Arianism rejected the equality of the Father and Son. The view was condemned at the Council of Constantinople (381) where it was asserted that the triunity of Godhead was fully expressed in the Trinitarian formula.

Magisterial Reformation: a general division within the sixteenth-century Protestant movement over the issue of the relationship or inter-relationship of the state and the church. Magisterial reformers viewed that state and church were integrally connected, each fulfilling necessary functions in the maintenance of societal cohesiveness, though differences can be observed. Luther saw the state as evil but necessary, Calvin the state as godly and the union of church and state a religious commonwealth.

Magyars: a tribal people from the East, the Hungarians who settled in the fifth century settled south of the Caucasus Mountains on the Don River. In the ninth century they settled in the Danube River region, claiming land formerly in the Carolingian Empire.

Mamelukes: an Egyptian slave-class of Turkish background peoples that rose to political power and inaugurated a period of Muslim-Mameluke control over Palestine and Syria from 1250–1517. They successful opposed the Khan invasions from the East as well as the Catholic Crusaders

from the West. Their political power declined with the emergence of the Ottoman Empire that control Palestine until the installation of the British Mandate in 1917.

Manichaeism: an early formidable threat to the Christian faith that combined elements of Christianity, Zoroastrianism, and Buddhism, and that thrived from the third through the seventh centuries. The influential Saint Augustine embraced the dualistic ideals of Mani prior to his acceptance of the Christian faith and subsequently those wrote against their teachings.

Marcionism: a second-century heretical group that combined some of the teachings of Christianity and Gnosticism with a dose of anti-Jewish religious appreciation. Led by Marcion, the sect accepted a series of dichotomies that sharply divided the Old Testament from the New Testament writings as well as disparaging Jewish-flavored books in the latter. Marcion argued for two gods in the writings, one good and one evil and a docetic, merely spiritual Christ. He made the church think about the creator-redeemer unity as well as the canon of sacred writings.

Margraves: a medieval title for a hereditary office that involved military jurisdiction and protection of a region or province. In sixteenth-century Germany, it had lost its military nuance and became a title for a higher class of nobility or lords, higher than a count (*Gr*af) and lower than a duke.

Marxism (Marxist Materialism): a philosophy developed by Karl Marx that centers around a materialist interpretation of history and the Hegelian dialectic model of social change. Marx and Lenin argued that the blight of the human condition is attributable to social and economic disparity, clearly the antithesis of the capitalistic, free enterprise approach to societal organization.

Mass (Eucharist, Sacrament of the Eucharist): a term, though uncertain of origin, used within the Catholic Church from the early seventh century for what had been generally designated as the Eucharist or Thanksgiving Offering, the liturgical service centered around the Lord's Table (a Protestant term). Only at the Fourth Lateran Council (1215) did the Mass become an unbloodied reenactment of Christ's once-for-all bloodied sacrifice by mandate.

Materialism (Philosophical): a term that suggests that all existence is subject to the categories of volume, shape, and proportion; that is, only matter exists and only the observable is real. This view of existence can easily be invoked to deny the existence of God and the spiritual since such cannot be observed. The view, however, does not take into account such recognized realities as gravity, an invisible force.

Maundy Thursday (Holy Thursday, Covenant Thursday): a celebration during Holy Week recognizing the events in Jesus's day prior to his crucifixion, emphasizing the Passover meal with the disciples and the institution of the New Covenant Lord's Supper, the episode of the Lord's garden agonies, his arrest by the Romans, and his confrontations with the Jewish leadership.

Melchiorites: see *Hoffmannites*

Mendicants: the term means "begging," indicating those who sustain their living through the benevolence of others. In a religious context, it indicates religious groups or orders that exist through charity so that in the belief that such a lifestyle is deeply spiritual, they invest their energies in the service of others through care and preaching. The largest mendicant orders in the Roman Catholic community are the Dominicans and Franciscans.

Methodism (The Methodist Church): A major Protestant tradition that emerged in the context of the eighteenth-century revivals in England under John Wesley and others. The founders desired to reform the Anglican community that they served in view of the detrimental inroads of religious rationalism, but the reformist societies separated from the Church of England in 1784 in the United States and in 1795 in England to form a separate denomination that now claims over seventy-million members worldwide.

Middle Ages (Medieval Period): a term that suggests the second period of the four periods within what is now designated the Common Era (CE) in the scholarly, secular community. It is usually defined as the period of European history stretching from the fifth to the fifteenth centuries, bounded by the classical period and the modern period, the era between the collapse of the Roman Empire in the West and the rise of the Renaissance.

Millenary Petition: a document of signatures by one thousand English Puritans requesting that their new monarch, James I (James VI of Scotland) abolish the episcopal governance of the Church of England and replace it with the presbyterial form of authority practiced in his native Scotland (1603). The king rejected the proposal saying, "No bishop, no king."

Modalism (Patripassionism, Sabellianism): the attempt to explain the Trinitarian existence of God by arguing for a strict singularity of God in person and attributes, but in a threefold manifestation. Often designated by a major proponent, Sabellius, God is seen as threefold in manifestation but singular in person. This explanation of the divine Trinity was consistently condemned in the fourth-and-fifth century ecumenical councils of the church.

Monophysitism (Eutychianism): an attempt

in the fifth-century Catholic Church to explain the relation of the deity of Christ to his humanity in the incarnate state by arguing an amalgam of the two characteristic sets into a third combination of the two. Condemned at the Council of Chalcedon (451), the view persisted in segments of the Christian churches in the East (Egypt, Ethiopia, Armenia, Lebanon), becoming known by this nomenclature. It, too, was condemned as heterodox at the Council of Constantinople in 553 leading to the first permanent schism in the professing church.

Monothelitism: a view of the incarnate Christ suggesting that he possessed a single will, not two (one human and one divine). It seems to have appeared as an attempt to bring the Eastern churches together against the formidable threat of Muslim insurgency. At the Third Constantinople Council (668), the Catholic Church condemned the view.

Montanism: a second-century movement in the church that sought to restore it to its first-century purity-the assumption being the church had drifted morally and spiritually, by emphasizing the extraordinary spiritual gifts of healing and perhaps ecstatic utterances and ecstasy. Some Montanists embraced the concept of continuative revelation through prophets, forcing the church to take up the issue of canon, or books to be read in the churches. The movement was condemned in the church, but it did have a prominent supporter in the great Tertullian.

Moravians (United Brethren): a Protestant religious group with roots in the fourteenth-century Hussite movement. In the eighteenth century, a group settled in the Moravian region of Germany where they were protected and led by German aristocrat, Nicholas Ludwig von Zinzendorff. The Moravians became leaders in the missionary movement of the church becoming the first church, as a singular church body, to send out missionaries.

Mystery Religions: religious cults that flourished in the Greco-Roman era and in the early Christian period, each having its own sacred rites and rituals. Secrecy characterized these religious expression with disclosure made available only to the "enlightened." Many of these were eventually persecuted when the Roman Empire under Theodosius I made Christianity the sole religion.

Münsterites (Münster Episode): a politically and religiously radical sect of Anabaptists in the sixteenth century aligned with the Zwickau Prophets in demeanor. Led by Jan Matthijs and John of Leiden, the group attempted to establish a sectarian, communal government in the city of Münster, Germany, 1534–1535, claiming it to be the "New Jerusalem." Leiden, who claimed to be the successor of the biblical David, assumed dictatorial prerogatives in the short-lived experiment. The political radicalism of the Münsterites was a turning point in Anabaptist history in that it thereafter sought to avoid political extremism.

Neo-Orthodoxy: an approach to theology in reaction to nineteenth-century religious Liberalism argued in methodology by Karl Barth of Germany. The movement generally viewed the Scriptures with greater confidence than did earlier movements, yet did not accord them with infallibility. Barth argued that the Scriptures become the Word of God at the intersection of the Spirit, the individual text, and the living Christ, meaning that his verification theory was subjective and piecemeal. Consequently, advocates of Barth's approach to revelation lack cohesiveness in understanding, and he proved to be only a temporary conservative reaction to progressive liberalism.

Neoliberalism (Realistic Theology): a theological movement that emerged in the United States in the 1930s within the liberal tradition that is critical of classic liberalism, particularly the component of triumphal, optimistic progressivism. The clarion call for this movement was the 1938 sermon by Harry Emerson Fosdick entitled "The Church Must Go Beyond Liberalism." Sometimes called Realistic Theology, its advocates, such as Walter Horton, John C. Bennett, and H. P. Van Dusen, interpreted the human condition in darker terms than their predecessors, yet remained solidly within the liberal tradition of understanding the person of Christ and human salvation.

Neoplatonism (Neo-platonists): a philosophically religious movement that arose in the third century, a synthesis of Platonic thought with Gnostic insights and Jewish theology in the tradition of the Alexandrian Philo. In essense it was a type of theistic monism. Neoplatonists, in contrast to Platonists who saw this world as a merely shadow of a greater invisible reality, envisioned ultimate reality in the infinite world of experience, thus eliminating the gap between form or substance and reality, by combining them.

Nestorianism: a teaching in the fourth-century church concerning the relationship between Christ's two natures in the incarnation. Nestorius accepted the full humanity and deity of Christ, but seemed to reject the concept of his unity, disjoining the natures and giving Christ two joined natures, joined morally but not organically. The view was condemned at the third ecumenical council held at Ephesus (431). Advocates of this view continued in existence for several centuries, extending their teaching into the Far East.

New Model Army: a term given to the military established by the English Parliament in 1645 that lasted through the Commonwealth period. The organization of the army was "new" in that it was mobile, not being restricted to one geographical region, and its soldiery was composed of full-time professionals, not local militia. Led by Oliver Cromwell, the army was composed of Puritan sympathizers and various religious sectaries.

Novatianism (Novatian Party, Rigorism): a third-century crisis in the early church caused by division of opinion concerning the treatment of Christians who had faltered in faith during the Decian persecutions. While Cyprian favored the readmission of such because he considered that the church was the only ground of salvation, the Novatians favored exclusion because they viewed the lapsed as in violation of the qualifying characteristic of holiness.

Orthodox Church (the Eastern Church): a major expression of the Christian faith, along with Roman Catholicism and Protestantism, that resulted from a separation from the Western Catholic churches, in the Great Schism, a devastating division in 1054, largely over the issue of the intrusion of the Western church in Eastern church affairs. When the term "Orthodox church" is used prior to the 1054 schism, it means those churches that possess what is considered correct faith and practice. In the fourth century and beyond, it refers to the affirmation of the findings of the ecumenical councils. The Orthodox community is composed of several independent churches, recognized along ethnic lines (for example, the Antiochian Orthodox Church, the Greek Orthodox Church, and the Serbian Orthodox Church) with leadership placed in the Patriarch of Constantinople, the second capital of the former Roman Empire, though the patriarchs in the various churches are seen as equal.

Ostrogoths: the eastern branch of the Goths (the western branch being the Visigoths), a Germanic tribe, which established a kingdom in Italy and the Balkans in the fifth century. Justinian I attempted to reclaim Italy as part of the empire but was largely unsuccessful.

Ottoman Turks: a Turkish-speaking people of Islamic faith that emerged as a ruling class gaining hegemony over the Seljuk Empire in the thirteenth century and governed the empire for over six hundred years. The Ottomans, expanding their lands captured Constantinople in 1453, destroying the last vestiges of the Roman Empire. They expanded the rule into the Holy Lands from 1517 until 1917.

Palatinate: a region in southwestern Germany bounded by the Neckar and Rhine rivers. In this area, with a center at Heidelberg, the Calvinist tradition became prominent in the sixteenth century as expressed in the Heidelberg Catechism.

Panentheism (Panentheistic Mystical Intrusion): a belief that God exists by interpenetrating nature. Thus, the natural realm is the habitation of God who is the animating force behind everything. Such a belief is found in Baha'i, Buddhism, Hinduism, and Sikhism, as well as in several Christian groups.

Passover: The great Jewish festival that celebrates the deliverance through blood-covering and miracle from Egyptian bondage in the fourteenth century BC, the grandest of miracles described in the Old Testament and a shadow of the true Passover Lamb who was sacrificed to bring deliverance to his people by becoming the true sacrificial lamb.

Patristics (Patrology): generally the term indicated the study of the earliest church fathers from the post-apostolic era to Augustine.

Peasants' War (Peasants' Revolt): an uprising of the economically strapped lower class in Germany, mostly in the southern and central regions, between 1524–25. Applying the religious upheaval of the day against authority structures the peasants envisioned a form of proto-liberationism. While Luther recognized the social inequities of the day and the plight of the poor, he greatly feared the consequences of anarchy and stridently opposed it. It ended in a disaster with thousands of peasants killed; it was the largest popular uprising in Europe prior to the French Revolution.

Pelagianism (Pelagians): a teaching promulgated in the fifth-century church concerning the nature of humankind and the human factor in salvation. Pelagius taught that Adam's first sin affected only himself and not the race except by setting a precedent that has been subsequently and voluntarily pursued universally. Rejecting original sin and inherent birth depravity, sin was defined as moral selfishness, remedied by resolve. Further, Pelagius rejected the divine initiatives of predestination, election, and foreknowledge, redefining the terms as predicated on human action. The view was condemned in the Catholic Church through the writings of Augustine and at the Synod of Orange (529).

Penitential System (Penance): A practice that arose in Irish Christianity through the writing of pentitential books that designated outward acts reflective of inward contrition for wrongdoing. In the medieval period in the emerging Roman Catholic community, penitentialism became a sacrament of grace acquisition, the "second plank," or remedy for sin, taught in the writings of Lombard and Aquinas, creedally stated in the findings of the Council of Florence in the fifteenth century, and dogmatized in the church at the Councils of Trent in the following century.

Petrine Priority: a view of authority within the medieval Catholic church in the western portion of the former Roman Empire based on such passages as Matthew 16:18 and John 21, supposing that Peter acted as head of the college of the apostles as vicar of Christ on the earth and that through apostolic appointment a series of successors have been appointed to lead the church in the papal office.

Picts: a Celtic people-group who lived in eastern and northern Scotland. They opposed the Roman conquest of their territories resulting in the protective barrier of the Hadrian Wall. Irish missionaries from the famous monastery at Iona christianized them in the seventh and eighth centuries.

Pietism: a movement that arose in Germany in the seventeenth and eighteenth centuries that opposed the rationalistic treads in the Protestant churches. Pietists, such as Spener and Francke, argued that true conversion was more than creedal assent; it was a change of heart, the affectional faculty of the invisible soul that integrally would lead to an interest in spiritual growth and missionary passion both nearby and abroad. The pietist movement became one of the sources of the modern Protestant missionary enterprise as well as the nineteenth century emerging evangelical movement rooted in the prior century's religious awakenings.

Plan of Union: a cooperative missions effort (1801) inaugurated by the Congregationalists and Presbyterians to combine finances and energy to establish schools and churches in the area north of the Ohio River to western New York. The plan was to build seminaries to be staffed by both denominations and that graduates by virtue of their ordination would be qualified to serve in either community. Through the endeavor, however, a schism developed in the Presbyterian community, and its beliefs became categorized as New England Congregational theology, a modification of historic Calvinist teachings.

Platonism (Platonic Idealism): a philosophical school of thought developed by Plato concerning the nature of reality, central to which is the distinction between what is perceptible, but not intelligible, and that which is intelligible but imperceptible. Plato argued that reality existed most fully before the forms and substance. The observable functioned as shadows or figurements of that greater, more real reality. Platonist thought has proved both a handmaid to Christian theology as well as a detriment in the hands of monastics, mystics, and transcendentalists who disparaged substance and form as less than real.

Pluralism: a perspective integral to postmodern, deconstructionist approaches to the nature of truth, it is a counter-response to the progressive optimism and utopian idealism of Enlightenment thought. Truth is private and individualized, a non-corporate concept of reality with all values as relative.

Political Liberation Theology: the application of the Christian gospel of spiritual deliverances to social, cultural, and political injustices and moral inequities. Often radically socialist in tenor, advocates envisioned the root of injustice in the capitalistic enterprise and fomented popular pressure, even violence, to create a leveling of societal authority.

Pope (Pontiff): a Latin term meaning "father." In the early church, the term was generally used of the bishops by Marcellius, bishop of Rome, and Cyprian, bishop of Carthage in the third century. However, beginning in the seventh century bishops of Rome sought to make it a technical religious title of the office of the highest authority claiming Petrine apostolic succession.

Postmillennialism: a view of "end times" that understands that the church through Christ is progressively triumphing, that the reign of

Christ is in the church, not in a geopolitical rule in space-time history. This rule, rather than a literal reign, will be brought to consummation in Christ's literal return to judge the nations, triumph over all his enemies, and share in the eternal state. In this view Christ's return to judge and redeem will take place after the millennium, the reign of Christ through the church.

Postmodernism (Deconstructionism/Ultramodernism): a view of reality expressed as a way of understanding values that rejected the assumptions of modernity, the three-hundred-year experiment and exploitation of the advances in the scientific and technology realms to secure a level of improved human condition through rationalistic devotion to the powers of the mind with its emphasis on human potential, optimism of success, and progressivism. Having lost faith in the Enlightenment agenda, as evidenced early in the writings of Nietzsche, this approach turned away from the mind, corporate consensus, and faith in progress to find solace in the inner self, private values, and individualistic tribalism.

Pragmatism: a theory for the establishment of human virtue and moral decisionmaking arguing that functional utility or favorable outcomes are the ground of choice making. It asks the question, "Will it produce a good or favorable outcome if a particular action is pursued?"

Premillennialism: a view of the end times that argues that Christ will return in two phases: initially to fulfill promises made through the ancient prophets to literally rule over his people, and will do so for a thousand years in an era of unprecedented spiritual, cultural, and social advance; and subsequently to judge the earth and its inhabitants, inaugurating the eternal, spiritual state. Some, though not all, premillennialists interpret their view through the overarching grid of dispensationalism, making the millennium a time of fulfillment of divine promises to God's ancient people Israel, based on the assumption that the Bible presents two distinct peoples of God (Israel and the Church), separate programs for each, and two destinies relative to promise fulfillment (the earth and heaven, one in time and one out of time).

Presbyterianism (Presbyterial Polity): A term that designates the polity of those churches in the Calvinist tradition that was crafted by Thomas Cartwright, the Puritan Cambridge University scholar in Elizabethan England, and enshrined in the Westminister Confession of Faith (1646). The governance of the church is in what is called the presbytery, a regional gathering of the sessions, the ruling elders and teachers, of the local churches.

Prescientific/Precritical Worldview: an approach to life, value, and meaning that deposits authority outside human dimensions of knowledge acquisition; it is adherence to the notion that metaphysics (what is ultimately valid and true) precedes epistemology (how one knows those things). The first priority is faith as a foundation that leads to understanding, not understanding (epistemology) seeking the structure of faith and truth. It is a worldview that asserts human frailty and incompetence and at the same time recognizes that knowledge must first be revealed before it is discovered. Often ridiculed as anti-intellectual and archaic, if not demeaning to the human self, it prevailed in the church from its inception until the inroads of the Enlightenment, with its optimistic assumption of human potential sustained an indelible influence.

Pretribulationalism: a view of end-time events that is associated with some forms of dispensationalist premillennialism. For advocates of this approach to futuristic events, those who embrace the concept of a literal reign of Christ on the earth for a thousand years, the issue is that of the seventieth week of Daniel 9, a seven-year period of precursory judgments on the earth. The question is: When will Christ return relative to this period? Pretribulationalists believe the Christ will return in the clouds to remove the church from the earth prior to an era of judgmental terror.

Process Theology: a recent development within the Protestant liberal tradition predicated on the scientific shift away from Newtonian physics to quantum physics discovered by Max Planck and deriving implications from Heisenberg's indeterminacy principle relative to subatomic particles and Einstein's relativity theory. In rejecting classic theism, advocates argue that there are two polarities in God, one sovereign and unchanging, and the other, evolutive and becoming, making it impossible for God to know nonrealities, meaning the future. God is grounded in the past but actively involved in the future by hoping or luring it into existence. When the future becomes the present, God can know it. This, it is proposed, makes God more compassionate and caring, thus less distant and detached. Grasping the reality of the past, God is fixed and determined; ignorant of the future God who is responsive to human needs.

Protestant (Protestantism): the term suggests a movement of resistance. In this instance, it was a rejection of the pelagian direction observable in the late medieval church, and a condemnation of the decline of moral integrity and pastoral compassion. The term was coined at the Second Diet of Speyer (1529) when it became apparent that Charles V's toleration of the Protestant movement in 1526 was about to be revoked. A conclave of cities that embraced Luther's teachings uttered a protest. Hence, the reforming movement came to be known as Protestantism.

Protestant Reformation: an attempt to reform the late medieval Catholic church. Contrary to its Roman Catholic nemesis, itself also a reforming endeavor, the Protestant reformers believed that moral correction and educational enhancement were only the superficial issues, though certainly important. The heart of the Protestant passion was the recovery of the gospel of the absolute grace of God expressed in the insight that divine righteous is reckoned solely because of the provision of Christ, not incrementally infused through sacramental obedience; that Christ's substitutionary death did not secure a possibility or chance of salvation (a chance being no chance at all) but that it accomplished all that is required for God in justice to declare the sinner justified and acquitted.

Quakerism (Friends): a Protestant religious group that arose in England in the 1650s, the Long Parliament era, founded by George Fox, that in contrast to the Puritan tradition advocated "inner light," that God often spoke to his people directly, not through the Holy Scriptures exclusively, in the context of "tarrying meetings" when the congregation sat in silence, the sexes segregated, awaiting a divine word to someone who then would relay it. Quakers rejected the professional minster, advocating lay ministry; called their places of worship "meeting houses," not churches; stressed equality of gender in ministry; embraced pacifism; and were aggressive in the dissemination of their religious ideals.

Quartrodecians (Quartrodecian Controversy, Easter Controversy, Passover-Easter Controversy): a term, derived from a Latin word meaning "fourteenth," applied to those Christians in the early church who followed the Jewish festival calendar and celebrated the crucifixion of Christ on the fourteenth day of the first month (Nisan) in the Jewish calendar, the day of Passover. There is evidence that this was the pattern of the churches into the fourth century until the time of John Chrysostom, bishop of Constantinople. The ecumenical Council of Nicaea (325) declared that Sunday following the Passover should be the day of celebration.

Racovian Catechism: a statement of the theological convictions of the emergent Socinian movement in Poland in 1605. The movement derives its name from its most prominent early advocates Lelio and Faustus Socinus who stepped aside from Christian orthodoxy to embrace an Arian conception of Christ and thus deny the Trinity of God. In retrospect, the Socinian Movement was a harbinger of the Enlightenment with its subjection of religious faith to reasonability and verifiability.

Radical Reformation: it is a general practice among scholars of the Protestant reforming movements of the sixteenth century to see two broad categories: what has been designated as the Magisterial Reformation and the Radical Reformation. The latter, quite variegated in goals and theology, rejected the concept of a state-church harmony and interconnectedness and was sometime called "free church movements." Those called the Anabaptists in the movement rejected the notion of a folk church entered through infant baptism and practiced the gathered church concept expressed by believer's baptism. The implication of such a theory was a denial of the role of the state and thus came the charge of treason that was declared at the Diet of Speyer in 1529.

Rationalism (Rational Worldview): an approach to the acquisition of knowledge that emerged in the Enlightenment that rejected medieval notions of external authority, whether it be the Scriptures, the institutional church, or both. Rationalists argued that all that can be known must meet the criteria of repeatability, verifiability, and worthiness of belief that would seem to reject the unseen and the possibility of the supernatural. As a method of knowing, rationalism is often appropriate; as a method of knowledge of all things it is deficient because it excludes the possibility that the existence of what the approach disqualifies is possible.

Realistic Theology: see *Neoliberalism.*

Real Monophysitism: see *Eutychianism.*

Religion: A set of values, perspectives, and assumptions about life and human destiny that shapes the ordering of our lives, explains the array of human experiences, and provides hope. For the ancients, however understood, it was expressed in the firm postulate of a transcendent being, called god, or beings, called gods.

Remonstrant Party (Arminian Party): a group of religious scholars in Calvinist Holland in the early seventeenth century, following the lead of Jacob Arminius, that believed the better defense of Calvinist faith against the invasive religious Enlightenment was in a revision of the Belgic Confession of Faith, the creedal standard of the churches. Struggling with the age-old dilemma of explaining the relationship between inability, responsibility, and culpability, the group prepared the "Five Remonstrances" in 1610 and appealed to the state to revise its confession. An assembly of divines from across Europe convened at the Synod of Dordt in 1618 and rejected all five revisions and issued a four-point statement in reply. Out of the rejection came a third tradition of Protestant interpretation, the Arminian one.

Renaissance: a cultural and intellectual movement that emerged in fourteenth-century Italy and sustained a discernible influence into the seventh century in Europe and spread throughout the seventeenth-century Europe that celebrated a resurgence of classical learning. It proved to be a strong intellectual impetus for the sixteenth-century reformations in that its focus on the humanities brought an emphasis on self-understanding. While it did not question medieval authority structures, it did question how they are embraced. Further, it was an impetus for the later Enlightenment Period that stressed the importance of individual belief and search to find it, but divorced it from medieval assumptions of authority. Thus, scholars think of the Modern Period as having two parts: early modern and late modern; eras that shared the same approach to knowledge through the humanities, but embraced diverse theories of authority.

Renaissance Humanism: a cultural and educational reform emphasis that emerged in the fourteenth and fifteenth centuries in reaction to medieval scholasticism, emphasizing personal affirmation of truth through a study of the sources of belief-structures, as well as the engagement in civic life through speaking and writing with eloquence and clarity. Its focus was on the study of the humanities with a new curriculum for university education, a shift from the scholastic preoccupation with rational explanation of the medieval faith to the readoption and prominence of the Aristotelian method.

Ritschlianism: an approach to reading the Bible championed by Albrecht Ritschl who believed that the Bible contained revelational material though encrusted with errant concepts engrafted into the text over centuries of transmission, even misperception by its writers. The Ritchlians proposed a method for recovering the essential message of the Bible that became popular in classic American liberalism with its christocentric approach. Simply put, all that was found in the Bible in accord with what Jesus would have said or done was valid; however Ritchlians, German or American, viewed Jesus as merely an inspired and inspiring person.

Roman Catholic Church: a movement that gradually emerged out of the increasingly moral, social, and theological divergences and controversies within the late medieval church. Like its counterpart the Protestant movement, proponents claim historic verification for its teaching ("that which has always and everywhere been taught in the church), though seriously flawed and lacking demonstrable consistency through the centuries. It seems that the defining definitional moments of the church were the Fourth Lateran Council, the Council of Florence (1439), and the enormously important formal creedalization and dogmatization of its teaching at the Council of Trent in the sixteenth century.

Roman Empire: The geographical, political, and social hegemony of authorities extending from the city of Rome. At its height it stretched from England to the north of the Sahara, from the Atlantic Ocean to the Indus Valley.

Romanticism (Romantic Movement, Romantic Philosophy): a movement in the latter half of the eighteenth century in reaction to the dangers of Enlightenment rationalism and the scientific revolution with its quest for truth primarily in the cognitive faculties with the consequential denigration or diminution of the affective and emotional faculties of the human makeup. The Romantic Movement, expressed religiously in transcendentalism and mysticism, finds the quest for meaning in humankind, though in a different faculty, the emotive and the intuitional, the balance or harmony with nature.

Sabbatarianism (Sabbatarian): a view developed among sixteenth-century Calvinist Protestants beginning with Henry Bullinger of Zurich and becoming a common emphasis within the Puritan tradition in England and North America. It is the perception and practice that Sunday is the new Sabbath-rest, a shadow fulfilled of the seventh-day rest from God's creative activities in Gen. 2:1–4. While the day was not to be spent passively, being a day for worship, catechism in the family, and the doing of deeds of love and mercy, it was a day set aside in trust of God's provision by refraining from wage earning.

Sabellianism (Modalism, Patripassionism): the attempt to explain the Trinitarian existence of God by arguing for a strict singularity of God in person and attributes, but in a threefold manifestation. This explanation of the divine Trinity was consistently condemned in the fourth- and fifth-century ecumenical councils of the church.

Saracens: a people-group, bedouins, who lived in desert areas in and around the Roman province of Arabia. Eventually, by the crusader period, beginning in the late eleventh century, the term came to encompass the Arab population that embraced Islam and occupied the Holy Lands.

Saxons: a confederation of Germanic tribes who migrated into Britannia (Great Britain) during the early Middle Ages. Later, the tribes were forged into a single nation under Egbert and Alfred the Great in the eighth and ninth centuries to more effectively resist the Viking intrusions.

Schmalkaldic League: an alliance of Lutheran princes and cities for the purpose of mutual defense from the threat of Charles V, the emperor of the "Roman Empire" who was motivated by Roman Catholic sympathies, given the revocation of religious toleration following the Diet of Speyer in 1529. Named for the city in which the alliance was created in 1531, the league did not formally accept the creed, the doctrines most essential to the Protestant Reformation, in which Luther envisioned orthodoxy being the primary voice in its construction. However, named the Schmakaldic Articles, it did become

one of the several Lutheran confessions incorporated into the Book of Concord (1580).

Schmalkaldic Wars: A series of clashes in 1546 and 1547 between the forces of Charles V, emperor of the Holy Roman Empire, and the Lutheran Schmalkaldic League. The result of the struggle was the defeat of the Lutheran forces at the Battle of Muhlberg. Though Lutherans faced defeat, their ideas continued to gain ever-wider audiences, so Charles V was compelled to grant their legal right to exist.

Scholastic Movement (Scholasticism, the Scholastics): an intellectual movement that emerged in Europe following the intrusive Viking disruptions reflective of the economic recovery in Europe. The context of its emergence was the realization that monastic education philosophy was outdated given philosophical advances in the Mediteranean world, specifically the dominance of the Aristotelian method in Spain and the East. The retooling brought about three phenomena: the emergence of the classroom as the center of the educational process, not the chapel; the writing of textbooks to synthesize vast sums of knowledge, the beginnings of systematic theology as later envisioned called "Summas"; and a new professional class, the scholar or teacher. The movement functioned as a servant of the church, not doubting its place or doctrine, seeking to show the rational coherency of it and, thus, providing a tool to explain and articulate the faith.

Scottish Common Sense Realism (Scottish Common Sense Moral Philosophy, Scottish Common Sense Political Philosophy): a product of the Enlightenment quest to establish a foundation for ethics and virtue in the context of the general disparaging of the traditional source of authority, the Scriptures, as the Enlightenment approach as a whole turned away from external authority to internal sources. In common sense realism, guidance was not derived from the cognitive faculties, but from the assumption of an innate, instinctual capacity not attainable by education or practice, instantaneously and inherently placed in all humans by nature or the God of nature. The fact that some truths were intuitive appeared to be evidence that moral truths were also. This school of thought was predominant in the early nineteenth century of the United States with its cultural embrace of equalitarianism and individualism. It become the glue for corporate moral values so necessary in a democratic view of popular self-government, thus replacing the role of religion, even though some saw it as a support and buttress of Protestant religion in the context of unwitting pluralism.

Second Kappel War (Second Battle of Kappel): a military engagement between Protestant Zurichers and nearby Roman Catholic cantons that proved a temporary setback for the Protestant cause in Switzerland with the death of Ulrich Zwingli on the battlefield (1531).

Second Plank (the Second Planck): a concept that seems to have been originally employed by Jerome, using a floating piece of wood as an illustration to describe the role of repentance as a restorative gift from God, the first plank being confession, the "planks" being a course of action after a "shipwreck" of baptismal innocence. In the development of sacradotalism in the medieval church and the development of the sacramental system of grace, the first step to safety was baptism, which removed inherited Adamic inability and guilt, leaving the saint to cope with acts of disobedience, not a blighted constitution. The second step was the sacrament of penance or confessional contrition that caused a restoration to innocence and a new beginning in the journey to redemption.

Secularism (Secularity): a term coined in the early nineteenth century to postulate a division between church and state, suggestive that the two spheres are separate and independent. The term has come to define a system of beliefs and consequent practices that are not informed by the traditions and conceptions of the place and value of religion. Clearly, it is not a synonym for inappropriate behavioral patterns; it embraces the assumption that values can be sustained in society without the necessity of religious values.

Semi-Pelagianism (Cassianism): a view concerning the issues of sin and grace in the church often identified with the teachings of the fifth-century cleric/monastic John Cassian. Cassian struggled to explain the relationship between ability, responsibility, and culpability (as well as freedom and sovereignty) by arguing for a matrix of causative, cooperative factors. He suggested that when God detects religious sincerity, clearly deficient to cause redeeming mercies, God can act in grace to supply what human effort can conceive but not accomplish. The view is a compromise of sorts between Augustinian inability—the necessity of uncaused, unmerited divine initiative in salvation—and the Pelagian view that humankind has the capacity to effect salvation by moral resolve and rectitude. The view was condemned at the Synod of Orange (529), but reemerged in the medieval church.

Severians (Monphysites, Monophysitism): another designation for those in the Eastern Empire who embraced a single nature in Christ, opposing the findings of Chalcedon. They were more generally known as verbal Monophysites, in distinct from ontological Monophysites, Severians were so named because the principal advocate of the position was Severus, patriarch of Antioch (512–519).

Shrine of the Black Virgin (Shrine of the Holy Lady, the Black Madonna): while there are many such shrines to the Virgin Mary, the particular one within the context of the sixteenth-century division of the Western Catholic Church into Roman Catholic and Protestant factions is the pilgrimage site in Einsiedeln, Switzerland, the second parish of the then Ulrich Zwingli. Housed in the Benedictine monastery, the shrine raised doubts about the authenticity of late medieval catholic truth claims, becoming a source of reformational dissent.

Simony: the practice, all too frequent, on the late medieval church of the buying and selling of ecclesiastical, spiritual offices. The term is derived from the biblical account of Simon Magnus who sought to purchase religious privilege (Acts 8). This moral and religious abuse proved a precipitating cause for the Roman Catholic and Protestant reformations in the sixteenth century.

Single Predestinarianism: a view of the order of the component parts of the eternal and single decree of God to redeem humanity. Advocates of this particular ordering suggest that God decreed human creation and the fall before the decree to redeem; that is, viewing the lostness of the race, God moved in compassion and love to avert the destiny of some in the context of having no obligation to any. It is the view that God did not predestine the reprobated to their state, but in choosing the elect out of the lostness passed over the others who would do as they please, evidencing the merit of condemnation.

Social Gospel Movement: an emphasis within the broader liberal tradition in the United States parallel to the progressive era (1890–1917) that sought to ameliorate social inequities through legislation. Advocates, such as Washington Gladden and Walter Rauschenbusch, suggested that sin was environmental and social in nature and propagation. The movement culminated in Rauschenbusch's *A Theology for the Social Gospel* (1917).

Socinianism (see also the Racovian Catechism in complete glossary): a teaching concerning the Trinity of God and the person of Christ that emerged in the sixteenth century and was capsulated in the Racovian Catechism of 1605. Socinians denied the divine trinity asserting that Jesus was less than God; it reflected a revival of Arianism and was the harbinger of the religious Enlightenment. This teaching was behind the rise of both Unitarianism and Deism in England and in North America.

Subdeacon: an office within the Roman Catholic community, the lowest of the sacred ordinations. The function of a subdeacon is to carry the chalice of wine to the altar, make preparation for the Eucharistic ceremony, and read the Scriptures. The office appears to have emerged in the medieval period.

Subordinationism: a view espoused in the early church by Origen, among others, prior to the Nicaea (325) and Constantinople (381) ecumenical councils, claiming that the Son is ontologically inferior to the Father, though not the view of Tertullian and Aristides. The latter spoke of a "triade of equal glories" and the former coined the term *Trinity*.

Supralapsarianism: an attempt to place in logical sequence the components of the eternal and single redemptive decree of God. Advocates of this perspective begin with the decree of divine election of some to life and others to eternal damnation followed by the creation decree of all people, the decree of the fall, and finally the decree to provide salvation for the elect.

Synod of Dordt: a gathering of church scholars in 1618 from across Europe under the authority of the Dutch government to reevaluate the

Belgic Confession of Faith, the creedal statement of the state-church, in light of the "Five Remonstrances" proposed by the Arminian Party. The synod rejected each of the proposed amendments and issued a four-point reply in affirmation of its Calvinist approach and interpretation of theology.

Taborites: with a designation derived from the fortress they established in 1420 a distance from Prague, this was a militant religious community that emerged in fourteenth-century Bohemia in sympathy with John Huss's complaints against the late medieval church. They were a Bible-based movement that insisted that the laity receive both the bread and the wine in the Eucharistic ritual and denied the Catholic view of its meaning, transubstantiation. The Taborites were crushed in 1452 when their fortress was captured by Catholic forces.

Theology of Being: an approach to Christian theology within the liberal tradition espoused by Paul Tillich (1886–1965) as a psychological mystical analysis of human self-understanding. According to Tillich, God is not a person, the concept being symbolic, but is the ground of our ultimate concerns (the concept of the Trinity being an ecclesiastical tool to suppress inquiring minds). The "persons" of the Trinity should be interpreted in the framework of human need. The "Father" is a symbol of care in the midst of human alienation; the "Son," of human inadequacy, finitude, and self-sacrifice; and the "Spirit," a synthesis of the two. The Trinity is a psychological human invention to secure stability in view of life's torments and exigencies.

Theology of Crisis (Theology of the Word, Barthianism): an approach to Christian theology expressed by perhaps the greatest theologian, if one is to use the criteria of influence rather than traditional orthodox conceptions in the twentieth century. Reacting against the anthrotheistic trajectory of nineteenth-century theology beginning with Schleiermacher, Barth strove to defend the transcendence of God. Barth reversed the previous century's attempts to discover God, arguing that God cannot be found by human contrivances; he is the God who can only be known by his prerogative of self-disclosure. This he does through an encounter with the living Word, the Christ, and in the written word, a portion of the Bible, by the Spirit in a moment of spiritual, revelatory crisis. In that remarkable instance, repeated numerous times, the Bible becomes the very words of God. The difficulty was not so much his conclusions at times, but his theory of verification of biblical truth.

Theology of Evolution: an approach to Christian theology within the liberal tradition that became popular in the 1960s and 1970s in the United States that fractured theology into a variety of individualized kerygmas, or messages. Teilhard de Chardin (1881–1955) combined evolutionary biology, paleontology, and Hegelianism to construct a theology. According to de Chardin, humankind has progressed over time toward a higher consciousness, the omega point, a collective, mystical unity in the body of Christ. God is the energizing power, a force, behind the evolutionary development of humans as spiritual beings.

Theology of History (Theology of Resurrection): an approach to Christian theology within the liberal tradition postulated by Hans Urs von Balthasar (1905–88). Adopting a Hegelian approach to the progress of history, his solution to the struggles within the human existence was the person of Christ; and thus Balthasar's approach to combining history, solution, and meaning into Christology. Christ is seen as the Lord and apex of history as Creator and Redeemer. Sympathetic echoes of Barth's approach to theology (his interests, starting points, and conservatism) can be detected in Balthasar.

Theology of Hope (Theology of Resurrection): an approach to Christian theology expressed by Jurgen Moltmann within the liberal tradition that focuses on the resurrection of Christ within a future *eschaton*. The ambiguities and tragedies of the human experience are to be understood in the Christian's embrace of a bright future based on the resurrection of Jesus Christ. Sin is living without hope; despair is a premature failure to find surety in hope. Ultimately, this creation will be transformed into a new creation. However, Moltmann understood the Trinity as modes of the expression of human freedom, hence his tendencies to liberationist and ecological interpretations of theology. The "Father" corresponds to political freedom, the "Son" to communal freedom, and the "Spirit" to spiritual freedom.

Tractarian Movement (Anglo-Catholic Movement, Oxford Movement, Puseyite Movement, Ultramontanism): a movement within the nineteenth-century English church enamored with the medieval church as an ideal and the return to the authority structures of the Catholic Church. Some questioned the validity of traditional authorities and some such as John Henry Newman returned to the Roman Catholic fold where he reached the status of cardinal. Called the tractarian movement because of a manifesto-type series of publications, "Tracts of Our Times;" Anglo-Catholic because of its High Church and Catholic orientations; Oxford movement because its intellectual center in Oxford, England; Puseyite movement because Edward Pusey was a prominent advocate; and ultramontonism (meaning literally, "beyond the mountains") because it found the solution to the ecclesiastical issues of the day in Rome.

Tübingen School of Higher Criticism (Historical Criticism): a movement centered in a coterie of German scholars at Tübingen University in the nineteenth century that pioneered work in literary criticism, particularly in the field of higher criticism, which was devoted to the study of the origin of the biblical texts to understand the background of their origins. Presuppositionally freighted with the assumption that the Bible was a product of a natural history and human writers, at best inspiring but not inspired, the German scholars of this school did not believe the Bible to be the eternal word of God.

Unitarianism: a religious movement that appeared near the end of the eighteenth century in the United States, though a century earlier in England. Influenced by the Enlightenment assumption of the nature of truth and knowability, it rejected the orthodox doctrine of the Trinity, viewed Christ as an example of humanity at its best, and explained salvation was the fruit of moral rectitude achievable through watchful care and the pursuit of passionate duty. In 1819 William Ellery Channing, pastor of Federal Street, Boston, delivered an address at the ordination of Jared Spark, then a Baltimore pastor and later president of Harvard College entitled "Unitarian Christianity," defining the movement with clarity and precision.

Vandals: a Germanic people group that conquered portions of Africa in the fifth century and sacked Rome in 455. Portions of Vandal North Africa were reclaimed in the sixth century by Emperor Justinian I after the collapse of the empire in west.

Verbal Monophysites (Severians): a view concerning the incarnate Christ. The Monophysites rejected the dual nature Christology decreed at the Council of Chalcedon (451), arguing that a person is a single nature and that Christ was not two persons (Nestorianism) and, therefore, possessed a single nature. Monophysites of this variety agreed in substance with the findings of Chalcedon, but disagreed with the language used in the Chalcedonian Creed.

Vikings (Norsemen): a Scandanavian people-group known for their longboats and seafaring exploration and conquest that reached North America, the Mediterranean, and Constantinople from the eighth through the eleventh centuries. The threat of Carolingian territorialism and increased population, but limited agricultural opportunities and resources, are frequently cited reasons for Viking expansion. The Vikings conquered much of England, establishing Danslaw, as well as kingdoms in Normandy and Sicily. They were hired mercenaries for the Slavic people who established the Varangian Kingdom with whom the Vikings blended. Numerous monasteries, including Iona and Landisfarne, were destroyed in the pillaging and looting and Europe was plunged into a nadir of darkness.

Visigoths: a branch of the Goths, a Germanic tribe that entered Europe after the defeat of a Roman army at the Battle of Adrianople (376), establishing rule on the Iberian Peninsula and in Italy in the fifth century. Though they initially were converts to Arian Christianity through the labors of Ulfilas (ca. 310–383), a missionary and Bible translator (*Silver Bible*), they accepted the Nicene faith in the sixth century.

Waldensians: an early protest movement founded by Peter Waldo in the twelfth century in northern Italy (and southern France) that was heralded by later Protestants as a precursor to the Reformation because it criticized the morals and teachings of the medieval Catholic Church. The Waldensians stressed the importance of the Bible and preaching much in the tradition of Wycliffe of England and Huss of Bohemia, though they predated them. Condemned by the Fourth Lateran Council (1215) under Innocent III, they were subsequently severely persecuted. In the Reformation era, the Waldensians joined the Calvinist tradition of Protestant reform through the work of William Farel, an early reformer in Geneva.

War of the Roses: a conflagration over dynastic succession to the throne of England between two rival branches of the Plantagenets, the House of Lancaster and the House of York, between 1455 and 1485. Henry Tudor (Henry VII) defeated Richard III of the House of York, married into the Yorks, and united the two houses. The Tudor dynasty of monarchs ruled England from 1485–1603, during the early Reformation of the church through the reign of Queen Elizabeth I. The War of the Roses derived its name from the flowers that adorned the rival houses: the York white rose and the Lancaster red rose.

Wat Tyler's Rebellion (Peasant Rebellion of 1381): a serious insurrection of the lower working class in England who had been reduced to grinding poverty and slave-like conditions. In retrospect, this most prolific class struggle in English history proved the harbinger of the end of feudalism and serfdom in the country. The rebellion was short-lived, though the Tower of London was assaulted and some of the king's officials murdered, and leaders were summarily captured and executed.

Westminster Assembly (Westminster Assembly of Divines): a gathering of divines from across Europe tasked with the restructuring of the Church of England after the collapse of the monarchy under Charles I in the Puritan Commonwealth era. Called by the Long Parliament from 1643–1649, and directed by William Twisse, the assembly produced a presbyterial church governance through the composition of the Westminster Confession of Faith, the Longer and Shorter Catechisms, a revision of the Thirty-Nine Articles, and the Directory of Worship. However, differences within the Puritan majority (variance of ecclesiastical understanding) and the presence of a strong Congregationalist Puritan faction in the military prevented the installation of the Presbyterian ecclesiology as the state religion. Nevertheless, the work of the assembly of divines has been deeply influential in the Calvinist communities worldwide.

Westminster Confession of Faith: a statement of the religious convictions held by the Reformed Tradition of the Protestant movement, as well as the high watermark in reformed confessionalism. Completed by the Westminster Assembly of Divines in 1646, the document was not accepted in England due to Congregational Puritan pressure, but it replaced the Scottish Confession of Faith written in the previous century by John Knox and remains the standard of Orthodoxy in most conservative reformed communities in the United States, even worldwide.

World Council of Churches: Formed officially in 1948 in Amsterdam, Holland, the WCC is an organization of 349 Protestant churches worldwide claiming a constituency of over 560-million people. Theologically latitudinal and socially oriented in its mission, the WCC serves through a variety of agencies that are concerned with global issues of hunger, racial and social inequity, and peace to name a few. Conservative Protestants have looked askance at the movement because of its theological latitude and largely social agendas that, while worthy, overshadow the central message of the gospel and the claims of Jesus Christ

Chapter Objectives

Introduction Objectives

- That the reader will describe why the study of church history is useful for the present and the future

- That the reader will distinguish between circular, linear, and progressive views of history

- That the reader will identify major figures in the study of history

- That the reader will describe the structure and meaning of history from the perspective of the church

- That the reader will identify the four main periods of church history by name and time period

- That the reader will identify the three major expressions of the Christian faith

Chapter 1 Objectives

- That the reader will identify the four main periods of the early church by name and time period

- That the reader will describe the origin of the church: its historical and social setting

- That the reader will describe early church structure and practices

- That the reader will identify major writers and records of the early church period

- That the reader will describe perspectives on the Trinity, Eucharist, and church leadership in the early second-century church

Chapter 2 Objectives

- That the reader will identify major periods of persecution under the Roman Empire

- That the reader will identify and define the heretical views that plagued the early church

- That the reader will identify the major apologists of the early church and their contributions to Christian doctrine

- That the reader will describe the development of the Biblical canon

- That the reader will gain insight into the development of the structure of the church

Chapter 3 Objectives

- That the reader will provide the reasons for the improving relations between Christianity and the Roman Empire

- That the reader will define the Trinity as well as alternative models declared to be heretical

- That the reader will describe the major accomplishments of the Councils of Nicaea, Constantinople, Ephesus, and Chalcedon

- That the reader will define the orthodox view of Christology as well as alternative models declared to be heretical

- That the student will delineate between the perspectives of Augustine and Pelagius on the effect of sin on humanity

- That the student will understand the importance of the revisionist Cassianian approach to salvation as well as the ramifications of the Synod of Orange in the medieval period

Chapter 4 Objectives

- That the reader will identify the causes and course of the growth of ecclesiastical authority in the early medieval church

- That the reader will describe why authority for the church came to be centered in Rome

- That the reader will define the iconoclastic controversy

- That the reader will describe the development of missionary activity in the early medieval church

- That the reader will recognize the influence of Islam on the development of Christianity

Chapter 5 Objectives

- That the reader will identify the causes for the collapse of the Carolingian kingdom

- That the reader will describe the influence of missionary activity in the middle medieval period

- That the reader will describe the increasing role of the papacy during the middle medieval period

- That the reader will identify the renewal and rise of monastic spirituality

- That the reader will identify the primary causes for the schism between the Orthodox and Western Catholic Churches

- That the reader will describe the causes for and the major events of the Crusades

Chapter 6 Objectives

- That the reader will identify the causes for the emergence of scholasticism

- That the reader will describe the influence of scholasticism on Christian thought

- That the reader will describe the institutional, spiritual, and doctrinal issues within the late medieval church

- That the reader will identify major forces for change within the late medieval church

- That the reader will describe the influence of Renaissance thinking on the approach to understanding Christian truth

Chapter 7 Objectives

- That the reader will demarcate the two periods of the modern era chronologically and understand the basis of the division

- That the reader will identify the primary causes of the Protestant reformations

- That the reader will define the goals of the Protestant reformations

- That the reader will describe the life of Martin Luther

- That the reader will describe the defining characteristics of Lutheran thought

- That the reader will have some grasp of the history of sixteenth-century Lutheranism

Chapter 8 Objectives

- That the reader will identify the two broad categories of the Protestant Reformations

- That the reader will distinguish the Reformed tradition from Lutheran theology

- That the reader will describe the lives and contributions of Zwingli, Bullinger, Calvin, and Beza

- That the reader will describe the spread of Reformed thought

- That the reader will understand the meaning, interests, and history of the Arminian tradition within Protestant faith

- That the reader will come to an awareness of the differences between the great Protestant traditions: Lutheran, Calvinist, and Arminian

Chapter 9 Objectives

- That the reader will distinguish the Radical Reformations from the Magisterial Reformations

- That the reader will describe the foundations and development of the Anabaptist movement in Europe and the Baptist emergence in England

- That the reader will identify the content, meaning, and development of the Church of England

- That the reader will describe the reasons for the emergence of the Puritan movement within the Church of England

- That the reader will identify other significant attempts to reform the late medieval church

Chapter 10 Objectives

- That the reader will distinguish between the Protestant Reformations and the Roman Catholic Reformation

- That the reader will identify the major decisions of the Council of Trent

- That the reader will describe the causes of the Thirty Years' War

- That the reader will describe the effects of the Thirty Years' War

Chapter 11 Objectives

- That the reader will identify the religious causes for the rise of Enlightenment thought

- That the reader will describe how pietism attempted to revitalize churches in light of the encroachment of the Enlightenment approaches to knowledge

- That the reader will describe the main features of Enlightenment thought

- That the reader will identify the major thinkers in the development of Enlightenment epistemology

- That the reader will describe the development of liberal theology in light of the encroachment of the Enlightenment approaches to knowledge

Chapter 12 Objectives

- That the reader will describe the emergence of conservative Christian scholarship

- That the reader will define the Broad Church movement in the Church of England

- That the reader will distinguish between High Church and Low Church practices

- That the reader will describe the major evangelical contributions of Low Church Anglicanism

- That the reader will understand the contributions of conservative Non-conformists in nineteenth-century England and their influence in North America

Chapter 13 Objectives

- That the reader will grasp the important contribution of Karl Barth to the redirection of European theology in the twentieth century

- That the reader will understand the impact of Rudolph Bultmann on the twentieth-century liberal tradition

- That the reader will understand the struggles in the Roman Catholic Church to maintain its traditional orthodoxy in the midst of modernism and postmodernism

- That the reader will describe the intent and development of the Ecumenical Movement worldwide

- That the reader will understand the development, impact, and contribution of the Charismatic movements in Europe and beyond

Chapter 14 Objectives

- That the student will understand the meaning of the various ways truth has been sought, capsulized, and embraced through the centuries since the advent of Christianity

- That the student will gain some insight into the structure of values and decision-making that characterize the public arena and how it is often antithetical to the Christian faith

- That the student will grasp the reality that the modern period was as detrimental to Christian affirmations as the postmodern period

- That the student will come to appreciate the struggles of Christian clerics and scholars to defend and propagate authentic Christian faith in a world of flux and change, reflecting on the notion that accommodation is required to maintain cultural relevancy but culture concession is dangerous

PERSON AND SUBJECT INDEX

I

Ibas of Edessa	125
Iconoclastic Controversy	172
iconography	444
Ignatius	65, 66, 68, 70, 75, 88
Immaculate Conception of Mary	246
Indulgence Controversy	286
infant baptism	150
infralapsarianism	177
Innocent I	136
Innocent III	207, 212, 220, 247, 384
Inquisition	390
International Missionary Council	484, 485
intertestamental texts	53
Investiture Crisis	204
Ionian Christianity	178
Irenaeus	66, 75, 80, 83, 84, 86, 88, 89, 90, 91, 112
Irish Potato Famine	452
Irving, Edward	454
Irvingite movement	455
Isidorean Decretals	170, 174, 204, 265
Islam	39, 181
first crusade against	206
Five Pillars	183

J

Jacob, Henry	348, 357
James, apostle	95
James I	381
James II	364
James IV	349
James of Viterbo	252
James, the brother of Jesus	60
James VI	359
James, William	505
Jane Seymour	350, 352
Jefferson, Thomas	408
JEPD theory	427
Jerome	97, 105, 129, 148, 176, 178
on death	167
Jerome of Prague	252, 262
Jerusalem Church	60
Jessey, Henry	348
Jesuits	335, 382, 390

Jesus Christ	
Chalcedonian formulation	124
christological controversies	117
oneness	84
Joachim of Flora	208
John, apostle	58, 64, 75, 95
John Cassian	130
John Chrysostom	138, 148
John Gratan	202
John, King of England	207
John of Chrysostom	105
John of Damascus	174, 216, 236
John of Harlicarnasses	124
John of Jerusalem	136
John of Leiden	365
John of Prague	282
John of Saxony	295
John Paul II	121, 217, 480
John Scotus Erigena	177
John X	200
John XI	200
John XII	200
John XXII	246, 250
John XXIII	260, 479, 488
Jonas, Justin	295
Josephus	60
Judaism	50, 51, 53
Judas Maccabeus	55
Juhasz, Peter Melius	333
Julian	115
Julian of Eclanum	135
Julian the Apostate	113
Julius Caesar	145
Julius II	255, 266, 285
Julius III	384
Justinian	125, 162, 168
Justinian I	124
Justin Martyr	53, 77, 80, 81, 83, 90, 91, 107
on Eucharist	94

K

Kantianism	421, 439
Kant, Immanuel	402, 405, 421
Categorical Imperative	408
Critique of Pure Reason	408

SCRIPTURE INDEX

6:3–4	60	20:28	61
6:5–6	60	22:16	62
6:7	57	22:22–29	51
6:8	60		
8:1	58	**Romans**	
8:12	60, 62	1:1–7	56
8:16	60	1:17	286
8:25	60	3:21–30	56
8:26–27	60	3:23–26	281
8:26–39	58	5:12	135
8:40	60	6:1–6	62
9:2	58	10:20	141
9:31	57	11:36	37
10:1–48	58	13:14	133
10:44–48	60	15:19	58
10:47	62	15:24	58
11:15	50	15:28	58
11:19	58	16:1–2	61
11:26	58	16:5	62
12:1–2	58	16:14	62
13:5	54	16:15	62
13:14	54		
13:32–42	54	**1 Corinthians**	
14:7	54	2:15	248
14:23	60	3:11–15	167
15:4	60	5:1	62
15:6	60	5:7	35
15:26	58	6:1–2	62
16:11–15	53	6:12–20	62
16:11–40	51	7:8	126
16:12–13	54	8:1–6	62
16:40	62	10:21	62
17:1	54	11:16–17	62
17:10	54	11:20	62
17:17	54	11:20–21	62
17:19–31	52	11:21	62
17:30	36	11:23–28	62
18:1–4	54	11:24–25	62
18:2	60	11:30	62
18:19	54	14:1–40	62
19:8–10	54	15:3–5	56
19:23	51	15:7	60
20:7	62	15:20–28	524
20:17	60	15:23	524
20:20	61	15:50–57	523